The Future of
Christian Mission in India

Missional Church, Public Theology, World Christianity

Stephen Bevans, Paul S. Chung, Veli-Matti Kärkkäinen
and Craig L. Nessan, Series Editors

IN THE MIDST OF globalization there is crisis as well as opportunity. A model of God's mission is of special significance for ecclesiology and public theology when explored in diverse perspectives and frameworks in the postcolonial context of World Christianity. In the face of the new, complex global civilization characterized by the Second Axial Age, the theology of mission, missional ecclesiology, and public ethics endeavor to provide a larger framework for missiology in interaction with our social, multicultural, political, economic, and intercivilizational situation; they create ways to refurbish mission as constructive theology in critical and creative engagement with cultural anthropology, world religions, prophetic theology, postcolonial hermeneutics, and contextual theologies of World Christianity. Such endeavors play a critical role in generating theological, missional, social-ethical alternatives to the reality of Empire—a reality characterized by civilizational conflict, and by the complex system of a colonized lifeworld that is embedded within practices of greed, dominion, and ecological devastation. This series—Missional Church, Public Theology, World Christianity—invites scholars to promote alternative church practices for life-enhancing culture and for evangelization as telling the truth in the public sphere, especially in solidarity with those on the margins and in ecological stewardship for the lifeworld.

The Future of Christian Mission in India

Toward a New Paradigm for the Third Millennium

AUGUSTINE KANJAMALA SVD

With a Foreword by Siga Arles

PICKWICK *Publications* · Eugene, Oregon

THE FUTURE OF CHRISTIAN MISSION IN INDIA
Toward a New Paradigm for the Third Millennium

Missional Church, Public Theology, World Christianity 4

Copyright © 2014 Augustine Kanjamala. All rights reserved. Except for brief quotations in critical publications or reviews, no part of this book may be reproduced in any manner without prior written permission from the publisher. Write: Permissions, Wipf and Stock Publishers, 199 W. 8th Ave., Suite 3, Eugene, OR 97401.

Copyright © 2008 *The New Community Bible*. Used by permission. Bombay: St. Pauls Publications.

Pickwick Publications
An Imprint of Wipf and Stock Publishers
199 W. 8th Ave., Suite 3
Eugene, OR 97401

ISBN 13: 978-1-62032-315-1

Cataloging-in-Publication data:

Kanjamala, Augustine.

The future of Christian mission in India : toward a new paradigm for the third millennium / Augustine Kanjamala.

xxii + 400 p. ; 23 cm. — Includes bibliographical references and index.

Missional Church, Public Theology, World Christianity 4

ISBN 13: 978-1-62032-315-1

1. Missions. 2. Public Theology. I. Arles, Siga. II. Series. III. Title.

BX1644 .K36 2014

Manufactured in the U.S.A.

Contents

Foreword by Siga Arles   *vii*

Preface   *xiii*

1. Seven Images of Churches in India   1
2. Varieties of Hindu Responses to Evangelical Mission   28
3. Violence against Christian Missions   95
4. Conversions of Marginal Communities to Christian Churches   116
5. From Confrontations to Dialogue and Partnership   163
6. Inculturation of the Indian Churches   186
7. The Spirit of God in Contemporary Social Movements   220
8. Christian Institutions at the Service of the Gospel   242
9. The Future of Missions in the Hindu Belt   262
10. Emerging Missions and Missiologies for the Future   289

Appendix: Christian Population in the States of India   345

Bibliography   347

Index   367

Foreword

THROUGH THE FELLOWSHIP OF Indian Missiologists (FOIM) it had been our privilege in India to be aware of the many committed to exploring relevant formation of what could be identified as "Indian Missiology." Our awareness of each other is mainly through the articles in Journals and the occasional books. A larger section of such literature is from the Roman Catholic scholars who by virtue of their celibate life could afford more time for research and writing. Surely Protestant scholars benefit from the hard work of the Catholic scholars. Beside literature, the face to face meeting and fellowshipping is enabled by our FOIM conferences. Friendships formed in such gatherings have enriched us to march together for shaping and reshaping the contours of the emerging Indian Missiology.

Among the precious friends that I discovered through the years, one who stands tall-both by physical and intellectual stature is Father Doctor Augustine Kanjamala, whose track record in terms of his writings, leadership roles, and articulations are superb. His time as the Director of Ishvani Kendra, Poona, was significant and now as he mentors doctoral scholars based at Mumbai University, he is a wealth of wisdom and contemporary scholarship. Here is one more offering from his research to enrich our journey into Indian Missiology, which I welcome with gratitude.

The author has put together ten chapters. The first six take us to in-depth consideration of the history of the church and mission in India, the responses from the Hindu majority and the Islamic minority, the amicable reception interspersed with occasional violence, the inculturation process, and the status of sustained dialogue. The author covers each section with masterful coverage of data and compiles something of a textbook for the history of the church and mission in India. Chapter 3 takes a look at the contemporary conflicts emerging from the cultural, social, political, economic, and religious angles. Again in so doing, he attempts to be as wide and thorough as he can, in bringing a lot of input from the church documents, news media, books, and conferences. Then in chapters 9–10 he goes to explore what he wishes to see as the future of Christian Mission

Foreword

in India. Here he predicts, proposes, and pushes for the sort of changes, priorities, and orientation for the church in mission in India.

The author gives a fair compilation of the Roman Catholic history and wisdom that provides an easy access to a systematic understanding of it for all his readers. Such compilation, I affirm, is sufficiently critical—not merely hagiographical. The author shows much courtesy in recounting the Protestant developments, often with appreciation, admiration, and accuracy. I commend the author for this ecumenicity in his approach. Quite often the Protestant missionaries, their stories, accomplishments, and writings are enlisted with acceptance. The commendation to Protestant efforts at Bible translation is echoed while identifying the failure within the Roman church to promote Scripture in the heart language of people. There is a broad and sweeping coverage of "the backdrop" with the Syrian and Protestant beginnings of the church, the geographic and demographic spread of the expanse of the church. It is further expanded with "the seven images" in the first chapter: (1) the Syrian; (2) the Latin and Protestant images; (3) the Adivasi / Tribal image; (4) the Dalit image; (5) the Patriarchal / Institutional Power image; (6) the Servant and Compassionate Image; and (7) the Persecuted Church image are identified.

"The Hindu Response to Evangelical Mission" in chapter 2 takes an extensive look at the beginnings of the Protestant mission history in the Calcutta sector with mission pioneers such as William Carey, Alexander Duff; with Hindu reformers and thought leaders such as Ram Mohan Roy, K. C. Sen, Vivekananda; early Christian converts who attempted the rudiments of Indian Christian theology such as Brahmabandhav Upadhyaya, K. M. Banerjee, Sadhu Sundar Singh, and the Educational contributions of both missionary pioneers and British officers. Father Augustine Kanjamala provides here a shorter version of an introduction to Indian Christian Theology—the chapter feels like a summary of the works of Kaj Baago, Robin Boyd, and M. M. Thomas in their concomitant works *Pioneers of Indigenous Christianity, Introduction to Indian Christian Theology*, and *The Acknowledged Christ of Indian Renaissance*, all published in 1969. His bibliography of this chapter is quite vast and inclusive.

A brief account of the emergence of the militant mode within Hindu fold—its roots, structures, ideologies—and its implications for democracy and secularism, its impact in terms of persecution of the Christian community in Orissa are found in chapter 3. Here the author pictures the unfortunate emergence of what he categorizes as "the two Indias," quoting from R. Guha in *Outlook*: "Contemporary India is home to pluralists and

Foreword

democrats as well as fanatics and sectarians; to selfless social workers as well as greedy politicians; to honest and upright officials as well as officials who are time-servers; to capitalists who distribute their wealth quietly as well as those who seek only to proactively display it. To redeem the republic, to bring the practice of Indian democracy closer to the ideals of Indian nationhood, is to valorize and support the first kind of Indian rather than the second."[1]

He also identifies a dangerous trend that is evolving—an "anti-minority bias among the judiciary and police." He quotes Christophe Jaffrelot from *Frontline*. As I live in Karnataka, I am very conscious of this in the recent years of BJP rule when there had been consistent attacks on Christian community, an apathy among the police since the BJP Home Minister was in favor of such attacks, and when the very Justice B. K. Somasekhara Commission report failed to rightly tackle the issues.

Chapter 4 analyzes "Conversions of Marginal Communities to Christian Churches." In a very helpful way the author traces the life, struggles, and rationale of the masses who flocked to the church. And in a precise and interesting way he contrasts Christianization from Sanskritization. Chapter 5 traces the movement forward "from Confrontation to Dialogue and Partnership." It provides a helpful summary of the history of developments from the Portuguese to the post-Vatican II periods, ushering in an age of ecumenicity. Chapter 6 specifically deals with "Inculturation of the Indian Church." The author's accounts of the "Six Ritual Families in the Catholic Church," the "Four Models of Inculturation after the Second Vatican Council," and the "Ashrams" prove significant contributions from this chapter. In chapter 7 he searches for the "Spirit of God in Contemporary Social Movements." Chapter 8 considers "How to transform Christian Institutions for the service of the Gospel." It interprets Good News and the Kingdom of God in relation to the institution of the church with its many institutions of service. The concern is vital to enable the presence of the church in mission to attest itself as "good news" to human community. It brings out the need for a renewal of mission methodology, mission praxis and mission training. Chapter 9 specifically studies the "Future of Mission in the Hindu Belt" in the light of the issues of Conversion, Baptism, and Ecclesiastical Realities.

The concluding chapter is a bold attempt to compile a prospectus for the "Emerging Missions and Missiologies for the Future." The core of the proclamation, the author identifies, was "Kingdom-centred" for Jesus,

1. Guha, "Will India become a Superpower?" 74.

Foreword

"Christ-centred" for apostolic mission, and "Ecclesio-centric" for the post-Constantine mission. In the modern times, the Kingdom-centred emphasis ought to be promoted. The author proposes a "new model of mission": (a) to interpret traditional mission theology with the help of Indian philosophical / religious categories and cultural idioms, including the idioms of the tribal cultures; (b) to search for new ways of organizing Christian communities and relating to people belonging to other faiths and ideologies; (c) to express new ways of feeling about mission, local peoples, and their cultures; and (d) to plan for new priorities in the realization of the various constitutive elements of mission. These could provide an integrated as well as a new vision of the mission, which would also demand a new life style and Christian witness.

In the emerging alternative model for mission, the highest priority proposed is the proclamation and working for the realization of the Kingdom of God; the missionary shall experience the conversion of the heart and mind and develop a "missionary spirituality" and be a saint—"contemplative in action"—to challenge the evils in Indian society reflecting the Kingdom values. Mission should lead to rising above ethnocentrism to dialogue with different religious traditions and to participate with the people in nation building. And two hermeneutical principles are enunciated to pass over from the past exclusivism to an all-inclusive mission.

The concluding paragraph is worth quoting: "And the Indian church is emerging as the most influential church in the third world, with its largest number of missionaries as well as creative theologians . . . Christian mission to all the people of India, with a preferential love for the poor, in the third millennium will be a very demanding vision. Facing these awesome opportunities and challenges in the twenty-first century we find inspiration and strength in the presence of the Risen Lord who promises to be with us always, until the end of the age." While highly appreciative of the work, I do wish to comment that though the author desires to deal with the future, he ends up overtly describing the past history and interpreting the present. This is a weakness in the content of the book. More chapters should have addressed the revision and reformulation of methodology and message. Augustine Kanjamala's scholarly compilation of a vast amount of facts and skilful interpretation to propose a pathway for the future of Christian mission in India is a helpful offering to the church in India.

As I am General Editor of the various series of books—Missiological Classics, Contextual, Pastoral, Literature series—from the Centre

Foreword

for Contemporary Christianity in Bangalore, I am delighted that here is one more pertinent book to enable the formulation of Indian Missiology. I recommend this to every student of missiology and every mission practitioner to take this as a guide to the process of inventing Indian Missiology.

Siga Arles, PhD
Director, Centre of Contemporary Christianity, Bangalore

Preface

IT IS CLAIMED BY a significant and influential section of the Indian Christianity that its origin dates back to St. Thomas the Apostle's mission in South India. After a huge gap of fifteen centuries opens the second chapter, the Portuguese colonial mission in the beginning of the sixteenth century with the fundamental teaching: *Extra ecclesiam nulla salus*. In the aftermath of the Reformation it took nearly two hundred years for the Protestants to arrive at a gradual realization that the mission of Jesus did not come to its end with the death of the Apostles and therefore all the believers in Jesus share in his mission. And the first Protestant Lutheran missionaries, under the patronage of the Danish King, Frederick IV, arrived in Tranquebar, Tamil Nadu, in the beginning of eighteenth century, followed by more powerful mission currents a century later. And the land of Bharat was woken up to some fresh air, in the views of one school, or to slavery in the opinion of the opposite school.

The personnel as well as economic investments in the huge enterprise was unquestionably phenomenal, not ignoring the human sacrifices and sufferings, physical hardships and psychological stresses, social ridicule and even martyrdom, starting from St. Thomas through de Britto to the recent martyrs of Kandhamal, Orissa. Did these heroes of faith achieve or actualize, in any significant measure, their grandiose vision and high hopes of converting the whole of the pagan India into Christianity? A century ago, at the peak of the mass conversion movement an evangelical missionary expressed his high hopes of conversions: "At the present rate of increase it would take another 160 years for India as whole to become Christian. The present rate is, indeed much faster than that of the Christian population in the first century of the Roman Empire." Similar hopes were also expressed in the beginning of the nineteenth century during mass conversions in Tinnevely, South India. It is estimated that today with a miniscule 3 percent of adherents to the original vision of the missionaries, 97 percent of the Indian people seek and find salvation through their own

Preface

religions, without any direct link with the Christian economy of redemption. And the same is equally true of all of Asia, the home of more than 60 percent of the sea of humanity, with the exception of the Philippines. It is sad, at the same time true, that such a huge humanity has rejected the Christian understanding of redemption, as the Jewish people refused to accept Jesus 2,000 years ago.

The Christian communities are concentrated mainly in three major regions—in South India (60 percent); the North East tribal belt (18 percent); and the Adivasi belt of erstwhile Chotanagpur (about 10 percent); and in some urban centres like Bombay its institutional visibility is high. Frustration and anxieties are experienced, but less expressed, particularly by the missionaries in the Hindu belt, the least responsive area, than those who labor in the tribal belt with relatively better responses. Such is the backdrop of the challenging and disturbing probe: What will be the future of Christian mission in India? Did the traditional understanding of the mission, i.e., *extra ecclessiam nulla salus*, fail in India? If so, why? What are the alternatives?

Crisis in the church and mission is not entirely new in the history of the Christian mission. Modernism, rationalism, liberalism, Marxism, and secularism were spreading their tentacles into the Christian faith, particularly in the West, starting from the Protestant Reformation period and accelerated from the middle of seventeenth century, reaching its high-water mark in the French rationalism and French revolution. The steel frame of the Catholic administrative mechanism rather successfully suppressed the challenges with stern objections and determination. *The Syllabus of Errors* (1864) of Pope Pius IX anathematized the position that "the Roman Pontiff can, and ought to, reconcile himself and come to terms with progress, liberalism and modern civilization." Again *Lamentabili Sane Exitu* (1907) and *Pascenti Dominici* (1907) listed and condemned modernist errors. The convocation of the Second Vatican Council (1962–1965) by Pope John XXIII opened the windows of the church for some fresh air. It seems it turned into a hurricane and ended up in a Runaway Church, at least in the first world. At the same time crisis is also an opportunity to respond creatively. The church history doesn't lack evidences of creative responses.

"Decree on the Missionary Activity of the Church" rediscovered the dynamic, biblically based Trinitarian *Missio Dei* (AG 2–5). The revised teaching of the possibility of salvation outside the church (LG 16), departing from the 1900 year-old teaching, created unprecedented confusion.

Preface

"Missionary activity is nothing else and nothing less than an epiphany or a manifesting of God's decree, and its fulfillment in the world and in world history, in the course of which God, by means of mission, manifestly works out the history of salvation" (AG 9). Less than a decade later the inability of a fractured Synod of the Bishops (1974) to produce a consensus document on Evangelization was a clear indication of the post-conciliar confusions. Attempts to avoid the term "mission" in the context of the post-colonial hostility, Christian missionary arrogance and superiority in Asia and Africa, and its replacement with the term "Evangelization" in *Evangelii Nuntiandi* (1975) of Pope Paul VI was short lived. The attempt to broaden the Christo-centric mission to the Kingdom-centred mission, i.e., "only the Kingdom is absolute" (EN 8), was replaced by the traditional Christo-centrism. Pope John Paul's encyclical letter *Redemptoris Missio* (1990) not only retrieved the traditional high Christo-centrism (RM 5) but also spelled out anxieties about the contemporary missionary crisis. "Missionary activity specially directed 'to the nations' (*ad gentes*) appears to be waning—Difficulties, both internal and external, have weakened the church's missionary thrust towards non-Christians—Missionary drive has always been a sign of vitality just as its lessening is a crisis of faith" (RM 2). "Is missionary work among the non-Christians still valid?" The pope was anxious that the new dimensions of mission, like inter-religious dialogue and human development, were blurring the traditional clarity of mission (RM 4). To those who were familiar with the clear and precise Christo-centric mission the Kingdom of God mission appears vague.

Starting with W. Buehlmann's prophetic book, *The Coming of the Third Church* (1976), there is a steady growth of literature on the future of the mission. Perception of future possibilities in a world that is changing in an unprecedented speed disrupts peoples' perspectives and creates bewilderment. Systematic practice of futurology—projecting statistical trend in order to construct realistic future scenarios—dates back to 1950s and is a distinctly social-scientific enterprise. Most forecasting depends on historical trends and patterns and projecting into the future. Given the complexity of variables involved, exact predictions are rare, especially in areas like religious beliefs and social attitudes. However attempts to chart future possibilities remain valuable as long as the limitations attached to them are not ignored.

Allow me to add a personal note. People ask: "Why do you write one more book on the mission when we have no dearth of books? What is lacking is people committed to the missions." My wide experience of traveling

Preface

across the length and breadth of the nation in the beginning of the 1990s in my capacity as the Secretary to the Commission for Evangelization, Catholic Bishop's Conference of India, to research into mission dynamics of the Catholic dioceses in the post-Vatican II period has deepened and enriched my perception of missionary activities as well as practical missiology at grass roots. Questionnaire surveys, group discussions and personal interviews with many priests, nuns and lay people, including non-Christians, in forty-five dioceses enhanced the quality of my quantitative survey. It was a rare opportunity and privilege for acquiring insights into and developing sensitivity to missionary challenges that can never be learned from books. I am deeply indebted to hundreds of people, including many bishops, who generously cooperated with the CBCI project. Some of its findings are already published, including the objections of the Hindu critics.

In the background of failures of missions, frustrations of missionaries leading even to mental breakdown, at least in a few cases, in the post-Vatican II struggle for a transition from a very rigid and narrow definition of mission to the broad description of Evangelization (EN), I arrived at the conclusion that these missionary crises are not isolated instances. My own personal search, starting with higher studies in Rome and four decades of teaching and researching for a relevant missiology for India is situated in this broader context. I discovered that many hearts are restless and are looking for meaningful answers to face the emerging complex challenges. Three more reasons, among others, will hopefully justify my humble attempt. One, many seem to be afraid of revealing their missionary predicament. Second, only a few are gifted to articulate their success and failures, joys and sorrows, anxieties and hopes, and the incongruence between the official missiology of the magisterium and the practical missiology of missionaries in the given antagonistic context of India. Finally, this book is also a gentle reminder of the huge sacrifices made by numerous missionaries for the people of this country, including the Hindu fundamentalist critics.

This discourse leads to the uncomfortable conclusion that, with around 3 percent social conversion, the Christian mission is a failure in India as well as Asia, in *quantitative* terms. This might sound pessimistic to the traditional ears. In contrast, I am glad to elucidate that the Christian mission was a success in *qualitative* terms. Mission publications and discussions in India have paid only a marginal attention to such a positive understanding. Four areas, among others, deserve better attention. One,

Preface

the radical restructuring of the Indian society, the object of virulent attacks of missionaries, through the abolition of many social evils and inhuman practices like Sati or widow burning, child marriage, temple prostitution, polygamy, untouchability, slavery, and so forth by the missionaries and British administrators, fired by the evangelical spirit of the eighteenth and nineteenth centuries. Two, more important were the contributions of English medium education with the modern scientific world view, a Western liberal-political philosophy combined with Christian values diametrically opposed to the Hindu world view. For the first time the idea of India was being constructed by the new intellectual elite, from the end of the nineteenth century. The transformation of the Indian mind was unquestionably the best fruit of the Christian-Hindu encounter. Three, the past Hindu-Christian encounter was not a one-way traffic. Missionaries were also evangelized by the Indian encounters. The recent change from an exclusive mission theology to an inclusive one was partly the fruit of the Hindu resistance, challenges, and resourcefulness. Four, the Protestant theologians, preceded by aborted attempts of a few catholic theologians, put the foundation for an Indian Christology and Indian Church. No honest scholar will dare to ignore that during the last two centuries Christian mission has been one of the catalysts for altering Indian society. And it is therefore logical to ask what difference will it make in the future?

The end of the Constantine Paradigm of mission logically leads to the end of the colonial mission and mission theology. The conquest model of the past is being replaced by the new Paradigm characterized by Witness, Dialogue, Inculturation, and Liberation. Dismantling of the Western colonialism by the middle of the twentieth century signaled the dismantling of colonial world vision that accompanied the western missionaries. Enlightened by successes and failures of the past mission it is not incongruent to conclude that Asia needs a new mission theology and fresh approaches. One of the reasons for the failure of the mission seems to be the Greco-Latin (Roman) interpretation of the person as well as the mission of Jesus. Are the Western interpretations of Jesus normative for Asia with its ancient philosophies, civilizations, and religions? Jesus was an Asian and Asia has yet to discover his original face. Was his face disfigured by the Constantine Council? It is the duty of the Indian theologians to articulate their faith in Jesus Christ with the philosophical, theological, and cultural resources of this country, being mindful of the limitations of frog in the well mentality. Theology is a human construct, a creative interpretation of the Word of God in diverse places and historical con-

Preface

texts. Indian theologians require freedom and space to venture into this new enterprise. In the recent decades new theologies are being created in Latin America, Africa, and Asia. The mission theology of the future will be a theology from below; it has to be a dynamic response to the dynamic context. A theology from above, detached from the context, tends to be static and irrelevant. The formulation of an Indian theology will also be a contribution to the universal church.

An interdisciplinary approach is the methodology employed in my search. Anthropology, sociology, church history, missiology, and the Scriptures, including Indian scriptures and comparative analysis can shed light on the moot exercise: What has happened to that hidden energy of the Good News that had powerful impact on India during the past nearly three centuries? In what way will that evangelical force continue to contribute in shaping India's destiny? How will the missionaries become genuine collaborators with all religions, and people of good will in promoting the Reign of God? Mission is an engagement with the world, its politics, economy, culture, and religion with the vision of Jesus.

With the recent positive and optimistic attitude to world religions and cultures it seems logical to appraise the past Christian definition of universal mission as narrow and ethnocentric, that is, mission of the Christians to all peoples and nations. In contrast, it will be argued, if all the people of the world are children of God, created in the image of God and recreated in the paschal mystery, with a single origin and the same destiny, as taught by the Second Vatican Council, then they all naturally do participate in God's single mission. With the past exclusivist understanding of salvation only through the church it was almost unimaginable to think that people of other religions, even no religion, could share in Gods single mission. In the unprecedented post-Vatican II context the exclusive mission of the past has little future. I believe that everyone born in to this world is called to contribute toward the realization of the Kingdom of God. Therefore the future of the mission becomes really bright and truly universal. Inclusivism and Universalism will be the defining character of the mission of the future.

Christian faith and mission articulated in the distant past with a static world view can't escape conflicts of encountering a more rational and dynamic world view. That tension is well articulated by Karl Rahner in the following words. On the one hand, "the church looking forward in hope must always be a church—of missionary planning"; on the other hand, "the church is the Sacrament of the unplanned future, because the future

Preface

is no other than the eternal incomprehensibility of God."[2] The future of the mission will be far more marked by tensions and doubts as a consequence of increasing intellectualization of the world in contrast to the mythological world-view in which the original mission was spelled out. The leap of faith becomes all the more audacious. Last, but not the least, the author acknowledges the limitations of the book that no single study can deal with the vast history and literature of nearly 2000 years of the Christian mission and its variegated impact on Indian thought, spirituality, religion, society, and life.

---

2. Rahner, "Perspectives on Pastoral Ministry in the Future," 196.

Acknowledgments

I AM DEEPLY INDEBTED to Professor Siga Arles PhD, for writing the Foreword with deep appreciation of my book and with an ecumenical spirit. I have earnestly attempted to incorporate some of the valuable recommendations of the erudite publisher of "Centre for Contemporary Christianity," Bangalore.

My mentor for a period of three and half a decades, i.e., during major seminary formation, higher education, and ministry, is gratefully remembered. The missionary spirit and global vision of late Engelbert Zeitler SVD deeply influenced and molded my vision, too. His life and services in India extended beyond the narrow domestic walls of his congregation to the Indian and Asian church, particularly in the post-Vatican II decades of *aggiornamento*. Sincere and thought provoking discussions and honest sharing of success and failures, doubts and frustrations of thousands of bishops, priests, religious women and men, and lay people during the evaluation of the Indian mission (1990–92) at their grass root locations, with the help of local evaluation teams, was a rare learning opportunity for me, as secretary to the commission for evangelization of the Catholic Bishops Conference of India. To these stoic missionary heralds, both foreign and Indian, who creatively and pragmatically blended the text, the Word of God, and the context in the missionary desert of India, this book owes no mean share of data and insights. Without the missionary ethos of the Society of the Divine Word that I naturally imbibed in the course of my life and interactions with missionaries, this book probably would not have seen the light of the day. Through my provincial superior, Lazar T. Stanislaus, who has taken very personal interest and provided all necessary support for the publication, I convey my hearty gratitude to my congregation.

Finally I feel deeply honored by the fact that Pickwick Publications is bringing out my book. It carries my humble effort to think in the contemporary anti-Christian Indian context and out of the traditional

Acknowledgments

Greco-Roman box. Thank you for this privilege. Let me also gratefully acknowledge the insightful editorial recommendations of Craig L. Nessan, one of the Series Editors of the same publications.

1

Seven Images of Churches in India

"The longer you can look back the farther you can look forward"
—Winston Churchill

The Context of India and Its Challenges

INDIA IS PERHAPS THE most complex nation in the world because of its nearly unimaginable pluralism and contrasting, often conflicting, diversities as well as affinities at every level. Today's population of over one billion originated from five distinct racial types and some degree of mixing, with the predominance of the Aryan race in the Indo-Gangetic plain in the North and the Dravidian race in the South. Eighteen official languages, including English, plus 1652 dialects belonging to five language families with twenty-five scripts, create a veritable tower of Babel. The geographical as well as linguistic isolation of innumerable communities in the early period, with hereditary occupations originally laid the foundation for the present day 3,000 ethnic core groups and 10,000 endogamous communities.[1] Such a social situation was gradually reorganized and legitimized as four broad Hindu castes by priestly authors of the Hindu sacred scriptures into Brahmins or priests, 8 percent; Kshatriyas or rulers, 16 percent; Vaishyas or commerce, 9 percent; and Sudras or peasants, 52 percent. About 15 percent were classified and treated as outcastes or untouchables. And religious communities like Muslims, Christians, Sikhs,

---

1. Singh, *Diversity, Identity*, 89, 102, 109.

The Future of Christian Mission in India

Buddhists, Jains, Jews, Parsees, and animists co-exist with the dominant Hindu community, nearly 80 percent.

In a country nearly as large as a continent is it right and just to speak of one Indian Church and one Indian Mission? While not denying that there are certain unifying all-India perspectives and realities, one is almost compelled to acknowledge that the regional realities and interests of the local churches and missions are more dynamic and challenging than that of the Indian church. For example, what is the relation between the Kerala Church in the South and the Jammu Kashmir Church in the North? Is there any influence of the Patna Latin diocese in Bihar in the eastern zone on the Rajkot Syrian diocese in Gujarat in the western zone? The similarities between the Tribal Church in the North—East and the Tribal Church in western India begin and end with the tasteless legal and Indian Constitutional phrase 'Scheduled Tribes.' And the same is true about the Dalit church in Punjab in the North and Dalit church in Tamil Nadu in the South. One might therefore find more justification in focusing on regional levels because missionary activities of the Church are becoming more effective at the linguistic and cultural levels.

The Christian missionaries arrived in India at different zones during different periods of mission history. And the major phases of the missionary movements can be broadly demarcated into the following periods. The Syrian church on the Malabar coast claims its origin, according to a strong oral tradition, to the mission of St. Thomas the Apostle who arrived at Cranganore port, near Cochin, in AD 52. Documented evidences of different waves of migrations of Christians from East Syria and Persia, starting in the third century are undisputed. Their peaceful and passive coexistence with indigenous people for more than a millennium was beneficially disturbed by two major confrontations, first, between the Latin Portuguese missionaries in the sixteenth and seventeenth centuries and second, between the Church Missionary Society (CMS) and the Jacobite church in the beginning of the nineteenth century.

The arrival of Vasco da Gama and the Portuguese in Calicut in 1498, the conquest of Goa in 1510 and the arrival of various missionary Congregations inaugurated the second and aggressive phase of the mission in India under the *Padroado*, the royal patronage system. The capture of Bassein, Salsette, Thane and Bombay and coastal towns in the following decades prepared the way for the Franciscan missionaries and others to establish small Christian communities in the western region.[2] In the

2. Meersman, "Latin Missions," 67–68.

Seven Images of Churches in India

aftermath of Reformation and subsequent preoccupation with denominational fights and political upheaval till the Peace of Westphalia in 1648 the Protestant awakening to missionary obligation was a slow process. The arrival of two German Lutheran Missionaries, under the patronage of the Danish King Frederick IV, fired by the Pietistic movement in Halle, Germany, in Tranquebar or Tarangambadi in Tamil Nadu, a Danish colony, in 1706 opened the first chapter of the Protestant Mission in India.[3] The entry of William Carrey and two of his missionary companions in Serampore, another Danish colony near Calcutta, in 1793 and the subsequent entry of large number of Protestant missionaries, after the prohibition of entry of missionaries into the territory of the East India company was lifted by the Charter of 1813, was the starting point of the "Great Protestant Century" in India.

The hallmark of the nineteenth and twentieth centuries was mass conversions, inaugurated first by the protestant missionaries, followed by the Catholics. Two German Lutheran Missionaries, C. F. Schwartz and T. E. Rhenius, inaugurated group conversions among the Shannars of Tirunnelveli, Tamil Nadu, at the end of the nineteenth century. More or less in the same period, the Protestant missionaries were pioneers in frontier territories of Chotanagpur and North—East India and the Catholic missionaries would follow them, with their characteristic caution. The undivided Punjab's successful evangelization was commenced by the American Presbyterians among the Chura and Chamar outcasts. Unfortunately missionaries failed to make any direct inroads into organized religions like Hinduism, Islam and Sikhism. However mission was not without its silver linings on Indian minds and social contours.

On Constructing Images

The nature of missionary activities and people's responses to them were deeply influenced by various factors, such as ethnicity, caste, class, culture and above all religions. Thus a variety of Christian communities were created across the length and breath of the country. Plurality dominates both the national as well as ecclesiastical ethos. "The singular thing about India that you can only speak of it in the plural. This pluralism emerged from the very nature of the country; it was made inevitable by India's geography and affirmed by its history."[4] In the context of such a glaring pluralism are we justified to speak about a single image of a Church in India? The idea

3. Jeyaraj, "History of Christianity," 200.
4. Nandi, "Visions of Nationhood," 39.

of one Indian Church is nearly a myth created by foreign missionaries when they reported to their home countries about their work in some unknown remote corner of India. Strictly speaking there is no Indian Church. All images, pictures and models—artistic, cultural and theological—are human constructs. The Indian Christian artist Mr. Jyoti Sahi, observes that many Indians cannot think of an Indian Christ. "For them Jesus has to be foreigner and hence white. They cannot just imagine a blue or a brown Jesus."[5] In the slave era the Blacks painted an African Jesus. Michelangelo's Jesus was modeled on Apollo. The Justification for creating different theological images of Jesus is found both in the Old as well as the New Testament.[6] The images of the Church in India are many which are constructed and reconstructed with the help of local cultural and religious building blocks. The creators of the image or identity of a community are two types. Every community in virtue of believing and behaving in a particular manner validates its subjective image. For the image to come about the group identities are defined in relation to that which they are not. This is an 'insider view'. It becomes socially effective by being acknowledged by the members. A community's image is also created by 'the outsiders' who label the group with their perceptions, true or imagined. The people of India, for example, were called (H) Indus by the Persians. This could be termed as an 'objective image', not in the sense of objective truth but the sense of images and perceptions of the observer or analyst. The images and stereotypes, particular notion of virtues or vices of people held by others, result in patterned social relationships or interactions of social distance or social closeness.

A shared culture is responsible for the creation of a particular image and the spirit of the individual as well as the community. Some of the cultural traits that are employed in the construction of the image are: shared ethnicity, shared beliefs like mythology of its origin, shared values and norms of conduct and behavior, common occupation, shared rituals and celebrations like the rites of passage, and shared experiences of joys, sorrows and other sentiments. The material culture that provide visibility and particular image of the community are, folk costumes and ornaments, worn specifically at public celebrations, traditional food and drink habits, particular music and musical instruments and dances, handicrafts, art and artists, printed floral pattern, community's heroes, saints and deities and places of worship and many other cultural symbols. Shared mother-

---

5. Sahi, "Many Indians," 25–26.
6. Milling, "New Trends," 78–95.

Seven Images of Churches in India

tongue or dialect is a powerful symbol of cultural unity and convenient tool for administration. At critical times cultural discourse "attempts to construct bonded cultural objects."[7] Thus the image of a community/church is continuously constructed, reconstructed and deconstructed. The image is not static, on the contrary, it is a dynamic historical process, not infrequently bound to a common territory. Cultural stuff is important and that "being a Catholic or a Protestant really means something to the people in question."[8] Being a Brahmin or an 'Outcaste' are images, created by the powerful upper castes and these images evoke many sentiments, both positive as well as negative.

Cultural traits are not absolutes nor simply intellectual categories but are invoked to provide identities to legitimate claims to rights. They are categories or weapons in competition over scarce social goods-power, material resources and status symbols. A community or a church is defined through its relationship to others, marked off through the boundary between 'us' and 'them.' These boundaries are zealously guarded and protected by its members as well as authorized watchdogs. Unauthorized boundary crossing is severely punished. For example inter-caste marriages in India are punished by ostracism, and, at times, even by brutal murder. If a Syrian Sudhist marries outside the community, he/she is excommunicated. Religious boundaries are also not infrequently, intimately bound together with ethnic boundaries. They evolve symbols which have the power for creating loyalty and the feeling of belongingness and security. "Since an identity—racial, ethnic, religious, sexual, gender and national—cannot exist in isolation and must take its meaning from the other, and because every individual possesses a number of identities not all of which are relevant in every context, a particular identity is situationally defined in the course of social interaction."[9]

Seven Images of Christian Communities of India

Christian missionaries arrived in India in different regions in different periods in history. The Word of God sown in different soils naturally yielded fruits of various kinds (Matt 13:18–23). Varieties of Christian communities were generated, promoted and preserved with the help of already

---

7. Eriksen, *Ethnicity*, 103.
8. Ibid., 56.
9. Campbell and Rew, *Identity and Affect*, 10.

existing cultural traits. In the construction of church images different combinations and permutations of the following factors are decisive.

1. How old is the particular Church? Is its origin in the distant past or in the recent period? What is the nature of its tradition?
2. What is the caste and ethnic background of different communities? For example, five races and their mixtures in India. Their social interactions and social distance.
3. The world view, life view and life style of the community.
4. Where do they fit into the economic and class structure of the Indian society? Is the church self-sufficient or economically dependent on foreign resources?
5. Who make decisions? Is the administration in the hand of the local people or outsiders? Bishops, religious superiors, heads of institutions and so forth.
6. Who is doing the theological thinking? Are they thinking in the context or is the theology imported from the West?
7. What is the geographical and cultural background of missionaries? Indigenous, Indian or foreign?[10]

The Syrian Church on the Malabar Coast: The First Church

The oldest Church, the Syrian Church on the Malabar Coast, also known as the St. Thomas Christians, with its traditional claim to apostolic and upper caste origin, could be called the first Church, not in any pre-eminence but from the point of its origin in history. According to Eusebius the church historian, Bishop Demetritus of Alexandria, sent Pantaenus, the head of the catechetical school in Alexandria, to India around 190 "to preach Christ to the Brahmins." Having returned he reported to have found Christians in Malabar who use the Gospel of St. Mathew for their liturgy.[11] The arrival of seventy two Christian families, under the leadership of the Nestorian merchant Thomas of Cana or Kanai Thoma and Bishop Mar Yausef, four priests and several deccans in 345 AD from East Syria, Edessa in Turkey, to Kodungallur or Crangannore, the capital of Chera kingdom on the Malabar coast, probably to escape religious per-

---

10. Kanjamala, "Understanding," 33–34.
11. Moffett, *History of Christianity*, 1:37.

Seven Images of Churches in India

secution in Persia between 340-80, was the origin of the Syrian Sudhist Community. They were surprised to know that the Christians here had no Bishop. Evantually they were brought under the Catholicose of the East at Seleucia—Ctesiphon, the capital of the Persian empire. Ten yeas later in 354 Theophilus 'the Indian,' being sent by the Roman emperor Constantine II to his native island and India, found the Indians "listening to the reading of the Gospel in sitting posture, and other things which were repugnant to the law."[12] The East Syrian liturgy of the Chaldean Catholic church was preserved until changes were introduced by the Latin Padroado church in the sixteenth century and by the Anglican Church in the Jacobite church in the last quarter of the nineteenth century.[13] The Christians here were deeply influenced by the Hindu caste culture. Their life style like the dress of women, ear-rings of men, long hair style of men, prenuptial rituals, marriage rites and family customs, Sraddha or rituals for departed souls, church buildings modeled after Hindu temples, landlord system and owning slaves nearly merged with the local culture.[14] But in their theological, juridical and liturgical practices they were under the Chaldean prelates and followed the 'Law of St. Thomas.' When the Portuguese missionaries arrived at the Malabar coast in 1498, they seriously doubted the Christian identity and image of the Syrian Christians which led to violent confrontation and split in the local Church. They were accused of being Nestorian Christians because of their dependency on the Persian church which was already well known as Nestorian.

The Anglican Church Missionary Society, originated in England in 1799, arrived in Calcutta in 1807 and reached South Travencore in 1813. The British colonel John Munro of Travencore, (1810–1819), a keen evangelical reformer, and the Anglican Chaplin Claudius Buchanan hoped to reform the Jacobite Church, and form an alliance for evangelization.[15] By 1816 three Anglicans, Rev. Benjamin Bailey, Joseph Fenn and Henry Baker, established themselves in the seminary in Kottayam. Rev. Joseph Fenn, engaged himself in the first translation of the Bible into the local language, Malayalam, and printed it in his press in 1829. And this was a historic contribution to the Kerala church which had failed to produce a

12. Ibid., 1:267.

13. Keay, *History of the Syrian*, 25–36.

14. Mundadan, *History of Christianity*, 1:154–74.

15. Keay, *A History of the Syrian Church in India*, 71. The Jacobites were "Monophysites" under the Jurisdiction of Mar Jacob, Baradai (d. 578), Bishop of Edessa, today's Urfa in Eastern Turkey. Monophysitism was condemned by the Council of Chalcedon in 451.

vernacular Bible for 1800 years. He had other publications to his credit, including the first modern Malayalam dictionary and grammar.

Deeply influenced by the CMS Abraham Malpan (1796–1845), teacher of Syriac Bible in the seminary, initiated the reformation of the Jacobite church. Reading and studying the Bible in the vernacular for the first time opened the eyes of the seminarians. Now their reforms included semi-autonomous Indian clergy, vernacular liturgy instead of the traditional Syrian liturgy, abolition of prayers for the dead and so forth. Reacting and rejecting the Protestant influences the Orthodox Metropolitan Dionysius IV in 1836 excommunicated Abraham Malpan and his companions who spearheaded the reform movement. With the support of the Anglican missionaries and the Travencore colonial authorities, Abraham Malpan sent his nephew Deacon Mathew to the Jacobite Patriarch Ignatius Mar Elias at Mardin in Syria and got him consecrated as Mathew Athanasios in 1842, who emerged as the leader of the movement. In 1875 the reformists, a small group of four parishes, with their leader Mar Athanasios, were excommunicated by the Syrian Orthodox Patriarch of Antioch. In 1887 the new group severed their umbilical cord with the CMS church to ensure complete independence. In the following year the Maramon Convention of the Reformed church began on the bank of river Pampa. The Reformed party, named itself Mar Thoma Syrian Church. The newly formed Mar Thoma Evangelical Association undertook vigorous evangelization among the Pulayas and Shanars in central Travencore, for the expansion and survival of the newly formed small church. This was a revolutionary step against the strong tradition of the caste-ridden Syrian church. Their Evangelical movement coincided with the mass conversion movement that was initiated by the CMS missionaries among the Shanar caste. Around 1900 the Syrian Christians in the Malabar coast numbered around 925,000 and were broadly divided into three–Roman Catholic, Orthodox and Reformed.[16] In 1900 CMS college was founded in Kottayam and with the establishment of CMS press in Kottayam Malayalam publications began to grow. The catholic *Nazrani Deepika* by Blessed Kuriakose Chavara in Mannanam, Kottayam, saw the light of the day after another four decades.

The Christian mission, indirectly, yet significantly influenced the reform movement among the Ezhavas of Travencore. Sri Narayana Guru (1856–1928) born in the socially despised Ezhava community was inspired by the selfless social service of the CMS to their Ezhava converts and their

---

16. Koilaparampil, *Caste in the Catholic*, 52–53.

economic development. He lived an ascetic life in the Hindu tradition and made all efforts to stem the tide of conversion to Christianity. He imposed on his Ezhava caste fellows abstention from the bloody Kali worship, animal sacrifices, Shamanism, witchcraft and other superstitious rites. He established a congregation of monks: Sri Narayana Guru Sangam. He taught "Whatever one's religion may be it is true as long as it makes better human beings." Hence conversions to Christianity are unimportant.[17]

Traditionally the Syrian Christians enjoy high social, economic and political status next to the Namboodiri Brahmins in the caste hierarchy. Due to rigid caste system, superiority complex, political patronage and restricted geographical mobility the Syrian Catholics in the southern corner of the country maintained a dormant and ghetto image until its encounter with the Padroado mission. The lack of missionary spirit is evident from the fact until the Vatican council no Syrian missionary Congregation was founded. Missionary Society of St. Thomas (1968) in Palai diocese was the first missionary society.[18] Today the Syrian Catholics constitute nearly 70 percent of Kerala Catholics and one fourth of India's catholic population; only 7 percent of the Kerala Catholics belong to the Syro-Malankara Rite with more traditional ritual characteristics. In 2005 there are nearly 3.6 million Syro-Malabar Catholics, or 70 percent; 1.3 million Latin Catholics, or 21 percent, and nearly 0.4 million Syro-Malankara Catholics or 7 percent in Kerala. Until very recently around 50 percent of the Indian priests and nearly 60 percent of the Indian women religious originated from this ancient church with its remarkable missionary spirit.[19]

The Latin Colonial Conquest Image: The Second Church

Like Christopher Columbus who reached America in 1492, Vasco da Gama (1469–1524) arrived in Calicut, Kerala, in May 1498. As per the Portuguese tradition his entourage included eight Franciscan Friars. The expansion of the mission in India under Padroado, the Portuguese royal patronage, more or less followed the route of the secular counterpart. The Portuguese got a cold reception from the Zamorin, the king of Calicut. Thus in 1503 they requested to establish a trade centre in Cochin, the very centre of pepper trade.[20] And they were gladly welcomed by the Raja,

17. Fuchs, *Rebellious Prophets*, 268–75.

18. Houtart, *Size and Structure*, 106.

19. Degrijise, *Going Forth*, 44–46. The growth of vocations in the young churches is recently altering the traditional structure of vocations.

20. Ames, *Vasco da Gama*, 45–62.

THE FUTURE OF CHRISTIAN MISSION IN INDIA

with the ulterior motive of checking the rival power of the Zamorin of Calicut as well as enriching the kingdom through trade. But he forbade missionary activities among caste Hindus and permitted the same among the marginalized communities. Without much delay missionaries began to arrive—the Franciscans (1500), the Jesuits (1542), the Dominicans (1553) and the Augustinians (1579). The most legendry among them was, of course, Francis Xavier (1506–52) who, after his arrival in Goa in 1542, visited Cochin several times and converted around 10,000 fishermen. In 1557, Cochin was made a diocese when Goa was elevated as archdiocese.

The Portuguese General Alphonso Albuquerque conquered Goa in 1510 from the Bijapur Muslim kingdom, with the support of the Vijayanagar Hindu empire. The colonial expansion was motivated both by "pepper and soul" as well as to create a united Christian alliance to control the Muslims who monopolized spice trade in Asia.[21] Conversion work in Goa was slow and peaceful in the beginning. But already before the arrival of the Jesuits Goa was transformed into a Catholic town by the Franciscans. The diocese of Goa was erected in 1533 with John d' Albuquerque, a Franciscan, as the first bishop. Already in 1572 Pope Gregory XIII acknowledged the archbishop of Goa as the Primate of the East. It became the hub of the Roman Catholic Mission in Asia as well as the largest diocese in the world, covering the vast territory from the Cape of Good Hope in South Africa to Macau in China and Funay in Japan. Goa was given the honorific title the "Rome of the East" due to the central role it played in the evangelization of the East. By 1886 the archbishop was elevated as the Patriarch of East Indies. After nearly Century, the title was relegated to Patriarch 'ad honorem' of the East Indies.[22]

Aggressive missionary methods were employed only after the arrival of Francis Xavier, the Apostle of the Indies, in 1542. Two missionary principles directed his apostolate. One, *"extra ecclesiam nulla salus"* was the unquestioned creed of the missionary who believed that the pagans would be damned in hell fire and it was the Christian duty to convert them and save them. Two, according to the *Padroado* agreement between the Pope and the King of Portugal in 1454 it was the duty of the king to actively promote the conversion of the enemies of Christ. Dom Joao III ordered the destructions of temples and to speed up the conversion process. For "God ordered and wished to continue to constitute Portugal as kingdom

---

21. Panikkar, *Asia and Western*, 30–31.
22. Kanjirakat, ed., *Catholic Directory*, 555–56.

Seven Images of Churches in India

for a great mystery of his service and for the exultation of the Holy Faith."[23] The Protestant Reformation in northern Europe and counter-Reformation headed by the Jesuits in southern Europe was the aggressive backdrop of the colonial mission. K. M. Panikkar accuses the Portuguese conquest 'the eight crusade.' In 1555 the Viceroy, to implement the mission command of the king, entrusted Salsette to the Jesuits and Bardez to the Franciscans. Ilhas was divided between the Dominicans and the Jesuits for missionary expansion. Many indirect methods were employed to attract converts. The Portuguese set up jobs and offices for converts and denying them to pagans. These privileges lasted for 400 years until the liberation of Goa in December 1961. Hindu religious practices were forbidden in the Portuguese territory. Laws were enacted to expel Hindus and Muslims from the conquered areas. By the order of 8th July 1644 converts were forced to wear western dress, and eat non-vegetarian food. They had to give up their original names and take up Portuguese names. In 1864 the Governor of Goa took the initiative to eradicate the local languages Marathi and Konkani and replaced them by Portuguese language and culture. Christianization thus was equivalent to Portugusization. Inquisition was another fearful method of conversion. Francis Xavier in 1545, three years after his arrival in Goa, wrote to the King of Portuguese Joao III to introduce the holy office in Goa to punish Jews, Muslims, Hindus and lax living Portuguese Catholics.[24] The number of those who suffered the brunt of inquisition is not exactly available since the Portuguese themselves destroyed many of relevant documents.

It would be a grave mistake to imagine that the Hindus passively accepted the conversion process. At every stage they vehemently resisted it and that was the reason why conversions were slow till 1550. When coercive methods were introduced, five Jesuits, including Joseph Acquaviva who had just returned from Emperor Akbar's Court, were murdered in "Cumcolim Revolt" in Salcctte on 25 July 1583.[25] In the course of the following century forty more revolts were made against Christian conversions.[26] On forced conversions Antonio Noronha, a former Judge of the High Court of Goa, wrote : "It is known how such rapid and extensive conversions took place: some by fear of physical force: others by moral cowardice, ... not a few to avoid the loss of their properties and interests;

23. Quoted by Subramanyam, *Exploration*, 132.
24. Priolkar, *Goa Inquisition*, 23–25; 92–113.
25. Xavier, *Goa*, 157.
26. Saksena, *Goa into the Mainstream*, 26.

The Future of Christian Mission in India

some with their eyes on lucrative jobs and almost none by conviction."[27] By 1779 out of a total population of 2,04,988, 90 percent were converted to the Catholic church. According to 1851 census out of a total population of 3,63,788, the Christians constituted 2,32,189 or nearly 64 percent. After a century it declined to 42 percent in 1951. The 2001 census records that the Christians constitute mere 3,59,568, nearly 27 percent, out of a total population of 1,343,998. And the Hindus Constitute 66 percent.

On the positive side, an English Jesuit Thomas Stephen (1549–1619), arrived in Goa in 1579 and settled down in Salsette, near Bombay, with 5000 converts. Having learnt the local languages, Marathi and Konkani and the popular vernacular style of Purana literature, he composed *Christapurana*, the story of Christ in Marathi and was printed in the Roman script in Goa in 1616. His literary style was inspired by the epic of Sant Dnyaneshwar (1275) and other Marathi poets. It was the story of the whole Bible, consisting of 10,962 poetic verses. It greatly appealed to Hindu converts who were accustomed to listening to the chants of Hindu Puranas. In 1956 the first Hindi edition was printed and in 2008 Nelson Falcao SDB edited and translated *Christapurana* in Marathi.[28] This was an historic step towards inculturation which the Portuguese authorities failed to appreciate. With nearly 450 years of Portuguese cultural influence, the Goan Church has a very distinct image and identity. A large number of Cardinals, Bishops, Priests and Religious hail from this tiny state, including the Missionary Society of St. Francis Xavier, popularly known as the Pilar Fathers, founded in 1878. Blessed Joseph Vaz from Goa (1651–1711) was a zealous missionary in Sri Lanka (1687–1711) and is therefore acclaimed the 'Apostle of Ceylon.'

The Parava fisher folk, on the 200 mile long Coromandal coast or Choramandalam in Tamil, whose main source of sustenance was pearl fishing, were ruthlessly exploited, including their women, by the Arabs who controlled the trade and paid revenue to the Pandyan rulers. It was this crisis situation that nearly forced them to accept Portuguese military protection on the condition of accepting Christianity *en masse*, around 10,000, without any catechesis, in 1536. Francis Xavier (1506–52), a few months after his arrival in Goa in May 1542, proceeded to the Coromandal

---

27. Quoted by Priolkar, *Goa Inquisition*, 55.

28. Correa, *Missionary Heralds*, 66–75.

The Jesuit missionaries were the first to introduce printing press in Goa (1556), Cochin (1577), and Quilon (1578). "A Tamil Catechism" (Lisbon, 1550) is the first known printed book in Tamil using the Roman Script. "Christiya Matatatwam" by Francis Xavier was printed in Tamil script in Cochin in 1557.

Seven Images of Churches in India

coast, accompanied by a few Tamil seminarians in Goa, to deepen the faith of the new converts. With the help of the Seminarians he prepared a Tamil catechism, "Christiya Matatatwam," containing the Our Father, the Ten Commandments, the Creed, Hail Mary, and a few other prayers which the people could easily learn by heart. In September he traveled to the west coast where he was reported to have baptized around 10,000 fisher folk in a month in Cochin and Quilon, ancient Syrian Christian centres. Francis Xavier's mission theology, a reflexion of the theology of the middle ages, is contained in his prayer for conversion of pagans: "Behold, Lord, to your dishonor, hell is being filled with them."[29] Further his method, "first baptize and evangelize later" would become the prominent missionary method in the following centuries in India. By April 1545 his missionary spirit drove him to Malacca and other missions in the far east.

The decline of the Portuguese power in India also marked the decline of their mission in the following centuries. The Calvinist Dutch captured Cranganmore, the centre of the Syrian Christians from the Catholic Portuguese in 1661 and Cochin, the centre of Latin Catholics in 1663, and destroyed all the Padroado Catholic institutions. The Duch conquest would extend to other Portuguese trading centers. Thus the Portuguese colonial rule was forced to withdraw into the small territory of Goa. During the past centuries, following the example of the illustrious missionary, Francis Xavier, numerous missionaries from Goa went out to different parts of the world. If Goa was the epicenter of missionary activities in the Padroado period today it has emerged as the epicenter of tourism in India.

In 1534 Bassein, near Bombay, was taken over by the Portuguese. Like in Goa the Franciscans, were the first missionaries here too. The most famous missionary of Bassein was Antonio do Porto, a Franciscan Friar who arrived in 1547. From Mount Poinsur in Salsette with 400 Catholics, the Franciscans branched of to the neighboring areas attracting more converts. Gonsalo Gracia (1557–97), a Franciscan missionary from Bassein, martyred in Nagasaki, Japan in 1597, is the patron of the Vasai diocese created in 1998. In 1534 King Bahadur Shah, Sultan of Gujarat, ceded Salsette, bounded by Thane, Kurla, Bandra and Bhyander to the Portuguese, an exchange for military protection against the Moghal emperor Humayun in Delhi. In 1538 Bandra, Kurla and Mazagoan were gifted to Antonio Pesso by the Portuguese Viceroy for his military services. In 1570 the area was donated to the Jesuits, honoring an early request of Francis Xavier for land to build churches, and the Jesuits continued to possess it in the following

---

29. Saldana, *Patterns*, 65, 121.

one century. Brother Manuel Gomes who arrived in 1573 is honored as the Apostle of Salsette because he was mainly responsible for the conversion of thirteen villages by the feast of Assumption in 1579. By 1600 the whole of Bandra, numbering around 6000 inhabitants, were converted. Most of them belonged to the lower strata of the society like fishermen, toddy tappers, farmers, salt pan workers, potters, and poultry keepers. The missionary methods in Bassein, Salsette, Bandra and other neighboring regions were not much different from that of Goa. As per Padroado agreement it was the duty of the King of Portugal to propagate the mission, pay for the maintenance of missionaries, together with the right to nominate bishops. By 1720 the total catholic population of Bassein, Salsette, Bandra, Bombay, Kalyan, and Thane was around 64,440.

In 1665 the Island of Bombay was handed over by the Portuguese, not without serious objection from the Jesuits, to England as it had been included five years earlier in the dowry of Catherine of Braganza on her marriage to Charles II of England. The decline of the catholic mission in Bombay and the neighboring territories was aggravated by the Maratha attacks starting in 1731 and the scandalous fight between the Padroado missionaries under the Archdiocese of Goa and the Propaganda missionaries under the Vicar Apostolic of the Great Mughal. To settle the bitter controversies Athanasius Hartmann, Vicar Apostolic of Patna, was sent as the administrator of Bombay in 1850. He paved the way for the Concordat of 1857 between the Holy Sea and the Portuguese king, defining their jurisdictions. And the concordat of 1953 was the end of two centuries of "double jurisdiction." The Propaganda Fide entrusted the area to the Capuchin and the Carmelite missionaries to heal the wounds of the conflicts and divisions. During nearly a decade of administration Hartmann envisaged a long time solution to the problems by educating the confused Catholics. He was instrumental in inviting the Jesuits in 1853 for the education of boys and the Sisters of Jesus and Mary for the education of girls.

After passing the Charter Act of 1813, permitting the entry of missionaries to the territory of East India company, the rush of the Protestant mission societies to Maharashtra included the Church of Scotland, Society for the Propagation of the Gospel, Church missionary Society, the Methodist Mission, The American Presbyterian Mission, Alliance Mission, Salvation Army and others. Direct preaching of the Gospel on streets, distribution of Christian literature, opening schools, vocational training institutions and hospitals were part of their services. A large number of outcaste Mahars and Mangs in Ahmednagar districts ac-

Seven Images of Churches in India

cepted the Christian faith. The American Presbyterian Mission opened a Model Mission hospital in Miraj. Likewise Nasik, Nagpur, Aurangabad, Solapur, Sangli, Kolapur, Satara and Poona became centers of Protestant Mission enterprises. The ruler of Kolhapur abolished caste practices in his state under the Christian influence. The American Marathi Mission founded the first college in Ahmednagar in 1947. Two American missionaries, Gordan Hall and Samuel Nott arrived in Bombay in 1812 under the auspices of American Board of Commissioners of Foreign Missions. Belonging to the American Marathi Mission they entered Ahmednagar district, in Maharashtra, in 1815. With the strategy of mission to interior villages Ahmednagar became the main centre of Protestant mission among the depressed castes. The Gospel of Mark in 1816 and the whole New Testament in 1826 were translated into Marathi by Gordan Hall. The Catholic mission is Ahmednagar was launched by Bishop Maurin of Bombay in 1878, six decades after the arrival of the Protestant missionaries. The area was entrusted to the German Jesuits. By 1950 the Christian population in the district grew to 76,000.[30]

Baptism of a few outcaste Vankars by the German Jesuits in 1890 marked the beginning of the Catholic mission in Gujarat. In 1899, during the severe famine, the missionaries undertook relief work in nearly a thousand villages, and many beneficiaries of the relief work embraced Catholicism. The German missionaries had to withdraw from the scene at the beginning of the First World War after which the territory was entrusted to the Spanish Jesuits in 1921. In 1934, there were, 8,884 Catholics. Owing to mass conversions, the number of Catholics grew to nearly 26,970 during the next fifteen years. The post-independence era witnessed a decline in the number of new converts. However, in 1960, the Jesuits began their work among the Tribals in South Gujarat and their work has been successful to some extent. From 1998 the persecution of Christians by the Vishva Hindu Parishad, Bajrang Dal and other Hindu fundamentalist groups have accelerated particularly in Dang district with 10 percent tribal Christians.[31] The Christians constitute only 1 percent of Gujarat's fifty one million population.

Emperor Akbar had permitted the Portuguese to establish a trade centre in Hooghly, Calcutta. The Jesuits built a church here in 1600. However the main missionary work in Bengal and Orissa was carried out by the Augustinians. The Dominicans too were actively involved in the mission.

30. Aguiar, *Making*, 20–38.
31. Mattam, "Catholic Church," 156–75.

The Future of Christian Mission in India

Within half a century the number of Catholics in the region increased to nearby 7600. With the arrival of the Dutch and the British in Bengal in the second half of the eighteenth century, the Portuguese power declined and the small Catholic community in the region lost their Portuguese patronage. The Bengal *Catholic Expositor* was launched in 1839 and after many changes it became today's *The Herald*. [32] The publication of *Light of the East* by the Jesuits on Christ and Vedanta contributed towards creating an atmosphere of Hindu—Christian Dialogue.

The majority of Christians in Karnataka are migrants. The Mangalorean Catholics are descendents of Catholic migrants from Goa in three major waves—in 1560 to escape inquisition, in 1570 and 1683 to escape the political upheaval created by Muslim invasions from Bijapur. One Hundred years later Tippu Sultan's persecution between 1784–99 and their captivity to Srirangapatnam led their dispersions, conversion to Islam, confiscation of land, which they could recover only partially after Tippu's death in 1799. Persecution also created a strong religious identity and conservative mentality among these Catholics. The dalit converts created in South Canara and North Malabar by the Italian Jesuits in the twentieth century could not be fully integrated into the local Church due to caste discrimination.[33] The latest data shows that nearly two million Catholics in Goa, Bombay, Vasai, Mangalore, Pune, and a few other cities trace their genesis to the Padroado mission. They constitute around 8 percent of the Catholics of India and can be considered the second Church, chronologically, of course.

The Protestant missionaries entered Karnataka in the beginning of the nineteenth century. The London Missionary Society arrived in Bellary in 1810, followed by the Wesleyan Methodist Mission in Bangalore and other areas, starting in 1821. The Basel Evangelical Mission arrived in Mangalore in 1834. These missionaries failed to make any significant number of converts: their major contribution was limited to the field of education and publication of a few dictionaries and grammer books. Most of the literary contributions to Kannada was made by the Protestant missionaries in the nineteenth century. John Hans of London Missionary Society was the first to translate the whole Bible into Kannada during 1810–1815. Rev. Williams Leev authored the *Kannada-English-Kannada Dictionary*. Rev. Thomas Hudson prepared An Elementary *Grammar of Kannada* in 1848. A pioneer journalist Hermann Moegling was the publisher of the

---

32. Pattery, "Catholic Mission," 261–72.
33. D'Souza, "Catholic Church," 96–114.

Seven Images of Churches in India

vernacular news paper *Kannada Samachara* in 1844.[34] Charbounnaux, E. L. the Vicar Apostolic of Mysore (1845-73) compiled a *Latin—Kannada Dictionary* in 1861 to help the foreign missionaries.

The first organized Protestant mission to India begins with arrival of two German Lutheran Missionaries in Tranquebar in 1706, at the persuasion of the Danish King, a student of Halle, Germany. As per the treaty between the Danish king Christian Frederick IV and Reghunath Nayak, king of Tanjavur, in 1720, Tranquebar, an area of fifteen square miles, was leased to the Danish East India Company till 1845. Bartholomew Zeigenbalg (1683-1719) and Henry Plutschau (1677-1746), students of the school of Pietism in Halle, were the new missionaries sent by the king. In their missionary approach the new missionaries were directed by three principles. One, the Bible should be translated into the vernacular; two, people should be educated in order to read the Bible, God's saving Word; three, for the successful preaching missionaries should also learn the mentality of the people. Ziegenbalg learnt Tamil language and wrote a Tamil Grammar, *Gramatica Damulica* in 1716. He translated the New Testament into Tamil, the first vernacular translation in India, and was printed in 1713. A translation of the whole Bible, a first in any Indian language, by another German missionary Philip Fabricus, had to wait till the end of the century in 1796. Bartholomew baptized nearly 400 outcastes and built a church before his death in 1719. The fruit of his hard labor was very unsatisfactory. In his disappointment before his death he wrote: "Since I know that my work often does not attain the looked for goal, at times such great sorrow and sadness overtake me that I cannot comfort my self and I experience many sleepless nights. Much patience is required in order to labor tirelessly for souls and not to be frightened away when work seems useless."[35] The Lutheran thrust to promote indigenous ministers is proved from the fact that in 1733 a prominent Sudra convert Aaron, in spite of objections from some quarters, received Lutheran ordination. Publication of Ziegenbalg's book *The Genealogy of the Malabar Gods* (1869) unfortunately saw the light of the day 150 years after his death due to serious objections of his teacher August Hermann Francke (1663-1727), at the university of Halle, who wrote to his student: "The missionaries were sent to exterminate heathenism in India, not to spread heathen non—sense all over Europe."[36] Such an attitude of the Lutheran Evangelical Missionaries

34. Anchukandam, "Christian Contribution," 116-21.
35. Smith, *The Serampore*, 293.
36. R. Boyd, *Introduction*, 88.

exemplified the prevalent missiology of the era and the pessimistic view of non—Christian religions.

The British East India Company had founded its trading centres in Surat, Gujrat, in 1609, Fort St. George, Madras in 1644, Bombay in 1655 and Fort William, Calcutta in 1696. By 1647 the company had twenty seven Indian posts. And the Anglican clergy came to India as chaplains to the company's employs and troops. As more Lutheran missionaries arrived and desired to expand their activities beyond the small territory of Tranquebar the Danish king refused to fund the projects. The Society for Promoting Christian Knowledge, the first Anglican Missionary Society founded in 1799 and the Society for the Propagation of the Gospel founded in 1701, took the responsibility for the new missionaries to serve in the British settlements as chaplains. The Anglican church was unable to provide enough chaplains to India since its priority was the pastoral care of huge migrants to the USA and the Lutheran pastors were ready to serve under the Anglican church in spite of a few doctrinal as well as liturgical differences. This was the beginning of the English Mission in collaboration with the German Lutheran Missionaries. Christian Friedrich Schwartz (1724-98), after serving twelve years in Tranquebar, served in Trichinopally (1762-78) as chaplain to the Company's soldiers. In the following twenty years he worked in Tanjavoor (Tanjore) mission. In 1788 he served as the Diwan or Prime Minister of the Tanjore king. He built a church and school in Ramnad. Between 1785 and 1805 Schwartz and the Tanjore missionaries with the dynamic support of catechist Vedamanikam, a shanar convert, inaugurated a mass movement by baptizing around 6,000 Shanars in Cape Comorin, which was part of the larger Tinnevelly or Tirunelveli mission. In 1800 the number of Lutherans in Tranquebar—Tanjore mission was around 20,000. His forty eight years of services in various capacities in South India, starting in 1750, made him "the most famous of all the missionaries who have worked in South India."[37] When Chaplain James Hough arrived in Palamkotta, Tamil Nadu, in 1816 he realized how the church in Tirunelveli was neglected after the mass conversion. He contacted Charles T. E. Rhenius, a German missionary in Madras under CMS, for assistance. Having arrived in 1820 his remarkable organizational skill injected a new life into the Christians of Tirunelveli. He organized the Christian villages around the church and school. The teachers in the school also functioned as catechists and local leaders, a pattern which will be imitated in Chotanagpur mission later. A serious

---

37. Frykenberg, "Raja-Guru," 483.

Seven Images of Churches in India

controversy erupted between the Lutheran missionaries and CMS regarding the ordination of experienced catechists. However, providentially, a schism was avoided by the death of Rhenius in 1838. Rhenius is revered as the second founder of Tirunelveli mission after Schwartz.[38] The eighteenth century Protestant mission in Tamil Nadu was dominated by the German Lutheran missionaries.

The Adivasi-Tribal Image: The Third Church

The Tribal church consisting mostly of the Adivasis of Chotanagpur and the tribal churches in the seven states in the N.E. Frontier India, constitutes the third church. Until recent decades the Adivasis, the original settlers of the land, lived isolated from the main stream of the Indian Society. The tribal population constitute nearly 9 percent of India's population, and 86 percent of them occupy the central mountainous belt of India. 641 tribal communities are identified by the Anthropological Survey of India.[39] Traditionally they were victims of exploitation by Muslims, Hindu rulers, landlords and others. There were eighty five tribal rebellions during a period of 150 years. When their rebellions did not achieve the expected results they turned to gods with religious revival like the Kabirpanthi Bhagat Movement in the second half of the nineteenth century, the Birsa Movement in 1895 and the Thana Bhagat Movement in 1914. The missionaries entered the scene in a situation of crisis and confusion when the Adivasis were looking for someone who would save them.

At the arrival of the Lutheran Evangelical Missionaries, founded in Berlin in 1836 by John Baptist Gossner, the British authorities in Calcutta advised them to work among the Adivasis of Chotanagpur. Having reached in Ranchi in 1845 they studied the sad plight of poor tribals who were being exploited for few centuries by the Hindu landlords and local rulers. After five years of preaching, village visits and legal aid to them four Oraons who used to visit Ranchi for court cases were baptized. Eventually the Adivasi response to the Lutheran missionaries was remarkable because they guided the people how to fight court cases against the oppressors. By 1880 the Lutheran harvest amounted to above 30,000.

Oobserving the success of the Lutheran missionaries, the Belgian Jesuit missionaries from Calcutta penetrated into the deep jungles of the Chotanagpur Plateau in 1885 and began their work where the number of Catholics was below one hundred. Because of their social involve-

38. Gibbs, "Anglican and Protestant," 231–32.
39. Xaxa, "Tribal Scene," 70–71.

19

ment, with the help of good lawyers, particularly in the protection of the Adivasis and their land from exploitation by the landlords and rajas, a mass conversion movement began under the leadership of Constant Leivens, S.J. Within a period of seven years about 73,000 tribals, mostly Oraons, Mundas and Kharias, accepted the new faith as an expression of gratitude to their new saviours. By 1931 the mass conversion movement created 391,000 Christians. Thousands of Santhals on the Bihar-Bengal border and Khonds in Orissa were converted by the Danish and American Baptist Missionaries. By 1930 the evangelization of the Santhal Parganas received a boost with the arrival of the Jesuits from Malta and Sicily. All these tribes are related to the Austro-Asiatic race and the Munda linguistic family, with the exception the Oraons who belongs to the Dravidian family.[40] The Norwegian L. O. Skrefsrud who arrived in the Santal Parganas in 1863 powerfully argued for the indigenization of the Santal Church. His publications included *The Grammar of the Santal Language* in 1873 and the translation of the New Testament in Santali in 1880.

The eight million tribals of North East India constitute 11 percent of India's tribal population and ethnically share close affinity with the Mongoloid race. The tribals in the North-East feel that their culture has nothing in common with the Hindu culture. They had been exploited by the Muslim rulers for a long time. Their life style was wild and violent, including practices like head hunting among the Naga tribe. They also periodically rebelled against the British occupation since 1833. The arrival of the Christian missionaries opened a new chapter in their life. Conversion to Christianity was significantly high with Welsh Presbyterian in the Khasi hills from 1842 and the English Baptist in Lushai hills and the American Baptist who went to the rescue of the Singhpho and the Naga tribe. Since the Protestant missionaries arrived first in the North-East, the British administrators who were aware of their traditional rivalries restricted the entry of the Catholic missionaries. However with the arrival of the Salesians of Don Bosco in 1922 the number of the Catholics in the N.E. rose from 5,000 to 55,000 in 1939. The Garos and the Khasi-Panars who constitute the bulk of the Catholic community in the N.E. follow the matriarchal and matrilineal system. A large number of Munda, Kharia and Oraon Catholics migrated from Chotanagpur to Assam as tea garden laborers with highest concentration in Dibrugarh diocese. There was a similar migration to the Andaman and Nicobar islands.

---

40. Kanjamala, *Religion and Modernization*, 56–91.

Seven Images of Churches in India

The Bhils, the second largest tribe in India, around five million, inhabit mainly South Rajasthan, Eastern Gujarat and Western Madhya Pradesh. The Church Missionary Society arrived in North Gujarat in 1880 while the Irish and American Missionaries reached South Gujarat in 1892. Unlike Chotanagpur and the North—East, there was no group conversion among the Bhils, probably because of their Hinduization and economic dependency on Hindus. At present nearly 20,000 tribal Christians here belong to twenty denominations, with highest concentration in Dang district of Gujarat where the Evangelical missionaries are actively engaged in direct evangelization. In the post-Vatican period the conversion motive is being mostly replaced by liberation theology except for the Pentecostal sects.

The Dalit Church Image: The Fourth Church

Nearly 16 percent of the Indian populations are Dalits. Known by different pejorative appellations like the untouchables, outcastes, the panchamas, the depressed caste, Harijan or Dalits, these people were the traditional slaves of the Indian Society. Since they performed all types of menial works for the society even their sights and shadows were believed to be polluting and impure. Ninety percent of them were landless laborers working for upper caste landlords under Hindu *jajmani*, patron—client system. The so-called holy cows and many other animals were given better treatment than to the untouchables by the caste Hindus. In the contemporary social discourse most of them prefer to call themselves *Dalits*, meaning, broken people. A mass movement of the Chura or sweeper caste and Chamar or leather workers in undivided Punjab from 1870-1920 created a large Christian community. In Andhra Pradesh in the south, the American Baptist missionaries, under the leadership of J. E. Clough, (1836–1910) came to the rescue of the Madiga caste or leather workers. In the eyes of the Brahmins who are strictly vegetarian, anyone engaged in leather work is considered impure and untouchable. Within five years more than 20,000 people were gradually accepted in the Christian faith and baptized. This was followed by a large number of conversion from the Mala or weaver caste into the Lutheran church. The mass movement resulted in more than one million Dalit converts by World War I. The Pulayas in Kerala, Mahars and Mangs in Maharashtra, Balahis in Madhya Pradesh, Dheds in Gujarat and the Chamars in Uttar Pradesh and Bihar embraced Christianity in the twentieth century in spite of organized opposition from the high castes who were losing their tight grip over the new converts.[41] However, in North India Dalit conversions, except in Punjab, did not have the characteristics of mass movement as in South India. In the middle of the nineteenth century the Lutheran and Anglican missionary efforts were directed to the Nadar community, toddy tappers from palmira trees, mainly in the districts of Tirunelveli in Tamil Nadu and Kanyakumari in Travencore. Converts also came from the Sambabar community in the same area.

Patriarchal and Institutional Image of the Church

With the emerging spread of the democratic spirit power sharing is becoming a sensitive issue in modern discourses. In the past, the vast majority of human societies, including India, were patriarchal and patrilineal with minor exceptions of matriarchy, like the Nairs of Kerala and the Khasis of Mehalaya. Power and wealth of the society were vested in the male members, particularly the head of the family or clan. In all religions the authors of Sacred Scriptures were men who legitimized patriarchy as natural. Women exercised little power in politics; they had no property rights; they enjoyed little space in religious fields. Most of their time was spent in the domestic sphere, i.e., in kitchen; and child bearing and rearing. They were second class citizens in the secular and ecclesiastical world. The church, after becoming the official religion of the Roman Empire in the fourth century, was organized according to the genius of the Roman social structures and laws. Thus the Roman Catholic Church evolved into a patriarchal and hierarchical organization. The pattern of the Jewish patriarchal society was conveniently adopted by the early Church, deviating from the vision and practices of Jesus. Priestly power was vested in the male and theological justifications were produced by the male theologians. Spirituality, that too was predominantly monastic in character, was practised and taught with male perceptions and orientations. The priestly, prophetic and kingly power of Jesus follow the male line, starting from the Pope, Bishops and priests. And the Western church was faithfully transplanted into India during the colonial era. However, in recent times a gradual development of feminist consciousness is emerging in a few educated catholic women. They are painfully aware of the need to struggle for justice, equality, freedom and human dignity of women in the Church. "Feminism struggles not against men but against the Kyriarchical structure of domination that affect both women and men."[42] Patriarchy in

41. Webster, *Dalit Christians*, 39–46.
42. Schüssler-Fiorenza, "Women, Mission," 150.

Seven Images of Churches in India

the Indian church is a natural reflection of the highly patriarchal ethos of India. For instance in the Indian Parliament today elected women constitute only 11 percent of the total members. In his encyclical letter, "The Dignity of Women," on 15th August 1998 Pope John Paul II pointed out that the present trend of growing feminism is a reaction to the lack of respect accorded to women.

After the mass conversion movement for nearly one and half Century, the institutionalization process is one of the major trends in the Churches. A certain amount of institutionalization is imperative for the preservation and propagation of the vision of the charismatic founder or leader. As a consequence a large number of ecclesiastical personnel are being absorbed into institutions. For instance, during the last six decades Catholic dioceses have grown from 56 in 1950 to 160 in 2004. In 2001 the numbers of educational institutions are as follows: Kindergarten schools 7,218 with 8,25,339 children; Primary schools 9779 with 30,19,094 students. Secondary schools 4,729 with 2,845,889 students; Christian colleges 271, including 161 Catholic Colleges, with 3,53,683 students. Dispensaries have increased twelve fold, recording 2,429 in 2001; hospitals have also increased eleven fold, numbering 737 in 2001; leprosaria 248; home for the aged 865; orphanages 2,112; centers for social education 4,969. There are a total of 14,672 institutions related to health ministry.[43] The institutionalization process which will be on the increase like bureaucratization in the wider society, is accompanied by two major challenges, among others. One, constant power struggles and conflicts to occupy prestigious offices in these institutions of power, money and status. The images of contemporary church administrators, like Chief Executive Officers, are replacing the traditional image of the missionary as a spiritual leader.[44] Decline in the quality of services is simultaneously reported. Secondly, mission *Ad Gentes* is on the decline, coinciding with the rational-liberal missiology of the post-Vatican II period. Late Varkey Cardinal Vithayathil, the CBCI president and head of the Syro-Malabar church, in his pastoral letter in December 2009 wrote: "In recent years there has been a decline in the exhalted position and recognition that priests use to receive traditionally in the church and the society." And he admonished them "to lead a spiritual and ascetic way of life" to face the challenges of the world.

---

43. Fernando and Gispert-Sauch, *Christianity in India*, 234–36.
44. Jones, *Jesus: CEO*, xiii–xv.

The Future of Christian Mission in India

The Servant and Compassionate Image

Avery Dulles, in *Models of the Church* portrays five dominant models of the church in the course of history: the Community, Institution, Sacrament, Herald, and Servant. The most inspiring image of Jesus in the Gospel is that of washing the feet of the disciples and then instructing: "You ought to wash one another's feet" (John 13:13-14). Saint Paul, employing the "Servant Songs" of Deutro—Isaiah, explains how Jesus assumed the form of a slave (Phil 2:6-9). Along with the powerful institutional image, the Servant image is very visible and much appreciated in India. The compassionate face of Blessed Mother Teresa represents the most known and loved image of missionaries. No Christian in India received as much media coverage and expression of deep appreciation, including Bharat Ratna, the highest civil award by the Indian Government, as Blessed Mother Teresa did during the last three decades of the second Millennium. The services of Missionaries of Charity and thousands of other missionaries since the nineteenth century, particularly nuns, serving the destitute and the poor in non-institutional set up portray the compassionate and selfless services of the Church in the country.

Most significantly, the Christians who constitute less than 3 percent of the total population run about 25 percent of the country's service centers. According to the CBCI Report 25 percent of the homes for orphans and widows and 30 percent of all the institutes of mentally and physically handicapped, leprosy patients and victims of AIDS are taken care of by the Christian community.[45] It is important to record that majority of the beneficiaries of these services are non-Christians, irrespective of caste, creed and class. Appreciating the selfless and humanitarian services of the Christian missionaries, particularly to scheduled caste and scheduled tribes, late Prime Minister of India, Pandit Jawaharlal Nehru observed: "The Christian Missionaries went to various tribal areas and some of them spent practically all their lives there. I do not find many instances of the people from the plains going to the tribal areas to settle down. Missionaries did a very good work and I am full of praise."[46] However there are fresh signs of hope. The number of Non Governmental Organizations serving the tribals and other marginalized communities have multiplied in the past two decades. On the demise of Blessed Mother Teresa on 5th September

---

45. Lobo, *Globalization*, 16.
46. Nehru, "The Tribal Folk," 4.

Seven Images of Churches in India

1997 I. K. Gujral, then Prime Minister of India observed: "A beacon of light and hope of millions of poor has gone out of our lives."[47]

On the arrival of this author at the entrance of the towering Lord Jaganath temple in Puri, Orissa, one of the four ancient as well as most holy centre of Hinduism, in the beginning of 1972, the warning at the entrance read: "Christians and dogs are not allowed." In 1975, Marian Zelazech SVD, a Polish survivor of Nazi concentration camp of Dachau, with prior missionary experience in Orissa, arrived here to initiate a new program. When he began to work with lepers in the outskirts of the town, its inhabitants were shocked. And the colony naturally expanded with more lepers; a mercy kitchen; and later a school for the children of lepers. Even some temple attendants—there are above 3000 of them like the Levites in Jerusalem temple—came for medical help at night to escape public eyes. After a decade, during the Christmas season, the main priest of the temple honored Fr. Marian with a gold cross and expressed deep appreciation for his inspiring service to outcast lepers. The traditional suspicion of missionaries gradually disappeared. The most important result was that he converted their hearts. His integral missionary method included the establishment of a Dialogue Centre, named Sotyo Sondhan Niketan and a Spirituality Centre, Ishopanti Ashram. A local Hindu poet Gangadhar Mishra, composed the following ode in honor of Fr. Marian when he expired on April 30, 2006.

> Immaculate and holy, Oh mother of mine
> Where are you running at day break?
> Is your Jagnath, not Universal?
> Does he dwell within the temple only?
> Does he not exist between the walls of the poor?
> Can he not be found in leper's colony?
> Where Father Marian,
> By the grace of Jesus Serve humanity,
> Stripped of all comfort?[48]

The Servant Church image is the best balancing act against the image of institutions of power. How much the institutional image tends to blur the prophetic image of the servant church differ from region to region. Yet it may not be an exaggeration to state that the Syrian churches in Kerala and the Padroado churches in Goa, Mangalore and major cities are highly institutionalized in contrast to the young churches.

---

47. Quoted by Moniz, *No Greater Service*, 2.
48. Quoted by Soreng, "India East Province," 239.

The Future of Christian Mission in India

A Persecuted Church Image

From St. Thomas the apostle in AD 72 through St. John de Britto in 1693 to the martyrs of Kandhmal in 2008 the Church in India has suffered persecutions periodically. But the recent wave of atrocities committed against Christians during the past one decade is unprecedented in Indian history. More than 50 percent of the violence committed against Christians in the post Independence period has taken place in the last one decade. Half of the recent persecutions occurred in Gujarat State alone, ruled by the Hindu Right wing party. The following shocking cases of atrocities and martyrdom has attracted the attention and reactions of the International community. The Australian Missionary Dr.Graham Staines, working with the lepers, and his two little sons were burnt alive in Orissa under the leadership of Dara Singh on January 23, 1998. The young priest, Arul Doss, working among the tribal people was allegedly murdered by the mob instigated by the same Dara Singh in Mayubanj district of Orissa in September 1999. Sr.Rani Maria, working for the welfare of the tribals, was stabbed to death by anti-missionary criminals in Udaynagar, Indore in February 1995. This was followed by the rape of nuns in Jhabua districts, M.P. In mid-January 2004 a few priests, sisters and lay people were badly manhandled by Hindu extremists in Jhabua district, Madhya Pradesh. "It is our government now, it is a government for the Hindus" shouted the attackers in Jhabua less than a month after the Hindu fundamentalist government had taken charge, under chief minister Miss Uma Bharati.[49] The latest incident is the murder of Sr.Valsa John belonging to the Sisters of Charity of Jesus and Mary, who was working and campaigning for the past twelve years against displacement and exploitation of Santal tribes in Pokur district of Jharkand state. She was brutally murdered at night on November 15, 2011 by a mob of thirty-forty people, allegedly instigated by mining corporate.[50] There have been many more incidents of martyrdom. Out of 193 atrocities committed against the Christians during 1997 to 2000, 44 percent were committed in Gujarat. Sixty percent of acts of violence like murder, intimidation, burning of prayer halls, Churches and burning of Bible took place in western India. South India suffered less than 20 percent of such atrocities.[51]

---

49. Kanjamala, "Democracy," 26.
50. *The New Leader*, December, 1–15, 2011.
51. Lobo, *Globalization*, 17, 22, 181–82.

Conclusion

By placing the accent on the regional missionary dynamics the author does not ignore the all-India dynamics of the Churches and their mission to the degree they participate in a common vision and mission for the realization of the Kingdom of God. Attention will be paid to the functioning of the Catholic Bishops' Conference of India and its Secretariats and the contributions of various commissions. Conference of Religious India is also committed to a common vision and collaboration with these Conferences. Ecumenical collaboration with the National Christian Council in India should have a high priority. Dialogues between the Catholic church, the Church of South India and the Church of North India is becoming more visible and effective. Missionary dynamics of the future will imply more interactions between different Christian churches and people of all religions and cultures. The seven images of the Christian communities portrayed above are neither exhaustive nor perfect. There is no perfect image, rather they are indicators. Each of them is identified by certain crucial distinguishing characteristics. Degrees of integration, i.e., relation of the part to the whole, conspicuously demarcates the boundaries of each community with its unique life style and patterns of behaviors. My attempt here intends to provide a more or less intelligible frame work, a map, or a broad picture for understanding the highly pluralistic as well as very complex Christian landscape of India.

2

Varieties of Hindu Responses to Evangelical Mission

WHAT ARE SOME OF the positive and creative responses of Hindus to the aggressive Evangelical proclamation of Jesus in the nineteenth century is the focus of this chapter. Hinduism with no historical founder, "may be described as an encyclopedia of religions rather than a religion . . . an amalgam of contradictory beliefs and practices held together in one by certain powerful ideas and a system of social regulations."[1] The Hymns of the Rig Veda, a collection of 1017 sacred songs and prayers, composed during 1500–900 BC; addressed to nature gods, was the origin of the Vedic religion. The social inequality and various sufferings were explained and legitimized by the theology of *Karma*, i.e., reward or punishment for conducts according to one's own caste duty, in the past lives, that predestine cycle of rebirths. Salvation from the endless chain of rebirths was the ultimate goal of life, rituals and right conduct. The Ultimate Reality is *Brahman*, the Supreme Soul. And the individual soul, *atman*, finds its true identity when it, after the cycle of rebirths, merges into the Ultimate Reality, like a river flowing into the sea and to become, *Aham Brahmasmi*, I am the Brahman. The philosophic speculations of India gave birth to the literature known as the Upanishads, around the sixth century BC. It emphasized that *Gnana*, knowledge, not ritual, is the best way to salvation. In the backdrop of dry and cold speculations of Advaita evolved the belief in incarnation and devotion, *Bhakti*, to a personal god as the best way to salvation as taught in the Bhagavad Gita of Lord Krishna. But Hinduism at its popular level, practiced by the illiterate masses, consisted of primitive animism, shamanism, totemism, magical practices and polytheism, with

---

1. Macnicol, *Living Religions*, 25.

Varieties of Hindu Responses to Evangelical Mission

thousands of gods and goddesses. Hinduism's elasticity, in contrast to the Semitic religions, is the secret of its survival without a central authority.[2]

In the battle of Plassey in June 1757 Robert Clive established the supremacy of Britain over the French. Charles Grant (1746–1823), a very powerful evangelical and civil servant in Calcutta for nearly forty years, unsuccessfully pleaded in the British Parliament in 1793 for the existing restrictions on the entry of missionaries into India to be abolished. Under the pressure of the Methodists, the Baptists and the Church of England Evangelicals, the entry of missionaries into India was finally legitimized in 1813.[3] These new missionaries arrived with the passionate question of salvation. The Evangelical and Pietistic missionaries were deeply anxious about the salvation of those who were not yet brought to the knowledge and experience of the Grace of Jesus Christ. They were deeply convinced in the literal meaning: "There is no other name under heaven given to the human race by which we are to be saved" (Acts 4:12). All the missionaries of that era further believed that humankind as a whole had fallen from grace. "There is no one just, not one" (Rom 3:10). "The upright one shall live by faith" (Rom 1:17).

Evangelism was a popular Protestant Movement, with multiform tributaries, which originated after the personal conversion of John Wesley (1703–1791) in 1738. Its distinctive features were: the intensification of the Christian life, associated with a deep sense of original sin and personal guilt; a call to conversion through personal repentance and moral transformation; a deep faith in the forgiveness of sin through the blood and atoning death of Jesus Christ on the cross; a commitment to social activism which springs from moral radicalism rooted in the sense of personal responsibility and accountability; preaching with an urgency to convert pagans. Ultimately a literal understanding of the Bible as the supreme authority in matters of faith and practices became the source of fundamentalism. Their world view was essentially pessimistic. In the backdrop of Lutheran pessimism of the world and the cold rationalism of enlightenment era German pietism was a breakthrough.[4] The Pietistic movement was also a statement that religion cannot be fully understood and expressed by reason alone.

Two major missionary forces in the beginning of the nineteenth century were: one, the German Lutheran Pietism promoted by Phillip

2. Radhakrishnan, *Hindu View*, 2–25.
3. Cairns, *Christianity*, 400–402.
4. Lewis, *Blackwell Dictionary*, xviii–xx.

Jacob Spencer (1635–1705) at Halle; His tract *"Affirming the Hope for Better Times"* introduced a radical missionary enthusiasm; two, John Wesley's Methodist movement in England, with an accent on personal conversion experience and an unprecedented sense of social responsibility. Methodism, the third religious awakening in England, after the sixteenth century Reformation and seventeenth century Puritanism, "was to Anglicanism what Pietism was to Lutheranism."[5] They expressed the joy of their personal conversion in the Holy Spirit by singing and praising God. The supreme goal of mission was the glory of God and other goals were secondary.[6] William Carey's, *An Enquiry into the Obligation of Christians to Use Means for Conversion of Heathens* in 1792 fired the imagination of the hyper-Calvinism. A voluntary organization, namely, "The Particular Baptist Society for Propagating the Gospel among the Heathen" was founded by him in Northampton in 1793. In the following decades because of Carey's influence numerous missionary societies came into existence in England and USA.[7]

Calcutta, the Epicenter of Hindu-Christian Encounter

The major modern Christian—Hindu encounter began after the arrival of the evangelical missionaries in Calcutta in the beginning of the eighteenth century. Attacks of the evangelicals on popular Hinduism forced them to search for Hinduism in its essence.

Arrival of the Baptist Missionaries

After founding the Baptist Missionary Society and enlisting the support of its members on June 13, 1793 William Carey (1761–1834) sailed to Calcutta, accompanied by his reluctant wife Dorothy and four children under nine, including a three week old baby, and two other companions. Many, including his father, considered him mad. They arrived in Hooghly and entered Sreeramapura or Serampore, the Danish colony, since he had no permission from the East India company to enter Calcutta.[8] Before his arrival two Moravian missionaries in Calcutta had already abandoned mission "because of total lack of response."[9] With the arrival of Joshua

---

5. Cairns, *Christianity*, 84–86.
6. Bosch, *Transforming Mission*, 257.
7. Kane, *Concise History*, 80–86.
8. Jeyaraj, *Bartholomaeus*, 200.
9. Balasundaram, "Carey William," 120.

Varieties of Hindu Responses to Evangelical Mission

Marshman (1768-1837), a school teacher in England, and William Ward (1764-1823), a printer by profession, in 1799, a new chapter in the Evangelical mission in India was opened. In the course of the mission history these would be known as the "Serampore Trio." "The Serampore Covenant" (1805), of the new mission, partly influenced by the Moravian missionaries, contained the Vision and Mission Statement of the Protestant missionary era in India.[10]

1. The human soul is of inestimable value and is in mortal danger of eternal punishment. But Christ can and will save.
2. We must gain all the knowledge we can of the Indian mind and of the Indian religions.
3. We must not offend Indian sensibilities by vaunting our English ways and attacking theirs.
4. We must "watch (for) all opportunities doing good" as in preaching, interacting and talking to all who will listen.
5. The great subject of our preaching must be "Christ the Crucified"
6. We must do everything necessary to win the confidence of the people
7. We must remember the importance of native leaders and building up Christian life of converts. We must value the work of female colleagues in their important work with women.
8. In all possible ways we must promote the development of Indian leadership on the formation of Indian churches led by Indian pastors.
9. We must labour with all our might in forwarding translations of the sacred scriptures in the language of Hindustan.
10. To be fit for these "unutterable important labors" we must be "instant in prayer and cultivation of personal religion."[11]

Because of its high idealism it failed. The Covenant was superseded by new agreements, under pressure of newly arrived young missionaries, and was dubbed, "Paper Constitution."[12] The Serampore missionar-

---

10. Smith, *Serampore*, 298.
11. Moffett, *History*, 2:257.
12. Smith, *Serampore*, 307.

ies divided their works into following categories: 1) Translation of the Scriptures; 2) printing and distributing Tracts and Portions of Scripture; 3) native schools to provide education at various levels; 4) direct proclamation of the Gospel; 5) acquainting oneself with indigenous cultures. The Bible was accorded maximum reverence and importance in the Protestant tradition, in contrast to the Catholic, because it was the only source of knowing God's inscrutable will and plan for man's salvation. Immediately after his arrival William Ward set up a printing press in 1799. By 1801, the first Bengali New Testament, translated by Carey, was printed. During the following three decades the New Testament was translated into eighteen languages; the whole Bible into six languages; and portions of the Bible in thirty four dialects.[13] Their missionary methods were also influenced by the Lutheran evangelical missionaries in Tamil Nadu nearly a century ago.[14] The assistance of local Hindus pundits were sought since the language proficiency of the missionaries was not up to the mark. In spite of their hard work and good will the qualities of translations were subject to severe criticism by the following generations. The Protestant mission, unlike the Catholic mission, was characterized by the Bible translations in all the mission territories. "Owing differing policies of the missionary work the Roman Catholics had played little part in this tremendous effort of translation, which was almost a Protestant achievement."[15] The first vernacular news paper in India, *Samachar Darpan* and English magazine *The Friends of India* were published by the missionaries. These exercised great influence on public life.

"The Baptist missionaries adopted two-pronged approaches to preaching: critical denunciation of indigenous religion and religious practices; and exhortation of the superior merits of Christ as the only Saviour from a sinful existence."[16] The Baptist criticism of ignorance's of Scriptures and domination of Brahmin priests was evidently continuation of their classic disparagement of Roman Catholic church. Many of the listeners also objected to public preaching, especially criticism of idol worship and ridiculing Brahmin priests who "are almost regarded as deities." They abused the missionaries and tore the tracts distributed into pieces and scattered them. Reacting to their claim of superiority people retorted: "God has created both Hindus and Museleman and had given them dif-

---

13. Moffett, *History*, 2:260.
14. Jeyaraj, *Bartholomaeus*, 290–93.
15. Neill, *History*, 254.
16. Mani, *Contentious Traditions*, 91–92.

Varieties of Hindu Responses to Evangelical Mission

ferent ways of life—All religions are the same."[17] Debating on miracles of Jesus some reacted. "Miraculous acts of Krishna far surpassed the miracles of Jesus."[18] Thus preaching and debating with the people was not only frustrating but also suffered periodic manhandling. Conversions of caste Hindus were almost nil. After fifteen years of labour Carey wrote: "The greatest burden was lack of conversions; want of success in my work. . . . often caused a great depression in mind."[19]

What is the use of printing the Bible if people are unable to read them? That the faithful should read the Scripture to learn the will of God, without depending on human agent, was one of the fundamental principles of Protestantism. The first English school and the first Bengali school, and first school for girls were founded, of course, with a small number of students, where girls were totally forbidden to be educated. The first "college for the instruction of Asiatic Christians and other youth in Eastern Literature and other Sciences" was opened by Carey in Serampore, in 1819 with nineteen Christian and eighteen non-Christian students for educating intellectual leaders. After ten years it was raised to the status of a University on the European model to confer Bachelor of Arts degree in Eastern literature and Western sciences and Bachelor of Divinity.[20] Assessing the greatness of William Carey Protestant Mission historian Anderson Kane wrote: "What Luther was to Protestantism, Carey was to the Christian missionary movement." In the beginning the twenty first century, with three and half a million members the Baptist mission comprises the single largest Protestant group in India.[21]

Dr. Alexander Duff : Pioneer of English Education.

Missionary of the Scottish Presbyterian Church to India, Alexander Duff (1806–78) arrived in Calcutta in 1830. The missionary strategy of the Presbyterians focused on discrediting the Orientalist School and promoting English medium schools and colleges with Western science and liberal thoughts of enlightenment. Their objective was to enlighten Indian youth with Western education and prepare them to accept Christianity as a better alternative to the unenlightened Hinduism. William Carey and his mission had already generated much interest among the youth

17. Ibid., 103, 105.
18. Sharma, *Sati*, 64.
19. Smith, *Serampore*, 289.
20. Ibid., 138.
21. Hedlund, "Baptist in India," 73–74.

for Western liberal education. Ram Mohan Roy too founded the Hindu College in 1817, eventually growing into Presidency University, partly to meet the need for modern education and to reform Hinduism and partly to counter conversion to Christianity. Duff soon opened an English medium school with five boys, and another English school for girls in 1834, with the help of Ram Mohan Roy and a few other liberal Hindus.[22] In 1831 Duff established the Christian College to challenge the intellectual and social inadequacies of Hinduism. According to his biographer, "The young Scot had vowed to kill Hinduism, and this he would do by striking at his brain."[23] He argued that the highest forms of education was Christian education, namely, a sound intellectual and scientific training, built on the moral and religious principle of Christ. And it was hoped that with scientific education Hindus would abandon superstitious Hinduism and spontaneously embrace Christianity. The number of students soon increased to 200. Duff's target was the youth, who were already influenced by Tom Paine's *Age of Reason* and rationalism of the eighteenth century. Everyday the morning school opened with the general assembly where the first act was to say the Lord's Prayer, followed by the Bible reading. In 1833 four high caste boys were baptized and later the number increased to thirty six. After listening to Alexander Duff's sermon, Krishna Mohan Banerji (1813–1885), a graduate and a teacher in the Hindu College was baptized in April 1832. He was Duff's first convert."[24]

As the 19th century debate between the Orientalists and the Anglicists were in progress Duff persuaded Governor General Lord William Bentinck that education in India should be in English rather than in Sanskrit or Arabic. With T. B. Macaulay's "Minute on Indian Education" (1835) English became the medium of education, without ignoring primary education in the mother tongue. The government policy demanded good knowledge of English for civil service employment, replacing the traditional Persian language. Duff is credited as the greatest of four early educationalists of the Scottish mission. With the establishment of the Scottish Church College in Calcutta Duff set a pattern for other mission colleges. From the very beginning of his mission in Calcutta Duff became a very controversial character by contravening the East India Company's policy of strict non-interference in Hinduism. Frontal attack on Hindu religious and social evils was his controversial method. Alexander Duff

22. Farquhar, *Modern Religious*, 20.
23. Smith, *Alexander Duff*, 49.
24. Ibid., 85–86.

spent thirty seven years in India, most of it in the field of education. He helped to change the face of the Christian education and is remembered as a pioneer of Christian higher education in India along with his contemporary Christian educators. He returned to his home country and was appointed to the first chair of the evangelical mission theology at New College, Edinburgh in 1867 at the age of sixty one. In the opinion of Eric Sharpe, a historian of phenomenology of religion: "In the 1830s and 1840s he had been the best known, best hated and best loved man in Calcutta . . . A country dominie of heroic proportions, Alexander Duff helped to change the educational face of India."[25]

Rediscovery of the Sanatana Dharma

The British Orientalists were the first scholars who endeavored to understand Hinduism for the sake of good administration. Later they were followed by many Hindus in order to defend their faith and identity.

Raja Ram Mohan Roy: The Father of Modern India

How did the Hindu society respond to Jesus Christ whom the missionaries preached as the only Saviour of the World is the most crucial question than their socio-educational activities. The first Indian exponent of Jesus and his mission was an affluent upper caste Bengali Brahmin, Ram Mohan Roy (1772–1833). He is acknowledged as the father of modern Indian renaissance. Influenced by Sufism his first book, *A Gift to Deists* (1804), written in Persian (Tuhfat-ul-Muvahiddin) with a preface in Arabic, was also a corrective to Hindu polytheism and idol worship. Marshman had already published a pamphlet in 1813, with the title, *Advantage of Christianity in Promoting the Establishment and Prosperity of the British Empire in India*. Roy's controversy with missionaries climaxed in the publication of, *The Precepts of Jesus, the Guide to Peace and Happiness, extracted from the Books of the New Testament ascribed to Four Evangelists* (1820), with translations into Bengali and Sanskrit. In nature and scope it was similar to *The Philosophy of Jesus*, compiled by Thomas Jefferson, a Deist, in 1804.[26] He was deeply influenced by the moral teaching of Jesus. "The consequence of long and uninterrupted researches into religious truth has been that I have found the doctrine of Christ more conducive to moral principles and more adapted for the use of rational beings than any other which have

---

25. Sharpe, "Duff Alexander," 328–29.
26. Guha, "Indigenous Christian," 80.

come to my knowledge."²⁷ For Roy the essence of the Gospel was Jesus' moral teaching. He rejected that Jesus was God; the doctrine of atonement for the sins of the world; the miracles are not true, but myths as in Hindu Scriptures where there are innumerable accounts of miraculous deeds of gods and goddesses. Holy Spirit is synonymous with the influence of God.²⁸ The passionate debates between the Baptist missionaries and Roy were inconclusive. The pattern of response of Roy would be repeated by Hindu intellectuals in the following centuries of missionary debates. "He was the first Indian to raise serious theological objections and in the process proposed his own version of Christianity, on the basis of a rational and monist interpretation of the Biblical evidence."²⁹ In my view Raja Ram Mohan Roy deserves the title, Father of Comparative Religion, an honour traditionally conferred on Max Mueller by Western scholars of religions.

Roy was deeply influence by the eighteenth century philosophy of Deism. Unsympathetic to the evangelical trends, the liberal thinkers of Calcutta formed the Unitarian Society. And finally the Brahmo Samaj, Society of Worshippers of Brahman, was founded in 1828 and a temple was constructed without images, in collaboration with Rev. William Adam, one of the Serampore missionaries, "for the worship and adoration of the Eternal Unsearchable and Immutable Being who is the Author and Preserver of the Universe." Their worship conducted on every Saturday evening resembled the Sunday services of the Protestant Christians in Calcutta. Deism was very popular among European rationalists in the eighteenth century and it also harmonized with the impersonal god of the Upanishads and the Vedanta philosophy of Sankaracharya. A rational approach to Hinduism would eventually eliminate, it was hoped, the social evils of Hinduism. The liberal Protestant theologians rejected the metaphysical pre-existent Second Person of the Trinity. And the Jesus of History, with great ideal of his ethical teachings crystallized in the Sermon on the Mount, was thought to be the foundation of the Christian faith. According to the new interpretation the Kingdom of God proclaimed by Jesus was not an other-worldly eschatological reality as traditionally preached but a perfect or new humanity that is gradually being reconstructed on earth.³⁰

---

27. Quoted by Farquhar, *Modern Religious*, 32.
28. Boyd, *Introduction*, 22–24.
29. Ibid., 25.
30. Baago, *Pioneers*, 71.

Varieties of Hindu Responses to Evangelical Mission

Roy's attitude to Christ was one of deep reverence as a messenger of God unparalleled in any other religion. In the long run the exalted rational Deism of Rammohan Roy had only a limited influence because the majority of Hindus, was naturally attached to the Vaishnavite bhakti marga, with personal devotion, verging on emotionalism. "Of all the religious movements of the nineteenth century Brahmo Samaj has without doubt, proved the most influential," observes J. N. Farquhar.[31] Having exerted long and honorable influence for a Century, it declined as other Hindu movements gained the upper hand from the beginning of the twentieth century.

Swami Vivekananda: The First Hindu Missionary to the West

Narendranath Datta (1862–1902), a student of Alexander Duff's Scottish Church college as well as a member of Sadharan Brahmo Samaj, became disciple of Swami Ramakrishna, (1834–86), a renowned mystic of Calcutta in 1893. He took the name Vivekananda and organized Ramakrishna mission in Belur, near Calcutta, in 1897 in order to spread the ideals of his Guru. The new religious community was organized almost like the Benedictine monastic communities. He said: "Christ was a Sannyasin (monk) and his religion is essentially fit for Sannyasins only—meant for those who hunger and thirst after righteousness."[32] It is this spirituality that brings Christ closer to the oriental heart. He even translated *The Imitation Christ into Bengali*. The outstanding character of this religious community was services to humanity, an aim quite foreign to the Hindu tradition. He said: "It is a man making religion we want . . . What vain gods shall we go and yet cannot worship the God we see around us"?[33] This is clearly a reformulation of St. John's teaching on the love of God and love of men. (1 John 4:20). Vivekanand's "Practical Vedanta" was an effort to turn the Vedantic inspiration this-worldly, instead of the world denying traditional Vedanta. Their schools, medical centres, social service centres, book shops and publications were clear imitations of Christian mission. The Sharada Math, named after the saintly wife of Ramakrishna, for Hindu women was inspired by the Convents of Catholic nuns since traditional Hinduism never promoted ashrams of women.

The Theosophical Society founded by colonel Olcott and Madam Blavatsky in New York in 1880 and later in Madras in 1882 had already declared the superiority of Indian Vedanta spirituality in the face of

---

31. Farquhar, *Modern Religious*, 29.
32. Quoted by Samartha, *Hindu*, 50.
33. Quoted in Macnicol, *Living Religions*, 119.

emerging materialistic and secular trends in the West. They hoped that Christianity could be redeemed by the Hindu spirituality.[34] With this backdrop it was not surprising that Vivekananda, the first Hindu missionary to America, addressed the participants of the World Parliament of Religions in Chicago on 11th September in 1893, as "brothers and sisters of America" and proudly announced: "If there is a religion which can claim to be the universal religion of the whole world it is ours and none else."[35] According to him Hinduism depends on universal principles and not tied to historic personalities like Jesus. He believed that the Christian mission has nothing to offer to India. In 1893 he wrote: "As regards to spirituality the Americans are far interior to us but their society is far superior to us. We will teach them our Spirituality and assimilate what is best in their Society."[36] In 1895 he went back to America and organized the Vedanta Society of New York. Later he travelled to many European countries to promote Hinduism. When he came back from Europe he was welcomed back like a triumphant conqueror. Many thousands of Ramakrishna missions are found today all over the world. Some compare him to St. Paul for his zeal for Hindu mission.[37]

Swami Dayananda Saraswati: Founder of the Militant Arya Samaj

Born in Kathiawar, Gujarat, Dayananda (1824–83) was a member of the orthodox Shivite Dashnami ascetic sect meant exclusively for Brahmins. To counter the attack of the missionaries and their aggressive proselytization in Punjab starting in 1870 Sarasvati made pilgrimages all over India and met many Hindu gurus and leaders. In 1873 he organized a debate with the representatives of all religions in Delhi to establish the supremacy of the Vedic religion over all religions. His fundamental view is that the Vedic religion alone is true and infallible and it is revealed by God. To revitalize Hinduism he founded Arya Samaj, the Society of the Aryans, in Bombay in 1875. His reform movement borrowed the methodology of the Lutheran Reformation. His motto, "Back to the Vedas" echoed Luther's motto, "Back to the Bible"; use of the common man's language-Hindi, instead of Sanskrit, in worship; conceding more religious authority to the

---

34. Veer, *Imperial Encounters*, 55–58.
35. Badrinath, *Swami Vivekananda*, 174.
36. Gambirananda, *History of Ramakrishna*, 71.
37. Fallon, "Swami Vivekananda," 363.

Varieties of Hindu Responses to Evangelical Mission

laity challenged the Brahmin priestly hegemony. He affirmed the principle of equality of all castes and sexes. He repudiated untouchability, a weakness of Hinduism which the missionaries exploited to their advantage. His major work *Satyartha Prakash*, The Light of Truth, (1875) is a reinterpretation of Hinduism for renaissance. He invites all men and women, contrary to tradition, to study the Vedas. He makes virulent attack on the Bible, particularly the abundant anthropomorphism in the Old Testament He instituted the rite of Shudhi, reconversion of all who left Hinduism.[38] "The Arya Samaj represents the militant strand from which, in particular, Hindu nationalism would spring forth."[39] The Arya Samaj organized itself, imitating various associations of Christianity. Arya Kumar Sabha or Young men's Arya Samaj, an imitation of the Y.M.C.A.; Stree Samaj or Women's Arya Samaj; Christian schools and orphanages. After the founder's death his collaborators founded the Vedic Salvation Army. Against his polemics Mahatma Gandhi wrote: "I have read *Satyartha Prakash*, the Arya Samaj Bible . . . I have not read a more disappointing book from a reformer so great—. He has unconsciously misrepresented Jainism, Islam, Christianity and Hinduism itself."[40]

Mahatma Gandhi: The Father of the Nation

The views of Dayananda and Mahatma Gandhi are examples of two opposite poles: extreme intolerance versus extreme tolerance of Christianity. The personality of Gandhi (1869–1948), defies classification. M. K. Gandhi's responses to Christianity passed through three stages. The first stage was marked by aversion. When he was a student in Rajkot the Irish Presbyterian missionaries, standing on the road, poured out abuses on Hinduism and their gods. Second, while studying Law for three years in London, he read the Bible, discarded the Old Testament; he was glad that the Theosophists in England were highly appreciative of Hinduism. While being a lawyer for a Muslim firm in Durban, South Africa, from 1893 he was deeply influenced by the reading of Tolstoy, Thoreau, the New Testament and the Bhagavad Gita. He was thrown out of a first class railway compartment since a European fellow traveler objected to the presence of a coolie. Fighting for racial equality of Indians in South Africa he developed his political philosophy and methodology of Satyagraha, or Truth; Ahimsa or Non-Violence; and Swadesh or Patriotism. In the final

38. Kuruvachira, *Hindu Nationalist*, 7–21.
39. Jaffrelot, *Hindu*, 14.
40. Quoted by Kuruvachira, *Hindu Nationalist*, 25.

stage he rejected Jesus as the Son of God but embraced his spirituality, particularly the Sermon on the Mount.[41]

His liberal and open attitudes to all religions were clarified in the course of his life and work in India. "I believe that all great religions of the world are true, more or less . . . And I admit . . . that even the Vedas, the Quran and the Bible are imperfect words of God because I believe that everything that the human hand touches are imperfect."[42] All religions are imperfect or more or less perfect. "Hence the conclusion that Christianity is as good and true as my own religion. But so also about Islam, or Zoroastrianism or Judaism."[43] "The message of Jesus Christ, as I understand it, is contained in the Sermon on the Mount . . . I regard Jesus Christ as one of the greatest teachers of mankind but I do not consider him to be the "Only Son of God."[44] When Gandhi was in South Africa he thought of becoming a Christian. Later he changed his mind. On conversion he said: "I was tremendously attracted to Christianity, but, eventually I came to the conclusion that there was nothing really in your scriptures that we had not got in ours and that a good Hindu also meant that I would be a good Christian. There is no need for me to join your creed to be a believer in the beauty of the teaching of Jesus or to try to follow his example."[45] "I am against conversion whether it is known as Suddhi by Hindus, Tabling by Mussalmans or proselytizing by Christians."[46] Gandhi debated with E.Stanley Jones, a prominent American Methodist missionary, V.S. Azariah, Bishop of Dornakal in Andhra Pradesh and many other Christian missionaries against social conversion. [47] All the modern Hindu leaders thus far examined as well as others like Sarvepalli Radhakrishnan (1888–1975), a brilliant exponent of Neo-Hinduism, Sri Aurobindo, (1872–1950), the promoter of integral Yoga and others, more or less, with some modification, followed the two trends introduced by Ram Mohan Roy: that is, uphold the Vedanta philosophy of Hinduism; two, service to humanity, an imitation of the Christian missionaries because Hinduism failed to develop a social philosophy. [48]

41. Oommen, "Gandhi's Early Christian," 158–83.
42. Gandhi, *Message*, 93.
43. Ibid., 97.
44. Ibid., 41.
45. Ibid., 23.
46. Ibid., 59.
47. For details on the debate on conversion, see Kim, *In Search of Identity*.
48. Radhakrishnan, "Hinduism," 350–51.

Varieties of Hindu Responses to Evangelical Mission

Caste Conversions to Christianity

In contrast to Ram Mohan Roy's response to Jesus Christ through Brahmo Samaj another radical response was the attempt, more or less successful, to evolve a synthesis of three major religious traditions. The Vedanta *Gnana Marga*, the Bengali *Bhakti Marga* of Chaitanya and the doctrines of Christianity as preached by the Baptist, Presbyterian and other missionaries in Calcutta. As illustrations a few cases are examined below.

Keshab Chandra Sen: Non-Baptized Believer in Jesus Christ

Born in a prominent Hindu family in Calcutta, Keshab Chandra Sen (1838–1884) joined the Brahmo Samaj at the age of 20 and took the name Jesu Das, servant of God. After reading *The Precepts of Jesus* he reached the conclusion that Jesus could provide the spiritual foundation for the progress of not only India but the whole of Asia that no other prophet of the world could. He strongly reacted to their barbarous masculine Christianity, a subject of discourse in colonial India that was dominating women, blacks and poor countries.[49] He further discovered that Jesus was not a foreigner as depicted by the Western missionaries; rather he was more akin to Oriental nature. He further protested against the denationalization and deculturation of native converts.

In 1861, K. C. Sen became a full time missionary of Brahmo Samaj.[50] In the following decade he was making serious and systematic study of Christianity which drew him closer to Christ with deep love and devotion. In 1866 Sen traveled to England and lectured on "Jesus Christ: Europe and America." He emphasized that Jesus was not Western, but Asian. Therefore he asks: "And was not Jesus Christ an Asiatic? Yes, and his disciples were Asiatics, and all the agencies primarily employed for the propagation of the Gospel were Asiatic. In fact, Christianity was founded and developed by Asiatics and in Asia."[51] From 1879 his deeper understanding of Jesus Christ was spelled out in "India asks: Who is Jesus Christ"? His answer: Christ is the eternal Logos. Following St. John's Gospel (John 1:1–18) and the Alexandrian Jewish philosopher Philo (BC 30—AD 45) he developed his theology. Christ is the eternal logos of the Father. The Spirit—Christ is spread in the universe as an emanation of the Divine reason. "Sum up all that is true and good and beautiful in the life of humanity, and you have

---

49. Veer, *Imperial Encounters*, 86–88.
50. Natrajan, *Century*, 10.
51. Quoted in Staffner, *Significance of Jesus*, 36.

the grand Logos of the early Christians, the Christ of universal Theism. Thus all reason in man is Christ-reason; all love (in man) is Christ-love; all power (in man) is Christ-power—. The holy Word, the eternal Veda, dwells in everyone of us. . . . Is not Christ then a mediating link between man and God ?"[52]

Another theological question raised was how to distinguish between the Hindu avatar, incarnation, an extension of pantheism, and the Christian incarnation where the Word became flesh. The Hindu scriptures are accused of pantheism, i.e., identification of all things with God. Hindu pantheism is the proud belief that man is God. In the opinion of Sen Christ's pantheism is a nobler and more perfect type. It is the conscious union of the human with the Divine Spirit. Christ's communion is active, not the passive pantheism of Hinduism. "It is the union of the obedient, humble and loving Son with Father."[53] Christ is not an avatar like myriad deities worshiped in India. His is not the Father in human form like the avatar of Hinduism, for example, Ram or Krishna. He is not the Fatherhood becoming man. Incarnation is the climax of the cosmic process of creation. The doctrine of absorption in the deity is one of those ideas of Vedanta Hinduism. The Hindu pantheism is fulfilled and perfected in Christ. Christ's pantheism is the active surrender of will. He fulfils what the Hindus always desired for. "I have not come to abolish but to fulfill" (Matt 5:17) is applicable not only to the Mosaic dispensation but to the Hindu dispensation too.

Sen, who was deeply influenced by the *Precepts of Jesus* by Roy, held the view that Jesus was not merely a teacher of religion or morality as Roy believed. Then what more did Jesus teach? "He was a teacher of Divine Sonship. His only object on earth was to raise mankind upward—to share in the light and glory of heaven. That was Christ's mission."[54] "The Father can teach us what He is . . . The Father cannot be an example of Sonship." "In him we see human nature perfected by true affiliations to the Divine nature. And in this affiliation we see the fullest realization of the purpose of Christ's life and ministry. He shows us—how we can exult our humanity by making it more and more divine, how while retaining our humanity we may still partake more and more of the Divine character."[55] In Jesus Christ Sen identified three distinguishing characteristics, more than what

52. Ibid., 52.
53. Ibid., 46.
54. Ibid., 51.
55. Ibid., 50.

Varieties of Hindu Responses to Evangelical Mission

Rammohan Roy was willing to concede. First, true character of Jesus: his extraordinary tenderness, humility, simplicity and lamb—like meekness (Isa 52:13—53:12); his mercy and forgiveness. Christ teaches us to forgive our enemies, to bless them that curse us and pray for them that despise us. He in his excruciating pain prayed for those who crucified him: "Father forgive them for they know not what they do" (Luke 23:34). Second the infusion of the Christian spirit brought in an enthusiasm for saving fellow sinners by carrying to them the New Gospel. The sense of sin and the urgent need for God's saving mercy was central to the Christian proclamation of the evangelical missionaries. Finally, the Christian attitude to society, to convert it into a household of God.[56]

In his 1882 lecture he confesses his faith in the Trinity. He was confessing his experience. God the Father creates all the wonders of the world through his almighty Logos or the Word. The Old Testament was the revelation of the Father. God Yehova is same as the Supreme of the Vedas. The primary creative force took the form of the Son in Jesus Christ. Divinity coming down to humanity is the Son. Divinity carrying up humanity to heaven is the Holy Spirit. He endeavored to harmonize the Western and the Eastern understanding of the Trinitarian mystery, with proper functions and attributes as follows.

Father	Son	Holy Spirit
The Creator	The Exemplar	The Sanctifier
The still God	The Descending God	The Returning God
'I am'	'I love'	'I save'
The Father above	The Son below	The Holy Spirit within
Truth	Goodness	Beauty
Sat	Chit	Anand
Truth	Consciousness	Bliss and Comforter

(Adapted to Boyd, An *Introduction to Indian Christian Theology*, 1969: 34–35).

According to K. C. Sen "the Trinity of Christianity corresponds with the Saccidananda of Hinduism." He declares "Saccidananda shall be India's God. She cannot be disloyal to the Trinity."[57] At the same time he rejected the popular Hindu Trinity as Brahma, the creator, Vishnu, the preserver and Shiva, the god of death. In his own words:

---

56. Farquhar, *Modern Religious*, 59–60.
57. Staffner, *Significance of Jesus*, 48.

> The Father, the Son, the Holy Ghost, the Creator, the Exemplar, the Sanctifier; the Truth, the Good, the Beautiful; Sat, Chit, Anand. Has not the Holy Ghost been described as the "Comforter"? Truly he is the heart's joy. Thus the Trinity of Christianity corresponds strikingly with the *Saccidananda* of Hinduism. Not three gods, but one God. Whether alone or manifest in the Son or quickening humanity as the Holy Spirit, it is the same God. Who can deny that there is an essential undivided unity in this so-called Trinity? . . . Let not lying lips say that Christ came to teach three Gods. One was his God, the same yesterday, today and for ever. How grand a conception of Three in One. How beautiful and sublime the thought when realized in consciousness . . . The Father above, the Son below, the Holy Ghost within.[58]

Reflexions on the Mystery of the Trinity, employing either the Western Greek philosophical categories or the Indian philosophical categories, were never without certain inadequacies. He speaks of a fundamental unity and a functional differences of the Trinity. The Father manifests Himself in creation and then in his beloved Son, Jesus. Thus God sends down his Divinity into the world through the Son: that Divinity reproduced in millions is carried by the Holy Spirit back into its source in heaven. When the Father works in us as the Holy Spirit, inspiring dead souls, we are converted and become new creatures. "Whether alone or manifest in the Son or quickening humanity as the Holy Spirit, it is the same God."[59] But remember the true Trinity is not three persons, but three functions of the same person. "Though there is a fundamental Unity in the Trinity, we must recognize and demarcate functional difference."[60] The Father cannot be an example of Sonship. Only the Son can show what the Son ought to be. In vain do I go to the Vedas or Judaism to learn Sonship."[61] "Divinity coming down to humanity is the Son. The Divinity carrying up humanity is the Holy Spirit." The descent of the Divinity into the world is through the humanity of Christ. Now all humanity must be lifted up to heaven in order that the redemption of mankind may be fulfilled. "The way to do it is Christ and the power to do it is the Holy Spirit. Nothing is possible unless the Holy Spirit touches the hearts. The Holy Spirit converts outward

---

58. Ibid., 48–49.
59. Ibid., 49.
60. Ibid., 54.
61. Quoted by Farquhar, *Modern Religious*, 66.

truths into inward purity."⁶² "I verily believe, when Jesus Christ was about to leave this world he made over the sacred portfolio of the ministry of the church to the Holy Spirit."⁶³

He realized that the English Christianity was too sectarian and narrow for large human hearts. He found the answer, probably, after a meeting with his contemporary saintly Ramakrishna Paramahamsa around 1875. The mystic Ramakrishna claimed that he had visions of the founders of all religions, including Jesus. He taught that all religions are essentially the same. The differences between religions are only on the social levels. It was this concern that prompted Sen to adopt a number of ceremonies and rites from both Hinduism and Christianity which became an integral part of the liturgy of his "New Dispensation." For instance Chaitanya's religious dance was introduced to express religious joy. He called God, Mother. He introduced the *arati* ceremony, the waving of lights, into Brahma ritual. In imitation of the 108 names of Vishnu, a Sanskrit hymn of praise, recounting of God was composed and used in the Liturgy of his new church.

Already in 1861 proposal for a National Church of Bengal was made by certain radical nationalist like Kali Charan Banerjee. Finally Twenty years later in January 1881, Sen, in the presence of his twelve disciple founded "The Church of New Dispensation."

"The glorious mission of the New Dispensation is to harmonize religions, he announced. Thus in October 1881 he wrote: Our position is not that truths are to be found in all religions; but all the established religions of the world are true . . . The glorious mission of the New Dispensation is to harmonize religions and revelations, to establish the truth of every particular dispensation, and upon the basis of these particulars to establish the largest and broadest instruction of a general and glorious proposition."⁶⁴ This grand vision has much similarity with the Mughal emperor Akbar's grand vision of the Din–Illahi or Divine Faith. Keshab promulgated the "Laws of Life" of the New Dispensation. Its concluding synopsis was: "My creed is the science of God which enlightens all. My Gospel is the love of God which serveth all. My heaven is life in God which is accessible to all. My church is the invisible Kingdom of God in which is all truth, all love, all holiness."⁶⁵

---

62. Staffner, *Significance of Jesus*, 54.
63. Ibid., 64.
64. Quoted by Farquhar, *Modern Religious*, 57–58.
65. Ibid., 73.

Another original theological insight of Sen was the doctrine of "Divine Humanity." In his 1879 lecture "India asks: Who is Jesus Christ?," he speaks of the divine humanity of Christ. He finds the answer in John's Gospel. "I and the Father are one" (John 10:30). "I can of my own self do nothing" (John 5:30, 36). "I am in the Father and the Father is in me" (John 14:1–14). The identity of Jesus Christ is his mystic union and oneness with the Father. Sen's interpretation of the Johnnine Gospel was quite spontaneous since it was much closer to the Indian mystical tradition. Jesus emptied his own self so utterly that he became a transparent medium in which God dwells and through which men can see God and know him. Jesus is the highest form of self—denial. Then he analyses the human condition of selfishness. "We, on the contrary, have each our hard selfishness ... I think, I preach, ... This is my virtue, my holiness, my prayer—these are selfish ideas which prevail universally among mankind ... root of our sins and weakness ... Jesus had not this self which is in all of us."[66] "Thus there is Christ before us as a transparent crystal reservoir in which are the waters of divine life."[67] Again quoting the Apostle Philip, Sen sees the divine transparency of Jesus through whom we see the Father (John 14:8–11). Jesus Christ has a human nature which is perfect because of its unity with the divine nature. He became an example of divinization of human nature. It is Divine—Humanity. Sen did not speak about the manner of the union of two natures, as was debated in the Council of Nicea against Arius in 325. Sen emphasized the process of divinization of the human nature by the self-emptying. Some critics were tempted to accuse him of Arianism.

The influence of the Baptist missionaries in Calcutta is clear from the fact, Sen accepted only two Sacraments—Baptism and the Lord's Supper—in contrast to the seven sacraments in the catholic church. He said: "Christ wants to baptize our hearts, not with cold water, but with the fire of religious and spiritual enthusiasm."[68] Real baptism, therefore, is the crucifixion of your evil inclinations and participation in Christ's death as St. Paul taught (Rom 6:3–4). If you have not crucified your own evil inclinations how can you say you have accepted the crucified Christ? The traditional Hindu asceticism blended well with the Pauline Christianity which the evangelicals were enthusiastically preaching. Sen and many of his companions who were believers in Christ were never baptized in the water because the traditional baptism of water would lead to the scandal

---

66. Staffner, *Significance of Jesus*, 41–42.
67. Sen, quoted by Thomas, *Acknowledged Christ*, 59.
68. Staffner, *Significance of Jesus*, 67.

Varieties of Hindu Responses to Evangelical Mission

of sectarianism and inter—church fights which were not rare in those days. It would have been too much to expect that unanimous appreciations of Sen would be pouring in from different quarters. The Unitarians and the rationalists said that Sen's thought was either mystic or romantic. The Scottish Presbyterian missionary J. N. Farquhar in 1929 wrote "He was not a systematic thinker, and his religious experience sprang from Christ."[69] "Keshab's deepest convictions were Christian beliefs, yet he was not a Christian," concluded Farquhar, for whom baptism was the decisive claim to being a Christian. K. C. Banurji, the registrar of Calcutta university, a respected Bengali Christian and a close friend of K. C. Sen believed: "Keshab died a Christian." In my opinion K. C. Sen, with all his theological limitations, deserve to be honored as "the father of the Indian Christian theology," after 1,800 years of existence of Christianity in India. This is his lasting legacy, though his church of New Dispensation gradually disappeared.

Brahmabhandav Upadhyaya: A Hindu-Catholic

Bhavani Charan Banerjee (1861–1907) born not far away from Calcutta, on 11th February 1861, was brought up in the strict Brahminical ideal and Sanskrit culture. His formal education was in the Scottish mission school as well as in the Metropolitan College, Calcutta. Already his uncle, Kali Charan Banerjee, a convert to Christianity, had generated in him a certain interest in the life of Jesus. Together with his friend Narendranath Datta, later known as Swami Vivekananda, he joined the Brahmo Samaj. At the invitation of a Brahmo Samaj friend he proceeded to Hyderabad, Sind, in July 1888 to teach in a school and as a preacher of the Samaj. His preaching of Jesus Christ stirred up controversy and he was forced to resign from the school. His ardent desire to follow Jesus reached a definitive stage with his baptism of water and Spirit, differing from Keshub Chandra Sen, in the Church of England, on February 20, 1891 and six months later was received into the catholic church in Karachi.

After baptism he began to publish a monthly journal, *The Harmony*, to write about the harmony between pure Hinduism and pure Christianity like Krishna Mohan Banerjee who had already published, *The Aryan witness* in 1875 to show many parallels between the Old Testament and the Vedas.[70] In order to explain the catholic faith in a language and terms intelligible to Hindus he started another journal, *Sophia*, Christ the Eternal

69. Farquhar, *Modern Religious*, 66.
70. Boyd, *Introduction*, 280.

Wisdom, in 1894 in consultation with a few Jesuit scholars. Having systematically studied how St. Thomas Aquinas (1225-1274) employed the Aristotelian philosophy to articulate the Christian theology in his *Summa Theologiae* he was convinced that "we must fall back on Vedantic method in formulating the Catholic religion to our country men."[71] He traveled extensively across India to lecture on his new ideas as well as to fight monism, theosophy of Mrs. Annie Besant, Dayananda Sarasvati, and the Vedanta philosophy propounded by his contemporary, Ramakrishna. Therefore he could write: "We hold with the Vedantists that there is one eternal essence from which proceed all things. We believe with the Vaishnavas in the necessity of incarnation and in the doctrine that man cannot be saved without grace. We agree in spirit with the Hindu law givers in regards to their teaching that sacramental rites are vehicles of sanctification." [72] Thus he tried to reconcile the traditional antinomy of two major Indian philosophical schools of Sankaracharya and Ramanuja.

Saccidananda Brahman and the Trinity

With his background of the Brahmo Samaj he was familiar with the unqualified understanding of God, Nirguna Brahman, as pure Consciousness. And he was also aware of 'The Thomist teaching that God is pure Being.' His mentor K. C. Sen had already introduced the concepts Sat, Chit, and Ananda in order to compare the Christian belief in the Trinity. i.e., the Father, the Son and the Holy Spirit. The crucial question is: How can man know, God the 'Nirguna Brahman' without the medium of relations? Upadhyaya's response is based on the revelation of Jesus that "God is self-related by means of internal distinctions that do not cast even a shadow of divisions up on the unity of his substance.... It is knowledge and nothing but knowledge which can distinguish the Knowing Self of God from His Known Self... God knows his own Self begotten in Thought and is known in return by Begotten Self ... It is this correspondence of knowing and being known, of cognition and recognition, which generates the relative distinction of subject and subject in the Absolute."[73] The unrelated and unknowable Brahman becomes internally related and therefore knowable is the explanation of the Christian Trinity. This 'Nirguna Brahman' 'begets' or produces 'Thought,' 'Intelligence,' 'Logos' or 'Cit' whereby he relates himself to himself. This Logos or Cit is Christ. Out of the Union of Sat

71. Ibid., 68.
72. Staffner, *Significance of Jesus*, 100-101.
73. Quoted in Baago, *Pioneers*, 39.

Varieties of Hindu Responses to Evangelical Mission

or Being, and Cit or Consciousness, proceeds the Ananda or Bliss. "God reproduces in knowledge a corresponding acknowledging Self-Image, and from this colloquy of Reason proceeds the Spirit of Love."[74] His beautiful Sanskrit hymn, *Vande Saccidanandam*, written in 1898, is not only an interpretation of God and the Trinity, but also an act of adoration.

I adore:

> The Sat (Being), Chit (Intelligence), Anandam (Bliss) the Highest goal, despised by worldings, which is desired by yogis (devotees).
>
> The Supreme, Ancient, Higher than the Highest, full, indivisible, transcendent and Immanent, One having triple interior relationship, holy, unrelated, self-conscious, hard to realize.
>
> The Father, Begetter, the Highest Lord, Unbegotten, the rootless principle of the Tree of Existence, the cause of the Universe, One who creates intelligently, the Preserver of the World.
>
> The Uncreated, Infinite Logos, or Word, supremely great, the image of the Father, One whose form is Intelligence, the Giver of highest freedom.
>
> One who proceeds from the union of Sat and Chit, the blessed Spirit, intense Bliss, the Sanctifier, One whose movements are swift, one who speaks about the Word, the Life-Giver.
>
> (Lipner & Gispet, *The writings of Brahmabandhab*, vol.I, 1991: 126–27)

The Christian Trinitarian explanation of Saccidananda, is an advancement of Sankaracharaya's Nirguna Brahma, the impersonal God. Having known the inner nature of God as Trinity from the revelation of Jesus Upadhyaya is endeavoring to make that belief reasonable to his Hindu believers. Once known by revelation, then the Trinitarian explanation as Saccidananda is found as the fulfillment of the Vedantic aspiration: "In the beginning this world was Being, one only without a second: It thought itself: would that I were many! Let me procreate myself." (C.U. 6:2). Rather than a theological speculation, for Upadhyaya, the Trinity is a delightful experience, that he confessed through his magnificent hymn *Vande Saccidanandam*. During the 38th International Eucharistic Congress in Bombay, 1964, Vande Saccidanandam, with Indian musical notation, was sung as the lead hymn.

---

74. Boyd, *Introduction*, 73.

How the 'Nirguna Brahman,' without name and form, (neti . . . neti) is related to the external world was another Vedantic concept that required reinterpretation in the Christian perspective. The Vedanta philosophy affirms that all that is not Brahman is Maya, i.e., an illusory manifestation of Brahman, caused by Avidya or ignorance. Upadhyaya reinterpreted the concept of Maya as follows: "All finite beings are Maya in the sense they are contingent beings. They have no right to exit . . . they exist by Maya by the habit of participating in the divine act. Maya is a divine overflow, resulting in the existence of creatures. By Maya, i.e., by God's power or Sakti "non-being" is brought into 'being.' That which is nothingness by itself is filled with the riches of being. Upadhyaya compared Maya to passive creation in the teaching of Thomas Aquinas. Only God is necessary Being; created being is not nothing, but contingent being; it does not exist by necessity. The created beings are "indeed darkness, falsity and nothingness," as St. Thomas taught.[75] And similarly Adi Sankaracharya , four hundred years before Thomas Acquinas, taught *Brahman Sathya, Jagad Mitya*. i.e., only God is Real and the world is unreal. In the words of Robin Boyd, "Maya has a double aspect, first creating man, and then showing the illusoriness of all man-made pleasures, so preventing the Jiva from resting in himself or anything finite."[76] The contingent being bears within itself the deep restlessness to return to the Absolute Being and prays: "From the unreal lead me to the Real; From darkness lead me to Light; From death lead me to Immortality."[77]

Upadhyaya defended the Hindu belief in multiple incarnations, like Lord Krishna and Rama. By special intervention God in his compassion descends into that individual being in order that he could fulfill his mission to restore order and justice. An avatar, incarnation, therefore, does not belong to the eternal being of God; he belongs to creation, and exists only for a time. The Hindu doctrine of Avatar, the earliest in any religious literature, is clearly found in the *Bhagavad Gita* where Lord Krishna teaches Arjuna: "Whenever there is a decline of righteousness, O Arjuna, and an upheaval of lawlessness, I appear from time to time for shielding the good and destroying the wicked and to establish righteousness" (*Bhagavad Gita* IV, 7–8). Upadhyaya would not object to his countrymen venerating ava-

---

75. Staffner, *Significance of Jesus*, 99. The world-relational definition of God, according to Sankaracharya; "Brahma is that from which these beings are born, that by which once born they live, that into which, when departing, they enter" (T.U.3.1.1).

76. Boyd, *Introduction*, 76.

77. Hume, *Thirteen*, 80. Asato ma sadgamaya; Tamaso ma Jyotir gamaya; Mrityor ma amritam gamaya. Om Shanti, Shanti, Shanti.

Varieties of Hindu Responses to Evangelical Mission

tars like Krishna, a great teacher of the lofty ideals of the *Bhagavad Gita*. As long as the uniqueness of Christ is upheld, veneration of Hindu deities, as an integral part of the national religious culture could be appreciated. Like Thomas Aquina's belief in natural theology Upadhyaya accepted the natural theology of Hinduism. But the avatara of Krishna belong to the realm of Maya, of contingent being. "Christ on the other hand, is beyond maya, for he is God himself, living in the eternal dialogue of the Trinity. He too appears in history as the man Jesus but his personality is eternally in the Godhead."[78] Thus belief in Krishna as an avatara, as Appasamy and a few other Indian theologians thought, can be very useful for formulating an Indian theology and does not constitute a threat to Christ the Incarnation.

After embracing Catholicism one of his mission was "to baptize the Hindu philosophy and employ it as stepping stones to the catholic faith." "Upadhyaya's most important contribution in his endeavour to lead India to Christ is his study of the relationship between the Hindu community and the Catholic church." observes Hans Staffner. For the first time he made a distinction between culture and religion. On dharma he distinguished between Samajdharma, Social obligations, and Sadhana dharma or personal religion. In Hinduism observance of certain customs like caste distinctions, dietary regulations are compulsory, but the Sadhana dharma leaves him free to choose one of the many ways. On the contrary the Catholics are bound by certain creeds but more free in social obligations. He and many other new disciples of Jesus vehemently opposed the European garb of Catholicism which cloaks and sublimates the Gospel of Jesus. He thus reached the conclusion that a Hindu can believe in Jesus Christ without severing his cultural communion with the Hindu community. In 1898 in an article titled, 'Are we Hindus?' he wrote: "By birth we are Hindus and shall remain Hindu till death. But as dvi-ja or twice—born by virtue of our sacramental rebirth we are Catholics." "But in regard to our immortal souls we are Catholics. We are Hindu-Catholics."[79] Already in 1883 another Bengali convert, Kali Charan Banerjee, had written; "We are Hindus as thoroughly Hindu as Christian. We have embraced Christianity, but we have not discarded our nationality."[80] Here the word 'Hindu' is defined more in cultural than in religious terms, observes Samartha.

Upadhyaya was far ahead of his time. The conservative catholic authorities for whom any religious practice that was non-European was

---

78. Boyd, *Introduction*, 76.
79. Staffner, *Significance of Jesus*, 99–101.
80. Quoted by Samartha, *Hindu*, 9.

devilish, failed to comprehend his vision. Msgr. L. Zaleski, the delegate Apostolic, instructed the Bishops to forbid the Catholics to read *Sophia* saying that the Christian creed was being misrepresented by unqualified persons. Unfortunately Rome was very harsh on his creative initiatives and forbade publication of his theological journals.[81] Sad to state that the Catholic authorities in Rome totally failed to learn any lesson from similar mistakes committed earlier with Robert de Nobili in Madurai. He undertook a lecture tour of Europe to meet eminent Christian scholars. Sadly he failed to get an audience with Pope Leo XIII. He was deeply disappointed. His interest in Catholicism began to wane. After the partition of Bengal in 1905 he plunged himself into radical political movement with Aurobindo Ghosh and companions. Soon he died after an hernia operation in the hospital on 27th October 1907. Upadhayaya firmly believed that the Western form of Christianity was neither the only possible nor the final. In the words of Alfons Vaeth, "He has begun new lines of thought and suggested new possibilities of interpreting the Christian Gospel in an Indian setting."[82] It is heartening to note that theologians like Swami Parama Ananda (1895–1957), Swami Abhishiktananda (1910–1973), Bede Griffiths (1906–2000) and a few others in the recent past have continued to carry on the vision of Brahmabandhaya Upadhyaya, in a more favorable ecclesiastical atmosphere.

Manilal C. Parekh on the Kingdom of God

Manilal Parekh's (1895–1967) religious journey from Jainism to Hinduism to Jesus Christ is marked by characteristics that merit special attention. Born in a Jain family in Rajkot, Gujarat, he embraced the *Bhakti marga* of Vaishnavism, i.e., belief in a personal god, a departure from Jainism that does not believe in the existence of god but believes in the existence of eternal souls—Jivas. During a prolonged illness he read T*he Bible*, and the *Imitation of Christ* by Thomas A. Kempis. He was much influenced by Saint Francis of Assisi, Leo Tolstoy and a few other Christian mystics. But conversion was viewed by many national leaders as both an anti-national activity as well as a pro-colonial gesture. Parekh, therefore, continued to remain a Hindu disciple of Jesus without baptism. Having overcome his apprehensions with the encouragement of a few Christian friends, finally at the age of thirty three he was baptized in the Anglican Church in Bombay and wrote. "It is essential because Christ has commanded it—baptism is

81. Lippner, *Brahmabandab*, 276.
82. In Boyd, *Introduction*, 67.

Varieties of Hindu Responses to Evangelical Mission

at least the most unequivocal and open confession of the discipleship of Christ . . . Thus baptism confers an *adhikar*, i.e., power, authority of the highest kind. Thus baptism makes the disciple of Christ at once a *shishya*, disciple, and *acharya*, Spiritual Guide and a prophet."[83]

His numerous publications, both in English and Gujarati, intended "to pay herewith my most humble tribute to Jesus Christ whose Hindu disciple I have been."[84] His Hindu understanding of the Kingdom of God proclaimed by Jesus Christ merits special attention. He believed, relying on the writing of the Jewish historian Flavius Josephus (AD 37-100), "there is a close resemblance between the teachings of the Essenes and those of Jesus."[85] The Essenes were a Jewish monastic community living along the north Western shore of the dead sea as well as Egypt in the inter—Testamental period. They had a community leader. Those who were admitted to membership after two years of probation, surrendered all their property to the common fund. They shunned sex and marriage. Prayer, meditation on the Law of Moses, and work in the farm were their main daily activity. They fled the world which was the source of all types of evils. They eagerly waited for the sudden appearance of the Kingdom of God and the reward for a few faithful and righteous ones. Their counterparts lived in world with less austerity, but closely associated with the monastic community.

Waiting in expectation for the arrival of the Kingdom of God was a dominant belief both among the passive Essenes and the militant Zealots during 30 BC—70 AD. The vision of the arrival of the Kingdom of God gradually evolved into diverse trends. In the first phase the expectation the messiah or saviour was pictured after David the ideal king, who unified the twelve tribes of Israel to establish the first Kingdom. Sadly after the division of the Kingdom and the subsequent fall of the Northern and Southern Kingdoms to the Assyrian ruler in 721 BC and to the Babylonians in 598 BC and 587 BC and the Babylonian captivity, the post-exilic prophets shifted the focus from the political Kingdom (Isa 11:2-4) to a spiritual Kingdom because Israel realized that it was an insignificant political power in comparison to its mighty neighbours.[86] However they failed to understand how could the suffering of the chosen people and the faithfulness of Yahweh be reconciled? There was a crisis of faith. A

---

83. Staffner, *Significance of Jesus*, 113.
84. Parekh, *Hindu Portrait*, vii .
85. Ibid., 71.
86. Ceresko, *Old Testament*, 315-24.

message of hope and consolation was given to them. Prophet Ezekiel, the Father of Judaism, and the unknown author of the second and third Isaiah assigned a difficult role to the Suffering Servant of God (Isa 42:6–7; 52:13 to 53:3–12). Here Parekh sees the new role of Israel. "In these passages we have a new conception of the role of Israel . . . It is a mission which, ethically and spiritually, is higher than anything the Jews had hitherto known . . . the destiny of the Jews was to be spiritual leader to the gentiles . . . by means of their suffering and devotion to God."[87] The shift is indeed radical from the root of Jesse (Isa 11:1) to the Suffering Servant of Yahweh. But it will be concluded with the royal rule or reign of God (Isa 60–62).

At the time of Jesus the messianic expectation had assumed two diametrically opposing currents. One, a political Kingdom that will be established after overthrowing the Roman domination by the political party known as Zealots. Second, a Spiritual Kingdom. John the Baptizer announced the "baptism of repentance for the forgiveness of sin" (Mark 1:2–4). And after the beheading of John, Jesus proclaimed "The Kingdom of God is at hand. Repent and believe in the Gospel" (Mark 1:15). And here Parekh's Hindu understanding at the Kingdom of God is very unique. "Looking to the tradition and the environment he had, Jesus was original in this—The idea of the Kingdom of God as stood in the mind of Jesus was somewhat akin to that of *Moksha*, emancipation . . . This was altogether new as far as the Jews were concerned."[88] However there are also significant differences. The Jews pictured an apocalyptic vision, with the victory of the transcendent God over the power of Evils; the Hindu rishis employed the immanent Vedantic mysticism to escape from the cycle of Karma and Rebirth. But both the Jews and the Hindus sought a religious solution to persecutions and release from the suffering of Sansara. Here he conjectures a possible link between the spread of Buddhism to West Asia and the origin of the Essene community and its apparent influence on early Christianity.

Parekh argues that Jesus clearly delinked his life, teaching and mission from the political Kingdom as anticipated by the common people. For instance, after the multiplication of the loaves when he realized the people were going to carry him away to make him a king he withdrew into the mountain alone (John 6:15). As the mother of James and John asked Jesus: "Will you let my two sons to sit on two thrones next to yours" (Matt 20:20–28), their requests were refused. In the last day of his life, dur-

---

87. Ibid., 309.
88. Ibid., 318.

Varieties of Hindu Responses to Evangelical Mission

ing the trial before Pilate, the Roman Governor of Judea, Jesus explicitly declared: "My Kingdom does not belong to this world" (John 18:36). One of the probable reasons why Judas betrayed Jesus was his growing feeling that Jesus was not the expected political messiah. During his public life Jesus did not speak against the Romans; on the contrary he advised them to pay taxes to them.[89] "On the whole Jesus is silent on the character and content on his Kingdom. The Lord's prayer, Our Father, partly explains it: 'thy Kingdom come; thy will be done on earth as it is in heaven' (Matt 6:10). The Kingdom meant to Jesus loving obedience on the part of man to the will of God."[90]

Jesus, of course, used the term Kingdom many times because it was too embedded in the consciousness of the people of Israel. In the Gospel Parekh found that Jesus had an awareness of the union with God which was unique. "No one knows the Son except the Father, and no one knows the Father except the Son and those to whom the Son chooses to reveal him and everyone to whom the Son wants to reveal him" (Matt 12:25-27; Luke 10: 21-22). "It is in this we find the foundation of the Messianic mission of Jesus . . . It is in this we find, formulated for the first time, that new relationship between God and man which is expressed by the term 'the Fatherhood of God' and which has been the greatest spiritual possession of mankind since his time . . . To be a Christian means to share this consciousness with Jesus, to enter and enjoy such a communion with God as Jesus had, a communion in which one is sure to feel the presence of the Spirit of Jesus also."[91] Parekh continues the characterization of the new Kingdom. "This is the Kingdom of God and none other. It belongs to all if only they would come to it with proper attitude. It is not the monopoly of so-called Christians alone: rather whoever have this consciousness are Christians. This is a spiritual relationship and fellowship with God as the Father and an integral part of the same is the sharing with all. It is this which was meant by the "Baptism of the Spirit."[92] "Jesus has undoubtedly given to the world a new kind of spiritual consciousness, which has been hitherto the greatest religious possession of mankind."[93] "I pray not only for them but also for those who will believe in me through their word, so that they may all be one, as you, Father, are in me and I in you, that they

---

89. Ibid., 486–92.
90. Ibid., 324.
91. Ibid., 374.
92. Ibid., 375.
93. Ibid., 442.

also may be in us" (John.17:20–21). "This relationship with God became the core of the Kingdom." Jesus prayed that his disciples too may experience similar communion with God. The superiority of the Incarnation of Jesus consists in his awareness of communion with the Eternal Father, with his essential attributes of love and forgiveness (Luke 15:11–32). "He (Jesus) felt himself to be the Son of God as none before him had done, and has since become a pattern of this filial relationship for his disciples and followers. This is the core of the religion taught by him and centred in him."[94] In this very act of becoming Son he became the Elder Brother of men as well.

Parek's Indian understanding of the Kingdom of God indeed is unique. "He represents the same line of thought as Upadhyaya, in fact moving to a more radical separation between Christian Spirituality and social ethic in the name of nationalism," opines M. M.Thomas.[95] To justify his understanding of the Kingdom of God, detached from social issues, he points out that St. Paul and the Christians tolerated slavery until the nineteenth century. "Jesus at most left a Messianic community and not church in the present sense of the term."[96] Unfortunately from the time of emperor Constantine the Roman Catholic church imitated the Holy Roman empire and the Protestant churches the ideal of the state church. "And by the end of his life, after his systematic study and the publication of *Christian Proselytism in India* (1947) he distanced himself from the idea of baptism that in those days seemed to disrupt the Indian social order by becoming a Firangi." He preferred the model of the secret discipleship of Nicodemus and Joseph of Arimathea (John 19:38–40). And he expressed deep appreciation for de Nobili's missionary method in Madurai who prudently distanced himself from disturbing the social order of those Hindus who became Catholics.[97] Parekh's interpretation of the Kingdom of God squarely matched the "other worldly" interpretation of classical Hinduism and the radical rejection of the world as Maya. By the end of his life he was moving towards Churchless Christianity. Unfortunately he showed little interest in the social precepts of Jesus which Ram Mohan Roy and many other Hindu reformers before him deeply appreciated. The social approach of Ram Mohan Roy and the spiritual approach of Parekh are two radically different Indian responses to the life and teachings of

---

94. Ibid., 447.
95. Thomas, *Acknowledged Christ*, 259–60.
96. Parekh, *Hindu Portrait*, 416.
97. Parekh, *Christian Proselytism*, 58–59.

Jesus. However eventually the Gandhian model emerged as a third pattern where the Hindu tradition and the Christian tradition were more or less successfully weaved together.

Pandita Ramabai: Jesus the Saviour of Womanhood

Which specific feature of the Gospel of Jesus inspired the conversion of one of the most revolutionary Hindu women of modern India is the question raised here. In the conservative ethos of the nineteenth century how did Pandita Ramabai (1858–1922), a south Indian woman, become a radical thinker and social reformer? Anant Shastri Dongre, a Chitpavan Brahmin, inspired by the Sanskrit education of women in Peshwa's court in Poona, dared to teach Sanskrit to his wife as well as his daughter Ramabai. When Ramabai and her brother reached Calcutta in 1878, culmination of their pilgrimage initiated by their father who died on the way due famine, the reformist and liberal atmosphere welcomed her as the ideal woman of the Vedic period, well versed in Sanskrit. K. C. Sen, the leader of Brahmo Samaj, asked her to lecture on the status of women in traditional Hinduism. It was a golden opportunity for her to read the *Vedas, Upanisads* and the *Dharmashastras* for the first time and discover the pathetic condition of woman, according to these sacred books. After listening to her very erudite Sanskrit lectures the Calcutta University Senate conferred on her the rare title 'Pandita,' Woman Sanskrit Scholar. In spite of conflicting views in the scriptures, all Hindu pundits and people agreed on two things. One, all women are bad, worse than demons as unholy as untrue; more dangerous than venomous snakes; and that they could not get *moksha* or salvation. Two, the only hope of their getting salvation was through the worship of their husbands, believed to be a woman's god. By faithful worship of the husband she hopes to be reborn as man in the cycle of rebirth. A woman has no right to study the Vedas. "My eyes were being gradually opened; I was waking up to my own hopeless condition as a woman. I became quite dissatisfied with myself."[98] She was determined to change the miserable condition of woman.

In June 1880 she contracted a civil marriage, outside her caste, with a Bengali lawyer. Their daughter, Manorama, was born in the following year. Sadly in the beginning of 1882 her husband died of cholera. Suddenly her social status became that of a Hindu widow, with no rights; she should shave her head, wear a white saree, use no ornaments and withdraw into her home or into one of the widow homes where such unfortunate women

---

98. Staffner, *Significance of Jesus*, 154–55.

were often maltreated, including sexual exploitation. Her liberal spirit revolted against such humiliations. Gradually she was transformed into the most controversial and revolutionary Indian woman of her times.[99] Madhava Govind Ranade (1842–1901) a member of the Prarthana Samaj in Bombay as well as a member of the Widow Marriage Association founded in 1866 and other reformers invited her back to Poona. Ramabai arrived in Poona in April 1882. With the support of some of the reformers, Pandita Ramabai opened the "Arya Mahila Samaj," Aryan Women's Association, in Poona and Bombay in May and November 1882 respectively with objectives of eliminating evils like child marriage, ill treatment of widows, and promoting of education of girls and so forth. As the spokesperson of 300 high caste women, Ramabai welcomed and addressed W.W. Hunter, the President of the Education Commission (1882) appointed by Lord Rippen, to enquire into the state of Indian education. She illustrated the pathetic situation of women in Maharashtra and India. According to the Census Report (1881), there were 23 million widows in the country, of whom 52 percent were below the age of ten; and only 0.5 percent were literate etc.[100] Her lecture in Marathi was so impressive that Hunter got it translated into English and it was distributed in both India and England.

She decided to travel to England, to cross the "black water," a sin in the eyes of the Hindus, to learn more about women's education and avail herself of some training in medicine to help the poor and sick women in the Indian villages. To raise fund for the travel she wrote the book, *Stree Dharma Neeti*, or *Morals For Hindu Women* in 1882. Her main source of knowledge was Sanskrit Scriptures and Literature, in addition to her own personal experiences. No woman in the past could have done a similar work since they were forbidden to learn as well as to read Sanskrit books. In addition to collecting funds, she prepared herself by learning English from the Anglican nuns in Poona and in return taught them Marathi. On 17th May 1883 she left for England with her daughter Manorama and Anandibai Bhagat, a student. They were welcomed and accommodated at St. Mary's Home, Wantage, Berkshire. While in Wantage she was deeply impressed by the services given to women in the Rescue Home. She enquired with the nuns what made the Christians to care for the "fallen women." In answer the nun read out the story of Christ's infinite love and compassion for the Samaritan women, from the Gospel of St. John (4:4–42) without despising her because Jesus came to save sinners. Later Ramabai wrote:

99. Chakravarti, *Pandita Ramabai*, 1–10.
100. Staffner, *Significance of Jesus*, 156.

Varieties of Hindu Responses to Evangelical Mission

"I have never heard or read anything like this in the religious books of the Hindus; I realized, after reading the fourth chapter of Saint John's Gospel, that Christ was truly the Divine Saviour he claimed to be, and none but he could transform and uplift the downtrodden women of India, and of every land." The Hindu laws and traditions were very harsh on women. "The Hindu Shastras do not deal kindly with these women. The law of the Hindu commands that the king shall cause the fallen women to be eaten by dogs in the outskirts of the town."[101]

The attraction that she had felt for Christianity in Calcutta, where she had read the Bible as a member of the Brahmo Samaj, was again resurfacing. The shock, pain, anxiety and confusion she suffered after the death of her five intimate family members, within a span of five months coupled with the experience of rejection of widowhood, seriously disturbed her faith in Hinduism. In Christianity Ramabai found the religion which treated women, including widows and fallen women, with respect and compassion. Attracted by Christ, the divine saviour of downtrodden women in India, she made a decisive break with the religion of her ancestors and was baptized along with her daughter on 29th September 1883. After her conversion Ramabai wrote: "I was comparatively happy, and felt a great joy in finding a new religion which was better than any other religion I had known before—I was hungry for something better than what the Hindu Shastras gave. I found it in the Christian Bible and was satisfied."[102] Many Hindus in India, including Vivekananda, who proclaimed the glorious Vedanta in the West, renounced her because Ramabai championed a discordant voice for the oppressed and subjugated women of her time.[103]

Then at the invitation of her cousin Anandibai Joshi, a medical student, she left for America in February 1886. During her two year stay in America she had the opportunity to travel widely, lecture on women's condition in India and get acquainted with various women's organizations working for their progress. Still in USA, in 1887 she published her best-known book, *The High caste Hindu Women*. On her return from America, with the help of some prominent Brahmins, "Sharada Bhavan" was inaugurated in Bombay in March 1889. The Sharada Bhavan was exclusively for Brahmin child widows. It was still too much controlled by Brahmin patriarchy to which Ramabai seriously objected. A severe famine in India during 1896–1900 created a large number of widows and orphans.

101. Ibid., 160.
102. Quoted by Sengupta, *Pandita Ramabai*, 139–40.
103. Chakravarti, *Pandita Ramabai*, 17.

The Future of Christian Mission in India

Ramabai recalled how her own parents died during the last famine. Her compassionate initiative of bringing many widows and orphans to Sharada Bhavan was opposed by the caste Hindus. Therefore she turned her back on the upper caste Hindu ethos and moved out of Bombay to establish "Mukti Sadan," House of Liberation, in Kedgaon, outside of Poona. Its objectives were the welfare of all widows and children of all castes, and religions. Soon the number of inmates began to swell. Gradually some of the inmates, after regular participation in prayer and worship, embraced Christianity. The girls did all types of works like weaving, dairy farming, cooking, gardening and running a printing press. She trained many girls as teachers, nurses, printers in the press she had opened. Out of the inmates eighty five shared in various administrative responsibilities of the community.[104]

From 1891 Pandita Ramabai felt a great urge to share her peace and happiness with more people "I can scarcely contain the joy and keep it to myself. I am like the Samaritan woman who left her water pot and went her way into the city and said to the men: come and see the man who told me all things I ever did. Is not he the Christ?—I have always found that it was the greatest joy of the Christian life to tell people of Christ and his great love for sinners."[105] Soon Mukti Sadan became a centre for prayer. In December 1901 about 1200 people were baptized.[106] The new Christians were not affiliated to any particular church. Ramabai said that she found "a Babel of religions in Christian countries. Each sect was different from the other." She therefore started a non-denominational institution, i.e., the Bible based Christianity. Singing Marathi Kirtans, composed by the Marathi Christian poet N. V. Tilak, was part of their worship.

She felt that the existing Marathi Bible was characterized by "Padri Marathi," Missionary Marathi and Sanskritized Marathi. She argued that the language of the original Bible was the language of the shepherds and peasants. With this in mind Ramabai began to study Hebrew and Greek in order to translate the Bible direcatly from the original. In 1904 she started the translations. When she was in England she had learnt to type-set at the press of the sisters, and now began to spend a great deal of time teaching the inmates to set type in Marathi, Hindi, English and later in Greek and Hebrew. She completed her translation in 1922, after two decades of strenuous work before her death in April in the same year, at the age of

---

104. Omvedt, "Pandita Ramabai," 168.
105. Staffner, *Significance of Jesus*, 164.
106. Sengupta, *Pandita Ramabai*, 283.

Varieties of Hindu Responses to Evangelical Mission

sixty four. And the Bible was finally printed in 1924 in her own press; 50,000 copies. Her own thirty seven publications included *Greek-Marathi Lexicon* and *Hebrew-Marathi Lexicon*. All the Marathi speakers must feel proud and deeply indebted to this great lover of the Bible. "Pandita Ramabai is the only woman in the world who has translated the whole Bible, single handed, from the original Greek and Hebrew," observes Padmini Sengupta. [107]

The above short survey of the Hindu converts who earnestly endeavored to answer the thorny question why they dared to leave their original religion and became disciples of Jesus Christ, in spite of serious objections and painful consequences, like expulsion from family and caste resulted in the creation of an indigenous Christian theology and is obviously sketchy and incomplete. But, for the first time, it put the foundation stone and showed the direction for further expansion and growth in the twentieth century. The contributions of the foreign theologians in India, unquestionably important, are not included for the sake of brevity. Among the founding fathers of Indian Christian theology study of other original thinkers will be unquestionably enriching.[108]

The Hindu—Christian encounter broadly gave rise to five distinct trends of thoughts and actions. The first school, having rediscovered the essential truth of Hinduism, either by their own search or with the help of Orientalist scholars, became open to the social precepts of Jesus for the purification of some of its degenerate social customs but rejected the theological content of the missionary preaching. The second school, enlightened by Western rationalism and liberalism, radically rejected Hindu religion, characterized by Brahmin priestly domination and dehumanizing social evils, and enthusiastically embraced Christianity, though not in large number. The third trend was marked by extreme Hindu fundamentalism, which displayed an equally aggressive hostility towards Christian proselytization and Western influence as subversive of the old order. And fourthly, the powerful social reform movements pioneered by charismatic Harijan and Adivasi leaders who began to challenge the traditional social order, with the help of western philosophy of liberty, equality, fraternity and human dignity. Finally, the Protestant Churches and sects introduced the idea that religion should become a personal choice, as opposed to religion by birth. The introduction of rationalism in religion was also simultaneously introduction of secularization in the country. And all these

---

107. Ibid., 238
108. Boyd, *Introduction*.

trends were directly or indirectly stimulated and inspired by the Christian mission, English education and the evangelical administrators. On the poor response of caste Hindus K. N. Subramanyam observes: "The only region in which Christians found high caste converts was Bengal and more were found in the Protestant community than among Catholics."[109] The Anglican chaplains belonging, both to the high church and low church, the Wesleyan Methodist Missionary Society, London Missionary Society the Danish Missionaries, the Moravians Missionaries were also laboring in various parts of Bengal after the change of the British policy in 1813.[110]

Western Education and Transformation of the Indian Mind

In the beginning of the eighteenth century almost all of India was illiterate. Persian, was the administrative language of the Mughal empire. The popular social ethos was characterized by ignorance, superstitions, and accompanying static socio-religious behavior in daily life, sustained by the opium of religion meticulously supplied by the Brahmin Priests. The new encounter with Western colonialism and Christian mission undoubtedly provoked a cultural revolution. The stimulating forces were almost exclusively Western; non-conformist evangelical missionary challenges, the British social reforms, English education with European science and liberal thinking. In the words of S. Natrajan, the editor of the *Indian Social Reformer*, "Three main channels through which modern ideas have found their way to India are British rule, English education and Christian Missions."[111] Because of the past exaggerated pre-occupation with quantitative analysis of the success of mission, a qualitative examination of the missionary contribution towards change of the traditional mindset of the Indian people drew only marginal attention. Therefore a qualitative interpretation of the impact of Christian mission through education is the primary focus here. In other words: how did the western education transform the mentality of the people? How the Indian mind and traditional pattern of thinking, its core value system, its culture and lifestyle were substantially altered, very slowly but unquestionably, at every strata of the population and society? The power of new ideas in changing individuals and societies for the better, usually originating outside the social system, is the subject of enquiry here.

---

109. Quoted by Moffett, *History*, 2:446.
110. Mitra, "Contribution of Christianity," 111–13.
111. Natrajan, *Century*, 5.

Varieties of Hindu Responses to Evangelical Mission

Missionary Education in South India

The beginning of basic education in India coincides with the arrival of the Danish—German Lutheran missionaries, Bartholomew Ziegenbalg and Henry Plutschau, in Tranquebar, Tamilnadu, in 1706. Two years after his arrival B. Ziegenbalg (1682–1719), the father of modern Protestant mission in India, following the Halle Pietist educational system of his homeland, Germany, opened two schools, one for boys and the other for girls, to impart Christian education. Opening the first girl's school in India was a revolution in the era. In 1715 the missionaries opened another school and seventy children joined it with the hope of securing employment in the European East India companies.[112] Christian F. Schwartz, (1724–98), the founder of the Tinnelvelly mission, was the most famous of all the Tranquebar missionaries in South India, under the aegis of the English Society for the Propagation of Christian knowledge. He himself was a teacher in a few Christian schools as he lived twenty years in Thanjavoor alone. Six English Schools were started by him in Madras Presidency between 1742–1772. He was the founder of the first High School, with his name, in the Presidency. Among his many converts a Maratha Brahmin lady, Kohila, built a church in Palayamkottai in 1785 and became famous as the "Mother of the Tinnevelly Church."

The scholar missionary Robert Caldwell (1814–1891), an Anglican from Belfast, having arrived in Madras in 1838, worked for half a century in the Tirunelveli or Tinnevelly mission and became another pioneer in the promotion of higher education. On the primitive method of education in the area he wrote: children sitting on the floor cross-legged, scantily dressed, were learning to write on fine sand spread out before them on the ground. Gradually they learn to write on Palmyra leaves with steel pen. In order to enforce work discipline the teachers were paid according to the number of pupils passed in the monthly exam, a pattern that was already operating effectively in South Travencore. Mrs. Martha Mault of London Missionary Society had already opened schools and hostels for girls in South Travencore as early as 1821.[113] Rev. Caldwell and his wife Eliza, with the financial support of the Ladies Association, a women's auxiliary of the Society for Promoting Christian Knowledge from England, founded two boardings: one for boys in 1841 and another for girls in 1844, with two hundred and sixty three boys and six girls.[114] The primary objective of ed-

---

112. Ghosh, *History of Education*, 294.
113. Kumardoss, *Robert Caldwell*, 103–6.
114. Ibid., 117.

ucation was to enable them to read the Bible; plus produce ideal Christian women. In the missionary hostels children of the upper castes and lower castes ate meals cooked by outcaste cooks and it was the beginning of a very challenging process of minimizing, if not overcoming, the rigid caste mentality. Caldwell also introduced mid-day meals to attract regular attendance. The lasting influence of this initiative can be gauged from the fact that the government of Tamil Nadu and a few other states even today continue the system.[115]

The renewal of the Charter Act of 1833 emphasized the promotion of Indian and Western knowledge through English education. With Sir Charles Wood's Educational Dispatch of 1854, the former government policy of Anglicizing the education of the upper castes was revised. Diffusion of Western knowledge to all classes of people by means of their own languages and higher education in English to the upper castes was the mark of the paradigm shift. So far all over India little was done for vernacular education except in Madras Province by the Christian missionaries. Demands for higher education, particularly for English education, encouraged Caldwell and his companions to establish two high schools for boys and girls, with some financial support of the government. Further in 1883 with the generous contributions of benefactors at home Bishop Caldwell college was founded in Tuticorin, the headquarter of Tirunelvelly as well as a seaport.[116] The publication of *A Comparative Grammar of Dravidian Languages* by Caldwell in 1856 would later influence the origin of the Dravidian Anti-Brahman cultural and political movement in Tamil Nadu. He was also the author of the controversial book, *A Political and General History of the District of Tinnevelly in the Presidency of Madras*.

An enquiry conducted in Madras in 1822 found that there were 12,498 institutions of all kinds, with 1,84,110 pupils, with an average of fifteen.[117] The government of Madras, in 1826 opened 100 new schools in rural districts. And English medium high schools were founded in Madras (1841) in Cuddalore (1853) and in Rajmundri (1853), implementing the new policy of the government.[118] In 1830 the Scottish Presbyterian Church established the General Assembly of schools in Madras. Rev. John Anderson opened an English medium school in 1837 which would later grow into the prestigious Madras Christian College. More schools were started by

115. Ibid., 131.
116. Ibid., 234–37.
117. O'Malley, *General Survey*, 645–49.
118. Mangalwadi, *Missionary Conspiracy*, 364–67.

Varieties of Hindu Responses to Evangelical Mission

him in Kanchipuram (1833), Chingelpet (1840), and in Triplicane (1841), including a school for girls.[119] In 1841 the Scottish Missionaries initiated the education of high caste Hindu girls at Madras. By this date 30,000 boys were being educated in missionary school, of whom about 3,000 were attending English schools. And the girls were offered equal opportunity. "By 1853 the missionary activity in education was almost equal to official enterprises which had 1,474 institutions with 67,569 pupils. If, however, the work of the Roman Catholic Mission were added to those of the Protestant organizations missionary work in education certainly exceeded the official enterprise."[120] This was a remarkable contribution of Christian missionaries to Tamil Nadu, perhaps, unmatched by any other part of India.

The London Missionary Society opened schools for the lower castes in Madras, Kumbakonam, Salem, Coimbatore, Nagarcoil, Attur and Erode. Society for the Propagation of Faith established vernacular schools and hostels in Madurai, Tanjore and Arcot in rural areas, targeting children of new converts. When the Wesleyan missionaries established schools and colleges in Nagapattnam they attracted large number of upper caste students who reacted to admissions of Paraiyar students both on the grounds of untouchability and the fear that educated Paraiyar would not be available for menials jobs. From 1880 the "Church of England Zenana Bible and Medical Mission" paid special attention to female education. The Zenana mission opened a new chapter in the Protestant mission which lacked women missionaries, unlike the catholic mission with religious nuns. By 1881 the Public Instruction Department realized that the beneficiaries of education were the upper castes and Eurasians. For instance the number of Paraiyar pupils in the primary school was only 2,740, including 254 girls.[121] The missionaries had frequently highlighted the government apathy towards the panchamas. The government order of 1893 sanctioned an additional stipend of Rs. two per month to each Paraiyar student. Separate schools were constructed in villages with large paraiyar population.[122] Since 1870 Tamil Nadu was blessed with more schools and colleges established by the Protestant churches for girls education than any other state in India.

---

119. Basu, *Nandanar's Childern*, 95–98.
120. Ghosh, *History of Education*, 338.
121. Basu, *Nandanar's Childern*, 169.
122. Ibid., 174.

The Future of Christian Mission in India

Calcutta and English Education of Upper Castes

Before the arrival of the British East India Company in Calcutta in 1690 and the arrival of the Danish Missionaries in Serampore in 1758 Portuguese was the *lingua franca* in sea-ports and European trade centres. The religious education of Hindus and Muslims consisted of memorizing Sacred scriptures with little critical methods. The Portuguese missionary as well as government contribution to Indian education was next to nil. The arrival of the Baptist missionaries in Calcutta in 1793 would mark radical shift in the educational system. The idea of promoting educational facilities to all classes of people was inspired by a pamplet entitled, *Hints for the Establishment of Native Schools* (1814) by the Serampore Baptist missionary Dr. Marshman. This document is considered revolutionary for that age.[123] English education was first introduced not as a result of state action but of private initiatives on the part of a few Christian missionaries, more especially the Baptist missionaries of Serampore and the private initiative on the part of a few enlightened Indians and not the British administration.[124] A government enquiry in 1846 revealed that less than 5 percent of the children in school going age attended schools. J. E. W. Bethune, head of the government schools, opened a girls' school in 1849 "to extend benefits of education to the other half (women)." And by 1889 Bethune school expanded to become India's first women's college. In 1819, some pious ladies in England, at the request of the Baptist missionaries in Calcutta, founded a Society for the Education of Girls in India. In 1823 Miss Cook of the British Foreign School Society established twenty three schools in Calcutta and in the surrounding villages, with about 500 Christian pupils, most of whom were from the lower castes.[125] On the state of female education in Bengal William Adam wrote in 1836: "A superstitious feeling is alleged to exist that the majority of the Hindu families, principally cherished by the women and not discouraged by the men, that a girl taught to read and write will soon after marriage become a widow."[126] As a consequence she would be burned alive on the pyre of her husband. An enquiry revealed that only 400 women out of forty million could write. It was the missionaries who initiated girl's education, with revolutionary consequences in the following decades.[127] In 1849 Pandit Ishwar Chandra

123. O'Malley," General Survey," 646.
124. Ibid., 649.
125. Ibid., 685.
126. Forbes, "Education for Women," 48.
127. Ibid., 87–88.

Varieties of Hindu Responses to Evangelical Mission

Vidyasagar (1820-91), a leading member of Brahmo Samaj, founded the first Hindu school in Calcutta for girl's education, including two high schools. The rapid change of attitude to girls' education was evident from the fact that enlightened Hindus began to establish free English schools at their expense, in Calcutta, Benares, Allahabad, Agra and Delhi.

Charles Grant after twenty three years of life and work in India, wrote a treatise: *Observation on the state of Society among the Asiatic subject of Great Britain, Particularly in the Respect of morals and on the means of Impressing it* (1797). For the betterment of a degenerating Indian Society Grant argued for introducing Western knowledge through English education.[128] Lord Thomas Babington Macaulay's (1800-1859) "Minutes on Indian Education," (1835), formulated the vision: "It is my firm belief that, if our plans of education are followed up, there will not be a single idolater among the respectable class in Bengal thirty years hence." He explained how to convert them into civilized English men and women: "We must at present do our best to form a class who may be interpreters between us and the millions whom we govern; a class of persons, Indian in blood and colour, but English in taste, in opinion, in morals and intellect. This object must be effected by means of the English language in the higher branches of instruction and by that of the vernacular languages of India to the great masses of people." Its goals further included, "uprooting demoralizing practices and crimes that had prevailed for ages in India." He, like Alexander Duff, cynically argued: "a single shelf of good European library is worth the whole native literature of India and Arabia."[129] In 1868 Max Mueller had written to the Secretary of State for India: "India has been conquered once. But it must be conquered, and that second conquest should be a conquest by education."[130] In March 1835 the Governor General William Bentinck's government decided, in the light of Lord Macaulay's education policy, to provide education through the medium of English and two years later Persian was abolished as the language of administration.

When the colonial secular policy, particularly after the Indian Mutiny in 1857, forbade the teaching of the Bible to non-Christians in schools and colleges teaching of English literature, secular humanism, enlightened liberal philosophy and modern science was envisaged as an adequate substitute to impart Christian morality and values and thus achieve the second

---

128. Ghosh, *History of Education*, 290-93.
129. Sullivan, *Macaulay*, 141-44.
130. Quoted by Shourie, *Missionaries in India*, 139.

goal of evangelization, i.e., civilizing the uncivilized.[131] The rapid spread of English education was achieved through three agents: missionaries, Government and progressive upper caste Hindus. The Indian openness and demand for English education and Western knowledge was evident from the sale of books in Calcutta in 1835: 32,000 English books, under 13,000 in Hindustani and Bengali, and only 1500 in Persian, Arabic and Sanskrit.[132] The popularity of English news papers, with foreign news, was on the rise. To speak English, to read English and write English were esteemed a mark of culture not only in the colonial era but also in the post-independence era because the contact with the West was highly refreshing for suffocated Indian minds. In the words of Indian sociologist M. N. Srinivas: "Evangelical Christianity is regarded characteristically Western, and it is indisputable that Christian missionaries played a crucial role in India's modernization."[133] The Catholic Church in India was very suspicious of the Protestant English education. However, witnessing the conspicuous impact of the Protestant college education in Calcutta the Jesuit missionaries cautiously entered into the new field of education by opening the first catholic college, St. Xavier's in Calcutta in 1860.

Education in Bombay and Western India

After the Maratha war in Poona in 1818, the British rule in Deccan was established and missionary activities were resumed in the Bombay Presidency. By 1822 the Honorable governor of Bombay, Mountstuart Elphinstone, took over the Bombay Education Society, established in 1815 by the church of England for the education of Anglo-Indian children. He was a pioneer of English education both for the Hindus and Parsees. When he retired in 1827, the leaders of these communities raised a fund in his honour and the Elphinstone College was founded to raise a class of persons qualified by their intelligence and morality for high employment in civil administration in India.[134] The American Missionary Society opened the first girl's school in Bombay in 1824. The Church Missionary Society opened their first Female school by 1826. Inspired by these examples two girls school were opened in Ahmedabad in 1851. The American missionary Society opened schools, in Ahmednagar, known as the Marathi mission. The London Missionary Society's Gujarat mission established

---

131. Mayhew, "Christian Ethic," 313.
132. Ibid., 313–23.
133. Srinivas, *Social Change*, 52.
134. Ghosh, *History of Education*, 331–33.

Varieties of Hindu Responses to Evangelical Mission

education institutions in Surat where the British East India had already established its first trading post as early as 1608. The Irish Presbyterian missionary Society opened both English and vernacular schools in the state of Kathiawar. By 1827 the Scottish Presbyterian missionaries were running eighty schools in South Konkan with around 3000 pupils. "Thus in every province of the Bombay Presidency missionary enterprise was at work."[135] The London Society for the Promotion of Female Education sent out women missionaries to work among the Parsee women. A few educated Hindus and Parsees took initiatives to open schools, particularity for girls.

Rev. John Wilson (1804-1875) of Church of Scotland and his wife Margaret arrived in Bombay in 1829. Margaret started the first Western School for the Indian girls in December 1929 and would continue to build another six in the following years. Wilson, after learning Marathi, founded the local Presbyterian church. He became the founder of the co-educational Wilson College in Bombay in 1832, with special emphasis on the education of women. Imitating the example of his counterpart, Alexander Duff, he conducted religious debates with educated Hindus, Muslims and Parsees. The missionaries of the Presbyterian Church of Scotland and American missionaries in Bombay and Western India were aggressively attacking Hindu idol worship, priesthood without spirituality, superstitious practices like astrology, caste system that denied human equality, numerous evils against girl child, widows and women in general. The evangelical revival in Scotland under the guidance of Methodist leaders like John Wesley insisted that the Gospel should have an impact on society. In 1839 the strength of students was reduced from two hundred and eighty four to fifty because of the commotion created by conversions of a few Parsee students. Notwithstanding after a few weeks most of the students returned to the college.

Debates held at the Scottish missionary John Wilson's home in Bombay in May 1830 between Wilson and the Hindu Pundits were published. The Hindu Periodical *Dharpan* started in 1832 by Bal Shashtri Jambekar, was the mouthpiece of Hindu defense and reforms in Western India. The American missionaries launched, *Dnyanodaya* or The Rise of Knowledge, in 1942, an Anglo-Marati periodical, conveying Christian beliefs as well as secular subjects like medicine and modern science. The scientific worldview, material development, social progress and secular values of the western Christian nation were presented as intrinsically

---

135. Mangalwadi, *Missionary Conspiracy*, 367-70.

linked to the Christian religion. In contrast India's failure to generate a rational science, political inability to maintain internal order and check external enemies, lack of economic development and misery of masses were attributed to Hindu doctrines. The conclusion was evident. India required a fundamental shift from the Hindu world view and doctrines to the Christian worldview and its doctrines. "The apparent connection of the Christian doctrine with objective truth about the world constituted a great polemical strength of missionary propaganda."[136]

Founding of a few organizations for social transformation testify to the direct impact of Christian mission and college education in Western India. *Paramahansa Mandali* or "Society for the Supreme Being," founded in 1849 by Dadoba Pandurang, a teacher of Elphinstone College, spelt out the following tenets of its beliefs which, without doubt, reflect the impacts of missionary debates with Hindu pundits.

1. God is one, and he alone is to be worshiped.
2. Religion consists in worshiping God with love and through moral conduct.
3. The Religion of Mankind is one.
4. Every individual has an independent right to consider for himself.
5. Daily and occasional religious ceremonies should be consistent with human reason.
6. The whole humankind is one caste.
7. Every human being is to be brought up and instructed in useful knowledge.

(Source, O'Hanlon, *Caste, Conflict*, 2002:99–100.)

Most of the above principles are similar to the principles enunciated by Brahmo Samaj in Calcutta. *Manavadharma Sabha* or "The Society for Human Religion" was founded in Surat by the founder of the above mentioned Mandali with similar guiding principles. Both organizations were secret societies because its members were afraid of reactions of the public. Parallelism between the ideological framework of Christian beliefs preached in the missionary propaganda and the ideas of the European radicals are evident in the doctrines and values of these new associations.

---

136. O'Hanlon, *Caste Conflict*, 56.

Varieties of Hindu Responses to Evangelical Mission

The branches of Mandali were founded in Poona, Satara, Ahmednagar, Belgaum, and Ratnagiri, covering the whole of Bombay Presidency. The social awareness generated by the Western education led to the creation of a Secret Society which met and discussed social problems and shared a common meal, cooked by an outcast and shared by the members of different religious communities. In 1867, under certain pressure from K. C. Sen, the members of the secret association founded *Prarthana Samaj*, a theistic Society, under the leadership of Dr. Atmaram Pandurang (1823–98), brother of Dadoba Pandurang, and a personal friend of Dr. Wilson. It established its branches in Poona, Kolhapur and Satara in Maharashtra. In South India out of twenty nine Samajes in the Madras Presidency eighteen were Prarthana Samaj. K. C. Sen had already founded Veda Samaj in Madras in 1864.[137]

The Catholic children, per law, were debarred from attending the Protestant schools and colleges because of the traditional enmity and doctrinal disputes. Being aware of the educational backwardness of the Catholics Vicar Apostolic Athanasius Hartmann of Bombay (1850–59) invited Religious Societies to meet the challenge. The Sisters of Jesus and Mary, opened a school for girls, near the Gateway of India. During the 1856–58 period the Jesuit missionaries were entrusted with the education of boys. St. Xavier's high school was built in 1856 on land donated by the government. The high school with the strength of 439 boys was elevated to a college in 1869 with eleven students.[138] In the initial period it was mostly attended by Hindu and Parsee students, so much so that it was popularly known as "Parsee College."[139] In Bombay too the founding of a catholic college was forty years behind the Protestants.

Some of the leading women religious congregations in the educational field in the nineteenth century were: Religious of Jesus and Mary (RJM), 1842 in Agra; Institute of the Blessed Virgin, popularly known as Loretto Sisters, in Patna, 1853; Daughter of the Cross from Liege, Belgium, in Bombay (1863) and Calcutta (1867). Canossian Daughters of Charity (1889); Holy Cross Sisters of Ingenbohl (1894); The Congregation of the Immaculate Heart of Mary in Pondicherry, in 1844; The Franciscan Presentation Sisters in Coimbatore, in 1853; Congregation of Our Lady of Dolors in Trichinapolly, in 1864; The Congregation of St. Anne in Madras in 1863; Sisters of St. Joseph of Lyon in 1906; Mission Sisters of Ajmeer in

---

137. Farquhar, *Modern Religious*, 77.
138. Minwalla, "History," 11–30.
139. Fuchs, "German Representatives," 86.

The Future of Christian Mission in India

1911.[140] The earliest Congregation of Brothers in India were: The Patrician Brothers in Madras in 1880; the Irish Christian Brothers in Delhi in1890; St. Gabriel Brothers in Pondicherry, in 1908. A Muslim ruler donated one of his palaces to the Sacred Heart nuns to open the first women's college in Western India, Sophia College, Bombay, in 1941, mainly for the education of Muslim girls.

Education in North—Western Province

Until 1800 there were only a few hundred Christians and no Christians schools in North-west India though the Jesuits from 1579, the Carmelites from 1773 and the Capuchins from 1784 were serving the Catholics attached to the army. Between 1800 and 1857 seven Protestant Mission Societies established mission stations and schools attached to them. With the support of Maharaja Ranjit Sing in Ludhiana the Presbyterian missionaries set up schools in Ludhiana (1834), Farukobad (1836), Ambale (1898), Lahore (1849), Dehra Dun (1853) and Rawalpindi (1856). The Church Missionary Society opened schools in Simla, Kotgarh, and Kangra in 1854. The Associate Presbyterian Synod of North America arrived in Sialkot in 1856 and took over a school that was started by the CMS in 1842. The Church of Scotland too arrived here in 1857 and opened two vernacular schools in the following year.[141]

An enquiry into the state of education in the North—Western Province in 1846 revealed that "on an average less than 5 percent of the youth who are of the age to attend schools obtain any instruction and that instruction which they do receive is of very imperfect kind."[142] By 1860 Delhi, Amritsar and Lahore had both the government as well as mission schools. At the same period Peshwar, Jullundhar, Ludhiana and Ambala only had mission schools, and no government school. Education of girls and Dalits was a major challenge since both the categories were strictly forbidden to learn by religious injunctions. However breakthrough was made by missionaries like in other regions of India. In 1836 a school was opened in Ludhiana for the orphan girls. The Society for the Propagation of the Gospel started a school for girls in Delhi in 1859. The CMS opened girl's schools in Amritsar, Kangra, Jandiala and Marowar in 1861. The Church of England Zanana Missionary Society (CEZMS) founded in 1880, was primarily responsible for running thirty mission schools with

140. Houtart and Lemercinier, *Size and Structure*, 139–40.
141. Webster, *Social History*, 41–48.
142. Ibid., 84.

Varieties of Hindu Responses to Evangelical Mission

1,254 women and girls. Facing many objections in 1880 nearly 9,000 girls, 4,000 in Government and 5,000 in Missionary schools, were attending schools, with certain amount of irregularity.[143] Up to 1881 no girl had yet passed the upper primary education.

In Delhi the Baptist missionaries pioneered the education of 558 Chamar children, attending thirty five schools. The American Presbyterians opened Dalit schools in Lahore. Another category was the Anglo—Indian schools. Bishop Cotton Public School for European and Anglo—Indian boys was opened in Simla, the summer capital of the British, in 1863. And the Congregation of Jesus and Mary began a girl's school here in the same year, mostly for the children of the British officers. And a boy's school run by the Vicariate Apostolic of Hindustan in Agra was shifted to Simla, in the same year. Every mission station in North—West India maintained at least one school. Missionaries made large investments in education because of the evangelical purpose. Upper caste parents were unwilling to send children to missionary schools where Christian instruction was mandatory. In order to make education affordable for the weaker sections of the society fees in the mission schools was lower than that of the government schools. According to the report of Director of Public Instruction in 1880 the number of students multiplied three times to reach the 100,000 mark. The government authorities found fault with mission schools, who received grant-in-aid program, that they failed to maintain good standard. In 1879–1880 the education department standardized education with three years of lower primary school, two years of upper primary, three years of middle school and two years of high school.

A small number of adult conversions, mainly in colleges, provoked serious protests, including withdrawal of students from a few schools. Arya Samaj in Punjab pressurized parents to withdraw students from mission schools. Some Muslim leaders too launched similar campaign to boycott mission schools and close their Zenanas to women missionaries who were engaged in medical services as well as Bible distribution during their visits. Mission schools were criticized for making Christian religious education compulsory in their schools yet the urban upper and middle classes were seeking western education in order to enter government services and professions. Rapid expansion of English medium schools by the Evangelical Missionaries in the Hindi belt between 1800–1857 was one of reasons for the Indian Sepoy Revolt of 1857. Therefore Queen Victoria's proclamation of 1858 disclaimed "any desire to impose our convictions on

---

143. Ibid., 89–90.

any of our subjects" and ordered British officials to abstain from interfering with Indian beliefs and rituals "on the pain of our highest displeasure."[144]

Progress of Education: Colleges and Universities

The government enquiry of 1835 found that not even one girls school was administered by the government. The government began to take some systematic step towards education only after Sir Charles Wood's dispatch of 1854. The girls' education passed through all stages of apathy, ridicule, criticism and finally acceptance. Whatever progress was made, particularly in girls' education, was the fruit of missionary initiatives. According to the Hunter Commission report (1882) out of 45–50 million children in the age bracket of five to twelve, in the total population of 200 million, only a little above 2.37 million were attending schools, i.e., about 5 percent. Only one out of twenty boys and one out of two hundred fifty girls attended primary school with extreme irregularity.[145] In 1901 after one hundred years of earnest efforts of all agencies, the literacy rate among primary level children increased to 6 percent and it was a breakthrough. The general literacy rate among women was an abysmal 1 percent, compared to 7 percent for men. Religious disparity in literacy was more shocking. Only three out of ten thousand Muslim women; four out of thousand Hindu women; and seventeen out of hundred Christian women were literate.[146]

A change in attitude towards education was more decisive than the numerical expansion. The Parsees were most open to Western ideas and English education, including girls' education. In 1913 out of ten high schools for girls' in Bombay, eight were being run by Parsees. The Parsee philanthropist and educationalist B. M. Malabari exclaimed: "How much we owe to Christian missionaries. We are indebted to them for the first start in the race of intellectual emancipation—. I feel bound to acknowledge the benefits I have derived from contact with the spirit of Christianity."[147] In spite of certain failures the missionaries unquestionably deserve to be credited with initiating a revolutionary process of democratizing education for all, particularly for outcastes, tribals and women, and breaking the monopoly of Brahmin priests.

With the opening of English colleges the Protestant missionaries trigged a revolution in the intellectual and cultural life of India. The Church

144. Quoted by Keay, *India*, 445.
145. Cunningham, "Education," 159.
146. Moffett, *History*, 2:442.
147. Quoted by David, "Mission," 244.

Varieties of Hindu Responses to Evangelical Mission

Missionary Society founded St. John 's College, Agra in 1835. After six years it opened Noble college Masulipattnam, Andhra Pradesh, in 1841. A few decade later the same Society started Edwards College in Peshwar in 1910. The London Missionary Society established Caldwell college in Tuticorin in 1883. Reid college in Lucknow was started in 1877. In 1881 the Society for the Propagation of the Gospel added a college department to their St. Stephen's High School, Delhi. In 1886 the Presbyterian Mission opened Forman College in Lahore. In 1893 the United Presbyterian Mission added a college to the existing school in Rawalpindi and named it Gordon College and the Church of Scotland opened Murray College in Sialkot in 1909.[148] The Muir Central College at Allahabad was opened in 1886. In addition many individual Christians occupied prominent positions in College and Universities and impacted policies.

All the first women's colleges were also administered by the Protestant missionaries. Of the premier women's colleges in India were: The Isabella Thoburn college, Lucknow, (1870) by the Methodist Episcopal church of America and Women's Christian college, Madras (1916) were deeply indebted to American women for their generous financial support; the Kinnaird college, Lahore, also financed by the American missionaries. The Sara Thaker college, Palamkottah, Tamil Nadu, was flanked by two pioneer schools, one for the deaf and one for the blind. Through out the nineteenth century and in the first quarter of the twentieth century women's education was an unprecedented major contribution of Christian missionaries. The Hocking Report (1932) establishes this claim. Christian Women's college thirteen; Teachers Training Schools, sixty seven; Girls High Schools, one hundred one; Girls Middle School, one hundred ninety seven. At her presidential address to the All India Women's Conference in January 1931 Dr. (Mrs) Muthulakshmi Reddi commended :

> I honestly believe that missionaries have done more for women's education in the country than government itself. The women's population of this country has been placed under a deep debt of gratitude to the several missionary agencies for their valuable contribution to the educational uplift of Indian women . . . Had it not been for these noble bands of Christian women teachers, who are the products of missionary training schools, even this much of advancement in the education of the Indian women would not have been possible; even at this day, in every province, we find the missionary women teachers working hard

---

148. Webster, *Social History,* 148.

The Future of Christian Mission in India

in the spirit of love and faith, in out-of-the-way villages, where Hindu and Muslim women dare not penetrate.[149]

After critically assessing the impact of English education, including a small number of conversions from upper castes, the Catholic Missionaries cautiously entered the field, of course quite late. Without making an enquiry into their large number of schools let me illustrate the case limiting to college education. The Catholic colleges established before 1900 were: St. Xaviers College Calcutta (1860), St. Xaviers College Bombay (1869), and St. Joseph's College, Trichiropolly (1883). St.Joseph's college was the only Catholic college in South India till around 1925. All of them were run by the Society of Jesus whose special charisma was education, both religious and secular. The Religious of Jesus and Mary established St. Bede's teacher—training college in Simla in 1904. The highest beneficiaries of college education, both by Protestants and the Catholics, were Hindus, Parsees, Jacobites, Marthomites and a small number of Dalit and Tribal converts. The relative absence of Catholic laymen in many fields like politics, economics, literature, science and others until Indian Independence was due to the closed mentality of the Catholic Church in India, with large manpower and huge financial resources, thanks to foreign missionaries. By 1900 out of fifty three colleges, founded and administered by the Christians, a minuscule minority of less than 2 percent of total population, speak volumes about their contribution to the intellectual transformation and the promotion of modernization of India. It is further observed that forty six of all the Christian colleges in India belonged to the Protestant churches. Unfortunately the Catholic church, was very reluctant to venture into English education because of their suspicion of the English Protestant liberal philosophy.

The founding of colleges by both Christian missionaries and the government in the first half of the nineteenth century had already prepared the background for establishing the first universities in India. In January 1857 Lord Canning passed the Act of Incorporation to establish three universities—Calcutta with eleven colleges, Bombay with two colleges, and Madras with one college—"to provide the highest test and encouragement to liberal education."[150] And the London University model was adopted by the new universities of India. Between 1857–1902 five universities-

---

149. Quoted by D'Silva, *Christian Community*, 99–100.
150. Ghosh, *History of Education*, 362.

Varieties of Hindu Responses to Evangelical Mission

Calcutta, Bombay, Madras, Punjab and Allahabad with 188 colleges were established.[151]

Medical missions and Medical colleges opened a new chapter at a later period. In 1835 John Scudder of the American Board of Commissioners for Foreign Missions, (ABCFM) set up the first medical missions in Madurai. In 1853 two of his sons moved to Arcot to serve in the same field. In 1854 the London Missionary Society opened at Neyyoor near Trivandrum, a hospital which would later grow into all India fame. In 1892 James Moro and his family set up the Ranaghat medical mission, in the malaria-ridden territory of Bengal. After the 1857 Mutiny when direct mission was under attack, medical work would become a means of access to the people. The Church Missionary Society opened many hospitals along the northwest frontier, at Dera Ghasi Khan (1876), Quetta (1885) and other towns. All patients and people who came to the hospital and medical centres were obliged first to listen to the reading of the Bible before receiving medical care which was free in most cases.

The American Methodist Clara Swain was the first woman doctor in India who opened a hospital for women at Bareilly in Uttar Pradesh in 1874. In the following year the American Presbyterian doctor Sara Seward opened a medical centre in Allahabad. A Medical Mission Training Institute of the United Presbyterian mission was started in Agra by Dr. Valentine in 1881. The North India School of Medicine for Christian women at Ludhiana by Dr. Edith Brown in 1894 expanded into a medical college, by the American Presbyterians. In the South Dr. Ida Scudder (1870-1960) of the Reformed Church of America, continued her father's medical work in India and opened a Medical College in Vellore, Tamil Nadu, for the training of women doctors in 1923. Medical mission was also the formal entry of women in to missionary activities on a large scale.[152] At the time of Indian Independence 90 percent of the nurses in India were Christian. But the Catholic women were prohibited to enter this field until 1920 when Anna Dengel began her work in Rawalpindi. The Society of Catholic Medical Missionaries was founded as late as 1936 when Pope Pius XI lifted the ban on women religious physicians. Again medical education was another area where the catholic church lagged behind the Protestants for a long time.

The missionaries invested large amount of foreign money and personnel in education with the primary objective of conversions. The

---

151. O'Malley, "General Survey," 656-58.
152. Neill, *The story*, 107-9.

The Future of Christian Mission in India

high hopes of missionaries and administrators fired by the evangelical spirit that a large number of Indians or high percentage of them, would be converted spontaneously under the impact of liberal education without proselytization and interference with religious liberty, were belied by the facts of history of conversion. Within half a century specially after the Indian Revolt of 1857, the evangelical expectations were frustrated, with minor exceptions. Serious debates and publications on 'educational evangelism' arrived at two major justifications to continue the educational apostolate. The first emphasized character building of the Indian students with Christian values, including manliness with highly disciplined program of athletics, gentleman's game like cricket, social services and strict moral code of conduct. Second, the changing political context of Indian Independence Movement from 1885 and the gradual introduction of local self-government schemes, required the formation of political leadership for the future. The Anglican C. F. Andrews (1871–1940), having arrived at St. Stephen's college, Delhi in 1904 and later becoming a close friend of M. K.Gandhi, R. Tagore and many other Indian political leaders, was one of the first missionary to argue that God's Spirit was incarnate in the national awakening and Indian Renaissance. Slowly but surely this view became a crucial element of the emerging new mission theology. He was convinced that the new awakening was due to the leaven of Christian thought and literature, at least in a measure, working silently beneath the surface for over a century. He strongly rejected western domination both in politics and ecclesiastical administration. He was also a great admirer of the Indian spirituality, Indian Ashrams, and supporter of the Brotherhood of the Imitation of Christ, based on the Franciscan ideal of poverty and simplicity.

Undoubtedly the spirit of the Gospel began to permeate the Indian society as a vital force. The enlightened citizens of the nineteenth century India, after acknowledging the authority of Western knowledge, instead of the religious authority of the Brahmin priesthood, dared to critique the religious traditions which were the objects of missionary attacks. They formed their own societies and program to purify and transform Hinduism from within. The English education has drawn the Indian mind into an entirely new world view and life view. "Along the line lie utterly new conceptions: freedom of speech and pen; criticism of authority, the questioning of accepted dogmas; the insistence on the right of man as opposed to his duties. The growing familiarity with these has brought a new spirit into the Indian life, the stirring of skepticisms instead of stagnant au-

Varieties of Hindu Responses to Evangelical Mission

thoritarianisms, a glimmering if not the fore runner of what we in Europe call democracy," wrote Lord Meston, in 1941.[153] One of the most decisive forces that more or less united most of the Indian educated class by the last quarter of the nineteenth century and helped in the construction of the new idea of India, was undoubtedly, English education. According to 2001 census ninety million Indians can use English as the first or second language and forty million use it as third language, totaling to one hundred thirty million. Knowledge of English language provide an edge to Indians in the global employment market, especially in the field of Information Technology. In the words of Indian historian M. J. Akbar: "Todays aspiring India feels an emotional continuity with the Raj not because of British rule but because of the English language . . . English is on the verge of dominance. The British were never as powerful as the language they left behind."[154]

Christian Mission and Social Transformation of India

As Indian philosopher S.Radhakrishnan rightly observes. "It is the pride of Hindu India that for centuries it has been able to produce individuals in every part of the country who embody the highest religious qualities—. It is the tragedy of India that while its culture produced individuals who had something undeniably attractive and superior, it did not develop a high civic or natural sense."[155] It is here that the Christian missionaries stepped in. The popular Hinduism of the nineteenth century was like the extremely polluted and dirty holy river Ganga which the Christian missionaries and the colonial administrators, with the support of enlightened Hindus, began to purify. "Christianity in India is not one among the several major religions practiced in this country, it has also been, during the last two centuries, a catalyst for altering social dynamics among . . . the people."[156] The Christian education coupled with social reform movements of the colonial administration, introduced a belated facelift to India. "A peculiarly arresting proof that Christianity has ruled the whole religious development of the last century is to be found in the social reform movements." [157]

---

153. Quoted in O'Malley, *Modern India*, vi.
154. M. J. Akbar, "History in Capital Letters," *India Today*, December 26, 2011, 13.
155. Radhakrisnan, "Hinduism," 350–51.
156. Mookherjee, *Ellusive Terrain*, 107.
157. Farquhar, *Modern Religious*, 442.

THE FUTURE OF CHRISTIAN MISSION IN INDIA

Rite of Sati and Its Abolition

The missionaries were most disturbed by various social evils, especially the horror of Sati—widow burning that was widely prevalent in Bengal and some other parts of India. The missionaries therefore initiated the process to abolish the barbarous religious act. "Sati was perhaps the most definite sign of Hindu depravity and Christian moral superiority evangelicals could get."[158] In 1803 Carey and the missionaries took a census of Sati within a radius of 30 miles from Calcutta. In 1813 an all India estimate of Sati was 33,000 of which 15,000 were among the Bengali bhadralok, elite society.[159] Carey made use of his position as a Professor in Fort William College to debate with the pundits how far the practice of Sati was approved by the Sacred books. Mrtyunjaya Vidyalankar, a much respected pundit, after analyzing different schools of Hindu laws, established that Sati was not an ordinance of the Shastras, Hindu laws. Sati rite was purely voluntary. "I regard woman's burning is an unworthy act and a life of abstinence and chastity as highly excellent."[160] Ram Mohan Roy too, in spite of his protest, helplessly witnessed the Sati of his brother's wife in 1811, began to campaign vigorously for the abolition of such a horrible custom. After Carey's three decades of crusade, with the support of missionaries and enlightened citizens, by the Regulation of XVII of 1829, Governor General Lord William Bentinck abolished the Sati rite, within the British provinces.[161] As the educated Indians began to distance themselves from the inhuman practices in villages a few Hindu widows continued the custom. Today India has at least 240 Sati temples, where rituals are still being conducted in memory of certain widows who had committed Sati not in the distant past. However the total eradication of the rite was a very slow process that it would take another 150 years, as late as 1987.[162]

Hindu Widow-Remarriage

The prohibition of Sati immediately created new problems. What happens to these widows since widows, even virgin child-widows of two years, were forbidden to remarry. Christian missionaries had already opened widow homes in Calcutta. Promotion of Hindu widow-remarriage was

---

158. Veer, *Imperial Encounters*, 43.
159. Fisch, *Immolating Women*, 233.
160. Quoted by Sharma, *Sati*, 50–51.
161. Ibid., 65.
162. *Times of India* (August 16, 2009) 16.

Varieties of Hindu Responses to Evangelical Mission

the next step of social reformers. Prompted by missionaries in October 1855 Ishwar Chandra Vidyasagar, the principal of the Sanskrit College in Calcutta, and an active member of Brahmo Samaj, led an agitation and submitted a petition to the government of India, demanding legitimation of Hindu widow marriage. He had delved deep into the Sacred books and established that widowhood was not enjoined by the Shastras. He himself conducted a few widow remarriages, including donation of monetary help. In the following year "Widow Remarriage Act" was passed .[163] Other Hindu pioneer of reforms were K. C. Sen and Sasipada Banerjee. In 1871 Banerjee, sailed to England with his wife, breaching the prohibition for a Hindu woman to cross the sea, in order to promote the cause. After his wife's death in 1887 he founded a House for Hindu widows. He himself promoted the remarriage of many widows and married a widow himself. He led the way for similar steps to be taken in Bombay and Poona.[164] One of the most prominent reformers in Maharashtra, M. G. Ranade (1842-1901), a member of the Prarthana Samaj and the general secretary of the Indian Social Conference (1887-1901), himself remarried twenty five widows in Bombay. He and his collaborators carried on vigorous agitation in Bombay in favour of marriages of Hindu widows. Soon some Hindu groups began to maintain Widow Homes in imitation of Christian practices. Pandita Ramabai, already a widow, opened Sarada Sadan, for Hindu widows in Bombay in 1889 and Mukti Sadan in Poona. Between 1906 and 1912 several Hindu Widow's Homes were founded throughout the country: for example, in Mysore (1907) in Bangalore (1910) in Madras (1912). The Deva Samaj in Ferozpore, the Arya Samaj in Jullunder and Digambar Jains in Bombay also established Widow's Homes. The Widow's Remarriage Acts alone would not change the situation drastically because many widows themselves, in addition to men, opposed the reform. Infant marriage, Sati, ban on widow remarriage and cruel treatment of widows were intimately rooted in Hindu beliefs, family system and social structure.

Child Marriage Abolition

It was the duty of the Hindu father, under the pain of sin, according to laws, to marry his daughter before her menses. Therefore most of the children were married before the age of five. The evils of child marriage included physical injury of girls and premature maternity. It was Keshub Chandra Sen, who turned the Brahmo Samaj into an all India mission

163. Natrajan, *Century*, 65.
164. Ibid., 42-47.

The Future of Christian Mission in India

with 124 branches and protested against many Hindu social evils, including child marriage and pleaded for education of girls. A Legislation in Calcutta in 1860, at the insistence of I. C. Vidyasagar, fixed the age of consent at ten years and the Arya Samaj, an anti-missionary organization, opposed child marriage in Punjab.[165] In spite of violent street protests in Calcutta the government of India passed the Age of Consent Act in 1881 whereby cohabitation with a wife under twelve years was prohibited. And B. M. Malabari, a Parsee reformer, influenced by I. C. Vidyasagar, with the support of the Prarthana Samaj as well as Christian missionaries, including John Wilson, mobilized public opinion in Bombay for the abolition of child marriage. He received much needed support when he visited England in 1890. In the following year a legislation in Bombay raised the age of consent from ten to twelve. A special marriage bill introduced in the Legislative Assembly of Delhi in 1911, in line with the Brahmo Samaj Act of 1872, with the provision of age of consent at fourteen years for girls and eighteen years for boys was defeated.[166] A Similar Act in Madras Council in 1914 was defeated; again it was defeated in 1918, owing to their conservatism.[167] A violent agitation against the Age of Consent Bill was led by the conservatives in Poona, under the leadership of B. G. Tilak, on the ground that early marriages of daughters was a religious obligation. There were, however, exceptions like Mysore and Baroda states which in 1890 and 1901 respectively adopted Civil Marriage Law and Infant Marriage Prevention Act respectively.

Sarada Marriage Restraint Act, introduced by Mr. Har Bilas Sarada in 1927 in Bombay, after three years of protest and delay came into effect in April 1930, penalizing parties for marriage when the girl was below fourteen and the boy below eighteen years of Age.[168] The 1931 Census reported that over twelve million girls were married before the age of thirteen. The social reform policy of the British government and missionaries has been in general in accord with the Christian principles. Yet the slow progress in the abolition of child marriage is evident from the fact that even today (2011) 48 percent of the marriages in rural India are contracted where the age of girls is below fifteen. It equally demonstrates the power of religious beliefs and traditions over government legislations. Change of mentality, it can be reasonably argued, cannot be achieved merely by legislation.

165. Ibid., 92.
166. Ibid., 129.
167. Ibid., 130.
168. Ibid., 140–41.

Effectiveness of any legislation equally demands supportive socio-cultural factors, particularly secular education and economic empowerment.

The Untouchables of India

The inhuman treatment of 16 percent of India's population, disturbed the moral conscience of the evangelical missionaries whose agenda included social reforms. Untouchables were the bonded slaves of India, without human rights and human dignity, almost like black slaves in America. The Hindu scriptures called them *Panchamas*, the fifth caste since they were outside the official caste system which organized the Indian society into four castes. Manu, the Hindu law giver called them chandalas or dog eaters. The British Census Report (1931) classified them as Exterior castes or Depressed Classes to accord a separate status for developmental allocations. In 1932 they were defined as "Scheduled Castes," a category which was later incorporated in the Indian Constitution. Mahatma Gandhi popularized the borrowed term, *Harijan*, children of god, first coined by the Gujarati poet Narsi Mehta, ignorant of its cryptic meaning, children of temple prostitutes. B. R. Ambedkar, spearheading their cause from the first half of the twentieth century, used the term *Dalit*, broken people, first introduced by the Indian reformer Jyoti Phule of Poona. Their menial work for the upper castes, like scavenging, leather work, grave digging, removing the night soil of the upper castes were seen as dirty and polluting. The belief of Brahmin priestly ritual purity, racial purity, and occupational purity were further hardened by their food habits like eating beef, carcasses, drinking country liquor and other licentious behaviors.[169] Their touch was considered polluting and therefore they were called untouchables. In Madras presidency they were forbidden to come out in the open because their sight was considered polluting; in Maharashtra they were forbidden to walk on the road in the evening because their long shadows would fall on and pollute the upper castes. Any outcaste who dared to defy numerous stringent rules for controlling them, were subjected various cruel punishments, including murder.

A small number of educated Hindus in the nineteenth century entertained the hope that under the British rule conversion to Christianity was the most promising means of raising the condition of the untouchables. The Indian Social Conference established under M.G.Ranade, a member of the Prarthana Samaj, in 1884 provided an all India common platform since the Hindu Society hand no common authority. Provincial

169. Webster, "Who is a Dalit?," 69.

The Future of Christian Mission in India

Conferences were organized in Bengal, Bombay, Madras, Utter Pradesh, Ahmedabad and Sind.[170] The Social Reform Conference in Calcutta (1901), the Bombay Presidency Social Reform Association (1903), the Madras Social Reform Association (1913) and the Social Reform Conference in Ahmedabad (1902) and others were the consequence of a dynamic follow up program. *The Indian National Reformer*, a journal with similar objectives, was launched in Madras in 1890. "The fear of Christianity has been the beginning much social wisdom in India," observes S. Natrajan.[171]

About 1890 an Ezhava reformist, Sri Narayana Guru, under the influence of the Christian missionaries, began to work for the transformation of his community. In 1903, the Sri Narayana Dharma Paripalana Sangam, Union for the Protection of Sri Narayana Religion, was founded near Trivandrum, the capital of Travencore. The founding of the Sanatan Dharma Sabha in Haridwar and Delhi; the Dharma Mahamandali in Bengal; the Bharat Dharma Mahaparishad in Madras worked towards the same goal. Under the initiative of the Arya Samaj an All India Sudhi Sabha, rite of purification, was started to reconvert the new Christians back to Hinduism. In order to coordinate the activities of all these new associations the Bharatha Dharma Mahamandala was formed at Muttra, Punjab in 1902.[172] In the same year the sweepers of Jullundur, after their conversion to Christianity started the Society, Valmiki Samaj to defend their rights. In 1906 the Depressed Class Mission Society was founded in Bombay to elevate the social and spiritual condition of the untouchables and the Society began to function from fifteen centres in the Presidency to remove all the disabilities imposed on them by religion and custom, like banning them admission to public schools, hospitals, court of justice, public offices and the use of public roads, public wells and so forth.[173] Educated in the Scottish mission school at Poona, Jotyrao to Phule (1826–90) and some of his friends were tempted to accept Christianity. In 1873, he wrote the book *Gulamgiri*, Slavery, and he dedicated his book to the people of America as a tribute for abolishing slavery in 1865. He said slavery in America was racial, but caste in India was religious." To fight the Brahmin domination he founded the Satyashodak Samaj, Truth—Seeking Society

---

170. Natrajan, *Century*, 215.
171. Ibid., 8.
172. Farquhar, *Modern Religious*, 316–19.
173. Natrajan, *Century*, 144–45.

Varieties of Hindu Responses to Evangelical Mission

in 1873, with the Christian principle: "All human beings are children of one God; hence they are my brothers and sisters."[174]

Dr. Ambedkar's Fight against Hinduism and Conversion to Buddhism

One of the most erudite scholar and crusader of the Dalits was Dr. Balasaheb Ambedkar (1891—1956) who, with the generous scholarships from the Maharajas of Baroda and Kolaphur, completed his higher education at Columbia University with Doctorate in 1916 and MSc in 1921 from London University. Against the backdrop of his life-long suffering as an untouchable belonging to the Mahar caste and his struggle for nearly quarter of a century for the basic human rights of the Dalits within the Hindu fold, he addressed 10,000 Dalits in Yevola in Nasik district in 1935, and declared his intention to change his religion. To the question, why conversion, he replied: "To get human treatment convert yourselves; convert for getting organized; convert for becoming strong; convert for securing equality; convert for getting liberty; convert so that your domestic life may be happy."[175] In the following two decades he made scholarly research and publications on Buddhism and Christianity with the intention of conversion. On Hinduism he reached the following conclusion: "Unfortunately, Hinduism, which is founded on the ideology of inequality and injustice leaves no room for development of enthusiasm.""So long as the untouchables continue to slave under the yoke of Hinduism, a diabolical creed— they can have no hope, no inspiration, no enthusiasm for a better life."[176] In 1935 Ambedkar met Bishop J. W. Pickett of the American Methodist church and asked for secret baptism. Ambedkar further said that he would recommend more dalits to become Christians. They even prayed together on the matter. Since Ambedkar wanted to be known as Hindu, although an unhappy one, Bishop politely refused secret baptism because of the strict rules of the Baptist church.[177] In another context Ambedkar expressed his deep appreciation of the social Gospel of Jesus. "Look at Jesus not from the stand point of theology but of society. If taken seriously, Jesus' unique message could not only save my people, but it could build the Kingdom

---

174. Joshi, *Jotirao Phule*, 25.
175. Quoted by Massey, *Dr. Ambedkar*, 31.
176. Ibid., 40.
177. Richard, *Exploring the Depth*, 36.

of God on earth."[178] After critically evaluating that the condition of dalit Christian had little impact on their social status, he abandoned the idea of conversion to Christianity. Therefore Christianity was not judged, shall we say unfortunately, his choice for conversion. His final choice therefore was for Buddhism. "Buddhism was acceptable to him because, though ancient, it satisfies the modern criteria of liberal democracy, humanism and scientific rationalism. But Buddhism also appeared satisfactory from the point of view of its religious—moral content. Paradoxically it can be argued that he rejected Hinduism because it rejected the Buddhist revolution."[179] Buddhism is the first "Protestant" religion in the world as it originated in the protest of Siddhartha Gautama, (563 BC–486 BC) against inequality of the Hindu caste system and Brahmin priest craft.

Therefore on October 14,1956, the conversion of Ambedkar and his Dalit followers in Nagpur created a history of the largest conversion event, larger than the conversion on the Pentecost. A senior Buddhist monk, Bhiku U. Chandramani (80), admitted him and his wife into Buddhism. Ambedkar, then, administered twenty two vows of neo-Buddhism, formulated by himself, to half-a-million Mahar Dalits in a public ceremony and thus converted them to Buddhism. In his address on the following day he announced: "I started the movement renouncing the Hindu religion in 1935 ... Buddhism is the religion of this country. It is more than two thousand years old. I feel sorry for the fact that I did not embrace this religion earlier.... The religion of Buddha has the capacity to change according to times, a quality which no other religion can claim to have."[180] Conversions to Buddhism still continues. Today neo—Buddhism has become a political ideology to struggle for social justice.

To what extent the "Iron cage of Casteism" is being broken is the crucial question. Some of the illustrious examples of breaking the iron cage of casteism are: late K. R. Narayan (1921–2005), President of India (1997–2002), K. G. Balakrishnan, the previous Chief Justice of India; Miss. Meira Kumar, the present Speaker of the Indian Parliament; Miss. Mayawathi, four time Chief Minister of Uttar Pradesh, the largest state in India, and many others who have climbed the social ladder. The contribution of Christianity in creating a new atmosphere of human dignity and equality is unparallel in Indian history because these values are not

---

178. Quoted by David, "Mission," 249.
179. Quoted by Massey, *Dr. Ambedkar*, 39.
180. Michael, *Dalits*, 143–47.

Varieties of Hindu Responses to Evangelical Mission

integral to Hindu philosophy.[181] In the words of a prominent Hindu, Sir Narayana Chandravarka of Bombay: "The ideas that lie at the heart of the Gospel of Christ are slowly but surely permeating every part of Hindu society and modifying every phase of Hindu thought."[182]

The above survey is incomplete, and merely indicative. Further enquiry into other reform movements should not ignore other evils like female infanticide, child marriage of boys, prohibition of castration of boys by eunuchs, polygamy, polyandry, the Zenana system, dowry system, temperance societies, the criminal tribes, renamed "de-notified tribes" in the post independence period, and abolition of slavery, devadasis, and temple prostitution and others which were part of the Indian society. The achievements of these social movements have been all embracing, if not spectacular. All the evangelical missionaries played their decisive role in India. And most of the British officers made no secret of their evangelical motivation. The transformative impact of the East-West encounter was succinctly ascertained by S. Natrajan, the editor of the *Indian Social Reformer* in 1938. "The British rule has transformed Indian life and thought more in one hundred years than Hindu and Muslims in several centuries. It has given a new direction to Indian history. It has filled our minds with hopes and aspirations undreamt before—. It has made us feel that we have a part in molding the future of humanity."[183] From the beginning of the eighteenth century the Protestant missionaries, in spite of stiff oppositions, challenged and upset the criteria of judgement, determining values, lines of thought and models of life which were contrary to the Gospel of Jesus. Unstinting credit should be accorded to them as pioneers of evangelizing the Indian culture while the Catholic missionaries followed the model of accommodation, starting with de Nobili, with the theology of salvation of souls, that nearly excluded the renewal of society. The post-Vatican theology of evangelization of cultures (EN 18–20) was already dynamically, at times aggressively, operative in the Protestant evangelical missionary commitment to social transformation.

---

181. Panikkar, *Human Rights*, 31–67.
182. Quoted by Farquhar, *Modern Religious*, 445.
183. Quoted by Gray, "Progress of Women," 482

The Future of Christian Mission in India

Conclusion: Merits and Demerits of Different Missionary Approaches

In conclusion a few fundamental questions deserve to be raised. In spite of nearly 2,000 years of Christian presence and mission in India why did the major churches or denominations almost fail to inspire or stimulate any significant socio-religious transformation of Indian religions and the Indian society which the nineteenth century evangelical missions and free churches achieved? Historically there had been, broadly speaking, four wholly separate streams of Christian missionary arrivals into India. First, the Syrian or St. Thomas mission; second, the Latin colonial mission; third, the Danish—Halle Lutheran Missionaries; fourth, the arrival of aggressive evangelical free churches. Of these four major missionary trends, distinct and unrelated to one another, or even inimical to each other in theology, missionary methods and cultural orientations, only the nineteenth century evangelicals were capable of generating a very conspicuous and distinct impact on India.

The origin of the St.Thomas church or the Syrian Christians in South India is shrouded in uncertain historical evidences and controversial conclusions. The apocryphal *Acts of Judas Thomas*, written in Edessa, dated by Harnack back to the third century, claim that St. Thomas the apostle, after landing in Kodungaloor in AD 52 founded seven Christian communities on the Malabar coast, by converting thousands of Brahmins and more people of other castes and he ordained bishops and priests. It is, further argued that in the second century a church came into being through migrants who arrived in Malabar from Persia. At the end of the second century, around 190, Pantaenus, the Alexandrian theologian, discovered a Christian communities here, including the Gospel according to St. Mathew and shockingly attributes the origin of the Christians to Apostle Bartholomew and not to Apostle Thomas, who was believed to have gone to Parthian Persia. A list of Bishops who signed the creed of the Council of Nicea in 325, included one who signed himself: "John the Persian, of the churches of the whole of Persia and of the great India."[184] Until the council of Nicea no Christian theologian from the West spoke of St. Thomas mission in India. Two contradicting traditions, the Alexandrian and the Syrian, from the second and third century are competing for the authenticity of St. Thomas' mission in India. All the later church fathers merely repeated the old claim without doubting since their motive was the preservation of the holy tradition. Critical and scientific enquiries into

---

184. Farquhar and Gavitte, *Apostle*, 66.

Varieties of Hindu Responses to Evangelical Mission

Apostolic tradition is a modern phenomenon coinciding with modern scientific temper. The major confusion results from the inability the locate precisely the 'India' that the ancient authors repeatedly mention.[185]

All the modern western critical authors doubt the authenticity of St. Thomas' mission in India. E. R. Hambye SJ, after his research, including archaeological excavations in Mylapore, and publication of St. *Thomas Christians in India* (1952) was not committed to a definitive view. L.A.Brown, research scholar in India and author of, *The Indian Christians of St. Thomas* (1956) concluded, India meant Parthia in Persia. C. B. Firth, after researching in Kerala, teaching and publishing *An Introduction to Indian Church History* (1960) was cautious about the claims of St. Thomas Christians. Cardinal Tisserant, French author of *Eastern Christianity in India. A History of the Syro-Malabar Church From the Earliest Time to the Present Day* (1957), seriously questioned the geographical location of the Apostle's preaching. One of the strong proponents of the St. Thomas tradition in Kerala is A. M. Mundadan CMI in his, *History of Christianity in India. From the Beginning to the Middle of the sixteenth Century* (1989). Another Syrian Christian author, E. M. Philip, *The Indian Church of St. Thomas*, in Malayalam, his mother tongue in 1929, was uncommitted to the theory that St Thomas ever came to India.

With this backdrop of mostly historical analysis, I would like to employ another methodology, cultural analysis. The probable migrant origin of the St. Thomas Christians, a highly emotional issue that touches the delicate nerve of powerful Syrian church identity, can be established by examining four core religious factors; one, the worshiping pattern; two, the church administration; three, indigenous theology; four, the life style and food habits.

Crucial questions include: Why do the St. Thomas Christians follow the Syrian liturgy? St. Thomas is said to have ordained local Bishops and Priests who in their turn failed to create an indigenous liturgy, preferably in Sanskrit or Tamil language which were probably the local languages, since the present Malayalam language of Kerala came into existence only around AD 800. One probable answer is that the Syrian liturgy was imposed on them and by the migrant Christians from Antioch and by the Persian hierarchy as the Latin liturgy was imposed on India by the Portuguese missionaries. Another answer to the question is: there were neither Brahmins nor Sanskrit language in existence here. The date of the Aryan arrival in Kerala is disputed. The period of Aryanisation began by

---

185. Kuriakose, *History*, 2-12.

the Kadamba Kingdom from the north of Kerala between 345–375. The Sanskrit language in Kerala reached its peak by the time of philosopher Shri Sankaracharya (700–750?), who was vigorously fighting the rapid expansion of Buddhism by developing his Advaita philosophy which, according to some critics, is cryptic Buddhism. In the early Christian era, when St. Thomas or St. Thomas missionaries arrived on the Malabar coast probably the only organized religion were Buddhism, and probably Jainism, starting around the third century BC.[186] Vast majority of the local people here were animist, which partly explains how missionaries from Persia were able to convert many local people, without resistance, similar to tribal conversions to Christianity in the nineteenth—twentieth century. The question, therefore, is which Brahmins did St. Thomas convert? Apart from the absence of historical evidence of the arrival of the Apostle Thomas, the cultural analysis, particularly the study of liturgical language and worship, suggest that the story of Apostle Thomas in Kerala is not historical, rather a tradition developed in a later period to affirm their improved social status. It was a form of Sanskritization.

It appears that the Christians in India depended on the Metropolitan of Basrah and on that of Rewardasir in South west of Iran since the fifth century. His title was the Catholicos—Patriarch of the East or East Syrian Church. There were bishops in Kodungallur, Quilon, Mylapore, Kalyan and Ceylon appointed by the Catholicos and send to India. In the eighth century the "Metropolitan and Director of the Holy Church of India" was residing in Kodungallur.[187] The administration of the local church coupled with foreign liturgy, further confirm the hypothesis that the St. Thomas Christians in Malabar and other parts of India originated partly from the migration from Antioch and partly by migration from Persia. A few students from Malabar were sent there to study theology. Around 470 the Metropolitan sent theological books, translated from Greek to Syriac, to India. By the middle of the sixth century the Indian church was well organized with Bishops, clergy and faithful, but dependent on the Nestorian Persian church. By the middle of the next century, the expanding St. Thomas church, had its own independent metropolitanate, with more than half a dozen bishops consecrated for India and the metropolitan of India outranked that of China and Central Asia.

The stone-crosses in South India, belonging to the seventh or eight century, with inscription in Phalavi, the ancient Persian, is another proof of

---

186. Nambudiri, *Aryans*, 45; Menon, *Survey*, 358.
187. Hambye, "Eastern Church," 33–34.

Varieties of Hindu Responses to Evangelical Mission

the close link between St. Thomas Christians in Malabar and the Nestorian Persian church.[188] Eight years before the arrival of the Portuguese in Malabar 1498, two Syrian monks were ordained bishops by the Catholicos Mar Simeon, patriarch of the East, and were sent to Malabar. They returned to Malabar and ordained many priests.[189] In my view, as a migrant community, the Syrian Christians passively adapted themselves to the new Hindu environment. They did not engage themselves in aggressive missionary activities; however, it can be concluded from the existence of significant Syrian community that they were engaged in some type of evangelization. The political record of granting them written permission to live and work in the area further confirm that they were treated by the local kings as foreigners.

While literature on aggressive Hindu reactions against advancing Buddhism is abundant no similar record against Christian conversion is available. Converting Buddhist temples into Hindu temples and gradual elimination of Buddhism from Kerala is well recorded.[190]

Creation of an Indian Christian theology is another test of the intellectual challenges. Why did the Brahmin converts, if any, in the early centuries of a Christian era, fail to create and defend their faith against the Kerala caste Hindus? The story of the nineteenth century Hindu—Christian encounter stimulated in the creation of the first Indian Christian theologians. It is reasonable to conclude, in the light of cultural encounters, that the early Syrian Christians of Malabar were not the 'sons of the soil,' on the contrary, they were migrants who adapted themselves quietly and passively to the new environment. Of course, later various civil favors were conferred upon them by the rulers and they would gradually rise in social hierarchy, claiming Brahman status. This process, known as Sanskritization, has been a legitimate cultural process operative in India, through the centuries. [191]

Another sociological factor in support of my argument is to enquire into favorable conditions for a significant number of conversions of people in Malabar. What was the religious traditions of the people in the early part of the Christian era? Apart from a small number of Jains and Buddhists, vast majority of the local people, according to the religious history of Kerala, were followers of Shamanism, a type of primitive rites

188. Moffett, *History*, 1:208.
189. Ibid., 503.
190. Menon, *Survey*, 77–79.
191. Srinivas, *Religion and Society*, 30.

and practices. They worshipped innumerable spirits, inhabiting trees and hills. The Dravidian people here worshiped gods and goddesses by offering them meat of sacrificed fowl and toddy. They built memorial stones in their honour and the heads of families offered sacrifices to propitiate their ancestors or angry spirits and gods.

It might have been rather easy to convert a group of people, with no systematic philosophy, as is seen in the mass conversion of tribals to Christianity. Strong resistance to conversion is manifested only where the following constitutive elements of an organized religion are dynamic and powerful. One, existence of a Sacred Book, believed to be given by God through an inspired author; two, priests or religious leaders who teach and interpret the holy book and write books to justify their office; three, a sacred place of worship where the faithful are periodically gathered at sacred periods; four, a strong sense of guilt or sin and fear of punishment, for being unfaithful to and abandoning the original gods and converting to another god/religion. A strong faith motivates even to die or accept martyrdom, hoping for higher rewards in the next life.[192]

A rather passive co-existence of the St. Thomas Christians, in the beginning and later claim to superior social status, inhibited their interactions with the lower castes. According to the 1901 Census, the Syrian Christians do not admit within their premises outcastes even after their conversion to Christianity. They failed to introduce any social transformation until the beginning of the twentieth century. Drawing inspiration from the Anglican missionaries in Travencore, "The Malabar Mar Thoma Syrian Evangelistic Association" made some attempts to convert people from the lower strata at the end of the nineteenth century. Servant of God, Kunjachan (1891–1973) of Palai diocese ventured into evangelization and social uplift of some outcastes in the second half of the twentieth century. As far as social reforms or revolutions are concerned, undoubtedly, the Communist government of Kerala during the past half Century, has achieved more than what the St. Thomas Christians could contribute for millennia. They failed to develop any Social Gospel like the evangelical missionaries in the nineteenth century.

The impact of the Latin missionaries on India, in comparison to the Protestant evangelical missionaries is, relatively better than that of the Syrian churches. Towards the social structure of the caste system, which was most oppressive, the Catholic missionaries in general took a lenient position that the caste is a civil issue and not a religious issue. The glar-

---

192. Luckmann, *Invisible Religion*, 63–66.

Varieties of Hindu Responses to Evangelical Mission

ing example of accommodation or adaptation was the mission theology of Robert de Nobili in Madurai mission, who said: "The holy spiritual laws which I proclaim do not oblige a man to renounce his caste." The view that caste was merely a social factor and had no religions significance has been largely accepted by the catholic missionaries until very recently. Such a policy ended in tolerating even separate sitting places for the upper caste Christians and untouchable converts in the churches and separate burial places even in the cemetery. It is not surprising that being unable to suffer the humiliation of discrimination a large number of new converts left the church and those who remain continue to fight for equality.

The failure of the Catholic missionaries, in comparison to the Protestant missionaries in the nineteenth century, to create an Indian Christian theology should be attributed to the conservative Catholic culture. The culture of the Evangelical churches and Free Churches was basically critical. Radical criticism and the questioning of the religious traditions, the rejection of priestly authority, trusting only in the authority of the Bible laid the foundation for a rational culture. The Reformation methods of the Protestant missionaries deeply influenced Indian Renaissance, starting with Rammohan Roy in Calcutta and spread to other parts of India. Those who accepted Jesus Christ, having rejected Hinduism and its social evils, were not only free to articulate but also obliged to construct an Indian Christian theology to legitimize their rejection of Hinduism and conversion to Christianity. Starting with Rammohan Roy, K. C. Sen the new upper caste converts across the country laid the foundation of an indigenous theology. In contrast, the Catholic culture was in general uncritical, adaptive and highly submissive to the Roman authorities. A passive culture of obedience to religious authorities like priests, bishops and popes could not provide a free atmosphere to creatively respond to the dehumanizing social context of India. The Indian Catholic Church with its sense of superiority and dogmatism failed to see anything good and noble in other religions and thus for centuries failed to create an Indian theology. Both the adaptation method of de Nobili and of Brahmabandab Upadhyaya was systematically suppressed. A few foreign catholic missionaries, made some attempt towards the formulation of an Indian catholic theology. The fate of some of modern theologians in the nineteenth century who dared to reinterpret traditional theology for modern men failed to see the light of the day. The official policy of the Vatican was to condemn such efforts with the treat of anathemas.

Another cultural argument against the claim of Brahmin background of St. Thomas Christians is their lifestyle and food habits. All Brahmins are strictly vegetarian. Eating meat was abominable to them. Suppose the Brahmins were converted to Christianity in the first century they would definitely have maintained this food habit. In every society changing the traditional food habits of its members is one of the most difficult challenges. The new Brahmin converts would never have tolerated the habit of eating meat, worse still the habit of consuming pork which is enjoyed as a delicacy by most of the Syrian Christians. Still worse, the habit of eating beef of holy cows.

All these arguments cumulatively lead to the conclusion that the claim of the Syrian Christians to Brahmin origin is false. And their claim to the preaching of St. Thomas the Apostle in Kerala, according to my analysis, is equally untrue. Most of the scholars discussing this issue in the past tried to argue from historical documents or archaeological evidences and have probably failed to resort to cultural analysis which is equally credible. A comparative analysis of the vision, missionary methods, success and failures of the Syrian Catholic church and Latin Catholic missionaries is made with reference to the success as well as failures of the Evangelical missionaries in the nineteenth and twentieth centuries with the hope of gaining better insights for the future. It is further appreciated that less authoritarian structures of the Evangelical churches provides better opportunities for creative thinking as well as creative action.

3

Violence against Christian Missions

WITH THEIR TRADITIONAL REPUTATION of tolerance recent violence against Christian missions is another controversial response of the Hindus. The fundamental issue that is being examined in this chapter is: How to understand India as a secular democratic nation scarred by frequent communal violences against minority religious communities and marginalized social groups? Is religious pluralism, particularly its fundamentalist version, the root of the conflicts and confrontations? Can India manage the growing chaos and culture of violence? Two major political events can shed light on the limping democratic process in contemporary India. One, the partition of Hindustan in 1947, the year of independence, into two nations produced an unprecedented violence and bloodshed. Nearly ten million uprooted Hindu and Muslim refugees crossed the boundaries of the two new nations. Probably around half a million people were brutally murdered and butchered in Hindu, Muslim and Sikh vengeance, mostly in Delhi, Punjab and Bengal. Forty million Muslims remained in the new India and eight million Hindus in Pakistan with unforgettable and unforgiving grievances on both sides.[1] And unfortunately history continues to be repeated in the following decades. Mahatma Gandhi, the Father of the Nation, fasting and praying for peace, was assassinated on 30th January 1948 for his sympathetic attitude to Muslims and the newly created nation of Pakistan. Against the backdrop of such communal violence the enlightened members of the Constituent Assembly, under its chairman Dr.Balasaheb Ambedkar, opted for a secular democratic Constitution, unlike the Muslim theocratic nation of Pakistan. The second factor is the unbelievable pluralism of India. The modern states in Europe and the U.S.A.

1. Watson, *India*, 159-61.

were created on the basis of a people of one language, one major religion and one culture. "The problem of India as a secular state is a complex one. The rich diversity of religious life as well as the legacy of communalism and partition, the influence of ancient Hindu values as well as the impact of the West, the leadership of a religious Gandhi and an agnostic Nehru, the tendency of traditional religions to regulate virtually every aspect of life and the tendency of the modern state to do the same—all of these factors and many others are part of the complex pattern. Problems frequently arise for which there is no clear parallel in western experience, which has contributed so greatly to India's political evolution in other respects."[2]

Origin and Expansion of Communal Politics in India

Spread of western values through liberal English education and the expansion of Christianity through mass conversions were perceived as the cause of decline of Hindu culture and values. Therefore for defense of religion political mobilization was seen as a necessity. It marks the beginning of communal politics in India.

The Hindutva Philosophy: Before Independence.

Organized anti-Christian animosity and violence in India has its root in the Hindu reformist movement, the Arya Samaj, founded in 1875 by Dayananda Sarasvati (1824–1883), and similar organizations during the following decades. As early as the American Presbyterian Mission in Punjab began to attack Hinduism and denounce its numerous superstitions and shocking social evils, Dayananda was infuriated by the Christian dogmatism and display of superiority coupled with street preaching and the assertion that salvation was possible only in Jesus Christ. His Hindu social reform movement adopted certain features from the Lutheran Reformation. His moto included, "Back to Vedas," like Luther's moto, "Back to the Scripture." He introduced a new rite of *Sudhi*, reconversion of Christians from the Chura outcaste. Swami Shradhananda, a Punjabi Arya Samajst, developed his plan for the reorganization of Hinduism in his book, *Hindu Sangathan—Saviour of a Dying Race* (1926). He provided the vision for the Hindu Mahasabha, the Great Hindu Organization, and proposed that the untouchables of Hindu Society should be integrated into Hinduism in order to dissuade them from conversion to Christianity.[3]

2. Smith, *India as a Secular State*, viii.
3. Jaffrelot, *Hindu Nationalist*, 20–22.

Violence against Christian Missions

Influenced by Lokmanya Tilak, a Congress extremist from Poona, V. D. Savarkar, another Maharashtrian, after imprisonment in the Andaman Islands for twelve years for terrorist activities against the British administrators, published his book *Hindutva. Who is a Hindu?* (1923), expounding the basic philosophy of the Hindu Nation. He argued that only those who are bound by the Hindu culture and uphold India as their *Pitrubhumi* or fatherland and *Punyabhoomi*, or holy land, enjoy full rights. "The Muslims and Christians whose holy land is far off in Arabia and Palestine, do not belong to this soil."[4]

He popularized the slogan: "Hinduise all politics and militarize Hinduism." In the Hindu Rashtra, Muslims and Christians have no place. The exclusivist Hindutva policy was radically opposed to the all inclusive philosophy of Indian National Congress. His follower, M. S. Golwalkar, the mentor of A. B. Vajpayee and L. K. Advani, further developed the philosophy of Hindutva in his book, *A Bunch of Thought*. He held the view, challenging the Christian superiority, that Hinduism is superior to other religions and cultures and ridiculed others saying that the Europeans were primitive hunters, eating raw, uncooked food while Hindus were composing the Sacred Vedas. "In this land Hindus have been the owners, Parsis and the Jews the guests, the Muslims and Christians the dacoits. Then do all these have the same right over the country"?[5] "The Muslims brutalized Hindus for 800 years and they like to eat the cow which we worship," he added. The Muslims and Christians must stay here, subordinated to the Hindu nation. They should claim nothing, "not even citizen's rights."[6] He vehemently opposed the idea of a secular India. The Hindutva movement was a desperate attempt to establish the diminishing power and glory of past Brahmin hegemony. They were unwilling to accept and recognize India as a multi-religious and multi-cultural country. The Hindutva ideology is nothing but 'Hindu chauvinism.'

Rashtriya Swayamsevak Sangh (RSS), founded by K. B. Hedgewar in Nagpur in 1925, provided the necessary organizational structure to the Militant Nationalism of Savarkar in Maharashtra and Aurobindo Ghosh in Bengal. He painfully realized that the organic fabric of the Hindu society, religion and culture and nation was being corroded and weakened by foreign powers, ideologies, cultures and religions. How to revive the whole Hindu Society was his anxiety. Educate and train the Hindu youth

---

4. Savarkar, *Hindutva*, 113.
5. Quoted by Guha, *India After Gandhi*, 26.
6. Quoted by Jaffrelot, *Sangh Parivar*, 73.

in Hindu social philosophy, Varnashramadharma, was his answer. Para—military training was introduced as part of the program. The foundation of Bhonsale Military School in Nasik, Maharashtra, by B. S. Moonje was part of the project. By this period many Hindus had arrived at the conclusion that India was repeatedly conquered by various foreign powers because of the lack of virility and military spirit. The RSS, the Hindu Rashtra in miniature, was a Hindu para-military group, which became Indian's most violent youth organization that eventually produced many Hindu extremists, including Mahatma Gandhi's assassin, Nathuram Godse and his companions. They were also great admirers of fascism of Mussolini and Hitler's Nazism. The RSS promoted ethnic pride in the Aryan conquest of India. After the murder of Gandhi, many of its prominent leaders were imprisoned and the organization was banned for a year because Prime Minister J. Nehru was convinced that Godse and his companions in Poona had refused to hoist the Indian tri-colour: instead they hoisted their own saffron flag. They had already made a few unsuccessful attempts to assassinate Gandhi in the previous years. The spread of Hindutva was intensified when the ban was lifted by Home Minister Patel who was a sympathizer of the RSS. Ridiculing M. K. Gandhi's non-violent independence struggle Dr. Kurtkoti, the Sankaracharya of Karweer Peeth in Maharashstra said in 1922: "Ahimsa undermines Hindu self-respect; passive and non-resisting sufferance is a Christian and not an Aryan principle." The view that in crisis and conflict situations Indians are less aggressive or less violent than any other nation would be a gross understatement. Abhinav Bharat, The Young India, founded by Savarkar in 1905, is recently being revived by some Hindu radicals to overthrow democracy, elected government and found the Hindu Republic or Hindu Monarchy.[7] These groups are secretly organizing themselves in different parts of India, and outside of India, like Nepal which was a Hindu nation until very recently.

After Independence : Jana Sangh and Other Hindu Organizations

After declaring its identity, as demanded by the home ministry, as a Hindu cultural organization for infusing Hindu values into public life, RSS was anxious to elicit the support of a political party that would be sympathetic to its vision of the Hindu Nation. M. S. Golwalkar and other R.S.S. leaders encouraged and actively supported S. P. Mookherjee, a disgruntled central

---

7. Koppikar, "Malegaon Chargesheet," 52.

Violence against Christian Missions

minister due to the pro-Pakistan policy of the Nehru government, to found a new political party to oppose the Congress government. A sympathizer of RSS as well as a member of the Hindu Mahasabha founded in 1915 to fight the Muslim League, Mookherjee thus emerged as the founder of the new party, Jana Sangh in 1951. Consequently, it won elections and formed governments in a few states in the Hindu cow belt. The Congress Party suffered a temporary set back. After the publication of *Report of the Christian Missionary Activities Enquiry Committee* in 1956, popularly known as the Niyogi Committee Report, a few state governments like Orissa in 1967 and Madhya Pradesh in 1968 were in the forefront of passing anti-conversion and cow protection laws at the insistence of the Jana Sang Party. The Jana Sang election slogans like, "A vote for the Jana Sang a vote for the protection of the cows," were most suited to arouse the traditional Hindu religious sentiments and even fanaticism.[8]

The partition of India and the subsequent Hindu-Muslim communal violence, a humiliating war with China in 1962, war with Pakistan in 1963 and many other socio-political factors continued to deeply wound the national and cultural pride of India, particularly the Sangh Parivar. The creation of Nagaland state in 1963 with a Christian majority population, and the demand for Jharkand state with a sizable Christian population in Chotanagpur region were seen as denationalization strategy of the foreign Christian missionaries. As soon as Pope Paul VI announced his plan to attend the International Eucharistic Congress in Bombay in 1964, Shiva Sankar Apte, a RSS catechist, founded Vishwa Hindu Parishad to unite all Hindu religious leaders for the protection and preservation of the Hindu society from the insidiously spreading clutches of alien ideologies. "The VHP was therefore created to endow Hinduism with a church like centralized structure and use this new ecclesiastical apparatus to counter Christian proselytizing—what was new, the involvement of a third group, the religious heads of several Hindu sects and monasteries."[9]

Bajrang Dal or the army of Hanuman, the youth wing of the VHP, was founded on October 7, 1984 and Vinay Katiyar, another RSS pracharak, was made its first convener, when procession of Hindu religious leaders was taken out with a goal of building Ram temple in Ayodhya. The three objectives of VHP was: Seva, Suraksha and Samskara—service, defence and training in cultural tradition. Its new strategy: direct attack and violence. "Might is the only law I understand. Nothing else matters

8. Jafferelot, *Hindu Nationalist*, 204–29.
9. Jafferelot, *Sangh Parivar*, 9.

to me. It is a war like situation as between Ram and Ravana," declared its founder.¹⁰ Togadia was supported and encouraged by the RSS in the production and distribution of Tridents to his followers to attack Muslims and Christians. Bajrang Dal is in the forefront of anti-Christian vandalism in many backward areas where Christian missionaries are working. In addition to reconversions of Christians violence became the second new strategy. Thus Hinduism under the impact of Christian conversions movement was becoming a converting religion. "VHP thus legitimizes conversion and transformed Hinduism from a religion whose following was based on birth to a religion based on association and direct absorption through purification—but it spread wide propaganda against conversion to Islam and Christianity and called for state intervention to stop the latter."¹¹ Their anti-Muslim and anti-Christian hatred is popularized with slogans like: *Pehele Kasai, Phir Isai, that is:* Finish first the Muslims, then the Christians. "Violence appears to be the swiftest and surest way to retain the loyalties of a cadre whose commitment could not otherwise endure their leaders compromises."¹² Like the Nazi youth, many unemployed youth, even from the tribal areas are being sent for training at Hindu centers in North India with generous pocket money. And on their return they are proud to show fruits of the training by periodic attacks on Christians or Muslims on flimsy grounds.

Decline of Democracy and Rise of Hindu Fundamentalism

The 1970s India witnessed separatist movements in Punjab, Kashmir, Assam and a few tribal areas in the North East. The emergency rule imposed by Prime Minister Indira Gandhi from June 1975 to March 1977, was Indian Democracy's darkest hour. In the post emergency election thus Jana Sangh would become a constituent member of the new coalition Janata Party which formed the central government under Prime Minister Morarji Desai, a Gandhian, in 1977. Reacting to the controversy over dual membership of some of the ministers, both in the Janata Party as well as in RSS, the ex-Jana Sanghis walked out of the government and Jana Sangh was reincarnated with a new name, Bharatiya Janata Party in 1980 under the leadership of A.B.Vajpayee, reasserting the traditional Hindu fundamentalist political ideology.¹³ Beginning with emergency rule, the Indian

10. Quoted by Katju, *Vishva Hindu*, 137.
11. Ibid., 128.
12. Rajgopal, *Politics*, 28.
13. Jaffrelot, *Hindu Nationalist*, 313.

Violence against Christian Missions

National Congress lost its traditional power and the ideology of secular democracy was seriously weakened. For over a decade from 1977—1990 five minority governments were in power at the centre. Unfortunately none of them provided political stability and peaceful social order. The communal party of the BJP, ideologically fortified by the RSS that had been kept under check for decades, began to raise its ugly head. In 1984 the first *Dharma Sansad*, association of the Hindu religious leaders, adopted a resolution demanding the liberation of Ayodhya, the capital of Hinduism. In July of the same year Sri Ramjanmabhoomi Mukti Yagna Samiti, Organization for the Liberation of the birth place of Lord Ram, was founded. The highly religious and emotive agenda was the long cherished construction of the Ram Temple in Ayodhya which was allegedly destroyed by the Mongol or Mughal conqueror Babur, "the tiger" and his general Mir Baqui who allegedly built the Babri Masjid in the same location around 1526. These and other acts of Hindu mobilization reached its climax in March 1990 when L. K. Advani, leader of the BJP, undertook an All India Ratha Yatra, starting at Somnath temple in Saurastra, Gujarat, once destroyed by the Muslim invader, Sultan Ghazni of Afghanistan, "the idol breaker," in 1023. Rousing these religious sentiments the Ratha Yatra criss-crossed the nation, covering 10,000 KMs,and mobilized Hindu anger at the grassroots.[14]

The Ratha Yatra of Advani across the country motivated more than 1,000,000 Kar Sevaks, or volunteers carrying bricks with name of Ram, Tridents, bows and arrows, to travel towards Ayodhya. On 6th December 1992, 15,000 strong Hindu militants led by the Hindutva leaders marched to the location in great hysteria and pulled down the Babri Masjid in Ayodhya, shouting slogans like, "Babri Masjid tor do," break down the Mosque, "Mandir yahin banayenge," the temple will be constructed here, while 25,000 para-military forces, majority of whom were sympathetic Hindus, stood like happy and silent spectators. The BJP ruled state government of Chief Minister Kalyan Singh in Uttar Pradesh as well as Congress ruled central government of late P. V. Narasimha Rao with his soft Hindutva, silently and tacitly approved the communal violence against the religious sentiments of over 120 million Muslims of India and many others outside India. The Hindu—Muslim communal rights that broke out across the country in the following two months claimed more than 2,000 lives and destruction of large amount of properties.[15]

14. Ibid., 416–17.
15. Guha, *India after Gandhi*, 638–39.

THE FUTURE OF CHRISTIAN MISSION IN INDIA

The Gujarat Carnage

It can be pointed out that following its rise to power in the centre in 1998, the BJP ruled states have been marked by increasing violence against Muslims and Christians.[16] Under the BJP government of Narendra Modi the Christians in Gujarat were also subjected to persecution. Out of 193 atrocities committed against them during 1997–2000, eighty five were in Gujarat, predominantly in Dang district with 10 percent tribal Christians. South India suffered only 20 percent of anti-Christian violences during the same period. Burning churches and Bibles, attacking priests, raping nuns, reconversion of tribal Christians to Hinduism as well as aggressive anti-missionary propaganda and protest meetings by the Sangh Parivar was the order of the day and paralyzed the Christian Community and its activities, which was the very goal of Hindutva forces, in the following years.[17] The Indians for whom secularism is the most important common value of the Republic ought to be worried since each communal attack weakens the democratic fabric and corrodes the spirit of secularism.

The anti-Christian organizations and their activities revolve around the following: 1) They have set up competing institutions in the area of health and education, especially in tribal areas; 2) relief and reconstruction during natural disasters and calamities; 3) printing and distributing anti-Christian literature and use of electronic media to demonize the minorities; 4) political mobilization of masses against Christians and Muslims; 5) celebration of Hindu festivals and religious events to attract tribals and Hinduize and Sanskritize their culture; 6) reconversion of new Christians and finally 7) employing violence and persecution of Christians.[18]

According to historian Ramchandara Guha, "India is both an unnatural nation as well as an unlikely democracy . . . Never before has a single political unit been constructed from such desperate and diverse parts . . . for India to be both united and untroubled would be a miracle. For it to be both democratic and free of conflicts would be doubly so."[19] The history of Independent India is one of fire being lit, doused and then lit again, adds Guha. In the words of political sociologist Ashish Nandy: "In India the choice could never be between chaos and stability, but between manage-

---

16. Ibid., 556–57.
17. Lobo, *Globalization*, 181–209.
18. Lobo, "Hindutva," 66.
19. Guha, "Great Indian Chaos," 74.

Violence against Christian Missions

able and unmanageable chaos, between human and inhuman anarchy, and between tolerable and intolerable disorder."[20]

Recent Attacks on Christians in Orissa State

Orissa with a population of thirty six million, according to the Census report of 2001, is one of the poorest states in the country. The people living below poverty line constitutes 50 percent. The socio-economic condition of Kandhamal district where recent violence occurred is far more worse. Out of a population of over 0.7 million in the district 70 percent are constituted of Kandha and Kui tribes and 17 percent Pana Scheduled Caste. The Scheduled Tribes and Scheduled Castes were traditionally engaged in certain degree of ethnic conflicts. The conversion of nearly three forth of the Dalit Panas to Christianity during the recent decades enhanced their development. The tribals observing their progress lately began to be attracted to the Christian mission. According to the 2001 Census report the Christian population has sharply increased to 13 percent (1,17,751) in contrast to 2 percent in 1961. For a hungry man food is God, said Mahatma Gandhi. When the starving and marginalized people were helped by the Christian missionaries it is not surprising that some of them were attracted to Christianity and moved away from the Hindu society that despised and ill-treated them worse them animals for centuries. The Hindus who were closely watching the missionary activities were alarmed by the trend since its social, cultural and political implications are obvious. When an outcaste Pana embraces Christianity the government denies those benefits which non-baptized Panas receive. [21]

Spread of Hindutva in Orissa

Being a criminal, accused of two murders in Titlagar, Orissa, the villagers chased away Laxmananda Saraswati, in the middle of 1960s. He escaped to Rishikesh, at the foot of Himalayas, and donned saffron and reappeared in Kandhamal district of Orissa in 1969. With the support of RSS he founded a new Vanabasi Kalyan Ashram and opened around 250 schools and social service centers for tribal children. Imitating the Christian missionary services to the tribals R. K. Deshpande had already founded Vanabasi Kalyan Ashram, an offshoot of RSS in 1952 to work among the tribals. Their education emphasizes study of the Vedas and

---

20. Quoted by ibid., 75.
21. Kanjamala, "Democracy," 15–30.

employs other methods of Sanskritization. Saraswati's Hinduaization process of the tribals was simultaneously accompanied by aggressive anti-missionary propaganda, reconversion of Christians to Hinduism by threats and an anti-cow slaughter drive. On reconversion he said: "The sooner the Christians return to the Hindu fold the better it would be for the country." Swami Laxmananda enjoyed the reputation and image of an anti-missionary fighter and anti-Naxel hero.

The growing political clout of Sangh Parivar in Orissa, a recent phenomenon, can be easily gauged from the following data. The RSS, with 6000 branches and 1,75,000 members is wide spread. The VHP has 1,50,000 primary members. The Bajrang Dal has 60,000 activists. BJP workers number above 4,50,000. Mohila Morcha, Durga Vahini, and Rashtriya Sevika Samati are three major women's organizations with 7,000 outfits in 117 locations. The 30,000 strong Bharatiya Kisan Sangh for farmers functions in 100 blocks. There are numerous other Hindutva outfits according to anthropologist Angana Chatterjee.[22] Through fifty five active affiliates the RSS is systematically penetrating every strata of the Hindu Society. In the past eight decades RSS has grown into a pan Indian fundamentalist religious organization, lending outside support and remotely controlling the BJP political policies as its founders envisioned. In 1985 the BJP won only one seat in the Orissa Legislative Assembly. At the time of the Kandhamal violence BJP occupied thirty seven assembly seats and headed eight ministries in the BJD-BJP coalition government under Chief Minister Naveen Patnaik of Biju Janata Party (BJD).

Hindu–Christian Violence

Traditionally a peaceful district, Kandhamal has now a history of Hindu-Muslim and Hindu-Christian conflicts during past four decades, after the arrival of Swami Laxmananda and his Hindu missionaries. In 1998 around 5000 Sangh activists attacked the Christian dominated Ramgiri-Udaygiri villages in the Gajapati district, setting fire to ninety two houses, a church and a police station. The Australian missionary Graham Staines and his two young sons, Philip, and Timothy, aged ten and six, were burned to death in the Keonjhar district while asleep at night in a vehicle in January 1999. Their crime, according to Dara Singh, the leader of Bajrang Dal and the violent mob he excited, was that Staine's twenty—five years of selfless services to the outcaste lepers were rendered with the ulterior motive of conversion. A young Catholic priest, Arul Doss, working among the Ho

22. Chatterji, *Violent Gods*, 165–70.

tribe, was murdered by a mob, instigated by the same Dara Singh, in the Mayurbanj district in September 1999. A catholic nun was raped in the same district. Their aggressive momentum was kept up by further violence against Muslims as well as Christians.[23] On 24th December 2007 while the Christians were preparing to celebrate Christmas, attacks were launched against the Christians by a crowd, headed by Swami Laxmananda. These atrocities, lasted a month, and ended in the death of 6 people, destruction of churches and prayer halls. Over 100 houses were destroyed and thousands were rendered homeless. Number of court files provide ample proof that Laxmananda was a saffron robed religious criminal, with the sinister agenda of wiping out the Christians in Orissa, like Hitler's ethnic cleansing of the Jews in Germany.

Fifteen years ago the Maoist Liberation Guerrilla Army, popularly known as Naxlites, under the leadership of Sabiasachi Panda, aged forty one, joined the Naxal movement in 1981 to organize and fight for poor exploited tribals and Dalits. He accused Swami Laxmananda for converting tribals to Hinduism by force and maintained that the tribals have their own distinct religion. Exactly eight months after the attack on Christians on Christmas 2007, the 84 year old seer and his four disciples were gunned down on 23rd August at 8.00 p.m. by thirty masked Maoist Liberation Guerrilla Army, pumping twenty two bullets from AK 47 guns, not without prior warning, for his fascist activities, as the Ashram was getting ready to celebrate Janmashtami, birthday of Lord Krishna. The Maoists owned up to responsibility of the murder. But VHP general secretary Pravin Togadia, denied it and accused the missionaries of having masterminded the murder of their revered Guru and at the same time the government was giving it a Maoist color.

The infuriated Sangh Parivar, in retaliation unleashed violent attacks, on thirty five Christian centres simultaneously, from the dawn of 24th August. A priest and nun working at the diocesan pastoral centre in Nuagoan block of the district were severely beaten up, stripped, and paraded semi-naked. The police and the public were mute spectators as the victims were pleading for help on bended knees. Later on 25th afternoon the young nun, 29, was taken to the nearby Jan Vikas building and was raped. "Two men stood on my hands and a third raped me, inviting more men to rape," stated the nun to the journalists. "Come let us rape her, at least hundred people should rape," shouted the attackers.[24] Miss

23. Kanjamala, "Democracy," 24–28.
24. Ibid., 27.

The Future of Christian Mission in India

Rajni Manjhi, a Hindu girl, 19, taking care of the catholic orphanage, in the Bargharh district, mistaken for a nun, was set ablaze and burned alive. She was in charge of the orphanage for the children of lepers. A few other priests were severely beaten and suffered burned injuries; ninety Christians were killed, including two pastors and three catholic priests. Nearly 250 churches and prayer halls were burned down. Over 4,655 Christian houses were either totally or partially reduced to ashes. Over 50,000 terrified Christians fled into forests to save their lives. Properties worth Rupees many millions were destroyed in nearly 300 villages. Over 22,000 men, women and children were living in refugee camps, mostly in forty schools. Birth and deaths are taking place in the crowded camps. Their mental agony and sufferings cannot be easily understood by others who have not visited this area.[25] The education of all the students in these schools were suspended. The rampaging mob, with guns, knives, lathis and other weapons, shouted, 'Jai Shri Ram," Victory to Lord Ram, "Jai Bajrang," Victory to Lord Hanuman, "Bharat Matha ki Jai," Victory to Mother India, "Yesu Christ Murdhabadh," death to Jesus Christ and so forth. VHP leaders justified the violence saying: "they deserve the treatment, they killed our Swamiji."

On 14th September Karnataka become the target of Hindu fundamentalists. Dakshina Kannada with a Catholic population of 1,65,000, Udupi, over 65,000 Catholics, Chickmangaloor, with 27,500 Catholics and other districts with small number of Christians have a history of 400 years. Politically, economically and socially these Christians enjoy good reputation. Twenty four churches and prayer centers in Karnataka were attacked and nearly 100 citizen were injured. Priests and nuns were attacked, including cloistered nuns who do not even come out of their convents. After Orissa, the Karnataka Christians suffered maximum number of attacks since the BJP government came to power here in June 2008, making history as the first saffron government in South India. The circulation of a booklet, "Satya Dharsani," vision of truth, by a Pentecostal sect, with criticism of Hinduism was alleged to have hurt the religious sentiments of Hindus. It is unfortunate that certain evangelical sects employ offensive missionary methods unacceptable both to the main line churches of India as well as Hindus. It is further alleged that these sects receive huge fund from their counterparts in the West.

---

25. Akkara, *Kandhamal*, 16–26.

Violence against Christian Missions

Proactive Initiatives of the Missionaries

Archbishop Raphael Cheenath of Bhubaneshwar, the capital of Orissa, on behalf of the Christians, particularly the Catholics, strongly condemned the dastardly acts and violent killings. A delegation of the CBCI, met the Indian President, Prime Minister and Home Minister and submitted a memorandum, appealing for reestablishment of law and order in the country. Article 355 of the Constitution of India states: "It shall be the duty of the Union to protect every state against external aggression and internal disturbances to ensure that every state is carried on in accordance with the provisions of this Constitution." To express protest and solidarity with the suffering Christians of Orissa, nearly 4,500 Catholic schools in the country remained closed on Friday 29th August. Archbishop Bernard Moras of Bangalore challenged the then Chief Minister B. S. Yeddyurappa of Karnataka: "The Christians are very hurt. If one of your temples are burned how you would feel?"[26] Ten human right activists headed by Swami Agnivesh met the Governor of Orissa, M. C. Bhandare, and requested him to visit the strife-torn area. A five-member team, headed by the former Chief Minister of Kerala Oommen Chandy, met the congress president Sonia Gandhi, Prime Minister Manmohan Singh and Home Minister Shivraj Patel and demanded a CBI enquiry on the violence against the Christian minority in Orissa. Prime Minister Manmohan Singh assured the Kerala delegates that a relief package to Orissa victims would soon be announced. Film director Mahesh Bhatt and delegates from different religious communities met President Pratibha Patel in New Delhi and discussed the Orissa violence and requested them to normalize the situation. The General Secretary of All India Christian Council, Dr. Abraham Mathai, vice chairman of the Maharashtra state minority commission, and other delegates, during the meeting with the Indian President demanded that organization like VHP and Bajrang Dal be banned. Numerous protest meetings were organized by the Christians across the length and breadth of country.

Only after the Prime Minister Manmohan Singh was confronted by a few political leaders during his visit to the USA and Europe at the end of September 2008, were certain serious steps taken to control the communal flare-up. The Prime Minister during his cabinet meeting on Friday 3rd October said, the communal violence in Orissa is a "national shame." Some of the central ministers demanded the dismissal of Orissa government and ban Hindu extremist groups under the "Unlawful Activities

---

26. Quoted by Kanjamala, "Democracy," 29.

The Future of Christian Mission in India

(Prevention Act) 1967." The seven day Dharna and prayer meeting at Jantar Mantar, New Delhi, beginning on September 26, 2008, witnessed an unprecedented demonstration of solidarity among the people of all faiths. Over 15,000 Christians, Hindus, Muslims, Sikhs, Buddhists, joined the peace and solidarity rally. The speakers included Swami Agnivesh, Central Minister Shri Lalu Prasad Yadav, Mr. Sitaram Yechury, of the Communist Party of India, Central Minister Oscar Fernandes, Chief Minister Smt. Sheela Dixit of Delhi and many others. In spite of numerous delegations of the archbishops, Christian leaders and prominent and enlightened citizens to the president, the prime minister, and the home minister of India and the chief minister N. Patnaik of Orissa prompt and decisive steps to curb the communal atrocities were shamefully tardy. Only after one month of communal flare ups were letters of warning sent to Orissa by the central government. The presence of 6,500 Special Police Force and several hundred Orissa State Armed Force, failed to control communal violence for two months.

Why did the central government and the state government fail to establish law and order at least for two months? Why was the Sangh Parivar afraid of a small Christian minority, constituting less than 3 percent of the Indian population, rendering yeoman services to the nation in the fields of education, health and social services, particularly to the poor and marginalized? Are they afraid of the liberation of the oppressed scheduled castes and scheduled tribes whom the missionaries educate and conscientize? The hidden agenda seems to be political. Before the national election Hindu violence is mobilizing its vote bank with a fear complex. In the 1960s the Jana Sangh party, supported by the RSS, employed religious grievance such as opposition to conversion to Christianity and cow slaughter to win some state elections in the cow belt. In 1989, BJP won eighty five seats in the parliament with the campaign to build Sri Ram temple in Ayodhya. In 1998, the BJP formed the central government with the support of two dozen regional parties. In the national election the BJP had managed to win nearly 25 percent of the national votes. After the demolition of the Babri Masjid in 1992 and retaliatory bomb attacks in Bombay and other places by the Muslims, the poor and marginalized Christians, whose vote bank is negligible, became the soft target of Hindu fundamentalists. In view of the next election the BJP was creating fear psychosis and unrest in the country, by provoking communal violence and hoping to win the election and capture power in the centre. Many concerned citizens are afraid that Orissa was going the Gujarat way: The Hindu laboratory. In the following state assembly election in the beginning of 2009 Chief Minister Naveen Patnaik's BJD party delinked its connection with BJP and won the election with thumping majority.

India: A Third-Class Democracy

All Indians should be happy that modern India is not ruled by the Hindu Laws of Manu. By the enlightened choice the framers of the Indian Constitution have created a Constitution with inviolable fundamental human rights. The Preamble to the Constitution of India reads: "We the people of India, having solemnly resolved to Constitute India into a sovereign socialist secular democratic republic and secure to all citizens; JUSTICE, social, economic and political; LIBERTY of thought, expression, belief, faith and worship; EQUALITY of status and opportunity; to promote among them all Fraternity assuring the dignity of the individual and the unity and integrity of the nation." India is a multi-religious nation with Hindu majority falling under three broad categories. At one end of the large spectrum, modern India is proud to have given birth to great sages like Swami Vivekananda, and numerous others who announced the exalted Advaita spirituality to the "brothers and sisters of America" in Chicago in 1893 during the World Parliament of Religions. He also upheld the view that Hinduism is superior to Christianity or any other religions. On the other hand, the so called tolerant ethos of India should be ashamed of those unenlightened, obscurantist and medieval Hindus of Orissa and other states, where many helpless and powerless Christians are forced to tonsure their heads, drink holy cow urine mixed with cow dung for purification and reconversion to Hinduism at gun and knife point. Is this what the "Freedom of Religion Act (1967) of Orissa" offers? And finally the moderate silent majority, while enjoying the benefits of Christian services in various fields, seems to be indifferent to the unknown, distant burning corners of India, as long as their peace is not directly disturbed. On the decline of Indian secular democracy late Indian jurist Nani Palkiwala observed: "India is a third class democracy with a first class Constitution."[27] On the one hand the Indian Constitution is secular *de jure*; on the other hand Indian elections and many political decisions at the local level are deeply impacted by caste identity and religious affiliations. Conversions therefore cannot be explained merely as religious acts; it has close political consequences. It is becoming clear that during the last quarter of a century soft Hindutva is on the rise.

27. Quoted by Guha, "Will India Become," 72.

The Future of Christian Mission in India

"In the words of Ramachandra Guha: "Contemporary India is home to pluralists and democrats as well as fanatics and sectarians; to selfless social workers as well as greedy politicians; to honest and upright officials as well as officials who are time-servers; to capitalists who distribute their wealth quietly as well as those who seek only to provocatively display it. To redeem the republic—valorize and support the first kind of Indian rather than the second."[28] We have two Indias that coexist side by side. While 700 million Indians survive with two dollars per person per day, of whom 250 million with one dollar per person per day, over 300 million Indians enjoy the fruit of modernization with a life style, culture and mentality comparable to that of the rich in Western Europe, U.S.A. and Japan. These economic elites, including Indian billionaires, successful non-resident Indians and the pro-capitalist mass media are misrepresenting Indian secular democracy and progress at international summits and high profile seminars. Both classes, by minimizing their rhetoric and directing their energy to reduce various conflicts and maximizing "human happiness index," should contribute to the progress of secular democracy where the focus will be development coupled with human dignity.

Freedom of Religion and Conversion

In India conversion is a very emotional and sensitive issue. The Indian Constitution (Art 25.1), influenced by The UN Universal Declaration on Human Rights (1948, Art. 18) and a few Western Constitutions, "guarantees that all persons are equally entitled to the freedom of conscience and the right freely to profess, practice and propagate religion subject to public order, morality and health and other provisions" of the Constitution of India. Are Indian politicians wrong when they, under the right to freedom of speech, persuade the poor and illiterate Indians to vote for their party? If the poor and illiterate tribals and dalits are capable to vote and choose their governments they are equally capable of choosing their religion. Is it surprising that many people are attracted to the Messiah, Jesus Christ, who was ready to suffer and die for them? Is it strange that the marginalized poor are attracted towards the missionaries who are serving them? They gladly and willingly distance themselves from humiliations heaped upon them by the dominant and oppressive Hindu Society. More important: in many instances conversion is both an act of protest and a movement towards social liberation. In the words of Dr. B. R. Ambedkar: "Choose any religion which gives you equality of status and treatment. I had the

28. Guha, "Will India Become a Superpower?," 74.

Violence against Christian Missions

misfortune of being born with the stigma of an untouchable—but I will not die a Hindu; for this is within my power."[29] The process of conversion initiated by the conversion of Ambedkar to Buddhism, together with half a million of dalits in Nagpur in 1956 still continues. Nearly one million dalits have embraced neo-Buddhism since 1956. Why? Because conversion is a legitimate act of social liberation from the oppressive Hindu caste structure. Simultaneously the act of conversion is a social statement of protest. Partly the Hindu caste system deserves to be blamed for these conversion to other religions. Freedom of conversion and freedom of worship is a fundamental human right.

In the ultimate analysis the Hindu-Christian confrontations in India is basically a confrontation of two world views and life views. The Hindu world view of pollution-purity, caste system, and denial of human dignity to scheduled castes and scheduled tribes in the modern rational world is an outdated world view. The conversion of dalits to Buddhism in Maharashtra, to Islam in Meenakshipuram in Tamil Nadu or to Christianity in different parts of the country is a revolt against the oppressive Hindu social system. Conversion has two distinct dimensions, i.e., internal and social. The Hindus approve conversion of hearts as do the Christians. With the outdated other-worldly Hindu life-view the social dimension of conversion is conveniently objected by the fundamentalist Hindus. In contrast, only the Christian world view, de jure, provides the foundation for liberty, equality, human dignity, human rights and conscience, the benchmark of modern civilization. An individual or a community can begin the conversion process from any one starting point i.e., personal or community and gradually grow into the second. In most cases the goal of conversion is achieved after a gradual socio-economic and educational development.

The Christians firmly believe that serving the poor and the marginalized is an integral part of their missionary vocation. Christian missionaries have a noble record of serving both the rich as well as the poor of this country irrespective of caste, class and religion. "The Orissa Freedom of Religion Act 1967" prohibits: "No person shall convert or attempt to convert, either directly or otherwise, any person from one religious faith to another by the use of force or by inducement or by any fraudulent means nor shall any person abet any such conversion."[30] The Christians fully support this position, as long as the Constitutional provision of freedom of religion is upheld. The present law is so vague that no one is able to establish

29. Quoted by Gore, *Social Context*, 126.
30. Quoted by Kim, *In Search*, 207.

The Future of Christian Mission in India

through objective and identifiable criteria which conversion is through force or fraud and which is through conviction, writes Mr. Michael Pinto, vice-chairman of the National Commission for Minorities.[31] "There are laws at least in six states against forced conversion, but can you cite a single case of conviction, leave alone the charge?," challenged Archbishop R. Cheenath of Bhuvaneshwar during his meeting with L. K. Advani and Mrs. Sushma Swaraj of the BJP party on October 8, 2008, in New Delhi. When pluralism of religions, cultures, languages, castes, class and political ideologies increases and adherents of these fail to cultivate an adequate spirit of tolerance, then the danger of conflict and violence tend to increase sharply. When the philosophy of hatred of "the other" is sown then they shall reap not only the harvest of violence but also murder and extermination of others.

The anti—Christian bias of the recent Supreme Court Judgement, on January 21, 2011 on Dara Singh and Humram, guilty of murdering the Australian missionary Graham Staines and his minor sons in Orissa, is clearly expressed as follows: "the intention was to teach a lesson to Graham Staines and his religious activities, namely converting poor tribals to Christianity." Because of the strong protest and appeal of the Christian community the Supreme Court of India was forced to expunge portion of its judgement, replacing it with the following sentence on January 25th "—We are of the opinion that the life sentence awarded by the High Court need not be exchanged (to death penalty) in view of the functional position discussed in the earlier para." Another portion of the ruling said, "It is undisputed that there is no justification for interfering in someone's belief by way of "use of force, provocation, conversion, incitement upon the flawed promise that one religion is better than the other." On January 25th the court accepted the following change: "This portion is now replaced with the following sentence: "There is no justification for interfering in someone's religious belief by any means."[32]

The Justice B. K. Somasekhara Commission, constituted to enquire into a series of attacks on priests, sisters, Christians and churches in Karnataka in September 2008 submitted its Report on 8th January 2011, after more than two years. The Report concludes that the district administration has failed, but not the state government. The miscreants have been identified as Bajrang Dal and the Hindu Jagaran Vedike but the Sangh Parivar has been explicitly exonerated. The Commission said there

---

31. Pinto, *Times of India* (October 8, 2008) 18.
32. Venkatesan, "Courting Anger," 49–50.

Violence against Christian Missions

were clear indication of conversions to Christianity. "It is not necessarily compulsion or fraud or coercion," adding that "the allegation that some persons involved in conversions are getting funds from foreign countries and misuse it for mass conversion of helpless people belonging to weaker sections is true." It further added that some attacks are true, but the Hindus have no role to play in any attack. Attackers mistakenly presumed that they would be protected by the party in power. The Commission failed to examine even a single state authority or a member of the RSS under whose close instruction these outfits carry on their attacks. The Karnataka Christian community in its protest meeting in Mangalore on February 20th 2011 rejected the Somashekhara Commission Report and demanded an investigation by the Central Bureau of Investigation.[33] On the increasing anti-minority bias among judiciary, Christophe Jaffrelot observes: "I think that we have seen over the last 10–15 years an increasing anti-minority bias among Judiciary and Police. You can see that in the recent Ayodhya and Dara Singh verdicts."[34]

The year 2008 was the worst year for Christians in their 2,000 years of existence in India. A week ahead of Christmas 2008 the government administration deployed 7,700 strong Central Reserve Police and Rapid Action Force, along with 22,000 state police personnel to guard Christian villages and churches in Orissa. Naturally the Christmas celebration was subdued and free of violence, but not free of fear and anxiety. These arrangements were the fruits of continuous social protests, political dialogue between the government authorities and the church representatives, and court cases for over a year. That the Christians could celebrate Christmas in 2008, 2009 and 2010 under police protection, is a clear indication of the fragility of Indian democracy and secularism. To the degree secular forces in the country are declining Hindu communal forces are escalating. Therefore religious conflicts in the future are expected to increase. The supreme court of India in the first week of January 2009 ordered the protection of the minority especially the Christians in Orissa. "We are a secular country. We cannot allow persecution of minorities," a Bench headed by Chief Justice K. G. Balakrishnan said. "We will not accept the persecution of minority. If the state government is unable to protect them its should resign," Justice Markandey Katju, one of the Judges hearing the Orissa case warned.[35] The recent violence against Christian missionaries in Orissa and

33. Jagadeesha and Narrain, "Samasekhara," 13–17.
34. Jaffrelot, "Sangh Parivar and New Contradictions," *Frontline*, March 25, 2011, 50.
35. Markandey Katju, in *Indian Express* (January 6, 2009) 5.

other parts of India, particularly violence against nuns, including rape and murder, has paralyzed missionary activities of the Catholic church since about 80 percent of the missionary work is being carried out by the nuns.

Swami Agnivesh, President of World Council of Arya Samaj, who was fed on anti-Christian diet in his youth and later changed his attitudes under the influence of his good friend, late Miss Nirmala Deshpande and others, writes:

> The lie of conversion by force and fraudulent means is being spread and perpetuated every where in India instigating people to take law into their own hands. Certain groups take pride in attacking the innocent member of the Christian community. It saddens me a great deal to see how this miniscule community, which renders far more service to the nation than representation in the Indian population, has become a victim of false allegations of "conversion by force and fraudulent means" of the poor masses of India. Right wing Hindu fundamentalist... have gone to the extent of burning innocent children alive, as in the case Timothy and Philip, and even raping the nuns—the holy nuns who have consecrated their lives to God and vowed to serve the poor and the downtrodden of our country.[36]

And the latest instance is the murder of a Keralite nun Valsa John, 52, of Sisters of Charity of Jesus and Mary, in Pachuwara village, Pakur district of Jharkand State, in her sleep in a hut with a recent tribal rape victim on November 15, 2011. For the past twelve years she had led partially successful agitations and negotiated a good rehabilitation and compensation package for around 500 displaced Santal tribal families with Panem Coal Mines Ltd. and timber mafia. She was seen a threat to illegal practices. The poor and exploited tribals and the missionaries who fight for justice are subjected persecution and martyrdom. The disturbing question is will they get justice?[37] 250 serious crimes and many more minor offences were committed against Christians during the year 2011 in the states of Karnataka, Gujarat and Madhya Pradesh, all ruled by the Hindu right wing party and in Chhattisgarh, Jharkand and Orissa with high concentration of tribals where the missionaries continue to serve the poor. According to Professor Ram Puniyani tribal communities have become easy targets of Hindu fundamentalists, with little fear of retaliation.[38] Young India, which is less than seventy years old, has miles to go before the realization of true

36. Agnivesh, "Forward," xv.
37. *The Indian Express* (November 2, 2011) 2, 5.
38. Puniyani, "2011: Year of Persecution," *The Examiner*, January 28, 2012, 19.

Violence against Christian Missions

democracy and secularism. "The only hope is that millions of enlightened and patriotic citizens will unite and come out and openly lead the fight against terrorism," opines George Menezes, ex-member of the Vatican Commission for the laity.[39] With Rabindranath Tagore therefore pray:

> Where the mind is without fear and the head is held high;
> Where knowledge is free;
> Where the world has not been broken up into fragments by
> By narrow domestic walls;
> . . . .—
> Into that heaven of freedom, my Father, let my country awake.[40]

---

39. Menezes, *The Times of India*, October 4, 2008, 11.
40. Tagore, *Gitanjali*, no. 25.

4

Conversions of Marginal Communities to Christian Churches

THE RECENT RENEWED ATTACKS on Christians and their institutions prompts one to throw some light on a very complex and sensitive subject of conversion to Christianity and clarify certain misunderstandings. In the face of extreme poverty, economic exploitation, powerlessness, and inhuman treatment meted out to outcastes and tribals for centuries, legitimized by Hindu scriptures and enforced by dominant castes, many of them were looking for and waiting for alternative ways and means to get out of the cruel system which they could neither change nor break. When the Christian missionaries appeared on the scene and offered them a new vision of life and liberation millions of these oppressed people believed that they had found the escape route they had been eagerly looking for and, therefore, embraced Christianity in large number. The central question raised here is this: Was their acceptance of Christianity reasonable and legitimate?

The Hindu Scriptures (*Manusmruti*, I, 87–91) divide the Indian society into four Varnas as God's will. The Sanskrit word for caste is Varna, colour, and is inherently racist.[1] In the traditional caste structure the high castes were in a position of power. That is to say, the Brahmins, priestly caste, controlled the value system, particularly religious values; the Kshatriyas, the rulers, had command over people and scarce resources; the Vaishyas, commercial caste too had a great share in the scarce resources of wealth. Major decisions in and for the whole society or country were made by these castes. The Backward Castes, scheduled castes and scheduled tribes

---

1. Singh, *Diversity*, 33–36; Hopkins, *Ordinance*, 18. These are not uncontested classifications.

Conversions of Marginal Communities to Christian Churches

shared little power or benefits; on the contrary, they were dominated by the three powerful upper castes. The position and function of each individual and caste group, they taught, were immutably fixed by three Hindu doctrine of *Karma*, every action with strict good or bad consequence and *Sansara*, the cycle of birth and rebirth according to the actions of the past life and *Dharma*, rules of each caste. One can achieve the ultimate goal of life, *Moksha*, or salvation from the endless cycle of birth and rebirth only by the strict observance of *Varnadharma*, an ethically determined cosmos.[2] Untouchability is a social behavior resulting from a belief of pollution. Ageless enimity between the pure and impure castes had been the root of unbridgeable social distance and perpetual tension and caste wars not only during the past centuries but also today.

Mass Conversions to Christianity

The British East India company strictly discouraged missionary activities for better commercial purpose. However from the beginning of the nineteenth century, under the pressure of the evangelicals in the British Parliament missionary activities were gradually introduced. After the Indian Mutiny in 1857 India came directly under the British rule. The religious policy of the crown, in principle, was one of non-interference. Unofficially many evangelical administrators supported the missionaries because they believed it was their Christian duty. For others it was politically advantageous. For example in 1889 the British Prime Minister Marquis of Salisbury, publicly stated: "It is not only our duty but is in our interest to promote the diffusion of Christianity as far as possible throughout the length and breadth of India."[3] Thus the missionaries enjoyed more freedom and support to propagate their religion, without creating disturbances. K. M. Panikkar, a staunch critique of Christian mission, wrote: "When their failure with the higher classes became more and more evident they diverted activities to the conversion of the untouchables and low castes."[4] In 1851 when a rather reliable account of Christian population in India was available the Roman Catholics numbered one million; independent Thomas Christians 250,000; Protestants 90,000.

---

2. Weber, *Theory*, 131.
3. Sundaran, *Encyclopedia*, 183.
4. Panikkar, *Asia and Western*, 49.

The Future of Christian Mission in India

Mass Conversion of the Adivasis of Chotanagpur to Christianity

The tribal population of India belong to 461 tribal communities and 86 percent of them are concentrated in the central belt, covering undivided Madhya Pradesh, 23 percent; Orissa, 22 percent; Gujarat, 15 percent; Rajasthan, 12 percent; Maharashtra, 9 percent; undivided Bihar, 8 percent; Andhra Pradesh, 6 percent; about 11 percent of the North Eastern region, traditionally known as Assam belt, is tribal. Among these seventy one tribal groups, amounting to 0.136 million are classified as "primitive" tribes.[5] Due to prolonged geographical isolation until the nineteenth century tribals developed their own culture distinct from Hindu caste culture. They claim that they are the original inhabitants of India, i.e., Adivasis, even before the arrival of the Aryans in India around 1500 BC. But gradually the caste Hindus found it profitable to exploit the lands of the Adivasis and their labor. For example the landlords treated them like bullocks to plough their fields and insulted them calling 'Kol,' Nigger.

Mass conversions among the tribals took place only in two regions—the Chotanagpur Adivasi belt and north-east tribal belt. The major aboriginal tribes of Chotanagpur among whom the Christian missionary work was quite successful were the Oraons, Mundas, Kharias, Santals and Hos. Around thirty tribes are spread out in the present states of Jharkand, Chattisgarh, northern Orissa and north West Bengal. The system of landlord system which was foreign to the tribal economy and administration was introduced by the British administration. This was the beginning of the prolonged and systematic exploitation of the people of Chotanagpur which reduced the majority to the status of tenants. A register of ancestral land was introduced by the British government in 1858 and it culminated in the Chotanagpur Tenures Act of 1869. A survey conducted by the British government among the Tribals of Ranchi in 1910 discovered that 90 percent land which the Adivasis owned earlier were unjustly robbed by the dominant groups of those who came from neighboring states.[6] Many times the tribal communities rebelled unsuccessfully against the exploitation and alienation of the land that was considered sacred since it was the resting place of their ancestors. The prolonged and systematic exploitation of the people of Chotanagpur generated great distress and provoked various rebellions.[7]

5. Xaxa, "Tribal Scene," 71.
6. Roy, "Effect," 373.
7. Fuchs, *Rebellious Prophets*, 22–53.

Conversions of Marginal Communities to Christian Churches

Christian missionaries entered the area in the midst of a socio-economic crisis and a religious revival movement. In 1844 four Gossner Evangelical Lutheran missionaries arrived in Calcutta from Berlin, where Rev. John Baptist Gossner (1773–1858), after breaking away from the catholic church, had founded this missionary society in 1836.On the advice of the British administrators they began to work in villages not very distant from Ranchi where they had come for court cases against the landlords. "It is interesting to note that the first four Oraons to be baptized by the Lutherans in June 1850 were Kabirpanthi Bhagats."[8] Since the missionaries began to advise them on court cases they became more interested in the life and teachings of the missionaries. The number of those people who began to follow the Christian religion grew rather rapidly. By the year 1880 there were over 31,200 Lutherans Christians spread out in 1,052 villages.[9] For the missionaries the translation of the Bible in the local languages was an urgent need for evangelization. In 1868 Rev. Hahn prepared a *Kuruk Grammar and Dictionary*. The Gossner mission started a printing press in Ranchi in 1882. Dr. Alfred Nottrot's translation of the Bible in Mundari in 1876 was a pioneering contribution to the Mundari language and literature. By 1950 the Independent Lutheran church of Chotanagpur and Assam increased to around 200,000 members.[10]

The rapid spread of the German Lutherans, the traditional enemy of the Catholics, disturbed the mission conscience of the Belgian Jesuit missionaries in Calcutta. Though a significant number of conversions took place among the adivasis around the Ranchi areas the most spectacular mass conversion movement was triggered by the twenty eight years old Flemish Jesuit, Constant Lievens (1855–93), the Apostle of Chotanagpur, who arrived in Torpa in March 1885. A Hindu officer with an Anglican wife said to him: "If you really desire the conversion of the natives, you have only to undertake the defense of their interests, specially in connection with the questions of their rights regarding land tenure and landlords services, and you will have as many converts as you desire."[11] Constant Lievens took the advice seriously. He studied the Munda, Oraon and Kharia dialects. He studied further the laws governing the land tenure, the extent and limitations of the rights of the Zamindars. He consulted magistrates and employed lawyers to help the people in their land disputes

---

8. De Sa, *Crisis in Chotanagpur*, 72.
9. Ibid., 77, 80, 101.
10. Mahato, *Hundred years*, 102.
11. Quoted by Bowen, *Father Constant*, 64.

through legal channels. As a result by 1887, ten landlords were jailed for their crimes. When the people saw his influence they were enthusiastic to seek more help. Some disgruntled Lutherans, including catechists and teachers, volunteered to become Leivens assistants. When the number of people seeking legal aid increased rapidly Fr. Leivens made a policy that he would help only Christians or those who wish to become Christians. They had nothing to lose by embracing Christianity; on the contrary, there was much to gain. It was a win—win situation. Leivens followed the policy of baptizing all who expressed the wish and catechizing them at a later period. He was helped by a handful of priests and a good number of village leaders, teachers and catechists who went around enrolling as well as gathering people in villages. These people Leivens baptized in crowds, merely by sprinkling holy water, contrary to the catholic law. Among the Adivasis decisions were traditionally made by the tribal leaders for the group and this practice was equally true in the case of mass conversions. The result was that within five years he and his small band of helpers baptized over 50,000 Adivasis and many thousands were registered for future baptism.

In the meantime, seeing the benefits of conversion to Christianity, large delegations from Barway, Gangpur in the northern part of Orissa, and other princely states were requesting for baptism. The catechists would visit these villages and enrole their names. Later Lievens and his ten companions priests like Dehon, Carton and Grosjean baptized them in large numbers. In the words of Bishop Stephen Neill: "It was not surprising that the simple people came to regard this vigorous, at times almost violent white man, riding about the hills on an elephant as a saviour sent from heaven."[12] Many missionaries seriously challenged his method and motives of people. Therefore in March 1892 his superiors in Calcutta objected to mass conversions and his work was suspended for a while. Soon he had to return to Belgium for medical treatment. When he died of tuberculosis before the age of thirty eight, 73,265 Catholics in India lost their saviour and liberator. But the wild fire of the mass conversion of the Adivasis was kept burning by other Jesuits in the following half a century.[13] Expressing appreciations for the liberative activities of these missionaries one of the adivasi Bishops recently said to this author: "Whatever may be the shortcomings of the foreign missionaries we must be grateful to them for bringing us out of the jungle."

12. Neill, *History*, 405.
13. Kanjamala, *Religion*, 62–74.

Conversions of Marginal Communities to Christian Churches

The concerns of the missionaries were not exclusively conversion of souls. Aware of the root cause of the Adivasi rebellions, "The Chotanagpur Tenancy Act" (1908), empowering to prevent land alienation of the tribal land by non-tribals, was drafted by Fr. J. B. Hoffmann and was entirely accepted by the British government. This Act was later expanded to the land ownership of the tribals even after Indian Independence. He also established "Catholic Mission Cooperative Credit Society of Chotanagpur" (1906) and "Chotanagpur Cooperative stores" (1913). A large number of families became beneficiaries and escaped the clutches of the landlords and moneylenders. The Catholic Saba founded in 1928 gradually evolved into Adivasi Mahasaba in 1929, covering the whole of Chotanagpur. It put the foundation of the Jharkhand movement and the creation of the state in 2000. He is also the celebrated author of the ten volume *Encyclopedia Mundarica* (1924-1938).

The Norwegian L. O. Skrefsrud (1840 -1910) of the Gossner Lutheran Mission who arrived in India in 1863 toiled in the Santal Parganas for half a century. He is one of the pioneers who powerfully argued for the preservation of the local culture and indigenization of the Santal church. His many publications included *The Grammar of the Santal Language* (1873) and the translation of the New Testament in Santali (1880). By the time of is death the adherents of the Scandinavian mission, to which he had turned off from the Gosner mission, numbered 15,000. The Society for the Propagation of the Gospel started work in Ranchi (1869). The Dublin University Mission entered Hazaribagh in 1892 and it started the first degree college, St. Columba's college, in 1899.[14]

Initiated by Alexander Duff Gonds of Madhya Pradesh was evangelized by the Free Church of Scotland. They are credited with a publication of a *Gondi Grammar* (1866). The Swedish Lutheran Mission, The Disciples of Church of Christ, The Evangelical Lutheran Church entered central India by the last quarter of the nineteenth century. The Korkus at the extreme western end of the Munda country came in contact with the Conservative Baptist Foreign Mission of the USA and the Zoram Baptist Mission during the same period. The Konds of Orissa and Andhra Pradesh, with custom of human sacrifice, were contacted by the American Baptists and the Roman Catholic Missionaries during the same period.[15] The Oxford educated Verrier Elwin (1902-64) arrived in India 1927. From 1932 he lived with Gond tribe of the Central Province and later moved

14. Mahato, *Hundred years*, 166-79.
15. Hrangkhuma, "Christianity," 15-22.

into the North East Frontier Agency. He is the author of forty books and 400 articles on Indian tribes. "The pen is the chief weapon with which I fight for my poor," he said. He was appointed to the Tribal Welfare and Research Unit by the Government of India.[16]

Mass Movement of Tribals in the North East

Until the middle of the nineteenth century 11 percent of the Indian tribal population lived in great isolation from the main land in the seven sisters states of the NE, six of them later reorganized, more or less, on the basis of a particular tribal identity. Ethnically they have more affinity with the Mongoloid race. With forty two major tribes and 150 minor tribes plus fifty major languages and nearly 200 minor dialects, penetrating their cultural worlds was the greatest challenge the foreign missionaries encountered.[17] The British occupation of the N.E., starting in 1833, and the introduction of various political and social reforms among different tribes caused a major cultural crisis. The social reforms of the British, disturbed the traditional order and resulted in a major cultural crisis.[18] Tribal revolts and rebellions naturally followed. Some of the instances of rebellions are; the Garo rebellion in 1852; the Synteng of Jaintia hills began their revolt in 1860, and 1861–63; the Manipur rebellion in 1891; the Kuki rebellion in Manipur in 1917–19 and the Naga rebellion of 1929–31. These and other rebellions were suppressed by the British might. Later their prolonged warring spirit forced the Independent India to create six tribal states, starting with the creation of Nagaland state in 1963, with 90 percent Christian population. And the struggles still continue.[19]

Among the numerous Protestant missions that began to penetrate into the North East tribal region the first was Rev. Krishna Pal of the Serampore Baptist Mission to Guwahati in 1813 and to Chirapunji in 1832. The Serampore mission translated the Bible into Assamese—The New Testament in 1819 and the Old Testament in 1833—using the Bengali script, which the local people did not follow. *The Khasi New Testament*, in the Roman script was ready in 1824. After a quarter of a century the Baptists had to discontinue the work but would return to Mizoram in 1903. The Welsh Presbyterians, formerly known as the Calvinist Methodist, after discontinuing with the London Missionary Society, arrived in Mehalaya

16. Guha, "Between Anthropology," 337.
17. Fuchs, "Races," 160–72.
18. Hutton, "Primitive Tribes," 432.
19. Stanislaus, "Tribal Movements," 192–94.

Conversions of Marginal Communities to Christian Churches

in 1841 and among the Karbis of Assam in 1880. The American Baptists entered upper Assam in 1836 and by 1870 they were among the head-hunting Nagas; and in Tura, Assam, in 1877; and among the Garos of Mehalaya in the same year. And they entered the Manipur in 1894. The Evangelical Lutheran Church arrived in Western Assam in 1870. The Church of God began their mission among the Khasis in 1902. The tribes of Tripura, currently dominated by migrant Bengalis, including those from Bangladesh, received the Gospel only in the twentieth century with the arrival of the New Zealand Baptists in 1938. Other mission agencies included the Salvation Army, the Seventh Day Adventists, the Pentecostal Mission and the Gossner Mission. Unlike the Portuguese Mission in Goa and the Danish Mission in Tamil Nadu, missionaries in the North East arrived without any political agenda.[20]

Though various Protestant Societies began to penetrate into North-East tribal areas in the beginning of the nineteenth century the mass conversion movement would not commence until the middle of the twentieth century.[21] The tribals were highly suspicious of the white missionaries since the British administration had disturbed their traditional administrative and social system. By 1918 number of Christians in Meghalaya, Mizoram, Manipur and Nagaland was only 48,000. In the mean time the missionaries were gradually winning the confidence of the people through their educational and medical services. The translation of the Word of God in local dialects was equally important. North East is a Babel of 240 dialects and languages which make the communication of the Word of God most difficult. Study of the local dialects as well as publications became an urgent need. William Pryse published *Introduction to the Khasi Language* (1855); Hugh Roberts authored *Anglo-Khasi Dictionary* (1871); and *A Grammar For Khasi Language* (1891). The Welsh Presbyterian F. W. Savidge and J. H. Lorrain translated the Bible into Mizo Language (1894) in the Roman script. They also prepared *Grammar and Dictionary of Lushai Language*.[22] Throughout the North East "the Christian missionaries were responsible for developing a written form of at least fifty languages."[23] Traditionally many Protestant denominations emphasized personal religious experience of conversion to be admitted to the church. Recognizing the tyranny of kinship, castes and tribes traditional missionary policy had to be aban-

---

20. Snaitang, "Christianity," 149–50.
21. Firth, *Introduction*, 267–76.
22. Plathottam, "Language Plurity," 209.
23. Downs, "Christian Conversion," 359.

doned. In contrast they shifted to the policy of baptizing first, mostly the whole community and Christianizing later. Historically, in spite of objections from some missionaries, this policy proved to be a success.

The progress of the American Baptists among the Nagas and the Welsh Presbyterian missionaries in the Khasi hills prompted the Catholic missionaries to enter the area which was earlier forbidden by the British administration, being well aware of the traditional enemy and conflicts between Protestants and Catholics. After the repatriation of the German Salvatorian missionaries during the First World War the Catholic mission became more dynamic with the arrival of the Salesians of Don Bosco in 1922, under the leadership of Fr. Louis Mathias the Prefect Apostolic of Assam. At this time there were only around 5,000 Catholics in Assam and Meghalaya. They began their mission work among the Khasi—Pnars, a matrilineal tribe, in the Khasi Jaintia hills of Meghalaya. Fr. Constantine Vendrame walked the length and breath of the Khasi hills to prepare new converts. It is estimated that he baptized over 30,000 Khasis.[24] He is recognized as the apostle of the Khasis, like Lievens in Chotanagpur. Today one third of the catholic population in the North east are Khasis. Their missionary activities were extended to the Garos, Boros, Rabhas, Tiwas Karbis, Dimasas, Tripuries. Most of the Garos easily welcomed the catholic church.[25] By 1941 the work of the Salesian missionaries attracted around 64,844 people to the Catholic Church. The tribals were attracted by the services of the missionaries particularly in the field of education through English medium schools and hostels. "The entire responsibility for running schools was given to missionaries by the government."[26] The Christian religion and English education became two major sources of new identity and unity for numerous divided and mutually hostile tribes. Conversion to the Catholic Church took place in large numbers from most of the tribes here. The rapid expansion of the catholic church is evident from the following records. Their number was 104,887 in 1959; 369681 in 1977; and above 1,000,000 in 2001.[27] The missionary dynamics and methods of the Salesians of Don Bosco deserve almost exclusive credit, not without the cooperation of many religious sisters, for the phenomenal expansion of the Catholic church in the North East as do the Jesuits for the

---

24. Menamparambil, *Introduction*, 25.
25. Koottuppallil, "Catholic Mission," 288–29.
26. Downs, "Christian Conversion," 390.
27. Houtart and Lemercinier, *Size and Structure*, 33.

Conversions of Marginal Communities to Christian Churches

genesis as well as growth of the Catholic church in Chotanagpur.[28] Over six fold expansion of Christian population from 6,00,000 (1951) to over 4, 000,000 was mostly the fruit of the labor of Indian missionaries though the British administration and foreign missionaries served as primary catalyst in the pre—independence era.

Mass Conversion of Outcastes to Christianity

About 16 percent of the population of India are classified as Scheduled Castes, suffering numerous social disabilities like untouchability, poverty and oppression by upper castes. Unlike the Scheduled Tribes, they have been part of the village system throughout the centuries. Traditionally they were landless bonded agricultural labors of landlords. Mass conversions of outcastes to Christianity occurred only in three Indian states—Punjab in the north, Andhra Pradesh and Tamil Nadu in the south. However small scale conversions are recorded in other states.

MASS CONVERSION IN PUNJAB

The arrival of seven Protestant Societies in North—West India between 1800–1857 marks the beginning of the Christian mission in this region. They are the Baptist missionary Society in Delhi (1818), the American Presbyterian Church, in Ludhiana (1834), the Church Missionary Society at Simla and Kotegarly (1840) and Amritsar (1850), the Society for the Propagation of the Gospel in Delhi (1854), the Associate Presbyterian Synod of North America in Sialkot (1855), the Moravian Brothers in Lehul, in the present Himachal Pradesh (1856) and the Church of Scotland in Sialkot (1856).[29] However the mass movement to Christianity commenced only after 1881, during which the following societies too entered: the Methodist Episcopal Church, in Lahore (1881), the Salvation Army at Lahore and Dhariwal, the Seventh Day Adventist and the Church of England Zenana Bible and Medical Mission Society. John C.Lowrie of the American Presbyterian church is considered to be the first missionary to Punjab in 1834. And four decades later the Belgian Capuchins arrived in Lahore, Amritsar and Jullundur Cantonment.

The gradual and remarkable response of the Dalits, particularly the untouchable Chura and Chamar castes in the undivided Punjab created a wave of mass movement. The Churas, engaged in occupations like scav-

---

28. Joshi et al., *Religious Demography*, 107–14.
29. Webster, *Social History*, 39–48.

enging, removing night-soil, sweeping public roads, agricultural labour, removing carrion, etc. were the most despised community. The Chamars, above the Churas in social status, were leather workers, weavers, and agricultural labourers. The 1891 Census recorded nearly 1.2 million Churas in Punjab.[30] With schools, medical services and other social activities the Protestant missionaries had already made entry points among the people in the first half of the nineteenth century. After the arrival of Andrew Gordon in Sialkot in 1855 the work of evangelization was expanded and intensified with street and village preaching. The baptism of certain Ditt, a Chura, near Sialkot, now in Pakistan, in 1873, is the beginning of dalit conversion. Because of his missionary spirit and wide contact as a hide dealer, Ditt was instrumental in bringing five hundred Churas to faith by 1884. In the following two decades, the united Presbyterian missionaries made over 10,000 converts, marking the beginning mass conversions. The Church of Scotland also gained some converts in and around Sialkot. The conversion movement soon became visible in the neighboring districts of Gujaranwala, and Gurudaspur. In 1881 the CMS in Batala received request for Christian instruction and a school. In 1881 mass conversion began to spread among the Churas of Lahore, Ferozpur and Hosiarpur districts. In central Punjab the American Methodists and the Salvation Army benefited from the movement. The Salvation Army with their utter simplicity of life and the message of racial equality attracted many converts in North—West Punjab. In 1889 the Belgian Capuchins in Sialkot moved into neighboring villages where some disgruntled Protestants, misguided by their catechists, volunteered to join the Catholic mission, as it happened among the Adivasi Protestant converts of Chotanagpur. In the eyes of illiterate and oppressed people, waiting for a rescuer, all the white missionaries were offering education, medical and social services to the poor Dalits and they preached a white God—Jesus—and for the people denominational differences made no sense at all. Some local Chamars too, though not in large number, influence by the Chura movement, accepted the new faith.[31]

In the initial stages of mass conversion changes among the converts were clearly social than spiritual. They were forbidden to work on the Sabbath as well as eating carrion. Faithfulness in marriage was strictly demanded. Fear of punishment by God in hell, a feature of evangelical preaching, was a strong motive in their social conduct and behavior.

30. Webster, *Dalit*, 8–12.
31. Webster, *Social History*, 169–76.

Conversions of Marginal Communities to Christian Churches

When the new converts were tempted to migrate from central Punjab to Chenab canal construction site for work all the missionary societies helped many new converts to obtain land and settle down in Christian villages, with churches, schools, boardings, dispensaries and social protection. Conversion and association with foreign missionaries improved their social status marginally. On the mixed motivations of huge outcaste conversion movement the missionaries themselves were aware of the following: "They saw the conversion movement as a basically social movement aimed at achieving a rise in social status and with it greater dignity and respect." "An untouchable becomes touchable by adopting Christianity." reported a missionary.[32] Strong reactions to mass conversions were naturally raised by the dominant community. The landlords were losing cheap labor in their fields. They began to persecute the new Christians by not paying them proper wages or even refusing to give them work. Arya Samaj introduced Shudhi rite in 1903 to reconvert them. "All India Shudhi Sabha" was established in 1911 to reconvert Christians to the original religion. Arya Samaj established their own rival schools, boardings, orphanages and other institutions to challenge the Christian expansion. Many missionaries were skeptical of mass conversion of the untouchables. For instance an American missionary compared it "raking in rubbish into the Church."[33]

For the Christian missions the period between 1800—1880 was the period of preparing the soil to sow the Word of God. The missionaries openly received moral and financial support from the British officials who were themselves, at least in a few instances, pioneers of new mission stations. The mass conversion movement began after 1880. The following data ascertains the dynamism of conversion to Christianity. The 1881 Census reported 3,914 Indian Christians in Punjab and its dependencies. In the following decade the Christian population grew to 19,750. During 1891–1911 the phenomenal expansion of new believers climbed to 1,63,994; plus 877 in the newly created North—West. Their denominational distribution per 1911 Census Report was as follows: 92,769 Presbyterians, nearly 57 percent of the total; 29,051 Anglicans; 18007 Salvation Army; 11,723 Methodists and 8,497 Catholics.[34] The Baptists and the Anglicans converts in Delhi came predominantly from the Chamar community. According to James Massey today there are more than 3,00,000 Christians on the

---

32. Ibid., 177–78.
33. Quoted by Massey, "Holy Spirit," 255.
34. Webster, *Social History*, 183.

The Future of Christian Mission in India

Indian Punjab and a larger number of Punjabi Christians on the Pakistan side. And 99 percent of them come from the dalit background; almost all the Churas of Sialkot district became Christians.[35] As per 2001 Census the Christians have a share of a little over 1 percent of the population of Punjab which is about the same as it was half a century ago. Their main concentration is in the four districts of Gurudaspur, Amritzar, Firozpur and Jalandhar.

Among the literary contributions of the missionaries a few deserve to be recorded. "Clearly translations and writing were major components of Presbyterian missionary work. John Newton . . . wrote the first comprehensive grammar of the Punjabi language in 1851 . . . and the first Punjabi Dictionary in 1854. . . . the Punjabi New Testament in 1868. Newton is today considered one of the fathers of modern Punjabi language."[36] Other early Punjabi Christian publications are: Padri Daud Singh, a Sikh convert (+ 1882) translated to The Gospel according to St. Mathew in Punjabi under the title, *Mangalasamachar* in poetic form. He is the first Christian Punjabi poet. "The story of Jesus Christ in Punjabi Verse," *Sat Swami Nihakalank Autar Prabhu Jisu Mashi Da Jas Dharam Pustak Anusa* by Tahil Singh was published in Lahore in 1900.[37]

Mass Conversion in Andhra Pradesh

The history of the Catholic mission in A.P. begins with the arrival of a few Franciscan Friars in Vijayanagar in 1530 and Bijapur in 1570. Two Italian Theatines, the Congregation for Evangelization, entered the Bijapur Muslim kingdom in December 1640. By 1720 they built two churches in Golconda near Hyderabad and Masulipatnam or Machilipatnam Sea Port for the pastoral care of small Catholic communities. Later their services were extended to Vizagapatanam and Srikakulam. The Augustianians who arrived in Masulipatnam and Golconda in 1652 left the place after handing them over to the Theatines by 1663. The services of all these congregations were mostly confined to pastoral care of foreign soldiers and employees of foreign companies, and not in evangelization. The French Jesuits entered Pondicherry, the French colony, in 1691 and it evolved into the headquarter of the Carnatic mission, covering the Telugu country, Tamil Nadu and part of Mysore state. Imitating the missionary method of de Nobili they were able to make a good number of upper caste converts

---

35. Massey, "Holy Spirit," 255.
36. Webster, *Social History*, 44.
37. Massey,"Punjabi Christian," 573–76.

Conversions of Marginal Communities to Christian Churches

in Guntur and Nellore districts. Before the suppression of the Jesuits in 1773, which gravely weaked the mission, the number of Catholics in this mission was around 10,000. Following the suppression of the Jesuits the Paris Foreign Missionaries reached the area and extended their work to Nellore in 1825. The most illustrious among them was Bonnard Clement (1796–1861) who arrived in Phirangipuram in 1827. After two decades of zealous labour in the Carnatic mission he was appointed Vicar Apostolic of Pondicherry in 1845. He played a major role in the formation of Indian clergy and the erection of the Latin Catholic hierarchy in India in 1886, based on his report of the Apostolic visitation of the Catholic missions of the East Indies between 1859–61. The Pontifical Institute for Foreign mission from Milan, arrived in Vijayawada in 1855. Visakhapatanam was the headquarter of the Missionaries of Francis de Sales of Annecy, France from 1845 and expanded their missionary services to the neighboring regions, of Nagpur in Maharashtra, Jabalpur, Khandwa and Bastar in Madhya Pradesh and southern Orissa. The Mill Hill Missionaries arrived in 1875 and worked in different parts of Andhra Pradesh. All these missions were strengthened by the generous services of many religious sisters, particularly in the fields of education and health. The Sisters of St. Joseph of Annecy for example arrived in Vizakapatnam in 1849 and opened schools, boardings and orphanages, accompanying the MSFS missionaries. The fact that the number of Catholics in A.P. was only 25,814 in 1900, after 400 years of missionary labor, tells a bleak story. At present their number is a little above one million. The missionaries published many Telugu books and liturgical hymns. The *Vedanta Saramu*, The Essence of Theology, was one of the major publications.[38] Some scholars opine that the catholic method of accommodation to upper castes, beginning with de Nobili, constrained their missionary expansion to Dalits.[39]

The American Baptist Mission in coastal Andhra Pradesh from 1840 seemed a failure until the arrival of Rev. John Clough (1836–1910) in Nellore in 1865 and his mission among the outcaste Madigas—leather workers. A few Madiga converts like Yeragundla Periah, whom Clough baptized in 1866 took the initiative to visit many villages and attract large number of converts by 1878; by the end of 1882 the membership had multiplied to 20,865. During the famine of 1876–79 Clough provided food and work to thousands of Madigas by digging three and a half miles of a canal, a contract he accepted from the government. In the following thirty

---

38. George, *Christianity*, 244.
39. Kumar and Robinson, *Legally Hindu*, 152–56.

years the number of the baptized increased over by 62,000. During the famine of 1871–1881 the Telugu Protestants multiplied fivefold to mark 77,000.

The American Evangelical Church entered Guntur in 1848. During the severe famine (1876–79) when thousands were perishing the Lutheran missionaries became the main relief workers. Attracted by the compassionate services of these foreigners nearly a million outcastes embraced various Christian denominations, mostly the Lutherans in the following decade. This was followed by the largest mass movement to Christianity in India. In the Godhavari—Krishna belt in the coastal region the number of outcastes was nearly 20 percent. Thus the majority of the Lutherans belonged to the Mala community while the Baptist mission was dominated by nearly 62,000 Madigas, mostly in Medak district.[40]

The CMS that was already engaged in very successful mission in Tinnevelly district of the Madras Presidency established its Telugu mission in Masulipattam in 1841 at the invitation of the British official who raised fund to support the missionaries. And the Society for the Propagation of the Gospel founded its mission in Cuddapa in 1842. An English medium school was set up in Masulipattam which was elevated to the rank of a college in 1893, with the name of the founder, Robert Noble. The baptism of a few Brahmin students in 1852 provoked temporary boycott of the school.[41] Unfortunately in mid-1930 the college was forced to close down due to lack of fund as well as students who opted for rival Hindu colleges in the neighboring area. In the Krishna-Godavari delta where CMS started its mission the number of Christians was 260 after twenty years of labor. During the famine time the number of baptism, increased to around 10,000. The missionaries vigorously preached against idol worship, bloody sacrifices offered to god Murgan, son of Shiva. The oppressed outcastes were glad to accept the religion of the powerful white rulers. Before baptism by total immersion in rivers or ponds they made baptismal vows, recited the creed, the Lord's Prayer, and Ten Commandments. After the baptism they put on the symbolic white dress and promised to preach the Gospel. Naturally the ritual was very dramatic and touching. Most of the converts belonged to the Mala and Madiga castes. Conversions from the tribal communities like the Waddars and Lambadis or Banjaras was not large. By 1912 the number of Anglicans in Dornakal area was around 56,000.

40. Webster, *Dalit*, 44–45.
41. Harper, *In the Shadow*, 177–79.

Conversions of Marginal Communities to Christian Churches

The large scale entry of the untouchables was not sympathetically viewed by some missionaries who looked at it as a pollution of the church. But most of the missionaries justified the programme, in the face of certain objections, quoting how God chooses the weak to confound the wise. "God chose the foolish of the world to shame the wise and God chose the weak of the world to shame the strong, and God chose the lowly and despised of the world, those who count for nothing to reduce to nothing those who are something, so that no human being might boast before God"(1 Cor 1:27–29). In 1935, 100,000 Christians in the Telugu region were affiliated to the following churches—United Lutheran Church, the American Baptist Telangana Mission, the Canadian Baptist Mission, the London Missionary Society and the Wesleyan Methodist Church of Medak. Regarding the non-Brahmin caste conversions the estimate was approximately 50,000 Sudras—mainly Kammas. Between 1900–1940 Andhra witnessed the fastest growth of Christians in India. Sadly their apostasy too was equally fast. The Telugu Protestants constituted nearly 30 percent the total Protestants in India in the same period.[42] The mass conversion movement among the outcastes was chiefly the work of the Protestant missionaries since the Catholic missionaries operated within the frame work of the caste system. "Unlike the dalit Catholics, therefore, the Lutheran converts here do not face caste based discrimination due to the absence of upper caste converts."[43] A sharp decline of converts, nearly 50 percent, during the following decades might partly justify the denigration of many converts as "rice Christians." Today the main concentration of Christians in the state are in the districts of Krishna, nearly 5 percent; west Godawari, nearly 4 percent and Guntur, 3 percent. At present only 1.5 percent of the state population is Christian.

Mass Conversion in Tamil Nadu

Around 1900, forty five rival Protestant missionary organizations, and ten or more denominations, were engaged in missionary activities in Tamil Nadu. The five largest Protestant missions were the Baptists, Anglicans, Lutherans, Presbyterians and Methodists.[44] The history of the Christian mission in Tamil Nadu passed trough three phases. One, mass conversion among the fisher folk of the Coromandel coast in the sixteenth century. Two, The Danish-Halle-mission from the eighteenth century. Three,

42. Ibid., 184–87.
43. Kumar & Robinson," Legally Hindu," 155–56.
44. Moffett, *History,* 2:434.

mass conversion mainly among the Shanar, toddy tappers and Paraiya out castes under the evangelical missionaries, starting at the end of the nineteenth century. In Madras Presidency 37 percent of Tinnevelly and 17 percent of Ramnad district's population was Nadars and Kanyakumari district in Travencore state had a concentration of 29 percent.[45] With a dynamic help of his zealous catechistic Vedamanikam, a Shanar convert, W. T. Ringeltaube, the successor of C. F. Schwartz, expanded his missionary work to Mailady, now known as Marthandam, not to far from Trivandrum, the capital of Kerala. Exploitation of the community by the upper castes,—Brahmins, Vellalas, and Nairs—especially the abuse of their women created the crisis situation.

Having improved their Socio-economic condition, by 1870 majority of the Shanars gave up climbing Palmyra trees and sought better occupation like shop keepers, traders, cultivators, and agriculturalist in their own newly acquired land. Important developments in the labor markets from the last quarter of the nineteenth century induced large number of Dalits to migrate to new tea and coffee estates in the country, and emigrate to British colonies like Sri Lanka, Burma, South Africa, Fiji, Malaysia and elsewhere. The number of those who joined the British army too was quite high. From 1875 they made a concerted effort to change their name to Nadar, Lord of the Land, and created a new mythology about their lost Kshatriya status. The women converts, under the leadership of Zanana women missionaries, defied the traditional injunction that forbade women to cover the upper portion of body. It coincided with the abolition of slavery by the proclamation of the king of Travencore in 1855. By the middle of the twentieth century nearly 35 percent of Kanyakumari district, 18 percent of Tuticorin district and 11 percent of Tirunelvely district in Southern Tamil Nadu had embraced Christianity. "In their response to the social and economic changes in the last century the Nadars have today become one of the most economically and politically advanced communities in South India."[46]

By 1849, the number of the converts to the Church Missionary Society (CMS) in Tinnevelly increased to 40,000 and to the London Missionary Society in South Travencore to 20,000. A severe famine of 1877 was also a factor for doubling the number of the converts by 1883. The Anglican church here, to which the majority were converted, functioned as two denominations, i.e., CMS and Society for the Propagation of the Gospel

---

45. Hardgrave Jr., *Nadars*, 270.
46. Ibid., viii.

Conversions of Marginal Communities to Christian Churches

(SPG). The most renowned Tanjavur Christian was Vedanayakam Pillai (1773-1864), for his powerful Tamil Christian thought and literature. The publication of *The Tinnevelly Shanars* in 1849 by Caldwell provoked violent reactions from the community for portraying their inferior social status. In Protest around 2500 new converts under their leader Sattampillai, broke away and inaugurated a new church, the *Nattar Sabai*, at Nazarath, Tinnevelly in 1857. Tirunelveli or Tinnevelly diocese in 1912 was the largest Anglican diocese in India under an indigenous bishop, V. S. Azariah.

The Paraiyar caste with 348 endogamous communities, was one of the four largest outcastes in India and the largest one in Tamil Nadu. They were born slaves who could be sold and bought by landlords. As agricultural laborers majority of them were attached to landlords.[47] Maximum number of converts during the mass movement emerged from the Paraiyars who for centuries yearned for some liberators. In the beginning of the nineteenth century CMS continue of to gain large number of Paraiyar converts in Poonamalle, Tripasore, and Vepery. The Society for the Propagation of the Gospel (SPG) was a late comer in Tirunelvelly in 1860. They began to set up schools and hostels in Madurai, Tanjore, Arcot, Tuticorin, Nazarath and Palamcotta. The Society for the Propagation of Christian Knowledge (SPCK), had already arrived in Madras and Cuddalore in 1792. The London Missionary Society and the Wesleyan Methodist Mission were founded to serve the lower-middle class people in England. Their mission among the Paraiyars of Tamil Nadu in the middle of nineteenth century in Salem, Attur, Coimbatore and Erode attracted more adherents than the high Anglican Church. The Anglican Episcopate was established in Madras in 1835.[48]

The Danish mission took over the Arcot mission in 1861 and set up most of their schools in rural areas in the vernacular medium in order to promote the education of rural converts. The American Dutch Reformed Church too arrived in Arcot. The American Lutherans with their fundamentalist inclination against the liberal Protestantism arrived in Madras in 1870 and South Travencore where mass conversion among the Shanars was already in progress. The policy of 'comity of mission,' a gentlemanly agreement to avoid overlapping, unhealthy rivalry and wasteful duplication, came into operation. Therefore the CMS handed over some of its mission stations to SPG.[49] Tamil Nadu witnessed group conversion move-

47. Webster, *History of Dalits*, 21-26.
48. Basu, *Nandanar's Children*, 90-95.
49. Ibid., 84-90.

ments, similar to the movements elsewhere in India, in the period of 1870–1930.

In Britain because of the pressure of the Evangelicals in the Parliament, the Slavery Abolition Act of 1833 was passed. Ten years later the Government of India passed the Slavery Abolition Act of 1843. The Madras Missionary Conference of 1850 argued that caste practice within the Christian church was sin.[50] The tyranny of caste mentality is established from the following practices. In Tamil Nadu most churches were divided by a partition, allotting one side for the outcaste converts and the other for the caste converts, mostly from the Sudra caste. For Holy Communion two separate chalices were used. Even after death, burials took place in cemeteries, divided into two or in rare cases into three sections. Many Sudra priests refused to enter homes of Paraiyars. As the Anglican Bishop Daniel Wilson of Calcutta (1833–58) ordered in 1834 that caste distinction must be abandoned decidedly, and immediately. Around 3,000 Vellalar Christians in Thanjavur and 700 in Vepery, after prolonged fight, joined the Leipzig Lutheran church with less rigid caste norms in 1842. The ecumenical collaboration that existed between the Lutherans and Anglicans for nearly a century suddenly came to its sad end because of the Anglican imprudence, both CMS and SPG, to grasp the power of caste mentality of the converts.[51] The Methodist Church in Trichinoppoly and Mysore state too upheld strict policy that caste practices would not be tolerated.[52] Reginald Heber, the second Anglican Bishop of Calcutta (1823–27) "argued that the Christians of different castes who sat separately were no worse than Christian masters and slaves of America or Christian gentry and servants in Europe who sat and worshiped separately."[53]

Bishop H. Whithead of Madras (1899–1923) maintained the view that Mass Conversion Movement was the manifestation of liberative movement of the Spirit of God.[54] His theology was seriously contested by some of his fellow missionaries. They continued to criticize the lack of quality even after many decades of conversions. Religion in itself, a very complex reality, is powerless to change a community without simultaneous changes in the socio-economic and cultural dimension of its total existence. "Max Mueller thus had a strong reason to purport as long ago as

50. Ibid., 90–91.
51. Thomas, "History," 487.
52. Gibbs, "Anglican and Protestant," 235–36.
53. Quoted by Fykenberg, "Rajaguru," 487.
54. Neill, *Story*, 118.

Conversions of Marginal Communities to Christian Churches

1869, that abolishing of caste 'would be one of the most hazardous operations that was ever performed in the political body.' He further suggested that even if caste dies 'as religious institution' 'as a social institution it will live and improve' . . . Mueller already uncovers the manner in which the economic and social aspect of the caste system are more powerful than the religious one."[55] Conversions of large number of poor and marginalized people were simultaneously marked by a shift in social loyalties. The people who were loyal and dependent on landlords for generations were now forced to shift loyalty and dependency on missionaries. Missionaries too felt the obligation to protect them from upper castes and empower them economically. They assumed a new role of becoming patrons. And the converts spontaneously created a new vocabulary; mai-baap: "you are our mother and father." And the dependency mentality of converts introduced a fresh challenge for both missionaries and new Christians. Missionary education enhanced opportunities for new jobs. The Madras Native Christian Association in its report of 1893 stated: "Christianity has wrought miracles in our midst. It has lifted many of us from the mire of social degradation; it has enlightened us, liberated us from the trammel of superstition and customs and planted in us an instinct of a free and noble humanity"[56] In 2001 Tamil Nadu with 7 percent Christian population has the second largest Christian population, 3,785,060, next to the Christian population of Kerala. In addition to these large scale conversions in three states there were also small scale Harijan conversion in different parts of India. At the beginning of the mass conversion movement only less than 1 percent of the Indian population was Christian. By 1931 it expanded to nearly 2 percent, that is, the growth rate of Christianity was over 250 percent during a period of fifty years. It further tilted the political balance since the government was introducing some kind of representative administration in the 1930s.Their numerical growth was 2.7 million, 8.3 million, 10.7 million, 14.2 million, 16.1 million, 22 million and 25 million, according to the Census reports of, 1901, 1951, 1961, 1971, 1981, 1991, and 2001 respectively.[57]

---

55. Quoted by Clarke, "Conversion to Christianity," 331.
56. Quoted by George, *Christianity*, 213.
57. Joshi et al., *Religious Demography*, 159.

The Future of Christian Mission in India

Some of the Reasons for the Success of Mass Conversions

What could have been some of the reasons for the remarkable success of the Christian mission among the Adivasis, Tribals, Dalits and other backward communities in various parts of India? Why did many of them respond readily to the call and message of missionaries, while other social groups in the same area, belonging to the Hindu caste communities, vehemently rejected similar appeal? Without answering these and other relevant questions our understanding of such a dynamic people's movement and its social consequences becomes inadequate. According to anthropologist S.Roy who researched the land problems of the Adivasis it was not merely an economic problem but also a religious problem since the land was a sacred place where the ancestors were buried and the place over which the ancestral spirits kept close guard. Their conversion to Christianity was considerably motivated by the protection of the land. Roy concludes: "When the Christian missionaries appeared in the country a large number of Kharias . . . along with a large number of Mundas and Oraons turned to the Christian faith. This they did, in most cases, in the hope of securing their agrarian troubles and oppressions and exactions of their landlords and usurious money-lenders . . . In fact it was their agrarian trouble which prepared the way for the Christian missions."[58]

Some of the missionaries were well aware of the socio-economic motivations of the people. However, they hoped that, after having won their confidence, gradually these new converts could be instructed properly in their new faith and purify their motives. To quote a missionary:

> It is not the preaching of the missionaries that has done it as practically all these converts declared themselves ready to embrace the Catholic religion before this religion had been explained to them at all . . . In every conversion that has taken place in Chotanagpur the points which tell are the same two; 1) the convert is an aboriginal, and he is in difficulties, suffering from oppression or in misery from some cause or other and requires the help or protection of the missionary . . . 2) these conversions are the means used by Divine providence to bring these poor ignorant aboriginals into the Church; the beginning is always a matter of material self-interest.[59]

---

58. Roy, "Effect," 377–78.
59. Schueren, *Belgian Mission*, 111–12.

Conversions of Marginal Communities to Christian Churches

The indirect connection between Christian missionary activity and colonial political power was an influential factor in the mass conversion. There was a considerable gap between the official policy of the Crown, and the actual practice of the British officers in India. It was the British officers who invited many missionaries to the tribal and other backward areas. Wherever it was advantageous to the political cause, they supported the missionaries. This is admitted both by the missionaries as well as by the government officials. On the help received from the government during the hard times of the First World War, one missionary writes; "with no men from home to replace the fallen ones and with no funds from the stricken fatherland to provide for the teachers and catechists it looked as if within a very short time the whole fabric must totter to pieces. That, it did not do so is due to the truly wonderful help the mission received in its hour of trial both from the government and private resources. Sir Charles Bayley and after him Sir Edward Bait, successive governors of the province saved the mission schools by making special and exceptional grants to keep them in full work."[60] The government officials too were well aware of the help and co-operation they were lending to the mission, as Earl Lytton, an official of the British Government, stated: "I can assure him there has been no lack of co-operation between the government and the work of the mission . . . We realize that these Belgian Fathers were doing our work, were saving our money . . . were educating children that were our responsibility and we were grateful to them for doing it."[61] When the Jesuit missionaries could not obtain permission from the Raja of Gangpur State, in the present day Orissa, to work there, only with the coercion of the Lt. Governor of Bengal was permission granted. Later the work of the missionaries was facilitated with the assistance received from the Dewan, an English administrator of Gangpur Raja. Father Veys, the Jesuit Superior in Calcutta, after his visit to Gangpur in 1929, wrote to the missionaries in Gangpur, "I am of the opinion that the whole Gangpur mission has contracted a heavy debt of gratitude towards Mr. Christian, the Dewan, a debt which the missionaries should not forget to pay in fervent prayers for the benefactor and his family."[62]

The status and prestige which the foreign missionaries enjoyed and the fact that Christianity was, at least in their experience, the religion of the ruling white class, who were considered superior, in the eyes of these

---

60. Ibid., 4.
61. Ibid., 20.
62. Vermeire, "Hinduism," 357.

simple people, influenced, at least to a limited extent, the desire to accept the religion of the powerful group. Some of the converts justified their conversion in the name of the Queen of England. Father Lievens reacted as follows: "We know some foolish men have used the expression: *Maharani ka hokum hai*, i.e., it is the order of the queen, but we have always checked and punished such men."[63] This phenomenon was identified not only in tribal areas but also in some other areas where mass conversion was taking place among the harijans. Bishop J. W. Pickett testified that he "has heard out-caste converts boast that the king-Emperor was their brother in Christian faith, and preachers have been known to counter the oft-repeated charge that only low caste people profess the Christian religion by referring to collectors, commissioners, governors, the viceroy and the royal family as Christians."[64] Such claims of social status encouraged mass conversion. The claim of superiority of Christian religion over Hinduism, no doubt, gave the converts a feeling of elation and superiority over their Hindu enemies.

The very structure of injustice that dominated the social condition of the poor people demanded change. In the face of oppression and exploitation the aboriginals were looking for justice as well as self-respect. They were very often treated as barbarous and uncivilized people. A Lutheran missionary reports the reactions of landlords: "These landlords in their insolent arrogance are not ashamed to tell the Kols: you are our bullocks; we keep you fed, why then should you not obey us and work for us."[65] Under such unbearable circumstances they were looking for justice as well as human dignity. "They could only achieve these goals as a community. And so when they were converted to Christianity, they came over either to obtain justice or because they had already obtained it."[66] According to Stephen Fuchs, an eminent anthropologist, social injustice was a major factor that influenced mass conversion. "And the reasons for the change of religion are evident: the refusal of the privileged class to grant social justice to the oppressed and exploited inferior communities. The conversion to Christian faith which preaches social justice and rejects economic exploitation would be fully justified. The dominating higher castes have to blame themselves for losing the aboriginals and low castes to the Christian

---

63. Quoted by De Sa, *Crisis in Chotanagpur*, 237.
64. Pickett, *Christian Mass*, 53.
65. Quoted by De Sa, *Crisis in Chotanagpur*, 82.
66. Ibid., 159.

Conversions of Marginal Communities to Christian Churches

Churches since they continue to refuse the tribals and low castes their basic human rights."[67]

The character and life style of the missionaries themselves considerably influenced the attitudes of the people. Most of the missionaries lived a simple and ascetic life, dedicated to the cause of their people. They devoted themselves totally to the social, economic as well as spiritual welfare of the people, identifying themselves with the life of the poor and unwanted. Most of them lived, at least in their early year of intense and active mission work, in mud houses, ate simple food, and showed no sign of comfort and luxury. People noticed how the missionaries traveled to interior villages, on horses or on foot in the hot sun, while they themselves remained indoors. Such an ascetic and dedicated life both revealed certain holiness and attracted many people to the missionaries and their religion. Charismatic and prophetic leaders like Francis Xavier in the Coromandel coast, Constant Lievens in Chotanagpur, Grossjean in Orissa, Vandrame in Meghalaya, J. E. Clough in Andhra Pradesh, Frederic Booth-Tucker in Central India, L. O. Skrefsrud among the Santals, Miss Catherin Ling among the Todas of Tamil Nadu, Father Caironi in northern Malabar, Pandita Ramabai in Poona, and many others were charismatic leaders in initiating and directing the mass movement. With great personal magnetism they attracted crowds. They challenged, in the name of God, the existing caste system, and economic system characterized by domination, by the powerful and rich castes over the powerless and poor harijans, tribals and other backward communities. By taking sides with the oppressed, upholding their human dignity, fighting and winning their court cases, protecting them from their enemies, the dominance relation in the Indian society was shaken. This change continued to influence the history of social development and modernization of the scheduled castes and tribes throughout the following decades.

The evangelical mission, with its origin in the Lutheran pietism of northern Europe and Methodism of England and the American colonies focused on conversion through personal repentance as well as commitment to eradication of personal and social evils. Majority of the Protestant missionaries in India were members of these voluntary missions societies. In addition enlightenment culture of Europe defined man as a free and rational being. The evangelicals among the illiterate tribals and other marginal groups encountered a radically different culture and mentality. For instance in tribal societies individual identity was almost non-existent.

---

67. Fuchs, "New Mission," 235.

The Future of Christian Mission in India

Their identity was ethnic identity. Major decision for the welfare of tribes and its members were made by the tribal Panchayat, meeting of five elders. Naturally during conversion movement the decision to abandon their tribal religious practices, at least in principle, and embrace Christian religion as a better solution to their social crisis was the unquestioned collective prerogative of the elders. Protestant missionaries with their strict demand for personal experience and decision for Christ had little choice than to fall in line with the local pattern of decision making. Both the missionaries and people had one undisputed goal—liberation from social oppression. Conversion thus was primarily a community exercise. As a converted community they found themselves powerful to fight the enemies. To the new converts missionaries and their social involvement appeared as a new social force in opposition to unjust zamindars and rajas. In villages where the Christians were in majority, they successfully fought, at times using unlawful force, their common enemy, and occupied the land on the claims of ancestral rights. The philosophy of personal choice however was progressively cultivated with the expansion of education, modern occupations and pride in personal income, replacing the common ownership of the land and collective earning. To the extend Reformation radically rejected the authority and power of the Catholic church and its religious mediators and exalted the priesthood of the laity it undoubtedly paved the way for modern individualism as well as its curses.

From the limited success of the Christian missionaries among the Hindus and their impressive success among the tribals and harijans one can deduce further reasons for mass movement. The total absence of a systematically developed philosophical and religious system among the tribals, and to a great extent also among the harijans, was a decisive factor in the expansion of Christianity among them. For them, no intellectual system or written tradition was ever developed by religious specialists, priests or other authorities, who prescribed strict norms and values for supporting the existing social structure, or forbidding an alteration in it in the name of sacred order or a divine law, as it was among Hindus whose sacred scriptures forbade a change in religion with the belief in Karma. In contrast, these marginal communities had no such intellectual or religious barriers to cross. They had very few interests to protect, mostly material interests. Here it is significant to note, that in the history of the Christian mission in India, as well as elsewhere, like Africa, success was achieved only among peoples and cultures who lacked a sophisticated philosophico—theological system with its priests or religious specialists as the custo-

Conversions of Marginal Communities to Christian Churches

dians of the traditions. Until recent times the tribals and harijans had few other alternative paths of liberation to choose, e.g., social ideologies like socialism, Marxism, communism, except Christianity which welcomed them whole heartedly. It can be further pointed out that those tribes which came in closer contacts with the caste Hindus and were Hinduized in different degrees in the course of history were little inclined to accept the call of Christian missionaries.

Taking into account these and other reasons, the whole Christian mass movement, especially of the nineteenth and twentieth century, could be understood as a Messianic movement or Millenarism that became quite successful. Certain social conditions that stimulate messianic movements and their characteristic features are:[68] 1) A society intensely dissatisfied with the social and economic conditions which it is forced to accept. It is a situation of political helplessness; 2) The existence of emotional unrest and frustrations of people expressed in hysterical manifestations and aggressiveness; 3) The appearance of a charismatic leader who inspires a new hope and commands obedience from the people; 4) As a test of the people's faith in the new movement, he demands a radical change in their life style, religion and ethic;. 5) They reject established authority and call for rebellion and revolution; 6) Threat of punishment of those who resist or non-cooperate with the movement; 7) Recalling of a "Golden Age" in the distant past and the expectation of a paradise here on earth in the near future. 8) Revival of certain native traditional values and rejection of foreign elements; 9) A powerful myth or ideology to provide satisfactory explanation and sustain the movement for a prolonged period.

The insurgence movements and demand for separate states in the post independence period was a consequence of "suspicion of the outsiders" and a violent reaction to Hindu domination. They were also vehemently against the Indian government which refused their demand for separate states demarcated by ethnic identity. "Becoming Christian was one way Mizos or people closely related to Mizos could make a political statement in places like Tripura, North Cachar of Assam and the Southern hills of Manipur . . . Christianity provided a new identity and a caring community beyond the traditional village limits."[69] Thus the Christian conversion was characterized by steep increase after the World War: from 12 percent in 1941 to 80 percent in 1981 in Nagaland; from one percent in 1941 to 53 percent in 1981 in Meghalaya; from 5 percent in 1941 to 30

---

68. Fuchs, *Rebellious Prophets*, 1–16.
69. Downs, "Christian Conversion," 393.

percent in 1981 in Manipur; and from 5 percent in 1941 to 30 percent in 1981 in Mizoram.[70]

For the purpose of a theoretical formulation all these reasons of change is summarized into, "Social Repulsion and Attraction" model. In the words of Archbishop T. Menamparambil who worked over half century in the N.E.:

> No wonder tribal communities with their democratic orientation, sense of equality, absence of inhibitions and complexes, habit of open and frank discussion, simplicity and directness, honestly and reliability felt a natural nearness to the missionaries who they understood as helpful, efficient and sincere ... they always felt some measure of distance from, and at times were threatened by the larger mainland society, loaded with caste hierarchy and honorific title, social distances, cultural taboos and food prohibitions, sophisticated conventions and unexplainable social subtleties.[71]

Social Repulsion-Attraction Model in Christian Conversion Movement

Dominant Groups In India and their Values & Social Relations	→Domination→ →Oppression→ →Exploitation→ →Inhumanity→ →Social rejection→ →Inequality→ →Injustice→ →Hatred→	Tribals, Adivasis, Outcasts And Their Possible Choices	→Service→ →Liberation→ →Protection→ →Human dignity→ →Social acceptance→ →Equality→ →Justice→ →Love→	Christian Missionaries And Their Dominant Values & Social Relations and Services

The oppressed and marginalized adivasis, tribals and harijans were caught up between the traditional exploiters on the one side and the liberative offer of the missionaries on the other. Intense crisis situation longs for messiahs or liberators. And their appearance are not frequent. Strike the iron when it is hot was a successful formula of the poor as well as the missionaries. Solicitude for justice, human rights and human dignity has a perennial appeal to all inhuman hearts and therefore anyone who dares

---

70. Joshi et al., *Religious Demography*, 105–13.
71. Quoted by Puthenpurackal, "Rising Sun," 109.

Conversions of Marginal Communities to Christian Churches

to challenge unjust structures, cultures, persons and situations will be respected, supported and followed as saviors or charismatic leaders.

Christianization as a Legitimate Alternative to Hinduization

The objective of this analysis is not merely to count the numerical increase of Christians and to explain the probable reasons for it but also to examine what impact such conversions made on attitudes, values, life view, pattern of behavior and structure of the group and the society at large. "The pertinent question is what difference does such outward affiliation to a universalistic religion mean in life . . . in the decisions he will have to make with reference to important problems and the crisis from birth to marriage, to making a living and to death."[72] M. N. Srinivas in his study of *Religion and Society among the Coorgs of South India* (1952) argued that one of the methods of social change among the lower castes was the improvement of their status through the process of Sanskritization. In line with the theory of Hinduization of tribals proposed by H. H. Risley, Srinivas argued that, "Sanskritization has been a major process of cultural change in India's history and it has occurred in every part of the Indian subcontinent. It may have been more active in some periods than in others, and some parts of India are more Sanskritized than others, but there is no doubt that the process has been universal."[73] In parallel to Srinivas' theory of social change through Hinduization or Sanskritization, I propose an alternative pattern of change, named Christianization. So far most of the sociologists and anthropologists use the term Sanskritization to include the general process of status improvement of backward communities belonging to all religions of India and they have failed to distinguish the content of changes, for instance, of Sanskritization and Christianization. It is my suggestion that social researches on change and modernization must maintain this distinction clearly and pay more attention than has hitherto been paid to the pattern of changes introduced through the process of Christianization.

Meaning and Nature of Sanskritization

Before illustrating the process of Christianization and the reasons for suggesting the new theoretical concept, I shall briefly expose the already accepted model, namely Hinduization. According to M. N. Srinivas,

---

72. Hsu, "Christianity," 223.
73. Srinivas, *Social Change*, 23.

> The caste system is far from a rigid system in which the position of each component caste is fixed for all time. Movement has always been possible, and especially able in a generation or two, to rise to a higher position in hierarchy by adopting vegetarianism and teetotalism, and by Sanskritizing its ritual and pantheon. In short, it took over, as far as possible, the customs, rites and the beliefs of the Brahmins and the adoption of the Brahminic way of life by a low caste seems to have been frequent, though theoretically forbidden. This process has been called "Sanskritization" in this book, in preference to "Brahminization," as certain Vedic rites are confined to Brahmins and the two other "twice—born" castes.[74]

As the social mechanism this process is chiefly characterized by the imitation of the life style of the higher castes, it could be called by different names linked to the castes of emulation. However, according to Srinivas, the most frequent models used by the low caste in their process of Sanskritization are the Brahminical model and the Kshatriya model and rarely the Vaishya model, because the three Varnas enjoy the status of the "twice-born" as only they are entitled to don the sacred thread at the ceremony of initiation which is interpreted as second birth. But among the twice—born varnas only the Brahmins are most particular about the performance of this rite and they may, therefore, be regarded as a better model of Sanskritization.

In the Indian Society traditionally social status was ascribed to individuals and groups according to caste hierarchy into which they are born. The low castes and tribes aspired to improve their social position and escape the social stigma through Hinduization. The method used in the process is the imitation of the ways of life of the dominant caste in a locality by the members of the lower castes. The model of emulation is the caste higher than the one with which the lower caste is in proximity. The locally available superior section of the population is imitated by the inferior section. In other words, the prestigious style of the area becomes the model of imitation. Traditionally, the Brahmins occupied the apex of status hierarchy in society. They enjoyed not only ritual superiority but also certain economic superiority. In the pre-British and princely India a popular mode of expiating sins and acquiring religious merits was to give gifts of land, house, gold and other goods to Brahmins or temples. Ownership of land further increased the great prestige the Brahmin already enjoyed as a member of the highest caste. A certain congruence between caste ranks

---

74. Srinivas, *Religion and Society*, 30.

Conversions of Marginal Communities to Christian Churches

and economic hierarchy would also suggest that generally land owners belong to higher caste, while tenants and laborers belong to low castes.

Another help for the Sanskritization of low castes was the acquisition of certain political power. When a particular individual or group gained political power they were gradually raised to the status of Kshatriya or warrior caste. For example, the Mughal empire organized its political system on a local, regional and imperial level and ruled through the help of many who shared political power. This was an opportunity, for the holders of office, to claim a high status and to get the gradual approval of Brahmins. So Brahmins were employed as family priests who invent for them a mythical ancestor or a god in the Hindu pantheon. Gradually they inter—marry with a higher caste with ancestry in the forgotten past. They assume new caste names, give up the traditional occupation and take up new occupations. For instance, according to H. H. Risley, the rulers of Chotanagpur region originally were tribal chiefs, who because of political influence and wealth, married caste Hindus and gradually acquired Kshatriya status. According to Srinivas one of the functions of Sanskritization is to bridge the gap between secular and ritual rank.[75]

The imitation of dietary regulations of the Brahmins was another step towards Sanskritization. This is, of course, the post-Vedic Brahmin model. In the Vedic period beef eating and liquor consumption was part of the Hindu culture. But under the impact of Buddhism and Jainism a more puritanical style of Brahmin life emerged. When a lower caste or tribe abstained from its traditional habit of eating meat or drinking liquor it gained more respectability in the eyes of the caste Hindus because caste system and social status was closely linked to dietary habits. Thus, among the non-vegetarians, fish-eaters regarded themselves as superior to the consumers of the flesh of sheep and goats, while the latter looked down upon the consumers of fowls, who, in turn, regarded beef eaters with great contempt. Not all meat eaters are traditionally consumers of liquor. It is again a mark of low caste.[76]

But the process had to cross many hurdles. It was controlled by the dominant caste and elders, the watch dogs of orthodoxy. They resented the members of low caste from taking over the hereditary occupation of another caste whose interest would have been hurt by an inroad made into their privileges. So the changes usually were introduced little by little and over a long period so that the transition avoided open conflict. The

---

75. Srinivas, *Social Change*, 28.
76. Ibid., 26.

slow process helps to relate their ancestry to unknown past.[77] The process admits different degrees which is the basis of different caste hierarchy. "It is true that when members of these tribes settle in the plains among the Hindu community they do become Hinduized. The natural desire to escape the taint of barbarism and raise themselves in the social scale forced them to claim equal status with their Hindu neighbours and the condition of recognition of their claim is the adoption of Hindu customs."[78] After the arrival of the Aryans in the Gangetic region around 1500 BC Hinduization of India was the result of a prolonged conversion process of various indigenous communities at different periods. Take the example of Kerala. According to scholars, until the third century AD probably there were no Hindus here. Adi Sankaracharya was primarily responsible for the Sanskritization of this southern most part of India. Thus on all India level Hindus had been the largest converters through centuries.

Meaning and Nature of Christianization.

The process of Christianization of low castes and tribes during the past two centuries has affected many million new Christians. Christianization is defined as a socio-religious process by which a large number of people from low castes or tribes first partly reject, at least in principle, their traditional supernatural system, ritual practices, life style and ethical behavior, and then, accept Jesus Christ, other supernatural beings and a symbol system, initially preached or presented by Western missionaries; a complex of rituals and sacraments, performed by specialized religious leaders; a new ethic and style of life—Western in certain cases—which, in turn, create a new sense of community or Universal Church. Generally, the process is made effective through education and other socio-economic programmes which enhance opportunities of employment in new occupations and services with better remuneration and higher social status.

The tribal religions were characterized by animism, known as Sarna among the Adivasis. Their traditional religious believes and rites were centred around worship of spirits. Though the supreme being is acknowledged as high God like Mahadev, Dharmes, Singbong and so forth the tribal preoccupation is with the world of spirits. They are more afraid of spirits than the supreme being who is too good to do any harm to his own creatures. So where do all evils originate? They are caused angry spirits. Thus the core of primitive religion is belief in innumerable spirits and

77. Ibid., 23.
78. Vermeire,"Hinduism," 8.

Conversions of Marginal Communities to Christian Churches

various bloody sacrifices offered to placate them. Fear of restless spirits—like ancestral spirits who were not properly placated by offering meat and liquor, women dying in child birth, youth killed by animals during hunting etc.—have power to create numerous misfortunes like draught, poor harvest, various illness and other natural calamities. One of the dreadful belief of tribals in India, not unlike tribals in other countries, is belief in witches, mostly women, who are believed to be possessed by evil spirits and do great harm to others in the village. Unexplained sickness, sudden death and other misfortunes are attributed to witches. Out of mortal fear and anxiety witches are murdered in the middle of the night. It is in this ethos exorcisms are in great demand. Priest who claim to have power to exorcise evil spirits are more in demand than priest for their sacramental power like forgiveness of sin. The Catholic tradition of praying for the dead, rejected by the Reformers, matched well with the primitive mentality. The Harijans worshiped deities of lower rank while caste Hindus worshiped deities of higher rank; for example Hanuman, the monkey god, is worshiped mostly by the Harijans and Rama is worshiped by upper castes in the same village. Hanuman was a servant of Rama; harijans are servants of high caste Hindus. A close affinity between the hierarchy of gods and the hierarchy in the society is usually observed. Hinduism too at the lower rung, not dissimilar to catholic tradition, has successfully incorporated tribal cultures in the course of Hinduization. Like those who fail to understand caste mentality fail to understand Hinduism so too those who fail to understand belief in spirits fail to comprehend tribal religions.

The introduction of Christian missions among the tribals provided an alternative world view. Jesus Christ, the incarnate son of God, was presented as the powerful liberator from the world of evil spirits. Jesus proved his divinity and superiority by casting out evil spirits from those who where possessed. The God of missionary was proved to be more powerful than spirits of tribal religions because they where not only saved from the power of evil spirits but also from social oppression, and their land was redeemed from landlords. The new world of supernatural beings included blessed Virgin Mary, Mother of God, according to the Catholics, who is venerated as the goddess of fertility. Female deities are numerous in the Indian religious tradition and without a female deity Christianity would have been viewed incomplete. The company of numerous angels and saints, as they were gradually catechized, performed various services to satisfy numerous mundane needs of converts. For example, St.Patrick would protect them from snakes that were many in the jungle. "Considering the evidence available we conclude that India's primitive religious type is amenable to Roman Catholicism and able to penetrate the hard core of Protestant Christianity."[79]

The Christian rituals, sacraments and worship were conducted in large beautiful churches built in the course of time, by richly adorned foreign priests amidst clouds of sweet-smelling incense, lighted candles, rhythmic ringing of bells and melodious music. It was a glorious transition from Shamanism of Sarna religion. The new rituals became the new source of identity and social status. The traditional agricultural feasts and processions were substituted by Christian festivals and processions. The evangelical worship was characterized by scripture reading, long preaching and joyful singing in English or vernacular languages, receiving their ritual services at important occasions like the rites of passage, added the prestige of the converts as Sanskritization was essentially related to the service of the Brahmin priests and Sanskrit Scriptures. Traditionally their women were marginalized at places of worship and rituals whereas Christianity gave them relatively better position in Church worship and membership in pious organizations and missionary services. Parish churches soon became a centre of community action, recreation and new social identity. In the course of time some of the coverts and their leaders visited prestigious Christian pilgrimage centres in Israel, the Holy land of the Christians, and in Europe which raised their position in the international organization of the Church. A certain number of indigenous priests and ministers were educated in European or American theological centres and universities. Even simple Christian villagers began to talk about their counter parts in Europe and America. Traditional narrow tribal or local world view was being broadened by a universal world view.

Introduction of new ethic and morality was an integral part of the process of civilizing mission. A puritanical ethic and new morality was rigorously imposed on the new converts, particularly by the evangelical missionaries. The tribal moral code was simple and centered around tribal customs. Traditionally their sexual mores and customs were not rigid. Sense of sin was restricted to the breaking of social norms. Family life was governed by practical morality. Divorce was easy and common. Polygamy existed among them and child marriage was not uncommon. In Chotanagpur, the North East region as well as in some parts of India a woman could be sold in the market by her father to a prospective husband or master. In sharp contrast, marriage and family life was held very sacred

---

79. Presler, *Primitive Religion*, 217.

in the Christian tradition and, according to the Catholic doctrine, it is a sacrament. Abolition of polygamy, insistence on monogamy, forbidding of premarital sex, exultation of the virtue of virginity and celibacy, open panchayat proceedings and punishment of sexual offenders were some of the new ethical norms and sanctions imposed on the new Christians. Further, youth dormitories were abolished, mixed dancing was strictly stopped and separate dancing, only on occasions of Christian festivals, were introduced as new disciplines. Men were asked to cut the tuft of hair on their head since it was associated with certain Hindu religious rites. A new standard of dressing, particularly for scantily dressed women, was introduced. Fight by the missionaries and government officials to cover the upper body of Nadar women in Tamil Nadu and Southern Travencore lasted a few decades. In some regions, particularly in the north-east, Westernization of dress became a status statement. Wearing scapulars by the Catholics was interpreted as equivalent to the sacred thread ceremony of twice-born Brahmins. Inculcation of new ethical standards and rules of conduct and behavior were achieved gradually and it evolved in to a new culture among these new Christians.

Dietary and food habits like consuming carrion were subjected to changes which had great significance in the eyes of caste Hindus. The most important improvement was controlling the habit of excessive consumption of alcohol. Many families were ruined and many suffered ill-health due to alcoholism. The new converts were encouraged to join the temperance society and to take temporary promises to abstain from alcohol, with religious sanctions. One of the fundamental reasons why the Adivasis, tribals and Harijans were given a low status in the caste hierarchy was their drinking habits, consumption carrion and permissive sexual behavior. Puritanism with which missionaries vehemently objected to these practices, though not always with prudence and sympathy, gradually but surely, brought about a new life style among the Christians which, in turn, raised their status in some degree, in the eyes of the dominant castes, and others in the wider society. Children educated in schools and living in boardings learned respectable style of dressing.

K. N. Sahay who studied the process of change among the adivasi Christians in Bihar describes the nature of the change in their self-image.

> Christianity has brought about a change of self-image and identity among the tribal converts. The immediate result is that the tribal converts begin to consider themselves different from the non-Christians and acquire a "sense of superiority" over

the latter. They dissociate themselves from the non-Christians, thinking that the latter are "inferior" people engaged in "spirit worship" which is not religion at all. On the other hand, as regards themselves, they think that they practice the best religion of the world; are on the right path and they will enter the Kingdom of God after Christian death. Also the tribal converts show an aversion for non-Christian tribals because the latter drink, speak filthy language, and have a vulgar tongue; they perform traditional dances in the company of girls which is immoral, and do not have proper manners or civic sense. The Christian converts consider themselves free from such vices and regard themselves better than non-Christians.[80]

"The destiny of India is now being shaped in her classrooms," wrote D. Kothari in *Report of the Education Commission* in 1966 which spelled out the philosophy of education for the new India. Thus destiny of millions of Tribals and Harijans was being shaped in thousands of schools, technical institutions and colleges which the missionaries founded for the first time all over the tribal and harijan regions of India. With the introduction of universal education for all—tribals, harijans, women and other backward caste—the Brahmin monopoly of knowledge was demolished by missionaries. The Christian contributions towards social change through education were in four distinct levels. First, providing educational facilities in remote villages long before the government agencies reached there with the facilities of primary education. Second, the organization of economic resources, scholarships, and hostels for the education of tribal and harijan children, particularly the gifted ones. Thirdly, providing moral support and motivation to the children where parents, particularly the illiterate ones, could not appreciate the benefits of education. Fourthly, the mission schools made every effort to provide moral and religious education in schools. The following data confirms the above view. The educational achievement of the backward communities must be appreciated in the background of social disadvantages they traditionally suffered. The Christian schools were opened to all irrespective of caste religion and sex. After the Parsis, Christians are the most educated community in India in spite of the fact that the majority of them belongs to SC, ST and backward communities. Praising the great contributions of Christian missionaries to the progress of Tribals late Prof. Munda, a non-Christian Adivasi and Vice Chancellor of Ranchi University observed: "For whatever changes one sees in India—if it were not for Christianity

---

80. Sahay, "Tribal Self-Image," 55.

we do not know were this movement of the tribal people would have been. They got whatever enlightenment, whatever education, whatever progress, whatever indication of sharing this new world that is coming up, all this would have been impossible without the work of this movement. Look at the areas of tribal people where there is no involvement, for instance, the entire central belt except where I come from."[81] Similar sentiment was expressed by an Adivasi archbishop during a national consultation: "What would have been the fate of Adivasis of Chotanagpur had not missionaries come to their rescue?."

Defending the cause of foreign missionaries who were ordered by the government of India to leave the country in the aftermath of the successful visit of late Pope John Paul II in 1986, Kushwant Singh, an eminent Indian scholar wrote:

> Who runs the best and cheapest schools and colleges in India? Answer: Christian missions. Who runs the best clinics and hospitals in India? Answer: Christian missions. Who do most of the social work among the backward tribes living in remote jungles? Answer: Christian missionaries. And the best among them are foreigners who have cut off all connections with their homelands to make India their home. Proselytization (making converts) is no longer their primary aim: it is only to serve the people amongst whom they live. Those who accuse them of being agents of foreign powers or meddling in Indian politics know full well that there is no truth whatsoever in these charges. What is more, they display a sense of gross ingratitude to a small group of people to whom the country owes so much. When they point their accusing fingers they should know they also point them towards people like Mother Teresa.[82]

According to M. N. Srinivas there existed a relation between Sanskritization and land ownership and political power. The combinations of these three were also important factors in the process of Christianization. "The existence of a certain amount of congruence between caste rank and agricultural hierarchy would mean that generally land owners belong to high caste while tenants and more especially landless laborers, belonged to lower caste."Further, a close link between land, political power, however, a caste or its local section, had to have a martial tradition, numerical strength and preferably also ownership of a large quantity of arable land.

81. Munda, "Non-Christian Tribal," 93.
82. Kushwant Singh, in *Sunday*, 10.

The Future of Christian Mission in India

Once it has captured political power it had to sanskritize its ritual and style of life and to lay claims to being Kshatriya. It had even to create an appropriate myth supporting the group's claim to Kshatriya status and the services of Brahmin priests."[83]

On the impact of the tribal Christians on political life in the N.E. a Church historian records: "In certain states like Nagaland, Mizoram, Manipur and Meghalaya, Church leadership has a very strong influence on the collective conscience of the people as well as a collective influence in major areas of government policy and decision making. The curbing of insurgencies in Mizoram and Nagaland was effected mainly through the efforts of the Protestant Church leadership. The program of control of drunkenness and of imposing prohibition by the people themselves have been successfully launched by the church leadership both in Nagaland and Meghalaya where the Protestant Churches are more influential."[84]

The above described transformation of a society through their conversion to Christianity was, to a considerable extent, the fruit of the dedicated work of the missionaries among these people for over a century. It has been praised both by the admirers as well as the critics of the Christian mission. Even staunch critics of the Christian Mission in India have openly admitted the great contribution of the Christian missionaries towards the development of these people. Indian historian K. M. Panikkar, a staunch critique of the Christian mission, honestly admitted the impact of the selfless services of missionaries on the framers of the Indian Constitution. "The work of the missionaries among the aboriginal tribes may be said to have created a tradition of social service which modern India has inherited. If the Indian Constitution includes special provisions for the welfare of the tribal communities and Adivasis, and if the Centre and the States are making concentrated efforts to bring them up to the general level of India, much of the credit for such activities must be given to the missionary."[85]

The enlightened architects of the Indian Constitution, under the chairmanship of Dr. B. R. Ambedkar, opted for a secular democratic Constitution. They were deeply influenced by the American, British and Swiss constitutions, shaped by Christian values, especially the fundamental human rights. The impact of the Western Christian Spirit on India through the Constitution is abiding. The makers of the Indian Constitution were

83. Srinivas, *Social Changes*, 42.
84. Kottuppallil, *Catholic Mission*, 296.
85. Panikkar, *Foundation*, 53.

Conversions of Marginal Communities to Christian Churches

also inspired by the selfless services of missionaries among the Scheduled Tribes and Castes. For instance the Constitution of India provides a number of positive welfare measures for Scheduled Castes and Scheduled Tribes which were already introduced by the British administration, Chief among them are: representation in the Parliament and State Legislatures; representation in the central and state services; scholarship for education, the Scheduled District Act of 1874, according to which tribal areas were treated as separate entities, is still incorporated in the Indian Constitution; the Untouchability (offence) Act of 1955 is a legislation under article 17 of the Constitution. It has been replaced by Civil Rights Protection Act of 1976. And the Mandal Commission Report (1978) further reinforces these affirmative steps.

The multidimensional as well as dialectical process of religious conversion is expressed as follows: "Conversion is paradoxical. It is elusive. It destroys and it saves; conversion is sudden and gradual. It is created totally by the action of god and it is created by the actions of humans. Conversion is personal and communal, private and public. It is both passive and active ... conversion is an event and a process. It is an ending and a beginning. It is final and open ended. Conversion leaves us devastated and transformed."[86] It is estimated that the process of Christianization in India has directly influenced the life of over 30 million Christians and many more millions through their numerous institutions of services. "The Lutherans embraced the Dalit identity because they find it socially and politically relevant for them. Christianity and the church have given the dalits the strength and voice to pursue their struggle and fight for their rights. . . . They are able to take on the battle against oppression by those considered upper castes."[87]

The indirect impact of Christianity on Indian Society can't be measured easily. However, in this context, it is only fair to mention that modern India's contact with Western civilization and Christian missionary activities has influenced the Indian society and its culture in a very remarkable way. Even today the post-Christian western civilization continues to influence the destiny of India. The forces that shaped India's life and culture are the result of creative synthesis of different cultures and religions for centuries. India was always open to other cultures, religions and philosophies, including Christianity, and she and her illustrious leaders have drawn inspirations from the Christian teachings and the way of

---

86. Clarke, "Conversion to Christianity," 192.
87. Robinson and Kujur, "Introduction In *Margins*," 15.

The Future of Christian Mission in India

life. The contribution of Christianity towards the modernization of various communities, and, perhaps, the whole nation, though only in a limited way, can be evaluated only in the context of this ongoing modern synthesis. And the Hindus too, imitating Christian missionaries, have accepted the idea of mission to western countries. The activities of the Ramakrishna mission, Hare Krishna mission and similar missions in Europe, America and elsewhere are illustrations.

Christianity is a minority religion in India and its direct influence and impact are limited to less than 3 percent of India's population. For instance, only less than 6 percent of tribal India have embraced Christianity during the mass conversion period and reaped the fruit of the process of Christianization. An accurate account of the mass conversion from the scheduled castes is not easily available since the census of India, in contrast to the recording of tribal Christians, does not record the number of dalit Christians. Based on various sources it is possible to estimate that from among them, about 6 percent have been Christianized.[88] The days of large number of conversion to Christianity is almost over. The present ratio of Christian population to the total population will not alter substantially. However, the indirect influence of Christianity in different regions, particularly where its presence is strong, both in number as well as institutions of services, cannot be overlooked.

Many Christian missionaries are making conscious and daring option for the poor. The following evaluation of the work of the Christian missionaries in Chotanagpur in the pre-independence era challenges the missionaries even today.

> Comparing the methods of Lievens with much of the work done by priests and religious today we notice another significant feature. Lievens and his companions were not afraid to adopt an approach that was bound to conflict with vested interests. Instead of directing their efforts to the landlords and encouraging them to have compassion on their tenants, they worked on the side of the oppressed—fostering their desire to take their destiny in their own hands ... Had their apostolate taken other forms, these Belgian Jesuits might never have experienced such opposition. Had they opened schools for the elite—they would surely have earned the gratitude and respect of those landlords who oppressed them so bitterly ... Had they promised an

---

88. The Census Report of 2001 on Christian population is unreliable since many Dalit Christians reported themselves as Dalit Hindus to escape the discrimination by the government that refuses to provide equal help to Christian dalits.

Conversions of Marginal Communities to Christian Churches

other-worldly reward for the sufferings these people were enduring, and preached a theology of fate and 'resignation to the will of God,' they might have succeeded in pacifying the tribals and turning away their attention from the real issues troubling them. But neither the Lutherans nor Lievens wanted such substitutes . . . They wanted Justice, and they came in large numbers. In their mass movement towards Christianity they seemed have been instinctively aware that there was power in numbers—consequently hope.[89]

Each religion has its own uniqueness and has a special contribution to make towards the understanding of the total religious experience of mankind and man's liberation. In the words of J. Nehru, the first Prime Minister of India: "But what I am concerned with is not merely our material progress but the quality and depth of our people . . . Can we combine the progress of science and technology with the mind and the spirit also? We cannot be untrue to science because that represents the facts of today. Still can we be untrue to those essential principles for which India has stood in the past throughout the ages. Let us then pursue our path of industrial progress with all our strength and vigour at the same time remember that, material riches without tolerance and compassion and wisdom may well turn out dust and ashes."[90]

Strength and Weakness of the Protestant and Catholic Missions.

A comparative analysis of the two distinctive missionary movements in India, particularly during the nineteenth and twentieth century, might throw some light for the benefit of the future. It is estimated with rather discrepant statistical reports that during the Mass conversion movement between 1881–1971 the Christian population grew from less than 1 percent to 3 percent in 1971. The Protestant missionaries in spite of their late entry compensated it with very impressive results, that is, from 91,092 Protestant conversions in 1881 to 5,000,000 in 1930 to 7,208,000 in 1971. The expansion of the Catholic population was not that impressive, that is, from 1,687,700 in 1881 to 8,108,943 in 1971. The Roman Catholics quadrupled their number while the Protestant Christians multiplied themselves eight times.[91] Unfortunately, contrary to the accusations of the

89. Narohna, "Preface," xiv–xv.
90. Quoted by Rao, "Some Problem," 104.
91. Computed by the author from Houtart and Lemericinier, *Size and Structure of the Catholic Church in India*; Neill, *Story of the Christian Church*, and Joshi et al., *Religious Demography of India*.

The Future of Christian Mission in India

Hindu fundamentalists, the Christian community has suffered marginal decline during the past three decades.

Glaring differences in the progress of mission are rooted, not excluding other socio-cultural forces, in two different missiologies. A sense of urgency added to the exasperate conviction that heathens in India were going to perish in hell-fire and their salvation depended exclusively on accepting Jesus Christ as the unique Saviour of the world. Their missionary focus was unambiguous, i.e., proclamation of Jesus in season and out of season. The social evils that the missionaries encountered further confirmed the evangelical understanding of Sin from which man is utterly incapable to redeem himself. The source of the Protestant fundamentalism was the authority of the revealed word of God, found in the Bible. Therefore Bible should be made available to everyone in their own language or dialect in order to understand God's inscrutable will. The Protestant missionaries were the first translators of the Bible or at least a portion of it in Indian languages/dialects. Study of the languages of the host communities necessitated production of Dictionaries and Grammar books. The happy consequence was that the foreign missionaries authored most of the Grammar books and Dictionaries of Indian languages and dialects. Establishing printing presses in India was another contribution of Mission. Until very recent times authority system for the laity in the Catholic church was vested in tradition and the teaching the magisterium and not in the Bible. For instance, after the Reformation and the Council of Trent the Catholics were discouraged to read the Bible.

Understanding strange customs, manners and mentality of people of different religions, cultures, castes and tribes was a pre-requisite for successful communication of the Word of God. Long before the modern anthropologists navigated the globe to investigate strange and curious customs and manners of distant nations missionaries were pioneers of anthropology. The Protestant research and publications in India, including that of the British administrators, surpassed that of the Catholic missionaries.

The Protestant missionaries became the trailblazers of English and western education in India. Numerous schools were opened across the length and breath of the country. By 1900, forty five colleges, both for boys and girls, were founded and the Scottish missionaries were in the frontier. The Catholics who were highly suspicious of the erroneous Protestant doctrines forbade their children entry to Protestant schools and colleges. After critically watching the influence and prestige of the Protestant col-

Conversions of Marginal Communities to Christian Churches

leges for a few decades, including a few converts from the upper casts, the Society of Jesus, was the first to cautiously open colleges in Calcutta, Bombay and Trichinopally. The number of the Catholic colleges was not even ten until the first quarter of the 20th century. The same was true of Catholic women's entry into medical profession. The first Catholic woman doctor would enter the field only six decades after Dr. Clara Swain, an American Methodist doctor, founded the first hospital in Bareilly, Uttar Pradesh, in 1874. Soon Protestant medical Colleges too were established. The first Catholic medical college saw the light of the day nearly a century later in Bangalore.

The Protestant missionaries were the first to venture into remote and inhospitable tribal terrain like the North-East and Chotanagpur. The mass movement of the Adivasis to Protestant churches inspired the Catholic church to enter the area, of course, a few decades later, and reap a better harvest. Very successful evangelization among the Dalits or the outcastes in Punjab, Tamil Nadu and Andhra Pradesh, starting in the middle of the nineteenth century was first launched by the evangelical missionaries. And the Catholic model emphasized the planting of the Church while the Protestant priority was preaching and baptizing. Fight against caste structure as unchristian was another first initiative by the Protestant and evangelical missionaries. The Catholic missionaries mostly tolerated caste system as a social evil because the primary goal of mission was salvation of souls and not social transformation.

The confrontation initiated by the Baptist Missionaries in Bengal and other states against many of the barbarous social evils like Sati, child marriage, widow remarriage, temple prostitution, castration of boys for the formation of eunuchs to serve goddesses, slavery of the outcaste and others, with the cooperation of the British administrators and a few educated Hindus, opened a new chapter in the social history of India. Sadly the sensitivity of the Catholic missionaries to social problems was far from conspicuous.

Training, educating and ordaining indigenous ministers was a priority for most the Protestant Societies. In the appointment of Indian Bishops too they were the first. Except in the case of the Syrian Catholic church the Latin Catholic Missionaries, in spite of repeated exhortation from the Propaganda Fide, were highly prejudicial against promotion of Indian clergy, with a few unenthusiastic exceptions in Goa, as well as the appointment of Indian Bishops. Indian Protestants ministers and laity were not afraid to communicate their protest against Western dominance, leading to the creation of over 150 indigenous churches, starting with the Hindu Church of Jesus Christ in Tinnevelly in 1858. The vow of obedience of all catholic religious congregations, including the special vow of the Jesuits to the Pope, inhibited even the thought of creative deviations from traditions.

The Christian participation in the Indian Independence Movement has poor record. When one examines the names of a few prominent Christians leaders, until the second part of the twentieth century, one notices that they came from the Protestant background and mostly the product of the Protestant colleges. Unfortunately the Catholics were discouraged to enter the field of politics.

It is true that missionaries in general despised Hinduism yet most of the Orientalist scholars of Hinduism belonged to the Protestant churches, starting with the British administrators. The foundation for an Indian Christian theology, articulation of Christian faith with the help of Indian philosophy, was laid by the Protestant scholars as well as Protestant converts from the upper castes from the middles of the nineteenth century. A few stray efforts in the field of inculturation and Indian theology by a small creative Catholic converts were insensitively suppressed by the Roman ecclesiastical authorities.

Those Catholic theologians who today cherish at least some familiarity with the Protestant theology, will not fail to discover that many innovative ideas of the Second Vatican Council, including key ideas in the Decree on the Church's Missionary Activity, (Ad Gentes), are cryptically borrowed from the Protestant theology without acknowledgement, filtered through the Catholic theologians of Northern Europe, the fountain of Reformation and subsequent theological debates and developments.

These significant difference, granted that these are not exhaustive, between the Protestant and Catholic approaches and methods leading to different outcome, spring from two distinctive religious cultures. The Protestant missionaries were the children of more independent, free, creative and adventurous world views and cultures of Northern Europe (and their migrants to the USA) in comparison to the Catholic missionaries who were highly cautious in thinking, and less openness to new ideas. Naturally they were controlled by fear of sanctions imposed by the ecclesiastical authorities at every level, local and universal. Well known Catholic theologian E. Schillebeekx maintains "that the hierarchical teaching authority of the Catholic church exerts an inhibiting and even paralyzing influence on the original thought of Catholic theologians" as well as her

Conversions of Marginal Communities to Christian Churches

missionaries.[92] Today, looking back, there are theologians as well as historians who assess that the Protestant Reformation, in spite of its initial good intentions, has now ended up as a runaway church.

Degrees of success and failures of the Protestant and Catholic missions are partly explained by the political powers which either supported or opposed them. By 1663 the Dutch drove out the Portuguese out of the Malabar coast and other parts to a small place named Goa. From that date the Portuguese power in India failed to rise to its formal status as the Rome of the East. The Dutch was in India for only a short period, but were violently anti-Catholic. The persecutions of the Catholic church and forced conversion to Islam in the South India by Tipu, the powerful Muslim Sultan of Mysore, in the last quarter of eighteenth century wiped away much of the fruits of the early Catholic mission. The suppression of the Jesuits for half a century from 1773 further aggravated the decline of the Catholic mission here. The supremacy of the British control of India from 1757, after the battle of Plassey, was highly favorable to the dynamic, at times aggressive, activities of the Protestant missionaries in the following two centuries as was the case of the Portuguese missionaries in the sixteenth and seventeenth centuries.

Despite these differences the missionaries, both the Protestant and Catholic, were the first organized bridge builders across the cultures of all continents. Rudyard Kipling's prediction on cultural distance: "Oh, East is East and West is West, and never the twain shall meet," is being disproved. The missionaries not only carried Christianity and Western civilization to the ends of the earth but also brought the great civilizations of the East to the people of the West. It was, undoubtedly, in the long run, an enriching contribution towards understandings of the complex human condition and world civilizations.

In the colonial era mass conversion to Christianity undoubtedly played a significant role in providing an alternative philosophy/theology of life, identity formation and upward social mobility. In the post-independence period, particularly in the emerging globalization scenario, most of the functions of Christianization are gradually being replaced by other ideologies and agents of identity and social change such as politicization of caste / tribe, the government's protective discrimination like reservations and services of NGOs. The Church in India is a miniscule minority. A vast majority of them—around two-third—are socially oppressed and marginalized, economically poor and exploited, politically powerless

92. Schillebeeckx, "Introduction," 1.

and manipulated, ethnically diverse, ritually divided, and intellectually inarticulate. There is however a minority within the church with opposite characteristics. Perhaps the foreign missionaries expected too much, reflecting the missionary atmosphere of the era, through social conversions and believed too much in the power and influence of Christianization.

In passim it should be noted that there are other agents of social transformation of the marginal communities. Dr. B. R. Ambedkar and his followers in the second half of the twentieth century opted for Buddhaization of the Dalits. Christophe Jaffrelot observes three trends of social transformation in the colonial India: Sanskritization or Hinduization; those communities which draw inspiration for change from the Hindu bhakti movement; finally, the anti-Brahmin movement that appeals to the Dravidian ethnic identity.

The political success of the Dravida Munnetta Kazhagam in Tamil Nadu from 1960s is seen as a dynamic route to progress. The Bahujan Samaj Party in Uttar Pradesh is deeply influenced by Neo-Buddhism of Ambedkar and Kanshi Ram, the founder of the political party. Gail Omvedt interprets that some of the lower caste movements in India have been akin to radical Marxism. Politicization of lower castes during the last quarter of Century, for example the manipulation of the Mandal Commission, is well recorded. All these differing routes have undoubtedly contributed towards the transformation of marginal communities in modern India. It was simultaneously an anti-Congress Party movement since the Congress was dominated by the Brahmins and other upper castes.[93]

Conclusion

It is true that some of the foreign missionaries in the past made severe attacks on the Hindu and Muslim religious beliefs and practices and deeply hurt their sense of pride and dignity. At the same time we have also ample evidences that many missionaries as well as European scholars deeply appreciated Hindu philosophy, culture and spirituality. Since the Christian mission theology and praxis have undergone radical changes during the last half Century, many of the recent renewed attacks on Christian mission, quoting the writings and examples of the colonial mission period, is like kicking the dead horse. These critics also demand that missionary activity must be subjected to public scrutiny. While granting the reasonableness of the suggestion the Christians are also equally aware that the government, which is sometimes biased by party ideology and religious

93. Basu, *Nandanar's Children*, xlii–xlix.

Conversions of Marginal Communities to Christian Churches

fundamentalism, is not the best judge. Are not people themselves the best judges? Of course subject to public morality, law and order.

The most radical missiological change for the last 100 years is the relegation of the church centred mission, i.e., conversion to the visible church, as the top priority at the middle of the twentieth century, to the third priority at the end of the century. According to a recent survey conducted by the author, for 85 percent of the Christian missionaries in India sociological conversion to Christianity is not an essential belief of their life and service.[94] On the contrary the Evangelical Fellowship of India strongly disagrees with such liberal view.

For Christians, particularly for the missionaries, the greatest religious revolution of this century is the discovery of other spiritual worlds, with their coherent meaning systems. Recognition of these religions, with positive attitudes of openness and program of dialogue and partnership, in contrast to the closed and aggressive approach of the past mission has laid the foundation for building a new civilization of Brotherhood and Sisterhood. A new awareness is being fostered that we all, belonging to different religions, cultures, castes, tribes, and nations, are children of One God—our creator, our father, our mother. We all are related to one another as members of one human family (NA 1).

One of the most significant social changes that has taken place in India in the post-Independence period is the growth of Dalit and Tribal awareness and identity. In the traditional Indian society knowledge, particularly religious knowledge, was the monopoly of the priestly caste. With the arrival of universal education for the first time introduced by missionaries, and other sources of informations and conscientization, the illiterate, ignorant, silent and dominated Dalits and Tribals have begun to challenge and protest against the existing unjust social structure. This is seen by some as a threat to the traditional domination of the high castes. The capture of political power by Dalits, Tribals and the Backward communities across the country during the past two decades is proof of the changing balance of power. They are demanding a legitimate share of the national cake of power, wealth and services. This new process is irreversible.

In the post-independence era the government as well as many other Non-Governmental Organizations are systematically working to help the SC, ST, OBC, women and children to enter into the main stream of the Indian society. And most of these people too are struggling to catch up

---

94. Kanjamala, "Trends and Issues," 260.

with modernization. The essential feature of modernization is rationality. Intellectualization of life in general—rational process of political life, industrial production, social life—demands similar intellectualization in the world of religion too. Otherwise the process will lead to intellectual incongruence and emotional tensions in people. In other words the logical consequence of modernization is that people of the "little tradition," i.e., those who are not part of a well articulated religious system, will abandon their primitive worldview and life view and look for a religious system which is rationally more tenable. Conversion, therefore, of these communities is almost a social necessity. The crucial question is: which world religion would they choose? Hinduism? Buddhism? Christianity? Islam? Sikhism? There are enlightened personal conversions to Christianity, of course small in number. My endeavour here is to demonstrate, through the analysis of conversion movement to Christianity and its subsequent impact on religious as well as socio-economic progress, that marginalized people's choice of Christianity was pragmatic, rational as well as legitimate. Further it is sufficiently demonstrated that Christianization is a better alternative to Hinduization for social liberation, not excluding spiritual liberation.

Assessing the long term impact of the Christian mass movement in the nineteenth to twentieth century it can be asserted without exaggeration that it laid the foundation for silent revolutions of three subaltern peoples' movements by the middle of the twentieth century, namely, scheduled tribe and adivasi movements, scheduled castes movements and Other Backward Class movements. Since the morning prayer said by the Missionaries of Charity of Blessed Mother Teresa, beautifully expresses the vision and mission of a majority of Christian missionaries of India today let me quote:

> Make us worthy, Lord,
> To serve our fellowmen throughout the world
> Who live and die in poverty and hunger
> Give them, through our hands this day their daily bread
> And by our understanding love, give peace and joy.
> . . . .
> Lord, grant that I may seek rather to comfort
> Than to be comforted;
> To understand than to be understood;
> To love than to be loved;
> For it is by forgiving that one is forgiven;
> It is by dying that one awakens to eternal life.[95]

---

95. Muggeridge, *Something Beautiful*, 151.

5

From Confrontations to Dialogue and Partnership

THE WAVE OF ATROCITIES committed against the Christians during the past few decades is unprecedented in Indian history. What is under investigation is the conspicuous influence of Hindutva ideology on a series of violence against a minority community like Christians. In the current atmosphere of growing fundamentalism of all religions is genuine dialogue possible? Do the past Christian missionary aggression and violence against Hindus and Muslims inhibit them to enter into genuine dialogue with Christians? Is there any other creative alternative than dialogue?

The Portuguese Mission in India

The Portuguese colonial venture and subsequent missionary encounters should be understood as extension of the Crusades which began in 1095. The Byzantine empire fell at the hands of Muslim Turks in 1453. The papal bull of Nicholas V in the following year stated: "We . . . by our apostolic letter concede to King Alfonso, the right, total and absolute to invade, conquer and subject all the countries which are under the enemies of Christ, Saracen or Pagan."[1] After the arrival of Vasco da Gama with such power and mission at Calicut on 7th May 1548, General de Albuquerque conquered Goa or Govapuri, in 1510.

Forced Conversions

The Conquest of Goa was propelled by the deadly combination of three most powerful drives of human beings—political, the conquest of a ter-

1. Panikkar, *Asia and Western*, 31.

The Future of Christian Mission in India

ritory; economic, control of spice trade in Asia, particularly in India; and religious, conversion of souls. During the first half of the century of Portuguese arrival in Goa, the missionaries employed persuasive method of conversion and this was not a success. Following the principle, *cujus regio, ejus religio*, i.e., the religion of the king shall be the religion of people, King D. Joao III ordered in the destruction of many temples and in speeding up conversion process.[2] The number of temples destroyed was calculated as follows: 116 temples in Ilhas, 176 in Bardez and 264 in Salsette. Majority of temples in villages were made of mud walls and thatched roofs. But there were also magnificent constructions. In the place of destroyed temples churches were built as it had happened in Rome in the fourth century. Many indirect methods were employed to attract converts from Hinduism. The Portuguese attracted new converts by granting favors like employment, tax exemption and denying these to the pagans. Hindu religious practices were forbidden in the Portuguese territory. Baptisms meant rapture with the convert's family, community, loyalty to society, culture and country and supposed new loyalty to the Portuguese rulers. By the order of 8th July 1644, converts were forced to wear western dress. Traditional vegetarianism was forcefully replaced by eating pork and beef, meat of the holy cow.

At every stage the Hindus vehemently resisted conversion and that was the reason why the process was very slow during the first half of the sixteenth century. In 1583, when the coercive methods were introduced, five Jesuits were killed in "Cuncolin revolt." In the course of the following centuries many more revolts would follow. Reconversion to Hinduism was introduced by taking a holy bath in the sea on the feast of Gokulashtami, birth of Lord Krishna, or sprinkling holy water from the river Ganges. All such attempts were suppressed by the political power of the Portuguese empire. Hinduism was practically wiped out of Old Goa within 200 years of Portuguese colonization. Ninety percent of coastal Goa was made Catholic. A Goan scholar's conclusion on forced conversion is worth quoting. "The Portuguese created a set of circumstances which rendered impossible the maintenance of Hindu symbolic life. The entire population became available to Christianity because their access to their own laws were cut off. Their decision to convert cannot be considered voluntary or pragmatic in a simplistic sense precisely because their own laws had been rendered inaccessible. Hindus were forced to consider the only option left to them—converting to Catholicism."[3]

2. Costa, *Missiological Conflicts*, 12.
3. Robinson, *Sociology of Religion*, 184.

From Confrontations to Dialogue and Partnership

The Inquisition

The office of the inquisition was an ecclesiastical tribunal that took cognizance of heresy, apostasy, schism like not acknowledging Jesus Christ as true God and Messiah; or irreverence to the Blessed Sacrament. Its aim was to bring the heretics to repentance or punishment in proportion to their offence. From the twelfth century, the repression of heresy, the goal of inquisition, was the business of both the Church and the state. Francis Xavier in 1545 wrote to the King of Portugal Joao III to introduce the Holy office of Inquisition in Goa. In 1560 Inquisition was established in Goa under the Dominicans.[4] The number of those who suffered the brunt of the inquisition is not easily available since the Portuguese themselves destroyed many of the relevant documents. According to C. J. Costa, the number of cases during the period of 1561 to 1774 were above 16,000; some were burnt at stake; some died in prison; some were sentenced to the galleys and other were absolved.[5] Many Hindus abandoned their property and migrated to other regions rather than give up their faith. Looking back on the abominable history of inquisition Archbishop Evora observed in Lisbon in 1879: "The inquisition was an infamous tribunal at all places. But the infamy never reached greater depths, nor was more vile, more black, nor more completely determined by mundane interests than at the tribunal of Goa, by the irony called Holy Office. Here the inquisitors went to the length of imprisoning in its jails all who resisted their advances and after having satisfied their bestial instinct there, ordering that they be burnt as heretics."[6]

The Syrian and the Latin Church Conflicts in Kerala

The Syrian Christians of Kerala, numbered around 1,00,000 when Portuguese missionaries arrived here in 1503. With the expansion of Islam in the middle-east in the seventh century their contact with the patriarchs of west Syria and Persia was minimal. The Episcopal succession from west Syria and Persia was interrupted, without extinguishing their loyalties to the Antiochean and Persian Patriarchs. They followed the "Law of St. Thomas." In many respect the community had adapted themselves to Hindu customs like dress, earring and Nambhoodri hair style for men, pre-nuptial rituals and marriage rites; tali for marriage, shradha for the

---

4. Priolkar, *Goa*, 23–25; 92–113.
5. Costa, *Missiological Conflicts*, 12.
6. Quoted by Priolkar, *Goa*, 175.

dead and so forth. The Syrian priests were married. The use of Syriac liturgy in churches built like temples was their only distinguishing identity as Christians. "In many respects it had become assimilated in manners and customs to the surrounding people."[7]

The Portuguese missionaries as well as the political authorities with the Roman orthodoxy defined by the Council of Trent (1545–1563) were shocked to note the strange manners and customs of the Syrian Christians and accused them of fifteen heresies. For example, the Syrian church did not recognize the authority of the Pope; denied trans-substantiation; in a land were wheat and vine were not available they used rice cake and the coconut juice to celebrate the mass; they did not practice auricular confession and extreme unction; allowed its priests to marry.[8] They were accused of being Nestorian Christians. They started an aggressive process of Latinizing the St. Thomas Christians who were almost ignorant of the Latin Rite church. With the arrival of archbishop, Alexio da Menezes in Goa in 1595, the conflicts accelerated. The "Law of St. Thomas" and the "Law of St. Peter" clashed. The process of Latinization of Syrian Christians reached its peak in the Synod of Udiamperur near Angamaly, the seat of the Syrian bishop, on 20th June 1599, attended by 153 priests, most of whom were newly ordained by the Archbishop da Menezes, 660 lay people and twenty deacons who understood little Portuguese; so the proceedings were translated into Syriac and some Malayalam. After six days of debates and fights the Syrian archdeacon was induced to sign decrees, including the Pope's supremacy. An arrogant Menezes burned most of the Syrian books. The Syrian Metropolitan was replaced by the Latin bishop, Francis Roz. The St.Thomas Christians were permitted to continue to use their own reformed Syriac liturgy.

The discontented and angry Syrian Christians appealed to Rome which were ignored. Responding to the cry of the faithful the Patriarch of Babylon sent bishop Ahatalla to them in 1652. On his arrival the Portuguese authorities seized him and deported him to Goa where he was tried by inquisition and burned at the stake. The controversy at its peak exploded when a large number of protesting Syrian priests and thousands of faithful gathered at Koonan Cross Churchyard, at Mattancherry, Fort Cochin, on 3rd January 1653 and holding on to ropes tied to the cross in front of the church took a solemn oath to abjure the foreign archbishop in Goa and Angamaly. After a few months they assembled some priests of

---

7. Neill, *History of Christian*, 143.
8. Moffett, *History*, 2:15.

From Confrontations to Dialogue and Partnership

their own and consecrated their own Archdeacon Mar Thomas. In the prolonged struggle the St. Thomas Syrian Christians were divided into three major warring parties—the Syrian Catholics loyal to Rome; the Jacobites loyal to the Patriarch of Antioch; the Nestorians are the east Syrians loyal to Baghdad.[9] The past fight between the Syrian Christians and the Latin Christians still continues to influence the ecclesiastical dynamics and atmosphere in Kerala even after 300 hundred years. The following case is an apt illustration. In 1764 the *Propaganda Fide* brought together to Verapoly the two minor seminaries which were functioning separately for the two Rites. In 1886 this seminary was raised to the status of a major seminary for the whole of Malabar coast, St. Joseph's Pontifical Seminary, Alwaye. In 1932 it was shifted to Mangalapuzha, with the philosophate in Carmelgiri. The administration was entrusted to the Spanish Carmelite missionaries. But the traditional cold war persisted. The tension between the Syrian and Latin staff and students reached a breaking point recently. There are strong feelings of resentment and discrimination on the part of the minority, 21 percent Latin Rite Catholics. In 1997 the major seminary was divided and separated into two major seminaries on the basis of two Rites, that is, Mangalapuzha seminary and Carmelgiri seminary for the Syrians and the Latins respectively. Cultural differences in terms of caste mentalities were the underlining cause for irreconcilable differences.[10] Many ecclesiastical institutions in Kerala function on the basis of Rites and a spirit of competition. As a marginalized or minority community grows in awareness as well as competence they begin to assert their rights for better sharing in the power structure. Constructions of institutions of services add visibility to their identity as well as status and prestige. The very same institutions in the course of time are tempted to become new centres of power struggles.

History of Hindu Militancy

To comprehend the historical roots of the nineteenth century Hindu militancy it is necessary to become aware that the Hindus were frequently attacked also by the Muslim and Buddhist rulers in the sixteenth century. Therefore different categories of militant Hindu organizations of Naga Sadhus and Sanyasis were already founded for physical training and self protection. These were later suppressed by the British administration. A crucial question asked by Hindu militant groups fighting for independence from the colonial rulers was: Why was India dominated for nearly eight

---

9. Keay, *History of the Syrian*, 50–55.
10. Ponnumuthan, "Pontifical Seminary," 561–62.

hundred years, first by the Muslims, then by the Christians? The western educated Hindus were becoming aware that they were made effeminate by a history of submission to the muscular Muslims and Christians. "The language of masculinity as a counterpoint to colonial emasculation has been crucial to . . . radical Hindu movements."[11] Questioning the masculinity and virility of Indians, partly attributed to child marriage, was undoubtedly very humiliating experience heaped upon an already subjugated nation.

The recent strategy of Hindu political organizations and cultural associations seeking the support of Sannyasis and Sadhus is rooted in the history of the Hindu militant monasticism. The Dasnami Sannyasis of Shivite tradition was founded by Sri Sankaracharya, in the eighth century, to check the spread of Buddhist monasticism. The Sannyasis with the vow of non-violence were caught up in a dilemma when Buddhist and Jain rulers and later Muslim Faqirs began to attack and kill them. In 1565, Madusudan Sarasvati, a Dasnami Sannyasi of Varanasi, sought the advice of Emperor Akbar (1556–1605) to solve the problem. He was advised to "initiate a large number of non-Brahmins into Sannyasi order and arm them for the protection of Brahmin Sannyasis."[12] "Around 1565 a large number of non-Brahmins who had no religious vows of non-Violence were initiated as Sannyasis and armed to fight Muslim Faqirs."[13] Full-blown soldiers' monasticism evolved and was institutionalized during Mughal rule. The creation of military orders and the militarization of monks and fakhirs were getting religious sanctions. Thus, during the Muslim rule in India, Hindu soldier monks fought sixty five battles against the Muslims, mostly in North India.

Swami Ramananda, a disciple of Ramanuja, who was opposed to Sankaracharya's school of thought and exclusive monasticism for the Brahmins, founded the Ramananda or Ramavat sect, to accommodate Sudras who were denied entry into Dasnami orders.[14] The rite of initiation into the fifth ashrama, *Panchamahashramavidhi*, the highest spiritual state, was characterized by total renunciation, after twelve years of training, when the Sannyasi abandoned even his water pot, the staff and the loin clothing. They were thus known as Naga Sadhus, naked monks. The militant Sadhus, recruited for the protection of the Brahmin Sannyasis and temple properties underwent physical training in the gymnasium. Each gymnasium had its own Naga Mahant or abbot and was independent. The

11. Veer, *Imperial Encounters*, 95.
12. Bouillier, "Violence," 32.
13. Quoted by "Pinch, Soldier Monks," 151
14. Ibid., 143.

From Confrontations to Dialogue and Partnership

Dasnami Naga Sannyasis were attached to six major Akharas. They were organized into armies and regiments and lived in fortified temples and were trained in wrestling and fighting with hand weapons like tridents and fire-tongs. Akharas were originally camps of fighting ascetics in the temple premises, which later developed into gymnasiums for the laity, with physical as well as moral discipline, including celibacy. In fact asceticism and organized violence is a long-standing historical combination. Ascetics of different persuasions-Vaishnavites, Shivites, Sikh or Muslims—continuously clashed during the Hindu bathing festivals, for the first dip at the most auspicious moment, determined by astrologers.[15] The doctrinal and caste differences provided sufficient reasons for inter-sect rivalries and battles between the Dasnami and Ramananda sects of Sannyasis. These belong to fifty two spiritual clans and out-numbered the Dasnami Sannyasis. The Hindu militant Sanyasis of the middle ages were in many respect similar to military religious orders, Militia Christi, for the crusades against Muslims in the Holy Land. A crucial question raised by the Hindu militant groups fighting for independence from the colonial rulers was: Why was India dominated for centuries first by the Muslims and then by Christians? T. B. Macaulay was most eloquent on this point. "The physical organization of the Bengali is feeble even to effeminacy."[16] According to the German philosopher Hegel: "Hinduism lacked masculine, world ordering rationality. Hindus were guided by feminine fantasies and imagination rather than by masculine reason."[17] Suspecting the masculinity and virility of Indians, partly attributed to child marriage, was unquestionably a very humiliating insult heaped up on a subjugated nation. Exceptions to these feminine stereotypes were the Sikhs, the Rajputs, the Pathans and the Gurkhas who displayed their fighting spirit on various political encounters.

Mass Conversions and Anti-Conversion Laws

"There is nothing in the past that in certain circumstances cannot provoke passion in the present."[18] Christian missionary activity in India in the nineteenth century was marked by mass conversions mainly from the outcasts and tribals who were marginalized and oppressed by the upper castes for millennia. Hindus, starting from the foundation of Arya Samaj and other extremist groups violently reacted to this socio-religious revolution and

---

15. Veer, *Imperial Encounters*, 99.
16. Ibid., 85.
17. Ibid.
18. Subramanyam, *Exploration*, 80.

promptly began to pass a series of laws, forbidding missionary activities and conversions. In 1936, the "Raigarh State Conversion Act" was passed against the Christian missionaries. According to the act, a person wishing to change his religion had to submit an application in a prescribed form to a government officer who would give permission or refuse. The Act made liable to punishment any person found guilty of misinterpretation, fraud, intimidation, coercion or undue influence in the matter of conversion. The law also forbade preaching in order to convert. The neighboring principality, following the example of Raigarh, passed "The Surguja State Hindu Apostasy Act of 1945," "Udaipur State Conversion Act" followed in the next year. All these principalities had witnessed large scale conversions among the adivasis of erstwhile Chotanagpur. "Freedom of Religion Act" was passed in Patna in 1942, where a large number of Harijans embraced the Church under the American missionaries. "Freedom of Religion Act" (1938) was passed by Bolangir state which was part of Bihar state but later merged with the state of Orissa in 1956.[19]

After Independence objections to conversions were most sharply and critically expressed in 1954 when the Government of Madhya Bharat, comprising the erstwhile princely states where anti-conversion laws were already passed, appointed an official commission to investigate social, economic and religious activities of foreign missionaries. On the one hand representations were sent to the Central Government that missionaries were converting illiterate aboriginals and other backward people through the use of monetary inducements and that it was creating widespread resentment among the Hindus. On the other hand, the missionaries denied these allegations and charged that local officials and other people were harassing the Christian coverts. At this juncture, Dr. M. B. Niyogi, a retired chief justice of Nagpur High Court, was appointed chairman of a six man committee to enquire into the allegations. The Enquiry Committee devoted several months to extensive tours from June 1954 to November 1955, and visited seventy seven mission centres and interviewed 1,130 persons, mostly in groups. They issued a questionnaire with ninety nine questions to many people of whom only a few replied. The findings of the enquiry were published in April 1956. The report included ten findings some of which are given as follows: It was accused that since 1950 there had been an appreciable increase in American missionaries working in India, and that a large sum of foreign money was spent on educational, medical, social and evangelical activities. Conversion was mostly brought about by undue influence, misinterpretations and not by conviction because of the

19. Soares, *Truth Shall Prevail*, 114.

From Confrontations to Dialogue and Partnership

various inducements offered for proselytization. On political involvement they stated that "there seems to be an unholy alliance between Roman Catholics and American money to save India from communism," that dominated her neighbor, China from 1948. As conversion muddles with the converts sense of unity and solidarity there was a danger of loyalty to their nation and the State being undermined. They further described the missionary activity as a form of western imperialism.[20]

The committee made nineteen recommendations to the Government. Some of them were the following: The missionaries whose primary objective is proselytization should be asked to withdraw. The large influx of foreign missionaries should be checked. Any attempt or effort, whether successful or not, directly or indirectly, to penetrate into the religious conscience of persons of another faith, so as to agree with the convictions of the proselytizing party, should be absolutely forbidden. It further recommended that a department of cultural and religious affairs in the State Government be created with power of censorship over literature intended for religious propaganda. All foreign money of missionaries should come through Government channels.[21] All the findings of the report, as well as detailed recommendations, were directly intended to stop every Christian missionary activity and to hinder the successful expansion of Christian missions as was lately happening. It is clear that these recommendations and many of the activities of the anti-Christian groups were contrary to the fundamental freedom of religion granted by the Constitution.

Jana Sangh, the erstwhile political wing of the RSS and a coalition partner in the Samyukta Vidhayak Dal government in Madhya Pradesh, passed the "Dharma Swatantra Act" or Freedom of Religion Act in 1968, to outlaw conversion to Christianity. In the same year Orissa state assembly passed "Freedom of Religion Act" along the recommendations of the Niyogi Report. In 1978, O. P. Tyagi, an earlier president of the Jana Sangh, introduced the "Freedom of Religion Bill" in the Parliament during the Janata Government in the centre and it could not be passed due to the collapse of the government. "Arunachal Pradesh Freedom of Religion Act" (1978), was a follow up of the O. P. Tyagi Bill. An anti-conversion law in Tamil Nadu in 2003 and a similar law in Gujarat in the same year, followed the recommendations of the Niyogi committee. These laws in various states provide the governments and other anti-Christians fundamentalist individuals and communities the legitimacy to harass the minority community of Christians to suit their political opportunism. Article

20. Niyogi, *Report of*, 131–32.
21. Ibid., 162–65.

25 (1) of the Fundamental rights in the Indian Constitution defines the "Right to Freedom of Religion: all persons are equally entitled to freedom of conscience and the right freely to profess and propagate religion." Fr. Stanislaus, a Catholic priest of Bhopal diocese, M.P. was prosecuted under the Madhya Pradesh Freedom of Religion Act for which the matter reached the Supreme Court. And the supreme court ruling of 1977 regarding the Freedom of Religion Act, judged: "What article twenty five (1) of the Indian Constitution grants is not the right to convert another person to one's own religion by an exposition of its tenets. . . . Article twenty five (1) guarantees "Freedom of Conscience" to every citizen and not merely to the follower of one religion and that in turn postulated that there is no fundamental right to convert another person to one's own religion because if a person purposely undertakes the conversion of another person to his religion as distinguished from his effort to transmit or spread the tenets of his religion that would infringe on the "freedom of conscience" guaranteed to all citizens of the country alike."[22] The supreme court judgement was in the light of the 1966 UN "International Covenant on Civil and Political Rights" which declared in article 18 (2) as follows: "None shall be subjects to coercion which would impair his freedom to have or to adopt a religion or belief of his choice." "This was considered necessary to allow for freedom of choice and at the same time to protect individuals from overzealous proselytizers."[23] The Supreme Court judgment in no way discourages anyone from making personal choice to adopt a religion of his / her choice. However when some Protestant sects take away our Catholics we accuse them of "sheep stealing" and constitute enquiry committees to bring them back to the true fold. I feel the objections of Hindus are, therefore, equally valid. Are not the Christian proselytizers, particularly the fundamentalists and evangelicals, insensitive to Hindu reactions to conversions? I believe that the Christians have a moral obligation to the wounded Hindu psyche, generated by the past colonial mission. Here I am not referring to conversions of tribals who believe that they are not Hindus.

Paradigm Shift in Mission: Confrontation to Dialogue

It is encouraging to note that emperor Akbar the Great during his tolerant and benevolent rule (1556–1605) initiated a path of dialogue in his "Ibadat Khana," house of worship, with various religious leaders of India. He invited theologians of Hindu and Muslims sects, Zorastrians,

22. Banerjee, *Religious Conversions*, 249.
23. Heredia, "Religious Conversions," 280.

From Confrontations to Dialogue and Partnership

Jains, Jews and Christians to discuss and understand better the tenets of all religions. Three Jesuit priests—Rudolf Acquaviva, an Italian, Antony Monserate, a Spandiard, and Francis Henrique a Persian—from St. Paul's College, Goa, after three months travel, arrived in Fatephur Sikri on 27th February 1580. Their great hope was to convert the Muslim ruler. They were under the respectful hospitality of the ruler for three years. During the period Akbar studied as well as conducted scholarly discussions on the Gospel and Christian religion with the learned Christian professors. Akbar's noble goal was to create a new religion, Din-Illahi, Divine Faith, incorporating all the inspiring elements from other religions. He had no intention whatsoever to embrace Christianity. The disappointed Jesuits returned to Goa after three years. Akbar's sincere and noble attempt, however, failed because of stiff opposition from his Muslim Ulemas, theologians. His liberal attitudes to other religions were practically and very personally proved by marrying Muslim, Hindu and Christian wives, including Maria Mascarenhas that changed into Miriam Makani. Some critical historians think that his Syncretistic Divine Faith was aimed at political convenience of ruling an empire with one religion. Historians are not sure whether he died the Muslim, Hindu or Christian. He also helped the Jesuit missionaries to construct their headquarter as well as a church in Agra.[24] In 1582 Akbar promulgated his new religion, Din Illahi. At the request of the emperor the Jesuit missionaries again visited his court in 1590 and 1593.

No religious or cultural situation can remain static or undisturbed because their contacts or encounters, peaceful or conflictual, compel them to self-examination and evaluation. Certain socio-cultural and religious forces that influenced the missionary thinking, therefore, merit attention. The beginning of the colonial mission was marked by imperfect knowledge of Non-Christian religions and superficial judgment based on outward manifestations. The encounter between science and religion already began with Galileo Galilei. The modern archaeological discoveries of ancient Mesopotamian and Babylonian records of creation and flood stories shed unprecedented light on cultural sources of inspired Biblical authors. The study of anthropology, the science of man and his culture in evolution, enhanced the appreciation of other cultures and alternative non-western life styles. Comparative study of religions led European scholars to the depth of philosophy, theology and spirituality of other religions, including Indian mysticism. The theory of evolution, proposed by Charles Darwin in 1859 was rejected by the church as "completely contrary to scripture

---

24. Smith, *Akbar the Great*, 150–60.

and faith."²⁵ By responding to these unprecedented challenges the Biblical scholars and theologians began to reinterpret sacred scriptures and traditional theologies. The liberal Protestantism of the nineteenth century took the lead. In contrast the Catholic church followed the policy of suppressing the liberals until the Second Vatican Council.

The rise of Orientalism and the impact of enlightenment contributed to changes of attitudes of Christianity to Hinduism. Between 1785–1802 the French Scholar Anquetil du Perron translated some of the Upanishads into Latin which deeply influenced Arthur Schopenhauer, one of the founders of Transcendental movement in Germany and later in America as a protest against New England Puritanism. William Jones, the founder of the Asiatic Society of Bengal (1783) tried to establish a common link between Sanskrit, Greek, Latin, the Gothic, the Celtic and old Persian and laid the foundation for the science of comparative philology and comparative religion which would be further developed by Max Mueller. In 1785 Charles Wilkins published a translation of the *Bhagavadgita*. Between 1828–1870 saw the flowering of the Oriental scholarship. "By the 1830, then, the encounter of Christianity with Hinduism was taking two contrasting characters. A minority among Christians had begun to look for, and found, common ground, though by-passing in the process a great deal of what had hitherto been regarded as vital to the Christian case."²⁶ Because religions of the world were becoming better known through research, study and translations of scriptures and religious literature. It marked the beginning of comparative study of religions.

In India Krishna Mohan Banerjee (1813–85), under the influence of Alexander Duff, was converted to Presbyterian denomination in 1832. Three years later he wrote The *Aryan Witness* to establish positive relation between Hinduism and Christianity. K. C. Sen (1838–84), an ardent unbaptized follower of Jesus, founded the "Church of New Dispensation," for harmonizing Hindu and Christian beliefs, rites, and cultures. Another follower of Jesus Christ, P. C. Mazoomdar (1840–1904) held the view that Jesus Christ completed and reconciled all revelations of the Spirit in the religious history of mankind. Brahmabandav Upadyaya (1861–1907), following the example of Thomas Aquinas, constructed an Indian theology of the Trinity, Sat-Chit-Ananda, employing the Vedanda philosophy. The Scottish missionary J. N. Farquhar (1861–1929), under the influence of liberal Protestantism and the evolutionary theory of the period wrote, *The Crown of Hinduism* and tried to establish that Christ himself was the

25. Kanjamala, "Arnold Janssen," 142.
26. Sharpe, *Faith Meets Faith*, 12.

crown of Hinduism. Jesus of history was seen as the consummation of all the religions of the world.[27] All these authors, both Indian and Western, rejected the traditional Protestant theology that there exists absolutely no link between what they called natural religion and the revealed religion-Christianity. The foundation for inter-religious dialogue was established, mostly by liberal Protestant scholars. When the World Parliament of Religions was held in Chicago in 1893 a few liberal Hindu thinkers, like K. C. Sen, P. C. Mazoomdar, and Swami Vivekananda attended it but the Catholics were forbidden to attend. No Hindu, with the exception of a few who embraced Christianity, accepted the fulfillment theology of *The Crown of Hinduism*. Chicago's Parliament was the celebration of liberal American theology, at the dawn of an American century. In the Chicago address, Swami Vivekananda, a disciple of mystic Sri Ramakrishna Paramahansa, declared: "Sisters and Brothers of America . . . I am proud to belong to a religion which has taught the world both tolerance and universal acceptance. We believe not only in universal tolerance but like to accept all religions to be true."

The Vatican Council II and Dialogue with Religions

After prolonged rejection of modernism, starting explicitly from the publication of the *Syllabus of Errors* (1864) and similar documents in the beginning of the twentieth century Pope John XXIII's initiative to open the windows of the Catholic Church to the modern world found new and unprecedented expressions in the Documents of Vatican II, particularly in the "Dogmatic Constitution on the Church" (L.G.), the "Pastoral Constitution on Church in the Modern World" (G.S.), the "Decree on Church's Missionary Activity" (A.G.), the "Declaration on the Relationship of the Church to Non-Christian Religions" (N.A.), and the "Decree on Religious Freedom" (D.H.). With the publication of the encyclical letter *Ecclesiam Suam* (1964), Pope Paul VI became the "Pope of Dialogue." He established the Secretariat for Non-Christian Religions in the same year. On the crucial missionary question of salvation of the Non-Christians the Council nearly reversed the traditional dictum, *extra ecclesiam nulla salus* and explicitly taught: "Those who through no fault of their own do not know the Gospel of Christ . . . but who seek God with a sincere heart may achieve eternal salvation." "—Nor shall divine providence deny the assistance necessary for salvation to those who . . . strive to lead a good life" (LG 16). It is rather puzzling to note that the Document failed to refer

27. Ibid., 22–31, 35–37.

to St. Peter who said to the house of Cornelius: "Truly, I realize that God does not show partiality, but in every nation everyone who fears God and does good is acceptable to him" (Acts 10:34–35).

Jacques Dupuis comments: "It needs to be underlined that Vatican II is the first council in the history of the church to speak positively of other religions."[28] Having recognized the world religions as source of salvation the church acknowledges the urgency of dialogue with other religions. *Nostra Aetate* "urges her sons to enter with prudence and charity into dialogue and collaboration with members of other religions and acknowledge, preserve and promote the spiritual and moral goods found among them" (NA 2). The council sees in these religious traditions, "a preparation for the Gospel" (LG 16); "seeds of the Word" (AG 11); "elements of truth and grace found among the Nations as a sort of secret presence of God" (AG 9). The council further affirms that Non-Christian religions contain "rays of that truth which enlightens all human beings" (NA 2). The council encourages dialogue even with non-believer (GS 92). Through these positive attitudes "the document, *Nostra Aetate* ends a sad chapter in the Christian history," observes Robert Graham.[29]

Indian philosopher S. Radhakrishnan (1888–1975), exponent of Neo-Hinduism, criticizes that the present teaching of the church has not made any substantial progress beyond what Justin the Martyr, Origen and other Fathers of the early church taught about the relation of Christianity to non-Christian religions.[30] In his numerous publications he repeatedly pointed out the root cause of conflict between Hinduism and Christianity. Hinduism firmly holds the view that all religions are equal: "Him who is One Real sages name variously"(Rg Veda, I, 164.46) and differences between religions are only nominal. On the contrary, the Christian view of religion is that Jesus Christ is the unique and ultimate revelation of God and all other religions are imperfect manifestations of man's search for God and the view that all religions are equal is false. According to Radhakrishnan these two uncompromising convictions are the root cause of conflicts. To quote, "Hinduism developed an attitude of comprehensive charity instead of a fanatic faith in inflexible creed ... Many sects professing different beliefs live within Hindu fold. Heresy hunting, a favorite game of many religions, is singularly absent from Hinduism."[31] "He was anxious to avoid religious conflicts and to establish peace by demonstrat-

28. Dupuis, "Theological Commentry," 124.
29. Graham, "Non-Christians," 658.
30. Radhakrishnan, *Religion*, 23–24.
31. Radhakrishnan, *The Hindu View*, 13.

ing that there existed a basic unity in man's religious experiences, but not in dogmas and outward expressions." "We cannot have religious unity and peace as long as we assert that we are in possession of light and others are groping in darkness . . . that very assertion is a challenge to fight—we can do so if we accept something like the Hindu solution which seeks unity of religions not common creed, but in common quest."[32]

An inclusive understanding of salvation was developed by the Alexandrian school of theology in the early church by Clement of Alexandria, Origen and others; Peter Abelard in the middle ages; Friedrich Schleiermacher in the nineteenth century and others were sidelined by other powerful theological schools. Bernard Lonergan and Karl Rahner in the second half of the twentieth century revived this school of missiology. Even before the second Vatican council Rahner developed the inclusive missiology under the offensive term, "anonymous Christians." He argued that even non-Christian religions contained grace-filled events and they were lawful religions. Therefore "Christianity does not simply confront a member of the extra-Christian religion as a non-Christian but as someone who can be regarded in this or that respect as anonymous Christians."[33] Under the inspiration of Rahner's theology of anonymous Christians, Raimundo Panikkar explored the hidden presence of Christ through the Advaita philosophy of India. He argued that Christ is already present in Hinduism and what is required is to unveil Him from the inside, and not presenting him from the outside. In the classical Hinduism, it is not the impersonal Brahman, but the personal Ishwara who is the cause of the world. Modifying this view Panikkar argues that Brahman is the ultimate cause of the world and Ishwara is none other than Christ, the Logos, the agent of creation, the mediator between Brahman and man. The task of the Christian mission is not to convert Hindus to Christianity but to make them realize the fundamental truth. Therefore, "Christianity and Hinduism both meet in Christ. Christ is their meeting place. The real encounter can take place in Christ because only in Christ do they meet."[34]

From among various objections to Rahner and Panikkar, the following recapture the sentiments of Hindus: "The Hindu is not going to thank you for even suspecting that he might be a Christian without knowing it— In dialogical terms it is fatal. What the Hindu undoubtedly respects, on the other hand, is the open and total commitment. He may not agree with

32. Ibid., 42.
33. Rahner, *Theological Investigation*, 5:126.
34. Panikkar, *Unknown Christ*, 6.

it but he does not, as a rule, despise it."³⁵ Further the Hindu can use the logic of Panikkar to argue for the *Unknown Krishna of Christianity*. After all, did not Lord Krishna say, "Yet even those who worship other gods with love and sacrifice to them fulfilled with faith, do really worship me . . . For it is I who of all acts of sacrifice am Recipient and Lord, though they do not know me as I really am" (*Bhagavad Gita* IX: 23). While the guilt-ridden Christian apologists are becoming enthusiastic about dialogue in the recent past Hindus and Muslims, in general, are responding to it coolly.

According to Panikkar, the problems of Hindu—Christian dialogue is ultimately rooted in two distinctive world views. All the Abrahamic religions—Judaism, Christianity and Islam-claim the central idea of being a chosen people. The concept of God in these religions is of a God totally other, the Holy. In contrast the Indian philosophical thinking is characterized by the principle of identity. According to the Indian perspective the all pervading and imminent binding force of everything is Brahman. India believes in the ultimate equality of all religions and sees different religions as different paths to realize the Ultimate Reality. No incarnation can exhaust the mystery of God. Every incarnation is partial and God is generous to enter human history whenever righteousness is in danger. Ultimately the Dialogue between Christianity and Hinduism is the question of two different world views. We are still in the process of searching to understand the riches which God in his generosity has bestowed upon all the Nations. Regarding his experience with the gentiles, St. Peter taught: "He (God) made no distinction between us and them." (Acts15:9). Like Peter we are called to undergo a painful conversion to recognize that God has no favorites. "I am submitting here to a common place agreed to by nearly everyone—intellectuals and common people alike—namely, a new degree of consciousness, a new epoch is dawning for humankind. We can see it as a crisis or a challenge, interpreting it from any view point we prefer-personal, depth psychology, sociological, theological or mystical."³⁶

Ten Types of Hindu-Christian Dialogues

Inter-Religious Dialogue is a very complex exercise. India provides an atmosphere of religious freedom unknown to the West which was distinguished rather for its persecution of the Jews and its crusade against Muslims. Religious freedom was unknown in Catholicism until the Second Vatican Council's belated, cautious and some what patronizing

---

35. Sharpe, *Faith Meets Faith*, 129.
36. Panikkar, "Crux," 86.

From Confrontations to Dialogue and Partnership

Declaration of Religious Freedom. Responses to the encounter between Christian missionaries and educated caste Hindus falls under three broad categories. First, the total rejection of Hinduism and acceptance of another, belief systems, religious or secular. Second, the total rejection of Christianity and a reassertion of Indian religion and identity. Third, interpret and adapt Hinduism to the challenges that were posed by Christianity as well as Western scientific and rational worldview. Further one is forced to discover the complexity of religious dialogue according to divergent dispositions and attitudes of partners in dialogue. Four types of dialogue with ten probable options are presented below.

Type A.

1. Conservative (Fundamentalist) Christians   Vs. Conservative (Fundamentalist) Hindus
2. Conservative Christians   Vs. Liberal Hindus.
3. Conservative Christians   Vs. Moderate Hindus.

Type B.

4. Liberal Christians   Vs. Conservative Hindus
5. Liberal Christians   Vs. Liberal Hindus
6. Liberal Christians   Vs. Moderate Hindus.

Type C.

7. Moderate Christians   Vs. Conservative Hindus
8. Moderate Christians   Vs. Liberal Hindus
9. Moderate Christians   Vs. Moderate Hindus.

Type D.

10. Secularized Christians Non-believers   Vs. Secularized Hindus Non-believers.

(Source: Sharpe, *Faith Meets Faith*, 1977: 132–49; Sharpe, "Hindu Christian Dialogue in Europe," 1989).

The above pattern of dialogues seems to be not simple as some believe, on the contrary, religious dialogue is very complex as well as difficult. Since the Abrahamic and Indian religions are rooted in contradictory philosophies and worldviews an in-depth dialogue seems to be nearly impossible. Even if these world views and religions are reinterpreted and modified to adapt themselves to modern challenges the patterns of dialogue are many and it is not easy to arrive at agreed upon conclusions. With better education and exposure to other religions through increasing international travels more and more Christians seem to be moving away from traditional dogmatism to Hindu tolerance and pluralism, respecting human freedom and human dignity of believers. Institutionalized religion, particularly among the youth, is declining. More than dialogues of religions today we are in need of dialogue of spirituality and religious experience. Religions usually tend to emphasize externals and theological differences while spirituality tend to accentuate the internal unity of all religions, ultimately rooted in One Spirit.

In the post-Vatican theology of Evangelization, relation between evangelizing mission and dialogue is rather unclear. Three types of attitudes to dialogue and mission are postulated. One, dialogue is opposed to Mission. This attitude underlies the objections of all those who do not want to get involved in dialogue because they believe that the traditional mission spirit is watered down or even destroyed by dialogue. The evangelical missionaries in general adhere to this position. They prefer the term evangelism to evangelization. Two, dialogue is not an end in itself but an instrument of the mission which ultimately aims at conversion in the traditional sense. "Proclamation is the foundation, summit and centre of evangelization" (DP. 10). This position confirm the Hindu suspicion of dialogue with "hidden agenda." Three, dialogue is an integral part of evangelization because evangelization is a complex reality, made up of varies elements: renewal of humanity, witness, explicit proclamation, inner adherence, entry into the community, acceptance of signs, apostolic initiative (EN.24).

Pope John Paul had already stated "The church proposes; she imposes nothing" (RM 39) Here proclamation is understood as a respectful invitation. "It is an invitation to a commitment of faith in Jesus Christ." (DP 10). The past Asian experiences of mission show that Asia has sadly rejected the invitation to enter "into the community of believers" through baptism. But the paradigm shift from the aggressive proclamation of the past to a respectful invitation should be deeply appreciated as progress. Unfortunately the Vatican documents, *Proclamation and Dialogue* (1991) in its concluding section has relegated the former status of the "Secretariat for Non-Christians" (1964) to that of the "Pontifical Council for Inter Religious Dialogue" to assert the superiority of the "Congregation for the Evangelization for the Peoples."

From Confrontations to Dialogue and Partnership

The Post-Vatican II Developments in Dialogue

Following the initial orientation given by the Vatican council the Asian church's subsequent development of the theology of dialogue is an unique contribution to the universal church. In the midst of all the world religions Christianity as a minority has nearly no other option than to be a church in dialogue with its neighbours.

Dialogue in Asia

The challenges of all the world religions found in Asia, have nearly forced to redefine evangelization in the Asian context. The Federation of the Asian Bishops' Conference held in Taipei, Taiwan, in April 1974 defined "Evangelization in Modern Day Asia" in terms of threefold dialogue with the religions of Asia; dialogue with the people, especially the poor; and dialogue with cultures.[37] Twenty years after the establishment of the Secretariat for Non-Christians its "Reflections and Orientations on Dialogue and Mission" (DM) in June 1984 defines dialogue thus: "It means not only discussion, but also includes all positive and constructive inter-religious relations with individuals and communities of other faiths which are directed at mutual understanding and enrichment" (DM 3). Dialogue demands a radical change of old attitudes towards other religions. "Dialogue is a manner of acting, an attitude and a spirit, which guides one's conduct. It implies concern, respect and hospitality towards others. Any sense of mission not permeated by such a spirit of dialogue would go against the demands of true humanity and against the teaching of Christ." The church's evangelizing mission in a broad sense consists of five elements: The presence and living witness of the Christian life; the concrete commitment to the service of mankind and activities for social development and liberation from unjust structures; liturgical life, prayer and contemplation; dialogue in which Christians meet the followers of other religions in order to walk together towards truth; and finally proclamation of the Good News of the Gospel (DM 13).

The universal presence and action of the Holy Spirit is further reaffirmed in John Paul II's Encyclical, *Redemptoris Missio*. Before its publication he had already made many international pastoral visits; visits to India in January-February 1986, including dialogue with various religious leaders in Madras on February 5, 1986. His inter-religious prayer for peace in Assisi on October 27, 1986 was to confirm that every authentic prayer

---

37. Rosales and Arevalo, *For All the People*, 14-16.

The Future of Christian Mission in India

is prompted by Holy Spirit who is present in every heart; RM (29) refers to three elements which together constitute the theological foundation of dialogue. These are: the mystery of the presence of the Spirit in creation and the unity of the entire human family, with a single origin and single goal: the divine plan has its centre in Jesus Christ; the mysterious presence of the Holy Spirit in the heart of every person. "The Church's relationship with other religions is dictated by a two fold respect; respect for man in his quest for answers to the deepest questions of his life, and respect for the action of the Holy Spirit in Man" (RM 29).

There are conspicuous differences and tensions between the Western and Asian theologies of dialogue. The western theologians who sit in comfortable air conditioned libraries and write books on dialogue, with no lack of footnotes from all sources, unfortunately, without prolonged exposure to people of other religions and existential angst fail to grasp the more sympathetic attitude of Asian Christians and theologians. Most of the western theologians seems to be engaged in "armchair dialogue."[38] The Asian Christians as well as theologians are well exposed to other religious neighbours from childhood onwards. They daily participate in the Dialogue of Life. After the Asian Synod of the Bishops (1998) having noted that Asia has two-thirds of the world population, with mere 3 percent Christians, John Paul II reaffirmed the importance of "dialogue as a characteristic mode of life of the Church's life in Asia" (EA 3), and renewed the commitment to dialogue in the following words:

> The Synod therefore renewed the commitment of the Church in Asia to the task of improving both ecumenical relations and inter-religious dialogue, cognizing that building unity, working for reconciliation, forging bonds of solidarity, promoting dialogue of religions and cultures, eradicating prejudices and engendering trust among people are all essential to the church's evangelizing mission on the continent. All this demands of the Christian community sincere introspection, the courage to seek reconciliation and a renewed commitment to dialogue. (EA 24)

John Paul II during his long pontificate not only wrote extensively on dialogue with religions but also repeatedly asked pardon for the past sins of the church. During his visit to the Synagogue in Rome in April 1986, his visit to Santo Domingo in October 1984, to Cameroon in August 1986 and to many Islamic countries, to Jerusalem on March 26, 2000 and many other visits, he continued to ask forgiveness for the sins of the Church

---

38. Klostermaier, *Hindu and Christian*, 41.

against other religions. He further asked pardon from the scientists on October 31, 1992 for the Galileo episode. Such brave and humble steps of the Pope illustrate that reconciliation and dialogue should go hand in hand.[39] The Galileo case was the symbol of the churches supposed rejection of scientific progress or dogmatic obscurantism. In the contemporary world dialogue is a three—way process of intellectual exchange and complementarity in which eastern and western religious and philosophical thought are joined by science. Each will approach the mystery of the universe from a different angle, not as the absolute truth.[40] Therefore late John Paul II wrote: "The church . . . admits . . . that scientific culture today requires to have mature faith, an openness towards the language and the questions of the learned, a sense of the orders of knowledge and different approaches to truth. In brief she desires that the dialogue between science and faith shall enter into an evermore positive stage even though it has known tensions historically."

Dialogue and Path of Mission in India

In the post-independence India the Christian mission is witnessing not only the development of a theology of dialogue but also some inspiring and daring experiments of dialogue. The French Benedictine monk Dom Henri Le Saux took the name Swami Abhishiktananda and lived like a Hindu hermit in the Himalayas, being aware of the suspicion felt by the Hindus; the English Benedictine monk Dom Bede Griffiths lived for over half a century in his ashram in Trichi, Tamilnadu and engaged in Hindu-Christian dialogue; the Scottish nun Sara Grant was the head of Christa Prema Ashram, Pune, an ecumenical dialogue centre; Vandana Mataji in Rishikesh, at the foot of the Himalayas; the German missionary Klaus Klostermaier spent many years in Vrindaban, engaged in study, research and dialogue, emphasizing 'dialogue in depth on the level of spirituality'; another German missionary, Guru Gyan Prakash in Bombay became a pioneer in dialogue and inculturation; late Amalorpavadass, was the founder of Anjali Ashram, Mysore, and a champion of dialogue and inculturation; R. Panikkar, drawing inspiration from Karl Rahner's theology of 'anonymous Christians' developed the theology of "The Unknown Christ of Hinduism" and Ama Swami, a pioneer in Christian-Buddhist Dialogue in Madurai, are some of the illustrious examples of dialogue with other religions. Further it is encouraging as well as inspiring that at

39. Accattoli, *John Paul II*, 107, 173, 271–80.
40. Sharpe, "Mission between Dialogue," 148–49.

The Future of Christian Mission in India

least a few Indian bishops participate in "live-together" seminars with the Hindus, Muslims, Sikhs and people of other religions in different ashrams and dialogue centres, like Varanasi, Mysore, Hyderabad and so forth. This incomplete list is merely a bird's eye view of attempts at Christian dialogue in a country with wounded memories of colonial and religious conflicts. The long history of Christian Missionary encounters in Asia, and the Hindu-Christian encounter in particular, are primarily responsible for the creation and promotion of theology of inter-religious dialogue and its practice. This is undoubtedly the Indian Church's unique contribution to the universal church and its mission.

The Catholic enthusiasm for dialogue is not necessarily reciprocated. In 1964 when Pope Paul VI's visit to Bombay for the International Eucharistic Congress was announced the Hindu fundamentalists accused that it was another attempt for conversion. Immediately the Vishwa Hindu Parishad, Association of Hindu religious leaders, was founded on August 29, 1964 by S.S. Apte to save Hinduism from Christianity and Islam.[41] Pope John Paul II's very successful pastoral visits to Bombay and other states in 1986 provoked strong reactions from the Hindu fundamentalists. They demanded the Pope to make a declaration of moratorium on conversions. The Pope held a dialogue meeting with a many Hindu religious leaders in Madras. Within a few months, under the pressure of the Hindu fundamentalists, the government expelled a few foreign missionaries who were rendering their selfless and peaceful services in India for many decades.

The converging focus of the emerging world religious consciousness, it seems, is the recognition of the presence of the Spirit of God in creation, in religions, in cultures and in human struggles for integral liberation. We are experiencing a radical shift in human consciousness and ultimate foundation of world unity from Christo-centrism to Pneumato-centrism. Since the Spirit was the driving force of Jesus from incarnation to resurrection to the creation of the new eschatological community, the paradigm shift seems to be justified. "The Spirit of God has been universally present throughout human history and remains active today outside the boundaries of the Christian fold . . . The Holy Spirit is the "point of entry' in to the life of the peoples, hence his immediate actions open up the way for distinct Christian theology of religions, no longer Christo-centric but Pneumato-centric."[42] The emerging Spirit centred vision is only partly dis-

---

41. Jeffrelot, *Hindu Nationalist*, 197.
42. Dupuis, "Religious Plurality," 329.

tinguished from the Christ-centred vision since both are inseparable in the Christian economy of salvation.

On the crucial role of dialogue in a religiously pluralistic world Hans Kueng wrote: "There can be no peace among nations without peace among religions; there can be no peace among religions without dialogue between religions; there can be no dialogue between religions without research into theological foundations. In today's world it is not enough to be religious, one has to be inter-religious."[43] All the people of good will are gradually, at times reluctantly, entering the new age of mutual mission, i.e., challenging as well as mutually changing their thinking, attitudes, feelings and activities; and a common mission and commitment to the creation of a new society characterized by justice, freedom, compassion; and a new humanity where the dignity of every child, man and woman is protected, promoted and respected. In a multi-religious and pluri-cultural India, wasting time and energy in religious violence and conflicts is most unfortunate. "The need of the hour is to bring down the walls that divide people and replace them with bridges that allow the followers of all religions to mix freely with one another."[44] We have arrived at an understanding, at least de jure, that not only Christianity but also all religions are imperfect co-pilgrims, walking and searching, in faith and hope, for the Ultimate Truth and Bliss. Dialogue therefore is not only an essential part of the Christian mission of evangelization but also an urgent path of the mission.

---

43. Hans Küng, quoted by Francis D'Britto, "Inter Religious Dialogue," *Examiner*, July 18, 2009, 22.

44. Jain, "For a Bold Vision," in *Times of India*, October 14, 2010, 20.

6

Inculturation of the Indian Churches

STUDY OF CULTURES BY anthropologists, with an unprecedented accent on plurality and diversity, in contrast to the European idea of culture as artistic refinement and urbane behavior, is a rather recent academic discipline, starting at the end of the nineteenth century. The Catholic missiologist Pierre Charles introduced the concept of inculturation in 1953, replacing earlier expressions like accommodation, assimilation, adaptation, indigenization or contextualization.[1] Every ethnic community is characterized by a distinctive culture, as people tend to do things together in a patterned manner; Sharing beliefs and customs with a world view at the centre, together with values and standards of judgments and conduct; common institutions; a distinctive mother tongue with shared proverbs, myths, folklores, and arts; a common history; a common land or territory; common occupation; shared rituals and celebration of rites of passage.[2] The material culture that provides visibility and particular image are folk costumes and ornaments, worn particularly at public and festive celebrations. Traditional food and drink habits, unique music, musical instruments, and dance, art and architecture sharpen the image. Culture cannot be understood as a value-neutral object of study because it provides an identity to communities and its members. It answers the basic questions: Who am I? Where do I belong? With strict cultural boundaries, it also tells who I am not. "Being a catholic or a Protestant really means something" to the people in question, for example in Northern Ireland, as being a Hindu or a Muslim in Jammu and Kashmir.

---

1. Quack, "Inculturation," 3.
2. Barrett, *World Christian*, 2:16.

For the sake of clarity and focus the above cultural description can be classified at three levels: 1) material cultural traits; 2) organized social relations: a) primary relations dominated by emotions, feelings and sentiments, for instants; family ,relatives and friends; b) secondary relations dominated by reason, or functional relations of institutions like economic institution, political institution and so forth to achieve certain goals and objectives; 3) fundamental premises, attitudes, values, norms and meaning system at the symbolic level or world view. Those who share a culture also share a world view and speak the same language both in the literal and metaphoric sense.[3] While the term 'inculturation' is of recent origin in the Christian mission theology one cannot deny the historical fact that the church always lived and progressed through mutual interactions between the Word of God and the cultures of the people to whom it was preached. "Culture has moved quite unexpectedly to the centre of people's aspirations and anxieties. It is linked with people's deeper level of identities, their historic memories, ethnic pride, their collective psyche, community ambitions, motivations, shared prejudices and fears."[4] The latest approach prefer the term, inter-cultural relations. Usually cultures create a sense of 'we feeling' and 'they feeling' that tend to divide the common humanity. They are understood and appreciated from two different perspectives: i.e., "the insider's view" and "the outsider's view."

Lessons From Church History

Colonial missionaries, believing in the superiority of the Christian culture and inferiority of non-Christian cultures, uncritically transplanted western churches into Asia and Oceania. The young churches of independent nations are today struggling to remove their western garb and don their local identity. In a fast globalizing world will inculturation of the local church be possible?

Confrontation with Pagan Culture in Goa

The history of Christian mission can be analyzed as a history of cultural and religious confrontations where colonial missionaries arrived with a conquest mentality. Until the arrival of the Portuguese missionaries in Goa in the beginning of the 16th century, Christianity, mostly concentrated in the Southern states of Travencore and Cochin, was marked by

---

3. Eriksen, *What Is Anthropology?*, 27.
4. Menamparambil, "Culture Has Moved," 20.

inculturated or even Hinduized, peaceful co-existence. The Portuguese colonial venture and subsequent missionary encounters should be understood as an extension of the crusades, started in 1095 in order to reclaim and reconquer the Holy Land from the Muslim control, and continued for nearly three centuries, generating an aggressive mentality and sense of superiority complex. The fourteenth century witnessed the creation of the "Military Order of Christ" for Christian soldiers. With the "two-sword' theology, i.e., the temporal order under the King and spiritual order under the Pope, the Portuguese king was made the "Grand master of the Order of Christ" with right and obligation to promote not only the Christian mission but also the Christian culture. King D. Joao ordered the destruction of temples to speed up conversion process. In the colonial era conversions and baptisms, demanded a complete rupture with convert's family, community, society, culture and nation. It demanded new loyalty to the Portuguese ruler and Portuguese culture. For instance, by the order of July 1664 converts were forced to wear western dress. They were forbidden to wear any dress or ornaments traditionally used by Hindus. They had to give up their original names and replace it by Portuguese names. In 1864 the Governor of Goa took the initiative to eradicate local language and replace it by Portuguese language.[5] The historical wounds inflicted on Hindus and the pejorative mentality perpetuated for centuries by the Goan Catholics and their descendants are major obstacles in current endeavors for inculturation.

At his arrival in Madurai in 1606, the twenty eight year old Italian Jesuit Roberto de Nobili was shocked by the great repugnance of high castes for the customs and manners of the *Pirangis*, foreigners. In the backdrop of the sixteenth century mass conversions among the Paravars, Mukkavars and other outcastes the term Pirangi also implied Christianity was the religion of uncultured low castes. Christianity was called "Piranghi Margam," the way of the foreigners. The church was foreign at every level. Eating meat, drinking alcohol, wearing leather shoes and similar habits of the missionaries were strongly detested by Hindus. And mission among them seemed a failure. Aware of the missionary method of adaptation by Matheo Ricci (1552–1610) in China and St. Thomas Christians in Travencore-Cochin, de Nobili dared, in stark contrast to the Portuguese in Goa, to adopt the culture and life style of the Brahmin Sanyasis. He noticed that the most respected men in India were Brahmin intellectuals coupled with their ascetic life style. He studied Sanskrit, the language

---

5. Xavier, *Goa*, 144.

of the Brahmin scholars and vernacular languages like Tamil and Telugu. Mastery of philosophical Hinduism, Saiva Siddhanta, too was part of his master plan to introduced a new chapter in Indian mission. In December 1607, twenty eight months after his arrival in India, he set up an ashram in the Brahmin quarter. His Hindu life style included vegetation food cooked by Brahmin cook and ate meal once a day. He took bath twice a day. He discarded his black cassock and put on saffron robe of Hindu Guru, wooden sandals, sandal paste on the forehead. He carried a water-gourd and a bamboo stick in the hand. He wrote as well as debated with the Hindu Pandits in Sanskrit. He told them he was not a Phiringi, on the contrary, an Italian Brahmin. He wore the sacred thread with a cross. His ascetic way of life made deep impression on his traditional enemies. It was estimated that during his thirty three years of ardent missionary work in Madurai around 1200 upper caste Hindus were baptized. The new converts were encouraged to maintain their Hindu traditions, like tuft of hair on head and sacred thread of twice-born castes and maintain social distance from the Phiringis as well as low caste converts to Christianity.[6]

The new experiment of 'accommodation' generated fierce opposition from other missionaries working with fishermen and low castes. The missionaries were divided into two categories, the *pandaraswamis*, working with the lower strata of people and *Brahmana Sannyasis*, working with the higher castes. de Nobili was accused of accommodating Hindu superstitions and diluting the purity of Christian tradition. In 1612 he was forbidden by his provincial, under pressure from other missionaries, to baptize. The intensity of the controversy can be gauged from the extreme case that some Portuguese ecclesiastical authorities tried and failed to subject him to inquisition. In 1610 the Portuguese visitation of the Jesuits in India reported about "the Scandal of Malabar." A group of theologians sent from Goa, after their investigation, reported that de Nobili's way of life was a negation of Christian faith. He was accused of compromising with paganism. His new converts gave the impression of a new Hindu sect. Therefore, they recommended that the movement should be suppressed under the pain of mortal sin.[7] After a decade of investigations and debates Pope Gregory XV in 1623 permitted de Nobili to continue the experiment, with caution. de Nobili's self defense addressed to Superior general Acquaviva, quoted the model of St. Thomas Christians in Kerala. After three decades of experiments of adaptation he was ordered to retire in 1639, and soon

---

6. Rajamanickam, "Founder of Madurai," 110–19.
7. Anchukandam, *Robert de Nobili*, 34.

due to ill health he became blind. In the meantime due to social pressure and absence of their shepherd many of the new converts returned to the original religion. When he died in 1656 de Nobili had already paid a high price for creating history for the first attempt in adaptation in the Indian mission, mostly at the level of external symbols and creation of a few theological vocabularies. The new experiment of adaptation was carried forward for a few more decades by his ardent admirers, in the midst of controversies, like John de Britto (1647–93) and Constantine J.Beschi (1680–1749), popularly known as Virmamunivar Swami. The "Malabar Rite Controversy," as it was known at that time, ended with its suppression by Pope Benedict XIV in 1744. Unfortunately it turned out to be the failed model of inculturation in India.

The Bible: The Primary Model of Inculturation

Inculturation and Adaptation in the Old Testament

If inculturation is a relevant concern for a living church one must search for its Biblical foundation. The Holy Bible, on the one hand provides certain insight into the process of inculturation and, on the other hand, it seems to be used as a fossilized immutable sacred power block of resistance to change. The Old Testament is the best example of adaptation or inculturation in the sense of borrowing religious ideas and cultural elements from the neighbours of Israel. The people of Israel were nomads and unsettled tribals for a few centuries before they settled down in Palestine (Deut 26:50; Ezk 16:3). In the process of writing various books of the Bible, the human authors, under the inspiration of Divine author, have generously borrowed myths, beliefs, rituals, temple architecture, laws, customs etc from the neighboring cultures and civilizations. Various concepts of God in the Bible—El, Elohim, and Yahweh—were borrowed from other tribes. For example the proto-semitic term denoting god is '*il* which probably means "the powerful one." In Hebrew it survived as '*el*, meaning god. In the Semitic world El meant the principle of divine power or god.[8] That the Hebrews borrowed the existing name of El with modification is clear from the following uses. In the Hebrew Bible, El of your fathers (Gen 49:5) and El of Israel (Ps 68:36) convey the same meaning. Another closely related term for the divinity is Elohim, the majestic plural for God. In the later period Israel named their God by the name Elohim, meaning the most high (Gen 14:18). *El-Shaddai'* (Gen 17:1, 28:3; Ex 6.3) was trans-

---

8. Luke, *Cultural Background*, 4.

Inculturation of the Indian Churches

lated as *Pantokrator*, the Almighty, in the Septuagint translation of the Old Testament, in Alexandria in the third century BC. During the tenth and ninth century BC the Israelites claimed to have their own separate god like other neighbouring tribes and he was named 'Yahweh,' that was revealed to Moses on Mount Horeb (Exod 3:14). Eventually the name Yahweh of Judah appears 6823 times and dominated the Old Testament theology, in contrast to Elohim, the god of the North that occurs only 2,500 times.[9] Only after prolonged conflicts, infidelity and competition with the polytheistic environment "Yahwehism" triumphed.[10] This was also related to the political triumph of the Judah. Until the writing of the book of Deutro-Isaiah, probably after the sixth century BC, the people of Israel had no clear idea of monotheism.

The creation story in the book of Genesis, the Elohist account in chapter one and the Yahwehistic account in chapter two are influenced by the pre-Abrahamic myths from neighbouring cultures. In the Mesopotamian cosmogony creation is portrayed as god Marduk's victory over goddess of Chaos-Tiamat.[11] The Babylonian myth of creation, from the Akkadian religious tradition, is found in the Epic poem Enuma Elis. In this account King Hammurabi (BC 1728–1686) is called by gods Anum and Enlil to promote the welfare of mankind. The concept of Sabbath, meaning rest, was borrowed from the Sumarian calendar where Sapattu or Sabatti, in Akkadian, was celebrated on fourteenth or fifteenth day of the month, on the feast of full moon.[12] While the stories of creation are borrowed, the theological interpretation is radically new: that is, Yahweh alone is supreme God and sun, moon, stars are his creation and they should not be worshipped.[13]

The story of the fall of humankind in Eve and Adam (Gen 3) is centered around the human anxiety about death and immortality. In the *Epic of Gilgamesh* the hero who lost his bosom friend, asks: "Shall not I, I too die like Enkidu?"[14] The Biblical narration is a modified answer to "the human condition defined by the inevitabity of death." "The tree of life and the tree of knowledge" (Gen 2:9) has allusion to "tree of truth and tree of life"

---

9. De Menezes, *God of Israel*, 86–88.
10. Imschoot, "Yahweh," 2614. Eliade, *History*, 161.
11. Eliade, *History*, 70–73, 162–65.
12. Emprayil, "Cultural and Idealogical," 33.
13. Kanjamala, "Inculturation," 169–70.
14. Prichard, *Ancient Near Eastern*, 88.

which were planted at the entrance to heaven in the Babylonian myth.[15] The sexual overtones of the story further indicate its link with fertility cult of in the land of Canaan. The direct and indirect reference to serpent is a reference to phallus and fertility in many cultures, including Canaan and India. In the story of the "fall of the first parents" the serpent tricks Eve, as a serpent in the Akkadian story steals the "plant of life."[16] Finally in the Genesis story the serpent, the devil, is conquered by the crushing of his head.

Reference could be made, without going into details of other borrowed myths and idea. These are the story of the great flood (Gen 6–8), borrowed from the Sumerian flood story (2600 BC); The story of King Sargon (2371–2230 BC) the founder of the Akkadian dynasty in Babylon, and the story of Moses' childhood (Exod 2:36) are very similar.[17] King Hamurabi's Laws (1728–1686 BC) which first shaped the Sumerian and Canaan cultures would later influence the Torah (Exod 20:2–17, Deut 5:6–21). Finally these and other steps of adaptation or inculturation in the O.T. is marked by two models. For Abraham is the symbol of exculturation, leave and go (Gen 12:1). Moses and the founding generation of Israel are symbol of critical assimilation.[18] Finally the Hebrew identity and religion was progressively constructed during a period of nearly 1,500 years by critically assimilating as well as rejecting numerous rich cultural items from a dozen major civilizations to which they were exposed. God has spoken to Israel and through their history to the whole world. On the inculturation of the Old Testament J.Wijngaards observes: "For the Israelites two-third of their religious practices and customs derived from Canaanite origins."[19]

Inculturation and Adaptation in the New Testament.

The culture of Palestine, a small territory situated between two great empires of Egypt and Mesopotamia, was shaped by various political and social forces. Judaism of the second temple period was formed by the Babylonian exile and the Persian rule (539–331 BC), the Hellenistic Culture (331–170) and the Roman domination (63 BC—70 AD). The Hasmonian self rule and the Maccabean revolts were against the Syrian and Roman rulers who

15. Eliade, *History,* 287.
16. Prichard, *Ancient Near Eastern,* 72–98.
17. Emprayil, "Cultural and Ideological," 27.
18. Legrand, *Bible on Culture,* 66.
19. Quoted by Saldhana, *Inculturation,* 20.

Inculturation of the Indian Churches

desecrated the Jerusalem Temple by installing the idol of Zeus and exploiting them with heavy taxes. In the emerging socio-political struggles three rival parties—the Pharisees, the Sadducees and the Essene sect—emerged during the Hasmonian period (134–63 BC) Jesus himself was a Jew who worshipped Yahweh, observed Jewish feasts and customs, a Jewish rabbi who gathered Jewish disciples and reinterpreted the Law and traditions of his religion. He belonged not the Israelite mainstream but to the despised "Galilee of the Gentiles."[20]

Jesus mission began with an encounter with an austere and uncompromising preacher in the desert, John the Baptist, who was announcing the advent of the Kingdom of God for which the Jews were eagerly waiting for centuries: "Repent the Kingdom of God is at hand" (Matt 3:2), said John. His life style and preaching was very close to that of the members of the Qumran community. Jesus was baptized by him and praised him as greatest of all the prophets. (Matt 11:7–19). The recent discovery of the Qumran scrolls near the Dead Sea Caves in 1947 and the Damascus Document in Cairo, north Egypt, shed unprecedented light on the life and activities of Judaism in the inter-testamental period. Three important religious movements that developed within Judaism during the Hasmonian independence (134–62 BC) influenced the preaching of John the Baptist, Jesus as well as his followers. These were the Pharisees' party; the Saducean party struggling for control over Judea and north Galilee; and the Essenes, withdrawing from the world. There is no direct reference to the Essene sect in the New Testament. Yet the study of the newly discovered scrolls reveal informations which were unknown for centuries. What is crucial is the challenges it threw up for fresh insights into the New Testament, particularly the life style of the early Christian community as recorded in the Acts of the Apostles and the Gospel of John.

The Qumran-Essene community originated from a group of 'Pious ones' who vehemently objected to the illegitimate usurpation of both the political and priestly office by Simon Maccabee (1 Macc 14:41–47) because he did not belong to the priestly lineage of Zadok (Macc 7:14–61). Simon Maccabee is identified as the "Wicked Priest" as opposed to the "Teacher of Righteousness." According to Philo, a contemporary of Jesus, the Essenes were introversionists who fled the cities "because of the ungodliness customary among the town dwellers."[21] They called themselves as 'the Remnant of Israel,' 'the True Israel,' and 'the New Covenant,' prob-

---

20. Legrand, *Bible on Culture*, 111–12.
21. Quoted by Lim, *Dead Sea*, 80.

ably with reference to "The new covenant with the house of Israel and the house of Judah" (Jer 31:31). Their 'soteriological exclusion' in the sense the group denies salvation to all the larger community. They withdrew to the desert to lead a common life of prayer, study of the sacred Law and work. The Qumran community organized themselves in groups of twenty-twenty five members and lived in man-made caves at Khirbert Qumran, near the Dead Sea along the north-western shore of the dead sea as well as in northern Egypt.

The Council of the community was consisted of a group of twelve men and three priests, well versed in legal matters, probably symbolizing the twelve tribes of Israel and three levetical clans. The community had a master who functioned as a spiritual leader, who instructed the members on the "precepts of the community" and examined their spiritual development. The Zadokite priests occupied a leading position in the organization because they came from the priestly line appointed to the first temple by King Solomon (1 Kgs 4:2). The agenda of their sessions included, among other things, admission or rejections of novices, whose probationary period was two-three years; the hearing of the infractions; punishment included, penance, and cut in rations or expulsion. Sins against the Torah of Moses were considered very serious. During the probationary period a novice is given a hatchet, loin cloth and a white garment. The community had a Bursar to whom the property and earnings of the novices had to be handed over, upon joining the community.

According to the Jewish teaching those engaged in holy war were forbidden to have sexual intercourse (1 Sam 21:4-5). The Qumran sectarians who believed that they were engaged in eschatological war against the children of darkness were required to maintain celibacy. Pliny the Elder wrote; "The Essenes have put the necessary distance between themselves and the insalubrious shore. They are a people unique of its kind and admirable beyond all others in the whole world without women and renouncing love entirely, without money and having for company only the palm tree."[22] The Essenes believed they were the faithful "remnant" in the eschatological days. "In the final stage ... God has chosen them for an everlasting covenant and all the glory of Adam will be theirs."[23] They believed in predestination that only a few are chosen for the everlasting glory. Only the full members were admitted to the common meal. Before the meal the priest first blesses the bread and the wine. It is quite possible that the meal

---

22. Ibid., 61.
23. Ibid., 103.

Inculturation of the Indian Churches

symbolized the eschatological banquet celebrated in the Day of Yahweh, according to Jewish belief (Isa 25:6). The members stayed awake together a third of each night to read, to study the Law and recite the blessings. During the day they engaged in manual labour. The urban branch of the Essenes, distinct from the celibate monks, were married, worked in business that brought them in contact with other Jews and gentiles. They too followed the Messianic rule: 'the rule of the congregation of Israel in the last days' to follow the institution called, 'The council of the community.' The two types of Essenes were united in doctrine and organization, but with distinct life style.

The Essenes and the Primitive Christian Community

The influence of the Essenes and their religious practices on the primitive Christian Community is a controversial subject. However most scholars today converge on the opinion that the Qumran community and their urban sectarians on the one side and the Jerusalem church and Pauline congregations on the other side, as distinct groups shared a common sectarian matrix. The sectarian matrix includes separation from the majority, organization into groups and religious ideas. Their common heritage was the Old Testament but their choice and interpretations of texts were very dissimilar. For instance, the Jewish apocalyptic literature taught that God would soon intervene in the affairs of the world to overthrow the forces of the Evil One and establish his Kingdom. The Christian core belief was that Jesus was the Son of God; after the resurrection he would return soon for the judgement of the world: "to await his Son from heaven, whom he raised from the dead, Jesus, who delivers us from the coming wrath" (1 Thess 1:9-10; 2 Thess 2:1-12). Later Paul in his letter to the Corinthians, on the celebration of the Lord's Supper, concludes with the anticipation of the second coming: "For as often as you eat this bread and drink the cup you proclaim the death of the Lord until he comes" (1 Cor 11:23-26). They eagerly prayed Maranatha: 'Come Lord Jesus come' (Rev 22: 20). To the disciples who wanted to know when the end will come, Jesus replied. "Truly I tell you, this generation will not pass away before all these things take place" (Matt 24:32-34).

The primitive church, like the Qumran group practiced community of possessions. "For those who owned property or home would sell them, bring the proceeds of the sale, and put them at the feet of apostles and they were distributed to each according to need" (Acts 4:34-35). When Annanias and his wife Sappira who failed to surrender the whole amount from the sale of property fell down and breathed their last, showing the power of Peter. On the question of celibacy, the teaching of Jesus (Matt 19:10–12) is repeated by Paul (1 Cor 7:7–8, 25–31). Both instructions were in the context of the imminent coming of the Kingdom. Paul's instruction both to the married as well as virgins is to be understood in the same eschatological spirit. "I tell you brothers, the time is running out" (1 Cor 7:29). "For the world in its present form is passing away"(v.31). The teaching and organizations of the primitive church portrayed in The Acts of the Apostles has unmistakable affinities to Qumran community because some of the new converts to Jesus' 'way' were already under the influence of the Essene religious culture. The existing religious culture was adapted to explain Jesus' teaching. The Qumran heritage of the Christian community and the New Testament cannot be easily ignored. However substantial differences between the primitive church and the Qumran group are established by the scholars.[24]

Two other most influential sects in Judea at the time of Jesus were those of the Sadducees and the Pharisees. How did Jesus interact with these subcultures is the subject of enquiry here. The name Sadducees, sons of Zadok, became dominant from the days of Ezekiel, "the father of Judaism," in the post-exilic period. They belonged to the privileged priestly class by birth. They were devoted to the strict fulfillment of the written Law, the Torah, with limited stress on oral traditions. According to them the sacred book consists of only five books, Pentateuch, revealed by God to Moses. The Sadducees provided the high priests and their advisers, the majority of the members of Sanhedrin, the supreme council of seventy, the commanders, the treasurer and other functionaries of the temple. Their seat of power was the temple of Jerusalem. The Sadducees were the party of the rich, the landed nobility, and the party of the property owners. To protect their privileges they were accommodative of foreign rulers. They were much influenced by the rational Hellenistic culture.[25] They denied the immortality of the soul because such a concept is not found in the book of the Law. They did not believe in rewards and punishments after death; nor in angels and spirits. He was not comfortable with the culture of Jerusalem, dominated by the political power, religious power and economic power of the upper class Sadducees. Jesus' Galilean culture was in conflict with the aristocratic culture of the Sadducees.

---

24. De Menezes, "Dead Sea," 85–102. Mckenzie, "Qumran Scrolls," in *The Dictionary*, 710–16.

25. Winter, "Sadducees and Pharisees," 51.

Inculturation of the Indian Churches

The second most influential sect at the time of Jesus was the Pharisees, the doctrinal party. The Pharisees called themselves "the separated ones" because they kept away from those who were ritually unclean. Later they were also called rabbis because they taught in the synagogues and were legal experts. In the N.T. scribes are mentioned in conjunction with the Pharisees. As laity they were opposed to the establishment of priests—the Sadducees. At the time of Jesus they and their supporters formed the biggest party of the Jews in the country, but politically less influential because they formed a minority in the supreme council, Sanhedrin. In the Gospel the Pharisees are represented as the most bitter opponents of Jesus. They are mentioned eighty seven times in contrast to fifty seven references to the scribes.[26] In contrast to the Sadducees, the Pharisees, borrowing the Babylonian and Persian ideas, came to believe in the resurrection of the dead and the last judgments of the righteous and sinners. The idea of the Kingdom of God or the universal reign of God was common to the Pharisees and rabbinic Judaism but not part of the thinking of the Sadducees. However the core belief of Judaism, in all sects and parties, was the belief in monotheism.

Jesus rejected the culture of Sadducees and Pharisees. Jesus warns his disciples against the leaven of the Pharisees and Sadducees (Matt 16:1–6; Mark 8:11ff.). His denunciations of the Scribes and the Pharisees include their hypocrisy, legalism, formalism and pride. The "Woes against the Scribes and Pharisees" in the Gospel of Mathew chapter twenty three are well known. There are twenty three accusations against them. These renunciations are better understood if they are situated in the context of the prophetic and rabbinic literature on hypocrisy among the Pharisees. These criticisms further echo the language of the prophets like Jeremiah and numerous woes of Amos against the northern Kingdom (Jer 8:8ff.; Amos 5:7–27; 6:1–14). "Dissent from his native culture stems from his very immersion in this culture. Jesus' prophetic attitude is not that of an outsider. Like Jeremiah and other prophets of Israel Jesus belongs to the culture which he transcends."[27]

The Jesus Movement: A Counter-cultural Movement

The NT presents the Scribes and Pharisees as anti-thesis of Jesus. Jesus the prophet was challenging the old system and announcing a counter culture, a new society or a new model of the Kingdom. A counter—culture is an

26. Legrand, *Bible on Culture*, 91–92.
27. Ibid., 83.

The Future of Christian Mission in India

end result of a sustained and systematic critique aimed at undermining the beliefs, ideas, values, rules and laws, symbolic language and behavior pattern of the dominant class and dominant culture in the society. A counter-culture provides alternative beliefs, thinking, rules, values, and symbols for new life style of the subordinate or oppressed group. Normally the group looks for a leader or a prophet in whom the counter-culture is already radically lived, made visible and attractive. Jesus the prophet from Galilee emerged as a threat to the high priests, the lawyers, the scribes, and the whole establishment of Judaism. Jesus acknowledged the teaching authority of the Scribes (Matt 23:2). Nicodemus, a leading Pharisee visited Jesus at night to listen to him (John 3). Jesus was in the home of a Pharisee named Simon (Luke 7:36–50). Jesus himself was called a rabbi by many and he does not forbid them to do so (Matt 26:25; Mark 10:51; John 26:16). But Jesus was radically different from others because he acted and spoke with authority (Matt 7:28–29; Mark 1:27). Since his teaching challenged and questioned their traditional piety and holiness they were gravely offended as well as humiliated. The Jewish accusations against Jesus included the following: Eating with sinners and out castes (Matt 9:11; Mark 12:13); performing miracles on the Sabbath, which is strongly forbidden (Matt 12:9–3; Luke 13:10–17); not keeping traditional customs and the ritual washing of hands before meals (Matt 15:1ff.; Mark 7:1ff.; Luke 11:37ff.); worst of all claiming equality with God (John 8:13; 5:19–47). Eventually the controversies were sharpened around his mission and his own personality claims like being, "Son of David" (Matt 22:42), and "the Son of God" (John 5:19–49).

In the inter-testamental period (200 BC—100 AD) Judaism longed for the coming of the Kingdom of God, that was understood either as a political, this—worldly kingdom of Israel or an other-worldly kingdom as understood by the Qumran Community.[28] The core of Jesus' alternative vision of the Kingdom of God is declared and taught in his sermon on the mount. The values and norms that he announced included a vision of an alternative society. Jesus gave a new and authoritative reinterpretation of the Law. The Laws given by Moses are modified by radical interpretation of Jesus. He becomes the new Moses in his Sermon on the Mount (Matt 5–7). For example: "You have heard it said, 'you shall not commit murder,' but I say to you, 'whoever is angry with your brother is liable to judgement." He continues to reinterpret the commandment on adultery and divorce. He abolished the prescriptions of ritual uncleanliness (Mark 7:1–23). He

---

28. Fullenbach, *Kingdom*, 33–34.

Inculturation of the Indian Churches

simplified hundreds of old Jewish rules and commandments into two laws of love (Matt 22:34-40; Mark 12:28-31). He reduced numerous Jewish prayers into a simple formula of "Our Father" (Matt 6:9-13; Luke 2-11).[29] Jesus severely criticized and rejected the value systems and life styles of the two dominant cultural groups in Israel. Equally he rejected the political interpretation of the advent of the Kingdom, to be established by violent methods of the fundamentalist Zealots, the contemporaries of Jesus.[30] They fought for decades with a radical zeal for the God of Israel, culminating in the Roman military operation in AD 66-73. Social unrests and political violence were regular features of the time of Jesus' mission and ministry. "Jesus movement grew in this atmosphere of social restlessness."[31] Jesus did not approve or support the political violence of the Zealots. He deliberately opted and preached the Kingdom of Love and non-violence, until his death on the cross (Luke 7:27-36; Luke 23:34). And initially the Jesus movement evolved into a counter-cultural community. Gradually from the fourth century it grew into a mighty Roman institution.

Six Ritual Families in the Catholic Church

In the incarnation the Word became flesh in a concrete culture, the Jewish culture. And the church, the body of Christ, following the same logic, should take flesh in different cultures of the world. The development of various local churches with very distinct and different characteristics is the proof that the "Word of God" planted in different cultural soils drew various nourishing cultural elements and produced different and dissimilar fruits. Let us examine the development of liturgical practices in the early centuries. The earliest liturgical practices were adopted from the traditions of late Judaism from which the first followers of Jesus emerged. But these would eventually modify to suit the cultural context and demands of their ever expanding new members. The origin, progress and existence of six Ritual families and twenty two autonomous churches or churches *sui juris* within the Catholic church provides the compelling proof of adaptation and inculturation in the early church as well as justification for rich pluralism. In the Eastern Rites there are five liturgical families, with twenty one autonomous churches—all of them Catholic. The names of these churches and the approximate number of Catholics belonging to each church are:

29. Wijngaards, *Background*, 263-72.
30. Baigent and Richard, *Dead Sea*, 298-99.
31. Legrand, *Bible on Culture*, 89.

THE FUTURE OF CHRISTIAN MISSION IN INDIA

I. *Alexandrian Family:* (1) The Coptic Catholic Church (243,000); (2) The Ethiopian Catholic Church(197,000)

II. *Antiochean Family:* (3)The Syrian Catholic Church (124,000); (4) The Maronite Catholic Church (3,107,000) (5) The Syro-Malankara Catholic Church or the West Syrian church (405,000)

III. *Armenian Family:* (6) The Armenian Catholic Church (369,000);

IV. *The Assyrian Family*: (7) The Chaldean Catholic Church (383,000); (8) The Syro-Malabar Catholic Church (or the East Syrian) (3,753,000);

V. *Byzantine Family* or *Greek Family:* (9) Belarusan, with no hierarchy (10,000); (10) The Bulgarian Catholic Church (10,000); (11) The Greek Catholic Church (2345); (12) The Hungarian Catholic Church (269,000); (13) The Italo-Albanian Catholic Church (61,000); (14) The Melkite Catholic Church (1,341,000); (15) The Romanian Catholic Church (764,000); (16) The Ruthenian Catholic Church (598,000); (17) The Slovak Catholic Church (226,000); (18) The Ukranian Catholic Church (7,322,000); (19) Krizevei (75,000); (20) Albanian: no parish; a few Catholics under Latin rite. (21) The Russian Byzantine Catholic Community in the Diasporas (3500). In addition to these thirteen Catholic Greek Churches thirty Orthodox Churches of the Greek family are dispersed throughout the world.

VI. *Latin Church* (22) The Roman Catholic Church (1.147 billion).[32]

The Indian Catholic churches are constituted of the Latin Church, the largest in number; the Syro-Malankara church, belonging to the Antiochean Family, the smallest in number and the Syro-Malabar church belonging to the East Syrian or Chaldean Family. The Syro-Malabar church is second largest Eastern Catholic Church, after the Ukrainian church. How did twenty two autonomous churches of sui juris evolve in the course of history is not within the scope of this investigation. What is more important is to realize and acknowledge that these beautiful pluralities were neither designed by Jesus nor planned by the Apostles of Jesus Christ. The dynamic interactions between the believing and worshipping communities with the local cultures produced them, of course, under the authority of the local elders or bishops. The role of the Roman authority in these developments was very minimal.[33]

32. Roberson, *Eastern Churches*, 161–215.
33. Chediath, "Eastern Christian," 51–53.

Inculturation of the Indian Churches

Alois Pieris identify combinations of four strands of philosophy, religious practices and cultures in the Christianization of Europe. They reflect the paradigms of indigenization in the West.

- The Latin model: incarnation of a non-Christian *culture*.
- The Greek model: assimilation of Greek *philosophy*.
- The North European model: accommodation to a non-Christian *religiousness*.
- The Monastic model: participation in a non-Christian *Spirituality*.[34]

The colonial missionaries to Asia and Africa unfortunately transplanted the Western model, without being sensitive to new cultures and people. The new churches are now struggling to allow the local church to grow in the soil of its culture. Are the Western theologies and liturgies normative for the whole world? Is the creativity of the young churches stifled by the Western model? "The various churches established in diverse places by the apostles and their successors have in the course of time coalesced into several groups . . . which preserving the unity of faith, enjoy their own discipline, their own liturgy and their own theological and spiritual heritage" (S.C.no. 23). However due to historical reasons many Eastern Catholic churches lost their heritage. The St. Thomas church in India was outside the Caesaro-Papist control until the arrival of the Latin domination from 1599–1896.[35] The chequered history of liturgical inculturation in the past in twenty two catholic churches can advocate that there is no reason why the dynamic process should not be carried on in the Indian church or elsewhere. The tendency of centralization and uniformity was a later development that lead to the gradual loss of relevance to the socio-cultural context. The lessons for inculturation today is to follow the wisdom of liturgical development from below, namely the local churches.

Four Models of Inculturation in India

Five hundred years of colonial mission in India, starting with the Padroado mission in Goa and continued with the Propaganda mission, was characterized by two dominant features: the destruction of cultures of the new converts, with minor exception, and the imposition of western culture on the new churches. The missionaries, with a few exceptions like de Nobili,

---

34. Quoted by Ariarajah, "Interreligious Dialogue," 69.
35. Koodapuzha, "Mission of St. Thomas," 131–48.

with the dominant mentality of the period, despised local cultures. In the post—colonial era new nations in Africa, Asia and Oceania began their struggle to rediscover their identity, not only politically but also culturally. Unfortunately, the Vatican Council has made no reference to tribal cultures, among which "the great missionary century" was successful. Liturgy—the public worship of the Christian community—is the core of the Christian life. In the liturgical renewal process the fundamental concern is now to make the Eucharist more meaningful through devout and active participation of the faithful. The Constitution of the Sacred Liturgy exhorts that the liturgy be adapted to the spiritual adornments, tradition and genius of different races and people, (SC 37–40). The struggles of the Indian Catholic church to creatively respond to the call of the council are now examined.

Liturgical Inculturation

With the promulgation of the Conciliar Document, "The Constitution on Sacred Liturgy" liturgical adaptation was considered urgent, because it seriously touches the identity of the church both in terms of her mystery as well as in terms of the world in which it lives and works (SC.7). The first General Body Meeting of the Catholic Bishops Conference of India in Delhi, in October 1966, provided broad guide lines for inculturation. "All liturgical adaptations must be based on the norms of the Constitution of Sacred Liturgy (SC 37–40)." The same meeting appointed late Fr. D. S. Amalorpavadass (1932–1990) as the founder—director of National Biblical, Catechetical, and Liturgical Centre (NBCLC), Bangalore, of which he took charge in February 1967. In the following decade he, together with many dynamic collaborators, played a very crucial role in liturgical inculturation in India.[36] The second All India Liturgical meeting, Bangalore, on January 27–31, 1969, prepared a long term plan for liturgical inculturation, consisting of four phases. (1) creating an Indian atmosphere through music, postures, decoration, objects and other elements of worship; (2) translation of liturgical rites into vernaculars and original composition of new texts; (3) use of scriptures of other religions; (4) compose a new Indian Anaphora.[37]

The first step towards inculturation was the introduction of twelve external elements for creating an Indian atmosphere of worship. With the recommendation of the Indian Bishops, fifty one Bishops out of seventy

36. Leeuwen, *Fully Indian*, 12.
37. Ibid., 70.

Inculturation of the Indian Churches

one, in March 1969 the Sacred Congregation for Divine Worship gave the approval on April 25, 1969, with the provision that it was left to the discretion of the Regional Council of Bishops and the local ordinaries to implement them.[38] The twelve items are, squatting posture, instead of standing; anjali hasta and Panchanga Pranam as forms of reverence; arati as form of welcome to the main celebrant; use of a shawl instead of the traditional liturgical vestaments; tray to keep the offering; oil lamps instead of candles; a simple incense bowl; touching objects to one's forehead instead of kissing them; Anjali hasta to share peace; spontaneous prayer of the faithful and maha arati at the doxology.[39]

AN ORDER OF MASS FOR INDIA: AN INDIAN ANAPHORA

Spurred by the post—Vatican enthusiasm for inculturation in the context of the three ritual churches in India, creation of "a basically common liturgy of the church in India," using Indian cultural and religious traditions and elements, was recommended.[40] In 1968, the Congregation for Sacred Liturgy published three new Anaphoras, in addition to the existing Roman Canon. "The Second All India Liturgical Meeting in January 1969 constituted a committee to compose a new Indian Anaphora, a basically common liturgy of the church in India." "The All India Seminar" (1969), in the light of liturgical renewal recommended by SC, exhorted to live an Indian way of life, spirituality and liturgy. The preparation for an Indian Anaphora was initiated in 1968. Passing through different stages of modifications it was finally approved by the CBCI meeting in Madras, in April 1972, receiving sixty votes out of eighty bishops present. The Indian anaphora is characterized by copious use of Indian objects and symbols, in addition to the use of vernacular language, as well as Sanskrit.[41] The third All India liturgical meeting in Bangalore on 28th November—4th December 1971, taking note of difficulties and differences of three Indian Rites, discussed how to respect and preserve their identity. The respective

---

38. Amalorpavadass, *Towards Indigenization*, 31.

39. *The Roman Missal* (2004), Bangalore, lxxv, published by the National Biblical Catechetical and Liturgical Centre, Bangalore, for the Commission for Christian Life (Catholic Bishops' Conference of India). Permission for the use of the twelve items mentioned on pages lxxv-vi. was granted by A. Bugnini, Secretary of the Sacred Liturgy, Vatican City, on April 25, 1969.

40. Gracias, *All India Seminar*, 327.

41. For the full text, see Amalorpavadass, *New order*, 20–53. The Indians anaphora is long and is for solemn occasions. A short version is prepared for the daily Eucharistic celebration.

rites were responsible for creating the new anaphora for different regions, on the principle that liturgy must evolve from below and answer the needs of the local people.

The general CBCI meeting held in Chennai on April 6–14, 1972 voted on the new text: but failed to secure the required majority. In the mean time serious objections were raised: Indian culture is Hindu culture and Indianization of liturgy amounts to Hinduisation. While many educated Hindus are discarding Indian culture and following Western culture, at least in different degrees, why should the Christians get converted to Hindu culture?[42] Objections and fears of the suppression of the existing three individual Rites and their identities were also weighty reasons. These were forwarded to Rome. The revised Indian Anaphora was sent to Rome with objections. Cardinal Knox, the prefect of the Sacred Congregation of Divine worship, in October 1975, forbade the use of the Indian Anaphora, and the reading from the Non-Biblical Scriptures in the liturgy.[43]

The Latin Bishops Conference held in Poona in 1992, approved the Indian Eucharistic prayer, with further modifications, by an overwhelming majority, ninety four out of ninety seven. Again it failed to get the Vatican approval.[44] To put it mildly, it is the rejection of the authority of Bishops of the local church established by the Second Vatican Council and an insult to the wisdom and prudence of Indian bishops and theologians. Sadly an inculturation process controlled from the top, it seems, has little future. All the hard work and sincere efforts of NBCLC and a few other regional centres for inculturation or adaptation of the Indian liturgy ended in failure and frustration. The Indian anaphora is currently used, periodically, in a few religious houses.[45] In contrast it should be noted that the emerging new churches and sects, freed from highly centralized control, are becoming better inculturated.

With regard to the Syrian Church, Pope Pius XI in 1934 initiated a process of liturgical reform to restore the oriental nature of heavily Latinized Syro-Malabar rite. A revised Eucharistic liturgy, drawing on the original East Syrian Sources, was approved by Pius XII in 1962. However there was strong resistance to this reform despite the reaffirmation of the 1962 rite by the Oriental Congregation in 1985. In 1998 Pope John Paul II gave the Syro-Malabar bishops full authority in liturgical matters in an

42. Amalorpavadass, *Towards Indigenization*, 55.
43. Leeuwen, *Fully Indian*, 79.
44. Thecknath, "Inculturation in India," 297.
45. Kanjamala, *Order of the Mass*.

Inculturation of the Indian Churches

effort to facilitate a resolution of the dispute between the traditionalists and modernists.[46] The traditionalists insist on the Chaldeanisation of the liturgy; on the contrary the progressive branch insist on the renewal of liturgy, responding to the cultural situation today. The status quo continues. Thus no progress has been achieved.[47] The Indian Mass prepared for the Latin Rite was adapted by the Syro-Malabar church with minor modifications in a few dioceses outside Kerala. "The order of the Holy mass of the Syro-Malabar church" was submitted to the Congregation for the Eastern Church for approval in October 1981. After the examination the Congregation in March 1983 replied that there was no "Indianization" but Latinization.[48] Further revisions in 1985, 1988, and 1996 ended with similar fate.

Ashram Model of Inculturation

Ashram tradition and life style in India—Jain, Buddhist, Hindu, and Sufi—has a history of over two millennia, centuries before the genesis of Catholic monastic system in Europe. Prominent modern Indian leaders like Mahatma Gandhi, Debendranath Tagore, Vinobha Bhave, Aurobind Gosh, Narayana Guru and many others established their own ashrams, to serve as a spiritual source of their life and activities. Unfortunately "the history of the church in India has no monastic tradition except for the de Nobili's experiment."[49] "All India Seminar. Church in India Today" (1969) recommended the establishment of ashrams to preserve and promote the mystical traditions of Christianity as well as Hinduism.[50] In April 1976 the CBCI standing committee mandated the Liturgical Committee to animate and promote the ashram movement. An All India Consultation in NBCLC, Bangalore, on June 7–11, 1978, attended by over 100 ashramites, describe:

> An ashram may be called a place of an intense and sustained spiritual quest, centered around a Guru, man or woman, recognized by others as a person of deep spiritual experience. In an ashram primacy is given to this relentless quest through sadhanas or specifically Indian practices. It is a place where above all people can experience God and live in an ever deepening

46. Roberson, *Eastern Churches*, 174.
47. Kurikosa, "Straight from the Heart," 12.
48. Pallath, "Syro-Malabar Church," 162.
49. Van Bergen, "Contemporary Christian," 177.
50. Gracias, *All India Seminar*, 346.

awareness of its presence. This is fostered by renunciation and detachment and an atmosphere of silence, peace and joy." Guru means one who removes (ru) darkness (gu) and leads to light. The Real Guru, spiritual guide, is the Antaryamin, the indwelling Spirit, Atman. The Sadhanas which one exercises are means to die to lower self and gradually find the true Self, the Atman.[51]

The Protestant missionaries were the pioneers of Christian ashrams in modern time. Bharat Ashram established by K. C. Sen near Calcutta in 1872, could be regarded as the first ashram, inspired by Jesus Christ as well as Sri Ramakrishna.[52] Sadhu Sunder Singh (1889–1921), educated in a missionary school, at Ludhiana, Punjab, burned the Bible, in revolt against Christian missionaries. In his restless he was contemplating to commit suicide. One night according to his testimony, Christ appeared to him and his heart was filled with joy and peace. Sunder Singh was baptized in Simla in the following year. For eight months he joined St. John's Anglican Divinity School. He refused to be bound by any church. He cut his hair: distributed his possessions to the poor; donned saffron rob. He wandered at the foot of the Himalayas. He was a wandering preacher of Jesus all over India. He made twenty trips to Tibet, which was closed to missionary activity. He was called the "apostle of bleeding feet." In 1920 he traveled to Britain, the USA and other European countries and challenged their materialistic out look. His interpretation of Jesus Christ was mystical. He wrote seven books and many articles on various subjects like Life of Jesus, prayer, meditation, spirituality, and other literary works based on his many visions. Sadhu Sunder Singh was an extraordinary and challenging Indian embodiment of the Gospel of Jesus Christ in the mystical tradition of India. "The ashram movement which in many ways is trying to acclimatize the Gospel in India, may be held to have arisen under the inspiration of Sadhu's example," opines Stephen Neill.[53] "If Brahmabandhav was a Christian Vivekananda, Sundar Singh might be called a Christian Ramakrishna." observes Baago.[54] "He became a bridge between Indian religion and culture on the one hand and the Christian evangelical faith and practice on the other by becoming a Christian sadhu."[55]

---

51. Vandanamataji, "Experiencing," 5.
52. Aleaz, "Keshub Chandra," 438–39.
53. Neill, *History*, 483.
54. Baago, *Pioneers*, 50.
55. Prakash, "Contributions of," 112.

Inculturation of the Indian Churches

N. V. Tilak (1862–1919), a Chitpavan Brahmin, born in the Konkan region of Maharashtra, captured by the personality of Jesus, became a Christian, in 1895 after his initial objection to Christian mission, and was ordained a minister of the Presbyterian Church. He was also ostracized by his wife and family members. He was deeply influenced by the Devotional Hinduism of Maharashtrian Hindu Saints like Namdev, Tukaram and Dyaneshwar. He wrote hundreds of Christian Marathi devotional hymns; sung them with Indian musical instruments. He became a Christian Sannyasi. He founded a Christian ashram in Satara in 1917 and developed the idea of Darbar of God where people of all religions come together as children of God. He referred to Jesus as the Guru, the Lord of Yoga and the head of the ashram. He addressed God as Father and Mother. His most reputed literary work is *Kristyan*, the story of Christ set in the poetic form of *Ramayana*, comparable to the seventeenth century *Kristhapuran* by Father Thomas Stephens.[56]

The Protestant Ashram, 'Christa Seva Sangh,' allied itself with M. K. Gandhi, was founded in Miri in Ahmednagar district, Maharashtra, in 1922 by Rev. J. Winslow, SPG missionary. In line with a few Protestant ashrams, for example the Kristhukulla Ashram, Thirupathur in north Arcot district, Tamil Nadu, 1921, it intended to respond to two modern Indian challenges: one, to give the Indian Church an Indian image; two, to become more sensitive to problems of rural poor. The society was determined by its engagement in India which naturally resulted in assuming simple Indian way of life. The material used for clothing had to come from Khadi industry, like in the Gandhian ashrams. The orange or saffron color referred to the Indian ideal of asceticism. The spirituality of the ashram is a blend of Indian bhakti marga and the Franciscan spirituality of poverty. St. Francis of Assisi was their patron. The ashram was shifted to Poona in 1928 and rechristened, Christa Prema Seva Ashram, Society of the Service of Christ's Charity. What is very unique about Christa Prema Seva Ashram is its ecumenical experiment headed by nuns, well versed in the Hindu philosophy and the ashram spirituality. A good number of Western seekers of Indian religious experience too visit the ashram.[57]

After the failed attempt of Robert de Nobili, one of the earliest attempts to introduce ashram life in modern India was that of a Bengali Brahmin convert, Bhavan Charan Banerjee. At his baptism in 1891 he took the name Theophilus. In 1894 became a Catholic Sannyasin with the name

---

56. Parkhe, "Poet Missionary," 65–72.
57. Taylor, "From Khadi to Kavi," 21–23.

The Future of Christian Mission in India

Brahmabandhu Upadhyaya.[58] Bishop Charles Felix Pelvat of Nagpur gave him the permission to start a Christian ashram, on the bank of the river Narmada, near Jabalpur. Soon the Bishop withdrew the permission owing to the pressure of Msgr. Ladislavo Zaleski, Apostolic delegate of India."[59] "In religion he was a devote Catholic, a Sannyasin, a pioneer who tried to establish an Indian monastery, who worked for an Indian theology—. It may not be too much to call him the Father of Indian Catholic theology."[60] With his untimely death in 1907 his dreams failed temporarily.

"Considered the mother house of the ashrams of Catholic initiative" Shanativanam was founded in Kulittalai, Tamil Nadu, on the bank of the holy river Kaveri by two French priests in 1950. Jules Monchain arrived in Thiruchirappally in 1939, from France, at the age of forty four, with a deep interest in Indian contemplative tradition and took the name Swami Anandam. And Henri Le Saux, a Benedictine monk, who was in contact with Monchain, came to India in 1948, at the age of 38. He changed his name to become Swami Abishiktanda. They were "responding to the call of Brahmabandhav Upadhyaya to the church of India to be truly Indian and abandon its western clothing," opines by Lipner.[61] The rule of St. Benedict became its starting point. The name "hermit of Sachidananda" spells out their objective. Like St. Benedict they took peace as their motto-Shanti Vanam. The vegetarian diet, sitting on the floor, and the orange robe became part of the life style. They adapted to the Hindu tradition of training, hospitality, poverty, asceticism, and a life of prayer. In 1957 Jules died and Abhshiktananda, influenced by the ideal envisaged by Upadhyaya and the example of de Nobili, emerged as a wandering mendicant. He argued that the Benedictine model of monastic stability is not suited to India, where the wandering renouncer is closer to the Indian mentality. For he believed the homeless existence and life of a wanderer will show that the church is not merely an institution. He moved into the Himalayas. His books, articles, above all his presence at "Church in India Seminar" in 1969 significantly influenced the recent vision for founding catholic ashrams. Bede Griffiths, an Anglican convert to Catholicism and later a Benedictine monk in England, came to India in 1955, at the age of forty nine. His life and literary output in the following four decades transformed Shanativanam into an international ashram.[62] Vandana

58. Lipner, *Brahmabandhab*, 199–201.
59. Ibid, 41. For details, see chapter 2 above.
60. Quoted by Mookenthottam, *Indian Theological*, 42.
61. Lipner, *Brahmabandhab*, 205.
62. Griffiths, "Christian Monastic Life," 132–33.

Inculturation of the Indian Churches

Mathaji, the founder of Jeevan Dhara Ashram in Rishikesh, at the foot of the Himalayas, observes: Bede Griffith's several theologico-spiritual books show a marriage between the Christian West and the Hindu India.[63]

The confluence of three spiritual traditions—Hindu, the Syrian and the Latin—is the unique feature of Kurisumala ashram in Kerala. Its history is traced back to the following traditions. The Order of the Imitation of Christ was founded in 1919 by a Jacobite Priest named Ivanios of the Malankara Orthodox Syrian Church in Serampore, following the rule of St. Basil of Caesarea, father of Eastern Orthodox Monasticism. Later as a Bishop, in 1930 he joined the Catholic Church, with many members of the Syro-Malankara church. His Bethany Ashram in Perunad, Kottayam, Kerala, made a synthesis of the monastic tradition of St. Basil, the Hindu ashram tradition as well as the Syro-Malankara Liturgical tradition. Serving the poor, particularly those from the lower castes, became an integral part of the ashram.[64] After his initial short stay in Santivanam, Fr. Francis Mahieu of the Order of Cistercians of the Strict Observance and Fr. Bede Griffiths of the Order of St. Benedict realized that the Syrian church had a rich monastic tradition and offered better possibilities for contemplative life. This conclusion was also influenced by Mar Ivanios. At the invitation of the Bishop of Tiruvalla, they founded Kurisumala Ashram in March 1958, synthesising three spiritual traditions.[65] In the ashram customs of dress, food and prayer etc. are borrowed from the Hindu traditions. Following the Sarvodaya ideal of Mahatma Gandhi, influenced by the Trapist monks in Durban, South Africa, it has also taken up work of agricultural uplift and cattle breeding. In order to collect and adapt the old monastic prayer of everyday of the Liturgical year, Francis, together with Jesuit church historian E. R. Hambye, traveled to Mossal, Iraq, to acquire and translate from Syriac into English the monastic Syriac prayer of Penqitho. *"Book of common Prayer: Prayer with the Harp of the Spirit"* were published in a four volumes, starting in 1980.[66] Bound by vows of stability, in addition to the observance of three religious vows the monks strive to follow the Cistercian spiritual heritage, started at Citeaux, France, by St. Bernard. "The Latin church has spread all over India in the last few centuries but it has shown little capacity to adapt itself to the traditions and customs of the Indian people. On the other hand the Syrian church has been in existence in India since at least the fourth century and has

---

63. Vandana Mataji, "Ashram Movement," 191.
64. Bergen, "Contemporary Christian," 184.
65. Francis, "Kurisumala Ashram," 22.
66. Mahieu, "Integrating the East," 36–37.

The Future of Christian Mission in India

shown considerable capacity for adaptation to Indian customs though, in modern times, it has been very much influenced by the Latin church, unfortunately."[67]

On two major trends among Christian ashrams, R. W. Taylor observes: There are among the protestants more 'Khadi' ashrams, oriented to social service while the Catholic ashrams tended to 'Kavi', geared more to Sannyasa and contemplation.[68] The growth of Catholic ashrams in the past half a century is encouraging. But the number of inmates will always remain small because the challenges of asceticism and monasticism, in its original vision are too demanding.

Proclamation of the Gospel in Indian Style

Born in Silesia, in February 1904, George Proksch SVD reached his mission destination, Indore, central India, in 1933, and was shocked by the 'foreign image' of the Church and the style of proclamation Ad Gentes. "The act of transmitting the message of Christ was conspicuously foreign in comparison to how traditional Hindu teachers and preaches carried their own message across," he wrote. This conviction was further reinforced by his personal encounter with Mahatma Gandhi, in Indore, in 1935. Gandhi's ascetical demeanor and image of a man of God was more eloquent than his political speech and unimpressive appearance.[69] Study of Sanskrit in Maharaja Sanskrit College in Mysore and Indian classical music in Lucknow in the following years qualified him to venture into proclamation of the Gospel in Indian style.

Being appointed to Bandra, Bombay, in 1946 he taught Hindi and Indian music, instead of Latin and Gregorian music that was in vogue, along with his pastoral responsibilities. In 1949, he established the Hindi-Sanskrit Sangam, with the collaboration of a few friends in Bombay to promote Indian culture. Later in 1955 he founded an ashram on a hillock in Andheri, Bombay, and took an Indian name, Guru Gyan Prakash. Soon a troupe of singers and dancers were gathered, with adequate technical and religious training, to present Jesus message of love and service to all, particularly the poor and the marginalized, as an unique *sadhana* to attain *moksha*. The first major opportunity to compose and present the Christian message in Indian art forms of music, dance and drama came on the occasion of the National Marian Congress in Bombay, in 1954. The

---

67. Griffiths, "Christian Monastic Life," 123.
68. Taylor, "From Khadi to Kavi," 19–20.
69. Proksch, "Gyan Prakash," 141.

Inculturation of the Indian Churches

folk as well as the classical dances and Hindustani ragas were melodiously blended in staging the Marian themes. His SVD superiors in India, all of them foreigners, initially failed to appreciate his unorthodox venture but Valerian Cardinal Gracias of Bombay became his ecclesiastical patron, ushering in a breakthrough. Guru Gyan Prakash created history when his ballet, "Eucharist and Charity" with Indian dancers, musicians and singers was performed in front of the Holy Eucharist, at the thirty seventh International Eucharistic Congress in Munich, Germany in 1960. In the pre-Vatican conservative climate of Germany, the reactions of 300,000 spectators ranged from extreme shock to spell-bound admiration.

But the finest hour of his dream of proclaiming the Gospel of Jesus in Indian style arrived when he staged *Anutam Prem*, No greater love, a ballet, at the International Eucharistic Congress in Bombay in 1964, in the presence of Pope Paul VI and around 50,000 spectators, Christian and non-Christian, with an impressive cast of 300 dancers, a choir of 1,000 singers and an orchestra of 100 musicians, trained by him. It created an unprecedented and entrancing experience and impact. While the majority of Indian Catholics and their clerical leaders found it very difficult to appreciate the new experiment, accusing him of Hinduisation of the Christian message, his patron Valerian Cardinal Gracias of Bombay was unambiguous in his words of appreciation: "perhaps Indians will lend a ready ear to the message of Christ if it is presented in the form that has for ages been the favourite means of expressing religious thoughts and sentiments."[70]

The new prophet of inculturation, long before the new vocabulary appeared in the theological and liturgical parlance, travelled extensively with his troupe and performed in India and abroad to create a new awareness that an Indian model of proclamation of the Gospel, in contrast to the western model, was possible. He was a prolific writer and composer in Hindi, the national language. Among his forty books are plays, dramas, musical compositions, translation of the book of Psalms with the blending of Indian and Western musical notations. *Mahakavya Isayana*, written after the model of the Hindu religious epic, is a classic, like *Kristayan*, in Marathi by N. V. Tilak. In him the East and the West were harmoniously blended. If today the idea of inculturation is more or less accepted without much resistance and controversy it is the fruit of the vision and struggle of a pioneer like Guru Gyan Prakash who was born in Germany a little more than a century ago and made India his home.

70. Quoted by Porksch, "Christ in Indian," 49–51.

The Future of Christian Mission in India

Popular Devotional Model of Inculturation

In spite of the good will and hard work of a small number of pioneers and experimental centres, inculturation efforts of the last four decades have nearly failed. "It must be sadly confessed that we have not done much in these two spheres, Dialogue and Inculturation. Not because we have not tried; we have not succeeded in any significant way" observed, Emeritus Simon Cardinal Pimenta of Bombay.[71] There was lack of unity among the bishops, priests and laity of the three liturgical Rites. This situation favored the Roman authority.[72] The Indian anaphora was characterized by the Sanskritic culture, replacing one dead language with another dead language. An objection is being raised that the Sanskrit culture is the culture of the oppressor in the caste hierarchy. It almost ignored the sub-cultural identities of the two-third of the Indian Church, i.e., dalits and the tribals. Is there a way out of the dilemma? Popular inculturation seems to offer a partial solution. The term 'popular' is contrasted with the 'elitistic.' In the Western church popular devotions and practices began to increase when the liturgy was in Latin, the language of the elite, and was highly structured and clergy centred. Illiterate common people began to satisfy their hunger for God, by taking recourse to rituals and places that were within their sense of the sacred and their reach. "It refers to the spontaneous and free action of the people which have no formal and structural shape in comparison to the well defined and structured performance of the elite in the society."[73]

With enthusiasm for liturgical renewal after the Second Vatican Council, totally dominated by the modern Western rational culture, traditional popular religious practices were discouraged. The liturgical prayers in general are abstract, other-worldly and far removed the immediate worries and concerns of the laity. In contrast, popular expressions of religious feeling in a particular socio-cultural context is symbolic and expressive, spontaneous and creative, festive and dramatic, immediate and mundane. While the official liturgy is celebrant-centred, and not people centred; more static than dynamic, popular devotions encourage spontaneity and emotionalism through body movements, clapping, singing, dancing, even crying and weeping. The common people, with little specialized religious education, are keen to find meaning of the mundane realities of life in celebrations of rites of passage like birth, puberty, marriage; crisis situations

---

71. Pimenta, *Memoirs*, 117.
72. Saldhana, *Inculturation*, 99.
73. Valentine, "Popular Devotion," 191.

Inculturation of the Indian Churches

like sickness, death, funeral; anxieties about infertility, draught, failure of crops, unemployment and so forth, through popular rituals, blessings, pilgrimages to shrines, devotions and novenas to the Blessed Virgin Mary and Saints, in the company of relatives and close friends, in contrast to the anonymity of large parish liturgy. Most of these popular practices are closely rooted in the Indian culture or Hindu religious ceremonies. Pilgrimages to holy places and fasting on special occasions and seasons are not exclusive to any particular religion. The inter-religious boundaries that are rigidly maintained in official liturgy of the church almost melt away in popular celebrations. It is the real bhakti marga of India. It is significant to recall that Jesus did not condemn popular preachers and healers of Galilee in contrast to his condemnation of Scribes and Pharisees. The Jewish religiosity of Galilee was more popular in character than that of the strict sects. It had a liberating impact on common people.

It is not infrequently observed, particularly in India and other developing countries, that there is a huge gap between the sophisticated theology of the official church and the popular beliefs and religious aspirations of the man and woman on the street. In a similar manner the highly structured formal liturgical celebrations of the church often fail to satisfy and answer the religious hunger and expectations of the laity, each with his or her own joys, and sorrows, anxieties, problems and frustrations of daily life. The popular religious rituals and celebrations in local idioms and cultures in a very personal and immediate context bridge the gulf between these two distant poles. The persistence of numerous religious practices, even some of those which are officially objected or even forbidden, fulfils a definite function with in the broad sphere of the religious world. And finally it offers the laity an opportunity to play central role, replacing the official role of the clergy. Popular devotions, with its strength and weakness, constitute the dominant spirituality of common folk.

With over a quarter of a century of life and experience in NBCLC, Bangalore, one of its former directors concludes: "Anything short of an inculturation from below will not become a movement of the church in India. Any inculturation that is not liberative of those who are oppressed and excluded will not pass the test of being fully Christian. Any inculturation worth our efforts should at the same time be an evangelization of cultures. An inculturation that is not dialogical will not take root in India. The risk of error should not constitute a valid obstacle for inculturating the Gospel."[74] Unfortunately the instruction of the *Propaganda*

---

74. Thekkanatt, "Inculturation in India," 302.

Fide (1659) had little consequence on colonial missionaries who imported their religious cultures into India. "For what is more absurd than to introduce France, Spain, Italy or any other part of Europe in to China."[75] And the dilemma continues.

Inculturation: A Vicious Circle

Contemporary globalization process, a form of new colonialism, unobtrusively tend to impose the modern western culture on other cultures, through numerous means, especially through mass media and marketing of western goods. Pope John Paul II identified the emerging global culture as the new Areopagus for missionaries (RM 37). The emerging phenomena of migration of peoples, particularly to towns and cities of the country or to developed nations, delinks oneself from one's own home territory; separates from family, kinship and ethnic circle; dissociates from traditional religio-cultural environment; minimizes the importance of mother tongue and increases the use of English. To those who try to understand and appreciate deep family ties, kinship relations and cultural bonds, something very characteristic of Indian culture the stressful socio-psychological consequences of migration become rather evident. The migrants pass through certain degree of disorientation, chaos, meaninglessness or anomie. In the cultural encounters the dormant, unexamined cultural and Christian identity suddenly awakes. Identity implies a sense of belonging and loyalty to the primary group with clear boundary. Unprecedented challenges to identity tend to generate identity crisis. In the new environment issues of culture and boundary crossing raise unprecedented questions. In the background of urban loneliness, anonymity, spiritual and emotional exhaustion, the parish or similar communities usually provide a comfortable framework for living the life meaningfully.[76]

The challenge of protecting the Indian Christian identity as a minority community in the all embracing ethos of the dominant Hindu culture, coupled with emerging global culture, is a new phenomenon. Will the struggle for inculturation diminish the Christian identity? An isolationist and static response to the emerging context can create only frogs in the modern well, with ghetto mentality. In the daily life the fact of dynamic adaptation and creative borrowing of cultural elements, without ignoring the core values of one's own religious tradition, is on the increase. However acceptance of material culture is usually a less controversial issue than

75. Quoted by Saldhana, *Inculturation*, 35.
76. Kanjamala, "Social Analysis," 1–28.

Inculturation of the Indian Churches

adapting to new value system. The viable alternative to isolation or confrontation seems to be a cautious adaptation and creative inculturation. In contrast to a few identity markers of the past, the single identity principle of the past, predominantly linguistic and religious, multiple identities with different accents in different situations, and multi-loyalties are the order of the day. If inculturation is an inescapable process in socio-cultural, economic and political spheres, then inculturation and adaptation in the religious field seems to be quite logical. Strict religio-cultural boundaries of the past are gradually getting blurred. Without expanding the cultural boundaries or breaking boundaries no progress is possible.

In the words of missiologist Robert Schreiter: "The postmodern concept of culture sees culture as a kind of force-field where identities are negotiated out of distinct, some times contradictory elements. . . . It is most evident under the impact of globalization and urbanization, in youth culture. Youth may constitute their identities out of elements of their parent's culture, either appropriating them or profiling themselves against them, with international youth music, style trends circulating in the urban sphere, and political elements gained from tensions in larger urban environment. Youth may end up having more in common with their peers internationally than with people immediately around them."[77]

Root of Resistance to Cultural Changes

Yet objections and resistance to inculturation of liturgy, Hinduization, according to those who oppose, both from the hierarchy as well as laity, is a fact of the Indian ecclesiastical life and history. Strong objections and protests by a group of educated and well placed laity, with the Padroado background, against the references made to Hindu and Muslim Scriptures in the footnotes of a recent Indian Bible translation is a good illustration.[78] Persistence of cultures and resistance to changes can explain, if not fully, the near failure of inculturation of liturgy, despite commendable hard work of a group of committed specialists for nearly four decades. Evolutionary sociology might shed some light on the dilemma. The collective memory of a community is the product of rather successful adaptation to the environment for survival. The lessons learned and wisdom accumulated by a community through trial and error methods in the long fights and struggle for survival, often in hostile environment, are faithfully handed over to the next generation. For instance at the level of biological survival

---

77. Schreiter, "Changed Context," 79.
78. *The New Community Bible* (Bombay: St. Pauls, 2008).

the food habits of a community, acquired in childhood, have preference over food habits acquired at a later age. The same is true with regard to language and other learnt cultural habits. The religious and social values that are interiorized in infancy and early stage of personality development are rarely abandoned even when one is challenged by other religions, cultures, even persecution. Resistance to conversions follows the same logic. Because these are planted and deeply rooted in the pre-rational and premodial emotional soil and have proved their credibility for successful and meaningful life. To extricate deep rooted traditions, particularly the sacred tradition, or religion is next to impossible.[79] For example, observe the religious attitudes and practices of a migrant Catholic community. Why do the Syrian Catholic migrants to Bombay or New York demand for Syrian priests, Syrian liturgy and even hierarchy. The Catholic Eastern churches in the Americas, Canada, Australia and other countries too make similar demands. In essence, theologically speaking, there is no difference between the Syrian Catholic Mass and the Latin Mass. Yet migrants, especially of the first generation, do not "feel and experience the religiosity and spirituality" offered through the Lain liturgy; i.e., through unknown language, say English, strange music, unfamiliar vestments, foreign liturgical symbols and atmosphere. It is an experience of uneasiness and cultural strangeness. It is a dry and meaningless liturgy to new comers. The first generation migrant Catholics are "hungry" for the primary religious feeling and experience of the childhood, the familiar cultural atmosphere. The collective memory recalls and yearns for first experiences, unconsciously and spontaneously inculcated through one's primary culture of origin and growth. However, it is also noted that the second and third generation Catholics, after being brought up in a new cultural environment, are less comfortable with the liturgical traditions of their parents or grand parents. Differences in cultural conditionings are the source of differences in responses to the new religio-cultural stimuli. Most people are unaware of the power of social conditioning and are happy with it. Worse still they see the whole world through their ethnocentric eyes.

To reverse the experience of the migrants let me invite the Latin bishops and priests in the host territory, who, in general, seems to be unsympathetic, with minor exceptions, to the "irrational" demands of the Syrian Catholics. For example during the CBCI biennial general meet-

---

79. Deunett, *Breaking the Spell*, 107. Berger and Luckmann, label the process as Internalization of Reality, through Primary and Secondary socialization. See *Social Construction of Reality*, 149–66.

Inculturation of the Indian Churches

ing where holy Eucharist are celebrated also in Syro-Malabar and Syro-Malankara Rites, the Latin bishops and a few commission secretaries, with the original Latin Rite back ground, participate in them out of courtesy and good will, but with a lot of discomfort. They endure it with the hope that the situation will pass away in a few hours. I can imagine the ordeal of these bishops if they are nearly forced, by whatever circumstances, to celebrate the Eucharist in the Oriental rite in Kerala, a totally foreign environment, for a few months continuously. The gist of my argument is this: these problems are not strictly theological; they are not religious. They are cultural: i.e., an encounter with unknown language, strange music, unfamiliar rituals and symbols that create irritation. What *Propaganda Fide* advised missionaries long ago are equally valid even today: "It is in the nature of men to love and treasure above everything else their own country and that which belongs to it. In consequence no stronger cause for alienation and hate than an attack on local customs, especially when these go back to venerable antiquity."[80] In short traditions and habits control the behaviors of uncritical and unreflective majority of members of a community. At the same time a very small creative minority, despite objections, becomes the agent of change.

I am strongly inclined to believe that uneasiness and aversion are experienced in the process of experimentation with the Indian anaphora and various steps of inculturation. The Catholic Church in India, in spite of some good will towards inculturation in official documents, is caught up in a vicious circle. The churches in India are quite comfortable with the Latin and Syrian Liturgies, though both are foreign in origin. All Christians in India today have inherited the colonial weight of the past. They are comfortable to worship in ways taught by foreign missionaries for centuries. The recent revival of the Tridentine Latin mass (2010) for certain occasions and lifting of excommunication of priests ordained by the ultra-conservative Archbishop Lefebvre fit into the same pattern. Similar mechanism is operative in seminary formation in India. Their long existence and mental adaptation, partly enforced in the case of the Syrian liturgy in the seventeenth century, nearly discredit the accusation that they are foreign. Another good example is the present status of English language in India. It has become Indian, with the Constitutional status. I am of the opinion that most of us who speak and write in favor of inculturation, after being systematically exposed to more than one languages and cultures, do not understood the enduring power of primary

---

80. Quoted by Allen, *Future*, 443.

cultural orientation and habits with strong resistance to changes, starting from food habits, languages, music, sacred rites, rituals and other learnt mental dispositions; especially those beliefs that are deeply rooted in the primordial fear of ancestral spirits, angry gods and the mysterious sacred cosmos. Prayer for the dead in most cultures is an excellent example.

The above analysis makes it clear that inculturation of the local church is a very complex and sensitive issue. A similar process is operative in inter-religious dialogue too. There is no shortage of literature on theology of inculturation. The sacred scripture, both the Old and New Testaments, written by hundreds of authors, in diverse cultural contexts and countries, during a period of over a millennium, is the most inculturated religious document. At the origin of Christianity the church of the Aramaic speaking Judeo-Christians in Jerusalem, Antioch, Asia Minor, the Latin church in Rome, the Greek speaking church in Alexandria and in Constantinople and the East Syrian church in Persia were conspicuously very different in cultures, in theological perspectives, liturgy, spirituality, ecclesiology and church organization. The six liturgical families, comprising twenty two Catholic churches today, celebrate pluralities, which developed gradually out of creative interactions with numerous local cultures with colorful elements. With the centralization process of the Catholic church, beginning with the fourth century, the original dynamism and pluralism in liturgy were stifled. And church began to identify herself with the European and Western cultures. In the colonial era missionaries spontaneously transplanted the Spanish church, the Portuguese church, the French church, the Italian church and other older churches to China, India, South America, Africa and other mission territories. And today these are continuation of colonial churches. Happily the colonial era has ended but the colonial churches refuse to give way to young churches.

In the post colonial era the young churches are struggling to overcome their Western image and establish their identity through inculturation of the local church. In this transitional period it creates a basic problem, at least in the mind of the old church. How the unity of the universal church is to be preserved vis-à-vis the plurality of local churches? There was a time when the Catholic Church thought that the unity will be preserved by the universal use of Latin language in liturgy and in seminary education. The post-Vatican vernacularization of liturgy, the first step in inculturation, has disproved such an anxiety. On the contrary by vernacularization a major aspect of inculturation is being successfully achieved. The rich plurality of liturgical rites in diverse Catholic churches, both Western and Eastern, established beyond any doubt that pluralism does not destroy

Inculturation of the Indian Churches

unity. Neither does the unity of the universal church depends on monolithic organization. True unity can and should be preserved at the level of faith in Jesus Christ and lives according to the values of his kingdom. More than theological speculations the existing plurality of Catholic churches that have evolved from below by dynamic interactions between faith and local cultures, throughout history, sheds enough light and justification for urgent inculturation of local churches. "The Kingdom which the Gospel proclaims is lived by men who are profoundly linked to a culture and the building of the Kingdom cannot avoid borrowing the elements of human culture or cultures"(EN.20). In the Post-Synodal exhortation, *Ecclacia in Asia*, John Paul II used the word "Culture" and related terms like "cultural" and "inculturation" 101 times. The four types of inculturation dealt in this chapter is by no means exhaustive, only illustrative.

7

The Spirit of God in Contemporary Social Movements

HISTORY HAS WITNESSED INNUMERABLE movements when a community or a particular interest group experiences dissatisfactions with the existing order of things. The unsatisfactory system generates stress in individuals as well as significant number of members of the community. If some solution to the perceived injustice, i.e., unfair share in power, wealth, status and privileges, is not addressed frustrations are bound to well up and the status quo is being disturbed. Struggles towards changes appear in different forms like panic responses, violent outbursts or organized social protests. It may be initiated by certain leaders or charismatic personalities in order to organize people to find a solution to the newly felt problems. "Movements are chief mechanism through which the deprived categories demonstrate their power. United by an ideology they create organizational devices to fight the evil and redress grievances. Once the social category develops commitment to a movement's ideology and organization, their mobilization may be relatively smooth . . . Therefore its crucial aspects are mobilization and institutionalization."[1] With the exception of analyzing conversion movements of tribal and dalit communities with religious concepts and categories most of social movements are subjected to interpretation of secular ideologies. Acknowledging its legitimacy, in contrast, I intend to identify in them certain sacred dimension at a deeper level, at least in a few instances and personalities. The focus here is not on the social teachings of churches nor on their social involvements. My attempt is to draw attention to the presence and activities of the Spirit of God in the whole world, outside the visible boundaries of the churches. "Since

1. Oommen, "Introduction," 21.

creation is the beginning of history the Spirit in a certain sense is a hidden power at work in history, guiding it in the ways of truth and goodness" (EA.15).

Marginalization of the Holy Spirit in the Catholic Tradition

Writing the preface of the book, *The Conspiracy of God*, L. J. Cardinal Suenens, a decade after the Vatican Council, observed: "Books on the Holy Spirit are rather rare in the Catholic Church of the Latin rite. The Fathers of the Eastern rites who were present at Vatican Council II never ceased to remind the rest of us that our preparatory schemes had failed to accord a sufficient amount of attention to the Holy Spirit."[2] The observation of Suenens, an outstanding and very influential theologian of the Council, summarizes the marginalized role of the Holy Spirit in the Catholic tradition and her spirituality for centuries. There is a conspiracy of silence among most Christians with the exception of Pentecostal churches. Granted that the situation has improved marginally in the recent times, with the growth of Catholic Charismatic movement in India, there is much to be desired.

Nobody has seen the Spirit and therefore She can be discerned only through Her fruits. The difficulty of the process of discernment of Her activities might be one of the reasons for the long ignored questions about Her. The following text from *Kena Upanishad*, expresses the problem well:

> Thither the eye does not reach. Or speech or mind. We do not know or understand how this can be taught. It is other than the known and beyond the known . . . That which cannot be expressed by words but that by which the word is expressed . . . That which cannot be taught by the mind but that by which, they say, the mind is taught . . . that which cannot be seen by the eye but that by which the eyes have sight . . . that which cannot be heard by the ear but by which the ears have hearing . . . that which cannot be breathed by breath but that by which the breath can breathe . . .[3]

Man in his present condition, a being of body and soul, with senses, intellect and intuition as sources of knowledge, feels the need to symbolize the invisible Spirit. In the Catholic tradition, thus, eight symbols are mainly used to speak about the Spirit: water, anointing with oil, fire, cloud

---

2. Haughey, "Preface," ix.
3. Hume, *Thirteen Principal*, 335–36.

The Future of Christian Mission in India

and light, the seal, the hand, the finger, and the dove.[4] Common people's deepest need for visible and tangible manifestations of the invisible Spirit explains crude anthropomorphism in religions except Islam. They seem to be quite satisfied and comfortable with their gods with imperfections, but more powerful than humans. The contemporary Catholic spirituality can be identified and distinguished in three basic types: Church and Christ centered Sacramental spirituality; the contemplatives who withdraw from the world and seek God in cloisters to be totally directed by the Spirit; and the spirituality of social action, particularly to the poor, marginalized and the oppressed, with a vision to transform unjust structures of societies according to the values of the Kingdom of God. Here it is important to keep in mind that any shift in theology introduces a corresponding shift in behavior with considerable social consequence. Within the Catholic tradition, the spiritual consciousness of the faithful as well as the spiritual masters are characterized by a regular oscillation between different key focuses of reference. Various spiritual exercises that maintain or deepen one's spirituality seem to be shifting along three reference points: God, Christ and the Holy Spirit. Unfortunately for most Catholics prayer to the Blessed Virgin Mary is more frequent than to the Holy Spirit. Dominant spiritual consciousness is centered around sacramental spirituality and popular devotions. Thanks to the recent charismatic movement, consciousness of the Holy Spirit is expanding.

If that is true, I believe that is so, then the other poles of reference become marginal and nominal. For illustration, how many Religious Congregations are founded in the name of God the Father or the Holy Spirit? Even to the members of those few Congregations dedicated to the Holy Spirit, their spirituality seem to be mainly sacrament-centered: for example Adoration of the Blessed Sacrament, devotion to the Sacred Heart of Jesus and other acts of piety are the main source of spirituality even among the Sister Servants of the Holy Spirit and the Sister Servants of the Holy Spirit for Perpetual Adoration. Among the laity, mainly marked by popular devotions, one of the main points of reference is the Blessed Virgin Mary and a few saints, differing from region to region. What I am trying to illustrate is that a spirituality distinguished by dominance of awareness of the Holy Spirit is rare. Even the contemporary Charismatic movement that endeavors to emphasize the power of the Spirit in the Christian life is characterized by these shifting references. My task of identifying and analyzing the work of the Spirit in various social movements

---

4. *Catechism*, 142–43.

The Spirit of God in Contemporary Social Movements

becomes more complex by the fact of ecclesiocentrism in outlook. In my earnest search to discern the presence, power and works of the Spirit in various contemporary social realities, from the point of methodology, one is forced to look beyond the walls of the visible boundaries of the Church we have created for our own security and easy manageability.

The post-Vatican understanding of the possibility of salvation outside the visible Church could be legitimately used to ascertain the presence and activities of the Spirit in the world and among peoples and nations of good will. But the task is not easy. Breaking the boundaries of our consciousness is more difficult than breaking the traditional boundaries of the Church. It seems to be a very dangerous attempt. Jesus dared to break the Jewish religious and social walls and He was crucified and buried outside the walls. "With His own body Christ broke down the wall that separated Jews and Gentiles as enemies . . . By his death on the cross Christ destroyed their enmity . . ." (Eph 2:14–18). One's own awareness is limited or protected by the walls of egocentrism, and ethnocentrism like family and kinship, cultural or language group, nationalism, religion, sect and so forth. Most people are comfortable with these protective boundaries and the awareness of reality prescribed by the specific world view and life view. Because of the fear of sanction for breaking the boundary walls, most of the Catholics are unable to discover the realities beyond narrow vision. The Spirit seems to be already bound by these human boundaries. The urgent challenge of contemporary mission is to cross the traditional ecclesiastical boundaries and pass over to other religions, cultures and ideologies. "The notion of 'passing over' is a fresh approach to our missionary vocation. It attempts to bring together the spiritual journey of the Christian Passover and the personal, cultural and even geographic 'passing over.'"[5]

The Holy Spirit in The Old Testament

To begin with, the Old Testament literature provides valuable pointers to the work of the Spirit in the world as well as among people who were considered not part of the chosen people. In the beginning of creation, as revealed in the Book of Genesis (Gen 1:1–2) the Spirit of God was actively present. As the earth was a vast waste, and darkness covered the earth, and the Spirit of God hovered over the surface of the earth. *Ruah* created cosmos out of chaos. By blowing the living breath into the nostrils, the first human being, Adam, was created (Gen 2:7). In spite of sin and chaos in the world, as well as among the people of Israel, the authors of

5. Barlage, *Following*, 43.

The Future of Christian Mission in India

Sacred Scripture constantly remind us of the salvific presence of the Spirit in creation. The Wisdom of Solomon says: "The Spirit of the Lord fills the whole earth and that which holds the whole thing together knows well everything that is said" (Wis 1:7). The work of the Spirit is understood, starting from *Genesis*, the first book of the Bible, to Revelation, the last book, as recreating and reordering everything, whenever and wherever, God's plan for the human family and the whole creation was disturbed or frustrated. "The former heaven and the former earth had passed away . . . Behold I make all things new" (Rev 21:1–5). The story of the Bible is the story of progressive liberation-salvation of the cosmos and humankind. The world is freed from chaos to become cosmos at creation (Gen 1–2). Israel is freed from slavery to become God's free people at Exodus (Exod 6: 2–7). Humankind is freed from sin-death to become children of God in the Resurrection of Jesus (1 Cor 15).[6]

That the Holy Spirit "spoke through the prophets" is part of the Christian faith. By contrast Balaam, who lived outside the non-Jewish society, is an example of the Spirit's activity among the non-Israelites (Num 23–24). As the people of Israel arrived in the plains of Moab, near the promised land, east of Jordan, Balak the king of the Moab prayed to the prophet to curse Israel. Balaam had a vision of the Almighty. "The Spirit of God came upon him and he uttered this prophesy" (Num 24:2). "A vision from the Almighty God. The tents of Israel are beautiful . . . Their king shall be greater than Agag . . . Whoever curses Israel will be cursed" (24:4–9). Balaam, a pagan, in the sight of the Israelites, blessed them thrice, instead of cursing. When the king demanded an explanation, he replied: "Even if you gave me all the silver and gold in your palace, I could not disobey the command of the Lord by doing anything of myself. I will say "only what the Lord tells me to say" (Num 24:13). This is a clear example that the Spirit of God reveals His will through the so called pagan prophets. Four oracles are attributed Balaam, the pagan prophet. The first of these (Num 23:7ff.) praises Israel for its distinction from other nation. The second (Num 23:18ff.) there is no misfortune or trouble for Israel. The third (Num 24:2ff) sees the future prosperity of Israel and victories over enemies. The fourth (Num 24:15ff.) sees the victories of Israel over Moab and Edom. However elsewhere he is mentioned as a teacher of false doctrine (Num 31:16).

Cyrus the Great, the founder of the Persian empire, is another example of how Yahweh makes a gentile an instrument to restore the Jewish

---

6. Soares-Prabhu, "Expanding," 37.

The Spirit of God in Contemporary Social Movements

people, after their Babylonian captivity. Nebuchadnezzar (605–562 BC) the king of Babylon, attacked, conquered Judah and deported thousands of Israelites together with their king Jehoiachin to Babylon in 587 BC (2 Kgs 24:14). This was a punishment for ignoring the covenant with Yahweh because of sins of King Manasseh. In 546 BC, Cyrus II began his campaign against Babylon and ended with its conquest in 539 BC. In the book of Deutero-Isaiah (ch. 40–45), Cyrus appears as the hope of the restoration of Judah and Jerusalem. It is Yahweh who grants Cyrus the conquests in order that He may restore His people Israel. This happened in 538 BC, 50 years after the Babylonians destroyed Jerusalem and Cyrus permitted the Jews to return to Jerusalem and rebuild the city and its temple (2 Chr 36:22ff.; Ezra 1:1–4). Cyrus agreed to give the sacred vessels of the temple, looted by Nebuchadnezzar, to those who went back. He also agreed to pay for the rebuilding of the temple. He appeared as a heaven-sent deliverer. Cyrus is called the "Shepherd of Yahweh" who accomplishes His will (Isa 44:28). He was given the grandiose title, "the Anointed of Yahweh" (Isa 45:1). This title was earlier reserved only for kings and priests.[7] I believe that such chosen instruments of God can be identified in our own times outside the new Israel, if we look without ethnocentric eyes.

A close scrutiny of Biblical literature shows that the myth of creation (Gen 1–2; 4–25), the flood, the union of gods with women (Gen 6:1–4) marriage of gods etc. were taken mostly from Mesopotamian and Canaanite myths of creation and were modified and integrated into Biblical motif with explicit polemic. The Code of the Covenant (Exod 20–23) borrows from the customary laws of the Canaanites. The majority of the Commandments of the Decalogue (Exod 20:2–17) are taken from the Near Eastern Codes but adapted to the social needs of Israelites. Some of the blessings and curses found in Genesis are literally borrowed from the Ugarite literature. Matters of temples, temple personnel, sacrifices and festival of the Israelites were borrowed from the Canaanites whose land they conquered and occupied. And then believed it as the fulfillment of promise God made to the chosen people. According to J. L. McKenzie, "the influence of the Canaanites upon the Hebrews in religion, culture and other human activities were incalculable."[8]

Three main Jewish liturgical feasts were adaptations of feasts borrowed from the Canaanites. The Passover celebration (Exod 12:1–28; Deut

---

7. McKenzie, "Cyrus," in *The Dictionary*, 167.
8. McKenzie, "Canaan, Canaanites," 118.

16:1–5) originally a pastoral feast, is taken from an Arabic Spring festival, in the first month of the year, 15th of Nissan (March–April). When the nomadic tribes broke camp to move into new pastures, the ritual originally consisted of the sacrifice of a young animal. The festival was historicized as the celebration of Exodus. Another feast, the Feast of the unleavened bread, Mazzoth (Exod 12:15–20), was a Canaanite harvest feast. The first fruit was offered to gods in thanksgiving. The Israelites began to celebrate it only after their entry into Canaan. The bread was made with the new flour and without leaven, for a week. The Feast of the Passover and Unleavened Bread were celebrated together (Exod 12: Lev 23:6) in remembrance of the exodus from Egypt, which took place at the same time of the year. The Feast of Weeks (Exod 23:14–17) from 15–21 of Tishri (September–October) fell seven weeks after the preceding feast. It is known as Pentecost, meaning, fiftieth day. It is the end of the harvest in summer and the time of formal offering of fruits. In Judaism the feast received a historical motif. This feast coincided with the arrival of Israel at Mount Sinai and the feast is observed in memory of the Covenant on Mount Sinai. The Feast of the Tents was celebrated in autumn (November-December) when Canaanite farmers gathered fruits and put up wine presses in make-shift huts. It was the Canaanite wine festival. The Israelites celebrated this feast to commemorate the protection of Yahweh in the desert where they lived in tents. The Israelites who wandered though the deserts naturally would not celebrate agricultural feasts until they settled down in Canaan. In the course of the following era most of their religious practices and customs were borrowed from the Canaanite religion.[9] And today the church has little difficulty to acknowledge them as a part of the Bible inspired by the Spirit.

Above all, monotheism, the most revolutionary religious idea, would appear only in the Second Isaiah (40–45) in the sixth century BC. Yahweh emerged as the Supreme God of the Israelites, after prolonged struggle against El, Elohim and other pagan gods. Monotheism of Israel has its origin probably outside Israel. Was it not inspired by the Spirit of God? There is no compelling reason to believe that these non-Biblical ideas were not inspired by the Spirit of God until they found their entry into the sacred scripture of the chosen people. However, the process is characterized by critical assimilation, rejecting many religious practices of the neighbours like idolatry (Deut 13:1–9) temple prostitution (Deut 23:18–19) and so forth. The question has been debated whether Moses taught monothe-

---

9. Wijngaards, *Background*, 132–34. For more details, see chapter 6 above.

ism, or worship of one god to the exclusion of others. Probably worship of Yahweh enhanced the development of monotheism.[10]

In the New Testament: "God Shows No Partiality" (Acts 10:34)

The working of the Spirit among the Gentiles was only reluctantly acknowledged by the early Christian community while it was easily recognized in the Pentecostal experience of the apostles and the new converts. For example, Cornelius, the Roman centurian, who was a pagan, received the Holy Spirit, before he was baptized. He was a religious man, highly respected by all Jewish people (Acts 10–11). In a vision he was directed to meet Peter from Joppa. The Spirit directed Peter to Cornelius and after some hesitation he met him, a gentile who was ritually unclean. Having met Cornelius and hearing about the vision he had, Peter spoke: "In truth, I see that God shows no partiality. Rather in every nation whoever fears him and acts uprightly is acceptable to him" (Acts 10:34–35). At the end of the speech Peter asks: "Can anyone withhold the water for baptizing these people who have received the holy Spirit even as we have." Then he ordered them to be baptized in the name of Jesus Christ (Acts 10:44–48). It created a serious controversy. Even the apostles and the new Christian community which had received the outpouring of the Spirit at Pentecost were blind to recognize the working of the Spirit in the gentiles (Acts 15:6–9). After much quarrel, arguments and reflection in the Jerusalem Council in AD 49, the controversy was settled under the guidance of the Spirit. "It is the decision of the Holy Spirit, and our decision" (Acts 15:28) that the new converts from the Gentiles need not be subjected to Jewish traditions. Receiving the holy Spirit at the Pentecost in itself did not guarantee that the Apostles would easily and naturally perceive the presence and working of the Spirit outside the visible boundaries of new Israel. The same blindness was repeated in the successors of the Apostles in the course of history. The traditional exclusive mentality of Christianity militates against the teaching of Apostle Peter (Acts 10:34).

After the first breakthrough by recognizing the presence and activity of the Spirit in the Gentiles, i.e., outside the new Israel, unfortunately, the following Christian centuries were characterized by ecclesio-centrism which failed to recognize the work of the Spirit outside its visible boundaries. "There is no salvation outside the Church" was a dictum of rigid interpretation for centuries until Pope John XXIII opened the windows of the church for some fresh air. Pope John Paul II has acknowledged, along with

10. McKenzie, "God," 739.

many others, that the council was the Second Pentecost (RM 86; TMA 18). In the views of Karl Rahner, the Church went through two decisive breakthroughs, with unexpected consequences. The first breakthrough was the Council of Jerusalem. But in the following centuries, the Church remained predominantly Greco-Roman. The second breakthrough in the missionary consciousness took place in the Second Vatican Council. To quote: "It means that the transition from one historical and theological situation into an essentially new one happened only once in the history of Christianity and is now set to occur for the second time in the transition from the Christianity of Europe (with American appendages) to an actual world religion."[11] The crucial question, in the present context of the renewed understanding of the Spirit in the world, is this: If the time span between the two breakthroughs was nearly 2,000 years, when will the third breakthrough, the millennium of the Holy Spirit occur?

We need, it seems, a third breakthrough, acknowledging and recognizing the presence and power of the Spirit in everything, as the underlying principle of life, love and truth in the face of diversities of dogmas, rituals and morals of organized religions. Unfortunately most of church leaders and Christians are slow to discover this hidden presence and power of the Spirit due to ignorance, sinfulness and ethnocentrism. In the words of Ishanand:

> "In our preoccupation with a narrow minded idea of election, we Christians often tend to be like Jonah and are very surprised, if not angry, at the notion of God's salvific love for all the nations" (Jonah 4:24–66). Sometimes we are inclined to reject any such idea, saying with St. Peter: "No Lord, for I have never eaten anything that is common or unclean" (Acts 10:15). What we must remember, therefore, is that all men have been, are and will be God's children, although from the beginning of history there have been prodigal sons and that His love for us is prior to our love for Him (1 John 4: 19) and that He seeks even those who do not seek Him (Romans 10:20).[12]

Holy Spirit in Contemporary Social Movements

In the last 150 years numerous social movements sprung up among the indigenous people all over India. Ethnologists were the first group

---

11. Rahner, *Theological*, 20:84.
12. Vempeney, *Inspiration*, 181–82.

The Spirit of God in Contemporary Social Movements

that showed interest in the primal religions. The world religions like Christianity, Hinduism, Buddhism and Islam while looking for converts from them, condemned primal religions as being totally under the influence of evil spirits. The work of the Spirit among them was least suspected. The Vatican Council paid no attention to the tribal religions while other religions and their spiritual heritages were recognized as a source of salvation for their sincere adherents (NA 2-4). The recent positive approach of the Church to primal religions itself could be understood as a sign of the working of the Spirit. The Office of Ecumenical and Inter-religious Affairs of Federation of Asian Bishops Conference in 1995 reflected on the Church's attitude towards indigenous people and the significance of the heritage of the primal religions. "When someone says that the tribal world view is essentially, 'life affirming' you have come to the central theme of tribal culture. They believe in a philosophy of vitalism, dynamism, and eagerness to live life with an enviable intensity."[13] Christians are also called to be evangelized by them and learn from them fresh insights in areas such as ecology, community life, and the celebration of life's joys and tragedies. "For the first time (1995) the Christian churches in Asia acknowledges that in the past the religious traditions and practice of indigenous people were treated unjustly and their adherents marginalized within the church."[14]

> The creator Spirit raises up leaders, prophets and kings in pursuance of his plan when human ingenuity comes to a standstill. This cosmic dance of the creator Spirit continues even today. This includes his dance with individuals and nations for He is the Lord of History. In the Christian understanding, with the Pentecost, this eternal play of the Lord is extended to every child born into this world. "In the last days, the Lord declares, I shall pour out my spirit on all flesh" (Joel 3:1-5; AA 2:17). But like in the past he raises up charismatic personalities and groups. Prophets were such individuals who were called to break new paths . . . In the ordinary events of the day they perceived the finger of God . . . they began to see life differently from the perspective of the Divine Spirit.[15]

13. Menamparambil, "Challenge," 19–20.
14. FABC, *Spirit at Work*, 26.
15. Srambical, "Arnold Janssen," 161–62.

The Future of Christian Mission in India

Thana Bhagat Movement: A Tribal Response to the Spirit

When the human spirit is crushed under the weight of suffering, injustice, oppression and dehumanization, it cries out to God and God hears their cry "I have witnessed the affliction of my people in Egypt and have heard their cry of complaint against their slave drivers" (Exod 3:7-8). This history repeats in every age. "In every age the poor have suffered because of the Cains and Pharaohs of the day."[16] Being moved by the Spirit, certain charismatic and prophetic personalities respond to their cry. Most of the tribal movements of India during the past 150 years are well documented. The Thana Bhagat Movement, a non-Christian tribal movement, is illustrated as an action of the Spirit of God among the poor. The Oraon tribe, along with other Adivasis, were one of the earliest settlers of Chotanagpur, currently better known as the Jharkand and Chattisgarh states. From 1765, the tribals were systematically exploited by outsiders like rajas, jagirdars, land owners and tax collectors. Most of the land of the Adivasis was taken away by these usurpers. In great distress, the Adivasis rose up in rebellion against the dhikus, foreigners. The Munda rebellions of 1811, 1819–1820, 1831, and the Oraon rebellion of 1820, 1832, and 1890 were some of the organized resistance against the land grabbing by the foreigners. These and other tribal rebellions were suppressed by the British administrations with brute power.

One Jatra Oraon of Chingri village, Gumla, Ranchi District, Jharkand, proclaimed he had a vision of God and the revelation was meant for all Oraons. He taught prayer and incantations for exorcising spirits and obstructing or destroying the evil spells of witches. From their incantations, "Tana Baba, Tana," meaning, pull out, father, pull out, used in their exorcism, they were nicknamed by others as "Thana Bhagats." The movement in the first half of the twentieth century was characterized by a mixture of religion and politics, opines Stephen Fuchs.[17] Self-purification of the tribe, or conversion, was seen as a precondition for salvation from their miseries. Many parallels to this movement can be seen in the life of the Israelites. The Spirit of God, it can be reasonably argued, through these messianic movements, was leading the Adivasis to freedom from oppression, and to the truth of one God and a life of upright conduct. The accounts of many similar messianic movements are well illustrated in *Rebellious Prophets* (1965). The fact that these movements, due to some reasons, did not grow to the status of national organization should not

---

16. Rayan, "Instruction," 247.
17. Fuchs, *Rebellious Prophets*, 27–45.

The Spirit of God in Contemporary Social Movements

tempt one to overlook the working of the Spirit in them. There are many Moses, big and small, in the lives of indigenous people all over the world. Following features of the movement, with different names like "Messianic movements," "Resistance movements" or "Revitalization movements," illustrate their objectives: a) Attempts to establish a new moral and religious order; b) express great solidarity and social cohesion which act as unifying force for groups; c) act as mediators between "Great tradition" and "little traditions" of India; d) helps in structuring a new social system.[18]

Dalit Movements for Liberty, Equality and Human Dignity

The liberation struggle of around 160 million Dalits of India during the last century followed two routes—religious and political. The Self-Respect Movement founded by E. V. Ramaswamy alias Periyar (1879–1973) in 1925 was an anti-Brahmin protest movement to defend and promote the Dravidian identity and Dravidian nation. It was later renamed the Dravida Munnetta Kazalagam (DMK) and is ruling the Southern State of Tamil Nadu for more than four decades.[19] The All India Scheduled Caste Federation established by Dr. Ambedkar in Nagpur in 1942 was reconstituted into Republican Party of India by his close associates in 1957 with the neo-Buddhist ideology. Its influence on dalit life in Maharashtra seems to be marginal.[20] On the contrary, the Bahujan Samaj Party, including all castes except the upper castes, was founded by Shree Kanshi Ram (1934–2008), a neo-Buddhist, in 1994. Kumari Mayawati (1956–) Ram's successor, who formed the government in Uttar Pradesh, four times, beginning with 1995, is the first Dalit chief minister in India.[21] She is credited for various social transformation of dalits in the state.[22] The rising power and influence of the Dalits in Indian politics, both in South and North India is part of a long drawn struggle for liberation and social justice, that does not exclude ugly features of politics like the liberation of Israel by Moses. The difficult challenge is how to read the signs of the time and the work of the Spirit, even if some of these movements refrain from explicit reference to gods. It is in the struggle for justice, for fullness of life, for the building up

18. Tirkey, "Thana Bhagat," 28–30.
19. Michael, "Dalit Vision," 102–8.
20. Ibid., 108–11.
21. Bose, *Behenji*, 100ff.
22. Swaminathan Aiyer, "Dalit Marching," in *Times of India* (September 26, 2010) 22; Aiyer, "Social Revolution," in *Times of India* (October 3, 2010), 16; and Aiyer, "Social Revolution," in *Times of India* (December 26, 2010).

The Future of Christian Mission in India

of a loving community that one may discern the activity of the Spirit. "All human communities are to be criticized by the Spirit of truth who convicts the world of sin. The Spirit continually encourages in and for the struggle, and at the same time points out and calls into question every move towards self-aggrandizement, power seeking for personal gain or new appearance of oppression even at the hands of those who were formerly oppressed. The Spirit of truth keeps the struggle honest and committed to the goal of justice for the least."[23]

Women's Liberation Movement

In the earliest period of human civilization—the hunting and food gathering period—human families as well as societies functioned with mother as the centre of authority, particularly for children. Hunting men were wanderers. With the invention of agriculture about 10,000 years ago human communities settled down in a definite land or territory. Man emerged as the protector, mainly due to superior physical power, of not only wives, children and slaves but also the absolute controller of land and property. This marked the gradual end of matriarchy and the beginning of patriarchy. Eventually the social order was legitimized by sacred scriptures, written by male priests. Now at the end of the industrial age, the patriarchal world order is gradually but surely breaking down, starting in the Christian West. The second phase of the feminist movement was gaining momentum in the USA and Europe in the mid 1960s. The United Nations Conference in Mexico (1975) was preceded by preparations for a decade. In India the freedom struggle marked the beginning of an awakening among women, at the call of M. K.Gandhi. The nationalist consensus symbolized in the Fundamental Rights Resolution of the Indian National Congress, 1931, postulated freedom, justice, dignity and equality for women and the Indian Constitution assured these rights. *Towards Equality. Report of the Committee on the Status of Women in India* (1974) drew attention to the continued "invisibility of women" as well on the emerging aspirations of women. Another remarkable achievement in recent years has been the 73rd and 74th Constitutional Amendments which provide for 33 percent representation for women in local bodies and urban areas. Increasing public protests by women's organizations against rape, anti-dowry agitation, Amendment of Dowry Prohibition Act in 1986, amniocentesis and sex selection, domestic violence against women and similar protests have rendered visibility and greater attention to women's liberation movement.

23. Brown, "Holy Spirit," 277.

The Spirit of God in Contemporary Social Movements

The Catholic church in India responded to the new challenges through the following initiatives. Streevani, Women's Voice, in Poona, was the first Catholic centre established in India in1982 to research on the issues of women in the Indian church. The CBCI General Body meeting in Poona in 1992 approved the founding of "Women's Desk" at New Delhi and in each diocese which was elevated to the status of full-fledged CBCI commission for women in 1996. Its programs are promoting empowerment of women both in the church the secular society.[24] In 2009 the Catholic Bishop's Conference of India issued the "Gender Policy of the Catholic church in India" with various guiding principles to create a just and egalitarian church. Unfortunately the Indian society is highly patriarchal with strong prejudices against girls and women because they are seen as an economic burden, chiefly due to the dowry system. The 2011 Census Report revealed that there are only 914 girls for every 1000 boys below the age group of six, in contrast the child sex ratio of 927 girls in 2001. Child Sex Ratio has declined in majority of the states. And the trend for the near future is not bright.[25] Numerous other crimes are committed against women, for instance, one rape every minute in India.

The task of keeping alive the experience of the Spirit that one receives is continuously challenged by patriarchal forces, both individual and social. What has happened to the position of women in the Church illustrates this struggle. The first Christian experience of the Pentecost was interpreted by Peter (Acts 2:17ff.) as fulfillment of the prophecy of Joel (2:28–30). "It shall come to pass in the last days, says the Lord, that I will pour out my Spirit upon all flesh and your sons and daughters shall prophesy." In the fellowship of the Spirit there are no more male privileges. The Kingdom of the Spirit is characterized by a new fellowship of free and equal disciples. Unfortunately history provides ample proof to demonstrate how churches deviated from the Pentecostal experience. In the Catholic tradition, patriarchal hierarchy, and male priesthood rule with the theology of one male Father, one Son, one Church with male pope. In the Reformation church, Christocentrism dominates the Church, i.e., Christ the head of the Church and man the head of woman (1 Cor 11:3–16). Women are expected to keep silence in the Church (1 Cor 14:34). They are excluded from ministry or spiritual office, although the male-female distinctions are not the decisive qualities of those baptized in the Spirit. "There is neither Jew, nor Greek—there is not male or female; for you are all one in Christ Jesus"

---

24. Kanjamala, "Streevani," 352–56.
25. Tharoor, *Hindustan Times*, May 26, 2011, 10.

(Gal 3:28ff.). Juergan Moltmann summarizes the present situation as follows: "Neither the patriarchal nor Christocentric concept of the church has any expectation that the Spirit will be experienced by men and women together and both repress the Pentecostal experience of the early church. If we want to do justice to the fellowship of women and men in the church, we must therefore come to have a new understanding of the church based on the shared experience of the Spirit."[26] The modern women's movement, in spite of certain aberrations of extremism, is a genuine struggle to recapture the life of justice, freedom and fellowship in the Holy Spirit, as experienced in the early Church. Do the patriarchal mindset sense the inspiration of God's Spirit in the liberative movement of women today?

Ecological Movements

We live in a time of increasing industrializations, globalization and consumerism. The continuous exploitation of raw material for unilinear development model threatens to destroy natural resources. In the 1970s environmental groups began to raise issues of clean air, water, and environment because more than ever today people are becoming aware that human life is intrinsically bound with natural world and the life of animals. Our planet is too precious to be sacrificed to greed. Ecology movements endeavour to demonstrate that modern technologies involve high environmental and social coasts. Survival of man and nature is the central concern and the movement is an attempt to shift values back to nature and man. The United Nations Conference on Human Environment at Stockholm in 1972 marked the beginning of an organized world concern. The U.N. Earth Summit in Rio de Janerio in 1992 dealt with global warming that affected the rich nations but ignored the problems of poor in the new situation. However the Vatican representative did not fail to question the scandalous pattern of consumption and waste of the industrialized rich nations. It was further pointed out that respect for human person and life itself is an expression of respect for the creator of the Universe. [27]

Hinduism, Buddhism, and Jainism believe in the essential unity of all that live. The Hindu tradition gives a sense of sacredness to the whole nature. It is expressed through the beliefs in holy mountain the Himalayas; holy river, Ganga; holy plant, Tulsi; holy animal, cow and so forth. These are symbols of sacredness of whole creation. The Chipko movement, among other movements, is the most well known ecological movement

26. Moltmann, *Source of Life*, 101.
27. Gosling, *Religion and Ecology*, 13–14, 58–63.

The Spirit of God in Contemporary Social Movements

in India. It was initiated by Chandi Prasad Bhatt and Sundarlal Bahuguna, followers of M. K. Gandhi's economic theory of village development and people's government. Chipko means "hug-the-trees" to protect them. It originated in the protest movement of village's in Uttarkhand in 1960s against the state policy of felling trees for commercial purpose. Bahuguna and Bhatt made nation wide padayatras, walking pilgrimage, to create better awareness of the issue, and inspired the state and the central government to enact laws in favor of environmental protection. The Chipko movement is the recipient of many national and international awards.

Man's reverence for creation is lost because of a secularized mentality. There is an urgent need to change the current attitudes and values. If we see God's Spirit in everything and all things are being prepared to become God's house the consequence is a cosmic worship of God's Spirit. The most high does not dwell in houses made by hands. As the prophet says: "Heaven is my throne and the earth is my footstool" (Acts 7:48–50; Isa 66:1). Perhaps the tribal sense of the sacred in nature—trees, plants, rivers, and mountains and animals is close to nature mysticism. And the ecological movement of today is an answer to the cry of the Spirit. Why does everything cry to the Spirit? Because She is the source of their origin (Gen 1:2). Ecological concerns are a protest against the destruction of life in God's Nature. "That is why we cry out for the Spirit that sustains the whole creation and wait for the spirit of new creation of all things. Our cry from the depths is a sign of life—a sign of divine life."[28]

Non-Governmental Organizations (NGO)

In a country like India, despite the recent reports as an emerging economic superpower, with 300 million people living below poverty line, there is no dearth of issues and problems. From 1990s, coinciding with India's economic liberalization, there has been a threefold jump in Non-Governmental Organization (NGOs), touching three million mark.[29] Aware of grass-root issues and pulse they empower people to find better localized solutions to their problems. People believe that civil activists do make a difference in tackling their problems. Many NGOs are being consulted by the government for designing as well as implementing its program, in addition to funding them. The major activities of NGOs are religious, 27 percent; community and social services, 22 percent; educa-

---

28. Moltmann, *Source of Life*, 124.
29. Singh, "Too much good will," 51.

tion, 21 percent; culture and sports, 18 percent; and health, 6 percent.[30] An area of suspicion is the source of funding as well as accountability. According to recent international enquiry two-thirds of the NGOs have only one paid staff, relying mostly on voluntary service, in non-profit making organizations. Only 8 percent of total donations originate from foreign funds. There are number of NGOs which can be considered illegal, perusing other than good works. "On the issue of relevance, however, many experts feel that despite the system exposing various rogue elements, by and large, they are able to voice the concern of the marginalized—or else would have no takers."[31]

The recent affiliation of a dozen Religious Missionary Congregations, both men and women, as NGOs to the United Nations signals a paradigms shift in mission theology. The words of Arnold Janssen, the founder of the Divine Word Society in 1894, become more relevant in the contemporary context. "We can no longer save the world with sermons and liturgy alone ... Perhaps you cannot avoid becoming politically involved."[32] Announcing the establishment of the NGO, "Vivat International" in November 2000, its objective was spelt out by SVD Superior General Antonio Pernia: "As an NGO we will have access to UN information resources and receive regular briefing ... have the opportunity to participate in the formulation of the policy and the development of UN documents ... will also be in a position to bring matter of concern before UN agencies ... We believe that the humanitarian goals of the United Nations are very consistent with our own goals and that collaboration with a UN can be an important way of working for the Kingdom."[33] It is logical to affirm that the Spirit of the Lord is on all who struggle and work for the liberation of the poor and oppressed (Luke 4:18). The recently appointed Bishop of Buxhar, Bihar (2009), with merely 25,000 Dalit Catholics, expressed his vision and mission in the following words: "The church in the real sense should be a leaven in the world. That is my ideal and motto." He is not enthusiastic about the traditional mission theology of conversions that was not very fruitful in the state of Bihar and other states in the Hindi speaking region. Therefore he added: "The Kingdom of God exists where there is humanity, life with dignity and freedom."[34] I believe that majority of missionaries

30. Mehra, *Strategic Research*, 18–19.
31. Nayar, "Navigators of Change," 46.
32. Quoted by Pernia, "VIVAT," 1.
33. Ibid., 2.
34. Kallupara, "Church as a Leaven," 3, 12.

The Spirit of God in Contemporary Social Movements

in the Hindu belt are in consonance with the emerging mission theology in India. Human right movements are on the rise after the Universal Declaration of Human Rights by the General Assembly of the United Nations on December 10, 1948.

Christocentric to Pneumatocentric Vision

Renewed Appreciation of the Presence and Activity of the Spirit

The number of local, regional, national, and international associations, organizations, and movements, NGOs, working and struggling for the promotion of life, liberty, justice, and human dignity are on the increase, e.g., the human rights movement, pro-life movement, rehabilitation of the displaced, refugees, prisoners, and prostitutes and so forth. Rather than recording and analyzing all in detail, what is significant and of meaning for missionary societies is to read the signs of the time and recognize the presence, inspiration and activities of the Spirit of God in all these. In the context of the darkness of sin and the night of unbelief, such discernment becomes more urgent. In the light of the above analysis the fundamental question is: Do we recognize the Spirit of God in creation and cultures of the peoples outside the visible boundaries of Church through the fruits of the Spirit? (Gal 3:22–23). The Spirit of life, freedom, justice, peace and righteousness is at work in different parts of the world through various groups and peoples of good will. If the fire of the Spirit burns in the struggles of the people throughout the world is not the Church challenged to acknowledge it? Is God not free to raise up, outside the Church, prophets and witnesses to the power of the Spirit? The answer is: The Spirit is free to blow where he wills (John 3:8). Jesus, who was always led by the Spirit, promised the Church: "When he comes, the Spirit of truth, he will guide you to all truth" (John 16: 13).

Beginning with the Second Vatican Council, there is, undoubtedly, a renewed openness on the part of the Church to discern the work of the Spirit in the whole world and articulate the new conviction in various official documents. Pope John Paul II said to a General Audience on September 9, 1998: "It must first be kept in mind that every quest of the human spirit for truth and goodness, in the last analysis for God, is inspired by the Holy Spirit. The various religions, arose precisely from this primordial human openness to God. At their origin we often find founders who, with the help of God's Spirit, achieved a deeper religious experience. Handed over to others, this experience took forms into the doctrines, rites and precepts of various religions."[35] The working of the Spirit is not only in individuals but also in society and history, peoples, cultures and religions (RM 28). These signs of hope include: "scientific, technological and especially medical progress in the service of human life, a greater awareness of our responsibility for the environment, efforts to restore peace and justice where they have been violated, a desire for reconciliation and solidarity among peoples, particularly in the complex relationships between the North and the South of the world" (TMA No. 46).

The Church's recognition of these signs of hope in the world only as the seed of the word (AG No. 11, LG No. 17) and a ray of truth which enlightens all men (NA 2) seems to fail to speak a new language and new psychology of the emerging new world. Some kind of a solution to the problem must be sought in the experience of the Spirit that is available to all, as Samuel Rayan suggests: "The Asian experience of the Spirit is more important than the texts created by the Spirit inspired people. The Spirit inspires not only religious texts but also secular ones like poems, plays, law, philosophies and all searching questions about meaning, values, relationship and ultimate concerns. The Spirit criticizes all texts and all interpretations of them. She challenges our creations . . . calls to fresh insights and new dreams and unsuspected depths and surprised praxis."[36] In the Asian Synod (1998) the bishops and theologians were speaking a new language for the Asian Church, quite different from the Agenda that was already prepared by the Vatican authorities. According to the report of John Prior, one of the secretaries, 76 percent of their interventions were centered around the Asian Church's dialogue with religions, cultures and poor where the Christians constitute less than 3 percent of the population.[37] The Asian Church's concern and involvement with these brothers and sisters outside the Church through dialogue with the poor is part of the emerging paradigm shift in the Asian mission theology.

The converging point of the emerging world consciousness, it seems, is the recognition of the Spirit of God by all people of good will in creation, in religions, in cultures and in human struggles for integral liberation. We are experiencing a shift in consciousness and ultimate point of reference to cosmic unity from Christology to Pneumatology. In the developed societies of the West more and more people are moving away from institutional Church, for various reasons, and are searching for a new spiritual experi-

---

35. John Paul II, in the newsletter *Petrus* (Mumbai: St. Pauls), 8.
36. Rayan, "Spirituality."
37. Prior, "Unfinished Encounter," 347.

The Spirit of God in Contemporary Social Movements

ence characterized by the fruits of the Spirit. The traditional Christians societies continue to maintain their spiritual consciousness with the help of institutions with their concrete and specific characteristics. As far as the Christian tradition is concerned it is undergoing a paradigm shift in theology and spirituality with its accompanying tensions, conflicts and anxieties. The shift is from Christocentrism to Pneumatocentrism. How can we justify the emerging trend? A close examination of the activities of the Spirit in the life of Jesus will hopefully provide the answer.

The Spirit and the Messiah

The Spirit of God was the dominant driving force in the life and works of Jesus of Nazareth. Yet because of the invisibility of the Spirit and the powerful visibility of Jesus, the Spirit was mostly marginalized and Jesus was given the major focus in the life and spirituality of the Church all through the centuries. Let me illustrate.

- According to Isaiah 11:2-3, the future ruler will be the bearer of the seven—fold gifts the Holy Spirit of. "The Spirit of the Lord shall rest upon him, a Spirit of wisdom and understanding, the Spirit of counsel and strength, a Spirit of knowledge and the fear of the Lord, and his delight shall be the fear of the Lord."

- The same concern is found again (Isa 42:1-3). "Here is my servant whom I uphold the chosen one with whom I am pleased; upon whom I have put my Spirit: He shall bring forth justice to the nation." In Isa 61:1-4, we see the Spirit of Yahweh rest on the One who is sent to bring Good News to the poor and liberation to those in captivity.

- At the Annunciation the Angel said, "The Holy Spirit will come upon you and the power of the Most High will overshadow you. Therefore, the child to be born will be called, the Son of the Most High" (Luke 1:35).

- At the Baptism: "Filled with the Holy Spirit Jesus returned from the Jordan and was led by the Spirit into the desert for forty days to be tempted by the devil" (Luke 4:1). Mark 1:12 states: driven into the desert by the Sprit. "The Spirit descended upon him in bodily form like a dove. And a voice came from heaven: 'you are my beloved son, with whom I am well pleased'" (Luke 3:22).

- At the beginning of the public ministry Jesus announces his manifesto in the Synagogue at Nazareth. "The Spirit of the Lord is upon me—" (Luke 4:18-19).

- During His public ministry, Jesus cast out demons with the power of the Spirit. "Since it is by the power of the Spirit of God that I cast out demons, the Kingdom of God has come upon you" (Matt 12:28).

- Holy Spirit and the glorified Christ: It was the Father—in response to Jesus' faithfulness until death—who raised Him to glory through the Spirit who gives life (Rome 8:11; Eph 1:19-20; 1 Cor 6:14; 2 Cor 13:4).

- Since He was filled with the Spirit, Jesus breathed on the disciples and said "Receive the Holy Spirit" (John 20:22). He became the medium through whom the Spirit is poured out on the Apostles and disciples at the time of the Pentecost. "The link between Jesus and the Spirit is so intimate that it could be said that Jesus did not just have the Spirit, but he was the Spirit in human form."[38]

Since the Spirit was the driving force of Jesus, the apostles, Paul, Barnabas (Acts 13: 2-4) and all the charismatic personalities in the Church as well as outside the Church the paradigm shift from Christocentrism to Spiritcentrism seem to be Justified. Only a few mystics, often in conflict with institutional church, are able to indicate this mystery of the Spirit, and the underlying unity of all. "The Spirit of God has been universally present throughout human history and remains active today outside the boundaries of the Christian fold. . . . The Holy Spirit is God's point of entry' into the life of the people; hence his immediate actions open up the way for distinct mode in the Christian theology of religions. No longer Christocentric, but Pneumatocentric."[39] In the beginning of creation the Spirit was at work (Gen 1:1); the incarnation of Jesus begins with the power of the Spirit (Luke. 1:35); the creation of the new Messianic community begins with the outpouring of the Spirit at the Pentecost (Acts 2:1-4). The whole history is moving towards the new heaven and new earth in the "Presentness of the Spirit."

The emerging Spirit-centered vision is only partly distinct from Christological vision, since both are inseparable in the Christian economy of salvation, yet, with the advantage of universal consensus; i.e., with peo-

38. Fuellenbach, *Throw Fire*, 366-404.
39. Dupuis, "Religious Plurality," 329.

The Spirit of God in Contemporary Social Movements

ples of all religions. This is an imperfect attempt to reinterpret and rediscover the truth that is already contained in the Christian tradition. In the backdrop of Montanism and subsequent polemics at the end of the second century serious attempts were made to minimize the role of the Holy Spirit in charismatic initiatives. Grappling with the fundamental question, who is Jesus Christ the councils of Nicea (325) and Chalcedon (451) marginalized the role of holy Spirit in the economy of salvation. And in the Apostale's Creed which is highly Christo centric, the holy Spirit gets only a passing mention: "I believe in holy Spirit." Concluding his study, *Christ in the Spirit*, Indian theologian Mohan Doss states: "In fact the aftermath of the Nicene Council diminished the significance of the role of the Spirit in Jesus and made increasing efforts to explain the union of Logos with flesh as the work of the Logos qua Logos. Further, once the Christology of Chalcedon (Logos-anthropos) became the definitive model for interpreting the significance of Jesus Christ any departure from this model was equated to be a departure from the faith. Thus the theological culture that prevailed from Chalcedon until the eighteenth century allowed no room for the revival of the early Christology."[40]

To repeat the fundamental question raised in the beginning of the chapter: what is the role of the Holy Spirit in millions of non-Christian men and women who render selfless services to less fortunate members of any community or Society. Take the example of around one million volunteers in 100 countries who work with the Sisters of Charity of Blessed Mother Teresa of Kolkata. Majority of them are not Christians. Are they not moved by the power of the Spirit? Is not the Spirit of the Lord upon them, bringing liberty to those oppressed by all type of afflictions? (Luke 4:18-19). I see therefore, no reason to doubt that the Spirit of God is operative in millions of selfless servants of contemporary social movements, irrespective of their religious affiliation or no religious affiliation.

---

40. Doss, *Christ in the Spirit*, 340.

8

Christian Institutions at the Service of the Gospel

SOCIAL SCIENTISTS OBSERVE THAT a mission, like other institutions, passes through three stages. Usually it begins with a charismatic person, inspired by a new vision or a dream for people in certain crisis or problems. Attracted by the enthusiasm, magnetism and moral authority of the founder more people join him, either out of curiosity or genuine conviction. The founding generation, in spite of certain objections and challenges from the watchdogs of the existing system, achieve remarkable success. Thirdly, in the following generations membership expands to wider territories. Then it becomes almost unavoidable to organize the movement with new norms, laws, polices and office bearers in order to achieve certain amount of stability, respectability and predictability without which social life would be chaotic. Simultaneously the institutionalization process carries the inherent danger of maintaining the status quo; original spontaneous behaviors become empty formalism; initial belief and religious experience become rigid dogmas; actions and personal relations may lose their excitement, vitality and idealism. After a period of mass movement, missions in India have become highly institutionalized. The process of institutionalization of missionary activities is on the increase and will be accelerated in the future with little possibility of escaping the modern secular culture of institutionalization and rational bureaucratization. Therefore the challenging concern is: how to transform church institutions into centres of Good News? Can they become agents of change, innovation, even a source of revolution as it was intended in the beginning by its founder-prophet, Jesus of Nazareth. The question is all

Christian Institutions at the Service of the Gospel

the more relevant in the emerging context of anti-institutional mentality of young generation.

The Gospel or the Good News

The word 'Gospel' is derived from the Anglo-Saxon word "god spell," standing for "good spell" or "good tale." In Greek, the New Testament language, the term is *eu* (good) *angelion* (message) while its Latin Vulgate Version by St. Jerome about AD 405 is *evangelium*.[1] The expression "New Testament," which occurs only once, is found in the first English translation in the King James version in 1611 and Douay-Rheims Catholic translation (1609–10). "This cup is the *new covenant* in my blood," found only in Luke 22:20. More recent translations render this term, as 'New Testament.' Paul spoke of the Old Covenant ratified by God at Sinai (Gal 3:15–18). Gradually the Gospel came to mean both the message and life of Jesus Christ, first orally taught in different communities and later written by or attributed to the four evangelists, distinct from other rival versions of the Jesus story. Therefore, they are not biographies or history. The oldest of these accounts, the Gospel according to Mark, starts as follows: 'The beginning of the *Gospel of Jesus Christ*' (Mark 1:1). 'Jesus came to Galilee, preaching the *Gospel of God*, and saying; 'The time is fulfilled, the Kingdom of God is at hand; repent and believe in the *Gospel*' (Mark 1:14–15). The Lukan use of prophet Isaiah, is a slightly modified version from prophet Isaiah, which was introduced in the context of Israel's political liberation after the Babylonian captivity (605–562 BC) by king Nebuchadnezzar, and their liberation by king Cyrus the Great of Persia in 538 BC. "How beautiful upon the mountains are the feet of him who brings *glad tiding*, announcing peace, bearing *Good News*, announcing salvation and saying to Zion. 'your God is king' (Isa 40:9). And the servant of Yahweh announces: "The Spirit of the Lord is upon me. Because he has anointed me. He has sent me to bring *glad tiding* to the poor" (Isa 61:1; Luke 4:18–19). Two fundamental questions are raised to seek the essence of the various expressions by different New Testament authors addressing different audiences. What did the Gospel signify to Jesus himself in his Galilean ministry? What did Gospel mean to the apostolic church?

The scripture scholars in general agree that the Good News preached in the apostolic church was the Gospel regarding the incarnate and redeeming Christ. For Paul "It (Gospel) is the power of God for the salva-

1. Grossouw, "Gospel," 888–95.

tion of everyone who believers." It was the church's confession of faith that Jesus was declared to be the Son of God with power by the resurrection of the dead (Rome 1:16). The church always worshipped him as the Lord and Redeemer, not merely honoring him as a prophet. In the primitive church—Peter, Paul, and the other apostles—were anything else than preachers of the Good News. Peter's speech at Pentecost (Acts 2:14–36) was concluded in the following words: "Therefore let the whole house of Israel know for certain that God has made him both Lord and Messiah, this Jesus whom you crucified." To the Sanhedrin which objected to his preaching Peter replied: "I cannot but speak" (Acts 4:20).

Immediately after the baptism by Ananias Saul began to preach in Damascus. "And he began at once to proclaim Jesus in the Synagogue that he is the Son of God" (Acts 9:20). He begins his letter to the Romans: "From Paul, a servant of Jesus Christ, called to be an apostle and set apart for the service of the Good News of God. *The Good News . . .* is about his Son, descended from David according to the flesh, but established as the Son of God in power according to the Spirit of holiness through the resurrection from the dead, Jesus Christ, our Lord" (Rom 1:3–5). Paul who was most conscious of his missionary vocation wrote that he was made to be "herald, apostle and teacher" of the Gospel (2 Tim 1:11). Proclamation of Jesus who is raised from the dead, obedience of faith, and salvation are inseparable in his missionary scheme (Rom 16:25–26).

The prophetic preaching in the Old Testament is the backdrop of the New Testament proclamation, *Kerygma*. In the New Testament the verb *Kerussein*, means to proclaim, to announce, to make known. What this verb implies is rather the solemn and official announcement of an event made in the name of God or Christ, an idea which is best conveyed by the word proclamation. In the New Testament the act of proclaiming, Kerussein, employed sixty one times, is more important than the herald, Kerux, found only three times, or even proclamation, Kerigma, eight times.[2] *Kerigma*, must be lived and made visible in a community, *Koinonia*, and witnessed in loving service, *Diakonia*. These three aspects, that is, *Kerigma, Koinonia,* and *Diakonia*, are integral elements of evangelization (Acts 2–6).

What was the Good News, that Jesus preached and asked his disciples to proclaim to the ends of the earth? What was the spiritual legacy which he intended to bequeath to mankind? It is commonly agreed upon by the Scripture scholars that the central concern of Jesus' words and deeds was

---

2. Koch, "Preaching," 688. Jongeneel, "Keryktics," 21–22.

Christian Institutions at the Service of the Gospel

the, "*Kingdom of God or the Reign of God.*" This expression repeatedly occurs in the Synoptic Gospels ninety times and again twice in John, six times each in the Acts and Paul and once in the Apocalypse.[3] According to the Gospel of Mark Jesus began his ministry in Galilee, proclaiming the Gospel of God. "This is the time of fulfillment. The kingdom of God is at hand. Repent and believe in the Gospel" (Mark 1:14–15). And he concluded his Gospel as follows: "Go into the whole world and proclaim the Gospel to every creature" (Mark 16:15). Though Jesus repeatedly announced the Kingdom of God or the kingly rule of God he never clearly told what it really was; nor did his listeners, mostly with Jewish background, asked for an explanation because the concept of the Kingdom of God was quite a familiar subject among the people of Israel, though with divergent interpretations among different listens.

The Old Testament Understanding of the Kingdom

The expression *Malkuth Yahweh* or the Reign of God, does not appear in the Old Testament but the idea is older. The core religious experience of the Jewish people is that Yahweh is the Lord who saves or liberates Israel from Egypt with mighty power manifested against the mighty Egyptian Pharaoh and his army (Exod 9–15; Ps 106:8–12; 118:10–14; 78:51–55; Isa 12:2). Yahweh reveals he is king by his numerous liberative activities in concrete historical situations. According to Samuel Rayan: "God's justice is concrete and contextual. In Egypt it meant liberation for the Jewish slaves, in the desert it meant bread for the hungry. In Galilee the justice of God's kingdom meant freedom and fellowship for outcastes and sinners. . . . The shape of justice and its demands have to be discerned and defined in each concrete historical situation."[4] The idea of king was wide spread in the ancient Middle-East among whom the Israelites lived. His sovereignty is exercised through the ruler chosen by God. People of Israel began to call Yahweh their king, from the monarchic period of king David (1000–961 BC; Ps 29;103). Isaiah's prophetic vision reveals the whole creation worships Yahweh, the king of the world (Isa 6:1–4). By the act of creation Yahweh is the king of the universe (Gen 1–2). This is the foundation of the Jewish belief in monotheism in contrast to polytheism of Israel's neighbor.

The political and colonial oppression of Israel by foreign powers like Assyria in 721 BC created the hope of their political liberation through

---

3. Whitaker and Goehring, *Eerdmans Analytical Concordance*, 579–80; Soares-Prabhu, "The Kingdom," 581–600.

4. Rayan, "Asia and Justice," 12.

a messiah, 'son of David.' The prophets like Isaiah, Jeramiah and Ezekiel hoped for the realization of the kingdom through the descendant of David. In the prophesy of Nathan (2 Sam 7:12–16) David is promised an eternal dynasty. Isaiah tells "a shoot shall sprout from the stump of Jesse" (11:1–9). But Davidic Messianism received a severe set back with the fall of Jerusalem and the Babylonian exile in 587 BC–538 BC. After the return from exile Davidic Messianism gave way to a new type of expectation, the apocalyptic vision. The situation out of which apocalypticism arose was the context of persecution and violent repression of the Jewish people, particularly in during the Hellenistic reform (198 BC–63 BC). The Authors of this type of literature were attempting to answer Yahweh's silence about their suffering. It pictures the final period of the world history in a catastrophe. In this vision power of Evil makes supreme struggle against God. The Jewish nation is represented as messianic leader and triumphs over the world. The prophesies of Zachariah and Daniel, characterized by apocalyptic literary style, portray contemporary history allegorically. For example, the images of the world empire and the kingdom of God in Prophet Daniel (7:9–14; 7:17–18), see the future kingdom of God as coming about through the wonderful intervention of God which will take place after a period of bitter tribulation. At least a certain dimensions of the Kingdom of God which Jesus proclaimed cannot be understood without reference to apocalyptic literature. In the inter-testamental period the Essenes vigorously separated themselves from the political and religious life of the Jews. They were preparing themselves by extreme ascetic life in the community of Qumran, expecting the day when God would set things right Himself.

The kingship of Yahweh was publicly manifested in liturgy in the temple, with the acclamation "Yahweh is king." The 'royal festival of Zion,' representing Yahweh's entry into Zion, commemorates the transference of the Ark (2 Sam 6:15; 1 Kgs 8:1–13) and is part of the celebration of the cultic kingdom of God. After the return from exile Nehemiah and Ezra rebuilt the temple in 515 BC. They adopted prophet Ezekiel's vision of Israel, written probably in the captivity, as a priestly people set apart from other nations to worship God rightly. They concentrated on Sabbath and proper worship in the temple. Judah was ruled by the high priest in the name of God. The role of land, functions of priests and high priest are central to this vision of the cultic kingdom. With these pluralistic interpretations in the Jewish life and literature; "the Kingdom of God is not a concept that can be precisely defined but a polyvalent symbol standing for all Israel's

Christian Institutions at the Service of the Gospel

hope for liberation. Each of the listeners of Jesus would have understood the 'Kingdom' in his own particular way."[5]

The New Testament Understanding of the Kingdom

When Jesus announced the arrival of the Kingdom (Mark 1:14-15), he was announcing that God's divine act of salvation is being fulfilled in his own deeds and life. From 63 BC Israel was ruled by the Roman procurators who were unsuccessful in dealing with the Jews in Palestine because they failed to respect the Jewish religious sentiments and acted in a highhanded fashion. A nationalistic group named Zealots introduced the strategy of holy war against foreign domination and their Jewish collaborators. Jesus lived in such an atmosphere. One of his apostles, Simon was a Zealot (Luke 6:15). Jesus, in contrast to the violence of the fundamentalist Zealots and the revengeful culture of the Sadducees, exhorted to love their enemies (Luke 6:27-37). Jesus does not fulfill the hope of the priestly kingdom by renewing the temple and its cult. On the contrary he predicts the imminent destruction of the temple (Matt 24:2). The prediction of the destruction of the temple meant destruction of the Jewish nation and its religion. It was a direct challenge to the high priest and the authority of the priests. Jesus and his apostles did not belong to the priestly clan. They belonged to marginal, despised lower class like the carpenters, fishermen, tax collectors, and so forth .None seem to have come from the upper or even the middle strata of the society.[6] He does not proclaim a new messianic Torah, whose observance, as the Pharisees expected, would bring about the "Kingdom of God." On the contrary he radically simplifies the Torah and the Jewish legalism into two commandments of love of God and love of neighbor (Mark 12: 28-34; Deut 6:5 and Lev 19:18). What then is the positive content of the kingdom which he announced repeatedly?

> For what Jesus proclaims in word and deed, in his saying and his parables, in his miracles and his table fellowship with taxcollectors and sinners, in his living out his life in availability and service and his laying it down in a freely accepted death (Mark 10:45), is always God's absolute and unconditional love for us—a love he himself has experienced in his foundational experiences of God as Abba. In announcing the Reign of God Jesus announces that God loves us; and in inviting us to "repent"; he

---

5. Soares-Prabhu, "Kingdom," 598.
6. Soares-Prabhu, "Class in the Bible," 85.

The Future of Christian Mission in India

invites us to accept that love and entrust our lives wholly to it, thus reversing the distrust of sin.[7]

God's kingdom comes not through political power which Jesus rejected at the time of his temptation in the beginning of his public life (Mark 4:1). He refused kingly rule during his ministry when the crowd tried to crown him king (John 6:15). At the end of his mission, when Pilot questioned him about his kingdom, he affirmed that his kingdom does not belong to this world (John 18: 33–37). "For him power is not the key. There can be no genuine liberation through the exercise of power, for power does not really free; it merely creates new structures of un-freedom. The only truly liberating force in the world is love and it is just this that Jesus offers when he proclaims the coming of the Kingdom."[8] The Kingdom that Jesus proclaimed was intimately linked to his experience of God.

Jesus Reveals God as Loving Abba

The O.T. image of God, YHWH, was the image of an angry, jealous and terrible God, with a minor exceptions found in a few prophets. Fear of spirits and gods is the dominant disposition found in all tribal religions. While the Jews were terribly afraid of uttering the name of God Jesus, in contrast, addressed him as *Abba*, the endearing Aramaic address of Jewish children. The N.T. refers to God 421 times, of these 183 address him, 'Father.' In the Gospels Jesus addresses God as Father 170 times, majority of these in John's Gospel. This is a radical departure from the Jewish culture.[9] Jesus taught his disciple to pray: Our Father (Matt 6:8–15; Luke 11:2–4). He also prayed that his disciples too would experience a new intimacy with God. "I pray not only for these but also for those who will believe in me through their word so that they may all be one, as you, Father, are in me and I in you, that they also be in us" (John 17: 20–21). In the view of a Hindu convert Manilal Parekh: "It is in this (in the *abba* experience) we find, formulated for the first time, that new relationship between God and man expressed by the term, 'the Fatherhood of God' and which has been the greatest spiritual possession of mankind since his time . . . to be a Christians means to share in the consciousness with Jesus, to enter and enjoy such communion with God as Jesus had, a communion in which one is sure to feel the presence of the spirit of Jesus also."[10]

7. Soares-Prabhu, "Expanding the Horizon," 45.
8. Soares-Prabhu, "Kingdom," 598.
9. Fuellenbach, *Kingdom*, 363–89.
10. Parekh, *Hindu Portrait*, 374.

Christian Institutions at the Service of the Gospel

The preaching of the Good News by Jesus and the proclamation of the early church expected in the imminent arrival of the kingdom (Mark 1, 1:14-15; Luke 4:14-21). But when the eschatological hope or imagery was not realized, eventually the Kingdom was identified with the church. The Reformers, however, insisted that the Kingdom is not identifiable with an institution. For example, for Luther it was synonymous with divine grace. In contrast, gradually the evangelical Calvinists, under the influence of the eighteenth and nineteenth century social conditions, expanded the Kingdom ideal to Christian community. Thus Christians believe that Jesus is the visible and tangible expression of God's liberative love. He is a sacrament of liberation. "Today this scripture passage is fulfilled in your hearing" (Isa 61:1-2; Luke 4:16-21). The proclamation and establishment of God's kingdom are the purpose of his mission "I was sent for this purpose." (Luke 4:43). Jesus Himself is the "Good News" as he declared in the synogue of Nazareth, anointed by the Spirit of the Lord. There is an identity between the message and messenger. He proclaims the "Good News" not just by what he says and does, but by what he is. Christ makes the kingdom present in himself (RM 13). The Reign of God which Jesus announced was an invitation to create a new world order.[11] The proclamation of God who loves all men and women must take flesh in history, must become history. The eschatological horizon of the kingdom of God also warns that any and every human achievement is incomplete and provisional in character. The tension between 'the already' and 'not yet' is an essential character of the unfolding of the Kingdom in history.

Critical Outlook of Jesus to Jewish Institutions

Jesus lived and preached in the Galilee of the gentiles which was inhabited by the heathens, barbarians and Syrian peasants who were crossed with Arab blood. So they were not considered pure Jews. Jesus was highly critical of the Jewish religion, society, its institutions and authority system. This was undoubtedly one of the major reasons why he was put to death by the Jewish authorities in connivance with the Roman rulers in the most painful and humiliating manner that existed in the Roman empire.

The Temple, Priests and the High Priest.

Jerusalem was the political as well as the religious capital of Palestine. Temple in Jerusalem was the heart of the Jewish life. The first temple was

11. Rhor, *Jesus' Plan*, 15-17.

built by king Solomon in 950 BC (1 Kgs 6-7 and 2 Chr 3, 4), and destroyed later by the Babylonian emperor in 586 BC. The second temple was built in 515 BC after the return from the Babylonian captivity (587-538). Nehemiah, the Jewish eunuch at the Persian court and Ezra, the priest, played key roles in restoring the temple (Ezra 6:3-13). Both adopted Ezekiel's vision of Israel as a priestly people (Ezek 40-42). They concluded their religious reform in the proper observance of Sabbath, proper worship in the temple. The temple and its sacrifices constituted a large part of Judaism. The temple was again destroyed by the Romans in 39 BC. The construction of the third temple by King Herod the great, starting in 19 BC was for appeasing the Jews and the process continued during the time of Jesus. The temple was not only a unifying force for the Jews but also a source of great wealth which attracted invasions from neighboring rulers. "The episode of the cleansing the temple is related in all four Gospels."[12] It was a violent protest against exploitation by priestly aristocracy and the institution of the temple. By this prophetic gesture Jesus condemned the priestly authorities and their corruption of the temple. The claim of Jesus that He was greater than the temple was seen by the temple authorities as arrogance and confrontation.[13] This was in the prophetic tradition of symbolic actions and John (2:19-22) regards the cleansing as sign of Jesus death. And the temple was later destroyed by the Romans in AD 70.

With hereditary priestly families (1 Kgs 2:26 ff.) Solomon appointed the priestly family of Zadok in charge of the temple (1 Chr 5:34). Three main functions of the priests were: he instructed the people in law; he offered sacrifices (Dt. 33:10); he uttered oracles (Deut 33:7-11). Priests were indispensable mediators, according to the Jewish religion, to enter into the sphere of the divine. That explains their status, power and influence. However the priests were often rebuked by the prophets for the misuse of their position and authority (Jer 2:8; Ezek 22:26; Hos 4:46). Prophet Jeremiah attacks them as deceivers of people (5:30-31, 6:13-14; 8:10-11; 23:11).

The high priest was the most important person in the Palestinian Jewish community after the post-exilic period. High priestly office was hereditary, Aaron being the first high priest. He was not only the head of the cult but also the head of the state. He was the Chief representative of the people to ruling offices of foreign power that ruled Palestine, like the Persians, Greek and Romans (Lev 21:16; Num 35: 25). He was the presi-

---

12. Mckenzie, "Temple," in *The Dictionary*, 877; Wijngaards, *Background*, 102-30.
13. Castelot, "Religious Institutions," 714-27.

Christian Institutions at the Service of the Gospel

dent of the assembly later known as Sanhedrin, council and supreme court. Composed of seventy members drawn from three groups, high priests, scribes or lawyers; the party of Pharisees and elders. They had power over life and death of their people, until the Roman period. The Roman administration removed capital punishment from their authority. They were the ruling party under the Hasmonian king (134–63 BC), the descendants of the Maccabees. Thus the high priestly families enjoyed political power, economic power and prestige (Mark 11:23; 12:6:2 Mark 1:10; 4:14). The religious and political power of the priesthood reigned supreme. At the time of Jesus, Caiaphas was the high priest of the year and Annas, the father-in-law of Caiaphas, was the ex-high priest (John 18:13–18) whom the Romans removed in AD 15.[14] The Sanhedrin's jurisdiction was limited to Judah. Its competence was both religious and secular, including power over capital punishment until the Romans removed it. Jesus, therefore, had to be brought to Pontius Pilot. Jesus predicted that his disciples too would be called before the council for preaching his Gospel (Matt 10:17; Mark 13:9) as it happened to Peter and John (Acts 4:5; 4;18) and many others in the course of history.

The Sabbath, Legalism, Pharisees and Sadducees

In Judaism Sabbath became one of the most important religious institutions. It is commanded by the Decalogue. The Rabbis argued that Sabbath was holy and to be strictly observed because even God observed Sabbath (Gen 2:3). How strictly and scrupulously the Sabbath had to be observed is evident, without doubt, from the penalty inflicted upon those who failed to observe it. Moses instructed that the violation of Sabbath be punished by stoning to death by the congregation (Exo 31:12–17; Num 15:32). The Rabbis enumerated thirty nine types of work which were prohibited on the Sabbath. A few petty examples: prohibition of lighting a fire, clapping hands, visiting the sick, a Sabbath day journey permitted was only 3000 feet. Following the prophetic tradition of criticizing priests and their rituals (Jer 5:30; 6:13–14; 8:10–11; Isa 1:13), Jesus challenged the legalism of Judaism. The Pharisees found fault with his disciples rubbing grain between their hands on the Sabbath. Jesus affirmed he was the Lord of the Sabbath (Luke 6:5). He was severe with the Pharisees who objected to healing on a Sabbath (Matt 12:4; Luke 6:2ff.; Luke 14:1–3). He reversed the existing order of the Sabbath by saying that Sabbath was made for man, not man for Sabbath (Mark 2:27). Without rejecting the Sabbath ob-

14. Ibid., 704–20.

servances as a whole Jesus pointed out that the rabbinical practices were mere human observances. By breaking the Sabbath on various occasions Jesus, not only challenged the Jewish religious system, but also made prophetic protests against their legalism and ritualism. He was uncompromising in his protest against the tyranny of Jewish legalism. His neglect of ritual ablution (Matt 15:1ff.) and other laxity in Sabbatical observances provoked them. It has always been felt that the charm and the power of the Gospel lie in the antitheses of the Law. Jesus never undermined the laws. But law could never be his last word. For Paul eloquently testified to "The Gospel of Grace" (Acts 20:24). The expression "Grace" and "Gospel" occur 90 and 60 times respectively in Paul's epistles.[15] The Syrian rulers of Judah (198–63 BC) looted the temple treasury and even auctioned high priesthood to the highest bidder. There was good deal of civil war during the Hasmonean rule, the descendants of the Maccabees 134–63 BC. It was during this period three parties came into existence—Pharisees party, Sadducean party, and the Essene group.

The Pharisees were the pious lay group in close alliance with the scribes whose main work was to copy and reproduce the scripture. Some among the Pharisees were 'teachers of the Law' and received the title of *'Rabbi'* or *'Raboni'.* They earned the name Pharisees, the separated ones, like Brahmins in India, by avoiding contact with the gentiles, sinners or Jews who did not try to be meticulous in the observance of the Law. To protect the holiness of the Law they emphasized complicated oral traditions in all its details which the common people were unable to grasp. They believed in resurrection, angel and spirit, which the Sadducees denied (Acts 23: 8) Israel under their law was a theocracy, a Jewish nation-state. They supported the Maccabeean revolt and were sympathetic to the revolutionary Zealots. The Pharisees were scandalized by Jesus' association and table fellowship with publicans, sinners, tax collectors and prostitutes (Matt 9:9–13; Mark 2:13–17; Luke 5:27–32; 7:36). The Pharisees, the lawyers and the priests, in spite of their mutual hostility, came together to fight their common enemy in the person of Jesus. Ritualism, legalism, public show of religiosity to attract public admiration, lack of deep spirituality and love for power, money and social status forced Jesus to accuse them of their hypocrisy. Their self—righteousness is castigated in the parable of the Pharisee and tax collector (Luke 18:9–14). Their religious legalism is unbearable (Matt 12:12; Mark 2:24ff; Luke 6, 2ff.). They are blind with their self-inflicted blindness (John 9:40). They commit unforgivable

---

15. Whitaker and Goehring, *Eerdmans Analytical Concordance*, 455–57.

Christian Institutions at the Service of the Gospel

sin against the Holy spirit (Matt 12:31ff.; Mark 3,28). Jesus abuses them as "hypocrites," "whited sepulchers," "blind fools," "serpents," "brood of vipers," looking devout while vicious in heart (Matt 23; Luke 11). Jesus calls them hypocrites twenty seven times, mostly in Mathew ch. 23. Saul who became Paul was an excellent example of a fanatic Pharisee (Acts 23:3-6). There were exceptions like Nichodemus (John 3) who was a good Pharisee. Some of the early Christians were converts from the Pharisees.

The Sadducees were the priestly and aristocratic party at Jerusalem. They resented the Pharisaic intrusion into priestly duty of interpreting the law. They accepted only the first five books of the scriptures, Torah. Theologically conservative, they did not develop new theology to meet the changing situations. Their political interest was for protecting the priestly and aristocratic privileges. Their religiosity was superficial and their life style was aristocratic. They hoped for the return of the priestly rule in Israel which would make them politically powerful rulers. The Sadducees strongly held the view: an eye for an eye.

Because there is a strong affinity between Jesus' attitude, teaching, and life style and that of the Qumran monastic community it is reasonable, I presume, to argue that he was once a member of the community. He discontinued in it because either he voluntarily left it or was dismissed for unknown reasons. His hostile and very offensive criticism of the temple, Sadducees, priests, high priests, and hypocritical Pharisees and scribes closely resembles the criticism of the 'Teacher of Righteousness' against the 'Wicked Priest' Jonathan of Jerusalem temple. Jesus too taught the imminent arrival of the Kingdom of God as did the monastic community. His views on celibacy was not as rigid as that of the Qumran community but definitely different that of Judaism. His teaching as well as practice of poverty was an anti-thesis of the luxurious life style of the Sadducees and of the high priest which the Qumran community severely criticized. Jesus habit of praying alone in the desert place at night might have been acquired from the night vigils of the Qumran monastery. One of Jesus unique instructions on pacifism and non-violence is very close to the pacifism of the Essenes. He never approved violence of his contemporary zealots in Galilee towards whom the Sadducees were sympathetic. His great appreciation of John the Baptist suggests that both of them were deeply influenced by the radical Qumran life style. Jesus never criticized the Essenes who were is contemporaries. The extreme ascetic ethical standard demanded of those who wished to enter the Kingdom of God, as taught in the Sermon on the Mount, is too close to the Qumran asceticism to ignore. And the Christian community portrayed in the Acts of the Apostle is a continuation of the life style of the Essenes. And there are many more similarities between the early Christian life style and that of the Qumran community. My hypothesis that Jesus spent a few years in the Qumran community will answer the traditional mystery where was Jesus between the age of twelve and thirty. It further sheds light on the question, "Where did this man get this wisdom?" (Matt 13:54–56). Jesus knowledge of the Old Testament and the inter—testamental Judaism was quite sophisticated. I believe that the same hypothesis will explain further the root of the Christian monasticism beginning in Egypt, though Jesus himself was not a monk. It further raises the question: how far the Catholic cloistered life is justifiable by either the teaching of Jesus or his own example?

In opposing and criticizing the institutional structures of Jewish religion Jesus shows that the concern of the kingdom is not limited to individual salvation but must challenge unjust power structures. His revolutionary interpretation of authority and power demands to be servant of all (Mark 10:35–45). Jesus condemned titles and honors (Matt 23:8–10). Before death his attitude to authority was manifested in the dramatic and prophetic gesture of washing the feet of his disciples (John 13:1–16). Unfortunately with the conversion of the Roman emperor Constantine in 313, a persecuted church began to be Romanized. In the course of the following centuries the vision of Jesus was over institutionalized. His challenges and criticisms of the Jewish religious institutions were nearly forgotten. "It seems that in her history the church has drifted back towards a too institutional self-understanding in vital spheres of her life and mission and, therefore, developed an over-institutional image which does much harm to her."[16] Deterioration of the institutionalized church reached its climax by the end of the fifteenth century. Therefore a radical anti-institutional revolution was brought about by the Protestant Reformation by Luther, starting in northern Europe. Provoked by and vehemently rebelling against the corruptions of highly institutionalized Roman Catholic church, its political power, religious authority, sacraments, rituals and traditions were almost totally rejected. The doctrine of salvation by faith alone rejected most of the sacraments and ritualism as means of salvation. Any veneration of images were banned as idol worship. Accentuating the priesthood of lay people, importance of clerical priesthood was seriously undermined by the Protestant churches. Unscriptural religious practices were abandoned. Thus the traditional religious institutions in Europe were radically restructured.[17]

16. Neuner, "New Spirituality," 89.
17. Cairns, *Christianity*, 267–354.

Institutionalization of the Indian Catholic Church

Institution is referred to organizations which contain people as in the case of schools, boardings, hospitals, social centres, monasteries, seminaries, convents, with specific atmosphere, rules, values, limitations on personal possessions, strict time table and subordination to the authority of the institutions. Another meaning of institution refers to entities which deal with interests and specific needs. In meeting various social needs, institutions are patterns of behaviors directed by well defined values and norms that become formalized and regularized. The development of attitudes, social habits, routine, for durability and stability which are necessary for social life creates recognizable patterns of behavior and results into institutions like family and kinship, religious institutions, economic institutions, and political institutions. The anti-thesis of institutionalization is anomie, a complete breakdown of normative order.[18] The charisma is made available to larger numbers through books on the founder or doctrines formulated in later councils. In the process it distances itself from the extraordinary personal qualities of the leader. Further by routinization there is the danger of compromise of the new vision and core values by adjusting to the world. The weakness of the charismatic movement is that it lasts only during the life span of the prophet and his close disciples who directly experienced the exceptional characteristics of the leader or founder. With the death of the first generation of founding members the new disciples fail to retain the original enthusiasm.

Without institutionalization, charisma in the long run, ends in failure. Institutionalization depends on a few conditions. One, designation of the successor by the original leader; two, the disciples and followers of the charismatic leader, after his death, designate a qualified successor; three, a new charismatic leader is designated on the basis of criteria that are thought to ensure the requisite charismatic qualities of the chosen one.[19] Contact with other societies and different religions and philosophies, leading to a greater awareness of one's own religion, compels to articulate and legitimize one's own religion. Finally the religious specialists develop a committed interest in defense of their system and followers.[20] According to Max Weber the initial institutionalization of charismatic authority gradually evolves into bureaucratization as the number of members multiply. Rational—legal authority, rather than personal quality, is the essence

18. Parsons, *Social System*, 39.
19. Bentix, *Max Weber*, 305.
20. Berger, *Social Reality*, 144–45.

of bureaucracy. Offices are occupied on the basis of merit measured by and professional qualifications. Their personal relationship with the office is defined by contract. Then emerges a system of supervision and control by a hierarchy of officers. While charisma is marked by high degree of personal qualities, these characteristics either partly or totally disappear from institutions, depending on the degree of bureaucracy and qualities of those in the office. Impersonality and empty formalism become its hallmark. Gradually the original idealism, meaningfulness, expression of sentiments and freedom might turn into rigid dogmas and legalism. Once institutionalized the initial idealism and spontaneous relationship may lose their excitement, warmth, vitality. Routine of office leads to impersonal and mechanical relations. Legalism and routinization that outlive their utility tend to kill the original spirit and turn into dead wood. Weber expressed anxiety and disenchantment of institutionalization and bureaucratization in the following words: "For the last stage of this cultural development, it might well be truly said: specialists without spirit, sensualists without heart, this nullity imagines that it has attained a level of civilization never before achieved."[21] Thus prophetic charisma and institutionalization are constantly marked by tensions, conflicts and contradictions. "Religion both needs most and suffers most from institutionalization."[22]

Varieties of Institutionalization of the Charism of Jesus

At the beginning of the third millennium Christians constitute nearly 33 percent of the world population. They are affiliated to six major ecclesiastico-cultural megablocs, to some 300 ecclesiastical traditions, and also to 33,820 denominations and paradenominations. The six mega blocs are Roman Catholic, Orthodox, Anglican, Protestant, Independent and marginal Sects.[23] The Pentecostal-Charismatic mega bloc, constituting of 20 percent Christian population, is the second largest group after the Catholic Church. Scholars like M.Weber, E.Troeltsch, M. Yinger and others attempted to typologise them into churches, denominations, sects and cults according to differing religious features and organizational structures. These features of course naturally overlap. Purity of religious beliefs and compromise with a world is a major distinguishing character. Thomas O'Dea identifies various paradoxes and dilemmas of mixed motivations

---

21. Weber, *Protestant Ethic*, 182.
22. O'Dea, "Sociological," 74. On institutionalization of the Indian Catholic church, see chapter 1 above.
23. Barret, *World Christian*, 1:7–10.

Christian Institutions at the Service of the Gospel

like promotions in the hierarchy of power, remunerations and status of members within the organization. In the modern rational cultural context religious intellectuals play a distinct role, differing from that of traditional prophets and priests.[24]

Being aware of the limitations of simplification of characteristics of numerous Churches, denominations established sects and cults the following typology of institutionalization of Jesus' Charism in the course of the centuries is constructed.

A Typology of Institutionalization of Jesus' Charisma

Variables	Catholic Church	Conciliar / Protestants	Sects / Established Sects	Cults
1. Doctrines:	Highly dogmatic	Fundamentalist Liberal interpretation	Low dogmatism	Free interpretation
2. Administration:	Bureaucratic	Formally organized/ democratic	Informal/ democratic	Informal/ personal
3. Norms:	Legalistic	Less legalism	Minimum rules, Persuasion	Blind obedience
4. Worship:	Sacraments/ Sacramentals	Word of God, two sacraments	Word of God/ Baptism in the Spirit	Word of God/ Baptism in the Spirit
5. Accommodation to world:	High	Low	Challenges accommodation	Rejection of this world
6. Asceticism:	To acquire virtues	Asceticism in the world	Withdrawal or Social Exclusion	Other-worldly
7. Membership:	By birth	By rebirth	By choice	By choice
8. Standard of admission:	Low	Low	High	High
9. Geography:	Universal	National	National	Local
10. Time span:	Millennia	Centuries	One generation	Short span
11. Relationship:	Impersonal	Impersonal	Personal/ Fellowship	Personal/ Fellowship

24. Robertson, *The Sociological*, 113–42.

The Future of Christian Mission in India

Variables	Catholic Church	Conciliar / Protestants	Sects / Established Sects	Cults
12. Commitment:	Low	Low	High	High
13. Reason / Emotion:	Highly rational	Rational	Emotionalism (clap, dance etc)	Emotionalism (in the Spirit)
14. Priesthood :	Ordained Priesthood	Priesthood of laity	Lay leaders (anti-clerical)	Prophets (anti-clerical)
15. Social Group:	Middle / Upper class	Middle / Upper class	Marginal groups	Marginal groups

(Adapted by the author, Bendix, *Max Weber*, 1962: 298–328; Robertson, *The Sociological Interpretation*, 1970: 113–42).

Freedom of belief, freedom of worship and freedom of organization are the root causes of emergence of numerous churches and sects. This trend will be on the increase in the future. And the highly institutionalized Catholic Church, it seems, will be the major loser to new sects and cults.

Anti-Institutional Atmosphere of Contemporary Culture

The emergence of counter-cultural groups nearly half a century ago in Western Europe and in U.S. was a historical event, spreading its irreversible impact and influence to other parts of the world. The student revolutions in the University campuses in the late 1960s under neo-Marxist banner radically challenged, questioned and revolutionized the then existing dominant Anglo-Saxon white Protestant culture, rigid structures of industrial institutions, stifling bureaucracy, traditional patriarchy and religious authority system. New codes of conduct, ideals, belief system, transcendental meditation, oriental gurus, unkempt long hair, unisex dress, dirty blue jeans, hippie movement and the Rock culture shocked the traditional society. "Make love not war" was the slogan against the U.S. war in Vietnam. Emergence of radical feminism was part of the new social philosophy of equality. Anti-institutionalism and anti-structural culture emerged as an attractive alternative for the youth.

New heroes and representatives of the young brave culture are John Lenon, Paul McCarthy, George Harrison, and Ringo Starr, Michael Jackson in his leather suits, Remo Fernandes, psychedelic rock of the 1970s, football hero like David Beckham, cricket star Sachin Tendulkar

Christian Institutions at the Service of the Gospel

and numerous music, film, sport stars of the new age culture. Fifty years after it gripped a generation of music lovers rock continues to offer a radical culture. "If you really want to understand an age, don't read its history, understand its most popular mythology. Because mythology is what truly embodies our most deeply-felt unarticulated aspirations and emotions. Our heroes reflect both who we truly are and what we wish we could be."[25] The new generation is apolitical and anti-institutional because, in their opinion these institutions are bearers and promoters of the traditional conservative, authoritarian, male dominated society. They are usually against authority, dogma, ritualism and formalism. They are not irreligious, on the contrary, the emergence and spread of charismatic movement conventions, mushrooming of Bible Study and prayer groups. T.V. evangelism or the growth of religious fundamentalism confirm that there is genuine hunger for God and fellowship, along with hunger for bread, freedom and human dignity. They are searching for truth and hate hypocrisy and corruption of those in power. They join a fellowship of their choice, breaking away from traditional churches. Their focus is not religion in the traditional sense, but on relationship. They try to follow the values of Jesus with least interest in sociological conversion, that requires one to leave the religion and culture into which they are born. 'Yes' to Jesus and 'no' to church, is a slogan of the anti-institutional youth culture. Jesus is very attractive to numerous genuine seekers of spirituality.[26]

Is the Good News of Jesus Christ the answer to mankind's perennial problems and their incessant search for answers? What is man? What is this sense of sorrow, of evil and death? Why is man so unhappy? Why is he so often unable to love and build loving relationships? Why is man often divided within himself? Why are nations waging wars? Why do the rich and the powerful dominate and oppress the poor and the weak? In the preceding pages I tried to show that the Good News of Jesus is his vision for a "new heaven and a new earth" which he proclaimed as the kingdom of God or reign of God. It is Jesus' alternative plan for a new world. In inaugurating the Kingdom and struggling for its realization he had to fight against anti-kingdom values and situations, including institutions of power and injustice. He gathered a community of disciples and commissioned them to proclaim the Good News to all nations. He founded a messianic community which expanded into a mighty institution, with innumerable supportive institutions. The quality of these institutions are

---

25. Singh, *Sunday Times of India* (July 18, 2004) 11.
26. *Sunday Express Eye* (July 4, 2004) 1, 4.

being repeatedly questioned and challenged throughout the centuries because they are easily tempted to deviate from the vision of Jesus. Pope John Paul in his encyclical letter on mission states. "No believers in Christ, no institution of the church can avoid this supreme duty: to proclaim Christ to all people" (RM 3). Missionary activity is for all dioceses and parishes, church institutions and associations (RM 2).

The role and function of the church in the proclamation of the Gospel, as envisaged by the Vatican council, could be analogously applied to each institution, the living and active unit of the body of Christ. The church should become a sacrament—a sign and instrument of communion with God and of unity among people (LG 1). It is "the universal sacrament of salvation"(LG 48). That it may be for each and everyone the visible sacrament of his saving unity (LG 9). The challenging question today is to examine whether church institutions are creditable and efficacious signs and agents of the new world order Jesus announced. While the church needs its numerous institutions as instruments of service and witness of love (AG. 12) particularly to the poor and marginalized, many of them unfortunately fail to be a place of "communion of life, love and truth" (LG 10).

Jesus' proclamation of Good News was primarily to the poor and He often challenged and questioned institutions and leaders of Jewish religion. To what extent contemporary church institutions and their leaders are agents and instruments of struggle for justice, particularly justice for the poor? Many of our prestigious institutions are turning into centres of scandals of open struggle and fight for positions of power, money and prestige. Having secured the chair, the unwillingness, at times open defiance to accept transfers, for example, are indication of failure to shine as centres of Good News. In a context of contemporary Indian political fighting and ruthless manipulations for power and corruption a new type asceticism of detachment from family and kinship, denial of greed and power will hopefully enhance the credibility of Christian institutions. I am afraid to illustrate the discontent, at times the anger of common people, against some of the Christian institutions, that they are like zero volt bulbs burning at night on long corridors of these mighty institutions. They seem to be opaque. Why are there not bright lights? (LG 1). Many office holders of institutions are often perceived as being alienated from common people and their daily struggles of life. On the contrary people-oriented, non-institutional ministries tend to become better carriers and bearers of the Good News. Levels and degrees of Luminous City of Good News should

Christian Institutions at the Service of the Gospel

be critically examined and regularly ascertained in thousands of Christian institutions across India.

These institutions could become centre of Good News to the extent the men and women in these institutions become shining carriers of Gospel values particularly love and compassion, in a society marked by intense struggle for power, economic corruption, hedonistic persuite of pleasure and other anti—kingdom forces. "In a world tormented and oppressed by so many problems, the one who proclaims the Good News must be a person who has found true hope in Christ" (RM. 91). By living the radical values of the Beatitudes, the Manifesto of Jesus according to Pope Paul VI, the missionary character of these institutions will concretely reveal that the Kingdom of God is being realized, at least in some degree. They become "some kind of a foreshadowing of the new age" (GS 25).

9

The Future of Missions in the Hindu Belt

POOR RESPONSE OF PEOPLE, failures and struggles of missionaries for a few centuries seem to surmise that the mission in the Hindu Belt is one of the most difficult missions in the world. The mission theology itself, in the process of religious encounters, is considerably challenged and changed. The Church is becoming aware that the dynamics of evangelization are conditioned to a remarkable measure by the economic, political, social, cultural and religious realities of the people among whom she lives and works. To the extent these secular realities become more complex in the course of human progress the mission of the Church too becomes more complex. The encounters between the missionaries and the people in Northern India had always been a bewildering story. Today in the light of modern cultural studies one is becoming more aware that the dynamics of missionary involvements are deeply conditioned by numerous socio-cultural forces like ethnicity, caste, class, religion and political objections. What is the impact of the missionary movements particularly in North India on the structure of the Christian population? What is the future of the missionary labor especially in the Hindu belt?

Indian demographer Asish Bose, with his excellent service record and wide experience with the Indian population, coined the pejorative acronym BIMARU in 1991, meaning 'sick.' The acronym stands for four Hindi speaking states—Bihar, Madhya Pradesh, Rajasthan and Uttar Pradesh. These were labeled sick states because they lag behind most demographically, economically, socially and politically compared to other states, particularly the four Southern states—Andhra Pradesh, Karnataka, Kerala, and Tamil Nadu with a combined population of 222 million or 22 percent of India's total population. "The Hindu rate of growth" was another

The Future of Missions in the Hindu Belt

term deployed by Economists to convey the stagnant and closed ethos of Hinduism. The total population of the four BIMARU states, according to 2001 census, was 365 million or 36 percent of the Indian population.[1] The BIMARU states, also known as the "cow belt" is the cradle of Hindu civilization. It is more correct to say that one is addressing not four sick states, but millions of sick minds. The decadent Hindu society in North India, in comparison to South India, was characterized by all that was perverse in popular Hinduism.[2]

It is not surprising that such a culture rejected new ideas like Westernization, modernization and Christianization. After nearly 500 years of mission merely less than 1 percent of the population, mostly from marginalized and powerless communities, welcomed Christianity. Hence the challenging as well as disturbing question: What is the future of the Christian mission in the Hindu belt? The predominantly tribal states of Chattisgarh, Jharkhand and Utterkhand created through the bifurcations of states of M. P. Bihar and U.P., respectively on November 1, 2000 are excluded from the following analysis of the Hindu region since their tribal isolation saved them from the evils of Hinduization.

Indian Ecclesiastical Realities in the Hindu Region

The origin of Christianity in North India is shrouded in myths and legends like its origin in South India. The spread of Christianity in the Roman empire and beyond the Roman empire in East Syria generated various apocryphal literature in the third century, trying to explain the origin of the new Christian communities in different parts of Asia. *The Acts of Thomas* written in Syriac between AD 180 and 230 narrates the story of Thomas the carpenter who was brought to the court of king Gundhaphar to build him a palace. The supposed mythology of Gundhaphar was partly dispelled by the archaeological discovery of some coins and a stone tablet in Peshwar and Punjab in Pakistan in the second half of the nineteenth century, with the inscription of King Gundhaphar who ruled, with his capital in Taxila, in Pakistan from around AD 19. His rule coincides with the traditional date of the arrival of the Apostle Thomas in India.[3] But

---

1. Bose, *From Population*, 113.
2. Weber, *Religion of India*, 143–44; 326–28; 336.
3. Farquhar, *Apostle Thomas*, 1–9.

The Future of Christian Mission in India

the "proof of the existence of a King Gundaphar does not guarantee the historicity of accounts of Thomas preaching in India."[4]

Among the church Fathers two contradictory traditions were held about the mission of Apostle Thomas in India. First tradition recorded in the *Syriac Didascalia Apostalorum* written around AD 250 maintains that Thomas went to India. A slightly modified Syrian tradition argued that an evangelist named Addai was the apostle of Eddessa in the northern part of Mesopotamia and Addai's disciple Aggaeus became a pioneer missionary in Persia. St. Ephrem, the Syrian (+373) composed hymns in honor of St. Thomas, whose relics were venerated in Edessa. Second, the Alexandrian tradition maintained the view that Thomas was a missionary in Parthia, in the Persian Kingdom with which Gundhapar was closely linked. Eusebius (260–340), the father of church history, upheld the Alexandrian tradition, received from Origen (+251). Origen was a student of Pantaenus, the head of the theological school in Alexandria, who visited India (ca. 190). The Alexandrian tradition held the view that the Gospel was preached in India by apostle Bartholomew and contradicts the Thomas tradition. Among these two traditions, the south Indian tradition, not proved historically, is fervently preserved by a vibrant Christian community, while the northern tradition has neither the claim of a Christian community nor any evidence of historical or archaeological discoveries. A third tradition argued that it was quite possible that St. Thomas, after preaching in North India, proceed to the South and established Christian communities in Kerala and Tamil Nadu.

Between 520–25 Cosmos Indicopleustes from Alexandria found a church in Thane, in Male (Malabar) and in the island of Taprobane, taken to refer to Ceylon by the Greeks, with Nestorian bishops appointed from Persia. Migrant Syrian Communities from Persia were also found scattered in Goa, Maharashtra (Chaul, Thane, Kalyan, Sopara) and Brouch in Gujarat. Rock inscriptions near Tankse, on the Eastern side of Leh, Kashmir, bear witness to Syrian Christian settlements.[5] Again a French Dominican Jordan Catalani de Severac (1285–1336) who arrived in Thane near Bombay, in 1321 found Nestorian Christians in Kalyan and a few other places in North India. It was reported by him that four Franciscan Friars in Thane were beheaded in April 1321 for their indiscreet teaching that Prophet Muhammad was the son of perdition and that he was now in hell and his followers would have similar end. This area was under the

---

4. Moffett, *History*, 1:30.
5. Hambye, "Medieval Christianity," 32.

The Future of Missions in the Hindu Belt

Muslim rule and it was the era of bitter antagonism between Muslims and Christians due to the crusades. Catalani was credited for creating small Christians communities in Thane, Sopara and Brouch. For his missionary zeal he was rewarded, being appointed Bishop of Quilon in August 1329. Unfortunately there is no record of his arrival in Quilon. According to some historians probably he died in Thane before reaching his destination.

The tradition that there was a Syrian bishop at Kalyan, appointed from Persia in the 6th century, is the reason why the Syro-Malabar Eparchy established in Bombay in 1988 is named the Eparchy of Kalyan.

The Colonial Mission in the Hindu Belt.

The origin of the Catholic Mission in the Hindu belt begins with the extension of the missionary activities of the Jesuits who arrived at the Moghul court in Fatehpur Sikri near Agra, in 1580. The Moghul emperor Akbar (1556–1605) who had invited them for a dialogue gave them land as well as money for their settlement. A church was built with the initiative of Fr. Jerome Xavier, a great-nephew of Francis Xavier, who stayed in the Moghul court for twenty years (1595–1615). However, the Moghul patronage was discontinued during the time of Shah Jahan (1627–58), the builder of the world famous Taj Mahal, to whom Jerome Xavier told that Prophet Muhammad was in hell and the fate of his followers would be no different. That was the end of the Muslim-Christian dialogue.[6] In 1631 he besieged the Portuguese settlement in Hugli, Calcutta, and carried away around four thousand Catholics to Agra and sold them as slaves.[7]

Raja Singh of Jaipur who was keenly interested in astronomy built observatories in Jaipur, Delhi and Mathura and he invited two Jesuits in 1740 to help him. The Raja himself met the expenses to build a church which attracted some Catholics to Jaipur. Though the new ruler himself did not encourage the missionaries to spread the Christian message, he donated money for the maintenance of priests. However, after his death in 1743 the next ruler had no sympathy for the Christians and the Christian community dwindled fast. At Marwar, 65 km south of Gwalior, Madhya Pradesh, the Raja sanctioned money to build a church and paid allowance to maintain a resident priest to take care of the Catholic soldiers and some Catholics who had migrated from Delhi and neighboring states. However, the mission here came to an end in 1778 when the Maratha ruler persecuted the Christians who fled to Bhopal and other towns. The Italian Capuchin

6. Saldhana, *Patterns*, 68.
7. D'Souza, *History*, 21.

The Future of Christian Mission in India

missionaries arrived in Agra in 1640. The Prefecture of Tibet-Hindustan was entrusted to them in 1703 under the *Propaganda Fide*.[8] After the suppression of the Jesuit Society in 1773, having worked for nearly 200 years in the Moghul empire, the northern part of the Vicariate Apostolic of the Great Mughal was added to the Prefecture of Tibet-Hindustan in 1784. Much later it was elevated to the status of Vicariate Apostolic of Tibet-Hindustan, with resident Vicar Apostolic in Agra from 1820.

The Tibet-Hindustan Mission of the Capuchins established a Christian Community in Lasha, in Buddhist Tibet, with the patronage of the ruler. When his successor began to persecute the Christians in 1745 the missionaries left for Katmandu in the Hindu Nepal Kingdom. Again because of persecution sixty two families and two priests moved out to Chuhari, near Bettiah town to become the first Christian community in north Bihar. In 1745 Raja Druva Singh of Bettiah requested Pope Benedict XIV to send Capuchin missionaries to his kingdom after Fr. Joseph Mary Bernini had healed the throat ulcer of the queen. A few converts were made among the outcaste Mushahar community and a church was constructed in 1751. Bernini, the apostle of Bettiah, believed that "a drop of ink makes millions to think." He eventually achieved the celebrated status of a scholar. He wrote seven volumes on Hinduism, *Adi Atma Ramahen*. He translated *Vishnu Purana* and *Ramayana* from Sanskrit into Italian. Francis Mary of Tours, the first Capuchin in Patna is the author of *Thesaurus Linguae Indiane*, the Latin-Hindustani Dictionary.[9] In their missionary debates the Brahmin Pandits accused that Christianity was worse than Muhammadanism and is to be abhorred.

Governor Maquirrum Khan of Patna, a Muslim, having become a Christian in Goa, where he had been Ambassador of Jahangir, imitating Akbar the Great, invited the Jesuit missionaries to Patna in 1620. There were already a few Portuguese Catholics in his army. A small church was built by John in 1620 and the foundation for a Catholic community was laid. However, due to the antagonism of some Muslims very little work could be done. The failure of Tibet-Nepal mission enhanced the importance of Patna, initially a stepping stone to Tibet, with a good number of Armenean and Goan Catholics. In 1846 Athanasius Hartmann OFM Cap. who was working in Gwalior was elevated as the first Vicar Apostolic of Patna, bifurcating the Vicariate Apostolic of Agra, which he administered with great missionary zeal between 1846–50; and 1858–65. In the interim

---

8. Lorenzen, *The Scourge*, 22–23.
9. D'Souza, *History*, 102–3.

The Future of Missions in the Hindu Belt

period Hartmann, a man great ability and holiness, was transferred to Bombay as Vicar Apostolic to settle the scandalous Padroado-Propaganda fights over territorial jurisdiction, churches and properties. The large territory of half a million square kms with twenty million people had only 2,700 Catholics. The small number of converts were ostracized and treated as an outcaste group. Only four priests were available to render minimum pastoral services to Catholic soldiers and they were given remunerations by the British Government. The travel facilities in those days were very meager. For instance travel from Patna to Bettiah by bullock cart or by walking took five days, covering an average of twenty miles per day.[10] It was nearly impossible to visit all the stations even once a year. After the French Revolution (1789), for fifty years the number of priests serving here between three and eight. Some of the missionaries failed to speak either good English or Urdu as a working alternative. The Catholic church, unlike the Protestant churches in India, made little efforts to ordain indigenous clergy because the foreign clergy, particularly the French, was very biased that Indians were incapable of rising to high intellectual as well as moral standard. Vocation for priesthood naturally develop only where there is an educated laity. Till the middle of the twentieth century the Roman Catholic contribution to promotion of education was marginal and they were banned to attend Protestant schools and colleges. During the administration of Hartmann the number of Catholics grew from 2,700–5,000; most of them were Chamar converts. The Indian Revolt of 1857 destroyed many churches, Christian institutions and murdered thousands of Christians, majority of whom were foreigners. And it was a great blow to the fragile mission in the North.

The Jagir or fiefdom of Sardhana, near Meerut, Uttar Pradesh, was donated to Walter Rainhart for his military services to Mughal emperor Shah Alam. After his death, his Muslim concubine Begum Samru, embraced the Catholic faith in 1781 with the new name, Begum Johana and thus Sardhana became an important hub of Catholic missionary activities in the following five decades.[11] Under the leadership of the Begum, the mission expanded and there were about 2,000 Catholics in Sardhana. She built a magnificent church in 1829 and appealed to the Pope to raise it as a diocese. With the appointment of Father Julius Caesar Scottie as the first and last Bishop of Sardhana in 1834 its importance increased temporarily. Another church was constructed in Meerut Cantonment in 1834 by the

10. Lorenzen, *Scourge*, 42.
11. Ibid., 263.

The Future of Christian Mission in India

Begum mainly for the Irish soldiers. However, after her death in 1836 the Christian community, instead of expanding, began to dwindle. As per last will she bequeathed an endowment of Rs. five million for the maintenance of the bishop and various charitable institutions she founded.[12]

The Agra and Patna Vicariates were conspicuous by the absence of Catholic schools while the Protestant missionaries were aggressively opening English medium schools. The growing influence of English education by the Protestant missions prompted the *Propaganda Fide* to entrust the Bengal mission to the English Jesuits at Calcutta in 1834. Soon women congregations too arrived to strengthen the Catholic mission, particularly education of girls. Bishop J. A. Borghi, Vicar Apostolic of Tibet-Hindustan mission and A. Hartmann of Patna were instrumental in inviting Loreto Sisters (1841), The Daughters of the Cross (1861), Institute of Blessed Virgin Mary to open schools and orphanages. The government granted some financial assistance to the Loreto Sisters in Calcutta in 1842 for the education of European girls of good family as well as education of Indian girls from poor class. The Congregation of Jesus and Mary arrived in Agra and opened a school in November 1842; opened another school in Sardhana in 1845. Institute of the Blessed Virgin Mary arrived in Bankipore, Patna, in 1853; opened a school and admitted students without any social discrimination.[13] In the course of the following century these nuns established numerous educational institutions across the length and breadth of the country and emerged as pioneer educators, particularly education of girls.

The Christian population of Bihar consists of three ethnic communities-Bettiah Christians in north Bihar; Dalit Christians in central Bihar and Tribals in South-east Bihar. "As among the tribals the first Dalits who approached the Catholic missionaries had been Protestant converts who had been left in the lurch by their pastors."[14] This case was by no means an exception. The mass movement of the Depressed Class to the Protestant churches in the beginning of the twentieth century spurred the American Jesuit missionaries of Chicago Province to venture into the new field in 1930s. It resulted in the conversion of nearly 50,000 Chamars. Among the Catholics one finds also a small number of Dusadhs, or weavers, Doms or funeral attendants and Mushars or rat hunters. When the American Jesuits started their work among the Chamars in Patna the oppressed Dalits were

---

12. Ibid., 45–46, 191.
13. D'Souza, *History,* 118–24.
14. Kalapura, "Dignity Discovered," 105.

The Future of Missions in the Hindu Belt

very glad to accept the invitation of the missionaries. A ninety year old catechist testified to this author: "When the white American missionaries in their white cassock entered the huts of untouchables, who used to be kicked around by the upper castes, and caressed our dirty children, we experienced an inexplicable joy of the Christian invitation that was offered to us. We gladly responded." The existence of about 55, 000 Dalit Catholics in northern regions of Patna is the result of their missionary struggle. The Dalit culture was a culture of silence and the Dalit experiences were the primordial experiences of fear, deprivation and inhumanity. The conversion experience was a process of gradual liberation. This was also the period when the Dalit movement in Maharashtra was becoming powerful under the leadership of B. R. Ambedkar who later embraced Buddhism. Many new Christians in Ahmednagar district, Maharashtra, followed Ambedkar's example. The Bettiah Catholics have maintained their distinct identity with a population of 13,000. The recently created Bettiah diocese (1998) accounts for 6,000 Catholics and the others have migrated to various urban centres.[15] Forty Protestant churches and sects in Bihar claim the membership of 1,57,100 Christians, including 3,300 caste Christians.

The Catholic mission in Madhya Pradesh owes its origin to the Jesuit military chaplain in Sirgarh, near Bhopal in 1750. A certain Philip de Bourbon of Navara, France, served emperor Akbar from 1560 and his descendents served different Mulsim rulers in various parts of India. The origin of the Catholic community here begins with some of the descendents of de Bourbon in 1743 and small number of converts. By 1770 there were 1500 Catholics. Alarmed by the increasing influence of Christians the local Brahmins attacked and killed around 400 Catholics at a Christmas celebration in 1778.[16] In the following decades the number of Catholics both by immigration and conversion increased to around 1,500. In 1871 Msgr. A. Hartmann of Patna appointed a resident priest and in following year a church was built. The scandalous life style of Bourbons who became Islamized, with many wives in Purdhas, dampened the work of the missionaries as did the scandalous life style of Portuguese soldiers particularly in the sixteenth and seventeenth century. The next mission to be opened in M.P. was Khandwa. The Missionaries of St. Francis de Sales in Jabalpur began to visit Khandwa, and built a small chapel in 1870. Kandwas was a cantonment as well as a railway station that attracted some Catholics, majority of whom were Goans. Eventually around 250 dalit Bhalais were

---

15. Kalapura, "Dignity Discovered," 77–78, 102.
16. Poruthur, *Glimpse of Mission* , 32–34.

received in the church. The sisters of St. Joseph of Chambery arrived in 1894 and opened a school for girls in a small bungalow, rented from the Railways. Another school was opened by the priests for the education of boys. With grant and donation from the railway a school and a convent were constructed. The educational apostolate of the sisters are being continued even today after a century. The Franciscan Missionary Brothers who arrived from Nagpur in 1901 began their tours of villages. Some of the late arrivals were the Norbertines or Fathers of the Abbey of Berne, Holland, in Jabalpur in 1929, the Divine Word Missionaries in Indore in 1932, and the Pallottines, The Society of the Catholic Apostolate, in Raipur in 1951.

The Rajputana mission was detached from the archdiocese of Agra and entrusted to the French Capuchins in 1890. After two years the Prefecture Apostolic of Rajputana-Malwa was erected. They also extended their missionary activities to the Bhils in Jhabua district and Barwani; to the Harijans in the Nimar, Madhya Pradesh in the beginning of the twentieth century. Bishop Fortunatus Henri Caumont, with the collaboration of Mother Mary Matilda, founded two women Congregations: Prabhu Dasi Sisters of Ajmeer in 1906 to work among rural women; and Mission Sisters of Ajmeer in 1911, to work among urban women. Sophia college in Ajmeer was founded for higher education of girls. In north India the Capuchins who established most of the Catholic centres over a period of 250 years were the most important missionary order

After two decades of correspondence and negotiations the *Propaganda Fide* entrusted part of the mission in central India to the Divine Word Missionaries in 1932. Indore, Mhow, Bhopal, Ujjain, Khandwa, Nimar, and the tribal areas of Jhabua and Thandla were detached from the dioceses of Ajmeer, Nagpur and Allahabad to create the new Prefecture of Indore in 1935 with Peter Janser as Prefect Apostolic. It covered a territory of 40,000 square miles, with nearly 13,000 Catholics, among six million people.[17] Dr. Stephen Fuchs SVD was the first Catholic missionary to make a systematic anthropological study of the Dalits, Bhalais, titled *Children of Hari* (Vienna, 1950). After a decade the Old Testament was translated into Hindi by Stanislaus Wald SVD. Tibet and Nepal which remained obstinately closed to missionaries for nearly 250 years, at last in 1950, agreed to receive missionaries for educational and medical purpose only.

---

17. Ibid., 60.

The Future of Missions in the Hindu Belt

Distribution of Christians in the BIMARU States

After 500 years of mission in the cow belt the presence of mere 6,75,915 Christians, according to 2001 Census Report, in a population of 365 million is like drop in the bucket and in numerical terms it is a total failure. Their distribution in four states is as follows: Bihar 2,20,100; Madhya Pradesh 1,70,381; Uttar Pradesh 2,12,578; Rajasthan 72,660. And the Catholic population numbers 3,74,650.[18] Its influence through various institutions and services will be illustrated below. Initially the mission in the Hindi belt mustered certain royal patronage and influence with the rulers. The result was a few individual conversions from the royal Muslim families. Most of the Catholic mission centers were started for the soldiers and other foreigners who had no roots in the local culture. "The thrust the mission work received in its early stages was lost largely due to . . . the mushrooming of chaplaincies and churches in railway colonies and military cantonments in the days of the British Raj, with the care of soul."[19] With a few personnel, limited resources and other problems mission failed to be a priority. The fate of many of these small communities was linked to the rise and fall of a certain princely rulers who in general supported missionaries with both land, construction of churches and financial remuneration for the maintenance of chaplains. The era was marked by appreciation and cooperation between rulers and Christian mission, in contrast to antagonism in the later period. The problem of Christian communities without deep roots in the local culture and loyalty to the local Church continues, to some extent at least, even today.

The vast majority of Christians in the Hindu belt belong to the scheduled castes. The image of the church among the general public is that Christian mission is for the Dalits and not for the caste Hindus. As almost all Dalit converts were landless their tendency in general to depend on the church and missionaries for economic help is quite evident. This tendency, in some sense, is a transfer of their past habit of dependency on landlords. These Christians suffer from double discrimination: that is, from government which refuses scholarships for education of children as well as job reservations which Hindu, Buddhist and Sikh Dalits enjoy as Constitutional rights; and in the church the traditional caste mentality continuous, often in subtle manner. In contrast the tribal Christians own land and were least influenced by the Hindu culture from which they maintained a safe distance. Most of the missionaries working with these

18. *Census of India 2001*, in Bantia, *First Report on Religion*, xxix, xxxiii.
19. Bhatt, "Catholic Mission," 178.

communities express a sense of disappointment or even frustration. If one is tempted compare the responses of tribal missions with Dalit missions, it could become worse. Since they lived on the margin of the Hindu community, they are to some extent influenced by traditional Hindu beliefs and customs. The dominant castes never wanted them to practice Hinduism, nor did they allow them to accept Christianity. However the new generation equipped with education and employment are marked by more positive attitudes.

Distribution of Missionaries and Institutions in the Hindu Belt

Majority of the missionaries in the Hindu belt do not hail from the local Church; the post-independence period the foreign missionaries were gradually replaced by missionaries from Southern and Western India. As the local churches are growing into their own identity and strength conflicts between the local churches and the missionaries from other regions are on the increase. The post-Vatican optimism and CBCI planning was the backdrop of establishing ten Syro-Malabar Rite dioceses outside Kerala. The old Rite conflicts of the colonial period continue to be operative even today in a subtle manner. At the twenty ninth General body meeting of the CBCI at Guwahati, Assam in February 2010, late Cardinal Varkey Vithayathil, Major Archbishop of Syro-Malabar church and the then CBCI president, expressed his concern as follows: "The unpleasant incidents of inter-ritual rivalry that take place sometimes makes me doubt if we are sufficiently educating our faithful, priests and religious in understanding our unity in diversity—. Justice has to be done to all the three ritual churches. Each *Sui juris* church getting its due has been my dream, a dream that remains unfulfilled."[20] The CBCI Evaluation Report (1995) based on 2,337 responses, on the statement: "The CBCI has not been playing an effective role in resolving or easing conflicts between the Churches / Rites," found the following responses: 66 percent agreed to the statement and another 30 percent agreed, "to some extent." Thus the Rite conflicts are doing much harm to the Indian Mission.[21]

Today only 1,776 priests are available for the evangelization of the Hindi belt. Out of these 317 are in Bihar with the highest concentration in Patna diocese. Four out of five dioceses have less than fifty priests each. 624 priests are spread out in nine dioceses of Madhya Pradesh. Two of them have less than fifty priests each. Uttar Pradesh, the largest state, has only

20. Vithayathil, "Presidential Address."
21. D'Souza, *Evaluation Report*, 273.

The Future of Missions in the Hindu Belt

695 priests. Out of nine dioceses here only Varanasi has nearly 150 priests. The whole of Rajasthan has only 140 priests in comparison to Delhi with over 200. Taking into consideration the number of 23,146 priests in India, the availability of priests in the Hindi region for 3,43,663 Catholics, is very low. And the total population of the four Hindi states is 365 million.

Out of over 1,00,000 nuns in India, only 5,567 are rendering their pastoral and missionary services in the Hindi belt. Nearly half of the Sisters serving in the Hindi belt are in Uttar Pradesh (2,658) with highest concentration in Meerut (518) and Varanasi (464). Madhya Pradesh has 1956 sisters with the highest concentrations in Bhopal (404) followed by 326 and 320 in Jabalpur and Indore respectively. This is followed by 838 Sisters in Bihar with the largest concentration in undivided Patna (193). In Rajasthan their number is 807 with a highest concentration in Ajmeer (478).[22] In most dioceses where evangelization is no more primarily centered around proclamation, administration of sacraments like Baptism, Eucharist, confessions, and so forth, nuns render equal, and in some cases, more services than priests. Nuns are the most visible signs and examples of Christian witness through their dedicated services in the field of education, health and other social institutions of service to the poor and unwanted. Unfortunately in many instances this fact is not openly recognized or appreciated and they are not given equality in status as well as in decision-making processes. Reading the present trend of vocations, the conspicuous presence as well as services of the nuns will continue for the coming decades. It is informed that certain ecclesiastical authorities in the South, the source of maximum vocations in the past, are discouraging missionary vocations for the Hindi belt. This attitude is aggravated by the recent violence against missionaries, specially the nuns, by the Hindu fundamentalists and communal forces. While the number of vocations for priesthood and sisterhood is steady, vocations for Brotherhood is not bright; for example, in the past twenty five years their number in India increased only marginally from 3,000 in 1984 to 3,398 by 2005, i.e., a growth of 400 in twenty five years. Unlike the priests and nuns proportionately more Brothers (262) are engaged in the Hindi belt. Vast majority of them are in the educational apostolate and are found predominantly in three states: sixty five in Bihar; ninety one in Uttar Pradesh and seventy six in Madhya Pradesh. Recent Census Reports reveal sizeable decline of child

---

22. Collated by the author from Kanjirakat, ed., *Catholic Directory of India 2005-6*, 35-41.

births in Kerala, Mangalore, Goa and Bombay which will lead to a significant decline in vocations.

During the last six decades the North Indian church has witnessed phenomenal institutional growth, without corresponding growth of the Christian communities. At the time of India's Independence, there were only six dioceses in the Hindi region. By 2005 they have increased to thirty three. These include six Syro-Malabar-rite dioceses which extended their missionary activities to the North after Vatican Council II, and the follow up of "All India Seminar. Church in India Today." The number of Christian colleges has grown from eight in 1950 to thirty three in 2005. Dispensaries and hospital multiplied from 190 to 326. Today there are 530 high and higher secondary schools in the region compared to sixty nine at the time of independence.[23] The growth of other Church institutions also follows the same trend. Because of the large number of Catholic institutions and the quality of services rendered to the public through these institutions, the Catholic Church's power and influence has spread far beyond its numerical strength. The numerical weakness is, in some degree, balanced by the number of institutions and the quality of dedicated services. The present trend indicates that the institutional expansion will be on the increase. The fast growth of evangelical and Pentecostal sects and cults during the past quarter of a century is probably a strong reaction to high degree of institutionalization.

Major engagements of missionary personnel in the Hindu belt fall under the following categories: a) running educational institutions, with increasing number of English medium schools; b) health services, mainly manned by nuns; c) administration of dioceses, seminaries, and formation houses; d) engagement exclusively in pastoral-missionary activities. Due to poor response of the people or minimum pastoral opportunities some of the priests in the Hindi region experience more frustrations than those who serve in the tribal missions; e) the religious, both men and women, who live and work in non-institutional set up, among the poor and marginalized in order to conscientize, empower and organize them and thus participate in their struggle for liberation and human dignity. The following picture of people and activities depict a major image of the emerging missions and mission theology in the Hindi belt. "The mud houses and the people who live therein remain the locus of the Kingdom . . . Kingdom is seen as a project, being shaped by human hands under the watchful eyes of God. . . ." The new mission demands new spirituality. "Experience

---

23. Ibid., 35–41.

The Future of Missions in the Hindu Belt

of the Divine in the midst of such events; contemplatives in the liberative action."[24] In the absence of strong religious motivation coupled with frustrations, number of those who abandon their vocation is increasing.

Missiological Reflections

The above statistical data reveal that Christian mission was a failure not only in the Hindu belt but also in the whole of India. In the past 130 years the Christian population in India increased from less than 1 percent (1871) to with 2.5 percent 2001. Though the missionaries, with a sense of failure among caste Hindus, diverted their attention to less sophisticated communities like the tribals and dalits the result was not very encouraging. For instance, probably only seventeen million Tribals and Dalits, out of a combined population of 250 million, might have embraced Christianity as an alternative route to liberation. In the last four decades the Christian population has marginally declined by 10 percent. What kind of missiological conclusions can be deduced from the above analysis of missionary efforts and results either in the Hindi belt or in the whole of India for 500 years?

Conclusion one: With less than 3 percent Christians, the result of proclamation and baptism of pagans to Christianity during 2000 years, in quantitative terms, Christian mission in India is a failure. Mass conversion has little future, on the contrary, during the past two decades Christian population has suffered minor decline. However Christianity's direct impact on nearly thirty million people and indirect impact, specially through their numerous institutional services on many more millions of Indians, should not be overlooked.

Conclusion two: In qualitative terms mission is assessed as a success. More important and enduring results are visible in following areas; (a) the impact of the Christian mission in the social transformation of India, through numerous reforms brought about by the British administrators, many of whom were moved by evangelical spirit, and the Christian missionaries, particularity the Protestants; (b) the intellectual transformation of India through Western scientific education, the study of Bible and Christian literature, liberal philosophy and other factors like industrialization, secularization and Westernization; (c) through the pioneering of education for all, including women, tribals and harijans; missionaries challenged and al-

---

24. Vellamkunnel, "Evangelization," 204–5.

tered the traditional Brahmin monopoly of education and knowledge; (d) The highly hierarchical caste structure was abolished, at least in principle, by the introduction of philosophy of equality, irrespective of religion, caste and sex; (e) a few caste converts, mostly among the Protestants, emerged as pioneers of Indian Christian theology, conspicuously absent for nearly 1,900 years.

Mission Deserts of the World among the World Civilizations

All the great religions of the world were born in Asia. Jesus Christ was born in Asia but compared to other continents Asia is least Christian, with exception of the Philippines. Jesus was a Jew, but not only his prophetic teaching was rejected in Israel but he was also exterminated by the Jews in collaboration with the Roman political authorities. Buddha was born in India, but Buddhism could not flourish in India where Hinduism was already well established but it spread mostly outside of India. Mohammad was born in Saudi Arabia and West Asia was subjected to Islam, Sunni and Shiite, not without eliminating Christianity by force.[25] An insignificant number of Christians in Asia, mostly from the marginal groups, makes this vast territory a missionary desert.

The failure of the Christian Mission not only to Hindus but to whole of Asia raises fundamental challenges and questions. Why mission was stubbornly resisted as encroachment on other religions and civilizations? Why the Christian mission could achieve certain measure of success only among the tribal and marginal communities of Asia? Is the "Constantine Model of Mission" where states and the church actively collaborated for the extension of mission in terms of preaching and baptizing pagans valid today? In the post-colonial period, what is the future of the Christian mission in India and Asia? The third millennium is witnessing a power shift from the traditional West to non-Western civilizations. The paradigm shift in mission, i.e., the centre of the world Christianity is shifting from the Atlantic region towards Pacific region, was already predicted by W. Buehlmann in his, *The Coming of the Third Church*.

The idea of civilization was developed by the French scholars of the eighteenth century in contrast to the idea of barbarism and savagery of primitive communities. The emerging school of anthropology was focusing on the study of tribal people in lower rungs of a more evolved western civilization. A civilized society is characterized by settled, urban, literate, complex and specialized labor force. The German scholars drew a dis-

25. Moffett, *History*, 2:xiii–xv.

The Future of Missions in the Hindu Belt

tinction between civilization which involved mechanical technology and material factors and culture (kultur), constituting values, ideals and higher intellectual, moral and artistic qualities, created, maintained and promoted by an elite minority in the society. Civilization is defined both by common objective elements such as race, language, history, religion, customs, institutions and by subjective self identification of people. Civilizations unique and particular essence is their long historical continuity, in spite of political, economic and social upheavals.[26] The Aztecs and Incas, ancient Greece and Roman empire, among a few others, are examples of extinct civilizations.

It seems that no well established religion with its own Holy Book, believed to be inspired by God, with its own well articulated philosophical-theological foundation, meaningful worship system, and priests or equivalent office bearers as the watchdogs of their religion, was ever conquered by another religion. All the well established living Asian civilizations—Sinic or Confucian, Japanese, closely linked to the Chinese culture, Hindu and Islamic—in spite of periodic internal and external threats like natural calamities or violent political conquests from outside, have stubbornly resisted any encroachment by the European civilization or Christianity and still continue to survive for millennia. Religion is a central defining characteristic of civilization and as Christopher Dawson argued: "the great religions are the foundations on which the great civilizations rest."[27]

The colonial expansion, started in the beginning of the sixteenth century reached its climax by 1920 when 85 percent of the world was colonized. By the beginning of the twentieth century the world was more one entity politically and economically than at any time in human history. The Western administrative systems were operative in most colonized nations. Civilization meant Western civilization.[28] Thus a multi-civilization systems emerged. Currently the four competing civilizations are: the Christian West with American and European values; China with its ethnic homogeneity and Confucian civilization, arching from the pacific to Africa; India, with its long religious history, is emerging as the third largest economy and soft power; and aggressive Islam with membership in the middle East, central Asian republics, East Asia, South Asia, and Eastern Europe. Will they, clash or cooperate for a better future?

26. Huntington, *Clash*, 40–43. Sharpe, *Faith Meets*, 53–55.
27. Quoted by Huntington, *Clash*, 47.
28. Ibid., 51–52.

The Future of Christian Mission in India

India was conquered and dominated by the Muslim and Christian powers for nearly eight centuries (1204-1947). In the colonial period missionaries were normally permitted to enter only those territories that were under the colonial domain of their nationality. "Pepper and Soul" were the goals of both the Asian conquerors and missionaries. Confronted with British colonialism and missionary attacks the wounded Hindu pride was challenged to search for its identity. The founding of Arya Samaj by Dayananda Saraswati in Bombay in 1875, the Hindu Mahasabha by Lala Lajpat Rai in Punjab in 1920, the Rashtriya Swayamsevak Sangh by Dr. K. B. Hedgewar in Nagpur in 1925, were the initial steps towards identity clarification. Who am I? Where do I belong? were compelling questions, seeking answers? All religions furnish people with a sense of identity and direction in life. The Indian religious renaissance was a reaction against corrosion of Indian religion and values because of conversion to Christianity and introduction of western values. A call to conversion to Christianity was equally a call to abandon one's own cherished sacred identity. V. D. Savarkar's book, *Hindutva. Who is a Hindu?* (1923) and M. S. Golwalkar's *We or Our Nation Defined* (1939) were aggressive attempts to answer the question of Hindu identity. Asserting nearly 4000 years old Hindu identity Savarker reformulated: "These are the essentials of Hindutva— a common nation or territory, a common race, the Aryan and common culture, Sanskriti—Sanskritic, including Sanskaras, i.e., rites and rituals ceremonies and sacraments that make the land a holy land."[29] The Hindu thinkers of this period were very much under the influence of the German school of civilization, the Aryan concept of race of Adolf Hittler's Nazism and Mussolini's fascism. People define their identity by characteristics that distinguish themselves from other groups as well as by what they are not. When I say, "I am a Catholic," it also implies that 'I am not a Lutheran' or 'I am not a Hindu.' "In an increasingly globalized world . . . there is an exacerbation of civilizational, societal and ethnic consciousness."[30] In the post-Independence India, Jana Sangh was formed by S. P. Mookherjee in 1951, with the RSS ideology and support of RSS leaders, as its political wing, with eleven regional branches. After 1967 Assembly elections Jana Sangh formed coalition governments in M.P, Bihar, U.P, Haryana, Punjab, and Delhi. It was the beginning of Saffronization of Indian politics. Promotion of Hindi as the national language, cow protection and reconversion of new Christians were part of their election manifesto.

---

29. Savarkar, *Hindutva*, 116.
30. Huntington, *Clash*, 68.

The Future of Missions in the Hindu Belt

A century ago at the peak of the Great Protestant Century church historian Julius Richter raised a very thorny question about the failure of mission in India. "The great problem of missionary work is: How can Christianity overcome and supplant native forms of religion? . . . What has been up to the present the attitude of Indian religions towards Christianity and what prospects are there for their ultimate overthrow?"[31] So far nobody has provided an adequate answer to his grave question. My view is that all scholars of mission failed to understand the self sustaining power of world civilizations. No world civilization is capable of conquering another world civilization. A civilization could be marginally and peripherally attacked and modified. Its core is indestrucable. India was politically conquered by Islam and Christianity for eight hundred years. But Hinduism survived and continue to flourish. And Hinduism, in the similar manner, will not succeed to overthrow Christianity, Islam and other civilizations.

In other parts of Asia too the expansion of Christianity was gravely arrested by: the persecution of Christians in Persia in the fourth century; in West Asia by the Muslim expansion from the eighth century, that climaxed in the fatal blow by Tamerlane at the end of the fourteenth century; in China in the eighth and ninth centuries and later by the Boxer rebellion of 1900; and the persecution of and extermination of a flourishing Catholic community in Japan at the end of the sixteenth century. And Christian missionaries were expelled from the Buddhist Tibet and Hindu Nepal in the eighteenth century. On the failure of Christian mission in Asia Joseph Neuner who taught theology in India for half a century and a Peritus in the Vatican Council observes: "The expansion of the European church to the world faced its worst crises and finally failed in Asia. On the Asian continent she encountered the ancient religions as they had developed within the great cultures of India, China, and Japan. She could neither conquer nor penetrate them." ". . . Forever the expansion of the church to the new world will be tragically associated with the colonial conquest, domination and exploitation of the new continents by the West."[32] Thus Asia was the greatest challenger of Christian mission in the past and will continue to be so in the future.

The Future of Christian Mission in India

The most significant result of past Hindu-Christian confrontations is the arrival at a win-win situation whereby both religions reexamined and

31. Quoted by Webster, *Historiography*, 30.
32. Neuner, "Inaugural Address," 19.

modified their initial positions, leading to mutual enrichment. "Win/win sees life as a cooperative, not a competitive arena. Win/win is based on the paradigms . . . that one person's success is not achieved at the expense or exclusion of the success of others."³³ And most situations in fact, are part of an interdependent reality and then Win/win is really the only viable alternative of the five." The five alternative paradigms are Win/win, Lose/win, lose/lose, win and Win/win.

A Win/Win Paradigm

A win/win paradigm is evident in the post-Vatican II missiology of the Catholic church, and major Protestant churches, excluding the Pentacostals and the Evangelicals. The shift from the traditional exclusive missiology to an inclusive missiology which recognizes the possibility of salvation of believers of other religions is radical. It is accepted by vast majority of the Indian missionaries. The transition from the traditional to new missiology is painful for many missionaries as well as ecclesiastical authorities in India. On the one hand the new theology is being formulated partly under the influence of Hinduism. At the popular level Christianity was seen as foreign and Western. This belief is reinforced by the Western theology that dominates India; by Latin and Syrian rite liturgy; Western architecture and art; Western hymns and prayers; Western life style and so forth. Certain efforts were made to correct this perception. Robert de Nobili in the sixteenth century initiated a process to create an inculturated church. Unfortunately he was forced by church authorities to discontinue his experiments. The Twentieth century witnessed fresh attempts. Names of a few prominent pioneers, without elaborating the content of their works, are mentioned. Non-baptized Christians like Keshub Chandra Sen; Catholic theologian Brahmabandhab Upadhyaya; Presbyterian J. N. Farquhar; The Bhakti school is represented by Sadhu Sundar Singh, Krishna Pillai and Narayan Tilak; theologians like Bishop Appaswamy and Raimundo Panikkar; Indian mystical tradition blended in the writings of Swami Abhishiktananda, Bede Griffiths, and Sara Grant; D. S. Amalorpavdas in liturgy; liberation theologian Samuel Rayan; dalit theologians like A. P. Nirmal and James Massey; tribal theologian like Bishop Nirmal Minz; Indian artist like Jyoti Sahi, and Indian feminist like Pandita Ramabai. And many more Indian scholars.

On the other hand, Hinduism was also purified and modified under the impact of Evangelical mission and Orientalist scholars from the end

33. Covey, *Seven Habits*, 207.

The Future of Missions in the Hindu Belt

of the eighteenth century and from the beginning of the nineteenth century. On the transformation that India experienced in its encounter with the Western civilization and missionary activities Indian historian K. M. Pannikkar observes:

> The inheritance that India has stepped into is only partly Hindu and Indian. The influence from the West is no less important. Modern India does not live under the laws of Manu. Its mental background and equipment, though largely influenced by the persistence of Indian tradition have been modeled into their present shape over a hundred years of Western education, extending practically every field of mental activity. Its social ideals are not what Hindu society had for long cherished but those assimilated from the West—The religious beliefs of Hinduism have been transformed substantially during the course of the last hundred years. In fact it will be no exaggeration to say that the new Indian state represents traditions, ideals and principles which are the result of an effective but imperfect synthesis between the East and the West.[34]

An enlightened openness to be influenced by the western philosophy, ideologies and technologies was a necessity since the Indian system was almost inherently incapable of generating them. Indian historian Ramachandra Guha opines:

> In my opinion there was little in the history and politics of the remote past that could have aided Indians in interpreting and confronting the profound changes that came in the wake of colonial rule. The necessity of a free press, the equality of women, the abolition of untouchability, the right of equal citizenship, the ending of mass poverty . . . these ideals and aspirations were beyond the experience and imagination of ancient or medieval scholars and rulers. Rather they were the product of the national and democratic revolutions that took place in the nineteenth and twentieth centuries and of the urban, industrial and social revolutions that accompanied them.[35]

All should be happy that the Gospel is freed from the 'Constantine Model' of Mission. The mission territories of Asia, Africa and Oceania should rejoice in its independence; yet unfortunately the third world churches continue to depend on western thinking, culture and resources.

34. Panikkar, *Foundation*, 15–16.
35. Guha, *Sunday Times* (October 17, 2010) 20.

The Future of Christian Mission in India

The unprecedented world political restructuring ushers in new opportunities for the young churches. The traditional model of mission emphasized sociological conversion of pagans by baptism and membership in the church, deviating from Jesus' proclamation of the Reign of God and call for inner conversion. Jesus addressed the Jews and said "The time is fulfilled and the Rule of God has come: change your hearts and believe the Good News" (Mark 1:14-15). There are eighty references to 'conversion' in the New Testament: *metanoia*, twenty two times and *metanoien* thirty four times. In the background of the Old Testament, conversion meant to "turn away from idols." It also meant a radical transformation of one's mind, a reversal of one's priorities. Repent means believe in the Good News of God's gratuitous gift of unconditional love. It does not mean change of religion.[36] And M. K. Gandhi was totally in agreement with this definition: "Conversion should mean a definite giving up of the evil of the old, adoption of all the good of the new and a scrupulous avoidance of everything evil in the new. Conversion, therefore, should mean . . . greater surrender to God, greater self-purification."—Conversion should not mean denationalization."[37]

And a shift in the Biblical foundation of the mission is being evolved. That is, from the mission command (Matt 28:18-20) to God's mission of Love (John 3.16). Mission is an overflow of experience of God's love and compassion. In the words of Soares—Prabhu, "Its (Church's) primary mission is that of promoting the growth of the Reign of God. . . . The church, will fulfill this mission by making God's love present in whatever way it can. This simple formula, I believe, describes adequately and accurately the primary mission of the church for where God's love is present, there the Reign of God grows."[38] The radical paradigm shift in Jesus is the shift from the Old Testament God of fear to the New Testament God of Love (1 John: 4.8). Jesus reveals his experience of God as loving Father.

Because Jesus of Nazareth was bound by time, space, culture and history there is an apparent tension between his being particular and universal. The Indian theologians and missionaries, in general, appreciate the position of *Redemptoris Missio* that the Holy Spirit is, "the principal agent of mission" (RM 22). He is present and active in the whole creation, in all religions and cultures, reconciling the traditional divisions and conflicts. Wherever, within the church or outside the church, one finds the fruits of

---

36. Legrand, "Conversion in the Bible," 18-20.
37. Gandhi, *Message of Jesus*, 26.
38. Soares-Prabhu, "Expanding," 47.

The Future of Missions in the Hindu Belt

the Holy Spirit—"love, joy, peace, patience, gentleness and self-control." (Gal 5:22-23)—there the presence and activities of the Holy Spirit is assured. These fruits of the Spirit are indications that God's love has been poured out not only into Christians hearts but also into the hearts of all who seek him with a sincere heart; and they too are children of God (Rom 5:5; 8:16:17; EA. no 15,17). The traditional narrow interpretation of these and similar scriptural passages, in my view, is ethno-centric. The universal operation of the Spirit in other religions and their saints is known from their fruits. "You will know them by their fruits" (Matt 7:20; Lk 6:44). Will it be fair to say that the fruits of the Holy Spirit is less shinning in Mahatma Gandhi, the Father of Indian Nation, than in Blessed Mother Teresa of Calcutta? In the first half of the twentieth century Christian missionaries were more challenged by the spirituality and moral authority of Gandhi than by his erudite discourse against conversions.

What took place between the Spirit of God and Gautama Buddha, Asoka and Muhammad when they received enlightenment or revelation? Rejecting the Biblical fundamentalism of Karl Barth, Hendrik Kraemer, and the sectarian definition of saints Indian theologians are open to identify saints in their own tradition. Saints in the Indian tradition emphasize personal experience of the Divine, that which is seen by the inner eye. Experience of God defies exact communication; expressing only through analogies and symbols. Names of a few popular Indian saints are: Kabir, Ravidass, Tukaraam, Meerabai, Guru Nanak, Tiruvalluvar, Sri Narayana Guru, Mahatma Gandhi, B. Ambedkar and many others. Can missiology claim any bright prospects for India and enter into meaningful dialogue without incorporating the spiritual and social resources of Indian popular saints? It is a sectarian and ethnocentric understanding to confine saints to a certain religion and fail to recognize the shining fruits of works of the Holy Spirit in saints of all religions.

Conversion and Baptism

The complexity of Indian pluralism of religions, cultures, castes, classes and tribes demands plurality of missionary approaches. More importantly the India of the twenty-first century is radically different from the India of the nineteenth century the missionaries encountered. Probably insisting on the quasi-failed model of the mission in India, i.e., social conversion and baptism promises little future. Jesus himself never baptized anybody and probably he never commanded anyone to do things which he himself did not do. If Jesus ever baptized anyone how is it that none of the four evangelists ever mention the event. On the contrary, John the evangelist made a special note that Jesus did not baptize. "The Pharisees heard that Jesus was attracting and baptizing more disciples than John, although Jesus himself did not baptize but only his disciples" (John 4:1–3). After reflecting on the mission in the Gospel of Mathew in the light of the great mission command (Matt 28:16–20), the mission discourse (Matt 10:1–42) and the exhortation to mission (Matt 5:13–16) Soares-Prabhu concludes: "There is, certainly, no suggestion in the Gospel that Jesus himself ever baptized or gave any great importance to this rite. To teach, on the other hand, is an utterly characteristic activity of Jesus in the Gospel."[39] And what about St. Paul, the apostle of the Gentiles? He hardly insisted on baptism. "Christ did not send me to baptize but to preach the Gospel" (1 Cor 1:17). Probably he had baptized just one family (ibid:1:16). In Ephesus Paul met some who had already received the baptism of repentance by John, but not the holy Spirit. So "when Paul laid (his) hands on them the holy Spirit came upon them and they spoke in tongues and prophesied" (Acts 19:6–7). For Paul baptism is the baptism in the holy Spirit, and not baptism of water.

Nonetheless I do not deny the significance of current practice of baptism, already in existence in the inter-testamental period, as a rite of passage. Every community prescribes a rite of passage for its new members. The Jews and Muslims follow the rite of circumcision. The Brahmins prescribe the donning of sacred thread, *dvi-ja*, second birth. Such a rite of passage is necessary and useful to socialize and enculturate the new members into the community. Every new born baby will fail to survive and grow into meaningful and successful life without the process of socialization, learning the art of living as a useful member of the community. It is further noted every socio-cultural rites, as long as they are not marked by sinful elements, are opportunities to enter into contact with the transcendent Absolute. And the community, the locus of the celebration.

As a controversial issue in the Indian context the subject of baptism demands deeper examination. In the new Testament three interrelated understanding of baptism can be discerned. The first is washing (baptism) "Now you have had yourself washed (baptized), you were sanctified, you were justified in the name of the Lord Jesus Christ and in the Spirit of our God" (1 Cor 6:11; 12:13). The second is that of dying and rising, which is strongly Paschal (Rom 6:3–11). Dying to sin is a participation in the death and resurrection of Christ. "Are you unaware that we who were baptized

---

39. Soares-Prabhu, "Following Jesus," 70.

The Future of Missions in the Hindu Belt

into Christ Jesus were baptized into his death? . . . So that, just as Christ was raised from the dead by the glory of the Father, we too might live in newness of life—We shall also be united with him in the resurrection." The third is about new birth. In the dialogue with Nicodemus, rebirth in the Spirit is mentioned three times and reference to water is made in passing or as a symbol of the Spirit. "Amen, Amen I say to you no one can see the Kingdom of God without being born from above" (John 3:3). "No one can enter the Kingdom of God without being born of water and Spirit" (John 3:5). And a third time Jesus repeats; "So it is with everyone who is born of the Spirit" (3:8). The relation between water and the Holy Spirit is clarified by John in the following discourse at the Feast of Tabernacles. "Let any one who thirsts come to me and drink. Whoever believes in me, as scripture says: 'Rivers of living water will flow from within him.' This he said in reference to the Holy Spirit that those who come to believe in him were to receive" (John 7:37–39). The tone of these texts are Pentecostal, fulfilling the prophesy of Joel: "Then I will pour out my Spirit upon all mankind" (3:1–5; Acts 2:17–21). The baptism of John with water was the preparation to receive the baptism of the Spirit. "I baptize you with water; he will baptize you with the holy Spirit" (Mark 1:8). All the three metaphors of washing, dying and rising, and new birth were employed in the early liturgies of the church. Baptisms were administered to adults on specific occasions like Epiphany, Pentecost and above all, Easter, preceded by long preparations and catechesis, lasting up to three years.[40]

That there is no intrinsic link between receiving the Holy Spirit and baptism of water is evident from the instance of pagan Cornelius. "While Peter was still speaking these things, holy Spirit came up on all who were listening to the Word . . . Then Peter responded: can anyone withhold the water for baptizing these people who have received the holy Spirit as we have received? He ordered them to be baptized in the name of Jesus Christ" (Acts 10:40:47–49; 11:15). This is evidence that people do receive the holy Spirit, even without the baptism of water. This conclusion is very important for recognizing the gifts of the holy Spirit even in those people who have not received baptism for whatever reason. In the Indian context the issue has raised unprecedented challenges.

And what about the baptism of Jesus? The baptism of John with water was only a preparation to receive the baptism of the Spirit (Mark 1:8). Jesus was baptized by John according to the social custom of the time and not for the repentance of sin. Jesus was circumcised according to the Jewish

---

40. Stevenson, "Bapitsm," 117–19; Baum, "Baptism," 66–78.

tradition. A physical imitation, or even a cultural imitation of Jesus is not required to be followers of Jesus. The Old Testament rites were either abolished or replaced by alternative rites in the New Testament. Circumcision of the heart (Rom 2:29) and baptism in the holy Spirit are the new rites. The baptism of Jesus in river Jordan was the symbolic invitation for his real baptism at the climax of his mission in the end. "Can you drink the cup that I drink or be baptized with the baptism with which I am baptized?" (Mark 10:38). Jesus asked this question to James and John on their way to Jerusalem and predicting his death and resurrection. His real baptism was the baptism of his passion and death and thus fulfilling the prophesy of the "Suffering Servant" (Isa 42:1–4). Gradually, from the Constantine era baptism degenerated into social and ritual baptism, replacing the baptism in the Spirit. The Christian baptism in its deepest sense is a participation in the baptism of Jesus and commitment to his mission. The Indian Theological Association states: "Participations in people's action for their liberation, with firm belief in God's presence in their midst and trust in his assistance is also an integral dimension of liturgy . . . In this perspective baptism becomes the commitment to a God who commits himself to his people and their struggle, and Eucharist become a celebration of this and their victory" (Isa 1:11–17; Amos 5:21–24).[41]

Change of Hearts, Minds and Society.

In the last two hundred years of Christian mission in India, there are many ardent believers in Jesus Christ, but refusing to be baptized in a particular church or denomination. Prominent among them are Keshub Chandra Sen, P. C. Mazoomdar, and K. Subba Rao. Currently Rao in Andhra Pradesh has the support of a large number of followers. Their rootedness in Hindu religion and culture forces them to be known as Hindu-Christians. They refuse to accept the view of radical discontinuity between Hinduism and Christianity. The Christa Bhakta movement in Varanasi, initiated by the Indian Missionary Society, attracting 50,000–60,000 believers in Jesus Christ per year for prayer, worship and listening to the Word of God, is an example of "Churchless Christianity" for today.[42] More crucial will be the transformation of the Indian mind, world view and life view. In the modern knowledge based society dissemination of knowledge and wisdom to the youth will determine, to a great degree, the future of India. If it is true that future of the nation is being shaped in her class rooms, as the Kothari

41. Parappally, *Theologizing in Context*, 87.
42. Author's interview with the staff, September 10, 2010.

The Future of Missions in the Hindu Belt

Report of the Education Commission envisaged then Christian educational institutions will substantially contribute in shaping the future of India. The civilizing mission to millions of Indians, in a positive sense, is not yet over; it has a bright future. The Christian missionary education policies during the past two centuries have passed through six different goals, adapting to changing contexts: a) discrediting popular Hinduism; (b) purification and civilizing the Hindu society; (c) preparatio evangelica; (d) deepening Christian faith and training Christian leaders; (e) preparing Indians for the emerging political leadership and (f) finally, in the post-Independence period, contributing towards nation building.[43]

Missionaries should be proud that the three contemporary subaltern movements-Dalit movements, Tribal movements, and Backward class movements—for liberation of the marginalized from all physical and social forces of oppression, owe their origin and inspiration to the challenging missionary movements of last 150 years. "It is here the church/Christians can play an enabling role in order to strengthen in future the solidarity movement of these subaltern groups of Indian society."[44] In contrast to the nineteenth century when missionaries were the only agents of liberation of these marginalized categories today the Christian mission is reduced to one of the many agents and therefore collaboration with other agents becomes imperative. The social impact of the Gospel of Jesus, as in the cases of Ram Mohan Roy and the members of Brahmo Samaj, Prarthana Samaj and other Samajes across the length and breadth of the country, is still attractive and meaningful. For M. K.Gandhi, Jesus was the supreme Satyagrahi, seeker God, and model of Ahimsa, non-violence. For Swami Vivekananda Christ was the Jivan Mukta. Pandita Ramabai discovered him as a great liberator of women. It is a matter of great satisfaction that all the builders of modern India, with minor exceptions, were deeply influenced by Jesus and his radical Gospel message, unparallel in other religious traditions. He continues to be irresistible to millions of people, including contemporary socialists and communists. The person of Jesus, his teachings and prophetic actions deserve to be widely made known.

The current missiology, unlike in the past, acknowledges the presence and work of God's Spirit in world religions, cultures and human history even before the arrival of the missionary in a particular place (AG.4). Yet it is not easy to search and discover His hidden presence. Today the prophetic mission of the church in India is to read the signs of the time

---

43. Webster, *Social History,* 182–272.
44. Massey, "Subaltern People," 40.

in the light of the Gospel; to inspire and invite all people of good will to struggle and fight together to overcome the power of Evil, in individuals and structures. The renewal of humanity, the goal of evangelization, is a complex process (EN 17, 18, 19). The missionaries are asked to die to the Western conquest and triumphalist model that continues to persist, at least in some degree, and exhorted to imitate the Servant model of Jesus. For example, Blessed Mother Teresa of Calcutta whose birth centenary was celebrated all over the world (2010) by people of all religions or no religion, is the most loved, appreciated and esteemed missionary of the twentieth century. She emerged as the gentle, yet powerful conscience keeper of the world for the utterly unwanted poor. Moved by her touching example, innumerable volunteers collaborate with the Missionaries of Charity. How is it that she was admired as a great missionary when Mother cleaned lepers and picked up the dying from the gutters of Calcutta but when her non-Christian volunteers do the same service they are labeled mere social workers? I believe that they too are missionaries. When Mother started her service to the poorest of the poor in the streets of Calcutta she was criticized for encouraging conversion to her faith. Her answer was: "I do convert. I convert you to be a better Hindu, a better Muslim, a better Protestant, a better Sikh. Once you have found God it is up to you to do with Him as you wish."[45] She believed conversion was God's work. There are instances where people of other religions, inspired by the touching example of Blessed Mother Teresa, embraced Christianity. The conversion of Malcolm Muggeridge, an Anglican journalist, after making a documentary film on Mother Teresa for the BBC, to Catholicism is a famous case. And he wrote the book on her, *Something Beautiful for God*. All the people of good will are now entering a new age of common mission, that is, all are equal partners and collaborators with God in the creation of a better world with the values of fullness of life, love, peace, justice, liberty and human dignity.

---

45. Chawla, "Pencil in the Hand," 28.

10

Emerging Missions and Missiologies for the Future

"Life can only be understood backwards but must be lived forwards"
—Søren Kirkegaard

Mission Trends until the Middle of the Twentieth Century

Protestant Mission Trends

UNLIKE THE ROMAN CATHOLIC church the Protestant churches are fragmented into denominational churches and these churches have seldom produced official documents on mission worth scholarly probing."[1] They are divided into a variety of denominations: Lutherans, Calvinists, Anabaptists, Anglicans, Methodists and others. After the Reformation lack of church interest in missions prompted certain individuals to establish independent voluntary mission societies. Some of the earliest missionary guidelines, rather than theology, in India were articulated by the German Lutheran missionaries in Tamil Nadu in the beginning of the eighteenth century and by the Baptist and other Evangelical missionaries in Bengal and other regions of India, from the beginning of the nineteenth century. Already in the beginning of the nineteenth century William Carey noticed the disadvantages of independent working of missionary associations and proposed to meet together and plan together for better missionary services. Unfortunately its realization required more time. From 1855 a few

1. Hrangkhuma, "Protestant Mission," 39.

The Future of Christian Mission in India

regional meetings of different missionary associations were organized in India. These were followed by decennial general missionary conferences held in Allahabad (1872), Calcutta (1882), Bombay (1893) and Madras (1902).[2] Similar conferences were also held in other parts of the world to promote interdenominational cooperation.

The first World Missionary Conference in Edinburgh in 1910 was the starting point of modern Protestant missiology and birth of ecumenical movement. It also marked the culmination of the "Great Protestant Century" of mission. The theme of the conference was: "Evangelization of the World this Century." And the sub title was: "To consider missionary problems in relation to the non-Christian world." At the end of the nineteenth century study of comparative religion or phenomenology as termed later, was gaining strength. In India the Orientalist scholars pleaded for sympathetic approach to other religions, differing from the traditional missionary attitudes. The presentation of Hinduism in Edinburgh was optimistic with the fulfillment theory of Farquhar. Among the topics of deliberations or debate in Edinburgh there was no mention of the theme of mission. The traditional understanding was least doubted by the members of the conference.[3] Among its 1215 delegates was a solitary Indian, V. S. Azariah from Tirunelvelly who read a paper on, "Cooperation between Foreign and Indian workers in the Younger Churches." At the closing speech John Mott, the brain behind the Conference, exhorted: "The end of the Conference is the beginning of the conquest."[4] Edinburgh witnessed the triumphalistic spirit of the west, including the Anglo-American Protestant conquest model of mission. At the end of the Conference a Continuation Committee was set up. Some of the visible fruits of Edinburgh was the formation of the National Missionary Conference in Calcutta in 1914 which was later renamed National Christian Council (1923). The formation of the World Council of Churches had to wait for a few decades (1948). After Edinburgh, a national survey of the mass movement was conducted by the American Methodist Bishop J. W. Pickett, under the auspices of the National Christian Council of India. "It seemed as if the non-Christian world was spread out before the eye of the world to be conquered."[5]

The high optimism of Edinburgh was shaken after World War I. When the recently formed International Missionary Conference met in

2. Ibid., 3–7.
3. Hedlund, "Future of Mission," 128.
4. Boyd, *Christian Encounter*, 6.
5. Ibid., 5.

Emerging Missions and Missiologies for the Future

Jerusalem (1928) with more participants from the mission countries, unlike the Edinburgh conference, its theme was: The Christian Life in relation to Non-Christian Religions. It welcomed "every noble quality in non-Christian persons and systems" as a ray of Christ. Jerusalem was more theological than Edinburgh. But it ended in bundle of theological contradictious.[6] To countract Jerusalem's uncertainty, Hendrik Kraemer (1880–1965), the Dutch missionary and theologian in Muslim Java, Indonesia, prepared *Christian Message in a Non-Christian World* for the International Missionary Conference in Tambaram, Madras (1938). It was also an answer to the ultra-liberal Protestant mission survey in India, Burma, China and Japan and edited by Harvard University philosopher W. E. Hocking, Rethinking *Missions: A Laymen's Enquiry after One Hundred Years* (1932).[7] Kraemer, following the neo-orthodoxy of Karl Barth, nearly restated that non-Christian religions are sinful man's attempt to find God. There is a radical discontinuity between non-Christian religions and the revelation of Jesus Christ. The Ultimate Reality can be known only by God's gratuitous revelation.[8]

Edinburgh had mere twenty delegates from the mission countries, out of a total of 1215. In Tambaram out of 471 delegates, half of them came from the young churches, including sixty one Indians. The composition of the delegates introduced a paradigm shift in the thinking.[9] Rejecting Kraemer's missiology, eminent Christian scholars of Hinduism from Madras Christian College and a few others upheld the position of continuity between non-Christian religions and Christianity. Christianity stands in definite relation with other religions. Many of the Indian participants, particularly the new converts like Vengal Chakkrai Chetty (1880–1958), Pandipeddi Chenchiah (1886–1959), A. J. Appasamy (1891–1975) and other members of the Rethinking *Christianity in India* (1938) resolutely refused to accept the discontinuity theory of Kraemer and his supporters. Some of the radicals even wanted to liberate the Indian church from Western captivity. In the words of Chakkrai: "Let there be no mistake about it, Christianity is not going to drive a wedge in national solidarity ... Let it be clearly understood we accept nothing obligatory save Christ. ... No scheme which is not born of the fervent emotion of the Indian,

---

6. Hedlund, "Future of Mission," 31.
7. Sharpe, *Faith meets Faith*, 82–87.
8. Ibid., 91–98.
9. Kalapati, "Edinburgh to Tambaram," 11.

which is not forgotten of his heart, can hope to thrive."[10] As a new convert he asserted that his attraction was not to Christianity but to Christ. P. Chenchiah argued how new Hindu converts have the advantage of influencing Hinduism from within and he was anxious to retain his cultural heritage. The confrontation was between the Calvinist exclusivism and the Indian inclusivism. This was a radical breakthrough and beginning of the new Indian mission theology. Broadly speaking the Indian theologians were upholders of the "fulfillment theology" introduced by Farquhar's *The Crown of Hinduism*. Tambaram marked the beginning of a paradigm shift in Indian Protestant missiology, while the conservative missiology continued to dominate.

The meeting of the World Council of Churches in New Delhi (1961) with the theme, "Dialogue with people of other Faiths and Ideologies," manifested an inclusive mentality. For the first time the Roman Catholic observers were present at the New Delhi meeting. All these meeting were marked by a certain decline of interest in direct proclamation and rise in interest in humanization. For instance the Uppsala, Sweden, meeting (1968) was dominated by the horizontal mission, with the enormous appeal of Johannes Hoekendijk, who interpreted the *Missio Dei* as recognition of God's reconciling activity in history. He argued that in the post-Christian, post-bourgeois, and post-religious world "other forces in history, possibly even secular men and women, unknown to themselves, are servants of the divine mission and instruments of human reconciliation in peace and justice."[11] At the Commission for World Mission and Evangelization meeting in Bangkok in 1973, in addition to the reflection on the theme, "Salvation Today," fight for the liberation of the young churches from the dominance of the western leadership became very conspicuous.[12] In the meantime the Church of South India was formed in Madras in September 1947, constituting of the Anglicans, Congregationalists, the Methodists and the Presbyterians. And the creation of the Church of North India followed in 1970.

Conflicts between the Evangelicals and Ecumenical Protestants characterized the Protestant theology after Uppsala meeting. Donald A. McGavaran, a leading evangelical missionary in Tamil Nadu for thirty years, became the founder of the "Church Growth Movement."[13] It was

10. Chakkarai, "Relation," 69.
11. Kool, "Post-Communist," 231.
12. Bevans and Schroeder, *Constants*, 262–63.
13. McGavaran, *Understanding Church*.

Emerging Missions and Missiologies for the Future

a reaction to the emerging openness to dialogue and human development that neglected the proclamation of the Gospel aimed at conversion and baptism. His method focused on particular ethnic or caste group movement. He significantly influenced the revival of the Evangelical movement, including the Lausanne Covenant. After the integration of the International Missionary Conference into the World Council of Churches in New Delhi, in 1961, the Commission on World Mission and Evangelization (CWME) of the World Council, being dissatisfied with the neglect of evangelism, created their own structures and held a few International Congress on Evangelization.[14] The International Congress on World Evangelization in Lausanne, Switzerland, in July 1974 brought together 2700 participants from 150 countries. The Lausanne Committee for World Evangelization was organized under the initiative of Billy Graham. It produced the Lausanne Covenant, a statement of fifteen articles of faith, including: "We enter into a Solemn Covenant with God and with one another, to pray, to plan and work together for the evangelization of the world."[15] An outstanding American evangelist, Hedlund, working in Madras, evaluated that LCWE as the most important evangelical gathering of the twentieth century. The Lausanne Covenant acknowledged the urgency of evangelizing the neglected two-third of the human race. It emphasized the need to believe, obey, proclaim and "make disciples of every nation." It was clearly a strong reaction to the radical horizontal mission in Uppsala and Bangkok. Between 1974-89 the Lausanne Committee for World Evangelization sponsored fifty four national and international conferences. The Lausanne Congress "was criticized for the way in which it had emphasized evangelistic mandate to the almost total exclusion of the church's calling in the area of justice and peace." The dichotomy was overcome in the Consultation on the Church in Response to human needs in Wheaton (1983) by a compromise formula: "We must therefore evangelize ... and press for social transformation."[16]

The Pentecostal Movement, born in Los Angeles, U.S.A., by Charles Parham, an American Holiness preacher, in the beginning of the twentieth century as a reaction to highly institutionalized church and the liberal Protestantism of the nineteenth century, is the largest Christian missionary movement, after the Catholic Church, in the twentieth century. And the Charismatic renewal born after World War II was part of the evangeli-

14. Jongeneel, "Ecumenical Theology," 173-75.
15. Scherer and Bevans, *New Directions*, 253.
16. Bosch, *Transforming Mission*, 407.

cal movement. Leading Charismatic Missionaries are now active both in the Roman Catholic Church, main line Conciliar Protestant churches and the free churches.[17] In India their main centres are in Bangalore, Chennai and Kolkata, Mumbai and many other cities. According to a recent survey there are about 2,500 Pentecostal and Neo-Pentecostal Churches in Chennai alone. The spread of evangelical churches predominantly in the urban centres is an indication that the educated and urbanized Christians are more inclined make options for new ways of worship. They follow the model of Mission according to the Acts of the Apostles. The evangelicals and the Pentecostal follow an exclusivist missiology, with no positive appreciation of other religions. Sad to note that some of the recent Hindu fundamentalist violence against the Christians are provoked by these aggressive sects.

The Catholic Mission Trends before the Second Vatican Council

In the backdrop of major Protestant Conferences on Mission, Popes began to periodically issue Encyclical letters on various subjects, including Christian mission. The twentieth century was marked by anti-colonial movements as well as horrors of two world wars, among other things. The anti-foreign and anti-missionary violence, starting with the opium war of 1839-42 in China, and the Boxer Rebellion (1899-1900) exterminated over 1,00,000 Christians, including hundreds of missionaries. After World War I (1914-18) in the colonized nations anti-missionary sentiments were on the increase. The western optimism of modernism was shattered. So Pope Benedict XV issued the first missionary encyclical letter, *Maximum Illud*, "On the Spreading of the Catholic Faith" (1919). In the backdrop of the Great Century of the Protestant missions Pope observed the rapid expansion of the Protestant missions as success of "servants of errors." Mission work was justified because the pagans were sitting in the darkness of sin. He advised the missionaries to "have compassion for the sad fate of this multitude of souls—sitting in the shadow of death, and to open the gate of heaven to those who rush to their perdition." He established the chair of missiology in Propaganda College, Rome. In the background of increasing attacks on foreign missionaries, training of native clergy, stressing good intellectual and spiritual formation, was advocated, in order to hand over the administrative responsibility. "Wherever there exists an

---

17. Parathazam, "Challenge," 59–61.

Emerging Missions and Missiologies for the Future

indigenous clergy . . . there the missionary work must be considered to have been brought to a happy close; there the Church is founded."[18] The distinction between mission and church is maintained. The idea that the whole church is missionary by nature was not yet born.

Pope Pius XI, esteemed as a great missionary Pope, promulgated his encyclical, *Rerum Ecclesiae*, "On promoting the Sacred mission" (1926) during the inter-war period. The problem of expelling missionaries from colonial territories continued. The Russian Revolution took place in 1917. The atheistic Marxism was spreading to Eastern Europe. The extermination of millions of innocent people under Stalin's totalitarianism was condemned. His personal vision of mission was the unification of all humanity under the headship of Christ (Eph.1:10). "For the church is not born for anything else but for spreading the Kingdom of God in the world so that the whole humanity participate in the benefit of salvation, so that the light of the Gospel, as also the good work of the Christian civilization may come to all humankind." Evangelization meant "adding to the Catholic church the greatest number of newly baptized." The success of the mission was measured by number of baptisms. Withdrawing the gentile races from the power of Satan was considered the greatest charity one can show. Mission to the elite was seen in the context of the wider society. History has proved that if the local leaders of the people are converted to Christianity then common people will follow the example. His keen effort to promote the indigenous church was proved in the following steps he took. At the time of his pontificate (1922–39) there were no mission dioceses with native bishops. He ordained forty native Bishops, including six in China and one in Japan by 1927. Promotion of the indigenous clergy who knows the people and language was given top priority. Training of catechists who know the local culture and dynamics was stressed. Pope inaugurated the World Mission Sunday and declared Saints Francis Xavier and Theresa of Lisieux as patrons of mission. He introduced the faculty of missiology in the Gregorianum University, Rome in 1932. Unfortunately he was not free from the racial prejudices. He referred to "heathens, particularly those who are still savages and barbarians."[19]

Pope Pius XII's Pontificate (1939–58) was contemporaneous with World War II. The encyclical letter *Evangelii Praecones*, "On promoting Catholic mission" was promulgated in 1951. On December 24, 1942 and June 2, 1943 he condemned the atrocities committed by Adolf Hitler and

---

18. *Catholic Encyclopedia*, 8:279–80; Vanchipurackal, *Why Missions?*, 34–39.
19. *Catholic Encyclopedia*, 2:412.

saved 37,000 Jews which was judged too little, according to his critics. Following the Louvain school of missiology he wrote "The ultimate aim of all missionary activity—is to plant the church firmly among the peoples of other land and to give them their own hierarchy, chosen from their own people." Regarding the people of other religions he wrote: "The missionary activity of the church proposes to purify and complete the religious and human values found in non-Christians religions." His encyclical letter *Mystici Corporis*, "Church, the Mystical Body of Christ" (1943) in Pauline term, is a radical departure from the traditional institutional model. It is Christ's mystical presence in the world. "Mission as Presence" received fresh attention in the post-war period when the influence of the church was conspicuously declining among Christians because of growing secularization. The near absence of missions in the Muslim countries prompted to emphasize the method of missionary presence. Pius XII's second mission encyclical letter *Fidei Donum*, "On the State of the Catholic Mission in Africa" (1957) was written to check the rapid spread of Islam and Protestant mission in Africa. "More priests in a particular region make it possible to plant the cross there today, while tomorrow this same land, filled by other workers than those of the Lord, will probably have become impervious to true Faith."[20]

Pope John XXIII's optimism towards the modern world remarkably changed the Catholic mission *ad extra* and *ad intra*. In *Princeps Pastorum* (1959) he encouraged Catholic lay participation in mission. He called the catechists the right hand men of missionaries. A foreign missionary in India wrote that catechists are the wheels on which missions run. Participation of the laity in the mission of church was a major thrust in the recent encyclicals. With this background Mr. P. C. Abraham established "Little Flower Mission League" in Bharanamganam, Palai diocese, Kerala, in 1947 and it was instrumental in active promotion of numerous priestly and religious vocations through over 2,500 units, with over one million members.[21] This lay movement immensely contributed to the rapid growth of missionary vocations in Kerala in the second half of the twentieth century. It was an exceptional contribution of a layman.

Gustav Warneck (1834–1919) the Father of the Protestant mission theology, defined mission as: "all the activities of Christianity aimed at the planting and organization of the Christian church among non-Christians. This activity is called mission as it is based on the missionary commis-

20. Quoted by Saldhana, "Mission Trends," 15–34.
21. Abraham, "St. Alphonsa," 128–31.

sion of the head of the Christian church carried out by the messengers (apostles, and missionaries) and has reached its goal as soon as the missionary work is no longer necessary." The main proponent of the Catholic mission theology and the founder of the Louvain school Pierre Charles S.J. (1883–1954) emphasized *Plantatio ecclesiae*, the planting of the church. Accordingly the formal object of the mission is "the establishment of the visible church in those countries where it is not established."[22]

The Catholic Missiology from the Council

The Second Vatican Council On Mission

In a rather pessimistic post-World War atmosphere, the newly elected seventy six years old Pope John XXIII, expected to be a short reign of a *papa di passaggio*, surprisingly announced on January 25, 1959 to convene an ecumenical council. To the 2,400 Council Fathers assembled in St. Peter's Basilica, Rome, after three years of preparation, Pope exhorted to look "to the present, to the new conditions and forms of life introduced into the modern world, which have opened new avenues to the catholic apostolate" and "to look to the future without fear."[23] The council that lasted three years, with interim preparatory time, from October 11, 1962—December 8, 1965, produced sixteen documents, including, the "Missionary Activity of the Church" (AG 1965). This document is intimately linked to four other documents; the "Dogmatic Constitution On the Church" (LG 1964); the "Declaration on the Relationship of the Church to Non-Christian Religions" (NA 1965); the "Pastoral Constitution On the Church in the Modern World" (GS 1965) and "Declaration on Religious Freedom" (DH 1965).

Probably for the first time the Catholic Church developed a biblically based dynamic Trinitarian foundation of the mission, *Missio Dei*.[24] The master idea of the document (AG) is taken from the Pauline description of the Father's plan for the whole humanity: "his loving design centred in Christ to give history its fulfillment, by resuming everything in him, all that is in heaven, all that is on earth, summed up in him" (Eph 1:9–10). In this sense the mission is highly Christo-centric. The Trinitarian theology is articulated in chapter one, Ad Gentes, nos. 1–5. The mission begins with the Father, the fountain of love. "The inner Trinitarian processions

22. Mueller, *Mission Theology*, 37–38.
23. Pope John XXIII, "Opening Speech," in *The Documents of Vatican II*, 714.
24. Wolanin, "Trinitarian Foundation," 38.

in the primodial fountain of love, *fontalis amor*, come forth ad extra in Christ's incarnation and in the mission of the Holy Spirit. It is these divine missions that the church derives its missionary form according to the saving design and decree of the Father."[25] And the missionary nature of the Church (AG 2) is rooted in the Blessed Trinity. There is only one mission, namely *Missio Dei*. A paradigm shift from the traditional mission command (Matt 28:18-20; Mark 16:15-18; Luke 24:46-49; John 20-23) to the mission of the love of the Father (John 3:16) is indicated. "If the "Missionary text" of the Greek patristic period was John (3:16) and that of medieval Catholicism Luke 14:23, then one may perhaps claim that Romans 1:16f. as "missionary text" of the Protestant theological Paradigm in all its many forms."[26] The ultimate source of the Mission of Christ and the Holy Spirit is the Love of the Father. But we know this Trinitarian mystery only from the revelation of Christ.[27]

The Council defined mission as follows with a distinction. The first is the missionary activity, the various modes, levels, and stages of the mission in different nations and circumstances. In contrast, the second, the mission of Christ, is one and the same always.

> "Missions" is the term usually given to those particular undertakings by which the heralds of the Gospel are sent out by the Church and go forth into whole world to carry out the task of preaching the Gospel and planting the Church among peoples or groups who do not yet believe in Christ. Their undertakings are brought to completion by missionary activity and are commonly exercised in certain territories recognized by the Holy See.
>
> The specific purpose of this missionary activity is evangelization and planting the Church among those people and groups where she has not yet taken root ... The chief means of this implantation is the preaching of the Gospel of Jesus Christ. (AG 6)

This definition is a balanced synthesis of the Protestant mission theology of the Muenster School of Gustav Warneck, whom the Catholic missiologists Joseph Schmidlin, the father the Catholic missiology, and the Louvain school of Pierre Charles closely followed. While Warneck emphasized the proclamation of the Gospel to people who do not believe in Christ, the conversion of mankind and salvation of souls of

---

25. Brechter, "Decree," 114.
26. Bosch, *Transforming Mission*, 240.
27. Lopez-Gay, "Proclamation," 92-95.

Emerging Missions and Missiologies for the Future

non-Christians, Pierre Charles' main emphasis was on planting the visible church among non-Christians. The heart and centre of missionary activity is the proclamation of Christ to Ad Gentes (no.13). The Christo-centric motive is again expressed in terms of love, and not the mission command (Cor 5:14). In the beginning was the "fountain like love" of the father from which flow the inter-Trinitarian "processions and missions."

The traditional ecclesiology, namely that "there is no salvation outside the church" is given a positive image: "The church is the Universal Sacrament of Salvation." (*Ecclesia Universale Salutis Sacramentum* (no.48). A new and positive attitude of the council to non-Christian religions, in contrast to the traditional negative attitude, and the new teaching on the possibility of salvation in other religions for those live according to their good conscience (LG 16) disturbed the conscience of a large number of missionaries who were struggling in Asia. The traditional geographical concept of the mission is maintained in the definition. If salvation is possible in other religions, then, what is the purpose of the mission, was the anxious question of many missionaries. To this conflicting problem neither the council nor later encyclical letters have yet given a satisfactory answer. Here the missionaries are speaking a faith language like the first witness of the Resurrection of Jesus. Overcome by the Easter experience they express it as unique. Their language was exclusivist like Peter: "There is no Salvation through anyone else" (Acts 4:12). This conviction was repeated by all the preachers and authors of the New Testament. Ultimately it is the language of faith: it is the language of Love. It is not the language of reason or the language of force. According to St. Paul, "the love of Christ impels us" (2 Cor 5:4). While stating the objective salvation of all in Christ, it fails to clarify, apart from the mission command, why the follower of Christ should engage in the mission of Christ. Perhaps the answer is one's own conviction of being called to participate in the reconstruction of the cosmic order under the headship of Christ: "Then I saw a new heaven and a new earth . . . Behold I make all things new" (Rev 21:1–5).

Catholic Missiology in India after the Council

The Second Vatican Council was predominantly an Euro-American Council. Out of fifty two members of the Preparatory Council there were only four colored members, including one from India. In the Council Hall out of 2,400 Council Fathers, 26 percent represented Asia, Africa and Oceania. Among 2,300 Bishops, there were only fifty one Indian origin

The Future of Christian Mission in India

Bishops.[28] Emphasizing the main sources of theological ideas one historian of the Council symbolically titled his book: *The Rhine Flows into the Tiber*. The first contact with the new ideas of Vatican II came through the Theological Seminar in Bombay in December 1964 on the occasion of the International Eucharistic Congress. Among the contributors were Hans Kueng and Raimundo Panikkar with the new theology of salvation of non-Christians. Hans Kueng further argued that salvation through the Church was not the ordinary way, but extraordinary way to salvation. The Bombay seminar sent shock waves to the Indian mission field, which was not yet adequately introduced to new reflections of the Vatican Council. Missionaries felt that their very vocation was threatened, and this time from inside the Church.[29]

After the closing of the Council one of the major concerns of the Catholic Bishops Conference of India was how to implement the vision of the Council. In October 1966, on the occasion of the CBCI meeting in Delhi the topic "Mission in India" was taken up and, announced an "All India Seminar of the Catholic Church in India." Its nearly three year preparation included fourteen regional seminars, forty nine diocesan seminars and many more seminars of various groups like eighteen seminars of seminaries, of educationalists and so on. Over 10,000 people participated in process at different places and different levels.[30] It culminated in "The Church in India Today in the Light of the Vatican Council" in Bangalore in May 1969. Six hundred delegates of the Indian Catholic church together with almost the entire hierarchy participated in this decisive event. Among the sixteen workshops, "Mission of the Church Today" was only one of the workshops, and failed to get sufficient attention it required. The seminar followed the definition given by the Vatican Document, AG. no 6. It further noted the decline of evangelical zeal due to the lack of conversions and baptisms.[31]

Reflecting on the "Church in India to Today" seminar, late Bishop J. R. Rodericks of Jamshedpur remarked: "As far as the workshop on Evangelization was concerned, the results, unfortunately, were not as good as one would have expected. What actually emerged from the seminar for our missionary activity was a strong desire . . . for a sound theology and

---

28. Wiltgen, *Rhine Flows*, 13; Brechter, "Decree," 87–95.
29. Neuner, *Christian Revelation*.
30. Zeitler, "Missionary Orientation," 115–33.
31. Gracias, *All India Seminar*, 331–38.

Emerging Missions and Missiologies for the Future

catechists of Evangelization relevant to the men of our times."[32] Therefore after three regional preparatory seminars in Hazaribagh, Bihar, in Bombay and in Ooty, Tamil Nadu more than a hundred participants from all over India, joined by a few theologian from other parts of the world, met in Nagpur in October 1971 for the first International Theological Conference on Evangelization. Considering the Indian context of religious pluralism and dehumanizing poverty, for the first time the concept of mission was widened so as to include dialogue and liberation as integral parts of the Church's Mission. The Nagpur Conference declared "The Mission of Church in India, therefore, has to be realized through evangelization. By Evangelization we mean the imparting of the Good News of salvation in Jesus Christ, through which men are enabled to share in the Spirit of Christ, who renews and reconciles them with God."[33] And then adds the paradigm shift. "The Christian community which finds itself in a pluralistic society, should be a community of dialogue with others. . . . It leads to a spiritual growth and therefore to a kind of deeper metanoia or conversion to God."[34] The document went on to emphasize the importance of Christian witnessing. The Bangalore Seminar had already stated that evangelization is not transferring people from one socio-cultural community to another community by rejecting ones on cultural roots. Being the Conference of theologians, the Nagpur Statement on Evangelization, Dialogue and Liberation is one of the finest expressions of a reflecting and thinking Church in India, opined late E. Zeitler, one of its organizers. The "All India Consultation on Evangelization in Patna" (1973), attended by 360 participants, including Bishops, priests, religious and laity, was an attempts to popularize the theology that was developed in Nagpur. In the context of India the consultation underlined the role of contemplation, witness, dialogue and liberation to arrive at a comprehensive understanding of mission theology.[35]

After many seminars, both national as well as regional, one finds little progress in the basic understanding of mission. However various reflections and deliberations on mission, evangelization, dialogue and liberation have created an unprecedented atmosphere for questioning and reflecting on key issues. For example the "Indian Theological Association" was founded in 1976 and every year its members reflect on key issues facing the church and mission and regularly publish its theological reflec-

32. Rodericks, *Church Extension*, 3.
33. Patrapankal, *Service and Salvation*, 6.
34. Ibid., 7–8.
35. H. D'Souza, *Life and Light*, 369–85.

tions.³⁶ *Research Seminar on Non-Biblical Scriptures*, Bangalore (1975); a national consultation on, *The Indian Church in the Struggle for a New Society*, Bangalore (1981); *Research Seminar on Shared Worship*, Bangalore (1988); are land marks in theologizing in India. In 1992 The "Fellowship of Indian Missiologist." was established. The founding of new theological journals of Scripture, Theology, Missiology, Spirituality and so forth in the post-Vatican era is clear proof of a thinking church in India. A number of institutions are established in various parts of the country to promote the emerging theological reflexions. The Indian mission that was totally dependent on western theology in the past is gradually emerging as athinking church and some of the ecclesiastical authorities in the West are uncomfortable with the new developments. The Indian church is now emerging as the most influential country in the Third World, with largest number of missionaries as well as creative theologians, in spite of objections from certain ecclesiastical quarters. A Nigerian theology student in Poona, India, recently made an interesting observation: "In India you have a thinking church; in Africa we have a dancing church."

The Evangelization in the Modern World (EN 1975)

Dissents, objections and confusions that followed the promulgation of the new inclusive missiology of the Council, almost radically different from the exclusivist teaching of the pre-Vatican era, compelled the Synod of the Bishops to search for a synthesis of rather scattered views, formulated during a three year period of the council. Ridiculing Karl Rahner's theological view on the salvific role of other religions, incorporated in LG (16), a Dutch theologian, teaching in Japan, wrote: "The anonymous Christian concept has done untold harms to the church by virtually removing any religious demand which might legitimately be made of non-Christians and by rendering the concept of conversion entirely superfluous."³⁷ He called Rahner an armchair theologian. Many foreign missionaries working in India shared their frustrations with this author about the new missiology.³⁸ While the Vatican Council was almost dominated by the Euro-American Council fathers the Synod of the Bishops (1974) was dominated by the third-world participants (EN 30). The participants from Latin America were imbibed with the Spirit of Liberation theology after

36. Parappally, *Theologizing*.
37. Straelen, *Catholic Encounter*, 97.
38. Kanjamala, *Religion and Modernization*, 297.

Emerging Missions and Missiologies for the Future

the Latin American Bishops' Conference in Medellin in 1968. The Asian Bishops and theologians, challenged by 97 percent of non-Christians in Asia, were pre-occupied with the theology of dialogue, with the deliberation of FABC, Taipei, April 1974. For the African delegates encounter between Christian ethic and African culture was the major challenge. Added to these, 80 percent the world population that was colonized and ruthlessly exploited by the Christian West achieved their independence by 1970. Hatred towards white colonizers and missionaries was still raging in the new nations. The Synod, therefore, made a conscious effort not to use the "dirty word mission" as far as possible, and replaced it with "evangelization," only with temporary success.

The fact that the Synod participants, with divergent experiences and socio-cultural backgrounds, failed to arrive at a consensus understanding of evangelization, betrayed irreconcilable divisions and crisis in the mission territories. The third world bishops and theologians challenged the traditional missiology of the West. Thus it became the prerogative of Pope Paul VI to draft the final document, based on conflicting debates in the Synod, and publish, *Evangelii Nuntiandi* in the following year. In the context of a global vision and global challenges evangelization is seen a "complex process made up of varied elements" (no. 24). Jesus Christ the first evangelizer, "proclaims a Kingdom, the Kingdom of God; . . . Only the Kingdom, therefore, is absolute, and it makes everything else relative" (no.8). "Evangelizing means bringing the Good News into all strata of humanity and through its influence transforming humanity from within and making it new . . . the church evangelizes when she seeks to convert, only through divine power of the message it proclaims, both the personal and collective conscience of the people and the activities in which they engage and the lives and concrete milieu which are theirs" (no. 18). Unlike in the past evangelization of man's cultures drew special attention in EN because contemporary anthropological insights expound that people are profoundly linked to a culture, right to their roots. Unless the culture is permeated by the values of the Gospel the building up of the Kingdom becomes next to impossible (no.20). In this process, it is the prophetic function of the church to challenge and upset lines of thought and inspiration and models of life, which are in contrast with the Word of God (no. 19). The Kingdom remains an abstraction unless it becomes visible in the person of Jesus. "There is no true evangelization if the name, the teaching, the life, the promises, the Kingdom and the mystery of Jesus of Nazareth, the Son of God are not proclaimed" (no. 22).

The Future of Christian Mission in India

The Latin American impact on EN is quite pronounced. The profound link between evangelization and human advancement—development and liberation is acknowledge. In evangelization one should not ignore the importance of "justice, liberation, development and peace in the world" (no. 31), but above all "liberation from Sin and the Evil one" (no. 9). The concept of liberation in EN is however toned down in comparison to the strong position accorded to it in the previous Synod of the Bishops on 'Justice in the World" (no. 6). "*Evangelii Nuntiandi* begins with Jesus the evangelizer (no. 7) and his proclaimation of God's reign (no. 8), leading to evangelizing church. The image of Jesus' prophetic personality and his mission to proclaim the Good News to the poor (Luke 4:18) has taken to the central stage in the Indian presentation of Jesus Christ. The Relevance of Jesus' message for the suppressed poverty ridden society has been realized deeply by a new generation of theologians."[39] However, the most disappointing section in EN is the unsympathetic attitude to Dialogue with world religions of Asia. Ignoring the positive spirit of Vatican Council (NA), and reacting to the strong stand of Asian participants under the leadership of late D. S. Amalorpavadass, EN stated: "the other religions do not succeed in establishing living relation with God even though they have . . . their arms stretched out towards heaven" (no. 53). Such a theological teaching seemed like a leaf from H. Kraemer's book (1938). Not withstanding this criticism the comprehensive teaching of *Apostolic Exhortation* of Pope Paul VI on evangelization is really inspiring.

In the course of mission history, two terms evolved with more or less the same meaning. The New Testament speaks of evangelizing or announcing the Gospel. The term mission has very late origin. In the sixteenth century, in the backdrop of Reformation and Counter-Reformation, St. Ignatius of Loyola (1491–1556) introduced the fourth vow of mission, *Votum Missionis* with unconditional obedience to the Pope, and wrote *Constitutions circa Missionis* (1544–45) whereby certain Jesuits were commissioned to non-Christian lands, with authority of the Pope, to propagate the catholic faith and establish the churches. Those who were sent with such goals were called 'missionaries' and the geographical territory termed mission territory. These mission territories were entrusted to the care of the Portuguese and Spanish kings, introducing the *Padroado and Padronato* systems. Simultaneously the mission was deeply intertwined with colonial expansions. The Protestants, who entered the mission field much later, not without political patronage, continue to maintain the

---

39. Neuner, "Mission Theology," 62.

Emerging Missions and Missiologies for the Future

Biblical term evangelization. In the new aggressive context evangelization, according to the Protestants, included the conversion of the Catholics and for the Catholics mission included the conversion of the Protestants.[40] The tension between these two concepts is evident in the publication of two papal documents, *Evangelii Nuntandi* (1975) and *Redemptoris Missio* (1990).

The Mission of Christ the Redeemer (1990)

On the twenty fifth anniversary of *Ad Gentes* and fifteen years after the publication of *Evangelii Nuntiandi*, John Paul II issued *Redemptoris Missio* in December 1990. The encyclical letter from the beginning to the end, projected a serious sense of anxiety because within the church there is "wide spread indifference" to mission (RM 36). A paradigm shift from proclamation ad gentes to dialogue with world religions and commitment to liberation of the poor and the spread of the new theological ideas raises the question, "Is missionary work among non-Christians still relevant? . . . why should there be missionary activity?" (RM 4). The quality of the Catholic life in Europe and America was at its low ebb, with less than 10 percent attendance in Sunday liturgy, for example. RM was also indirectly responding to the emerging missiology of the Kingdom of God in Asia where proclamation of Christ was becoming cryptic because of virulent attacks on missionaries, particularly in India. The office of the Catholic Bishops Conference of India, in New Delhi, had already received warning letters from the Vatican authorities, Rome, against the alarming new missionary trend. "Missionary drive has always been a sign of vitality, just as its lessening is a sign of crisis in faith" (RM 2), observed the Pope.

The encyclical strongly and repeatedly teaches that an explicit proclamation of the Gospel of Christ aimed at "conversion and baptism" (47) is "the permanent priority of mission" (RM 44). It is distinct from pastoral care and new evangelization of non-practicing Christians, mostly in traditional Christian countries (RM 33). Holy Father's strong Christo-centricism is the unique character of the encyclical. The modern New Testament scholarship has already established that the core of Jesus' proclamation was the Kingdom of God. Jesus spoke about the Kingdom nearly one hundred times.[41]

The traditional Christological controversies, are revisited again in the modern times. What is the nature of the union between the Word, who

40. Mueller, *Mission Theology*, 30–31.
41. Kanjamala, "Redemptoris Missio," 198–99.

was in the beginning with God, who become flesh in Jesus Christ? (John 1:2,14). What is the relation between "Jesus of history" and the" "Christ of Faith"? (RM 6). The encyclical is reaffirming the unity that is traditionally taught. Christ is none other than Jesus of Nazareth: the Word of God made man for the salvation of all.

The tension between the proclamation of the Kingdom, as Jesus did, and the proclamation of Christ by the apostles is resolved as follows. "The preaching of the early church was centred on the proclamation of Jesus Christ, with whom the Kingdom was identified. Now, as then, there is a need to unite *the proclamation of the Kingdom of God* (the content of Jesus own Kerigma) and *the proclamation of the Christ event* (the Kerigma of the Apostles). The two proclamations are complementary" (RM 16). But many who speak about the Kingdom are silent about Christ, says the Pope (RM 17); many seem to be confined to mere theocentric preaching as well as praxis. There is an urgent need to establish the unity, "Christ not only proclaimed the Kingdom, but in him the Kingdom itself became present and was fulfilled" (RM 18).

I try to understand this tension in the following manner. Is not an abstract preaching the values of the Kingdom—a kingdom of a truth and life, a kingdom of holiness and grace, a kingdom of justice, love and peace—a cold appeal to the intellect with little attraction for the heart? Let me picture it in another way. Are you really touched by the idea of love or by the person who actually loves you in the concrete life situation? Is the sermon on compassion or the person who is compassionate to you in your difficulties is more appreciated and preferred? Are not the missionaries who in their daily life fight for justice and human dignity, even though imperfectly, really dearer to victims of injustice and inequality than those who deliver excellent lectures on the same theme? Is not Mother Teresa of Calcutta and thousands of little known Mother Teresas, in whom the love and compassion of Christ is made visible and tangible in a remarkable degree more appreciated by millions of people all the world over than many eloquent preachers of love and compassion? If this is true, and I believe it is, then mere proclamation of the kingdom is not enough. Human hearts long to see and experience these values actualized in daily life situations. As St. John writes, "What we have heard, what we have seen with our eyes, what we looked upon and touched with our hands concerning the Word of life—we proclaim now to you" (1 John 1:1–3). It is in Him the values of the Kingdom are given visible expression and realization. The proclamation of the Kingdom of God by Jesus Christ and its manifestation in the

Emerging Missions and Missiologies for the Future

life, preaching , death and resurrection of Jesus Christ are two sides of the same coin. The two are intrinsically related . The one without the other is not adequately understood. To pose an opposition between the two is a pseudo-intellectual exercise. Jesus is the best visualization of the values of the Kingdom. He is the noblest communication of God's Love and concern for the broken world.[42] Therefore Jesus must be seen ,heard and touched in today's missionaries who are called to continue the mission of Jesus.

The major signs of the presence of the Kingdom of God are identified as follows: 1) Fellowship, a loving and sharing community; 2) Freedom. freedom from sin as well as from the cruel forces of nature and domination of people; 3) Justice. The prophets repeatedly taught that justice is more important than the noise of their solemn assemblies (Amos 5:23-24) In the words of prophet Micha, "do what is just, to love tenderly and live in humble fellowship with your God."[43] The Kingdom of God missiology is of recent origin as far as the Catholic tradition is concerned, in contrast to the Protestant missiology which focused on the expansion of the Kingdom of God and the Kingdom of Christ. And it got only one passing reference in *All India Seminar. Church in India Today*, Bangalaore, 1969.[44] However in the following decades the kingdom of God missiology would emerge as the major trend in India.

Following the Trinitarian pattern of the mission, chapter three teaches that "the Holy Spirit is the Principal agent the Mission." "The Holy Spirit remains the transcendent and principal agent for the accomplishment of this work in the human spirit and history of the world" (no.21). This is testified by the Pentecostal experience and subsequent proclamations (Acts 1:8; 2:17-18). The Acts of the Apostles record six summaries of early missionary discourses (RM 24-25). The mission of the Spirit is universal and operative beyond the visible community of church. During his pontificate John Paul II under took pastoral visits to non-Christians countries, including India, in 1986. His prayer meeting for Peace at Assisi in October 1986 with the representatives of all world religions strengthened his conviction in the presence and working of the Spirit in the world and in all Religions.

The first three chapters of RM expound the Trinitarian pattern of proclamation. It could be argued that as an adequate understanding of the Trinity is nearly impossible, except through faith, so also the preaching

---

42. Kanjamala, "Understanding Evangelization," 31.
43. Soares-Prabhu, "Kingdom of God," 601-7.
44. Kanjamala, "Evaluation," 21.

of the Trinitarian mission is almost difficult. The history of theology and history of missions point to the fact that when one of the three models, Kingdom-Centred, Christ-Centred and the Spirit-Centred, is accentuated the other two models suffer from marginalization. Such different emphases are found also in the Gospels, Acts of the Apostles and the Epistles (RM 23–25). Late Joseph Neuner, a peritus in the Council, regrets the theological method of the encyclical: "RM begins with "Jesus Christ the only Saviour," which is the Second article of the creed: "I believe in Jesus Christ," not with the first: 'I believe in God the Father.' Such an approach is a deviation from the council's Trinitarian frame, that is: the universal love and saving design of God the Father for all people, which is realized in Jesus Christ and fulfilled through the Holy Spirit (LG 2–4; AG 2–4)."[45] And how far RM is relevant for Asia? "To many in Asia RM appears to be primarily a response to the missionary crisis in Europe and America. It does not take seriously the Asian and Indian theological reflections . . . In essence, however, this encyclical, despite its many good and valid elements, only indirectly and then inadequately address problems and life experience of Asia, home of all the major world religions."[46] Let me quote the criticism of a historian of religions: "To the non-Christian reader, despite the mildly radical language that is used from time to time, both documents (RM and PD) sound (dare one say?) positively old fashioned."[47] In the backdrop of the Lausanne Covenant (1974) and the Manila Manifesto (1989) the Evangelical Protestants welcomed RM enthusiastically.

In the beginning of 1986 Pope John Paul II made a very extensive as well as triumphant pastoral visit to India . In the aftermath of this missionary event a good number of foreign missionaries were expelled from India on flimsy grounds. After the publication of the encyclical *Redemptoris Missio* the Hindu fundamentalists sent their strong written objections to it to the headquarters of CBCI, New Delhi. Sensing that RM was not enthusiastically received the Prefect of the Congregation for the Doctrine of Faith, Joseph Cardinal Ratzinger published, *Dominus Jesus*, "On the Unicity and Salvitic Universality of Jesus Christ and the Church." It was subjected to grave criticism by the Catholics, Protestants and Buddhists.[48]

Three broad types of mission theologies are operative in contemporary India. One, the official teachings of the church: mission documents of

---

45. Neuner, "Mission Theology," 54.
46. Kanjamala, "*Redemptoris Missio*," 202.
47. Sharpe, "Mission Between Dialogue," 164.
48. Rausch, *Introduction*, 60–61.

Emerging Missions and Missiologies for the Future

Vatican Council and the post-Vatican mission encyclical letters of recent Popes, Synods of the Bishops, and the collective teaching of the FCBC and CBCI. Two, in contrast to above official teachings, the grass root missionaries, struggling with numerous challenges of life situations, develop their own praxis and practical missiologies. This trend is discovered through the CBCI national survey. Three, the missiology of seminary professors and scholars in general, with minor exceptions, differ from the above two types. Sad to note, fear of sanctions by ecclesiastical authorities nearly compels most of them to be cryptic in their teaching and publications.

From its origin pluralism is an essential characteristic of Protestant Churches, theologies and missiologies. The World Council of Churches, founded in 1948, with 300 member churches, "is a fellowship of churches which confess the Lord Jesus Christ as God and Saviour according to the scriptures and therefore seek to fulfill together common calling to the glory of the one God, Father, Son and Holy Spirit."[49] After the United Nations declaration of Decade of Development in 1960 the WCC's social involvement became more radical than that of the Roman Catholic Church. Passion for mission in the 'traditional' sense is nearly dead among the Catholics as well as the Conciliar Ecumenical Churches which together constitute nearly 80 percent of the world Christian population.

Evangelization is the sole focus of Evangelical churches. The evangelicals do not constitute a monolithic block. "It is a loose coalition of individual persons, missions and evangelism agencies, and institutions sharing common theological position and with a common missionary and evangelical purpose."[50] The Lausanne Covenant (1974) marked the highpoint of evangelical missiology. While the WCC is radically committed to social transformation the evangelicals are radically committed to evangelism. One of their weaknesses in India is that they preach mostly to "stolen sheep." The Pentecostal Movement, starting in the beginning of the twentieth century and the Evangelical Movement, starting in the post-War II period, were in fact a return to the earliest model of mission in the Acts of the Apostles. It emphasizes baptism by the holy Spirit and making disciples by God the Holy Spirit. Their aggressive evangelism is Bible centred, and their strategy is spirit inspired. Focus on faith healing, laying of hands and exorcism are some of their distinctive characteristics.

---

49. Quoted by Scherer and Bevans, *New Directions*, x.
50. Ibid., xvii.

The Future of Christian Mission in India

Mission Theology of the Indian Missionaries.
Today's rapidly changing scenario provokes serious questions about mission. What is happening to proclamation of the Gospel of Jesus Christ in the post-Vatican Council II period? What do the missionaries in the field think about the relationship between proclamation and inter-religious dialogue; between proclamation and human liberation? What new methods of evangelization are initiated or emphasized by the missionaries because of new theological orientations and directions given by the Catholic Bishops Conference of India and national as well as regional mission institutes and their renewal program? What are some of the contradictions and tensions between missionary vision on the one hand and praxis on the other? Which are the main theological and missiological trends that are being taught, circulated and published by Indian theologians? Is missionary work among non-Christians still relevant if salvation is possible in other religions?

Being the secretary to CBCI commission for Proclamation, I, in collaboration with the diocesan secretaries, conducted a national survey in forty five sample diocese out of 130, in the twelve ecclesiastical regions of all the three ritual churches, during 1993–94. My analysis below is based on the data collected from 1,690 priests, 4,127 sisters, and 9,050 lay people. Over 15,000 people actively participated in the massive survey by answering questionnaires, through group discussions, and personal interviews. The near consensus that emerged from forty five independent diocesan surveys, with minor local variations, confirms the validity of the methodology of the survey. My examinations of strong resistance to conversions and other socio-cultural changes during the past 200 years make it quite evident that people strongly resist changes, more so in the field of religious beliefs and practices. Hence I believe that the use of twenty year old data is justified.[51]

As per the CBCI survey on Evangelization around 66 percent of priests and 70 percent of religious sisters maintain that all religions are means of salvation for their sincere followers. In contrast, a minority, 16 percent priests and religious sisters continue to subscribe to the traditional view.[52] The majority of the lay people, 58 percent, who have little opportunity to be updated with the new theology uphold the traditional views on mission. "No salvation outside the Church" was the axiom taught by St. Cyprian of Cartage (d. 258), and further reinforced by St. Augustine of

51. Kanjamala, *Mission Trends.*
52. For the survey statistics, Kanjamala, "Trends and Issues."

Emerging Missions and Missiologies for the Future

Hippo (354–430), and Bishop Fulgentius of Ruspa (647–533), a disciple of St. Augustine, all three of them bishops from North Africa. It was strictly interpreted and adhered to by the Church and defined in the Council of Florence (1438–1445): "The Roman Catholic Church firmly believes, professes and teaches (sic) that outside the church no one, neither pagan nor heretics, nor schismatic can attain eternal life, but will go to the everlasting fire which was prepared for the devil and his angels."[53] Unfortunately a small number of Catholics as well as most of the evangelicals and members of sects still continue to hold on to this grim view. For them conversion of pagans, an unfortunate term, and baptism into the Church is the top priority.

Among the three major motivations of evangelization—Church-centred, Christ-centred, Kingdom of God centred—Christ-centred mission is the most powerful motive among Catholic missionaries. Around 70 percent of the missionaries on the all India level consider that making Christ known is their first priority. The second priority of the missionaries is the promotion of the values of the Kingdom of God, 65 percent. The link between these two approaches is clear to most of the respondents. The Vatican Council's teaching that God's saving love extends to sincere followers of all religions has been accepted by most of our respondents: 66 percent of the clergy and 74 percent of religious sisters. Religious sisters, in responding to the questionnaire, in general expressed more liberal attitudes and opinions, probably due to lack of any systematic indoctrination, unlike the clergy who undergo prolonged seminary formation.

While the vast majority of priests and nuns, 84 percent, are gradually moving away from the traditional ecclesio-centric approach to the mission, a very small minority seems to be closer to the traditional position. Such a difference is one of the sources of tensions and even serious conflicts. In a few dioceses the problem of conflicting perceptions is further exacerbated by the fact that there are significant regional differences in the perception of the source of salvation as well as goals of mission. The church-centred mission gets only the third priority. Merely 16 percent of the missionaries, priests and nuns, consider this as most important. The main exception to this trend is the North East where church-centred mission gets a higher rating, 36 percent, because this is a responsive area in the traditional sense. Nearly half of the tribal population in the N.E. has embraced Christianity in the second half of the twentieth century. The national missiological survey uncovered two distinct trends. The mind-

---

53. Neuner and Dupuis, *Christian Faith*, 237–38.

THE FUTURE OF CHRISTIAN MISSION IN INDIA

set of the old churches, i.e., the Syro-Malabar, Syro-Malankara and the Padroado churches, more or less persist and resist any change, in contrast to the mindset of the new churches born out of the missionary laborers of the nineteenth and twentieth centuries. One of the main reasons for the difference might be that the young churches are less rooted in traditions. They are also less powerful in terms of numbers, economic resources and institutions.

Tensions and Conflicts in the Mission

The findings of CBCI national survey on mission in various dioceses confirm the anxiety of John Paul II on the decline of missionary spirit (RM 2). On the All India level only 33 percent of the missionaries are happy with the missionary atmosphere in their dioceses, that means 67 percent are dissatisfied. However, a higher level of satisfaction was expressed in the Chotanagpur region, 45 percent of the priests and 36 percent of the nuns; and in the North East, 56 percent of the priests and 76 percent of the nuns. The decline in the missionary spirit is, to some extent, due to other modern social and cultural forces. "The dampening of missionary zeal is due ultimately... to the fact that the power of the Word is choked by the cares of the world and the delight in riches (Matt 13:32) that is, by consumerism and the lure of power and money among those who should be servants of the Word," observes the final statement of the CBCI consultation on Evangelization in Poona.[54] The President of the Vatican Secretariat for Evangelization, in his address to the Cardinals in Rome on 4–5 April 1991, accused India of being the epicenter of new heresies.[55]

Serious conflicts between pre-Vatican and post-Vatican II theologies of mission are observed in many dioceses. This is one of the major sources of conflicts, for example, between Bishops and priests; between senior priests and junior priests; between priests and catechists; between Rome and the Indian Church. The conflict between traditionalists and modernists seems to be on the increase in the context of growing scientific rationalism and individual freedom. While the missionaries, along with the official Church, recognize and uphold the centrality and uniqueness of Christ's redemptive acts on the one hand, and the possibility of salvation outside the visible Church on the other hand, no clear answers to the question regarding the relation between these two theologies are articulated. Because of the prolonged tensions and conflicts about 10 percent

54. Kanjamala, *Paths of Mission*, 294.
55. Tomko, *L'Osservatore Romano*, April 15, 1991.

Emerging Missions and Missiologies for the Future

of priests in a few dioceses resigned from their priesthood or migrated to other dioceses abroad. But it is a clear indication of the serious frustration not only of those who have left but also of some of those who continue to work in these dioceses. Unfortunately, the spirit and morale of these dioceses are waning. The sprouting of numerous small sects, both in the cities as well as in villages, seems to be an attempt to find alternative expressions of religious needs like certainty and anchor in the Word of God, experiencing peace, joy and fellowship in small communities, in contrast to impersonal worship in large parishes.[56] Church centered missionary approach gets low priority among the missionaries in the Hindi Belt and comparatively high priority in the North East. Missionaries also expressed a corresponding sense of satisfaction, dissatisfaction or frustration during the author's personal interviews with them.few missionaries are ready to venture into frontier areas with poor amenities. The young missionaries of today manifest various characteristics of the emerging "soft culture" in contrast to the "tough culture" of earlier missionaries. The future of the mission will depend to a considerable degree on committed laity who are in strategic position to influence every sphere of the society with the values of the Gospel (LG 33; GS 3). And the laity, in the views of some Indian lay theologians are either "sleeping giants" or "domesticated giants." The Indian Catholic church seems to be very clerical, with little space for the laity.

Regionalism and ethnocentrism in the Church and mission is on the increase. Dalit conflicts, Tribal re-awakening, Rite conflicts and tensions between the missionaries from the South and the indigenous people in the North are gradually increasing. The recent Christian Dalit Liberation movement, inaugurated in 1985 to fight for equality in the church has become a controversial and encouraging sign. Its impact is slowly but surely spreading from Tamil Nadu to Pondicherry, Andhra Pradesh and other neighboring states, challenging the marginalization and oppression of the dalit Christians by the upper caste Christians who constitute the dominant minority. For example, eight members of the Tamil Nadu Oppressed People's Movement demolished a 200 year old 800 feet wall that divides Christian cemetery in Trichi diocese. The division of the cemetery is based on members of untouchable Christians and caste Christians. The Dalit Christians are not allowed to enter non-dalit section.[57] Worse still, there exist cemeteries with three divisions, at least in a few parishes: for the up-

56. Parathazam, "Challenge," 17–20.
57. *Times of India* (October 29, 2010); Dorairaj, *Frontline* (February 25, 2011) 38.

per castes; for the Adi Dravidars; and for the Arunthathiars. Millions of Dalits and Tribals who were silent sufferers for centuries are becoming aware of their oppressive condition and are demanding their rights, at time using violence as one of the methods, influenced by Maoism.

Signs of Hope

Tensions, confusion of vision, breakdown of values, in individuals as well as institutions, are undoubtable indications of transition from the traditional system to a not yet clear and stable system. The crisis situation is also a time of creative opportunities. Granted that there are certain crises in the Indian mission, the post-Vatican era is also characterized by many signs of hope. For over two-thirds of the missionaries, the priority in mission is to make Jesus Christ known and to work for the realization of the values of the kingdom of God. Openness to other religions and cultures is on the increase and it reduces the social distance and conflicts between Christian missionaries and people of other religions. The radical commitment of some missionaries to the poor and the oppressed, moved by the spirit of compassion and service and without any ulterior motives of social conversion, is another challenging trend. They "rejoice with those who rejoice, weep with those who weep" (Rom12:15). Missionaries in India should be proud and happy that the Gospel is being preached to the poor and they have made significant contributions to restore human dignity to those who were suffering the pain and humiliation of dehumanization for centuries.

During my public debate with Mr. Arun Shourie, author of *Missionaries in India*, (1994) in Hyderabad on Christian mission this author asked: "Indian Christians constitute only less than three percent of the population. They are manning a large number of schools and educating twelve percent of students of this country. Ninety nine percent of the students, in the Hindi belt, are Hindus, Muslims and others. In many schools Christian students constitute only one percent. How many non-Christians here are converted to Christianity? None. The Christian dispensaries and hospitals take care of nearly fifteen percent of sick people in the country, irrespective of religion, caste or class. Nearly thirty five percent of lepers, destitute and orphans take refuge in Christian social institutions. I wonder why the Hindus who constitute nearly eighty percent of the population don't assume a proportionate responsibility?"[58]

---

58. Goel, *Arun Shourie*, 23–24.

Emerging Missions and Missiologies for the Future

The following are some of the major social trends in India that the Christian missionaries initiated long before the origin of the Liberation Theology. a) Dalit liberation movement; b) Tribal liberation movement; c) Women's liberation movement. It must be kept in mind that every quest of the human spirit for truth and justice, is inspired by the Holy Spirit. The people of "little traditions" achieved a new identity by becoming members of the universal church. Many tribal and dalit communities which were traditionally divided, even fighting against each other, are now being united under the umbrella of the Church. In such situations mission has undoubtedly worked as an agent as well as sign of unity.[59] The number of those who adopt new and creative forms of missionary methods is on the increase. The survey of nearly one hundred "Catholic Inquiry Centres" shows that between 40,000–50,000 adults of other religions are deepening their knowledge of Jesus Christ through correspondence courses per year.[60] Around 1,500 letters received annually from listeners of programmes of "Radio Veritas," Manila, in Hindi, Bengali, Telugu and Tamil show that thousands of Indians of all religions are listening to the Gospel of Christ regularly.

The number of Indian missionaries going to foreign countries is on the increase. The recent CBCI survey (2011) provides the good news that the Indian Catholic Church has become a global mission sending church. The presence of 8,868 Indian missionaries are recorded in 166 countries of the world. These missionaries include 6,543 religious sisters, 1,940 religious priests, 226 diocesan priests, and 159 religious Brothers. They are inspiring signs of an unprecedented missionary spirit because "missionary drive has always been a sign of vitality" of the church (RM 2). Of all the third-world Churches, the Indian Catholic church and mission seems to be the most dynamic, with its emerging theological articulations, large number of dedicated missionary personnel and Indian contemplative spirituality, sustained by the rich and ancient religious and cultural atmosphere of India. The recent foundation of Mission Society of St. Thomas the Apostle (1968), Heralds of Good News, Khammam Diocese, Congregation of the Little Flower (1947) Kristiya Sannyasa Samaj (1955) are encouraging signs of growth and flowering of missionary spirit.[61] The number of Women Congregations of Indian origin is much higher.[62]

59. Kanjamala, "Spirit of God," 140–45.
60. Nediyakalayil, "*Report of the Association*," 6.
61. Houtart, *Size and Structure*, 106.
62. Ibid., 138.

The Future of Christian Mission in India

One of the most radical missiological changes in the last half a century in the Catholic Mission has been the relegation of the Church-centered mission, the first priority at the beginning of the twentieth century, to the third priority at the beginning of the twenty first century. The views, attitudes and methods of the Indian missionaries today are closer to the teaching of Pope Paul VI in his *Apostolic Exhortation. The Evangelization in the Modern World* than the traditional stand taken by Pope John Paul II in *The Mission of the Redeemer*. The views and opinions elicited from over 15,000 respondents of the CBCI survey confirm this conclusion. For Christians, particularly for the missionaries, the greatest missionary revolution of last one century is the discovery of other spiritual worlds, with their coherent meaning system. Recognition of these religions, with positive attitudes of openness and programmes of dialogue and partnership, in contrast to the closed and aggressive approach of the colonial mission, has laid the foundation for building a new civilization of Brotherhood and Sisterhood. We are all related to one another as members of one human family. We are entering a new age of Common Mission. Since the responsibility for shaping the future of humanity rests on all, we cooperate with people of all religions and no religions to find answers to all contemporary problems. The paradigm shift identified in the CBCI research is the beginning of a "Copernican revolution" in the Indian mission: that is, the heart of the mission is no more the church, but the Rule of God.

Change of World Views and Change of Missiologies

"A world view is a set of presuppositions or assumption which we hold, consciously or unconsciously, about the basic make up of our world."[63] Each world view is constituted of five basic assumptions: the nature and character of Ultimate Reality: the nature of the Universe; the nature man, including the question what happens to man after death; what is the basis of morality; and what is the meaning and finality of human history. When one or more of these basic assumptions are challenged or modified, for different reasons, the world view encounters a crisis situation.

The history of a rather static theology in general or mission theology in particular until the First World War and the radical changes introduced thereafter, both in the Catholic as well as Conciliar Protestant mission theologies in the second half Century, provide ample evidence of reluctant adaptations to a fast changing world views. A transition from the

---

63. Sire, *Universe*, 17–18.

Emerging Missions and Missiologies for the Future

old missiology, formulated with the static world view, to new missiologies formulated with dynamic world views is conflictual and painful. While the traditional western Christian world view was theistic the eastern world view is monistic or pantheistic. These world views have little in common. An animist world view, one of the oldest, believes that all things have souls. In a geocentric world view earth was centre of everything. In contrast, in the heliocentric world view, first proposed by Nicolas Copernicus and further established by Galileo Galilee, sun is the centre of the cosmos. Later discoveries of thousands and thousands of galaxies, with millions of stars, have invalidated the traditional mechanical world view. The evolutionary world view of Charles Darwin argued that human beings are the end result of a very long process of evolution through the principles of 'natural selection' and adaptive strategy of 'survival of the fittest.'[64] What are the consequences of numerous scientific and technological discoveries of last few centuries which challenge or modify one or more than one constitutive element of the world view? "Quite literally we live in a world fundamentally different from that of the nineteenth century, let alone earlier times."[65]

In the scholarly views of David Bosch, Walbert Buelhmann, Arnulf Camps, Marcel Heyndrik, Allen J. L. (Jr.) and others contemporary missions and missiologies are deeply challenged, influenced and altered by the following currents of thoughts.

We live in a pluri-centric rather than Western dominated world which continue to influence the global politics, economics, culture and religion. Societies everywhere seek their own cultural identities and reject slavish imitation of western models. Inculturation of the local church, a major theme in contemporary missiology, implies at least certain rejection of the western garb. The local church should divest itself of its foreignness, both externally as well as internally, namely in mentality and theology.

Freedom of religion and greater awareness of other world faiths compel Christians to evaluate their own traditional pejorative attitudes towards other faiths and enter into respectable dialogue. Today world religions are breaking their own geographic boundaries through internal and external migrations. The consequence is the emergence of dynamic pluralism, replacing the past static pluralism.

We inhabit a shrinking 'global village' with finite resources and this calls for growing mutual interdependence. Rapid expansion of technolo-

---

64. Heyndrix, *Towards Another Future*, 119–30; Schaeffer, *Christian World*, 165–82.
65. Bosch, *Transforming Mission*, 189.

gies and uncontrollable spread of informations and knowledge from different parts of the world, without any synthesis or unifying world view, leads to disorientation and confusions. It is identified as post-modernism.

Humans are for the first time aware of their capacity to destroy the earth and make it uninhabitable for future generations.

The scientific and technological achievements of the West, in spite of certain amount of criticisms, is becoming universal. The scientific spirit enhances intellectualization and rationalization of every sphere of life.

Simultaneous decline of religious world view leads to growth of secular world view. One cannot, however, deny that there exists certain hunger for spirituality and meaning of life, manifested in two different trends. One, search for mysticism, including eastern mysticism, and an aversion towards institutionalized and ritualized religion; two, a rapid growth of Pentecostalism—from 6 percent in the mid 1970s to 20 percent of the Christians in 2010.

The structure of oppression and exploitations are today being challenged as never before. Justice for the poor and option for the poor have become powerful motivations for various social movements.

Further noted is the paradigm shift from traditional "other-worldly" to "this-worldly" religion. There is an unprecedented awareness and responding to the concrete living conditions of suffering people. The new focus is on humankind in contrast to the past focus on God. The growth of numerous international and national agencies working for human welfare is conspicuous: the World Food Organization, the World Health Organization, UNESCO, Bread for the World, Oxfam, Misereor, Catholic Relief Society and so forth. Nearly three million NGOs in India render various services to the poor since the government fail to attend to them satisfactorily. All humanitarian involvements are rendered irrespective of nationalities, religions, castes, class, sex and race. The only criteria for involvement is human need and human dignity.

Care of ecology and environment has become an international concern. Ecology is not only a human concern but also a religious issue because it is also an expression of respect and reverence for the creator and his creations.

Fighting for equality of gender, rejecting traditional patriarchal exercise of authority, both in the secular and religious sphere, is on the increase. It is universally recognized as a struggle for human dignity.

"The Coming of the Third Church" is an exclusively Christian issue. In the beginning of the twentieth century 85 percent of Christians and

77 percent of the Catholic population were living in the affluent northern hemisphere. A century later less than 40 percent of the Catholics are found in the North. Most of them are merely Sacramentalized without being evangelized. In the prediction of W. Buelhmann (1976) the power shift is from the Atlantic region to the Pacific region. But the third Church is a poor church and power shift is mostly in terms numbers.

The above world views and philosophies can be summarized in three categories: one, pre-rational or pre-critical; two, rational or critical; three, post-rational or post-modern. The new constellation of these and other associated scientific, social, cultural, and religious forces create an unprecedented global ethos.[66]

It is therefore crucial to ask and identify what is the unifying factor in all the above authors with diverse, social, political, philosophical and religious background? They all are seriously committed to human dignity and human rights, specially of the least, the last and the lost. Man is seen as the centre of the emerging new civilization. "Universal Declaration of Human Rights by United Nations General Assembly on 10th December 1948," after witnessing the horrors and tragedies of the World Wars, put the foundation of the new civilization. All people of goodwill are exhorted to contribute towards the construction of the new world order, traditionally called the Kingdom of God. The mission of the future will be realized by millions of people of good will working in the secular world. It will be the mission of the lay people (GS 2,40). To be relevant and meaningful to rapidly changing and challenging world trends the understanding of mission is being reformulated in the recent decades "Both the church in general and the Christian mission in particular are today faced with issues and invited to grow in directions which were unthinkable within the parameters of former paradigms of theology and ministry."[67]

The rapidly changing world views and life views pose new challenges to today's missionaries. The fundamental difference between the India of the nineteenth century, characterized by notable missionary expansion, and the twenty-first century is in the degree of prosperity, in the degree of education, the knowledge available through modern communication technology. The defining mark for today's young generation is new aspirations. They are looking foreword to colleges and universities that offer

---

66. Buelhmann, *Coming*, 86–87; 129–60; Buelhmann, *With Eyes*, 11–18; 102–113; 143–157; Camps, *Patterns in Dialogue*, 5–10; Toffler, *Power Shift*, 450–60; Allen Jr., *Future*, 436–39.

67. Scherer and Bevans, *New Directions*, ix.

degrees and job opportunities and not 'jail bharao', fill the jails, the call of M. K. Gandhi, leader of Indian Independence Movement. As per Census Report 2001, 55 percent of Indians are below the age of twenty five and they grew up in an era of Information Technology and globalization. For instance mobile phones were introduced in India in 1995 and today 75 percent of Indians own them. Thirteen million students are enrolled in Indian universities per year. Around 2,00,000 Indian students register themselves in foreign universities per year. The number of youth migrating to the USA, Canada, England, Australia and other prosperous nations for education and employment is accelerating. The illegal and adventurous migration of unqualified youth to these countries further illustrate the mentality of the two Indias, the rich and the poor. They are also restless and angry for many reasons, including wide spread corruption in public life. Young India no more subscribes to the traditional philosophy of *Maya*, i.e., the world is unreal. On the emerging secular meaning of the Gospel, Professor Jongeneel of the University of Utrecht wrote: "The negative valuation of secularization in the Mission Conferences of Edinburgh (1910), Jerusalem(1928), and Tambaram (1938) yielded to a "Yes to the Secular" in Mexico City in 1963. This "Yes to the World" produced joy in the heart of many but at the same time disturbed not only evangelical theologians but also some members of the World Council of churches."[68] And the Catholics too no longer believe that they are "exiled in the valley of tears" as they used to sing in the Marian hymn, *Salve Regina*.

Imagining another Future

The main goals of traditional mission were: 1) Proclaiming Jesus Christ, baptizing non-Christians, and making members of the Church for the salvation of souls; 2) planting the Church where it did not exist and ensuring its institutional growth; 3) sanctification of life through sacramental life and acts of charity. In a rapidly changing and challenging context and near failure of mission, at least in numerical terms, the Indian mission should imagine and envision an alternative model for the future. Some of the hallmarks of the alternative model could be:

- To interpret traditional mission theology with the help of Indian philosophical / religious categories and cultural idioms, including idioms of the tribal cultures. The crucial question is: to what degree the Asian church should be bound to the Greco-Latin theology?

---

68. Jongeneel and Engelen, "Contemporary Currents," 438–39.

Theology is the reflexion of the local church which is involved in the life of the contemporary society, it is the reflexion on Christian experience in the light of the Word of God. "This is the reason why an Indian theology cannot be developed or formulated by non-Indians, living abroad however competent and eminent they may be in theological erudition, however much we may profit by their insights and contributions."[69] And on the limits of the Greco-Latin theology a German scholar who lived and studied in Vrindaban, the heart of Hinduism, writes: "Greek Christology has not exhausted the mystery of Christ though it has helped the church the better to see some aspects of Christ. Indian wisdom, too, will not exhaust the mystery of Christ. But it would help the church in India to understand Christ better and let him to be understood: the knowing of Christ as the revelation of Brahmavidya-Christ the desire of the eternal hills."[70]

- The Special Assembly for Asia of the Synod of Bishops in Vatican from 18th April to 14th May 1998 identified some of the images of Jesus that would appeal to the heart of Asia, in contrast to the traditional Euro-ecclesiastical Christ of theological doctrines. "Among them were Jesus Christ as the Teacher of Wisdom, the Healer, the Liberator, the Spiritual Guide, the Enlightened One, the Compassionate Friend of the Poor, the Good Samaritan, the Good Shepherd, the Obedient one" (EA no. 20). Jesus who unjustly suffered on the cross, who forgave and prayed for those who persecuted him, is a great source of meaning and consolation for large number of suffering people of Asia. The attempt of the Synod is appreciated as a pedagogical step in presenting Jesus to Asia, responding to the cultural sensitivities of the Asian people. The construction of an Asian theology, answering the question: 'who do people say the Son of Man is ? (Matt 16:13), will naturally require time and freedom in the context of very complex Asian experience. The struggles and experiments of the past Asian and Indian theologians warn that the path ahead will not be easy. And theologizing in context is not merely repeating century old formulas.

- To find new ways of organizing the Christian community and relating to members of sister churches and people of other faiths or no faith. Currently the Indian churches, particularly the Roman Catholic

---

69. Amalorpavadass, "Theology," 32.
70. Klostermaier, *Hindu and Christian*, 118.

church, is caught up in the Roman model of institutionalization. The crucial question is how far the Indian church is growing into a local church. The local church should be more than an administrative territorial subdivision of the universal church. The incarnation of the mystery of the church in the context of the dynamic history and culture of the people of post-colonial India is the unprecedented challenge. For instance how far an Indian diocese is different from an Italian or German diocese?

- Religious pluralism, a strong character of India, and the modern democratic culture will appreciate a more decentralized church. The incredible Indian pluralism further contributes towards the creation of religious tolerance. It is becoming clear that anxieties about social conversion is not an Indian phenomenon as it was for the colonial missionaries. Unfortunately such an anxiety is being perpetuated by the aggressive evangelical sects, who, not infrequently, are confronted by equally fundamentalist Hindus.

- To express new ways of feeling and relating with other communities. The caste mentality of Indians is, unfortunately, highly exclusivist. It is further colored by regionalism. Normally positive feelings are expressed only to people of one's own caste or tribe. The Christian vision is a challenge to rise above ethno-centrism and a call to universal brotherhood/sisterhood. Jesus expressed this new relationship by his table fellowship with Zacchaeus the tax collector (Luke 19: 1–10), a woman of the street (Luke 7:36–50), and the hungry crowd in the desert place (Mark 8:1–9; Matt 15:32–39), and many others. And the Eucharistic celebration is the sacramental expression of the new fellowship he intended to establish, according to the Trinitarian model. Further it is an invitation to celebrate the new fellowship in the pluralistic world.[71] According to the Gospel of John the Eucharistic celebration is a radical challenge to wash one another's feet (John 13:14–16).

Qualitative Model of Mission

The alternative model may be envisaged as a *qualitative* model of mission in contrast to the traditional *quantitative* model for measuring missionary success. The future of the mission in India in all likelihood is not going to

---

71. Bevans and Schroeder, *Constants in Context*, 362–66.

Emerging Missions and Missiologies for the Future

be marked by a great increase in quantitative terms such as numbers of converts, but in quality. Numerical conversion and numerical strength, which was the top priority during the colonial mission, is not outright rejected here; but it might have only a limited relevance and scope in the future. How should we understand the emerging alternative model?

First. Mission begins with credible witnesses. Jesus Christ is the supreme witness, who said to Pilate: "For this I have come to the world to bear witness to the truth" (John 18:37). And before his ascension the apostles were given the mission: "You shall be my witness . . . to the end of the world" (Acts 1:8). Missionaries who have not experienced God as unconditionally loving and forgiving (Luke 15:11–32) and are therefore often unable to communicate this experience of God, are not credible messengers and ambassadors of Jesus Christ. In this regard the last chapter of RM, "Missionary Spirituality," is very crucial. "The missionary is a universal brother / sister" (RM 89). Majority of the missionaries are signs of universal brotherhood and sisterhood, struggling to grow out of one's own narrow loyalties like family, caste, linguistic affiliation and religion. This was more conspicuous in the case of foreign missionaries. The exhortation that "the missionary must be a contemplative in action" (RM 91) is very appropriate and attractive in the Indian religious ethos with a predilection for contemplation and mysticism. "Modern man listens more willingly to witnesses than to teachers, and if he does listen to teachers, it is because they are witnesses" (EN 41).

Second. Proclamation and working for the realization of the Kingdom of God are the highest priorities in evangelization. However, that in no way undermines the centrality of the proclamation of Jesus Christ. In the Risen Lord who proclaimed the Kingdom, we have the concrete initial unfolding and realization of the Kingdom and its actualization in history through the Spirit. India is a country that loves and respects the person of Jesus and his message of love, compassion, forgiveness, and selfless sacrifice. The message of Jesus is universal; i.e., to be offered with love to all and as an invitation to respond freely. In the past the response of India to Jesus, with minor exceptions, was unambiguous: Yes to Jesus and no to the church.

Third. The future missionary methods in India should abandon the past model of power and conquest. What then is the alternative model? "You are the salt of the earth . . . You are the light of the world . . . It is set on a lamp stand where it gives light to all in the house just so your light may

The Future of Christian Mission in India

shine before others, that they may see your good deeds and glorify your heavenly Father" (Matt 5:13–16). This is a peaceful model, provoking no controversy. "The new paradigm invites us, I suggest, to shift our attention from church growth to church life. The 'great mission' read in the light of Mission Discourse of Mt. 10 and the exhortation to mission in Matt 5:13–16, is to be understood, not as a mandate to an aggressively militant mission, obsessed with 'making disciples' (Church Growth) but as an invitation to follow Jesus in mission (Church Life)."[72] The "great mission commission" text (Matt 28: 18–20) is now being overshadowed by the mission of the "great love of the Father" (John 3:16; 15:13; 20:19–23). Our mission is to make God's love present, in whatever way we can, especially wherever it is least present. According to Wilbert Shenk, "Evangelicals are increasingly turning to John 20:19–23 as the foundational text for missionary mandate."[73] "Peace be with you. As the Father has sent me, so I send you.—Receive the Holy Spirit. Whose sins you forgive are forgiven, and whose sins you retain are retained."

Fourth. A new awareness is being fostered that we all, belonging to different religions, cultures, castes, tribes race, languages and nations are ultimately children of one God. We are all related to one another as members of one human family. We are entering an age of common mission, that is to say, everyone is called to contribute towards the realization of the common vision: fullness of life, love, and light that Jesus promised will be gradually realized like the growth of a mustard seed (Luke 13:18–21).

Fifth. Jesus, the radical prophet, was highly critical of Jewish institutions like temple, sacrifices, ritualism, Sabbath, scribes and pharisees, priests and high priest. He challenged their legalism by performing acts of mercy on Sabbath to reveal that salvation is a free gift of God and not the fruit of perfect observance of laws. The ten commandments and over 600 Jewish laws and regulations were simplified into two commandments—love of God and love of neighbor, including enemies. He asked them to worship God in spirit and truth. As children of God all are treated equal, abolishing social distinctions like Jew and Gentile, male and female, slave and free. In other words, rejecting the prevalent socio-religious system and structures he was preaching the mission of liberation: liberation from fear of spirits and gods; liberation from ritualism and legalism; liberation from structures of domination and oppression. Instead he assumed the

72. Soares-Prabhu, "Following Jesus," 86.
73. Shenk, "Mission for the 21st Century," 50.

Emerging Missions and Missiologies for the Future

servant model. He warned against the danger of wealth or mammon. Jesus was demanding a paradigm shift from highly institutionalized religion of external observances to a life of inner conversion and spirituality. Here one shall not fail to distinguish that throughout history Christianity, functioned at two models, i.e., the monastic model like the Essenes and the 'secular' model. The prophetic model is characterized by at least four elements: 1) a strong sense of being called (Jer 1:5-8); 2) an urge to denounce evil and announce God's good news; 3) as a consequence the prophet might become a suffering servant (Isa 52—53:12); Jesus took the form of a servant (Phi 2:6-9; Isa 42ff.); the prophetic function might often lead to martyrdom; 4) and eventually it leads to restoration and glorification (Isa 54:1-17; Phi 2:9).

Salvation of the Unevangelized

The core of the Christian mission, both the Catholic as well as Protestant, revolved around the two fundamental beliefs that the whole of humankind had sinned in Adam and were under the condemnation of God. Thus all the gentiles and pagans were depicted as the 'children of wrath' (Eph 2:3), 'having no hope and without God' (Eph 3:12). However the humankind would be redeemed if it believes in the atoning death of Jesus Christ and his resurrection. The New Testament theology of Salvation was an extension of the Old Testament belief that the Jews were a chosen people and worshippers of one true God (Deut 7:6-9; 26:16) and the pagans were idol worshipers (Jer 10:8-10; Is 44:9-20; Ps 115:4-8). Such an exclusive religious belief and tradition was further hardened by the strict belief and observances of the Essene Community, that withdrew from the world and lived a very ascetic and austere life, expecting the imminent end of world. Their core beliefs were, among others; one, the gentiles are God's enemies; two, only a few elect like them would be saved when God appears in the imminent future.

In the beginning of the Christian era the question of salvation become more complex with the final revelation in Jesus Christ. New questions included: what about the salvation of those who lived before the incarnation of Jesus Christ? What about the pagans who not only refused to believe in him, but also severely persecuted the followers of the new messiah? What is the destiny of innocent children who die without baptism? Their answer was more or less in line with the Old Testament and the Essene Teaching: Predestination of a few who are saved and others who are excluded from the salvific plan. Naturally in the early church more than

The Future of Christian Mission in India

one theological school competed for true answer. Theological conflicts as well as ecclesiastical conflicts were inevitable in the course of following centuries. One of the predominant beliefs that gained acceptance in the New Testament was that though Jesus died for the salvation of all human beings but the opportunity for salvation is restricted to a select few only. All the New Testament authors taught and wrote about this fundamental belief. For example, St. Peter filled with the Holy Spirit announced: "There is no salvation through anyone else, nor is there any other name by which we are to be saved" (Acts 4:12). The believers in Jesus Christ claimed that they were the New Israel. So Peter would justify it with reference to the original identity of Israel. "You are a chosen race, a royal priesthood, a holy nation, a people of his own so that you may announce his praises" (1 Pet 2:9; Exo 19:5). St. Paul demanded an explicit confession of Jesus for salvation: "If you confess with your mouth that Jesus is the Lord and believe in your heart that God raised him from the dead you will be saved" (Rom 10:9). The Gospel of Mark end with the mission command of Jesus to the eleven. "Go into the whole world and proclaim the Gospel to every creature. Whoever believes and is baptized will be saved. Whoever does not believe will be condemned"(Mark 15:16). Though St. John's Gospel begins with the Universalism of the Logos, "which enlightens everyone"(John 1:9) concluded with exclusivism: "I am the way and the truth and the life. No one comes to the Father except through me"(14:16). Multiplication of Scriptural texts is superfluous as exclusivism was the dominant thrust of the mission history.

A few of the early Church Fathers like Clement of Alexandria (155–215) and his disciple Origen (185–254) in north Africa maintained a more optimistic view that all people will be saved in the end because the power of Christ's salvific sacrifice excludes none. In another context St. Cyprian of Carthage, in north Africa, summarized this theology in the dictum, "Extra ecclesiam nulla salus"[74] to condemn the separatists who had left the mother church, which was symbolically explained as leaving the Ark of Noah. In a later period the axiom was extended to all the unbaptized, including innocent children, who died without baptism. After the Edict of Milan of the Roman emperor Constantine in 313 and the elevation of Christianity, until then a persecuted religion, as the religion of the Roman empire, the theology of exclusion from the church was interpreted rigorously by St. Augustine of Hippo (354–430). He was the proponent of the theology of Original Sin, that is, in the first sin of Adam the whole

---

74. Sanders, *No Other Name*, 146–49.

Emerging Missions and Missiologies for the Future

of humanity is condemned to damnation. Rejecting the optimism of the Alexandrian theology of salvation of all, Augustine, with his pessimistic life experiences, engaged himself in various polemics against Gnosticisms, Manichaeism, Donatism and Pelegianism. Augustine taught the doctrine of limited atonement. Interpreting various Biblical data, either in the Old Testament or in the New Testament, he demonstrated that there were three classes of human beings: 1) those to whom the Gospel was never preached because it was foreknown that they would not believe; 2) those to whom it was preached even though God foreknew that they would not believe; and 3) finally those to whom the Gospel was revealed and did believe.[75] Augustine was deeply influenced by the legalism of Tertulian of Cartage (160–225), the first systematic theologian of the church, who upheld the justice of God, that is, the sinful humanity must pay for its sin against the majesty of God. St. Ambrose of Milan (339–97) whose eloquence converted Augustine, declared that all those who die without baptism would go to hell.[76] Augustine reinforced the existing theology that the church, instituted by the Apostles was holy and perfect and the only source of holiness. Those who are cut off from the church and its sacraments are also cut off from Christ. Once baptized the new Christians become and object of ecclesiastical discipline and they can be forced to fulfill what they have promised (Luke 14:23). Later the concept of force was extended and legitimized in the conversion of non-Christians. Augustine's theology of baptism, church and salvation dominated Western theology until very recently.[77] St. Ambrose in the second half the fourth century, St. Augustine in the beginning of the fifth century, Pope Gelasius in the same century, and St. Gregory in the second half of the sixth century taught that the state was the 'Secular Arm' of the church. These teachings legitimized the "two sword" theology. The Reformers, Luther, Calvin, Zwingli and others followed Augustine's theology of restricted salvation. Calvin taught that salvation is a matter of unconditional election by the sovereign and mysterious will of God. The theology of dual predestination rigidly believed that the elect would be saved and others would be condemned to hell. Calvin, like Luther, taught that justification comes from faith alone. Calvinism faced its strong opposition in the theology of Jacobus Arminus (1560–1609) in Holland who taught that man is free to resist the grace of

---

75. Ibid., 51–56.
76. Ibid., 74.
77. Bosch, *Transforming Mission*, 215–23.

election.[78] Thus the unfortunate marriage of the church and state, inaugurated by Constantine and ratified by the early theologians and popes, ended in a happy divorce only at the conclusion of the twentieth century.

Models of Exclusive-Missionaries

Ishanand Vempeny identifies varieties of missionaries generated by exclusive missiology.[79]

Political missionaries: The Edict of Milan issued by co-emperors Constantine and Licinus in 313 transformed the persecuted Christianity into the official and glorious religion of the mighty empire. The Edict of Constantinople (529) prohibited the existence of paganism and pagan worship because pagans and heathens were thought to be inferior to Christians. There is a general consensus among scholars that the Christian population grew from 10 percent in AD 300 to 57 percent in AD 350 in the Roman Empire.[80] The use of political savagery in the conversion of the Saxons by Charlemagne, the emperor of the Holy Roman Empire (771–804) is part of the shameful history of conversion of Europe.[81] Deviating from the "two sword" theory Spain brought together the "cross and the sword" to convert the pagans in the Americas. And the Portuguese mission in Goa used both sword and inquisition to speed up conversions at the order of the Portuguese king. Reformation in North Europe would not have succeeded had it not been for the powerful support of kings. And later the protestant mission was actively promoted by the kings, with minor exceptions.

Street Preachers: The evangelical missionaries in India in the nineteenth century were aggressive street preachers. They focused more on abusing Hindus and their idol worship than preaching God's love and reconciliation with the world. And the infuriated listeners at times manhandled them.

Exclusive Salvation-Sellers: "You must be born again to be saved" is the core message of the evangelical preachers. They reject both the Kingdoms of God theology as well as dialogue with people of other religions.

78. Witte, "Calvinism," 247–51.
79. Vempeny, "Conversion," 24–45.
80. Stark, *Rise of Christianity*, 6–7.
81. Neill, *History*, 78–82.

Emerging Missions and Missiologies for the Future

Bible Peddlers: There are some who believe in the magical power of the Bible. Its printing and free distributions, for example, in public places like markets and railway stations, ignoring whether the recipients would read it, is part of their missionary methods.

Miracle Workers: One of the attractions to Charismatic and Pentecostal preachers is their claims to healing and miracles. The skeptics question whether most of healings are result of mass psychology or genuine faith healing.

Quixotic militant outfit missionaries: These use different army titles like "The Salvation Army," founded by the Methodist minister William Booth-Tucker, or "Army of Christian Liberation." In the age of military crusade to the holy land military religious orders like Militia Christi, Knights Templar, the Hospitallers and others were founded, for the defense of faith, motivated by the spirit of pilgrimage, indulgences and martyrdom.

Missionaries of apocalyptic eschatology: At the occurrence of natural calamities like earthquake, flood, and war some missionaries appear preaching repentance and conversion, telling that these natural calamities are signs of the end of world as predicted in the Bible. For instance after a violent earth quake and death of thousands of people in Chirapunji, on the Southern slop of Khasi hill, Mehalalya, in 1897, the Khasi conversions doubled in a year from 2,101, that was the meager fruit of sixty years of missionary work.[82]

From the traditional exclusivism to inclusivism or universalism is the new paradigm shift in missiology. Serious challenges are being raised, particularly in the modern era, how to reconcile God's infinite love for the humanity with the damnation of majority of people who are non-Christians. The most crucial question is: ultimately who has the final victory? Christ or Satan? "God wills everyone to be saved" (1 Tim 2:4). St. John also teaches such universalism. "Christ is the expiation for our sins, and not for our sins only but for those of the whole world" (1 John 2:2). The most important scriptures text on universalism is found in Paul's own teaching. If the first Adam brought sin and death for all his offsprings, without their choice, then logically, the Second Adam brought righteousness and justification to all the people, without their decision. "For if, by the transgression of one person, death came to reign through that one how much more will those who receive the abundance of grace and the gift of justification

---

82. Downs, "Christian Conversion," 386.

came to reign in life through one person Jesus Christ. In conclusion, just as through one transgression condemnation came upon all, so through one righteous act acquittal and life came to all" (Rom 5:17–18). Equally powerful universalism is taught in 1 Cor 15:22–28. Paul believed that there will be no longer any enemy of the Kingdom, only loyal subjects. In the last days Christ will achieve his goal "When every thing is subjected to him then the Son himself will (also) be subjected to the one who subjected every thing to him, so that God may be all in all" (1 Cor 15:28). It is the faith of all Christians that the whole of humanity is recreated and renewed in Jesus Christ (Eph 1:10). This is the foundation of the Christian anthropology. This new humanity is the meeting point for all people of good will.

Rejecting Christian exclusivism, Indian philosopher Radhakrishnan wrote: "All truth about God has its source in God. The conception of a unique revelation of a chosen people is contrary to the love and justice of God . . . In the new world order such a view of spiritual monopolies has no place."[83]

Two Hermeneutical Principles of Inclusivism

All the scriptural texts on exclusivism and inclusivism should be distinguished between the ontological and epistemological necessity of Christ for salvation. There is no simple solution to the controversy because these two conflicting teachings are biblically tenable and scripture texts are always subjected to more than one interpretations. It is not easy to harmonize them. However let me propose two hermeneutical principles to arrive at a solution, if at all it is possible. One, various books of the Bible were written by numerous authors during a period of over one thousand years, addressing different people, and answering conflicting contexts, in a variety of religio-cultural worlds—Canaanite, Babylonian, Assyrian, Egyptian, Persian, Greek and Roman. However the overriding theme of the Bible is God's creation of the world, humanity's fall and sin in Adam and the final definitive recreation of humanity and the cosmos in Jesus Christ. All scriptural texts and events must be interpreted with reference to this master plan. According to the Bible the mission of God begins with creation (Gen 1:1) and culminates in the final recreation of the "New heaven and New Earth" (Rev 21:1–4). The Bible contains a series of creative and liberative acts of God in the midst of recurring chaos in the beginning (Gen 1–2); creating Israel as a "Contrast Community" (Gen Chapters 12–50; Ex 6: 2–7), after the chaos caused by the sin of Adam

83. Radhakrishnan, *Basic Writing*, 39–40.

Emerging Missions and Missiologies for the Future

(Gen 3; Gen 4–11), leading to exile and slavery. God in his faithfulness overcomes sin and evil and begins to establish a new order in the person of Jesus Christ. Ultimately universalism or Salvation of all is founded in the unlimited atonement and gratuitous grace in Christ. It is the Christian belief that the first Adam will not triumph over the second. Finally the Devil is conquered by Christ's victory won in the power of the resurrection (1 Cor 15). And the new humanity is created.

The second principle for interpreting and harmonizing certain paradoxical Biblical texts is to examine them in the light of God's infinite and unconditional love and compassion. It is almost unimaginable for the modern people, in contrast to the primitive ethnocentrism of the Old Testament, to picture an angry God, letting millions of humans being condemned into eternal hell fire. The New Testament exclusivism is the unfortunate theological continuation of the Old Testament exclusivism, maintained and perpetuated by one powerful school of theologians in the early church. In contrast universalism and inclussivism is founded on the unlimited atonement of Christ, the universal salvific will of God and the sovereign love of God.[84] I believe that the vision of Jesus rejected all the anthropomorphic and primitive understanding of the God of Israel, Yahweh. In the backdrop of the Abba experience of Jesus the exclusivist and unloving portrayal God therefore should be understood or interpreted as human words. Jesus excluded none from his all embracing love. The Vatican council acknowledged that God's Word is communicated through human words or human languages that are immersed in particular cultures. Passed on orally first, much of the earliest Christian traditions, recorded in the Bible is only of human origin. However drawing a delicate line between what constitutes the rule of faith, or the revelation of Christ, recorded under the inspiration of the Holy Spirit, and what constitutes mere human tradition, is a sensitive and formidable issue (DV no. 10,12). Yet the believing and teaching church trusts that the Holy Spirit continues to lead her to the fullness of truth (John 16:13). Universalism and inclusivism, in my opinion, is the fullness of truth of the universal God, the God of all people, and not the God of Israel. The Abba experience of Jesus that God is unconditionally loving and forgiving (John 3:16; 1 John 4:11; Luke 6:35–36) was made visible to humankind through the unconditional love and forgiveness of Jesus. It was the self-sacrificing love of Jesus Christ, climaxing in his death on the cross. By loving his own "to the end," he manifested his own love which he received from the Father (John 13:1)

---

84. Sanders, *No Other Name*, 97.

And the missionary service is an extension of the Trinitarian love (John 15:12). In Paul the love of God and the neighbor are seen as one unity (1 Cor 13). The Christian love, Agape, therefore, should be distinguished from other forms of love like *eros*, sensual love, and *philia*, friendship.

The Second Vatican council cautiously maintained the view that salvation is possible and available even to the unevangelized (LG 16; GS 22). The evangelicals and the Pentecostals in general reject universalism and inclusivism. The Frankfurt Declaration (1970) is a clear example. The Laussane Covenant (1974) left the issue undecided. However, it is good news to note that many of the contemporary evangelicals, addressing the unlimited atonement merited by the death of Jesus, do not follow Augustine and Calvin.[85] For instance Hendrik Kraemer in tune with Karl Barth was reluctant to uphold the traditional rigid view on the unevangelized.[86] All Salvation is the work of one God. In the words of Indian theologian Amaladoss: "As Creator and Redeemer God's action embraces the whole universe. . . . It (God's saving action) manifests itself in a unique way in Jesus, the incarnate Word. In Christ' death and resurrection God commits God's self in a special way and God's saving action in the world enters a decisive stage. But God's action in Christ must not be separated from God's ongoing action in history in the Word and in the Spirit."[87]

Models of Inclusive Missionaries

Missionaries of charity and compassionate services: The best known example is the Missionaries Charity of Blessed Mother Teresa who take a fourth vow to serve only the destitute. Blessed Damien of Molokai (1840–89), who himself died of the most dreaded disease, leprosy, after his selfless service of lepers for seventeen years, in the island of outcast lepers, is one of earliest example of heroic missionaries. No religion in the world has created as many missionaries of destitute as Christianity. Jesus in his parable of the Last Judgement (Matt 25:31–46) teaches that salvation, the goal of traditional mission, is determined by your love for the "least of my brothers and sisters," and not by religious affiliation or observance of laws and rituals. If Saint Francis Xavier was the model of many Catholic missionaries in the colonial period, Blessed Mother Teresa of Calcutta will be one of the best models for the future.

---

85. Ibid.,30.
86. Ibid.,77.
87. Amaladoss, "Kingdom," 34.

Emerging Missions and Missiologies for the Future

Missionaries of integral development and liberation: The number of missionaries working for the integral development of poor in India, particularly tribals, dalits and slum dwellers, no more as *preparatio evangelica* as in the past, but as an integral part of evangelization, is on the increase. One of the recent means employed in order to fight for justice is providing legal aids by qualified priests and nuns in the Supreme Court of India. Responding to the Vatican document, "Instruction on certain aspects of the Theology of liberation" the National Assembly of the Conference of Religious in India (CRI, 1986) stated: "But as Christian, we see in Jesus the visible expression of that liberative Love. He thus became for us the greatest sacrament of liberation."[88]

Missionaries of prison ministry: It was initiated in Trichur district, Kerala, a few decades ago. Visiting prisoners, listening to their stories, giving counseling, conducting prayer services by priests and nuns are integral part of their services. Currently it is functioning under the CBCI Commission for Justice, Peace and Development. These new missionaries, undoubtedly, are prophets of the contemporary church. A small number of nuns and lay missionaries, are engaged in rehabilitating sex workers into the main stream of the society. Such a ministry was unimaginable in India a few decades ago.

Missionaries of Quality Education: The impact of Christian education on Indian society was already established in the previous chapter. Their popularity becomes more conspicuous when Hindus and people of other religions establish English medium schools with such brand names as, "St. Jesus Convent School," or "Missionary Convent School." Marriage advertisements in news papers often add the qualification of girls as "convent educated."

Missionaries of Dialogue with other Religions for Peace and Harmony[89]

Missionaries of Christian Ashrams and Spirituality to Enhance the Indian Image of the Church[90]

Missionaries of Witness and Martyrdom: The noun witness, *martyres* occur thirteen times in the Acts. It is witness to the good news of the reign of God in Jesus Christ—in his incarnation, his life, his crucifixion and

---

88. Arokiasamy, *Liberation*, 256.
89. See chapter 5, "From Confrontations to Dialogue and Partnership."
90. See chapter 6, "Inculturation of the Indian Churches."

resurrection (Acts 13:31; Luke 24:48). The proclamation of faith, beginning with its founder Jesus, suffered martyrdom. And hence Tertullian's dictum, "the blood of Martyrs is seed" (of the church). The mission in India has suffered much persecution, particularly in the second half of the last century.

The fact that the Vatican authorities issued warnings against these unorthodox trends points that the paradigm shift is not smooth and it will naturally take time to gain ground. "Instruction on certain Aspects of the Theology of Liberation" issued in September 1984, "Instruction on Christian Freedom and Liberation" in March 1986, and the anxieties expressed in *Redemptoris Missio* (no.4) exhibit tension between the official orthodoxy and praxis at the grass-root level.[91] The emerging mission theology of inclusion or universalism is gradually shaping, not without suspicion and objections, new models of missionaries, particularly in Asia. The crucial difference between the exclusive and inclusive missiologies and their missionaries is this: the former was, at least in principle, "other-worldly," i.e., salvation of soul while the latter is assertively "this-worldly." The number of "exclusive missionaries," it seems, is on the decline, at least in India and Asia; they have little future. On the contrary, the "missionaries of inclusivism" are on the increase, gradually and steadily, with better future.

Universal Mission of all the Peoples of the World

It was always believed and professed that the church is universal and her mission is universal. With the past negative attitudes towards non-Christian religions it was logical that earlier missiologists would hardly ask whether these world religions had any mission at all. In the radically new atmosphere of positive appreciation of world religions, cultures and peoples unprecedented questions need to be raised. The missiology of the Vatican Council was predominantly Euro-American, both in the geographical and in the theological sense. The past history of mission proves that it has only very limited relevance for Asia, with its predominantly non-Christian ethos. Some of the Indian theologians assess the traditional Christian universality as hegemonic in the sense that mission meant to go out and convert all non-Christians. The new context of the Asian mission demands a reverse catholicity: "The incoming universality is the movement by which Christianity receives the ways of the Spirit

---

91. Rayan, "Instruction on Christian," 226.

Emerging Missions and Missiologies for the Future

from other religions."[92] And it will be gradually realized through a process of dialogue. It sounds like one-way traffic. Therefore the new question is this: how does two-third of non-Christian humanity, participate in God's plan of creating a "new heaven and a new earth" (Rev 21:1)? Is it a right question to ask if all the peoples of the world share in this great mission? Is it correct to believe that only Christians have a mission and other people of God are excluded from participating in God's mission? I would like to answer in the affirmative: all the people of God or all the children of God, created in the image of God and recreated in the Paschal mystery, are entrusted with a mission. They all participate in the universal mission of God in different ways.

One, the whole human family has one origin and one destiny. The all inclusive vision of the Vatican council teaches: "For all people comprise a single community, and have a single origin since God made the whole race of men dwell over the entire face of the earth. One also is their final goal: God. His providence, His manifestation of goodness and his saving designs extend to all men . . . (and) the nations will walk in his light" (NA 1).

Two, in the Trinitarian plan of salvation, God's love became visible in the incarnation of Jesus Christ, his life, his activities, death and resurrection. His mission is being fulfilled in history through the Holy Spirit. If the original plan of God was rejected by the Sin of the first Adam, it was perfected in the second Adam, Jesus Christ. If all became sinners in the first Adam, then all people were justified in Jesus Christ (Rom 3:9–25). The blessings of the past missionary services have explicitly reached only one-third of humanity. The majority of humanity, however, participate in God's unconditional love implicitly. "All this holds true not only for Christians but for all men of good will in whose hearts grace works in an unseen way. For since God died for all men and since the ultimate vocation of man is in fact one, and divine, we ought to believe that the Holy Spirit in a manner known only to God offers to every man the possibility of being associated with this paschal mystery" (GS 22). Elsewhere the same council taught that every person who lives an upright life, according to his conscience, will attain salvation (LG 16). All these are confirmed by the teaching of St. Peter, who said: "In truth, I see that God shows no partiality. Rather, in every nation whoever fears him and acts uprightly is acceptable to him" (Acts 10:34–35). And St. Paul too wrote to the Romans: "For there will be glory, honor, and peace for everyone who does good, the Jew first and then Greek. There is no partiality with God" (Rom 2:10–12).

---

92. Wilfred, *Asian Public Theology*, 348.

The Future of Christian Mission in India

Three, the Trinitarian mission is being carried forth in human history through the Holy Spirit. The Holy Spirit who was traditionally marginalized in the Catholic mission and spirituality is being better recognized in recent times. In the back drop of John Paul's address to the representatives of non-Christian religious leaders in Madras on February 5, 1986 and similar addresses elsewhere, he held a day of prayer and fasting for peace with representatives of major religions of the world in Assisi in October 1986.[93] And the Holy Spirit is present not only in individual human heart but also in creation and human history. After the Synod of the Asian Bishops in Rome in May 1998 and while releasing the "Post-Synodal Apostolic Exhortation Ecclesia in Asia" in New Delhi in November 1999 John Paul II affirms: "The Holy Spirit is present from the first moment of creation ... and is always present in the world and its life-giving force. Since creation is the beginning of history, the Spirit is in a certain sense a hidden power at work in history, guiding it in the ways of truth and goodness" (EA.15). Spelling out a few pointers, without elaborations, how different persons and categories of people become partners, being aware or unaware, of the silent unfolding of the new heaven and earth is attempted below.[94]

ONE. *All human life originates and develops in families, the cradle of civilizations.* Parents, by participating in the generative process, become noble channels through which God's life and love flow from generations to generations. Families that cherish, promote and transmit human, cultural and religious values, first and foremost through their own lived examples, and then by teaching their own children, become strong building blocks of human civilization. The Indian civilization was preserved and promoted through three fundamental units: joint family, caste and village which were intimately related and united. However radical changes are being ushered in today. For instance women are becoming more conscious of their human dignity and claim equal rights and duties in the domestic and public arena. From early childhood contemporary culture exerts unprecedented influence on education and formation of children.

TWO. *Parents and teachers together shape the minds of most people in the world.* Teachers generously dedicate their whole lives to leading curious minds to a better understanding of a fascinating world. They are being led from darkness of ignorance, superstitions and dead habits to truth and ultimate light of God. The mind and reason is being led forward into

---

93. Accattoli, *John Paul II*, 173.
94. Abbott, *Documents of Vatican II*, 717–37.

Emerging Missions and Missiologies for the Future

ever widening thought. And the journey of the youth to greater heights of scholarship is being continued under the inspiration of erudite and brilliant college and university professors who question and challenge traditional wisdom. Not only the future of the nation but the future of humanity is intertwined with the expansion and spread of knowledge and wisdom. It is the youth who receive the torch from the hands of teachers and transform the society of tomorrow with fresh vision.

THREE. *Workers of the world through varieties labors actualize their god-given potentialities and serve humanity.* Without adequate opportunities for work their hidden qualities fail to flower. Through productive, distributive and service sectors they serve their neighbours and make available everything necessary for a truly human and dignified life. Food, pure drinking water, clothing, shelter, health services, travel services, transport, training in skills, press and media, leisure and recreation and so forth are requirements of fullness of a more dignified and excellent life (GS 26). And all these workers should enjoy the right to self-determination and freedom from capitalistic and feudalistic exploitation. Justice, liberty and dignity of the workers whose immense services, often obscure and marginal, are better promoted by the social teachings of the church.

FOUR. *And the field of medicine.* What will be quality of modern life without the dedicated and patient services of numerous doctors, physicians, nurses, and their collaborators who live their total life at the service of healing, alleviating pain, wiping away tears from millions of eyes and restore life to its original state. By protecting and promoting life the whole medical fraternity become the most esteemed and respected collaborators with God's plan of sharing fullness of life with the human family. A major part of the ministry of Jesus was focused on healing all types of illness. It is our conviction that all those who dedicate their lives to the genuine service of the sick share in the mission of "the man of sorrows" nailed to the cross.

FIVE. *The human person, constituted of body, mind and soul, seeks assistance for good mental health and growth in emotional maturity.* The intrinsic link between health of mind and body is being better understood by modern psychology, psychoanalysts, psychiatrists, and counselors who are being sought after more than ever in the modern stress inducing unhealthy atmosphere. Wounded hearts and minds are being helped to achieve wholeness. In contemporary India the number of Christian institutions for personality development, counseling and healing are more than the centres for the study of missiology.

SIX. *Scientists, explorers, and thinkers throughout ages keep seeking to fathom the mysteries of the universe.* They search for truth because the cosmos is rational. Most scientists believe that they come closer to the mystery of God through the mystery of the universe. As sincere searchers of truth, religion and science, in the last analysis, cannot be enemies as it unfortunately happened sometimes in the past, but humble companions. "In every true researcher of nature there is a kind of religious reverence." wrote Albert Einstein.[95] In the words of Albert Bernhard Nobel "they have conferred the greatest benefit on mankind." While modern science has immensely contributed to transform the quality of life, unfortunately the very scientific process is inherent with the possibility of creating catastrophic instruments of destruction. Here lay the immense responsibility of scientists towards future of humanity.

SEVEN. *Poetry and literature.* In the 'Introduction' to Nobel Laureate Rabindranath Tagore's *Gitanjali*, W. B. Yeats wrote in 1912: "A tradition where poetry and religion are the same thing." Poets enable human hearts, tempted to pessimism, to inspirations; authors of great literature delve in the riches of human hearts and promote highest values; musicians assist people to sing God's glory and majesty; architects construct magnificent churches, temples, mosques and other places of worship; artists resist the wear and tear of life through promoting beauty; artist's of the world apply their talents for the promotion of truth, goodness and beauty of God.

EIGHT. *Rulers of nations are entrusted with the responsibility of promoting order and peace in the society.* Their duty includes enacting just laws, recognizing that ultimately God alone is the source of all authority. They are called to dedicate their lives towards the promotion of common good. Lawyers and judges are entrusted with the delicate vocation and mission of administering justice to all, rich and poor, powerful and weak, without fear or favor and thus participate in God's justice.

NINE. *International Organizations.* Learning from the accumulated wisdom of human history, that man's evil passions beget brutal wars and untold suffering and misery, modern nations fervently and vigorously engage themselves in the pursuit of international peace and protection of

---

95. Quoted by D'Souza, *What Is Great*, 99.

lives. International organizations like the United Nations Organization, founded after witnessing man's indescribable inhumanity against humanity in the two world wars, that are engaged in promoting peace and cooperation in solving critical problems and promoting human progress and development deserve sincere appreciation and unreserved cooperation in their difficult global mission.

TEN. *World Civilization of Human Dignity.* Manifest in the program and services of various organizations and groups are tendencies characteristic of contemporary culture and impulses towards unification in economic, political and cultural realms of life and the movement towards liberation and human dignity. The emerging new world civilization is centered around human dignity and fundamental human rights which can be ultimately traced to the teaching and person of Jesus Christ. "All things on earth should be related to man as their centre and crown," taught the Vatican Council (GS 12).

ELEVEN. *Search for Ultimate Meaning.* Unprecedented developments and progress in science, technology, medicine and other fields of empirical knowledge are pushing many modern men and women towards meaningless precipice. The human advancement is simultaneously scared by struggles, sufferings, despairs, hopelessness and meaninglessness. People seemed to be confused and disoriented. Many ask: Does God exist? What is man? What is the meaning of suffering of innocents? There are reasons enough for contemporary agnosticism and atheism.[96] The number of people traveling from affluent West to the East in search of God—experience or Nirvana, seems to be on the increase. And the Indian Gurus traveling to the West are complimenting new religious demands. Contemporary men and women seem to be more restless than St. Augustine who prayed: "You, O Lord, have made us for yourself and our hearts are restless until they rest in you." All the founders of religions, their philosophers and theologians, have seriously and sincerely attempted to help the human family to discover extra-sensory truth, the existence of the trans-empirical Ultimate Reality which is named differently by different religions. They all share in God's mission of elevating humanity to Himself. All founders of religions, prophets, sages and saints of all times and nations are Gods servants, guiding the human family to its ultimate destiny. Divine providence is directing all people of good will to a new order which is oriented towards the fulfillment of God's inscrutable design, despite apparent human failures.

96. John Paul II, *Crossing the Threshold*, 27–44.

The Future of Christian Mission in India

The church is entering the new era with a radically redefined concept of mission as well as missionaries of the secular world.

TWELVE. *In the present era the human family is moving into a planetary society.* "Discarding the exaggerated dualism of the past centuries the church now manifests a new awareness" that "it is an essential part of the Christian mission to humanize and thereby Christianize political, social economic, cultural and technical life."[97] In all these services the church has a single intension: "to re-establish all things in Christ, in heaven and on earth" (Eph 1:10). "And the Spirit of God . . . who with a marvelous providence directs the unfolding of time and renews the face of the earth is present in this evolution" (GS.26).

Conclusion: Finally Why Mission?

If all people have the opportunity to be saved without an explicit encounter with Jesus Christ, then, what is the necessity of the Mission? Questions, confusions and anxieties about proclamation of the Gospel and baptism are intensified in the recent decades. Without exhaustive treatment of motives of mission, once more, they are recapitulated.

ONE. Exactly a month before the opening of the Vatican Council in a radio-television address, Pope John asked: What is the relevance of the church to the needs and problems of the Christians and non-Christians in the modern world? And he himself answered and said that the church has responsibilities and obligations bearing directly on every phase of life—starting from daily bread to spiritual food. That is *missio ad extra*.[98] The missionaries in India, therefore, should continue to ask: Church of Jesus Christ what is your relevance for contemporary India? As long as there is suffering in the world, the world is in urgent need of men and women who are willing to compassionately hear the cry of suffering humanity (Exo 3:7–10). What do you name them (Missionary?) is secondary. They are universal servants of humanity.

TWO. The greatest missionary challenges of the postindustrial, postChristian and postmodern era is the unprecedented sprouting of unbelievers and practical atheists. No doubt the number of faith seekers too are increasing. The decline of religion and religiosity, a highly disturbing feature

---

97. Rauch, "Foreword," ix.
98. Wiltgen, *Rhine*, 206.

Emerging Missions and Missiologies for the Future

of developed countries is, slowly but surely, denting the traditional religious spirit of developing countries, as an extension of globalization. In the new context of multiple conflicts, contradictions and dichotomies of life search for the ultimate meaning system does not disappear. Religions always played a strategic role in creating sacred cosmos for protecting humanity against the nightmare of chaos. Therefore the Christian mission will assume a new role, that is, to become one of the major partners, not an exclusive one as it was believed in the past, with other religious and secular partners, in constructing the ultimate meaning of human existence and the universe.[99]

THREE. The Missionary Command of Jesus, *Missio Christi* (Matt 28:18-20; Mark 16:15; Luke 24:47; John 20:21; Act 1:8), is normative for all Christians. Bible is God's infallible word. The believer humbly obeys his commission. It is the language of faith. Among the evangelicals *Missio Christi* is the only Biblically legitimate form of mission. They reject the Mission of the Church, *Missio Ecclesiae*, as the unique salvific institution. They reject *Missio Dei* too as mission for all mankind.[100]

FOUR. Apart from the missionary command experience of God is an equally powerful motivation for missionary commitment. Through the sacraments of baptism every Christian participates in the mission inaugurated by Jesus. Those who have experienced the Good News of God's unconditional love and compassion feel an urge to share it with others who have not yet shared in the peace and joy in Christ. Mission is an overflow of the Christ-experience. For St. Paul it began with his conversion experience and not with the mission command in the Scripture. Mission for him became an irresistible urge. "Indeed the love of Christ urges us" (2 Cor 5:14). Again, "If I preach the Gospel there is no reason for me to boast, for an obligation has been imposed on me and woe to me it I do not preach it" (1 Cor 9:16). And similar was the convictions of St. Peter before the Sanhedrin (Acts 4:20), other apostles after the Pentecost-experience, and multitude of heroic and illustrious evangelizers in the course of history. The missionaries are merely humble servants of the *Missio Dei*, for the historical realization of the Reign of God.

Five. There is an urgency of calling and awakening people to repentance (Mark 1:15; Matt 4:17; Luke 24:47) in every place and time because of

---

99. Berger, *The Social Reality*, 34–37.
100. Matzen, "Standing under," 173–76.

man's sinfulness. Though God is unconditionally forgiving there are always prodigal sons and daughters who continue to rebel against the love of the Father (Luke 15:11-16). The pervasiveness of sinfulness of all men and women and social structures continue to fracture human affairs horribly. The story of Cain murdering his brother Abel is the prototype of murder, violence, hatred, jealousy and other innumerable evils that continue to destroy humanity. It is always in need of reconciliation which God offered in Christ. "And all this is from God who has reconciled us to himself through Christ and gives us the ministry of reconciliations" (2 Cor 5:18-19). And Pope Paul VI beautifully recapitulates: "And the purpose of evangelization is therefore precisely this interior change and if it had to be expressed in one sentence the best way of stating it would be to say that the church evangelizes when she seeks to convert, soley through divine power of the message she proclaims, both the personal and collective conscience of people, the activities in which they engage and the lives and concrete milieux which are theirs" (EN 18). This integral transformation or liberation must take place at three levels, personal, socio-historic and cosmic. All people of good will who are seriously concerned with shaping the future of humanity can ill afford to ignore the vision, prophetic challenges, inspiring teaching, words and deeds of Jesus Christ. On the future of mission W. Kaspar writes:

> Our future can be no other than the reign of God. It is the *eschaton*, which is not only at the end but which is breaking in even now, shaping the present and enlisting the resources of man. Eschatological statements, therefore, are not speculations about a distant future but about a future that is here are now approaching and determining the present. Eschatology is a ferment of continuous unrest that keeps history for ever in motion, prevent it from being complacent and self-righteous about the *status quo* so that it always opening up to new goals and ever greater future. It is not without reason the categories of *exodus*, *metanoia* and hope are closely connected with the eschatological message of the Old and New Testament.[101]

The recent paradigm shift from the ecclesio-centric to the Kingdom-centered mission offers a new vision. Therefore the future of the Christian mission is as bright as the Reign of God. There should be no room for pessimism and sense of hopelessness. And the Indian church is emerging as one of the most influential church in the third world, with its largest

---

101. Quoted by Mueller, *Mission Theology*, 68-69.

number of missionaries as well as creative theologians. We are equally aware that we are a "little flock" (Luke 12:32), a pilgrim people, having participated in the mission of the Father, the Son and the Spirit, marching in solidarity with the whole human family of God towards the new heaven and a new earth. We are also conscious that the Christian mission to all the people of India in the new millennium will be a very demanding vocation. To face these opportunities and challenges we find inspiration and strength in the promise and the presence of the Risen Lord (Matt 28:20).

Appendix

Christian Population in the States of India

"Demography is destiny." — Augustus Comte

Indian States	Christian Population	Percentage
Andaman & Nicobar Islands	77,178	21.7
Andhra Pradesh	1,181,917	1.6
Arunachal Pradesh	205,548	18.7
Assam	986,589	3.7
Bihar	2,63,154	0.6
Chandigarh	7,627	0.8
Chhattisgarh	401,035	1.9
Dadra & Nagar Haveli	6,058	2.7
Daman & Diu	3,362	2.1
Delhi	130,319	0.9
Goa	359,568	26.7
Gujarat	284,092	0.6
Haryana	27,185	0.1
Himachal Pradesh	7,687	0.1
Jammu & Kashmir	20,299	0.2
Jharkhand	1,093,382	4.1
Karnataka	1,009,164	1.9
Kerala	6,057,427	19.0
Lakshadweep	509	0.8
Madhya Pradesh	170,381	0.3
Maharashtra	1,058,313	1.1

Indian States	Christian Population	Percentage
Manipur	737,578	34.0
Meghalaya	1,628,986	70.3
Mizoram	772,809	87.0
Nagaland	1,790,349	90.0
Orissa	897,861	2.4
Pondicherry	67,688	6.9
Punjab	292,800	1.2
Rajasthan	72,660	0.1
Sikkim	36,115	6.7
Tamil Nadu	3,785,060	6.1
Tripura	102,489	3.2
Uttaranchal	27,116	0.3
Uttar Pradesh	212,578	0.1
West Bengal	515,150	0.6
India	24,198,016	2.35

(Source: *Census of India* 2001. *The First Report on Religion*, xxix, xxxiii.)

Bibliography

Abbott, Walter M. *The Documents of Vatican II*. New York: Guild, 1966.
Abraham, P. C. "A Sister in White Habit." In *Saint Alphonsa*, edited by Alexander Paikada, 128–31, Kottayam: Rashtra Deepika, 2010.
Accattoli, Luigi. *John Paul II: Man of the Millennium*. Bombay: St Pauls, 2001.
Adhav, S. M. *Pandita Ramabai*. Madras: Christian Literature Society, 1979.
Agnivesh, Swami. "Foreword." In *Christianity, Hindutva, Conversion*, by Dominic Emmanuel, xii–xvii. Delhi: Indian Society for Promoting Christian Knowledge, 2011.
Aguiar, Benny. *The Making of Mumbai: The History of the Metropolis and its Catholic Past*. Mumbai: St. Pauls, 2012.
Akkara, Anto. *Kandhamal: A Blot on Indian Secularism*. Delhi: Media House, 2009.
al-Faruqi, Ismael R. "Islam." In *Historical Atlas of the Religions of the World*, edited by R. Ismael al-Faruqi and D. E. Sopher, 237–281. New York: Macmillan, 1974.
Aleaz, K. P. "Keshub Chandra Sen." In *A Dictionary of Asian Christianity*, edited by Sunquist, Scott W. et al., 438–39. Grand Rapids: Eerdamans, 2001.
Allen, John. L., Jr. *The Future of the Church: How Ten Trends are Revolutionizing the Catholic Church*. New York: Doubleday, 2009.
Amaladoss, Michael. "The Kingdom, Mission and Conversion." In *Mission and Conversion: A Reappraisal*, edited by Joseph Mattam and Sebastian Kim, 31–48. Mumbai: St Pauls, 1996.
Amalorpavadass, D. S. "Indigenization and the Liturgy of the Church." *International Review of Mission* 65, no. 258 (1976) 164–76.
———. *New Order of the Mass for India*, Bangalore: National Biblical Catechetical & Liturgical Centre, 1974.
———. "Theology of Evangelization in the Asian Context." In *Service and Salvation: Nagpur Theological Conference on Evangelization*, edited by Joseph Pathrapankal, 19–39. Bangalore: Theological Publications in India, 1973.
———. *Towards Indigenization in the Liturgy*. Bangalore: National Biblical, Catechetical & Liturgical Centre, 1972.
Ames, Glenn J. *Vasco da Gama: Renaissance Crusader*. New York: Pearson Longman, 2005.
Anchukandam, Thomas. "De Nobili Robert 1577–1656." In *Encyclopedia of Philosophy*, edited by Johnson Puthenpurackal, 1:378–82. Bangalore: Asian Trading, 2010.
———. *Robert De Nobili's Responsio (1610): Vindication of Inculturation and Adaptation*. Bangalore: Kristu Jyoti, 1996.
Ariarajah, W. "Interreligious Dialogue as an Intercultural Encounter." In *Towards an Intercultural Theology*, edited by Martha Frederiks et al., 63–78. Bangalore: Centre for Contemporary Christianity, 2010.
Arokiasamy, S. and George Gispert-Sauch. *Liberation in Asia. Theological Perspectives*. Anand: Gujarat Sahitya, 1987.

Bibliography

Ashok, Kumar M. and Rowena Robinson. "Legally Hindu: Dalit Lutheran Christians of Coastal Andhra Pradesh." In *Margins of Faith: Dalit and Tribal Christianity in India*, edited by Rowena Robinson and J. M. Kujur, 149–67. New Delhi: Sage, 2010.
Baago, Kaj. *Pioneers of Indigenous Christianity*. Madras: Christian Literature Society, 1969.
Badrinath, C. *Swami Vivekananda: The Living Vedanta*. New Delhi: Penguin, 2006.
Baigent,Michael, and Richard Leigh. *The Dead Sea Scrolls Deception: The Explosive Content of the Dead Sea Scrolls and How the Church Conspired to Suppress them*. New Delhi: Random House, 2006.
Balasundaram, F. J. "Carey William." In *A Dictionary of Asian Christianity*. edited by Sunquist, Scott W. et al., 119–21. Grand Rapids: Eerdamans, 2001.
Banerjee, Nath B. *Religious Conversions in India*. Delhi: Harnam, 1982.
Bantia, Jayant Kumar. *The First Report on Religion Data*. New Delhi: Registrar General and Census Commissioner, 2001
Barlage, Henry. *Following the Word: Mission, Spirituality and Formation*. Rome: SVD Generalate, 1988.
Barrett, David B., editor. *World Christian Encyclopedia: A Comparative Survey of Churches and Religions in Modern World*. 2 Vols. New Delhi: Oxford University Press, 2005.
Basu, Sekhar R. *Nandanar's Children: The Paraiyans Tryst with Destiny in Tamil Nadu 1850-1956*. New Delhi: Sage, 2011.
Baum, Gregory. "Baptism." In *Encyclopedia of Theology: A Concise Sacramentum Mundi*, edited by Karl Rahner, 66–78.London: Burns & Oats, 1981.
Bendix, Richard. *Max Weber: An Intellectual Portrait*. London: University Paperbacks, 1966.
Bergen, Van. "Contemporary Christian Experiments in Ashram Life." *Journal of Dharma* 3, no. 2 (1978) 174–94.
Berger, Peter L. *Social Reality of Religion*. Norwitch: Faber & Faber, 1973.
Berger, Peter L., and Thomas Luckmann. *The Social Construction of Reality: A Treatise in the Sociology of Knowledge*. Harmondsworth, UK: Penguin, 1966.
Bevans, Stephen B., and Roger Schroeder. *Constants in Context: A Theology of Mission for Today*. Bangalore: Claretian, 2004.
———. *Mission for the 21st Century*. Chicago: Chicago Centre for Global Ministries, 2001.
Bhatt, Dhiranand. "Catholic Mission in the Region of Uttar Pradesh." In *Integral Mission Dynamics: An Interdisciplinary Study the Catholic Church in India*, edited by Augustine Kanjamala, 176–92. New Delhi: Intercultural, 1995.
Bosch, David J. *Transforming Mission: Paradigm Shift in the Theology of Mission*. New York: Orbis, 1993.
Bose, Ajoy. *Behenji: A Political Biography of Mayawati*. New Delhi: Penguin, 2008.
Bose, Ashish. *From Population to People*. Delhi: Census Commissioners, 1988.
Boullier, Veronique. "The Violence of the Non-Violent. Or Ascetics in Combat." In *Violence and Non-Violence: Some Hindu Perspectives*, edited by Denis Vidal et al., 27–63. New Delhi: Manohar, 2003.
Bowen, Francis J. *Father Constant Lievens: The Apostle of Chota Nagpur*. London: Ouseley, 1936.
Boyd, A. J. *Christian Encounter*. Edinburgh: Saint Andrew, 1961.
Boyd, Robin H. *An Introduction to Indian Christian Theology*. Madras: Christian Literature Society, 2009.
———. *Kristavidya: A Theology for India*. Madras: Christian Literature Society, 1977.

Bibliography

Braun, Herbert. "The Qumran Community." In *Jesus in His Time*, edited by Hans J. Schultz, 66–74. Philadelphia: Fortress, 1980.
Brechter, Suso. "Decree on the Missionary Activity." In *Commentary on the Documents of Vatican II. Vol IV*, edited by Herbert Vorgrimler, 87–181. London: Burns & Oates, 1968.
Brown, John P. "Holy Spirit in the Struggle of the People for Liberation and Fullness of Life." *International Review of Mission* 79, no. 315 (1996) 35–45.
Buelhmann, Walbert. *The Coming of the Third Church*. Liverpool: St Pauls, 1976.
———. *With Eyes to See: Church and World in the Third Millennium*. Bangalore: Claretian, 1992.
Burrows, William R. *Redemption and Dialogue: Reading Redemptoris Missio and Dialogue and Proclamation*. New York: Orbis, 1999.
Cairns, Earle E. *Christianity Through the Centuries. A History of the Christian Church*. Thiruvalla: Suvartha, 2004.
Campbell, John R., and Allan Rew. *Identity and Affect: Experience of identity In a Globalizing World*. London: Pluto, 1999.
Camps, Anulf. *Partners in Dialogue. Christianity and Other World Religions*. New York: Orbis, 1983.
Castelot, John J. "Religious Institutions of Israel." In *The Jerome Biblical Commentary*, edited by Raymond Brown et al., 703–35. Bangalore: Theological Publications of India, 1968.
Catechism of the Catholic Church. Bangalore: Theological Publications in India, 1994.
Ceresko, Antony R. *The Old Testament: A Liberation Perspective*. Bombay: St Pauls, 1993.
Chakkarai, V."The Relation between Christianity and Non-Christian Faith." In *Rethinking Christianity in India*, edited by G. V. Job, 65–79. Madras: Sundarisanam,1939.
Chakravarti, U. *Pandita Ramabai: A Life and Time*. New Delhi: Critical Quest, 2007.
Chatterji, A.P. *Violent Gods: Hindu Nationalism in India's Present Narratives from Orissa*. Gurgaon: Three Essays, 2010.
Chawla, Navin. "A Pencil in the Hands of the Lord." *The Week* 28, no. 40 (2010) 26–29.
Chediath, Geevarghese. "Eastern Christian Churches." In *Indian Christian Dictionary*, edited by Jose Panthplamthottyil, 51–53. Kottayam: Rashtra Deepika, 2000.
Clarke, Satyanathan. "Conversion to Christianity in Tamil Nadu: Conscious and Constitutive Community Mobilization towards a Different Symbolic World Vision." In *Religious Conversion in India: Modes, Motivation and Meanings*, edited by Rowena Robinson and Clarke Satyanathan, 323–50. New Delhi: Oxford University Press, 2003.
———. "Introduction." In *Dalit Theology in the Twenty-first Century*, edited by Clarke Sathianathan et al., 1–16. New Delhi: Oxford University Press, 2010.
Colaso, Cletus. "The Magisterium on Mission". In *Realizing the Missionary Mandate. A Case Study of the Divine Word in India 1932-79*. 34–44. Bangalore: Asian Trading Corporation, 1998.
Correa, Francis. *Missionary Heralds of India*. Mumbai: St Pauls, 2010.
Costa, Cosme J. "Catholic Mission in the Archdiocese of Goa and Daman." In *Integral Mission Dynamics: An Interdisciplinary Study of the Catholic Church in India*, edited by Augustine Kanjamala, 128–47. New Delhi: Intercultural, 1995.
———. *Missiological Conflict between Padroado and Propaganda in the East*. Pillar: Pillar, 1997.
Covey, Stephen R. *The Seven Habits of Highly Effective People*. London: Simon & Schuster, 1989.

Bibliography

Cunningham, J. R. "Education." In *Modern India and the West. A Study of the Interaction of their Civilizations*, edited by L. S. S. O'Malley, 138–87. Oxford: Oxford University Press, 1968.

Daniel-Rops, Henri. *Daily Life in the Times of Jesus*. New York: American Library, 1964.

David, M. D. "Christianity in Western India." In *Indian Christian Directory*, edited by Jose Panthaplamthottyil, 114–15 Kottayam: Rashtra Deepika, 2000.

———. "Mission, Intercultural Encounter and Change in Western India." In *Missiology for the 21st Century*, edited by Roger E. Hedlund and Paul J. Bhakiaraj, 240–50. Delhi: Indian Society for Promoting Christian Knowledge, 2004.

De Menezes, Rui. *The Cultural Context of the Old Testament*. Bangalore: Theological Publications in India, 2005.

———. "Dead Sea Scrolls and Early Christianity." *Vidyajyothi: Journal of Theological Reflection* 67, no. 1 (2003) 85–102.

———. *God of Israel or God of All*. Mumbai: St Pauls, 2010.

de Sa, Fidelis. *Crisis in Chotanagpur*. Bangalore: Redemptorist, 1975.

De Smith, Richard, and Joseph Neuner. *Religious Hinduism*. Mumbai: St Pauls, 1997.

De Souza, Alphonse. "Catholic Church in Karnataka" In *Integral Mission Dynamics*, edited by Augustine Kanjamala, 89–95. New Delhi: Intercultural, 1995.

Degrijise, O. *Going Forth. Missionary Consciousness of the Third World*. New York: Orbis, 1984.

Desrochers, John. "Communalism, Hindutva and Terrorism." *Integral Liberation* 12, no. 4 (2008) 311–36.

Deunett, David. *Breaking the Spell: Religion as a Natural Phenomenon*. London: Penguin, 2007.

Dhingra, Malhotra R. *Non-Governmental Organizations and Protection of Human Rights*. New Delhi: Deep & Deep, 2010.

Dorairaj, S. "Caste Divide." In *Frontline* 28 no. 4 (2011) 38–42.

Doss, Mohan. *Christ in the Spirit: Cotemporary Spirit Christologies*. New Delhi: Indian Society for Promoting Christian Knowledge, 2005.

Downs, Frederick S. "Administrators, Missionaries and a World Turned Upside Down: Christianity as a Tribal Response in North East Asia." *Indian Church History Review* 15, no. 2 (1981) 99–113.

———. "Christian Conversion Movements in North East India." In *Religious Conversion in India: Modes, Motivations and Meaning*, edited by Rowena Robinson and Clarke Satyanathan, 381–400. New Delhi: Oxford University Press, 2003.

D'Silva, Louis. *Christian Community and the National Mainstream*. Poona: Spicer College, 1985.

D'Souza, Daniel. *A History of the Church in North India*. Mangalore: St. Annes Friary, 1982.

D'Souza, Dinesh. *What's so Great About Christianity*. Mumbai: Jaico, 2008.

D'Souza, Herman. *Light and Life We Seek to Share: All India Consultation on Evangelization*. Bangalore: Secretariat for Church Extention Commission, 1973.

D'Souza, Patrick. *Catholic Bishop Conference of India Evaluation Report: Retrospects and Prospects*. New Delhi: Evaluation Committee, 1995.

Dulles, Avery. *Models of the Church*. Dublin: Gill & McMillan, 1978.

Dumont, Louis. *Homo Hierarchicus: Caste System and its Implications*. London: Paladin, 1970.

Bibliography

Dupuis, Jacques. "FABC Focus on the Churches' Evangelizing Mission in Asia Today." *Vidyajyoti: Journal of Theological Reflection* 56, no. 9 (1992) 449–68.
———. "Religious Plurality and Christological Debate." *SEDOS Bulletin* 28, no. 11(1996) 329–33.
———. "A Theological Commentary: Dialogue and Proclamation." In *Redemption and Dialogue. Reading Redemptoris Missio and Dialogue and Proclamation*, edited by William Burrows, 119–58. New York: Orbis,1993.
Eliade, Mircea. *A History of Religious Ideas.* Vol. 1. London: Collins & Son, 1979.
Emprayil, Thomas. "Cultural and Ideological Conditioning of the Old Testament." In *Bible and Mission in India Today,* edited by Jacob Kavunkal, 17–37. Mumbai: St Pauls, 1993.
Eriksen, H. Thomas. *Ethnicity and Nationalism.* London: Pluto, 2002.
———. *What is Anthropology?* Jaipur: Rawat, 2008.
Eriksen, Hylland, et al. *A History of Anthropology.* London: Philo, 2001.
FABC. *The Spirit at Work in Asia Today.* Federation of Asian Bishops' Conference Paper no. 81. Hong Kong: 1996.
Fallon, P. "Swami Vivekananda." In *Religious Hinduism,* edited by Richard De Smet and Joseph Neuner, 361–65. Bombay, St. Pauls, 1996.
Farquhar, J. N., and G. Gavitte. *The Apostle Thomas in India According to the Acts of Thomas.* Kottayam: St. Thomas, 1972.
Farquhar, Nicol J. *Modern Religious Movements in India.* London: Macmillan, 1929.
Fernando, Leonard, and George Gispert-Sauch. *Two Thousand Years of Faith. Christianity in India.* New Delhi: Penguin, 2004.
Firth, Cyril B. *An Introduction to Indian Church History.* Madras: Christian Literature Society, 1976.
Fisch, Jorg. *Immolating Women: A Global History of Widow Burning from Ancient Times to the Present.* Delhi: Permanent Black, 2006.
Forbes, Geraldine. "Education for Women." In *Women and Social Reform in India*, edited by Sumit Sarkar and Tinika Sarkar, 1:82–112. New Delhi: Permanent Black, 2011.
Francis, Acharya. "Kurisumala Ashram." *Third Millennium* 11, no. 2 (2008) 18–31.
Frykenberg, Robert E. "Raja-Guru and Sishiya-Sastriar: Christian Friedrich Scwhartz and his Legacy in Tanjavur." In *Halle and the Beginning of the Protestant Christianity in India,* edited by Andreas Gross et al., 1:471–96. Halle: Franckesche Stiftungen, 2006.
Fuchs, Stephen. *The Aboriginal Tribes of India.* New Delhi: McMillan, 1973
———. *At the Bottom of the Indian Society.* New Delhi: Munshiram, 1981
———. "German Representatives in the Catholic Church in Bombay." In *Bombay and the Germans*, edited by Walter Leifer, 77–100. Bombay: Shakuntala, 1975.
———. "A New Mission Method for India." In *Verbum SVD* 13 (1972) 225–35.
———. "The Races of Northeast India." In *Indian Missiological Review*, 12 no. 3-4 (1990) 160–72.
———. *Rebellious Prophets: A Study of Messianic Movements in India.* Mumbai: Asia, 1965.
Fuellenbach, John. *The Kingdom of God.* Indore: Satprakashan, 1994.
———. *Throw Fire.* Indore: Satprakashan, 1999.
Gambirananda, Swami. *History of Ramakrishna Math and Ramakrishna Mission.* Calcutta: Advaita Ashrama, 1983.
Gandhi, Mohandas K. *The Message of Jesus Christ.* Mumbai: Bharatiya Vidya Bhavan, 1971.

Bibliography

George, K. M. *Christianity in India Through the Centuries.* Secundarabad: Authentic, 2009.
Gerth, H. H., and C. Wright Mills. *From Max Weber: Essays in Sociology.* London: Routledge, 1970.
Ghosh, Suresh C. *The History of Education in Modern India 1757-2007.* New Delhi: Orient BlackSwan, 2009.
Gibbs, M. E. "Anglican and Protestant Mission 1706-1857." In *Christianity in India: A History of Ecumenical Perspective,* edited by H. C. Perumalil and E. R. Hambye, 211-47. Alleppey: Prakasam, 1972.
Goel, Rama S. *Arun Shourie and his Christian Critic.* New Delhi: Voice of India, 1995.
Golwalkar, M. S. *We or Our Nation Defined.* Nagpur: Bharat, 1947.
Gore, M. S. *Social Context of an Ideology: Ambedkar's Political and Social Thought.* New Delhi: Sage, 1993.
Gosling, David L. *Religion and Ecology in India and South-East Asia.* London: Routledge, 2001.
Gracias, Valerian. *All India Seminar: Church in India Today.* New Delhi: Catholic Bishop Conference of India, 1969.
Graham, Robert A. "Non-Christians." In *The Documents of Vatican II,* edited by Walter Abbotts, 656-59. New York: Guild, 1966.
Gray, H. "The Progress of Women." In *Modern India and the West,* edited by L. S. S. O'Malley, 445-83. Oxford: Oxford University Press, 1968.
Griffiths, Bede. "Christian Monastic Life in India." *Journal of Dharma* 3, no. 2 (1978) 122-35.
Grossouw, W. "Gospel." In *Encyclopedic Dictionary of the Bible,* edited by F. Louis Hartman, 888-950. New York: McGraw-Hill, 1963.
Guha, N. "Indigenous Christian Movement in Bengal." In *Christianity is Indian: The Emergence of an Indigenous Community,* edited by E. Roger Hedlund, 78-99. Delhi: Indian Society, 2010.
Guha, Ramachandra. "Between Anthropology and Literature: The Ethnographies of Verrier Elwin." In *Anthropology in the East. Founders of Indian Sociology and Anthropology,* edited by Patricia Uberoi et al., 330-59. New Delhi: Permanent Black, 2010.
———. "The Great Indian Chaos Theory." *Outlook* 49, no. 1 (2009) 66-74.
———. *India After Gandhi: A History of the World's Largest Democracy.* London: Picador, 2007.
———. "Remaking India." *Sunday Times of India,* October 17, 2010, 20-21.
———. "Will India Become a Superpower?" *Outlook Exclusive,* January 2009, 1-79.
Hambye, E. R. " The Eastern Church." In *Christianity in India: A History of Ecumenical Perspective,* edited by H. C. Perumalil and E. R. Hambye, 30-38. Alleppey: Prakasam, 1972.
Hardgrave, Robert L., Jr. *The Nadars of Tamilnadu: The Political Culture of a Community in Change.* Mumbai: Oxford University Press, 1969.
Harper, Billington S. *In the Shadow of the Mahatma: Bishop V. S. Azariah and the Travails of Christianity in British India.* Grand Rapids: Eerdmans, 2000.
Haughey, John C. *The Conspiracy of God: The Holy Spirit in Men.* New York: Image, 1973.
Hedlund, Roger E. "Baptists in India." In *The Oxford Encyclopaedia of South Asian Christianity,* edited by Roger E. Hedlund, 1:73-74. New Delhi: Oxford University Press, 2012.

Bibliography

———. "Theological Trends in Mission in the 20th Century." In *Missiology for the 21st Century: South Asian Perspective*, edited by Roger E. Hedlund and Paul Bhakiaraj, 120-43. Delhi: Indian Society for Promoting Christian Knowledge, 2004.
Heredia, Rudolf C. "Religious Conversion in a Secular and Pluralistic World." In *Cultural Challenges in Christian Mission in the 21st Century*, edited by Michael Sebastian and Kuriala Chittatukalam, 250-89. Delhi: Media, 2008.
Heyndrikx, Marcel. *Towards Another Future: On Christian Faith and Its Shape between Yesterday and Tomorrow*. Louvain: Eerdmans, 2006.
Hiebert, P. G. *The Gospel in Human Contexts: Anthropological Exploration for Contemporary Missions*. Grand Rapids: Baker Academic, 2009.
Hopkins, Edward W. *The Ordinance of Manu*. New Delhi: Oriental Books, 1970.
Houtart, Francois, and Genevieve Lemericinier. *Size and Structure of the Catholic Church in India: The Indigenization of an Exogenous Religious Institution in a Society in Transition*. Louvain: Universitate Catholique de Louvain, 1982.
Hrangkhuma, Francis. "Christianity Among the Tribes of India. An Overview." In *Christ Among the Tribals*, edited by Francis Hrangkhuma and Joy Thomas, 16-34. Bangalore: Fellowship of Indian Missiologists, 2007.
———. "Impact of Indian Missionary Conferences on Edinburgh 1910." *Dharma Deepika* 14, no. 1 (2010) 3-9.
———. "Protestant Mission Trends in India." In *Mission Trends in India Today: Historical and Theological Perspective*, edited by Joseph Mattam and Sebastian Kim, 37-54. Mumbai: St Pauls, 1997.
Hsu, Francis L. K. "Christianity and the Anthropologists." In *Anthropology and Archaeology. Essays in Commemoration of Verrier Elwin 1902-64*, edited by M. C. Pradhan et al., 203-28. London: Oxford University Press, 1969.
Hume, Robert E. *The Thirteen Principal Upanishads*. London: Oxford University Press, 1968.
Huntington, Samuel P. *The Clash of Civilizations and the Remaking of World Order*. New Delhi: Penguin, 1996.
Hutton, J. H. "Primitive Tribes." In *Modern India and the West*, edited by L. S. S. O'Malley, 417-19. London: Oxford University Press, 1968.
Jaffrelot, Christophe. *The Hindu Nationalist Movement and Indian Politics 1925-1990*. New Delhi: Penguin, 1999.
———. "Hindu Nationalism and Welfare Strategy: Seva Bharati as an Education Agency." In *The Sangh Parivar: A Reader*, edited by Christophe Jaffrelot, 211-24. New Delhi: Oxford University Press, 2005
———. *India's Silent Revolution: The Rise of the Lower Castes in North India*. Delhi: Permanent Black, 2003.
———. "Sangh Parivar and New Contradictions." In *Frontline* 28 no. 6 (2011) 47-50.
Jagadeesha, B. N., and A. Narrain. "Samasekhara Commission Report: Inconsistencies and Contradictions." *Economic and Political Weekly* 46, no. 9 (2011) 13-17.
Jeyaraj, Daniel. *Bartholomaeus Ziegenbalg: The Father of Modern Protestant Mission*. New Delhi: Indian Society for Promoting Christian Knowledge, 2006.
———. "The History of Christianity in India." In *Missiology for the 21st Century: South Asian Perspective*, edited by Roger E. Hedlund and Paul Bhakiaraj, 195-211. Delhi: Indian Society for Promoting Christian Knowledge, 2004.
John Paul II, Pope. *Crossing the Threshold of Hope*. London: Jonathan Cape, 1994.
———. *Post-Synodal Apostolic Exhortation: Ecclesia in Asia*. Bombay: Pauline, 1999

Bibliography

———. *Redemptoris Missio. On the Permanent Validity of the Church's Missionary Mandate*. Mumbai: St Pauls, 1991.

———. *Tertio Millennio Abveniente*. Mumbai: St Pauls, 1994.

John XXIII, Pope. "Opening Speech to the Council." In *The Documents of Vatican II*, edited by Walter M. Abbotts, 711–19. New York: Guild, 1966.

Jones, Beth L. *Jesus: CEO*. New York: Hyperion, 1995.

Jongeneel, Jan A. B. "Eccumenical Theology of Mission." In *Missiological Encyclopedia, Part I*, edited by Jan A. B. Jogeneel, 173–77. Bangalore: Centre for Contemporary Christianity, 2006.

Jongeneel, Jan A. B., and J. M. Van Engelen. "Contemporary Currents in Missiology." In *Missiology: An Ecumerical Introduction*, edited by F. J. Verstraelen et al., 438–57. Grand Rapids: Eerdmans,1995.

Joshi, A. P., et al. *Religious Demography of India*. Chennai: Centre for Policy, 2005.

Joshi, T. L. *Jotirao Phule*. New Delhi: National Book, 1996.

Kalapati, Joshua. "Edinburgh to Tambaram; A Paradigm Shift in Mission?" *Dharma Deepika* 14, no. 1 (2010) 10–14.

Kalapura, Jose. "Dignity Rediscovered: Christians in Eastern India." In *Indian Christian Directory*, edited by Jose Panthaplamthottiyil, 102–6. Kottayam: Rashtra Deepika, 2000.

———. "Margins of Faith: Dalit and Tribal Christians in Eastern India." In *Margins of Faith: Dalit and Tribal Christianity in India*, edited by Rowena Robinson and J. M. Kujur, 75–96. New Delhi: Sage, 2010.

Kallupara, Sebastian. "Church as a Leaven in the Wider Society." *Satyadeepam* 6, no. 12 (2009) 3, 12.

Kanjamala, Augustine. "Arnold Janson and Dialogue with Cultures." In *Arnold Janson and Spirituality for our Times*, edited by Chacko Thottumarickal, 137–74. Indore: Satprakashan, 2002.

———. "Challenges of Cultural Conflicts Affecting Missionary Activities in India." In *Cultural Challenges in Christian Mission*, edited by Sebastian Michael and Kuriala Chittattukulam, 109–37. New Delhi: Catholic Bishops Conference of India, 2008.

———. "Christian mission and Violence in India: An Interpretative Understanding of Hindu Fundamentalist Violence against Christian Missionaries in India." In *Mission and Violence: Healing the Lasting Damage*, edited by Patrick F. Gesch, 29–47. Madang: Divine Word University Press, 2009.

———. "Christianization as a Legitimate Alternative to Sanskritization." *Missiology: An International Review* 14, no. 1 (1986) 21–36.

———. "Crusade against the Missionaries." *Ishvani Documentation and Mission Digest* 13, no. 1 (1995) 87–94.

———. "Democracy, Secularism and Pluralism in India." In *Violence Against Christians in India: A Response*, edited by Augustine Kanjamala and Michael Sebastian, 10–39. Mumbai: Institute of Indian Culture, 2009

———. "Emerging Mission Trends in India." *Verbum SVD* 41, no. 3 (2000) 451–70.

———. "An Evaluation of Evangelization in the period after All India Seminar on Church in India Today" In *The Church in India after the All India Seminar 1969: An Evaluation of the Life and Ministry of the Catholic Church*, edited by Paul Puthanangady, 7–40. Bangalore: National Biblical, Catechetical, Liturgical Centre, 2000.

———. "From Confrontation to Dialogue" In *In the Service of Mission*, edited by Manjally Thomas, et al., 278–95. Shillong: Oriens, 2006.

Bibliography

———."The Future of the Christian Mission in the Hindi Belt." *Verbum SVD* 34, no. 1 (1993) 45–68.

———. "Inculturation: A Biblical Model." *Verbum SVD* 46, no. 2 (2005) 163–78.

———. *Integral Mission Dynamics: An Interdisciplinary Study of the Catholic Church in India.* New Delhi: Intercultural, 1995.

———. "New Directions of Christian Mission in the Changing Context." In *Promise of Indian Pluralism and Solidarity*, edited by Joy Thomas et al., 199–226. Delhi: Indian Society for Promoting Christian Knowledge, 2011.

———. *An Order of the Mass for India.* Poona: Ishvani Kendra, 1988.

———. *Paths of Mission in India.* Mumbai: St Pauls, 1996.

———. "Redemptoris Missio and Mission in India." In *Redemption and Dialogue: Reading Redemptoris Missio and Dialogue and Proclamation*, edited by William R. Burrows, 195–205. New York: Orbis, 1993.

———. *Religion and Modernization of India: A Case Study of Northern Orissa.* Indore: Sat Prakashan, 1981.

———. "Seven Images of the Church in India" In *The Church in India in the Emerging Third Millennium*, edited by Thomas D'sa, 27–44. Bangalore: National Biblical, Catechetical & Liturgical Centre, 2005.

———. "Spirit of God in the Contemporary Social Movements." In *Spirit of God and Mission Spirituality for the New Era*, edited by P. A. Augustine, 125–60. Indore: Sat Prakashan, 1999.

———. "Streevani and Empowerment of Women." In *History of the Divine Word Mission in India*, edited by Augustine Kanjamala, 352–56. Indore: Sat Prakashan, 2007.

———. "Trends and Issues in Evangelization in India: Facts, Figures and Views." *Jeevadhara: A Journal of Christian Interpretation* 24, no. 142 (1994) 251–70.

———. "Trends in Numerical Conversions." In *Integral Mission Dynamics: An Interdisciplinary Study of the Catholic Church in India*, edited by Augustine Kanjamala, 611–16. New Delhi: Intercultural, 1995.

———. "Understanding of Evangelization Today." In *National Assembly Report 1990: Role of Religious in Evangelization in the Indian Context*, edited by Bro. John SG, 23–38. Delhi: Conference of Religious of India, 1990.

———."Unity and Universality as a Goal of Inter-religious Dialogue." In *Mission and Dialogue*, edited by Leonard Mercado and Jim Knigh, 174–85. Manila: Divine Word, 1989.

Kanjirakatt, Benny, ed.. *The Catholic Directory of India 2005-6.* Bangalore: Claretian, 2006.

Kane, Herbert J. *A Concise History of the Christian Mission.* Grand Rapids: Baker, 1981.

Katju, Manjari. *Vishva Hindu Parishad and Hindu Politics.* Hyderabad: Orient Longman, 2003.

Kavunkal, Jacob and Francis Hrangkhuma. *Bible and Mission in India Today.* Bombay: St Pauls, 1993.

Keay, F. E. *A History of the Syrian Church in India.* Delhi: Indian Society for Promoting Christian Knowledge, 1960.

Keay, John. *India: A History.* Noida: HarperCollins, 2004.

Keyes, Nelson B. *The Story of the Bible World.* New York: Hammond, 1959.

Kim, Sebastian C.H. *In Search of Identity: Debates on Religious Conversion in India.* New Delhi: Oxford University Press, 2005.

Klostermaier, Klaus. *Hindu and Christian in Vrindabhan.* London: Student Christian Movement, 1969.

Bibliography

Koch, R. "Preaching." In *Encyclopedia of Biblical Theology*, edited by Johannes B. Bauer, 2:686–93. London: Sheed & Ward, 1970.
Koilaparampil, George. *Caste in the Catholic Community in Kerala*. Cochin: St. Theresa's, 1982.
Koodapuzha, Xavier. "Mission of the St. Thomas Christians: An Ecclesiastical analysis of Mission in the Indian Context." *Ephrem's Theological Journal* 4, no. 2 (2000) 131–48.
Kool, Anne-Marie. "Post-Communist Europe: From Intercultural Theology to Missiology." In *Towards an Intercultural Theology: Essays in Honor of Jan A.B.Jongeneel*, edited by Martha Fredericks et al., 225–46. Bangalore: Center for Contemporary Christianity, 2010.
Koppikar, S. "Malegaon Charge sheet." In *Outlook* 49 no. 4 (2009) 52–55.
Kothari, D. S. *Report of the Education Commission 1964-66*. New Delhi: Ministry of Education, 1966.
Kottuppalil, George. "Catholic Mission North East India." In *Integral Mission Dynamics: An Interdisciplinary Study of the Catholic Church in India*, edited by Augustine Kanjamala, 288–300. New Delhi: Intercultural Publications, 1995.
Kraemer, Hendrik. *The Christian Message in a Non-Christian World*. Bangalore: Centre for Contemporary Christianity, 2009
Kumar, Ashok, and Rowena Robinson. "Legally Hindu: Dalit Lutharans Christians of Coastal Andhra Pradesh." In *Margins of Faith. Dalit and Tribal Christianity in India*, edited by Rowena Robinson and J. M. Kumar, 149–68. New Delhi: Sage, 2010.
Kumaradoss, Vincent. *Robert Caldwell: A Scholar-Missionary in Colonial South India*. New Delhi: Indian Society for Promoting Christian Knowledge, 2007.
Kuriakose, M. K. *History of Christianity in India: Source Materials*. Delhi: Indian Society for Promoting Christian Knowledge, 2006.
Kuruvachira, J. *Hindu Nationalists of Modern India. A Critical Study of the Intellectual Genealogy of Hindutva*. Jaipur: Rawat, 2006.
Leeuwen, Van Gervin. *Fully Indian and Authentically Christian*. Bangalore: National Biblical, Catechetical & Liturgical Centre, 1990.
Legrand, Lucien. *Bible on Culture*. Bangalore: Theological Publications in India, 2001.
———. "Conversion in the Bible." In *Mission and Conversion: A Reappraisal*, edited by Joseph Mattam and Sebastian Kim, 17–30. Mumbai: St Pauls, 1996.
———. *Mission in the Bible: Unity and Plurality*. Poona: Ishvani, 1992.
Lewis, Donald M. *The Blackwell Dictionary of Evangelical Biography, 1730–1860*. 2 Vols. Oxford: Blackwell, 1995.
Lim, Timothy H. *The Dead Sea Scrolls: A Very Short Introduction*. New York: Oxford University Press, 2005.
Lippner, Julius. *Brahmabandhab Upadhyaya: The Life and Thought of a Revolutionary*. New Delhi: Oxford University Press, 2001.
Lipner, Julius, and G. Gispert-Sauch, eds. *The Writings of Brahmabandab Upadhyaya*, 1. Bangalore: The United Theological, 1991.
Lobo, Lancy. *Globalization, Hindu Nationalism and Christians in India*. New Delhi: Rawat, 2002.
———. "Hindutva: Cultural Nationalism as Cultural Intolerance." In *Cultural Challenges in Christian Mission*, edited by Michael, Sebastian and Kuriala Chittatukalam, 60–78. Delhi: Media House, 2008.
Lohff, Wenzel. "Pietism." In *Sacramentum Mundi: An Encyclopedia of Theology*, edited by Karl Rahner et al., 24–25. London: Burns & Oates, 1969.

Bibliography

Lopez-Gay, Jesus. "Proclamation." In *Following Christ in Mission. A Foundational Course in Missiology*, edited by Sebastian Karotemprel, 91–100. Mumbai: Pauline, 1995.
Lorenzen, David N. *The Scourge of the Mission*. New Delhi: Yoda, 2010.
Luckmann, Thomas. *The Invisible Religion: The Problems of Religion in the Modern Society*. London: Collier-Macmillan, 1970.
Luke, K. *The Cultural Background of the Old Testament*. Bangalore: Claretian, 2002.
Luzbetak, Louis J. *The Church and Cultures: New Perspectives in Missiological Anthropology*. New York: Orbis, 1989.
Machieu, Martha. "Integrating the East and the West: Life and Vision of Francis Mahieu Acharya." *Third Millennium* 11, no. 2 (2008) 32–42.
———. *Kurisumala: Francis Mathieu Acharya, A Pioneer of Christian Monasticism In India*. Kalamazoo, MI: Cistercian, 2008.
Macnicol, Nicol. *The Living Religions of the Indian People*. New Delhi: Oriental, 1979.
Mahato, S. *Hundred Years of Christian Missions in Chotanagpur*. Ranchi: Chotanagpur Christian, 1971.
Mangalwadi, Vishal. *Missionary Conspiracy: Letters to a Postmodern Hindu*. Mussoorie: Nevedit, 1996.
Mani, Lata. *Contentious Traditions: A Debate on Sati in India*. New Delhi: Oxford University Press, 1998.
Massey, James. *Dr. Ambedkar: A Study in Just Society*. New Delhi: Manohar, 2003.
———. "Holy Spirit led Mission in North India." In *Missiology For the 21st Century*, edited by Roger E. Hedlund and Paul Bhakiaraj, 251–59. Delhi: Indian Society for Promoting Christian Knowledge, 2004.
———."Punjabi Christian Writer's Response to the Gospel." In *The Oxford Encyclopedia of South Asian Christianity*, edited by Roger Hedlund E., 2:573–76. New Delhi: Oxford University Press, 2012.
———. "Subaltern People and the Rise of their Movements." In *A Vision of Mission in the New Millennium*, edited by Thomas Malipurathu and Stanilaus Lazar, 23–41. Bombay: St Pauls 2001.
Mattam, Joseph. "Catholic Church in Gujarat." In *Integral Mission Dynamics*, edited by Augustine Kanjamala. New Delhi: Intercultural, 1995.
Matzken, R. H. "Standing Under the Missionary Mandate." In *Missiology: An Ecumenical Introduction*, edited by F. J. Verstraelen et al., 172–76. Grand Rapids: Eerdmans, 1995.
Mayhew, A. I. "The Christian Ethic and India." In *Modern India and the West*, edited by L. S. S. O'Mally, 305–37. Oxford: Oxford University Press, 1968.
McDermott, Robert A. *Basic Writings of S. Radhakrishnan*. Mumbai: Jaico, 1975.
McGavran, Donald A. *Ethnic Realities and the Church Lessons from India*. California: William Carey Library, 1979.
———. *Understanding Church Growth*. Madras: Christian Literature Society, 1972.
McKenzie, John L. *The Christian Task in India*. London: Macmillan, 1929.
———. "The God of Israel." In *The Jerome Biblical Commentary*, edited by Raymond Brown et al., 736–47. Bangalore: Theological Publications in India, 1980.
McKenzie, L. John. *Directory of the Bible*. London: Geoffrey Chapman, 1968.
Meersman, Archilles. "The Latin Missions under the Jurisdiction of Padroado." In *Christianity in India: A History in Ecumenical Perspective*, edited by H. C. Perumalil, and E. R. Hambye, 65–81. Alleppey: Prakasham, 1972.

Bibliography

Mehra, Vivek. *Strategic Research and Political Communications for NGOs.* New Delhi: Sage, 2009.

Menamparambil, Thomas. "The Challenge of Cultures." In *Evangelization among the Indigenous Peoples of Asia: A Report of a Conference on the Concerns of the Indigenous Peoples,* 3–20. Hua Hin, Thailand, September 3–8, 1995. FABC Paper no. 80, Hong Kong.

———. "Culture has moved to the centre." In *Cultural Challenges in Christian Mission,* edited by Michael Sebastian and Kuriala Chittattukalam, 20–37. Delhi: Media House, 2008.

Menon, Sreedharan A. *A Survey of Kerala History.* Madras: Viswanathan, 1991.

Meston, Lord. "Foreword." *Modern India and the West,* edited by L. S. S. O'Malley, v–viii. Oxford: Oxford University Press, 1968.

Michael, Sebastian M. *Dalits' Encounter with Christianity. A Case Study of Mahars in Maharashtra.* Delhi: Indian Society for Promoting Christian Knowledge, 2010.

Milling, D. H. "New Trends in New Testament Studies." *Religion and Society* 48, no. 1 (2003) 78–96.

Minwalla, Sabanam. "History." In *St. Xavier College: Celebrating Diversity from 1869,* edited by Sabanam Minwalla, 11–31. Hyderabad: Pragati Art, 2010.

Mitra, Sudhan K. "Contribution of Christianity to Bengal." In *Indian Christian Directory,* edited by Jose Panthaplamthottiyil, 111–13. Kottayam: Rashtra Deepika, 2000.

Moffett, Samuel H. *A History of Christianity in Asia.* Vol 1. Bangalore: Theological Publications in India, 2006.

———. *A History of Christianity in Asia.* Vol. 2. New York: Orbis, 2005.

Moltmann, Juergen. *The Source of Life: The Holy Spirit and the Theology of Life.* London: Student Christian Movement, 1997.

Mookenthottam, Antony. *Indian Theological Tendencies.* Studies in the Intercultural History of Christianity 21. Bern: Lang, 1978.

Moniz, John. *No Greater Service: Mother and Mahatma.* Mumbai: St Pauls, 1998.

Morrison, Ken. *Marx, Durkheim, Weber: Formation of Modern Social Thought.* London: Sage, 1997.

Mudge, Luwis S. "Calvin John." In *Jesus: The Complete Guide,* edited by Leslie Houlden, 150–54. London: Continuum, 2006.

Muggeridge, Malcom. *Something Beautiful for God: Mother Teresa of Calcutta.* London: Collins, 1971.

Mukherjee, Meenakshi. *Ellusive Terrain: Culture and Literary Memory.* New Delhi: Oxford University Press, 2008.

Mueller, Karl. *Mission Theology: An Introduction.* Berlin: Reimer, 1987.

Mundaden, Mathias A. *History of Christianity in India.* Vol. 1, *From the Beginning up to the Middle of the Sixteenth Century.* Bangalore: Church History Association, 1989.

Munda, Dayal R. "Non-Christian Tribal Response to Christian Mission." In *Paths of Mission in India Today,* edited by Augustine Kanjamala, 93–106. Mumbai: St Pauls, 1996.

Nambudiri, Narayan. *Aryans in South India.* New Delhi: Inter-India, 1992.

Nandi, Proshanta. "Visions of Nationhood and Religiosity Among Early Freedom Fighters of India." In *Sociology of Religion in India,* edited by Rowena Robinson, 39–53. New Delhi: Sage, 2004.

Natrajan, S. *A Century of Social Reform in India.* Bombay: Asia,1959.

Nayar, Lola. "Navigators of Change." *Outlook* 51, no. 5 (2011) 44–48.

Bibliography

Nediyakalayil, Varghese. "Report of Association of Catholic Enquiry Centers." New Delhi: 2010.
Nehru, Jawaharlal. "The Tribal folk." In *The Adivasis*, 1–8. New Delhi: Ministry of Information, 1955.
Neill, Stephen. *A History of Christian Missions*. Middlesex: Penguin, 1975.
———. *The Story of the Christian Church India and Pakistan*. Madras: Christian Literature Society, 1972,
Nelson, Thomas. *The New American Bible*. Nashville: Catholic Bible, 1987.
Neuner, Joseph, ed. *Christian Revelation and World Religions*. London: Burn & Oates, 1967.
———. "Inaugural Address." In *A Vision of Mission in the New Millennium*, edited by Thomas Malipurath, 15–22. Mumbai: St Pauls, 2000.
———. "Mission Theology after Vatican II." In *Paths of Mission in India Today*, edited by Augustine Kanjamala, 49–63. Bombay: St Pauls, 1996.
———. "Mother Teresa's Charism." *Vidyajyoti: Journal of Theological Reflexion* 65, no. 3 (2001) 179–92.
Neuner, Joseph, and Jacques Dupuis. *The Christian Faith in the Doctrinal Documents of the Catholic Church*. Bangalore: Theological Publications of India, 1991.
Neunheuser, Burkhard. "Baptism." In *Sacramentum Mundi. An Encyclopedia of Theology*, edited by Karl Rahner et al., 136–44. London: Burns & Oates, 1968.
Niyogi, N. B. *Report of the Christian Missionary Activities Enquiry Committee*. Nagpur: Government Printing, 1956.
Nongbri, B. L. "Christianity and Khasi Language and Literature: A Historical Analysis of the Interaction of Christianity with Traditional Culture." In *Christianity and Change in Northeast India*, edited by T. B. Subba et al., 177–93. New Delhi: Concept, 2009.
Naronha, Alvino. "Preface." In *Crisis in Chota Nagpur*, edited by Fidelis de Sa, vii–xviii. Bangalore: Redemtorist, 1975.
O'Connor, Daniel. "Lutherans and Anglicans in South India." In *Halle and the Beginning of the Protestant Christianity in India, Vol II*, edited by Andreas Gross et al., 767–82. Halle: Franckesche Stiftungen, 2006.
O'Dea, Thomas F. "Sociological Dilemmas: Five Paradoxes of Institutionalization." In *Sociological Theory, Values and Socio-cultural Change*, edited by Edward A. Tiryakian, 71–89. New York: Free, 1963.
O'Hanlon, Rosalind. *Caste Conflict and Ideology: Mahatma Jyotirao Phule and Low Caste Protest in 19th Century Western India*. New Delhi: Cambridge University Press, 2002.
O'Malley, L. S. S. *Modern India and the West: A Study of the Interaction of their Civilizations*. London: Oxford University Press. 1968.
Omvedt, Gail. "Pandita Ramabai: Women of the Kingdom of God." In *Awakening Faith* 21 no. 4 (2008) 162–69.
Oommen, George. "Gandhi's Early Christian Encounters." *Indian Church History Review* 43, no. 2 (2009) 158–83.
Oommen, T. K. "Introduction. On the Analysis of Social Movements." In *Social Movements: Issue of Identity*, edited by T. K. Oommen, 1:1–46. New Delhi: Oxford University Press, 2010.
Pachuau, Lalsangkima. "Church-Mission Dynamics in North east India." In *Missiology for the 21st Century*, edited by Roger E. Hedlund and Paul Bhakiaraj, 212–90. Delhi: Indian Society for Promoting Christian Knowledge, 2004.

Bibliography

Painadath, Sebastian. *Solitude and Solidarity: Ashrams of Catholic Initiative.* Delhi: Indian Society for Promoting Christian Knowledge, 2003.
———. "The Spiritual and Theological Perspectives of Ashrams." *Vidyajyoti: Journal of Theological Reflection* 65, no. 3 (2001) 214–80.
Pallath, Paul. "Syro-Malabar Church and Inculturation." *Ephrem Theological Journal* 4, no. 2 (2000) 149–75.
Panikkar, K. M. *Asia and Western Dominance: A Survey of the Vasco da Gama Epoch of Asian History.* New York: John Day, 1953.
———. *The Foundation of New India.* London: Allen & Unwin, 1963.
Panikkar, Raimundo. "The Crux of the Christian Ecumenism: Can Universality and Chosennes be held Simultaneously." *Journal of Ecumenical Studies* 26, no. 1 (1989) 82–99.
———. "Hinduism and Christ." In *Spirit and Truth,* edited by Ignatius Viyagappa, 112–22. Madras: Aikiya Alayam, 1985.
———. *Human Rights As a Western Concept.* New Delhi: D. K. Print World, 2007.
———. *The Unknown Christ of Hinduism.* London: Darton, Longman & Todd, 1964.
Parappally, Jacob. *Theologizing in Context: Statements of Indian Theological Association.* Bangalore: Dharmaram, 2002.
Parathazam, Paul. "Pentecostal Churches." In *Indian Christian Directory,* edited by Jose Panthaplamthottiyil, 59–60. Kottayam: Rashtra Deepika, 2000.
Parekh, Manilal C. *Christian Proselytism in India.* Rajkot: Harmony, 1947.
———. *A Hindu's Portrait of Jesus Christ.* Rajkot: Harmony, 1953.
Parkhe, Camil. "Poet missionary: Rev. Narayan Vaman Tilak." In *Contributions of Christian Missionaries in India,* edited by Camil Parkhe, 65–72. Anand: Gujarat Sahitya, 2007.
Parsons, Talcott. *The Social System.* New Delhi: Amerind, 1972.
Pattery, George. "Catholic Mission in West Bengal". In *Integral Mission Dynamics,* edited by Augustine Kanjamala, 261–72. New Delhi: Intercultural, 1995.
Paul VI, Pope. *The Evangelization in the Modern World.* Mumbai: St. Pauls, 1975.
Pernia, Antonio M. "VIVAT: Let there be Life." In *Arnoldus Nota,* 1–2. Rome: SVD Curia, 2011.
Phan, Peter C. "Crossing the Borders: Spirituality for our times from an Asian Perspective." *Sedos Bulletin* 35, nos. 1–2 (2003) 8–19.
Philip, T. V. "Protestant Christianity in India Since 1858." In *Christianity in India: A History in Ecumerical Perspective,* edited by H. C. Perumalil and E. R. Hambye, 267–99. Alleppey: Prakasham, 1972.
Pickett, Waskom J. *Christ's Way to India's Heart: Present day Mass Movement to Christianity.* Lucknow: Lucknow Publishing House, 1938.
———. *Christian Mass Movement in India.* Lucknow: Lucknow Publishing House, 1969.
Pimenta, Simon. *Memoirs and Milestones.* Mumbai: Printania, 2010.
Pinch, William R. "Soldier Monks and Militant Sadhus." In *Making India Hindu: Religion, Community and Politics of Democracy in India,* edited by David Ludden, 140–61. New Delhi: Oxford University Press, 2005.
Plathottam, George. "Language Plurality and Ethnicity: Identity and Change in North East India." In *Christianity and Change in Northeast India,* edited by T. B. Subba et al., 158–73. New Delhi: Concept, 2009.
Ponnumuthan, Selvister. "Pontifical Seminary, Carmelgiri." In *The Oxford Encyclopedia of South Asian Christianity,* edited by Roger E. Hedlund, 2:561–62. New Delhi: Oxford University Press, 2012.

Bibliography

Poruthur, Anto. *Glimpses of Mission History: Central India*. Indore: Sat Prachar, 1993.
Prabhupada, Swami. *Bhagavad Gita as It Is*. New Delhi: The Bhaktivedanta Book, 2003.
Prakash, Surya P. "Contributions of Sadhu Sundar Singh to the Indigenous Christian Movement in India." In *Christianity is Indian: The Emergence of an Indigenous Community*, edited by Roger E. Hedlund, 111–26. Delhi: Indian Society for Promoting Christian Knowledge, 2000.
Presler, Henry. *Primitive Religions in India*. Bangalore: Christian Literature Society, 1971.
Prichard, J. B. *Ancient Near Eastern Texts Relating to the Old Testament*. Princeton: Princeton University Press, 1969.
Priolkar, Anant K. *The Goa Inquisition*. Bombay: Mumbai University Press, 1991.
Prior, John. "Mission for the 21st Century in Asia: Two sketches, Three Flash-Backs and An Enigma." In *Mission in the 21st Century*, edited by Stephen Bevans and Roger Schroeder, 68–109. Chicago: Chicago Centre for Global Ministries, 2001.
———. "A Tale of Two Synods." *Sedos Bulletin* 30, no. 9 (1998) 219–24.
———. "Unfinished Encounter." *Verbum SVD* 41, no. 3 (2000) 347–61.
Proksch, George. "Christ in Indian Dress." In *Word in the World*, edited by John Boberg et al., 49–51. Steyl: Steyler, 1964.
———. "The Gospel in Indian Dress." In *Word in the World*, edited by John Boberg et al., 59–62. Steyl: Steyler, 1975.
———. "Gyan Prakash Sangam." In *Lead Me to Light*, edited by Clarance Srambical 141–44. Indore: Sat Prakashan, 1975.
Puthenpurakal, Joseph. "The Rising Sun: Christianity's Contribution to India's North Eastern Region." In *Indian Christian Directory*, edited by Jose Panthaplamthottiyil, 107–10. Kottayam: Rashtra Deepika, 2000.
Quack, Anton. "Inculturation: An Anthropological Perspective." *Verbum SVD* 34, no. 1 (1993) 3–17.
Radhakrishnan, Sarvepalli. *East and West in Religion*. London: Allen & Unwin, 1996.
———. *The Hindu View of Life*. London: Allen & Unwin, 1974.
———. "Hinduism and the West." In *Modern India and the West*, edited by L. S. S. O'Malley, 338–53. Oxford: Oxford University Press, 1968.
———. *Religion in a Changing World*. New York: Humanities, 1967.
Rahner, Karl. "Perspectives on Pastoral Ministry in the Future." In *The Church of the Future*, edited by Walbert Buehlmann, 185–97. New York: Orbis, 1986.
———. *Shape of the Church to Come*. London: Indian Society for Promoting Christian Knowledge, 1972.
———. *Theological Investigations*. Vol. 5. London: Darton, Longman & Todd, 1966.
———. *Theological Investigation: Concern for the Church*. Vol. 20. London: Darton, Longman & Todd, 1981.
Rajamanickam, S. "Founder of Madurai Mission. Robert De Nobili." In *Christianity in India. Its True Face*, edited by R. A. Sundaram, 110–19. Tanjavur: Don Bosco, 1981.
Rajgopal, A. *Politics After Television. Hindu Nationalities and the Shaping of India*. Cambridge: Cambridge University Press, 2001.
Rao, Raghavendra K. *Babasaheb Ambedkar*. Delhi: Sahitya Academy, 1998.
Rao, V. K. R. V. "Some Problems confronting Traditional Societies in the Process of Development." In *Tradition and Modernity in India*, edited by A. B. Shah and C. R. M. Rao, 70–105. Bombay: Manaktalas, 1965.
Rauch, James S. "Forword." In *The Gospel of Peace and Justice: Catholic Social Teaching Since Pope John*, edited by Joseph Cremillion, ix–x. New York: Orbis, 1976.

Bibliography

Rausch, Thomas. *Pope Benedict XVI: An Introduction to his Theological Vision*. New York: Paulist, 2009.
Rawlinson, H. G. "Indian Influence on the West." In *Modern India and the West*, edited by L. S. S. O'Malley, 535–66. New York: Oxford University Press, 1968.
Rayan, Samuel. "Asia and Justice." in *Liberation in Asia. Theological Perspectives*, edited by S. Arokiasamy and George Gispert-Sauch, 3–15. Anand: Gujarat Sahitya, 1978.
———. "Flesh of India's Flesh." *SEDOS Bulletin* 8, no. 12 (1976) 393–98.
———. "Instruction on Christian Freedom and Liberation: Some Reflections on the Document." In *Liberation in Asia. Theological Perspectives*, edited by S. Arokiasamy and George Gispert-Sauch, 225–54. Anand: Gujarat Sahitya, 1987.
———. "Spirituality of the Mission in the Asian Context." *SEDOS Bulletin* 27, no. 7 (1997) 194–206.
Ray, Shovan. *Backwaters of Development in Six Deprived States of India*. New Delhi: Oxford University Press, 2010.
Richard, H. L. *Exploring the Depth of the Mystery of Christ: Subba Rao's Eclectic Praxis of Hindu Discipleship to Jesus*. Bangalore: Centre for Contemporary Christianity, 2009.
Richardson, Janet. "The 21st Century: Challenge to Mission." *SEDOS Bulletin* 16, nos. 5–6 (1988) 85–89.
Roberson, Ronald. *The Eastern Christian Churches. A Brief Survey*. Bangalore: Theological Publications In India, 2004.
Robertson, Ronald. *The Sociological Interpretation of Religion*. Oxford: Blackwell, 1970.
Robinson, Rowena. *Christians of India*. Jaipur: Sage, 2003
———. *Conversion, Continuity and Change: Lived Christianity in Southern Goa*. New Delhi: Sage, 1998.
———. *Sociology of Religion in India*. New Delhi: Sage, 2004.
Robinson, Rowena, and Sathianathan Clarke. *Religious Conversion in India. Modes, Motivations and Meaning*. New Delhi: Oxford University Press, 2003.
Robinson, Rowena, and Joseph Kujur. *Margins of Faith: Dalit and Tribal Christianity in India*. New Delhi: Sage, 2010.
Rohar, Richard. *Jesus Plan for a New World: The Sermon on the Mount*. Mumbai: St. Pauls, 2009.
Rosales, Gaudencio B., and G. G. Arevalo, *For all the People of Asia. Federation of Asian Bishops Conferences Documents from 1970 to 1991*. Querzon City: Claretian, 1992.
Roy, Chandra S. "The Effect on the Aborigines of Chotanagpur of the Contact with Western Civilization." *Journal of Bihar and Orissa Research Society* 67, no. 4 (1931). 358–94.
———. The *Kharias*. Ranchi: Bar Library, 1937.
———. The *Mundas and Their Country*. Calcutta: Bar Library, 1912.
———. The *Oraons of Chotanagpur*. Ranchi: Bar Library, 1915.
Sahay, Kesari N. "Tribal Self-Image and Identity." In *Tribal Heritage of India*, edited by S. C. Dube, 1:8–57. New Delhi: Vikas, 1977.
Sahi, Jyoti. "Many Indian Christians cannot Think of an Indian Christ." *The New Leader* 117, no. 1 (2004) 25–26.
Saksena, R. N. *Goa into the Mainstream*. New Delhi: Abhinav, 1974.
Saldhana, Julian. *Inculturation. Mumbai*: St Pauls, 1997.
———. "Mission Trends in the Official Documents of the Catholic Church." In *Mission Trends Today*, edited by Joseph Mattam and Sebastian Kim, 15–36. Mumbai: St Pauls, 1997.
———. *Patterns of Evangelization in Mission History*. Mumbai: St Pauls, 1988.

Bibliography

Samartha, S. J. *The Hindu Response to the Unbound Christ*. Madras: Christian Lit-erature Society, 1974.
Sanders, John. *No Other Name: An Investigation into the Destiny of the Unevangelized*. Grand Rapids: Eerdmans, 1992.
Savarkar, Veer D. *Hindutva. Who is a Hindu?* Mumbai: Veer Savarkar, 1969.
Schaeffer, Francis A. *A Christian World View of the West*. Westchester, IL: Crossway, 1986.
Scherer, James A. and Stephen Bevans, B. *New Directions in Mission and Evangelization*. New York: Orbis, 1992.
Schllebeeckx, Edward. "Introduction." In *Breakthrough: Beginning of the New Catholic Theology*, by Mark Schoof, 1-5. Dublin: Gill & MacMillan, 1970.
Schnackenburg, Rudolf. "Kingdom of God." In *Encyclopedia of Biblical Theology*, edited by Johannes B. Bauer, 2:455-70. London: Sheed & Ward, 1969.
Schreiter, Robert. "The Changed Context of Mission: Forty years after the Council." *Verbum SVD* 46, no. 1 (2005) 75-88.
―――. "Mission into the Third Millennium." *Missiology: An International Review* 18/1 (1990) 3-12.
Schueren, T. van der. *The Belgian Mission of Bengal*. 3 Vols. Calcutta: Thacker, Spink, 1922.
―――. *Moral and Intellectual Uplift of the Aboriginal Races of Chotanagpur*. London: East & West, 1928.
Schüssler-Fiorenza, Elizabeth. "Women, Mission and Catholicity of Theology." In *The Church in Mission*, edited by Thomas Malipurathu and Lazar Stanislaus, 147-80. Anand: Gujarat Sahitya Prakash, 2002.
Schultz, Hans J. *Jesus in His Time*. Philadelphia: Fortress, 1980.
Sengupta, Padmini. *Pandita Ramabai Saraswati: Her Life and Work*. London: Asia, 1970.
Sen, Mala. *Death by Fire. Sati: Dowry Death, and Female Infanticide in Modern India*. New Delhi: Penguin, 2001.
Sharma Aravind et al. *Sati: Historical and Phenomenological Essays*. Delhi: Motilal Benarsidass, 1998.
Sharma, R. B. *Christian Mission in North India 1813-1913*. Delhi: Motilal, 1988.
Sharma, Sangeeta. "Indian Renaissance and Reinterpretation of Tradition: Dayanand's Construction of the Vedic Age." *Indica* 42, no. 1 (2005) 65-80.
Sharpe, Eric J. "Duff Alexander." In *The Blackwell Dictionary of Evangelical Bibliography. 1730-1860*, edited by Donald M. Lewis, 328-29. Oxford: Blackwell, 1995.
―――. *Faith Meets Faith. Some Christian Attitudes to Hinduism in the Nineteenth and Twentieth Centuries*. London: Student Christian Movement, 1977.
―――. "Mission between Dialogue and Proclamation" In *Redemption and Dialogue*, edited by William R. Burrows, 161-72. New York: Orbis, 1993.
Shenk, Wilbert. "Mission for the 21st Century: A Protestant Perspective." In *Mission in the 21st Century*, edited by Stephen Bevans and Roger Schroeder, 43-58. Chicago: Chicago Centre for Global Ministries, 2001.
Shourie, Arun. *Missionaries in India*. New Delhi: ASA, 1994.
Singh, K. S. *Diversity, Identity and Linkages: Exploration in Historical Ethnography*. New Delhi: Oxford University Press, 2011.
Singh, Pragya. "NGOS: Too much Good Will." *Outlook* 51, no. 5 (2011) 50-51.
Sire, James W. *The Universe Next Door*. Downers Grove, IL: InterVarsity, 1976.
Smart, Ninian. *Historical Atlas of the Religions of the World*. Delhi: Oxford University Press, 1999.
Smith, Christopher A. *The Serampore Mission Enterprise*. Bangalore: Centre for Contemporary Christianity, 2006.

Bibliography

Smith, Vincent A. *Akbar the Great Mogul 1542–1605*. Delhi: Reprint, 1989.
Smith, Donald E. *India as a Secular State*. Princeton: Princeton University Press, 1967.
Smith, George. *Alexander Duff: The Missionary to India*. London: Hodder & Stoughton, 1899.
Snaitang, O. L. "Christianity and Change Among the Hill Tribes of North East India." In *Christianity and Change in North East India*, edited by T. B. Subba et al., 146–57. New Delhi: Concept, 2009.
Soares, Aloysius. *Truth Shall Prevail: Reply to Niyogi Committee*. Mumbai: Catholic Association, 1957
Soares- Prabhu, George. "Class in the Bible: The Biblical Poor as a Social Class." In *Liberation in Asia: Theological Perspectives*, edited by S. Arokiasamy and George Gispert-Sauch, 65–92. Anand: Gujarat Sahitya, 1987.
―――. "Expanding the Horizon of Christian Mission: A Biblical Perspective." In *Paths of Mission in India Today*, edited by Augustine Kanjamala, 33–48. Mumbai: St Pauls, 1996.
―――. "Following Jesus in Mission: Reflection on Mission in the Gospel of Mathew." In *Bible and Mission in India Today*, edited by Jacob Kavunkal and Francis Hrangkuma, 64–92. Mumbai: St Pauls, 1993.
―――. "The Kingdom of God: Jesus Vision of a New Society." In *The Indian Church in the Struggle for a New Society*, edited by D. S. Amalorpavadass, 579–608. Bangalore: National Biblical, Catechetical and Liturgical Centre, 1981.
Soreng, Ignatius. "India East Province." In *History of the Diving Word Mission in India 1932–2007*, edited by Augustine Kanjamala, 140–260. Indore: Satprakasan, 2007.
Srambical, Clarence. "Arnold Janssen, A man of the Spirit: His Relevance for Our Times." In *Spirit of God and Mission Spirituality*, edited by P. A. Augustine, 161–94. Indore: Satprakasan, 1999.
Srinivas, M. N. *Religion and Society Among the Coorgs of South India*. London: Oxford University Press, 1952.
―――. *Social Change in Modern India*. California: University of California Press, 1973.
Staffner, Hans. *The Significance of Jesus Christ in Asia*. Anand: Gujarat Sahitya, 1985.
Stanislaus, Lazar T. "Tribal Movements and Contemporary Resurgence." In *Christ Among the Tribals*, edited by Francis Hrangkhuma and Joy Thomas, 185–210. Bangalore: Fellowship of the Indian Missiologists, 2007.
Stanley, David M., and Raymond E. Brown. "The Kingdom of God" In *Jerome Biblical Commentary*, edited by Raymond E. Brown et al., 782–84. Bangalore: Theological Publications of India, 1980.
Stark, Rodney. *The Rise of Christianity*. San Francisco: HarperCollins, 1996.
Stevenson, Kenneth. "Baptism." In *Jesus: A Complete Guide*, edited by Leslie Houlden, 117–22. London: Continuum. 2005.
Straelen, van Henry. *The Catholic Encounter with World Religions*. London: Burns & Oates, 1966.
Subrahmanyam, S. *Exploration in Connected History*. New Delhi: Oxford University Press, 2005.
Sullivan, Robert E. *Macaulay: The Tragedy of Power*. New Delhi: Orient Black Swan, 2010.
Sundaran, N. *Encyclopedia of Social Work*. New Delhi: Ministry of Information, 1968.
Tagore, Rabindranath. *Gitanjali*. New Delhi: Macmillan India, 1995.
Taylor, Richard W. "From Khadi to Kavi: Toward a Typology of Christian Ashrams." *Religion and Society* 24, no. 4 (1977) 19–37.

Bibliography

Thekkedath, Joseph. *History of Christianity in India: From the Middle of the Sixteenth Century to the end of the Seventeenth Century*. Bangalore: Church History Association of India, 1982.
Theckanath, Jacob. *The Asian Image of Jesus*. Bangkok: Federation of Asian Bishops Conference, 2000.
———. "Inculturation in India: Review and Prospects in Pluri-Cultural Context of India." In *Cultural Challenges in Christian Mission in the 21st Century*, edited by Michael Sebastian and Kuriala Chittattukalam, 290–304. Delhi: Media, 2008.
Thomas, M. M. *The Acknowledged Christ of the Indian Renaissance*. Madras: Christian Literature Society, 1976.
Thomas, Job. "History of the Protestant Christianity in Tirunelveli." In *Halle and the Beginning of Protestant Christianity in India*, edited by Andreas Gross et al., 1:497–525. Halle: Franckesche Stiftungen, 2006.
Thumma, Anthoniraj. "Ambedkar and the Christians." *Vidyajyothi: Journal of Theological Reflection* 57, no. 8 (1993) 449–70.
Tirkey, C. A. "The Thana Bhagat Movement: The Oraon Quest for Liberation." *Indian Missiological Review* 19, no. 2 (1997) 27–32.
Tofflelr, Alvin. *Power Shift*. New York: Bantam, 1991.
Valentine, Joseph. "Popular Devotion and Liturgy." *Shepherd's Voice* 1, no. 3 (2002) 191–204.
Vanchipurackal, George. *Why Missions?* Bangalore: Claretian, 1989.
Vandana, Mataji. "Ashram Movement and the Development of Contemplative Life." *Vidyajyoti: Journal of Theological Reflection* 47, no. 4 (1983) 179–92.
———. "Experiencing the Divine Indweller in the Cave of the Heart." In *Solitude and Solidarity: Ashram of Catholic Initiative*, edited by Sebastian, Painadath, 2–6. Delhi: Indian Society for Promoting Christian Knowledge, 2003.
van Imscoot, P. "Yahweh." In *Encyclopedic Dictionary of the Bible*, edited by Louis F. Hartman, 2614–15. New York: McGraw-Hill, 1963.
Vatican Secretariat for Dialogue. *An Attitude of the Church Towards Followers of Other Religions*. Mumbai: St Pauls, 1984.
Veer, Peter van der. *Imperial Encounters: Religion and Modernity in India and Britain*. Delhi: Permanent Black, 2001.
———. "Writing Violence." In *Making India Hindu*, edited by David Ludden, 250–69. New Delhi: Oxford University Press, 2005.
Velamkunnel, Joseph. "Patna: A Mission Molded from Mud Houses." In *Integral Mission Dynamics: In Interdisciplinary Study of the Catholic Church in India*, edited by Augustine Kanjamala, 193–207. New Delhi: Intercultural, 1995.
Vellappallil, Thomas. *History of the Bhil Catholic Church*, Vol. 1. Indore: Arnold Seva Sadan, 1999.
Vempeny, Ishanand. *Inspiration in the Non-Biblical Scriptures*. Bangalore: National Biblical, Catechetical and Liturgical Centre, 1973.
———. *Conversion: National Debate or Dialogue?* Anand: Gujarat Sahitya Prakash, 1999.
Venkatesan, V. "Courting Anger." *Frontline* 28, no. 4 (2011) 49–56.
Vermeire, M. "Hinduism among the Oraons." In *Our Field*, 1–4. Kurseong: St. Mary's, 1938.
Vithayathil, Varkey. "Presidential Address: CBCI General Body Meeting." Unpublished paper, Guwahati, 2010.
Watson, Francis. *India: A Concise History*. Singapore: Thames & Hudson, 1992.

Bibliography

Weber, Max. *The Protestant Ethic and the Spirit of Capitalism*. London: Unwin University Books, 1971.
———. *The Religion of India*. New York: Free, 1958.
———. *The Theory of Social and Economic Organization*. New York: Free, 1968.
Webster, John C. B. *The Dalit Christians: A History*. Delhi: Indian Society for Promoting Christian Knowledge, 1972.
———. *Historiography of Christianity in India*. New Delhi: Oxford University Press, 2012.
———. *A Social History of Christianity: North West India Since 1800*. New Delhi: Oxford University Press, 2007.
———. "Who is a Dalit?" In *Dalits in Modern India. Visions and Values*, edited by S. M. Michael, 68–79. New Delhi: Vistar, 1999.
Whitaker, Richard E., and James E. Goehring. *The Eerdmans Analytical Concordance to the Revised Standard Version of the Bible*. Grand Rapids: Eerdmans, 1988.
Wijngaards, John. *Background to the Gospels*. Bangalore: Theological Publications in India, 2007.
Wilfred, Felix. *Asian Public Theology: Asian Path to Catholicity*. Delhi: Indian Society for Promoting Christian Knowledge, 2010.
Wiltgen, Ralph M. *The Rhine Flows into Tiber*. New York: Hawthorn, 1967.
Wind, A. "The Protestant Missionary Movement from 1789 to 1963." In *Missiology: An Ecumenical Introduction*, edited by F. J. Verstaelen et al., 237–52. Grand Rapids: Eerdmans, 1995.
Wingate, Andrew. "Indian Christianity." In *Jesus: A Complete Guide*, edited by Leslie Houlden, 382–88. London: Continuum, 2003.
Winter, Paul. "Sadducees and Pharisees." In *Jesus in His Time*, edited by Hans J. Schultz, 47–56. Philadelphia: Fortress, 1980.
Witte, Johannes. "Calvinism." In *Sacramentum Mundi. An Encyclopedia of Theology*, edited by Karl Rahner et al., 1:247–52. London: Burns & Oates, 1969.
Wolanin, Adam. "Trinitarian Foundation of Mission." In *Following Christ in Mission*, edited by Sebastian Karotemprel, 37–49. Mumbai: Pauline, 1995.
Xavier, P. D. *Goa: A Social History 1510–1640*. Panaji: Prabhakar Bhide, 1933.
Xaxa, Virginius. "Tribal Scene in India Today." In *Understanding Tribal Culture for Effective Education*, edited by Joseph Anikuzhikattil et al., 70–78. New Delhi: Catholic Bishop Conference of India, 2003.
Zeitler, Englebert. *Church in India Today: Personal and Resources*. New Delhi: Catholic Bishops Conference of India, 1969.
———. *Ever Ancient, Ever New. A Report on the all India Seminar on the Church in India Today*, New Delhi: Organizing Committee, 1969.
———. "Missionary Orientation Given by the Indian Church after Vatican II." In *Engelbert Zeitler SVD: A Man of Vision*, edited by Augustine Kanjamala, 115–34. Poona: Ishvani Kendra, 1993.

Index

Aaron, 250-51
Abelard, Peter, 177
Abhinay Bharat (Young India), 98
Abhishiktananda, Swami, 52, 183, 208
Abraham Malpan, 8
Abraham, P. C., 296
accommodation, 189
Acquaviva, Rudolf, 173, 190
Act of Incorporation, 76
Acts of Judas Thomas, 88
Acts of Thomas, 263
Adam and Eve, 191-92
Adam, William, 36, 66
Addai, 264
Adi Sankaracharya, 50
Adivasi Mahasba, 121
Adivasi-Tribal Image, 19-21
Adivasis of Chotanagpur, 118-122
Adivasis, rebellion, 230
Adivasis, tribals, low status, 149
Advani, L. K., 101
Age of Consent Act in 1881, 82
Aggaeus, 264
Agnivesh, Swami, 107, 114
Agra, 266
  school, 268
Ahatalla, Bishop, 166
Ahimsa (Non-Violence), 39
Ahmednagar, 14, 15, 71
  first college, 15
Akbar, M. J., 79
Akbar the Great (1556-1605), 172-73, 265, 269
Akharas, 169
Albuquerque, Alphonso, 10
alcohol, 149
Alexandrian liturgical family, 200, 264

Alexandrian school of theology, on salvation, 177
Alfonso, King, 163
All India Consultation on Evangelization in Patna, 301
All India Ratha Yatra, 101
All India Scheduled Caste Federation, 231
All India Seminar, Church in India Today, 307
All India Women's Conference, 75-76
Alliance Mission, 14
Ama Swami, 183
Amalorpavadass, D. S. (1932-1990), 183, 202, 305
Ambala, education in, 72
Ambedkar, Balasaheb (1891-1956), 83, 95
  conversion to Christianity, 85
  fight against Hindusim and conversion to Buddhism, 85-87
Ambedkar, B. R., 110, 152, 160, 269
Ambrose of Milan, 327
American Baptist Mission, 129, 131
American Baptists, 123, 124
American Board of Commissioners of Foreign Missions (ABCFM), 15, 77
American Dutch Reformed Church, 133
American Evangelical Church, 130
American Marathi Mission, 15
American Missionary Society, girl's school in Bombay, 68
American Presbyterian Church, 73, 125
American Presbyterian Mission, 14, 15

367

Index

Amritsar, education in, 72
Ananda (Bliss), 49
Ananda, Parama, 52
Anandam, Swami, 209
Anaphora, Indian, 204–5, 212, 217
Andhra Pradesh, 21
    fastest growth, 131
    Mala and Madiga castes, 130
    mass conversion in, 128–31
    tribal groups, 118
Andrews, C. F., 78
Anglican Church, 18
Anglican Church Missionary Society, in Calcutta, 7
Anglo-American conquest model, 291
animism, 146, 317
"anonymous Christians," 177
Antaryamin, 206
Anti-Christian organizations, 102
Anti-Conversion laws, 170
Anti-Institutional culture, 259
Antiochean liturgical family, 200
Anutam Prem (ballet), 211
apocalyptic eschatology, missionaries of, 330
apocalypticism, 246
Apostolic Exhortation, 316
Apte, S. S., 184
Aquinas, Thomas 175
Acquaviva, Joseph, 11
Arcot mission, 133
Armenian liturgical family, 200
Arminius, Jacobus, 327
Arunachal Pradesh Freedom of Religion Act (1978), 171
Arya Samaj (Society of the Aryans), 38, 39, 73, 82, 96, 127, 278
The Aryan Witness, 47
Aryan Women's Association, 58
Aryanisation, 89
asceticism, and organized violence, 169
Ashram model of inculturation, 205–10
Asia
    dialogue in, 181–83
    image of Jesus in, 322

rejection of Christian understanding of redemption, xiv
    Special Assembly for Asia, 322
Asian Bishops, 303
Asian, Jesus as, 41
Asian Synod (1998), 238
Asiatic Society of Bengal, 174
Assam belt
    separatist movements, 100
    tribal groups, 118
Assamese, Bible translation, 122
Associate Presbyterian Synod of North America, 72, 125
Association of Hindu religious leaders (Vishwa Hindu Parishad), 184
Assyrian liturgical family, 200
atheists, 340, 341
Atman (individual soul), 28, 206
Augustine of Hippo (saint), 310–11, 326–27, 340
Augustinians, 10
Aurobindo Ghosh (1872–1950), 40, 97
Avatar, Hindu doctrine of, 50
Avidya (ignorance), 50
Ayodhya, Ram Temple, 101
Azariah, V. S., 40, 133, 291

Babri Masjid, 101
Babylonian captivity (605–562 BC), 243
Backward castes, 116–17
Bahadur Shah, King, 13
Bahuguna, Sundarlal, 235
Bahujan Samaj Party, 160, 231
Bailey, Benjamin, 7
Bait, Edward, 137
Bajrang Dal (army of Hanuman), 99, 104, 112
    anti-Christian vandalism by, 100
Baker, Henry, 7
Balaam, 224
Balahis, 21
Balak, 224
Balakrishnan, K. G., 86, 113
Bandra, 13, 14
    missionary methods, 14
Banerjee, Bhavani Charan, 207–8
Brahmabhandav Upadhyaya, 47–48

Index

Banerjee, Kali Charan, 47, 51
Banerjee, Krishna Mohan (1813-85), 174
　Aryan Witness, 175
Banerjee, Sasipada, and reforms, 81
Banjara tribal community, 130
Banurji, K. C., 47
baptism, 46, 283-86, 295
　of Jesus, 285-87
　by Lievens, 120
　of outcastes, 130-31
　of Parekh, 52-53
　refusal by believers, 286
　of the Spirit, 55
　prayers before baptism, 130
Baptist missionaries
　arrival of, 30
　in Calcutta, 66
　in Delhi, 73
　and social evils, 157
Baptist Missionary Society, 125
Bardez, 11
Barth, Karl, 332
Bartholomew (Apostle), 88, 265
Basel Evangelical Mission, 16
Bassein
　missionary methods, 14
　taken over by Portuguese, 13
Bayley, Charles, 137
Beatitudes, 261
Belgaum, 71
Belgian Capuchins, 126
Bellary, London Missionary Society in, 16
Benedict XV (pope), 294
Bengal, 62
　Catholic community, 16
　Evangelical missionaries in, 289
　medical mission, 77
Bengali, New Testament, 32
Bentinck, William, 34, 67, 80
Bernini, Joseph Mary, 266
Besant, Anne, 48
Beschi, Constantine J. (1680-1749), 190
Bethune, J. E. W., 66
Bettiah Catholics, 269
Bhagavad Gita, 28, 50

translation, 174
Bharat Ashram, 206
Bharat Ratna, 24
Bharatha Dharma Mahamandala, 84
Bharati, Uma, 26
Bharatiya Janata Party, 100
Bharatiya Kisan Sangh, 104
Bhatt, Chandi Prasad, 235
Bhatt, Mahesh, 107
Bhils, 21
Bhonsale Military School (Nasik, Maharashtra), 98
Bible
　Genesis, 191
　Genesis 1-2, 224, 225, 330
　Genesis 1:1, 330
　Genesis 1:1-2, 223
　Genesis 1:2, 235
　Genesis 2:3, 251
　Genesis 2:7, 223
　Genesis 2:9, 191
　Genesis 3, 191-92, 330
　Genesis 4-11, 330
　Genesis 4-25, 225
　Genesis 6-8, 192
　Genesis 6:1-4, 225
　Genesis 12:1, 192
　Genesis 14:18, 190
　Genesis 17:1, 190
　Genesis 28:3, 190
　Genesis 49:5, 190
　Exodus 2:36, 192
　Exodus 3:7-8, 230
　Exodus 3:14, 191
　Exodus 6:2-7, 224, 330
　Exodus 6:3, 190
　Exodus 9-15, 245
　Exodus 12, 226
　Exodus 12:1-28, 225
　Exodus 12:15-20, 226
　Exodus 19:5, 326
　Exodus 20-23, 225
　Exodus 20:2-17, 192, 225
　Exodus 23: 14-17, 226
　Exodus 31:12-17, 251
　Leviticus 19:18, 247
　Leviticus 21:16, 250
　Leviticus 23:6, 226

369

Index

Bible (*continued*)
  Numbers, 224
  Numbers 15:32, 251
  Numbers 23-24, 224
  Numbers 23:7, 224
  Numbers 24:2, 224
  Numbers 24:4-9, 224
  Numbers 35:25, 250
  Deuteronomy 5:6-21, 192
  Deuteronomy 6:5, 247
  Deuteronomy 7:6-9, 325
  Deuteronomy 13:1-9, 226
  Deuteronomy 16:1-5, 225-26
  Deuteronomy 23:18-19, 226
  Deuteronomy 26:16, 325
  Deuteronomy 26:50, 190
  Deuteronomy 33:7-11, 250
  Deuteronomy 33:10, 250
  1 Samuel 21:4-5, 194
  2 Samuel 6:15, 246
  2 Samuel 7:12-16, 246
  2 Samuel 11:1-9, 246
  1 Kings 2:26, 250
  1 Kings 6-7, 250
  1 Kings 8:1-13, 246
  2 Kings 24:14, 225
  1 Chronicles 5:34, 250
  2 Chronicles 3, 4, 250
  2 Chronicles 36:22, 225
  Ezra, 246, 250
  Ezra 1:1-4, 225
  Ezra 6:3-13, 250
  Psalm 68:36, 190
  Psalm 78:51-55, 245
  Psalm 106:8-12, 245
  Psalm 115:4-8, 325
  Psalm 118:10-14, 245
  Isaiah 1:11-17, 286
  Isaiah 1:13, 251
  Isaiah 11:1, 54
  Isaiah 11:2-3, 239
  Isaiah 12:2, 245
  Isaiah 40-45, 226
  Isaiah 40:9, 243
  Isaiah 42, 325
  Isaiah 42:1-3, 239
  Isaiah 42:1-4, 286
  Isaiah 42:6-7, 54
  Isaiah 44:9-20, 325
  Isaiah 44:28, 225
  Isaiah 45:1, 225
  Isaiah 52—53:12, 325
  Isaiah 52:13-53:3-12, 54
  Isaiah 52:13-53:12, 43
  Isaiah 54:1-17, 325
  Isaiah 60-62, 54
  Isaiah 61:1, 243
  Isaiah 61:1-2, 249
  Isaiah 66:1, 235
  Jeremiah 1:5-8, 325
  Jeremiah 2:8, 250
  Jeremiah 5:30, 251
  Jeremiah 6:13-14, 251
  Jeremiah 8:8, 198
  Jeremiah 8:10-11, 251
  Jeremiah 10:8-10, 325
  Jeremiah 31:31, 194
  Ezekiel 16:3, 190
  Ezekiel 22:26, 250
  Ezekiel 40-42, 250
  Daniel 7:9-14, 246
  Hosea 4:46, 250
  Joel 2:28-30, 233
  Joel 3:1-5, 229
  Amos 5:7-27, 198
  Amos 5:21-24, 286
  Amos 5:23-24, 307
  Amos 6:1-14, 198
  Jonah 4:24-66, 228
  Micah 6:8, 307
  1 Maccabees 7:14-61, 193
  1 Maccabees 14:41-47, 193
  Wisdom of Solomon 1:7, 224
  Matthew, 341
  Matthew 3:2, 193
  Matthew 5-7, 198
  Matthew 5:13-16, 324
  Matthew 5:17, 42
  Matthew 6:8-15, 248
  Matthew 6:9-13, 199
  Matthew 6:10, 55
  Matthew 7:20, 283
  Matthew 7:28-29, 198
  Matthew 9:9-13, 252
  Matthew 9:11, 198
  Matthew 10:17, 251

Index

Matthew 11:7-19, 193
Matthew 12:4, 251
Matthew 12:9, 198
Matthew 12:12, 252
Matthew 12:25-27, 55
Matthew 12:28, 240
Matthew 12:31, 253
Matthew 13:18-23, 5
Matthew 13:32, 312
Matthew 13:54-56, 254
Matthew 15:1, 198, 252
Matthew 15:32-39, 322
Matthew 16:1-6, 198
Matthew 16:13, 321
Matthew 19:10-12, 196
Matthew 20:20-28, 54
Matthew 22:34-40, 199
Matthew 22:42, 198
Matthew 23:2, 198, 253
Matthew 23:8-10, 254
Matthew 24:2, 247
Matthew 24:32-34, 195
Matthew 25:31-46, 332
Matthew 26:25, 198
Matthew 28:16-20, 284
Matthew 28:18-20, 282, 298, 324, 341
Matthew 28:20, 343
Mark, 243, 251, 326
Mark 1, 249
Mark 1:2-4, 54
Mark 1:8, 285
Mark 1:10, 251
Mark 1:12, 239
Mark 1:14-15, 243, 245, 247, 282
Mark 1:15, 54, 341
Mark 1:27, 198
Mark 2:13-17, 252
Mark 2:24, 252
Mark 2:27, 251
Mark 3:28, 253
Mark 4:14, 251
Mark 7:1, 198
Mark 7:1-23, 198
Mark 8:1-9, 322
Mark 8:11, 198
Mark 10: 38, 286
Mark 10:35-45, 254

Mark 10:51, 198
Mark 12:6, 251
Mark 12:13, 198
Mark 12:28-31, 199
Mark 12:28-34, 247
Mark 13:9, 251
Mark 15:16, 326
Mark 16:15, 245, 341
Mark 16:15-18, 298
Luke 1:35, 239
Luke 2-11, 199
Luke 3:22, 239
Luke 4:1, 239
Luke 4:14-21, 249
Luke 4:16-21, 249
Luke 4:18, 236, 304
Luke 4:18-19, 240, 243
Luke 4:43, 249
Luke 5:27-32, 252
Luke 6, 252
Luke 6:2, 251
Luke 6:5, 251
Luke 6:15, 247
Luke 6:27-37, 247
Luke 6:35-36, 331
Luke 6:44, 283
Luke 7:27-36, 199
Luke 7:36, 252
Luke 7:36-50, 198, 322
Luke 10:21-22, 55
Luke 11:37, 198, 253
Luke 12:32, 342
Luke 13:10-17, 198
Luke 13:18-21, 324
Luke 14:1-3, 251
Luke 14:23, 298
Luke 15:11-16, 341
Luke 15:11-32, 323
Luke 15:14-32, 56
Luke 18:9-14, 252
Luke 19:1-10, 322
Luke 22:20, 243
Luke 23:24, 199
Luke 23:34, 43
Luke 24:46-49, 298
Luke 24:47, 341
Luke 24:48, 333
John 1:1-18, 41

371

Index

Bible (*continued*)
  John 1:2, 306
  John 1:9, 326
  John 1:14, 306
  John 2:19–22, 250
  John 3, 198, 253
  John 3:1–5, 285
  John 3:3, 285
  John 3:5, 285
  John 3:8, 237, 285
  John 3:16, 282, 298, 324, 331
  John 4:1–3, 284
  John 4:4–42, 58–59
  John 5:19–47, 198
  John 5:19–49, 198
  John 5:30, 36, 46
  John 6:15, 54, 248
  John 7:37–39, 285
  John 8:13, 198
  John 9:40, 252
  John 10:30, 46
  John 13:1, 331
  John 13:1–16, 254
  John 13:13–14, 24
  John 14:1–14, 46
  John 14:8–11, 46
  John 14:16, 326
  John 15:12, 331
  John 15:13, 324
  John 16:13, 237, 331
  John 17:20–21, 56, 248
  John 18:13–18, 251
  John 18:33–37, 248
  John 18:36, 55
  John 18:37, 323
  John 19:38–40, 56
  John 20–23, 298
  John 20:19–23, 324
  John 20:21, 341
  John 20:22, 240
  John 26:16, 198
  Acts, 253–54
  Acts 1:8, 307, 323, 341
  Acts 2:1–4, 240
  Acts 2:14–36, 244
  Acts 2:17, 229, 233
  Acts 2:17–18, 307
  Acts 2:17–21, 285
  Acts 4:5, 251
  Acts 4:12, 29, 299, 326
  Acts 4:18, 251
  Acts 4:20, 244, 341
  Acts 4:34–35, 195
  Acts 7:48–50, 235
  Acts 9:20, 244
  Acts 10–11, 227
  Acts 10:15, 228
  Acts 10:34–35, 176, 227, 335
  Acts 10:40, 285
  Acts 10:44–48, 227
  Acts 11:15, 285
  Acts 13:2–4, 240
  Acts 13:31, 333
  Acts 15:6–9, 227
  Acts 15:9, 178
  Acts 15:28, 227
  Acts 19:6–7, 284
  Acts 20:24, 252
  Acts 23:3–6, 253
  Acts 23:8, 252
  Romans 1:3–5, 244
  Romans 1:16, 244, 298
  Romans 1:17, 29
  Romans 2:10–12, 335
  Romans 2:29, 286
  Romans 3:9–25, 335
  Romans 3:10, 29
  Romans 5:5, 283
  Romans 5:17–18, 330
  Romans 6:3–4, 46
  Romans 6:3–11, 284
  Romans 8:11, 240
  Romans 8:16, 283
  Romans 10:9, 326
  Romans 10:20, 228
  Romans 12:15, 314
  Romans 16:25–26, 244
  1 Corinthians 1:17, 284
  1 Corinthians 1:27–29, 131
  1 Corinthians 6:14, 240
  1 Corinthians 7:7–8, 196
  1 Corinthians 7:25–31, 196
  1 Corinthians 9:16, 341
  1 Corinthians 11:3–16, 233
  1 Corinthians 11:11, 284
  1 Corinthians 11:23–26, 195

Index

1 Corinthians 12:13, 284
1 Corinthians 13, 332
1 Corinthians 14:34, 233
1 Corinthians 15, 224
1 Corinthians 15:22-28, 330
1 Corinthians 15:28, 330
2 Corinthians 5:4, 299
2 Corinthians 5:14, 341
2 Corinthians 5:18-19, 342
2 Corinthians 13:4, 240
Galatians 3:15-18, 243
Galatians 3:28, 234
Galatians 5:22-23, 283
Ephesians 1:9-10, 297
Ephesians 1:10, 295, 330
Ephesians 1:19-20, 240
Ephesians 2:3, 325
Ephesians 2:14-18, 223
Ephesians 3:12, 325
Philippians 2:6-9, 24, 325
1 Thessalonians 1:9-10, 195
2 Thessalonians 2:1-12, 195
1 Timothy 2:4, 329
2 Timothy 1:11, 244
1 Peter 2:9, 326
1 John 1:1-3, 306
1 John 2:2, 329
1 John 4:8, 282
1 John 4:11, 331
1 John 4:19, 228
1 John 4:20, 37
Revelation 21:1, 335
Revelation 21:1-4, 330
Revelation 21:1-5, 224, 299
Revelation 22:20, 195
Bible peddlers, 328-29
Bible translation, 32
Bihar-Bengal border, conversions, 20
Bihar state, 262-63
   Christian population, 268, 345
   Christians in, 271
   tribal groups, 118
Biju Janata Party (BJD), 104
Billy Graham, 294
BIMARU states, Christians in, 271-72
Bishop Caldwell college, 64
Bishop Cotton Public School for European and Anglo-Indian boys, 73

BJP, 104
   in elections, 108
   violence against Muslims and Christians, 102
Blessed Virgin Mary, Catholic prayers to, 222
Blessed Mother Teresa, 24, 162, 288-89
Blessed Kuriakose Chavara, 8
Bombay, 14, 68-72
Bombay Education Society, 68
Bombay Presidency Social Reform Association, 84
Booth-Tucker, Frederic, 139
Booth-Tucker, William, 329
Borghi, J. A., 268
Bose, Asish, 262-63
Bourbon, Philip de, of Navara, France, 269
Boyd, Robin, 50
Brahman Sathya, 50
Brahman (Supreme Soul), 28
Brahmana Sannyasis, 189
Brahminical model, 144
Brahminization, 144
Brahmins (priestly caste), 1, 116
   imitation of dietary regulations of, 145
   and leather work, 21
   as vegetarian, 94
Brahmo Samaj, 36, 41, 47
British Census Report, on depressed classes, 83
British East India Company
   and missionary activity, 117
   trading centres, 18
British, social reforms, 122
Brown, Edith, 77
Brown, L. A., *Indian Christians of St. Thomas, The*, 89
Buchanan, Chaplin Claudius, 7
Buddhism, 276
   Ambedkar and, 86
   Hindu reactions against, 91
Buelhmann, W., 319
   The Coming of the Third Church, xv, 276
bureaucratization, 255-56
Byzantine liturgical family, 200

373

Index

Caiaphas (high priest), 251
Caironi, Father, 139
Calcutta, 66-68
    Anglican Church Missionary Society in, 7
    Belgian Jesuit missionaries from, 19
    Hindu-Christian Encounter, 30-35
    Portuguese in, 2
    sale of books, 68
Calcutta University Senate, 57
Caldwell, Robert, 63
Calvin, John, 327
Canaanites, influence on Israelites, 225-26
Canadian Baptist Mission, 131
Cape Comorin, 18
Carey, William, 3, 80, 289
    in Calcutta, 30
    An Enquiry into the Obligation of Christians to Use Means for Conversion of Heathens, 30
    on lack of conversions, 33
Carmelgiri seminary, 167
Carmelite Missionaries, 167
Carnatic mission, 128
caste system, 144
    Catholic missionaries and, 157
    Christian vision and, 322
    conversions to Christianity, 41-62
    de Nobili, 190
    discrimination, 16
    education of, 65
    and partition in churches, 134
    and partition in cemetries, 134
    rigidity, 9
Catalani de Severac, Jordan (1285-1336), 264-65
Catherine of Braganza, dowry of, 14
Catholic Bishops Conference of India (Delhi, 1966) xvi, 27, 202, 300, 305
Catholic children, 71
Catholic Church, 256. *See also* Vatican Council II (1962-1965)
    Christians in India and, 90
    educational institutions, 23
    Holy Spirit marginalization in, 221-23
    Indian, 68, 200
    missiology, 297-302
    mission, 65
    mission trends before Second Vatican Council, 294-97
    ordination of indigenous clergy, 267
    patriarchal and hierarchical organization, 22
    ritual families in, 199-201
    Vatican Council II, 175
    and women's issues, 233
Catholic Mission Cooperative Credit Society of Chotanagpur (1906), 121
Catholic missionaries, 124
    and castes, 92-93
    schools, 76
Catholic missions
    in Andhra Pradesh, 128
    strengths and weaknesses of, 155-160
Catholicism
    religious freedom in, 178-79
    Upadhyaya and, 51
Caumont, Fortunatus Henri, 270
CBCI
    Evaluation Report, 272
    survey on Evangelization, 310
celibacy, Jesus and, 254
cemetery division, 313-14
Census Report (1881), on widows in India, 58
Census Report (2001), 154n88
    on Christian population in the States, 345, 346
Chaldean Catholic church, East Syrian liturgy of, 7
Chamars (leather workers), 21, 126
Chandramani, Bhiku U., 86
Chandravarka, Narayana, 87
Chandy, Oommen, 107
Charbounnaux, E. L., 17
Charismatic movement, 222, 293-94
Charlemagne, 328
Charles, Pierre, 186, 297, 299
Charter Act of 1813, 14
Charter Act of 1833, 64
Chattisgarh state, 230

374

Index

Cheenath, Raphael (Archbishop of Bhubaneshwar), 107, 112
Chenchiah, P., 292
child marriage, 148
　abolition, 81-83
Child Marriage Law (Mysore), 82
Child widows in 1881, 58
Children of Hari (Fuchs), 270
China, 277
Chipko movement, 234
Chirapunji, Serampore Baptist Mission in, 122
Choramandalam in Tamil, exploited by Arabs, 12
chosen people, 178
Chotanagpur, 3, 19
　Christian missionaries in, 154-55
　exploitation of people, 118
　missionaries' satisfaction, 312
　social status of rulers, 145
Chotanagpur Plateau, 19-20
Chotanagpur Tenures Act of 1869, 118
Chotanagpur Cooperative stores (1913), 121
Chotanagpur Tenancy Act, 121
Christ in the Spirit (Doss), 241
Christa Bhakta movement, 286
Christa Prema Ashram, 183
Christa Seva Sangh (Protestant Ashram), 207
Christapurana, 12
Christia Prema Seva Ashram, 207
Christian ashrams, 206
Christian communities in India
　Adivasi-Tribal Image, 19-21
　Concentration of, xiv
　Dalit Church Image, 21-22
　Latin Colonial Conquest Image, 9-19
　patriarchal and institutional image, 22-23
　persecuted church image, 26
　servant and compassionate image, 24-25
　Syrian image on the Malabar coast, 6-9
Christian Dalit Liberation movement, 313

Christian-Hindu encounter, xvii
Christian identity, 214
Christian institutions, anger against, 260
Christian Message in a Non-Christian World (Kraemer), 291
Christian missionaries
　arrival in India, 2, 88
　priorities, 161
　and women's education, 75-76
Christian missions in India
　crisis in, xiv
　failure vs. success, xvi-xvii
　and social transformation, 79-94
Christian population in India, (in 1851), 117, 345-46
Christian Proselytism in India, 56
Christian rituals, 148
Christian West, 277
Christianity
　analysis of conversion movement, 162
　caste conversions to, 41-62
　expansion limits, 279
　Gandhi on, 40
　and Hinduism, 174
　increasing after World War, 141-42
　mass conversions, 117-43
　and modernization, 154
　population increase in Orissa, 103
　and treatment of women, 59
Christianization, 143
　as alternative to Hinduization, 143-55
　influence of, 153
　meaning and nature of, 146-55
Christians
　persecution by low pay, 127
　in Punjab, statistics on expansion, 127
　and serving the poor, 111
"Christiya Matatatwam" (Tamil catechism), 12-13
Christocentrism, 233
　pneumatocentric vision and, 237-39
Chuhari, 266
Chura (sweeper caste), 21, 125-26

375

Index

"Church in India Today in the Light of the Vatican Council, The" (Bangalore, 1969), 300–301
Church Missionary Society (CMS), 2, 14, 21, 125, 132–33
   female school, 68
   hospitals, 77
   St. John's College, 75
Church of England Zanana Bible and Medical Mission Society, 72, 125
Church of God, 123
Church of New Dispensation, 45, 47, 174
Church of North India, 27, 292
Church of Scotland, 14, 72, 75, 125, 126
Church of South India, 27, 292
churches, 148, 299
   all-India dynamics, 27
   caste mentality in, 134
   cultures and development of, 199
   growth of local church, 322
   history lessons on inculturation, 187–90
   in India, 302
   in India, images of, 4
   role in proclamation of Gospel, 260
   unity of universal, 218
Churchill, Winston, 1
Churchless Christianity, Parekh and, 56
Cit (Consciousness), 49
Civil Rights Protection Act of 1976, 153
civilization, 276–77, 337
   of human dignity, 340
Clement, Bonnard, 129
Clement of Alexandria, 326
clergy, indigenous
   ordination, 267
   promotion, 295
Clive, Robert, 29
Clough, J. E., 21, 129, 139
CMS. *See* Church Missionary Society (CMS)
CMS college, 8
Cochin, 10, 13
   trade centre, 9

Code of the Covenant, 225
colleges, growth, 274
colleges and universities, 74
colonial political power, Christian missonary activity and, 137
Coming of the Third Church, The (Buehlmann), xv, 276
comity of mission, policy, 133
Commission for World Mission and Evangelization (Bangkok, 1973), 292, 293
communal politics, origin and expansion of, 96–103
community's image, 4
community, collective memory of, 215
Comparative Grammar of Dravidian Languages (Caldwell), 64
compassionate services, missionaries of, 332
Concordat of 1857, 14
Concordat of 1953, 14
Conference of Religious India, 27
Congregation for Evangelization, 128
Congregation for Sacred Liturgy, 203
Congregation of Jesus and Mary, 268
Congress party, 100
consciousness, breaking boundaries of, 223
Conservative Baptist Foreign Mission (USA), 121
Constantine, 326
"Constantine Model of Mission," 281
Constantine Paradigm of mission, end of, xvii
Constitution. *See* Indian Constitution
Constitutions circa Missionis, 304
Constructing images, 3–5
contemporary culture, anti-institutional atmosphere of, 258–261
conversion movement, xiii, 142
conversions, 110–15, 153, 283–86. *See also* mass conversions
   to Christian churches, 116–62
   as community exercise, 140
   forced, 163–65
   impact of, 143
   of marginal communities, 116–62
   paradoxes of, 153

Index

as primary objective in education, 77–78
reference in New Testament to, 282–83
religious freedom and, 110–15
resistance to, 216
sectors in strong resistance to, 92
Copernicus, Nicolas, 317
Cornelius, 227, 285
Coromandel coast, 131
  mass conversion among fisher folk, 131
Cosmos Indicopleustes, 264
Costa, C. J., 165
Council of Chalcedon (451), 241
Council of Jerusalem, 228
Council of Nicea (325), 88, 241
Council of Trent, 166
counter-culture, 197–98
cow protection laws, 99
Cranganore, 2, 6
creation story, 191
  Holy Spirit's presence in, 224
Crown of Hinduism, The (Farquhar), 174–75, 292
Crusades, 163, 188
Cuddapa, 130
cultural change, resistance to, 215–19
cultural conditionings, differences in, 216
cultural traits, and identities, 5
cultures 187, 280
  description levels, 188
  destruction in converts, 201
  plurality and diversity, 186
  postmodern culture, 216
"Cumcolim Revolt," 11, 164
Cyprian of Cartage (saint), 310–11, 326
Cyrus II, 225
Cyrus the Great, 224–25

da Gama, Vasco, 2, 9
Dakshina Kannada, 106
Dalit Panas, conversions, 103
Dalits
  Christian mission for, 271
  as Christians, 268–69
  conversions, 22, 111

converts, 16
growth, 161
movements for liberty, equality, and human dignity, 231–32
school for, 72
struggle for human rights, 85
Damascus Document, 193
Damien of Molokai, 332
Danish-Halle mission, 131
Danish Missionaries, 62
Dara Singh, 26, 112
Darwin, Charles, 173
Dasnami Sannyasis, 168
Datta, Narendranath, 37, 47
Daughters of the Cross, 71
  schools and orphanages, 268
Davidic Messianism, 246
Dayananda Saraswati, Swami (1824–1883), 38–39, 96, 278
de Britto, John (1647–93), 190
de Nobili, Robert (1577–1656), 250–52, 93, 188–90, 280
de Severac Jordan Catalani, 265
dead, Catholic tradition of praying for, 147
Deism, 36
deity, absorption in, 42
Delhi, education in, 72
Demetritus of Alexandria, 6
democracy
  decline of, 100
  in India, 109–110
Dengel, Anna, 77
dependency mentality of converts, 135
Depressed Class Mission Society, 84
Desai, Morarji, 100
Deshpande, Nirmala, 114
Deshpande, R. K., 103
Dharma, 117
Dharma Mahamandali, 84
Dharma Sabha, 84
Dharma Sansad, 101
Dharma Swatantra Act, 171
Dharpan (Hindu Periodical), 69
Dheds, 21
Diakonia, 244
Dialogue
  four types, 179–80
  in Asia, 181–83

377

Index

of church, with other religions, 176
differences in Western and Asian theologies, 182
  in India, 183-86
  and mission path in India, 183-85
  post-Vatican II developments in, 182-85
  Vatican II on, 175-76
dictionaries of Indian languages, 156
dietary habits, 149
dignity, Dalit movements for, 231-32
Din-Illahi (Divine Faith), 173
Dionysis IV, 8
Disciples of Church of Christ, 121
Divine Humanity, Sen's doctrine of, 46
Divine Word Society, 236
divinization of human nature, 46
divorce, 148
Dnyanodaya (Rise of Knowledge), 69-70
do Porto, Antonio, 13
Dom Joao III, 10
Dominicans, 10
Dominus Jesus, 308
Dongre, Anant Shastri, 57
Doss, Arul, 104-5
  murder of, 26
Doss, Mohan, *Christ in the Spirit*, 241
Douay-Rheims version, 244
Dravida Munnetta Kazhagam (DMK), 160, 231
Duff, Alexander, 33-35
Dulles, Avery, *Models of the Church*, 24
Dupuis, Jacques, 176, 241
Durga Vahini, 104
dying to sin, 284-85

East India company, missionaries in territory of, 14
Eastern Christianity in India (Tisserant), 89
Eastern Gujarat, 21
ecological movements, 234-35
ecology, 318
Edit of Milan (313), 328
education, 33, 124
  in Bombay and Western India, 68-72
  in Calcutta, 66-68
  Christian contributions towards social change, 150-51
  Christian missionary policies, 287
  by Christians, 314
  college and universities, 74-76
  goals of, 287-88
  by missionaries in South India, 63-65
  missionaries of, 333
  in North-Western Province, 72-74
  philosophy of, 150
  progress, 74
  in South India, 63-65
  Protestant missionaries and, 156-57
  standardized, 73
  women religious and, 71
Educational Dispatch of 1854, 64
Edwards College, 75
El, 190
El-Shaddai,' 190
elections in India, 109
Elias, Ignatius Mar, 8
Elohim, 190
Elphinstone, Mountstuart, 68
Elwin, Verrier, 121-22
England, Ramabai travel to, 58
English colleges, impact, 74-75
English education, 34
  in Calcutta of upper castes, 66-68
  impact of, 78-79
  justification for, 78
  rapid spread of, 68
English language
  for education, 67
  in India, 79
English Society for the Propagation of Christian Knowledge, 63
enlightenment, 174
enlightenment culture of Europe, vs. tribal societies, 139
Enuma Elis, 191
environment, 318
Epic of Gilgamesh, 191
equality, Dalit movements for, 231-32
eschatology, 342
Essene sect, 53, 193-95, 246, 254, 325

Index

and primitive Christian community, 195-97
ethics, introduction of, 148-49
ethnic community, distinctive culture of, 186
Eusebius (260-340), 6, 264
Evangelical Fellowship of India, 161
Evangelical Lutheran Church, 121, 123
Evangelicals, 68
  churches in Indian urban centres, 294
  conflicts with Ecumenical Protestants, 292
  reject inclusivism, 332
Evangelii Nuntiandi, xv, 303, 304, 305
Evangelii Praecones, 295-96
evangelism, 29
evangelization, 296, 304, 309
  cultures, 87
  dialogue and mission in, 180
  failure to produce consensus document, xv, 304
  goal of, 288
  in modern world, 303-5
  motivation of, 311
  redefining in Asian context, 181
evil spirits, 147
evolution theory, 173
evolutionary world view, 317
Evora, Archbishop, 165
Exclusive missiology, 327-28
exclusivism, 326
  missionary models, 328-30
  New Testament vs. Old, 331-32
explorers, 338
Extra ecclesiam nulla salus, xiii, 326
Ezekiel, 54
Ezhavas of Travencore, reform movement, 8

Fabricus, Philip, 17
Falcao, Nelson, 12
families, 336, 340
famine in India
  1876-79, 130
  1896-1900, 59-60
Farquhar, J. N., 37, 47

Crown of Hinduism, The, 174-75, 292
Feast of Tents, 226
Feast of unleavened bread, 226
Feast of Weeks, 226
Federation of the Asian Bishops' Conference, 181
  Office of Ecumenical and Inter-religious Affairs, 229
Fellowship of Indian Missiologists (FOIM), vii, 302
female deities, in Indian religious tradition, 147
feminine stereotypes of Hinduism, 169
feminism, 22
Fenn, Joseph, 7
Fidei Donum, 297
Firth, C. B., *An Introduction to Indian Church History*, 89
Flavius Josephus, 53
flood, 192
food habits, 149
forecasting, xv
foreign missionaries, status and prestige, 137-38
Forman College, 75
Francis Xavier (saint), 10, 11, 12, 139, 165, 332
  mission theology, 13
Franciscan Missionary Brothers, 270
Franciscans, 10
Francke, August Hermann (1663-1727), 17
Frankfurt Declaration (1970), 332
Frederick IV (Danish king), xiii, 3, 17
Free Church of Scotland, 121
freedom of religion, 178-79, 317
  and conversion, 110-15
Freedom of Religion Act, 170
Freedom of Religion Act (1967) (Orissa), 109
Freedom of Religion Act (1968), 171
Friends of India, The, 32
Frustrations of missionaries, xvi, 17, 33
Fuchs, Stephen, 138, 230
  Children of Hari, 270
fulfillment theology, 292
Fulgentius, bishop of Ruspa, 311

Index

fundamentalism, 29
future, imagining, 321–22
Future of Missions in the Hindu belt, 263
Future of Christian Mission, 343
futurology, xv

Gajapati district, Sangh activists attacks, 104
Gandhi, Indira, 100
Gandhi, Mahatma (1869–1948), 39–40, 83, 98, 210, 232,
   assassination, 95
   conversion and, 40, 283
   Jesus and, 240
   synthesis of religion and politics, 56
   three types of responses to Christianity, 39–40
Gangadhar Mishra, 25
Garos, 20
Gelasius (pope), 327
gender equality, 318
"Gender Policy of the Catholic church in India," 233
Genealogy of the Malabar Gods, The (Ziegenbalg), 17
General Assembly of schools, 64
Gentiles, Holy Spirit's presence in, 227
geocentric world view, 317
Ghosh, Aurobindo, 52
Gift to Deists, A (Roy), 35
girls schools, 63, 65, 72–73
   in Calcutta, 66
   government and, 74
global village, 317–18
globalization, inculturation and, 214–19
Gnana (knowledge), 28
Goa, 10
   archbishop as Primate of the East, 10
   conquest of, 163–64
   printing press in, 12n28
God
   as Father, Sen on, 43
   fear vs. love, 283
   love and compassion, 331
   as loving Abba, 248–49, 331

Godhavari-Krishna belt, 130
Godse, Nathuram, 98
Golconda, 128
Golwalkar, M. S., 98
   Bunch of Thought, A, 97
   We or Our Nation Defined, 278
Gomes, Manuel, 14
Gondi Grammar, 121
Gonds, Alexander Duff, 121
Gordon, Andrew, 126
Gordon College, 75
Gospel, 243–49
   secular meaning, 320
"Gospel of Grace," 253
Gossner Mission, 123
government, failure of law and order, 108
grace in Christ, 331
Gracia, Gonsalo, 13
Graham, Billy, 293
Grammar and Dictionary of Lushai Language (Lorrain and Savidge), 123
grammar books, 156
Grammar for Khasi Language, A (Roberts), 123
Grammar of the Santal Language, The 121
Grant, Charles, 29, 67
Grant, Sara, 183
Greek liturgical family, 200
Greek-Marathi Lexicon, 60
Gregorianum University, faculty of missiology, 295
Gregory XIII (pope), 10
Gregory XV (pope), 189
Griffiths, Bede, 52, 183, 208, 209
Grossjean, 139
Grossner, John Baptist, 19, 119
Guha, Ramachandra, 102, 110, 281
Gujarat Carnage, violence, 102–3
Gujarat state
   Catholic mission in, 15
   against Christians, 114
   crimes against Christians, 114
   persecutions in, 26
   tribal groups, 118
Gujral, J. K., 25

Index

Gulamgiri (slavery), 84
Gundhaphar, and St. Thomas mythology, 263–64
guru, 207
Guru, Sri Narayana, 84
Guwahati, 122

Hahn, Rev., 119
Hall, Gordan, 15
Halle Pietist educational system, 63
Hambye, E. R., 209
  St. Thomas Christians in India, 88
Hammurabi (BC 1728–1686), 191
Hammurabi's Laws, 192
Hans, John, 16
Hanuman (the monkey god), 147
Hare Krishna mission, 154
Harijan, 21, 83
  low status, 149
The Harmony (journal), 47
Hartmann, Athanasius, 14, 71, 266–67, 269
health ministry
  by Christians, 314
  institutions, 23
Heber, Reginald, 134
Hebrew-Marathi Lexicon, 60
Hedgewar, K. B., 97–98, 278
Hegel, philosopher, 169
heliocentric world view, 317
hell, fear of, 126
Henrique, Francis, 173
Heralds of Good News, Khammam Diocese, 315
Hermeneutical principles, 331–32
Herod, 250
heroes of youth, 259
High Caste Hindu Women, The (Ramabai), 59
high priest, 251–52
higher education, demand for, 64
Hindi-Sanskrit Sangam, 210
Hindu belt, 263–75
  colonial mission, 265–70
  distribution of missionaries in, 272–75
  future of missions, 262–63
  priests available, 272–73

Hindu caste system, and conversion, 111, 190
  and status, 144
Hindu castes, 1
Hindu-Christian dialogues, 51–52
  trends of thoughts and actions, 61
  types, 178–80
Hindu-Christians, 286
Hindu-Christian encounter, 30
  five trends, 61–62
Hindu Church of Jesus Christ, 158
Hindu College, 34
Hindu families, views on women's education, 66
Hindu fundamentalism, 100–101
  persecution of Christians, 15
Hindu Jagaran Vedike, 112
Hindu laws
  of Manu, 109
  and women, 59
Hindu Mahasabha, 278
Hindu militancy, history of, 167–72
Hindu militant Sanyasis, 169
Hindu pantheism, 42
Hindu region, 264, 266
  distribution of missionaries in, 273–76
  mission in Hindu region, 266–71
Hindu Scriptures, *Manusmruti* on caste (Varna), 116
Hindu widow, social status, 57
Hinduism, 276
  described, 28
  on equality of religions, 176
  masculinity and, 169
  of nineteenth century, 79
  rational approach, 36
  responses to evangelical mission, 28–94
  sacredness of nature, 234–35
Hinduization, 143–44, 215
  Christianization as alternative, 143–55
Hindus
  forbidding change in religion, 140
  in Pakistan, 95
  resistance to conversion, 11–12, 164
Hindu- Catholics, 51

381

Index

Hindustan, partition, 95
Hindutva philosophy, 96–98
  spread in Orissa, 103–4
Hindutva (Who is a Hindu?, Savarkar), 278
Hints for the Establishment of Native Schools (1814) (Marshman), 66
History of Christianity in India (Mundadan), 89
Hocking Report (1932), 75
Hocking, W. E., *Rethinking Missions*, 291
Hoekendijk, Johannes, 292
Hoffman, J.B., 121
Holy Spirit, 307, 336
  affirmation of universal presence and action of, 181
  appreciation of presence, 237–39
  in contemporary social movements, 220, 228–37
  fruit of, 283
  marginalization in Catholic tradition, 221–23
  in New Testament, 227–28
  in Old Testament, 223–27
  Roy on, 36
  and truth and justice, 315
  and water, 285
Hooghly, Calcutta, Portuguese trade center in, 15
hope, 314–16
  signs of, 238
hospitals
  growth, 274
  for women, 77
Hough, James, 18
Hudson, Thomas, 16
humankind, fall of, 191–92
human family, 341
Hunter, W. W., 58
Hunter Commission report (1882), 74
Hymns of the Rig Veda, 28
Hypocrisy of Pharisees, 253–54

Ilhas, 11
images, of Christian communities in Inda, 5–26
  of Jesus in Asia, 322

incarnations, Upadhyaya defense of belief in, 50
inclusive missiology, 331
inclusivism, xviii
  hermeneutical principles of, 330–32
  models of missionaries, 332–34
inculturation, 186
  Ashram model, 205–10
  Bible as model, 190–99
  globalization and, 214–19
  gospel proclamation in Indian style, 210–11
  lessons from church history, 187–90
  liturgical, 202–3
  models in Europe, 202
  models in India, 201–14
  in the New Testament, 193–95
  in the Old Testament, 191–93
  order of mass for India, 203–5
  popular devotional model, 212–14
  a vicious circle, 215–16
  resistance to, 216–20
Independent Lutheran church of Chotanagpur, 119
India, 277
  challenges of, 1–3
  Christian population by states, 345–46
  colonial period, 278
  Dutch vs. Portuguese in, 159
  economic conditions, 110
  future of missions, 279–283
  social trends, 315
  today's young generation, 319–20
  win/win paradigm, 280–83
Indian Anaphora, 203–5
Indian Catholic Church, 200
  institutionalization in, 23, 255–61
Indian Christians of St. Thomas (Brown), 89
Indian Church of St. Thomas (Philip), 89
Indian Constitution, 109, 152–53
  Article 355, 107
  freedom of conscience on religion, 110
  on freedom of religion, 172
Indian Eucharistic prayer, 204

Index

Indian Independence Movement, 78
  Christians and, 158
Indian mind, Western education and transformation, 62–79
Indian Missionaries abroad, 316
Indian Mutiny in 1857, 67, 117
Indian National Congress
  inclusive philosophy, 97
  loss of power, 100
Indian National Reformer, 84
Indian Social Reformer, 87
Indian Parliament, elected women in, 23
Indian Sepoy Revolt of 1857, 73, 78, 267
Indian Social Conference, 83
Indian Theological Association, 286, 301–2
indigenization in West, 201
Infant Marriage Prevention Act (Baroda), 82
Inquisition, 11, 165
Institute of Blessed Virgin Mary, 71
  schools and orphanages, 268
institutionalization, 242
  of charism of Jesus, 256–59
  in Indian Catholic Church, 23, 255–61
  of religion, 180
inter-religious dialogue, 178
International Congress on Evangelization, 293
International Covenant on Civil and Political Rights (UN), 172
International Eucharistic Congress, 49, 211
International Missionary Conference (Jerusalem, 1928), 290–291
International Missionary Conference (New Delhi, 1961), 293
international organizations, 338–39
International Theological Conference on Evangelization (Nagpur, 1971), 301
An Introduction to Indian Church History (Firth), 89
Irish Presbyterian missionary Society, 69

Iron cage of Casteism, examples of breaking, 86
Isabella Thoburn college, 75
Ishwara, 177
Islam, 277. See also Muslims
Israelites, 191
  deportation to Babylon, 226

Jacobite church, 2
  reformation, 8
Jaffrelot, Christophe, 113, 160
Jagad Mitya, 50
Jagir (fiefdom of Sardhana), 267
Jahan, Shah (1627–58), 265
jajmani (patron-client system), 21
Jambekar, Bal Shashtri, 69
Jana Sangh, 98–100, 171, 278
Janata Party, 100
Janser, Peter, 270
Janssen, Arnold, 236
Jantar Mantar, New Delhi, Dharna and prayer meeting, 108
Jeevan Dhara Ashram, 209
Jefferson, Thomas, 35
Jeremiah, 250
Jesu Das, 41–47
Jesuits, 10, 128–29, 137
  education by, 71
  at Moghul court in Fatehpur Sikri, 265
Jesus, 193, 276, 282
  Abba experience of, 248–49, 331
  Ambedkar on social Gospel, 85–86
  and baptism, 283–84
  baptism of, 285–86
  Christian core belief in, 195
  as evangelizer, 304
  and evil spirits, 147
  Good News of, 259–60
  images of, 4, 24, 321
  incarnation of, 42
  influence of, 287
  Jewish accusations against, 198
  missionary command of, 341
  and new world order, 249
  outlook on Jewish institutions, 249–54, 324–25
  parable of Last Judgment, 332

383

Index

Parekh on awareness of union with God, 55
prayer, 56, 248
Roy's attitude to, 37
and Sadducees and Pharisees, 198
and salvation, 335
Sen on, 42–43, 46
Sermon on the Mount, 198–99
Spirit in life of, 239–40
Western interpretations vs. Asian, xvii, 321–22
as witness, 323
Jesus Movement, 197–99
Jewish institutions, Jesus' outlook on, 249–54
Jewish liturgical feasts, 225
Jewish temple, 249–51
prediction of destruction, 247
Jhabua districts, rape of nuns, 26
Jharkand state, 230
demand for, 99
Jivas (eternal souls), 52
Joao III, 164
Joao, King D., 188
John d'Albuquerque, 10
John Paul II (pope), 151, 181–83, 306, 308, 340
"Dignity of Women," 23
Ecclacia in Asia, 219
Redemptoris Missio, xv
John the Baptist, 54, 193
John, Valsa, murder in Pakur district, 114
John XXIII (pope), xiv, 175, 227, 296, 297, 340, 341
Jones, E. Stanley, 40
Jones, William, 174
Jongeneel, Jan, 320
Joseph of Arimathea, 56
Jotyrao to Phule, 84
Judaism
Jesus' criticism of institutional structures, 254
social forces impacting, 192
Jullundhar, education in, 72
Justice B. K. Somasekhara Commission, 112–13
justice, of aboriginals, 138

justification by faith, 327

Kalyan, 265
Kanai Thoma, 6
Kandhamal, conflicts, 104
Kandhamal district, 103
Kane, Anderson, 33
Kannada, Bible translation into, 16
Kannada-English-Kannada Dictionary (Leev), 16
Kannada Samachara, 17
Kanshi Ram, 160
Karma, 28, 117
Karnataka
Christians in, 16, 113
crimes against Christians, 114
Protestant missionaries in, 16
violence in, 106
Kashmir, separatist movements, 100
Kaspar, W., on future of mission, 342
Kathiawar, 69
Katju, Markandey, 113
Katmandu, 266
Kena Upanishad, 221
Kerala, 90, 146
Syrian and Latin church conflicts in, 165–67
Kerala Catholics, 9
Kerussein, 245
Kerygma, 245
Khandwa, mission in, 269
Kharias, conversions, 20
Khasi hills, 20
Khasi New Testament, 122
Khasi-Panars, 20
mission work by Catholics, 124
Khonds, conversions, 20
Kingdom of God, 303, 319
attraction of, 307
expectation for, 53
Hindu understanding of, 53–56
human culture, 220
Judaism and, 198
New Testament understanding, 247–49
Old Testament understanding, 245–47

384

Index

Parekh's Indian understanding of, 56
proclamation of vs. proclamation of Christ, 306–7
signs of presence, 307
working for realization, 323
King James Version, 244
kings
 idea of, 245
 support of Christianity, 328
Kinnaird College (Lahore), 75
Kipling, Rudyard, 159
Kirkegaad, Soren, 290
Klostermaier, Klaus, 183
Kohila, 63
Kodungallur, 6, 90
Koinonia, 244
Kolhapur, caste practices abolition, 15
Konkani, initiative to eradicate languages of, 11
Koonan cross, Mattancherry, 167
Korkus, 121
Kothari, D., 150
Kottayam, 8
Kraemer, Hendrik, 332
 Christian Message in a Non-Christian World, 292
 discontinuity theory of, 292
Krishna-Godavari delta, 130
Krishna Mohan Banerji, 34
Kristiya Sannyasa Samaj, 315
Kristyan (Tilak), 207
Kshatriya model, 144
Kshatriya (warrior caste), 1, 145
Kshatriyas (rulers), 116
Kueng, Hans, 185, 300
Kumar, Meira, 86
Kurisumala Ashram, 209
Kurla, 13
Kuruk Grammar and Dictionary, 119

Lahore, education in, 72
laity, Indian Catholic Church and, 313
Lambadi tribal community, 130
Lamentabili Sane Exitu (1907), xiv
land
 ownership of, 144–45
 problems of the Adivasis, 136

landlord system, in tribal economy, 118
languages and dialects, 1
 for education, 34
 Persian, 62
Latin American Bishops' Conference (Medellin, 1968), 303
Latin Bishops Conference (Poona, 1992), 204
Latin Catholics, in 2005, 9
Latin Kannada Dictionary (Charbounnaux), 17
Latin liturgical family, 200
Latinization of Syrian Christians, 166
Laussane Covenant (1974), 294, 308, 309, 332
Laxmananda, Swami, 104
 Christmas attacks, 105
lay participation in mission, 297
Le Saux, Henri, 183, 208
Leev, Williams, Kannada-English-Kannada Dictionary, 16
Leipzig Lutheran church, 134
liberation, 324
 missionaries of, 332–33
liberty, Dalit movements for, 231–32
Lievens, Constant (1855–93),19–20, 119–20, 138, 139
Light of the East, 16
Ling, Catherin, 139
liquor, 145
literacy rate, in 1901, 74
literature, 338
liturgical practices, 199–201
 inculturation, 202–3
local churches, 2
local dialects, 123
Lokmanya Tilak, 97
London Missionary Society, 16, 62, 63, 65, 131, 132, 133
 Caldwell College, 75
 Gujarat mission, 68
 hospital, 77
 London University model, 76
Lonergan, Bernard, 177
Loreto Sisters, schools and orphanages, 268
Lorrain, J. H., 123

385

Index

Lowrie, John C., 125
Ludhiana, education in, 72
Lushai hills, 20
Lutheran Evangelical Missionaries, 19
Lutheran missionaries, xiii, 18
Lutheran pessimism, 29
Lytton, Earl, 137

Macaulay, Thomas Babington (1800–1859), 67, 169
Madhya Bharat, objections to conversions, 170
Madhya Pradesh, 26, 262–63
   Catholic mission in, 269
   Christians in, 271
   crimes against Christians, 114
   Freedom of Religion Act (1968), 171
   nuns in, 273
   tribal groups, 118
Madiga converts, 129
Madras Christian College, 64
Madras Missionary Conference of 1850, 134
Madras Native Christian Association, 135
Madras, schools, 64
Madras Social Reform Association, 84
Mahakavya Isayana, 211
Maharashtra
   Dalit movement in, 269
   tribal groups, 118
Mahars, 21
Mahieu, Francis, 209
mai-baap, 135
Makani, Miriam, 173
Mala (weaver caste), 21
Malabar coast, Syrian church on, 2, 6–9
Malabar Rite Controversy, 190
Malabari, B. M., 74, 82
Malayalam language, Bible translation, 7
Malkuth Yahweh (Reign of God), 245
Malpan, Abraham, 8
Manavadharma Sabha (Society for Human Religion), 70

Mandal Commission report (1978), 153
Mandali, branches of, 71
Mangalapuzha, 167
Mangalasamachar, in Punjabi, 128
Mangalore, 16
Mangalorean Catholics, 16
   persecution of, 16
Mangs, 21
Manila Manifesto (1989), 308
Manipur, 152
   Christians in, 123, 142
Manjhi, Rajni, 106
Manu (Hindu law giver), 83
Maoist Liberation Guerrilla Army, 105
Maquirrum Khan of Patna, 267
Mar Thoma Syrian Church, 8
Maramon Convention of the Reformed church, 8
Marathi, 12
   initiative to eradicate languages of, 11
   mission, 68
Marathi Kirtans, 60
marginal communities
   agents of social transformation in, 160
   conversions to Christianity, 116–62
Marshman, Dr., Hints for the Establishment of Native Schools, 66
Marshman, Joshua, 31
Marthandam, 132
martyrdom, missionaries of, 333–34
Marwar, 265
Marxism, 295
Mary (mother of Jesus), 147
Mascarenhas, Maria, 173
masculinity, 169
mass conversions, 3
   of Adivasis of Chotanagpur, 118–22
   of Tribals in the North east, 122–24
   anti-conversion laws, 169–72
   reasons for success, 136–42
   in Andhra Pradesh, 128–30
   in Punjab, 125–28
   in Tamil Nadu, 131–35
Massey, James, 127

Index

Masulipatnam, 128
Masulipattam, school in, 130
material culture, 4
Mathai, Abraham, 107
Mathaji, Vandana, 208-9
Mathew Athanasios, 8
Mathew, Deacon, 8
matriarchy, end of, 232
Mault, Martha, 63
Maximum Illud, 294
Maya, 50
Mayawati, Kumari (1956-), 86, 231
Mazagoan, 13
Mazoomdar, P.C. (1840-1904), 174, 286
Mazzoth, 226
McGavaran, Donald A., 293-94
McKenzie, J. L., 225
meat, eating, 145
medical colleges, 77, 157
Medical Mission Training Institute, 77
medical missions, 77
medicine, 338
Meerut Cantonment, church construction, 267-68
Meghalaya, 141, 152
  Christians, 123
Mehta, Narsi, 83
Menamparambil, T., 142
Menezes, Alexio da, 166
Menezes, George, 115
mental health, 337
Messianic movement, social conditions stimulating, 141
Meston, Lord, 79
Methodist Church, 30, 126
  mission, 14
  policy on caste practices, 134
Methodist Episcopal Church, 75, 125
militant outfit missionaries, 329
Mill Hill Missionaries, 129
ministers, training and ordaining indigenous, 157
minority religious communities, violences against, 95
miracle workers, 329
miracles, debating on, 33
Missio Dei, xiv, 298, 341

Missio Ecclesiae, 341
missiology
  paradigm shift in, 329
  shift from exclusive to inclusive, 280
  third world challenge to Western traditional, 280, 303
mission, 242, 304-5
  alternative model, 321-23
  definition, 296-99
  encyclical letters, 295-97
  of future, 319
  failed, 280
  in the Hindu belt, 264-70
  methods, 155-66
  future in Hindu belt, 262-63
  future in India, 279-83
  goals of traditional, 320
  qualitative model, 322-25
  reasons for, 341-43
  tensions and conflicts, 312-14
  trends, 290-98
  universal, 334-40
  universal participation in, xviii
  Vatican Council II definition, 299
The Mission of the Redeemer, 306
Mission Sisters of Ajmeer, 270
Mission Society of St. Thomas the Apostle, 315
mission theology, xviii
  of Indian missionaries, 311-13
  shift in, 236
mission trends, Catholic, 295-98
mission trends, Protestant, 290-94
missionaries
  aggressive methods, 10-12
  attacks on, xvii, 294-95
  categories, 189
  character and lifestyle of, 139
  conclusions about efforts, 275-76
  conferences, 290
  distribution in Hindu belt, 272-75
  entry into India, 29
  forces influencing thinking, 173
  institutionalization of activities, 242
  major activities, 274
  mission theology of, 310-14
  models of exclusive, 328-30
  models of inclusive, 332-34

387

Index

practical missiologies of grass root, 309
priorities, 311
problem of work, 279
restriction on, 171
satisfaction of, 312, 313
shift of loyalty and dependency, 135
Missionaries of Charity of Blessed Mother Teresa, 24, 289, 332
morning prayer, 162
Missionaries of Francis de Sales of Annecy, 129, 270
missionary drive, xv
missionary spirit, 9
Missionary Society of St. Francis Xavier, 12
Missionary Society of St. Thomas, 9
Mizo Language, Bible translation, 123
Mizoram, 152
  Christians in, 123, 142
modern ideas, in India, 62
Modi, Narendra, 102
Moegling, Hermann, 16
Mohila Morcha, 104
Moksha (emancipation), 54, 117
Moltmann, Juergan, 234
monastic model, 325
Monchain, Jules, 208
monks, 9
monotheism, 191, 226
Monserate, Antony, 173
Mookherjee, S. P., 98-99, 278
Moonje, B. S., 98
morality, introduction of, 148-49
Moras, Bernard, Archbishop of Bangalore, 107
Moravian Brothers, 125
Moravian missionaries, 62
Moro, James, 77
Moses, 192
Mott, John, 290
Mueller, Max, 67, 174
Muggeridge, Malcolm, Something Beautiful for God, 288
Muhammad, 265
Muir Central College, 75
Mukti Sadan (House of Liberation), 60
Mueller, Max, 134-35, 175

Munda rebellions, 230
Mundadan, A. M., History of Christianity in India, 89
Mundas, conversions, 20
Munro, John, 7
Murray College, 75
Muslims
  antagonism of, 266
  destruction of temples, 101
  in India, 95, 168
  leaders' boycott of mission schools, 73
  tribal exploitation by rulers, 20
Mystici Corporis, 296
mythology of *Acts of Thomas* and Gundhaphar, 364

NBCLC, Bangalore, 203
Nadar, 132
Naga Sadhus (naked monks), 169
Naga tribe, 20
Nagaland, 122, 141, 152
  Christians, 123
  creation of, 99
Nagapattnam, 65
Nagpur Statement on Evangelization, Dialogue and Liberation, 301
Namboodiri Brahmins, 9
Nandy, Ashish, 102
Narayan, K. R., 86
Nathan, 246
National Christian Council in India, 27
National Church of Bengal, Kali Charan Banerjee, 45
National Missionary Conference (Calcutta, 1914), 290
Nationalism of Savarkar (Maharashtra), 97
Natrajan, S., 62
  Indian Social Reformer, 87
Nattar Sabai, 133
natural calamities, and end of world, 329-30
Naxal movement, 105
Nazrani Deepika, 8
Nebuchadnezzar (605-562 BC), 225, 243

Index

Nehemiah, 246, 250
Nehru, Pandit Jawaharlal, 24, 98, 155
Neill, Stephen, 120
neo-Buddhism, dalits and, 111
Nepal, 270
Nestorian Christians, 6, 265
Nestorian Persian church, link between St. Thomas Christians and, 91
Neuner, Joseph, 279, 309
new birth, 285
New Delhi, 293, 294
New Testament, 243
  Holy Spirit in, 227–28
  inculturation and adaptation in, 192–95
  translations, 32
  translation into Assamese, 122
  translation into Bengali, 32
  translation into Hindi, 271
  translation into Kannada, 16
  translation into Malayalam, 7
  translation into Marathi, 15
  translation into Mizo, 123
  translation into Mundari, 119
  translation into Punjabi, 128
  translation into Santali, 121
  translation into Tamil,17
newspaper in India, 32
Newton, John, 128
Nicholas V (pope), papal bull, 163
Nicodemus, 56, 253, 285
Nirguna Brahman, 48, 50
  as pure Being and pure Consciousness, 48
  and external world, 50
Niyogi Committee Report, 99, 171
Noble, Robert, 130
Noble college Masulipattnam, 75
non-Christian religions, pessimistic view of, 18
non-governmental organizations (NGO), 235–37
Noronha, Antonio, 11
North East India, 19
  tribals, 20
North Gujarat, 21
North India
  church growth, 274
  Dalit conversions, 22
  origin of Christianity in, 263
North Malabar, 16
North-West India, Protestant Societies in, 125–28
Nostra Aetate, 176
Nott, Samuel, 15
Nottrot, Alfred, 119
nuns in India, 273
  violence against, 114
nurses, in India, 77

O'Dea Thomas, 256
Old Testament, 331
  Holy Spirit in, 223–27
  inculturation and adaptation in, 190–92
Omvedt, Gail, 160
Oraon tribe, 230
  conversions, 20
Order of the Imitation of Christ, 209
organizations, international, 338–39
Orientalism, rise of, 174
Origen, 264, 326
Orissa, 103–4, 109
  attacks on Christians, 103–9
  conversions, 20
  Freedom of Religion Act 1967, 111
  police to guard Christian villages Christmas 2008, 113
  socio-economic condition, 103
  tribal groups, 118
outcastes, 21
  mass conversion to Christianity, 125–42
  Syrian Christians and, 92

pacifism, 253
Padroado agreement, 10
Padroado missionaries, fight between Propaganda missionaries and, 14
Padroado-Propaganda fights, 267
Padroado (royal patronage), 2
pagan culture, Christian confrontation with, 187–90
Pal, Krishna, 122
Palai diocese, 9

389

Index

Palestine, culture of, 192
Palkiwala, Nani, 109
Pampa, 8
Panchamahashramavidhi, rite of initiation into, 168
Panchamas, 21, 83
Panchayat, tribal meeting of five elders, 140
Panda, Sabiasachi, 105
pandaraswamis, 189
Pandurang, Atmaram, 71
Pandurang, Dadoba, 70–71
Panikkar, K. M., 11, 117, 152, 281
Panikkar, Raimundo, 177–178, 183, 300
Pantaenus, 6, 88
pantheism, 42
Paradigm shift in mission, 173–75
Paraiyar caste, 65, 133
Paramahansa Mandali (Society for the Supreme Being), 70
Parekh, Manilal, 52–57, 248
   baptism, 52–53
   Hindu understanding of Kingdom of God, 53–56
   Christian understanding of Kingdom of God, 55–56
   Core of the Kingdom, 56
parents, 336
Parham, Charles, 293
Paris Foreign Missionaries, 129
Pascenti Dominici (1907), xiv
Passover celebration, 225–26
Patna, 266
   school, 268
Patnaik, Naveen, 104, 109
patriarchy, 22–23
   end of, 232
Paul (saint), 24, 252, 326, 329–30
   and baptism, 284
Paul VI (pope), xv, 99, 175, 303, 304, 342
   Apostolic Exhortation, 316
peace, 185
Pelvat, Felix, 208
Pentecost, 226, 233
   apostles' experience, 227
   Pentecostal movement, 294

Pentecostal-Charismatic mega bloc, 256
Pentecostal Mission, 123
Pentecostal Movement, 293, 309
   growth, 318
   and universalism and inclusivism, 332
Periyar (1879–1973), 231
Pernia, Antonio, 236
Perron, Anquetil du, 174
Persian language, 62, 67
Peshwar, education in, 72
Peter (saint), 178, 227, 326
   on Pentecost, 233
Pharisees, 193, 196, 197, 252–54
   Jesus and, 251–52
   hypocrisy of, 253–54
Philip, E. M., *Indian Church of St. Thomas*, 89
Philo, 41
Philosophy of Jesus, The (Jefferson), 35
Phule, Jyoti, 83
Pickett, J. W., 85, 138, 291
Pieris, Alois, 201
Pietistic movement, 29
Pilar Fathers, 12
Pinto, Michael, 112
Pirangis, 189
Pius IX (pope), *The Syllabus of Errors* (1864), xiv
Pius XI (pope), 296
Pius XII (pope), 296–97
Plantatio ecclesiae, 298
Plassey, battle of (1757), 29
Pliny the Elder, 194
pluralism, 1, 3–4, 95–96, 322
Plutschau, Henry (1677–1746), 17, 63
pneumatocentric vision, Christocentric vision and, 237–39
poetry, 338
Political and General History of the District of Tinnevelly (Caldwell), 64
political kingdom
   Jesus delinked from, 54–55
   vs. spiritual Kingdom, 53
political life, 152
political missionaries, 328

Index

polygamy, 148
Pondicherry, 128
Pontifical Council for Inter-religious Dialogue, 181
Pontifical Institute for Foreign mission, 129
Poona, 71
  Aryan Women's Association in, 58
poor, attraction towards missionaries, 110
Portugal
  king's agreement with pope, 10
  mission in India, xiii, 163-67, 188
  power decline in India, 13
Portuguese, 66
Portuguese territory, Hindu religious practices forbidden in, 11
postmodern, 318, 319
Power, political, 248
Prabhu Dasi Sisters of Ajmeer, 270
"Practical Vedanta" (Vivekanand), 37
Prakash, Guru Gyan, 183, 210-11
Prarthana Samaj, 71
preaching, Baptist missionaries approach to, 32
Precepts of Jesus, The (Roy), 35, 42
Presbyterian Mission, 75
  conversions, 126
Presidency University, 34
priests in Jerusalem, functions of, 250
Princeps Pastorum, 296
printing press in India, 156
  in Goa, 12n28
prison ministry, missionaries of, 333
Proclamation and Dialogue (1991), 181
Proksch, George, 210
Propaganda Fide, 14, 167, 217, 266, 268, 270
prophetic model, 325
proselytization, 171
Protestant missionaries
  impact of, 87
  mission trends, 289-94
  in North-Western India, 72
  strengths and weaknesses of, 155-60
Protestant Reformation, 254

Pryse, William, *Introduction to the Khasi Language*, 123
Pulayas, 21
  evangelization among, 8
Puniyani, Ram, 114
Punjabi Christians, 128-29
Punjab, separatist movements, 100
Puri, Orissa, Lord Jaganath temple, 25

Quantitative/qualitative analysis, 62
Quantitative/qualitative success, xvi
Qumran-Essene community, 193-94
Qumran monastic community, Jesus and, 254-55
Qumran scrolls, 193

rabbis, 198
racial types, 1
Radhakrishnan, Sarvepalli (1888-1975), 40, 79, 176-77, 330
radical missiological change, 161
Rahner, Karl, xviii-xix, 177, 302
Rai, Lala Lajpat, 278
Raigarh State Conversion Act, 170
Rainhart, Walter, 267
Rajasthan state, 262-63
  Christians in, 271
  nuns in, 273
  tribal groups, 118
Rajputana mission, 270
Ram, Shree Kanshi (1934-2008), 231
Ramabai, Pandita (1858-1922), 57-62, 81, 139, 287
  Conversion and baptism, 59
  Marathi Bible, 60-61
  Mukti Sadan, 60
Ramakrishna mission, 37, 154
Ramakrishna Paramahamsa, 45
Ramananda, Swami, 168
Ramaswamy, E. V. (1879-1973), 231
Ramananda or Ramavat sect, 168
Ranade, Madhava Govind (1842-1901), 58, 81
Ranaghat medical mission, 77
Ranande, M. G., 83
Rani Maria, 26
Ranjit Sing, Maharaja, 72
Rao, K. Subba, 286

391

Index

Rashtriya Sevika Samati, 104
Rashtriya Swayamsevak Sangh (RSS), 97
Ratha Yatra of Advani, 101
rationalism, 61
Ratnagiri, 71
Ratzinger, Joseph Cardinal, 308
Rayan, Samuel, 238, 245
Rebellious Prophets, 231
rebirths, cycle of, 28
Reddi, Muthulakshmi, 75-76
Redemptoris Missio (1990), xv, 305, 308
Reghunath Nayak, 17
Regulation of XVII of 1829, 80
Reid College, 75
relationship boundaries, 5
religions
  boundaries, 5
  in civilization, 277
  comparative study, 173-74
  Gandhi on, 40
religious communities, 1-2
religious disparity in literacy, 74
religious freedom, 178-79, 317
Religious of Jesus and Mary (Agra), 71
religious world view, decline of, 318
renewal of humanity, 288
repentance, 282, 341-42
Report of the Christian Missionary Activities Enquiry Committee, 99
Report of the Education Commission (1966), 150
Rerum Ecclesiae, 295
Rethinking Missions (Hocking), 292
Rethinking Christianity in India, 292-93
Rhenius, Charles T. E., 18,3
Ricci, Matheo, 188-89
Richter, Julius, 279
and overthrow of religions,279
Ringeltaube, W. T., 132
Rishtriya Swayamsevak Sangh, 278
Risley, H. H., 143, 145
rite of passage, 284
Ritual Families of the church, 200-201
Roberts, Hugh
  Anglo-Khasi Dictionary, 123

A Grammar for Khasi Language, 123
Rodericks, J. R., 300
Roman Catholic Church. *See* Catholic Church
Roy, Ram Mohan (1772-1833), 34, 35-37, 93
  and Sati, 80
Roy, S., 136
Roz, Francis, 166
RSS, 98. *See also* Rashtriya Swayamsevak Sangh (RSS)
  growth, 104
Ruah, 223
Rulers of nations, 339

Sabbath, 126, 191, 251
Saccidananda Brahman, 48-52
Saccidananda, Christian Trinitarian explanation of, 49
Saccidananda of Hinduism, 43
sacraments, 148
  Sen and, 46
Sacred Congregation for Divine Worship, 203
Sacred Scriptures, men as authors, 22
Sadducees, 193, 196, 254
Sadhana dharma, 51
Sahay, K. N., 149-50
Sahi, Jyoti, 4
saints in Indian tradition, 283
Salesians of Don Bosco, 20
  missionaries, 124
Salsette, 11-14
  missionary methods, 14
salvation, 223, 299, 311-12
  Alexandrian school of theology on, 177
  exclusivist understanding of, xviii, 10
  by faith, 254
  in Hinduism, 28
  and Jesus, 335
  New Testament theology of, 326-27
  of non-Christians, 300
  of unevangelized, 326-28
Salvation Army, 14, 123, 125, 126, 127, 329
salvation-sellers, 328

Index

Samachar Darpan, 32
Samajdharma, 51
Samru, Begum, 267-268
Sanatana Dharma, 35-40
Sangh Parivar, 102, 105, 112
  political clout, 104
Sanhedrin, 198, 251
Sankaracharya, Shri, 49, 90
Sannyasis, 168
Sansara, 117
Sanskrit language in Kerala, 89-90
  teaching to women, 57
Sanskritic culture, 212
Sanskritization, 91, 104
  improvement through, 143
  and land ownership and political power, 151-52
  meaning and nature of, 143-46
Santal Church, 20
Santhals, conversions, 20
Sara Thaker College, 75
Sarada, Har Bilas, 82
Sarada Marriage Restraint Act (Bombay), 82
Sarasvati, Dayananda, 48
Sarasvati, Madusudan, 168
Saraswati, Laxmananda, 103
Sardhana, Catholic missionary activities in, 267
Sarna (animism), 146
Sat (Being), 49
Satara, 71
Sat-Chit-Ananda,(the Trinity), 43, 175
Sati, rite of, 80
Sattampillai, 133
Satyagraha (Truth), 39
Satyartha Prakash, The Light of Truth, 39
Satyashodak Samaj, Truth-Seeking Society, 84-85
Saul (Paul), 244
  as Pharisee, 253
Savarkar, V. D., Hindutva (*Who is a Hindu?*), 97, 278
Savidge, F. W., 123
Scheduled Castes, 83, 125
Scheduled District Act of 1874, 153
Schillebeekx, E., 158

Schleiermacher, Friedrich, 177
Schopenhauer, Arthur, 174
Schreiter, Robert, 215
Schwartz, Christian F., (1724-98), 3, 18, 63
scientific culture, John Paul II on, 183
scientists, 339
Scotland, 69
Scottie, Julius Caesar, 267
Scottish Church College (Calcutta), 34
Scottish missionaries, 65
Scottish Presbyterian Church, 64
  schools in South Konkan, 69
Scudder, Ida (1870-1960), 77
Scudder, John, 77
Second Vatican Council. See Vatican Council II (1962-1965)
secularization, 61
self-image of Adivasi Christians, 149-50
self-respect, 138
Self-Respect Movement, 231
Sen, Keshab Chandra, 41-47, 48, 57, 71, 81, 93, 174, 206, 286
  on Jesus, 41-42
  New Dispensation, 45
  reaction to, 47
  and reforms, 81
  on the Trinity, 43-44
Serampore, 3, 30
Serampore Baptist Mission, 122
Serampore Covenant, 31
Serampore Trio, 31
serpent, 192
service centers, run by Christians, 24
Seventh Day Adventists, 123, 125
Seward, Sara, 77
Shamanism, 91-92
Shanars
  change, 132
  evangelization among, 8, 132-33
Shanativanam, 208
Sharada Bhavan, 59
Sharada Math, 37
Shardhananda, Swami, *Hindu Sangathan—Savior of a Dying Race*, 96
shared culture, 4

Index

Sharpe, Eric, 35
Shenk, Wilbert, 324
Shiva Sankar Apte, 99
Shourie, Arun, 314
Shudhi, rite of, 39
Simon Maccabee, 193–94
Simon the Zealot (apostle), 247
sin, dying to, 284–85
Sing, Ranjit, 72
Singh, Kushwant, 151
   appraisal of Christians, 151
Singh, Manmohan, 107
Singh, Padri Daud, 128
Singh, Raja, 265, 266
Singh, Sadhu Sunder, 206
Singhpho tribe, 20
Sisters of Charity of Blessed Mother Teresa, 162
Sisters of St. Joseph of Annecy, 129
Sisters of St. Joseph of Chambery, 270
Skrefsrud, L. O., 20, 121, 139
Slavery Abolition Act of 1833 (Britain), 134
Slavery Abolition Act of 1843 (India), 134
Soares-Prabhu, 284
social awareness, Western education and, 71
social institutions, 314
social movements, Holy Spirit in, 220, 228–37
Social Reform Conference in Ahmedabad, 84
Social Reform Conference in Calcutta, 84
social repulsion-attraction models, conversion movement in, 142
social status
   in Indian society, 144
   and mass conversions, 138
social transformation, 80, 87
   through education, 150
   Ambedkar's fight against Hinduism and conversion to Buddhism, 85–87
   child marriage abolition, 81–83
   and Christian mission, 79–94
   Hindu Widow-Remarriage, 80–81

   needed reforms, 87
   Sati abolition, 80
   untouchables of India, 83–85
   widow-remarriage, 80
Society for the Education of Girls in India, 66
Society for the Propagation of Christian Knowledge (SPCK), 133
Society for the Propagation of Faith, 65
Society for the Propagation of the Gospel (SPG), 14, 18, 75, 121, 125, 130, 133
   in Delhi, 125
Society of Catholic Medical Missionaries, 77
Society of Jesus, colleges, 76, 157
Society of Worshippers of Brahman, 36
Solomon, 250
Something Beautiful for God (Muggeridge), 288
Sonship, 44
Sophia College (Bombay), 72
Sophia, forbid Catholics to read, 52
South Canara, 16
South Gujarat, Jesuits in, 15
South India, 90
   anti-Christian violence, 102
South Rajasthan, 21
South Travencore, Anglican Church Missionary Society in, 7
Spencer, Phillip Jacob, *Affirming the Hope for Better Times*, 30
SPG. *See also* Society for the Propagation of the Gospel (SPG)
spirits, tribal preoccupation with, 146–47
spiritual kingdom, vs. political Kingdom, 53
spirituality, 223
   dialogue of, 180
   male perceptions in, 22
Sri Narayana Dharma Paripalana Sangam (Union for the Protection of Sri Narayana Religion), 84
Sri Narayana Guru Sangam, 8–9

Index

Sri Ramjanmabhoomi Mukti Yagna Samiti (Organization for the Liberation of the birth place of Lord Ram), 101
Sri Sankaracharya, 168
Srikakulam, 128
Srinivas, M. N., 68, 143-44, 151
  Religion and Society among the Coorgs of South India, 143
St. Bede's teacher-training college (Simla), 76
St. Columba's college, 121
St. Jerome Vulgate version, 244
St. Joseph's college, 76
St. Thomas Aquinas (1225-1274), 48, 50
St. Thomas Christians, 6-7
  cultural analysis, 89-94
  lack of Social Gospel, 92
St. Thomas Christians in India (Hambye), 89
St. Thomas church in India, 201
St. Thomas church, uncertainty of origin, 88-94
St. Xaviers (Calcutta), catholic college, 68, 76
St. Xaviers College Bombay, 76
Staffner, Hans, 51
Staines, Graham, 26, 104, 112
Stanislaus, Fr., 172
statistics
  on Christian expansion in Punjab, 127
  Christian population by states, 345-46
  on missionaries in Hindu belt, 272-75
Stephen, Thomas (1549-1619), 12
stone-crosses, 90-91
Stree Dharma Neeti (Morals for Hindu Women) (Ramabai), 58
Street preaching, 32-33, 96
street preachers, 328
Subramanyam, K. N., 62
Subaltern movements, 288
Sudhi, reconversion rite, 96
Sudras (peasants), 1

Suenens, L. J. Cardinal, *The Conspiracy of God*, 221
suffering
  awareness of, 318
  and human spirit, 230
Suffering Servant, 24, 54, 286
Sumerian flood story, 192
Supreme Court Judgement, anti-Christian bias, 112
Swadesh, in M. K. Gandhi's politics, 39
Swain Clara, 77
Swedish Lutheran Mission, 121
Syllabus of Errors, xiv, 175
symbols, in Catholic church, for Spirit, 221-22
Synod of the Bishops, xv, 302-3
  Special Assembly for Asia (1998), 321
Synod of Udiamperur, 166
Syriac Didascalia Apostalorum, 264
Syrian Christians, 91, 165
Syrian church, 2, 264
  liturgical reform, 204
  liturgy, St. Thomas Christians and, 89-90
  on Malabar coast, 6-9
  Latin church conflict, 165-67
Syrian Sudhist Community, origin of, 7
Syro-Malabar Catholics, in 2005, 9
Syro-Malakara church, 200
  dioceses, 272
Syro-Malankara church, Catholics in 2005, 9

Tagore, Rabindranath, 115, 339
  Gitanjali, 338
Tamil catechism, "Christiya Matatatwam," 13
Tamil language, 17
Tamil Nadu, xiii, 3, 131-35
  Christian population, 135
  German Lutheran missionaries in, 289
  Oppressed People's Movement, 313
  Paraiyar converts, 133
  Protestant mission in, 19
  Shanar converts, 132

395

Index

Taprobane, church in Ceylon, 265
Tarangambadi, 3
Taylor, R. W., 210
Teachers, 336
Telugu region
   Christians in, 131
   mission, 130
temples, destruction by Portuguese, 164
Temple in Jerusalem, 251
Tertulian of Cartage, 327
Thana Bhagat movement, 230–31
Thane, 13
   church founded in, 264
theology, xvii–xviii
Theophilus "the Indian," 7
Theosophical Society, 37
Thesaurus Linguae Indiane (Latin-Hindustani Dictionary), 266
Thomas of Cana, 6
Thomas the Apostle
   contradictory traditions, 264
   Indian Christianity origins and, xiii, 2
Tibet, 270
Tibet-Hindustan Prefecture, 266
Tilak, B. G., 82
Tilak, N. V. (1862–1919), 207
Tinnevelly district, 130, 133
Tinnevelly mission, 63
Tinnevelly Shanars, The (Caldwell), 133
Tippu Sultan, persecution of Christians, 16
Tipu, suppression after 1773, 159
Tirunelveli, 133
Tisserant, Cardinal, Eastern Christianity in India, 89
Togadia, Pravin, 100,105
Torah, 192
Towards Equality. Report of the Committee on the Status of Women in India (1974), 232
Tranquebar, xiii, 3, 18
   Lutheran missionaries, 17
Transcendental movement, 174
Transformation of India, 87
tribal Christians, 122–24

   impact of, 152
tribal church, 19
tribal groups
   central theme of culture, 229
   growth of awareness and identity, 161
   mass movement in North East, 122–25
   population in India, 118
   rebellions, 122, 230
tribal religions, 146
   Vatican Council and, 229
tribal terrain, missionaries in territory of, 157
Trichinopally, 18
Tridentine Latin mass, 217
Trinitarian mystery, Sen on, 43–44
Trinity, 48–52, 298, 307–8
Trinity (Sat-Chit-Ananda), 49, 174
truth, apparent connection to Christian doctrine, 70
Tuticorin, 64
twice-born, 144
Tyagi, O.P., 171

Ultimate meaning, search for, 340, 342
Ultimate light of God, 337
Ultimate Reality, 28, 178, 316
unbelievers, 340
unevangelized, salvation of, 325–28
Unitarian Society, 36
United Lutheran Church, 131
United Nations,340
   Conference on Human Environment (Stockholm, 1972), 234
   Decade of Development, 309
   Earth Summit (Rio de Janerio, 1992), 234
   humanitarian goals, 236
   Universal Declaration of Human rights, 110, 320
United Presbyterian Mission, 75
Universal mission, 335–41
   Christian definition, xviii
   silent unfolding of, 337–41
Universalism, xviii, 329, 331
Universal servants, 341
Universe, nature of, 316

Index

Unknown Christ of Hinduism, The, 177–78
Unknown Krishna of Christianity, The, 178
universities in India, 76–77
untouchability, 39, 117
Untouchability (offence) Act of 1955, 153
untouchables, 1, 21, 83–85. See also Dalits
  integration of, 96
Upadyaya, Brahmabandav (1861–1907), 47–51, 175
  Incarnation, 50
  Maya and contingent being, 50
  Vande Saccidanandam, 49
Upanishads, 28
Uttar Pradesh, 262–63
  Christians in, 271
  nuns in, 273

Vaeth, Alfons, 52
Vaishnavism, Bhakti marga of, 28, 52
Vaishya model, 144
Vaishyas (commerce caste), 1, 116
Vajpayee, A. B., 100
Valentine, Dr., 77
Valmiki Samaj, 84
Valsa John, 26
Vanabasi Kalyan Ashram, 103
Vande Saccidanandam, 49
Varnadharma, 117
Varnashramadharma, 98
Vatican Council II (1962–1965), xiv, 158, 175–78, 228, 229, 237, 332
  Catholic missiology in India after, 299–302
  Catholic mission trends before, 295–97
  on mission, 297–302
Vatican Secretariat for Non-Christians, 181
Vaz, Joseph, 12
Vedamanikam, 18, 132
Vedanayakam Pillai (1773–1864), 133
Vedanta Hinduism, 42
Vedanta philosophy, Upadhyaya's opposition to, 48

Vedanta Saramu, The Essence of Theology, 129
Vedanta Society of New York, 38
Vedic religion, 38
Vedic Salvation Army, 39
vegetarians, Brahmins as, 94
Vellalar Christians, 134
Vempeny, Ishanand, 328
Vendrame, Constantine, 124, 139
vernacular education, 64, 67
vernacularization, 218
Vicariate Apostolic of Hindustan in Agra, 73
Vicar Apostolic of the Great Mughal, 14
Vidyalankar, Mrtyunjaya, 80
Vidyasagar, Ishwar Chandra, 66, 81, 82
Vijayanagar, 128
Vijayawada, 129
Vinay Katiyar, 99
Violence
  anti-foreign and anti-missionary, 294
  attacks on Christians, 26, 103–9
  communal, 101
  Hindu-Christian, 104–6
  by Hindus, 95
  against missionaries, 273
  proactive initiatives of missionaries, 107–9
Virmamunivar Swami, 191
Visakapatnam, 128, 129
Vishwa Hindu Parishad (Association of Hindu religious leaders), 99, 184
Vithayathil, Varkey Cardinal, 23, 272
Vivat International, 236
Vivekananda, Swami, 37–38, 47, 109, 175, 287
  Hindu Missionary, 38
Vizagapatanam, 128
Votum Missionis, St.Ignatius, 305

Waddar tribal community, 130
Wald, Stanislaus, 271
Ward, William, 31, 32
Warneck, Gustav, 297, 299
water, and Spirit, 285

397

Index

We or Our Nation Defined (Golwalkar), 278
Welsh Presbyterians, 122
Wesley, John, 29, 30, 69
Wesleyan Methodist Church of Medak, 131
Wesleyan Methodist Mission, 16, 133
Wesleyan Methodist Missionary Society, 62
Wesleyan missionaries, 65
Western civilization, India's transformation by, 281–82
Western colonialism, dismantling of, xvii
Western education, 62
  In Bombay, 68–71
  In Calcutta, 66–68
  In North-Western Province, 72–73
  In South India, 63–65
western imperialism, missionary activity as, 171
Western India, 68–72
Western Madhya Pradesh, 21
Western theology, in India, 280
Whithead, H., 134–35
widow burning, 80
Widow Marriage Association, 58
Widow Remarriage Act, 81
Wilkins, Charles, 174
Wilson, Daniel, 134
Wilson, John, 69, 82
Wilson College (Bombay), 69
Wiltgen, Ralph M., *The Rhine Flows into the Tiber*, 300
Winslow, J., 207
witches, 147
witness, missionaries of, 333–34
women
  Amendment of Dowry Prohibition Act (1986), 233
  being sold by their fathers, 148
  Christianity and, 148
  education of, 57
  Hindu views on, 57
  Kyriarchical structure and, 22
  Liberation movement, 233
  Nadar, 132, 149
  religious congregations, 71
  second class citizens, 22
  tribal, 148
women doctors, training, 77
Women's Christian College (Madras), 75
women's colleges, 75
  in Western India, 72
Women religious congreagations, 71
women's liberation movement, 232–34
Woods, Charles, 64
work, prohibition on Sabbath, 251
workers of the world, 338
world civilizations, 277–78
  and human dignity, 339
  mission deserts among, 276–79
  overthrow of, 279, 280
World Council of Arya Samaj, 114
World Council of Churches, 290, 309
  meeting in New Delhi (1961), 292, 293
World Missionary Conference (Edinburgh, 1910), 291
World's Parliament of Religions (Chicago, 1893), 109, 175
world views
  change in, 316–20
  confrontation of Hindu-Christian, 111
  unifying factor in, 320

Xavier, Jerome, 265

Yahweh, 191, 193, 245
  kingship of, 246
Yausef, Mar, 6
Yeats, W. B., 338
Yeddyurappa, B. S., 107

Zacchaeus, 322
Zadokite priests, 194
Zaleski, L., 52
Zamorin, 9
Zealots, 54, 247
Zeitler, Engelbert, xxi, 302
Zelazech, Marian, 25
Zenana mission, 65, 72

Ziegenbalg, Bartholomew, (1683–1719), 17, 63

Zoram Baptist Mission, 121